LOAN

PS.7204

12 FEB 2018

Benefit

Rebates

2013-14

RIES
ENT
AY

d Martin Ward

D0280512

99

Guide to Housing Benefit
Peter McGurk and Nick Raynsford, 1982-88
Martin Ward and John Zebedee, 1988-90

Guide to Housing Benefit and Community Charge Benefit
Martin Ward and John Zebedee, 1990-93

Guide to Housing Benefit and Council Tax Benefit
John Zebedee and Martin Ward, 1993-2003
John Zebedee, Martin Ward and Sam Lister, 2003-12
Sam Lister and Martin Ward, 2012-13

Guide to Housing Benefit and Council Tax Rebates
Sam Lister and Martin Ward, 2013-14

Sam Lister is policy and practice officer at the Chartered Institute of Housing
(email: *sam.lister@cih.org*) and a founding director of Worcester Citizens Advice
Bureau and Whabac. He has specialised in Housing Benefit and Council Tax
Benefit since 1993.

Martin Ward is an independent benefits consultant and trainer (e-mail:
mward@info-training.co.uk). He maintains a web-site which gives convenient
access to relevant legislation and other useful sources – *www.info-training.co.uk*
He has specialised in Housing Benefit and Council Tax Benefit since the schemes
were introduced.

The authors each assert the moral right to be recognised
as an author of this work

ISBN 978 1 903595 94 7

Edited and typeset by Davies Communications *(www.daviescomms.com)*

Printed and bound by Ashford Colour Press, UK

Shelter

Shelter helps over a million people a year struggling with bad housing or homelessness – and we campaign to prevent it in the first place.

We're here so no-one has to fight bad housing or homelessness on their own.

Please support us at *shelter.org.uk*

For more information about Shelter, please contact:

88 Old Street
London
EC1V 9HU

Tel: 0300 330 1234
shelter.org.uk

For help with your housing problems, phone Shelter's free housing advice helpline on 0808 800 4444 (open from 8am to 8pm on Mondays to Fridays and from 8am to 5pm on weekends: calls are free from UK landlines and main mobile networks) or visit *shelter.org.uk/advice*

Chartered Institute of Housing

The Chartered Institute of Housing (CIH) is the professional body for people involved in housing and communities. We are a registered charity and not-for-profit organisation. We have a diverse and growing membership of over 22,000 people – both in the public and private sectors – living and working in more than 20 countries on five continents. We exist to maximise the contribution that housing professionals make to the wellbeing of communities.

Chartered Institute of Housing
Octavia House
Westwood Way
Coventry
CV4 8JP

Telephone: 024 7685 1700
E-mail: *customer.services@cih.org*
Web site: *www.cih.org*

Contents

Preface

This guide explains the rules about housing benefit and council tax rebate as they apply from 1st April 2013, using the information available on that date.

We welcome comments and criticisms on the contents of our guide and make every effort to ensure it is accurate. However, the only statement of the law is found in the relevant Acts, regulations, orders and rules (chapter 1).

This guide has been written with the help and encouragement of many other people. Much material remains as written by John Zebedee. This year we thank the following in particular:

Mary Connolly, Helen Highwater, Colin Hull, Michael Iyekekpolor, Phillip J. Miall, Jonathan Reid, Mark Rodgers, Linda Davies and Peter Singer (editing and production) as well as staff from the Department for Work and Pensions and the Rent Service. Their help has been essential to the production of this guide.

Sam Lister and Martin Ward

April 2013

List of tables

Table		Page

Table		Page

Abbreviations

The principal abbreviations used in the guide are given below. A key to the footnotes can be found in chapter 1 in table 1.4.

CTB	Council tax benefit
CTC	Child tax credit
CTR	Council tax rebate
DSD	The Department for Social Development in Northern Ireland
DWP	The Department for Work and Pensions in Great Britain
EP	Extended payment
ESA	Employment and support allowance (including ESA(C) and ESA (IR))
ESA(C)	Contributory employment and support allowance
ESA(IR)	Income-based employment and support allowance
GLHA	The DWP guidance local housing allowance
GM	The DWP HB/CTB Guidance Manual
HB	Housing benefit
HMRC	Her Majesty's Revenue and Customs
HMCTS	Her Majesty's Courts and Tribunals Service
HRA	Housing revenue account
IB	Incapacity benefit
IS	Income support
JSA	Jobseeker's allowance (including JSA(C) & JSA(IB))
JSA(C)	Contribution-based jobseeker's allowance
JSA(IB)	Income-based jobseeker's allowance
NI	Northern Ireland
NIHE	The Northern Ireland Housing Executive
OG	The DWP HB/CTB Overpayments Guide
SAR	Second adult rebate
SDA	Severe disablement allowance
SI	Statutory instrument
SMI	Support for Mortgage Interest
SR	Statutory rules (Northern Ireland)
SSI	Scottish Statutory Instrument
UC	Universal credit
UK	England, Scotland, Wales and Northern Ireland
WTC	Working tax credit

Key to footnotes

Each reference applies to Great Britain only unless otherwise stated.
If prefixed by 'NI' (e.g. NIAA) it applies to Northern Ireland only.

AA	The Social Security Administration Act 1992 [section number]
art	Article number
CBA	The Social Security Contributions and Benefits Act 1992 [section number]
CPR	The Housing Benefit and Council Tax Benefit (Consequential Provisions) Regulations 2006, SI No. 217 [regulation number]
CPSA	The Child Support, Pensions and Social Security Act [section number]
CTP	The Council Tax Reduction Schemes (Prescribed Requirements) (England) Regulations 2012, SI No, 2885 [regulation number]
CTPW	The Council Tax Reduction Scheme and Prescribed Requirements (Wales) Regulations 2012, SI No, 3144 [regulation number]
CTR	The Council Tax Reduction Schemes (Default Scheme) (England) Regulations 2012, SI No. 2886 [paragraph number of the schedule to those regulations]
CTRW	The Council Tax Reduction Schemes (Default Scheme) (Wales) Regulations 2012, SI No. 3145 [regulation number]
CTS	The Council Tax (Scotland) Regulations 2012, SI No. 303 [regulation number]
CTS60+	The Council Tax Reduction (State Pension Credit) (Scotland) Regulations 2012, SI NO 319 [regulation number]
DAR	The Housing Benefit and Council Tax Benefit (Decisions and Appeals) Regulations 2001, SI No. 1002 [regulation number]
DAR99	The Social Security and Child Support (Decisions and Appeals) Regulations 1999, SI No. 991 [regulation number]
EEA	The Immigration (European Economic Area) Regulations 2006, SI No. 1003 [regulation number (UK reference)]
FTPR	The Tribunal Procedure (First-tier Tribunal) (Social Entitlement Chamber) Rules 2008, SI No. 2685 [rule number
HB	The Housing Benefit Regulations 2006, SI No. 213 [regulation number]
HB60+	The Housing Benefit (Persons who have attained the age for state pension credit) Regulations 2006, SI No. 214 [regulation number]

IAA99	The Immigration and Asylum Act 1999 [the section number (UK reference)]
LGFA	The Local Government Finance Act 1992 (as amended) [section number]
NIAA	The Social Security Administration (Northern Ireland) Act 1992 [section number]
NICBA	The Social Security Contributions and Benefits (Northern Ireland) Act 1992 [section number]
NICPR	The Housing Benefit (Consequential Provisions) Regulations (Northern Ireland) 2006, SR No. 407 [regulation number]
NICPSA	The Child Support, Pensions and Social Security Act (Northern Ireland) 2000 [section number]
NIDAR	The Housing Benefit (Decisions and Appeals) Regulations (Northern Ireland) 2001 SR No. 213 [regulation number]
NIDAR99	The Social Security and Child Support (Decisions and Appeals) Regulations (Northern Ireland) 1999 SR No. 162 [regulation number]
NIED	The Housing Benefit (Executive Determinations) Regulations (Northern Ireland) 2008 SR No. 100
NIHB	The Housing Benefit Regulations (Northern Ireland) 2006, SR No. 405 [regulation number]
NIHB60+	The Housing Benefit (Persons who have attained the age for state pension credit) Regulations (Northern Ireland) 2006, SR No. 406 [regulation number]
NISR	Statutory Rules of Northern Ireland (equivalent to Statutory Instruments in GB)
NISSCPR	The Social Security Commissioners (Procedure) Regulations (Northern Ireland) 1999, SR No. 225 [regulation number]
reg	regulation [regulation number]
ROO	In England and Wales, The Rent Officers (Housing Benefit Functions) Order 1997, SI 1984; in Scotland, The Rent Officers (Housing Benefit Functions) (Scotland) Order 1997, SI 1995; in both cases followed by article number or schedule and paragraph number
sch	Schedule
SI	Statutory instrument [year and reference number]
SR	Statutory rules [year and reference number (apply to NI only)
TCEA	Tribunals, Courts and Enforcement Act 2007
UTPR	The Tribunal Procedure (Upper Tribunal) Rules 2008, SI No. 2698 [rule number]

1 Introduction

1.1 Welcome to this guide, which describes housing benefit (HB) and council tax rebate (CTR). The guide applies throughout the UK from 1st April 2013, and is used by administrators, advisers, claimants, landlords and appeal tribunals.

1.2 HB helps people pay their rent throughout the UK, and their rates in Northern Ireland. CTR helps people pay their council tax in Great Britain: it is new this year (and replaces the former council tax benefit). HB and CTR are an important source of income for many households: some basic statistics are given in table 1.1.

1.3 This chapter contains:

◆ a summary of the HB and CTR schemes;

◆ changes to the schemes including the introduction of universal credit;

◆ the benefit figures, terminology and references used in this guide; and

◆ HB and CTR administration, law, guidance and proper decision-making.

Summary of the HB and CTR schemes

Who gets HB and CTR?

1.4 In broad terms, the main rules about who can get HB and CTR are:

◆ nearly everyone with low or lowish income and capital can get HB if they pay rent (unless they are on universal credit: para. 1.9) and/or in Northern Ireland rates (chapter 6);

◆ many people with low or lowish income and capital can get CTR if they pay council tax (chapter 6) – but the rules about CTR vary across Great Britain (paras. 1.11 and 1.14);

◆ to get HB or CTR the claimant has to make a claim – and keep the claim going by providing details of changes in their circumstances (chapters 5 and 17);

◆ HB and CTR are only payable on the claimant's normal home, but there are rules for people who are temporarily absent or are liable for rent on two dwellings (chapter 3);

◆ there are limits on how much rent can be met by HB (chapters 7 to 9);

◆ some groups of people cannot get HB or CTR no matter how low their income is; for example, some care leavers, most full-time students and certain migrants (chapters 2, 20, 21 and 22); and

◆ the rules about HB and CTR often vary between pension age and working age claims (para. 1.20).

Table 1.1: Key HB and CTB statistics

HB claims in Great Britain on 1st November 2012

Number of cases	5.05 million
Average weekly payment	£89.27

Main CTB claims in Great Britain on 1st November 2012

Number of cases	5.90 million
Average weekly payment	£15.68

Composition of HB caseload in Great Britain on 1st November 2012

In receipt of passport benefit	64.2%
Recipients aged under 65	74.0%
Local authority tenants	28.7%
Housing association tenants	38.4%
Private tenant LHA cases	27.0%
Private tenant non-LHA cases	5.8%

HB caseload in Northern Ireland on 1st June 2012

All claims	162,240
Claims where claimant aged 65+	36,500

◆ Source: DWP, Single Housing Benefit Extract (SHBE):
DSD Statistics and Research Agency

HB, CTR and the 'passport benefits'

1.5   The state 'safety net' of benefits is designed to make sure citizens have enough money to live on. For claimants not on universal credit (para. 1.8) it has the following two halves.

1.6   Four benefits – often called the 'passport benefits' – can help meet basic living needs (such as food, heating and mortgage interest – but not rent, rates or council tax):

- ◆ income-based jobseekers' allowance (JSA(IB));
- ◆ income-related employment and support allowance (ESA(IR));
- ◆ income support (IS); and
- ◆ guarantee credit (part of state pension credit).

1.7   Help with rent, rates and council tax can be met by HB and CTR. People on one of the passport benefits get maximum help, but many other people qualify for some help.

Table 1.2: Summary of changes after April 2012

SI 2012/1267 4th June 2012	Decisions of the former appeal tribunals and commissioners may be superseded. Has retrospective effect to 3rd November 2008.
SI 2012/3040 1st January 2013	New LHA figures take effect from 1st April each year. The former 'anniversary date' reconsiderations cease on 31st December 2012.
SI 2013/358 1st April 2013	Introduction of CTR. For details see paras. 10.21-30 and table 10.2.
April 2013	Universal credit (UC) pilot scheme commences in parts of Greater Manchester. New rules for assessing UC cases in CTR.
SI 2012/3040 1st April 2013	Size limitations commence in working age social sector cases, with protections in the case of bereavement. Working age over-large registered HA (and LA) lettings now referred to rent officer. In LHA cases, a reduction in actual rent can trigger a reduction in eligible rent.
SI 2013/665 SI 2013/666 1st April 2013	Concessions to size criteria for foster carers and certain households where a related non-dependant is a member of HM armed forces away on operations.
SI 2012/2994 SI 2013/546 1st April 2013	Introduction of overall benefits cap, administered via HB, for many working age claimants: £350 per week for single claimants, £500 for lone parents and couples (para. 6.31).
SI 2012/3040 1st April 2013	LHA rates no longer based on live rental market evidence but on historic LHA rates uprated by CPI.
SI 2013/443 2nd April 2013	Disregard introduced for new local welfare provision replacing the social fund, and related changes.
October 2013	Introduction of universal credit replacing HB and passport benefits for certain new working age claims initially, and eventually all new working age claims. HB continues alongside universal credit for existing claims (the 'legacy caseload').
April 2014	End of tax credits scheme. All new claims for child and in-work support become claims for universal credit.

October 2014	Introduction of housing credit element of state pension credit replacing HB for all new pension age claims for housing benefit and/or pension credit.
October 2013 to October 2017	Gradual 'natural migration' of legacy HB caseload to universal credit/state pension credit arising from major changes of circumstance (e.g. moving home or changes in household size).
2015	Block transfer of legacy HB caseload starts.
March 2015	Rules about support for mortgage interest revert to pre-2009 position: waiting period increases from 13 to 39 weeks; eligible loan limit for working age claims reduces from £200,000 to £100,000.
October 2017	Final block transfers of legacy HB caseload take place. HB scheme ends.

HB, CTR and universal credit

1.8   Universal credit (UC) is a new benefit for working age claimants (para. 1.20). From 15th April 2013, UC applies (as a pilot scheme) only in certain parts of Greater Manchester. The government then intends to introduce it nationally over four years from October 2013. To begin with, UC is available only to new claims made by working age claimants who are out of work. For them it replaces:

+ the passport benefits (JSA(IB), ESA(IR) and IS);
+ child tax credit; and
+ HB for most types of letting (paras. 2.8).

For further planned changes relating to UC (and related changes to pension credit), see table 1.2.

1.9   Universal credit can help meet basic living needs (such as food and heating) and also rent or mortgage interest – but not council tax or rates. In most cases, claimants on UC cannot therefore get HB towards their rent; but can get CTR to help meet their council tax, or HB towards their rates in Northern Ireland.

How much HB and CTR?

1.10   HB is a national scheme applying throughout the UK. It is worked out on the claimant's 'eligible rent' – and/or in Northern Ireland their 'eligible rates':

+ in social sector lettings, the eligible rent normally equals the rent payable on the claimant's home (reduced in certain cases if the home is larger than the claimant needs), apart from any charges included in the rent for services which HB cannot meet (chapters 7 and 9);
+ in most private sector lettings, the eligible rent is a fixed 'local housing

allowance' figure depending on where the claimant lives and the size of accommodation needed (chapters 8 and 9);

+ in Northern Ireland, eligible rates equal the rates payable on the claimant's home (chapter 11).

1.11 CTR varies across Great Britain. It is worked out on the 'eligible council tax' payable on the claimant's home (chapter 10). In Scotland and Wales this means 100% of the council tax. In England it can mean 100% of the council tax or (in some authorities' areas) a lower figure (para. 6.5 and see para 1.14).

1.12 The amount of HB/CTR a claimant qualifies for then depends on the following main things (chapter 6):

+ whether the claimant (or partner) is on a 'passport benefit' (para. 1.6);

+ if they are not on a passport benefit, how much income and capital the claimant (and partner) have (chapters 13 to 15);

+ if they are not on a passport benefit, how much they (and their family) are treated as needing to live on, known as their 'applicable amount' (chapters 4 and 12);

+ whether the claimant (or partner) is of 'pension age' or 'working age' (para. 1.20);

+ the circumstances of other adults in their home, known as 'non-dependants' (para. 1.13).

1.13 HB and CTR can be reduced because a non-dependant is expected to contribute towards the rent, rates or council tax (chapter 6). However, in England and Scotland, there is also a less common type of CTR known as second adult rebate that depends not on the claimant's circumstances but on those of a non-dependant (paras. 6.25-36).

1.14 For CTR, how the above factors (paras. 1.11-13) are taken into account varies between England, Wales and Scotland. In England (and to a lesser extent in Wales) it also varies from one authority to another. Details of how the variations can operate are given throughout this guide: the key points are summarised in table 10.2 and paragraphs 10.21-30.

Awards and appeals

1.15 HB and CTR are administered by local councils (para. 1.25) or in Northern Ireland by executive agencies of government. Once they have assessed HB/CTR, they should notify the decision (and any later changes to it) to the claimant and sometimes others (paras. 16.9-12).

1.16 There is a right to ask the council to reconsider its decision about HB/CTR, and to appeal to an independent tribunal (chapter 19). This includes decisions about how much HB and CTR is awarded, how it was calculated, when HB/CTR starts, including decisions about backdating (chapter 5), and what happens when HB is overpaid (chapter 18).

Using this guide

1.17 The HB and CTR rules in this guide are the ones applying from 1st April 2013. The rules change frequently. The main changes since the last edition of this guide are given in table 1.2, which also outlines the government's plans for future changes.

HB/CTR and other benefit figures

1.18 The various figures used in calculating HB and CTR are up-rated each April together with other social security benefits and tax credits, usually in line with inflation. For the exact dates this year, see table 1.3. For the main figures for HB/CTR and other benefits this year, see table 12.1 and appendix 4.

Table 1.3: April 2013 up-rating dates

For HB in all cases	Monday 1st April 2013
For CTR (former CTB cases transferred to CTR)	Monday 1st April 2013
Most other state benefits	Week commencing 8th April 2013 *
Tax credits	Saturday 6th April 2013 *

* These changes are taken into account for HB/CTR on 1st April 2013 but see also paras. 13.157 and 17.39.

Terminology used in this guide

1.19 In this guide, the following terms are used:

+ 'authority' means any of the public authorities which administers HB/CTR (para. 1.25);
+ 'tenant' is used to describe any kind of rent-payer (including, for example, licensees);
+ 'housing benefit' (HB) means any form of HB for rent or (in Northern Ireland) rates;
+ 'rent rebate' means HB for rent for a council or NIHE tenant;
+ 'rent allowance' means HB for rent for anyone else;
+ 'council tax rebate' (CTR) means any of the forms of CTR available in Great Britain including the less common kind called 'second adult rebate' (referred to in the law as 'alternative maximum CTR');
+ 'council tax benefit' (CTB) means the former scheme which CTR replaced on 1st April 2013;
+ 'state pension credit' refers to either type of pension credit – 'guarantee credit' and 'savings credit';

- 'guarantee credit' is used to refer to any award of pension credit which includes an amount of guarantee credit – whether it is paid with or without the savings credit;
- 'savings credit' is used to refer to awards of pension credit which consist solely of an award of the savings credit;
- 'pension age' and 'working age' are defined below (para. 1.20 and table 1.4).

'Pension age' vs 'working age' claims for HB/CTR

1.20 Many HB and CTR rules are different between pension age and working age claims. The main differences relate to entitlement to CTR (table 10.2), backdating HB and CTR (paras. 5.51-57) and the assessment of income and capital for HB and CTR (para. 13.8).

1.21 The main dividing line is the qualifying age for state pension credit (SPC). The law refers to people below that age as being 'working age', people above it as 'pension age'. The qualifying age for SPC is increasing from 60 (before April 2010) to 66 (from April 2020). During the 2013-14 financial year it rises from (approximately) 61½ to 62. A complete list of qualifying ages is given in appendix 7.

1.22 However, people on JSA(IB), ESA(IR), IS or universal credit (UC) are counted as 'working age' regardless of their actual age. And, due to slight differences between HB and CTR law, some couples can fall into either age group. Table 1.4 shows which claimants count as 'working age' or pension age'.

Table 1.4: Pension age or working age claim?

Single claimant/lone parent

• under SPC age	HB/CTR: working age claim
• at or over SPC age:	
• not on JSA(IB)/ESA(IR)/IS/UC	HB/CTR: pension age claim
• on JSA(IB)/ESA(IR)/IS/UC	HB/CTR: working age claim

Couple/polygamous marriage

• both/all under SPC age	HB/CTR: working age claim
• at least one at or over SPC age:	
• neither on JSA(IB)/ESA(IR)/IS/UC	HB/CTR: pension age claim
• one on JSA(IB)/ESA(IR)/IS/UC	HB: working age claim CTR: pension age *or* working age claim (para. 1.22)

• Appendix 7 gives a complete list of the qualifying ages for state pension credit ('SPC age').

T1.4   HB5; HB60+5; NIHB5; NIHB60+5; CTP3; CTR3; CTPW3; CTRW3; CTS12; CTS60 I 12

Abbreviations and footnotes

1.23   The tables at the front of this guide (following the contents page) give:

◆ a list of the abbreviations used in the text; and

◆ a key to the abbreviations used in the footnotes.

The footnotes throughout this guide refer to the law governing HB and CTR. For CTR we have generally included the English references in the footnotes, with Welsh and Scottish equivalents in appendix 8. All the references are to the law as amended.

1.24   For example, the footnote for this paragraph (which is actually about the definition of a non-dependant) refers to regulation 3 of the Housing Benefit Regulations 2006, regulation 3 of the Housing Benefit (Persons who have attained the qualifying age for state pension credit) Regulations 2006, the two Northern Ireland equivalents, and the six CTR equivalents, all ten of which are similar.

Administering the HB/CTR schemes

Who administers the HB and CTR schemes?

1.25   HB was first introduced throughout the UK in 1982-83. CTR is new this year, replacing the CTB scheme which (along with council tax) was introduced in 1992-93. They are administered mainly by local councils (which are largely reimbursed for this by the government: chapter 24). There are different arrangements for this in different parts of the UK:

◆ in areas in England with two layers of local government (county and district/borough), HB/CTR are administered by the district/borough councils – also known as the local housing authority;

◆ in the rest of Great Britain (areas with one layer of local government), HB/CTR are administered by English unitary authorities and London boroughs (including the Common Council of the City of London), Welsh county and county borough councils, and Scottish local councils;

◆ in Northern Ireland, HB for rent and rates for tenants is administered for tenants by the Northern Ireland Housing Executive (NIHE) and for owners by the Land and Property Services. More details and exceptions are in table 1.5.

The overall effect is that a particular claimant's HB and CTR are almost always administered by the same authority. But if an authority has properties in another area, the tenants there claim HB from their landlord authority, but CTR from the authority for the area they live in.

1.24   HB3; HB60+ 3; NIHB 9; NIHB60+ 9; CTP 9; CTR 9; CTPW 9; CTRW 9; CTS 3; CTS60+ 3

1.25   AA 134(1),(1A),(1B),(2), 139(1),(2), 191; NIAA 126(2),(3)

Table 1.5: Which agency administers HB in Northern Ireland

Land and Property Services	Northern Ireland Housing Executive (NIHE)
Owner occupiers	NIHE tenants
Partners of sole owners	Housing association tenants
Former partners of sole owners	Tenants of private landlords
Former non-dependants of sole owners	People with a life interest
	People in co-ownership schemes
	People in rental purchase schemes

• The same agency also administers rate relief and lone pensioner allowance.

Arranging for someone else to administer HB/CTR

1.26   Authorities in Great Britain (but not Northern Ireland) may arrange for HB (but not CTR) to be administered on their behalf by another authority or by a number of authorities jointly. The latter is a frequent occurrence.

1.27   Authorities can contract out the administration of HB and CTR to private companies (in other words, pay them to do part or all of their work). They do this under the Deregulation and Contracting Out Act 1994 and the Contracting Out (Functions of Local Authorities: Income-related Benefits) Regulations 2002/1888. When contractors make decisions on claims, they must submit a daily 10% random sample of claims for the authority to check.

Good administration

1.28   Under the Local Government Act 1999 authorities in England and Wales are required to provide the best value they can, achieve continuous improvement and publish their plans for how they will perform.

1.29   The DWP sets authorities 'performance indicators' relating to HB (checks on how well they do their work). The key indicators for 2013-14 are:

• a 'right time' indicator – which is the average time to process claims and changes to entitlement; and

• a 'right benefit' indicator – which is the number of changes to entitlement in a year.

The DWP inspects a small number of authorities each year and reports on their

---

1.26   AA 134 (1A),(5), 191

1.29   AA 139A-139H
       www.dwp.gov.uk/local-authority-staff/housing-benefit/performance-and-good-practice/

administration generally and on the prevention and detection of fraud. The HB Good Practice Guide provides guidance to help authorities manage their services efficiently and is available online [www].

Maladministration

1.30   In individual cases of bad authority administration, the claimant (or someone else) can complain to the Local Government Ombudsman. Guidance on how to complain, what constitutes maladministration, and recent Ombudsman's reports on HB (and CTR and CTB), are available online [www].

HB and CTR law

Acts of Parliament

1.31   The Acts giving the basic rules of the HB scheme are the Social Security Contributions and Benefits Act 1992, the Social Security Administration Act 1992 and their Northern Ireland equivalents, and also (as regards decision-making and appeals) the Child Support, Pensions and Social Security Act 2000.

1.32   The Act giving the basic rules of the CTR schemes is the Local Government Finance Act 1992 (as amended by the Local Government Finance Act 2012).

1.33   The Data Protection Act 1998 controls the use of, and access to, information about an individual held on a computer or any other retrievable filing system. This Act does not stop disclosure when other law requires it (section 35 of the Act) but authorities are under a duty to protect personal information (GM chapter D3).

1.34   Other Acts affecting HB and CTR include the Immigration and Asylum Act 1999 (e.g. s.115 about migrants), section 87 of the Northern Ireland Act 1998 (making the social security system UK-wide), the Human Rights Act 1998, various anti-discrimination laws, the Local Government Finance Act 1982, the Deregulation and Contracting Out Act 1994 and the Local Government Act 1999.

Regulations, orders and rules

1.35   The regulations, orders and rules giving the detail of the HB and CTR schemes are all passed under the Acts mentioned above and are listed in Appendix 1. They are known technically as Statutory Instruments (SIs) and in Northern Ireland as Statutory Rules (SRs).

Obtaining the law

1.36   The public has the right to see copies of the relevant legal material (plus details of any local scheme: para. 23.17) at an authority's principal office.

1.30   www.lgo.org.uk (England), www.ombudsman-wales.org.uk (Wales)
        www.spso.org.uk (Scotland), www.ni-ombudsman.org.uk (Northern Ireland)

1.37   The Acts, regulations, orders and rules are available online [www]. For the consolidated legislation, see the DWP's *The Law Relating to Social Security,* volume 8 parts 1 and 2 (also called 'the blue volumes') which are available online [www]. The Child Poverty Action Group's (CPAG's) annual publication, *Housing Benefit and Council Tax Benefit Legislation,* also contains all the law in Great Britain plus a detailed commentary including references to case law.

Proper decision-making

1.38   This part of the guide explains how an authority should go about making decisions on HB and CTR by working through the following steps:

* identifying what the relevant facts are in any particular case;
* properly considering the evidence that does exist, if the facts are in doubt or in dispute;
* establishing the facts 'on the balance of probability' if this is necessary;
* correctly interpreting the relevant law and applying it to the facts of the case; and
* arriving at decisions that can be understood in terms of the relevant facts and law.

Relevant facts

1.39   The only facts which are relevant to the authority are those which affect the HB/CTR schemes:

* sometimes the facts are clear and not in dispute. For example, it may be agreed by the claimant and the authority that the claimant has a grown-up son living with him;
* sometimes facts are unclear or are in dispute. For example, the claimant may say the son is not living with him (but other things suggest he is);
* sometimes there is no evidence of the facts at all. For example, the claimant may have left all of the 'your household' section of his HB/CTR application form blank.

1.40   The law uses two ideas to deal with uncertainty about the facts: 'burden of proof' and 'balance of probability'. Lawyers argue about what these mean, and which applies when, but it is possible to distinguish them in a general way.

Burden of proof

1.41   The 'burden of proof' is the idea that it is up to someone to prove their side of a dispute. It is used when there is something that has to be shown to be

---

the case in order for HB/CTR law to apply at all. Two examples are:

* when a claimant first makes a claim for HB/CTR, there is at the outset no evidence – and so it is for the claimant to support the claim by supplying the authority with all the evidence it reasonably requires (para. 5.13);

* when the authority says that a recoverable HB overpayment has occurred, the authority must have evidence to support this (para. 18.11).

1.42   The 'burden of proof' is also used when a decision cannot be made by the 'balance of probability' because there is no evidence either way, or the evidence that does exist is exactly balanced. In these cases the side with the burden loses unless they can supply evidence that adjusts the balance of probability in their favour.

Balance of probability

1.43   The 'balance of probability' is the idea that in the end a decision has to be made or nothing would ever get done. It is used when there is a disagreement about the facts. In such a case, the authority must consider the available evidence to decide what the true position is. The evidence each way must be weighed up and the 'facts' of the case are those supported by the greater weight of evidence. There does not have to be absolute certainty. It is because HB/CTR decisions are matters of civil law that the appropriate test is the 'balance of probability' (not 'beyond reasonable doubt', which is a test used in criminal law).

Examples: Relevant facts and balance of probability

1. The claimant and the authority agree that the claimant's grown-up son is living with him.

    The facts are not in dispute, so the facts are that the son does live there.

2. The authority receives reports from its HB/CTR visiting officer that a claimant's grown-up son is living with him and has been there on four consecutive visits, on one occasion coming down from his bedroom when the visiting officer arrived. The claimant says his son is not living there, but it is his correspondence address. He also says he does not know where the son is living.

    The facts are in dispute, but it is suggested here that, weighing up the evidence, it is more likely than not that the son is living there. So the facts are (on the balance of probability) that he is.

3. Following on from 2, six months later, the son makes his own claim for HB from another address and the authority accepts that he is living at that other address.

    Following this change of circumstances, the facts are no longer in dispute, so the facts are that the son is not (any longer) living with his father.

Applying the law

1.44   The HB and CTR schemes are governed by law passed by Parliament (paras. 1.31-37). The starting point for applying the law is that it means exactly what it says – though many words have special meanings in HB/CTR (as described in this guide) and precedents can affect how the law is interpreted (para. 1.46).

1.45   Having worked out which piece of law applies and what it means, it must then be applied to the case in hand. For example, whether or not a claimant's son counts as a non-dependant can only be answered by considering the legal definition of 'non-dependant' and applying it to the facts. Part of the definition is that the person must 'normally reside' with the claimant. So if the facts are that the son normally resides somewhere else but visits the claimant from time to time, then as a matter of law he cannot be a non-dependant.

Precedents from courts and Upper Tribunals

1.46   When there are 'precedents' (also called 'case law'), these should be followed. A 'precedent' is a binding decision by a court or an Upper Tribunal (para. 19.67) on a case which is relevant to the case in hand. For example, in deciding whether a person 'normally resides' with a claimant (para. 1.45) there is a precedent in the decision *Kadhim v Brent LBC* (para. 4.45) which may well have a bearing on other cases. Generally speaking, precedents from one part of the UK are regarded as binding in other parts of the UK (for example Great Britain precedent is taken into account in Northern Ireland: *C001/03-04(HB)*); precedents from HB and from the former CTB scheme are very likely to be taken into account in similar CTR decisions; and precedents from other parts of the social security system may be binding on similar HB/CTR decisions (e.g. on backdating: para. 5.58).

1.47   Case law from the courts is given throughout this guide, and a list is given in appendix 2 (which also gives details of how to find the case law online). Most Upper Tribunal decisions are available online [www]. Since 1st January 2010 Upper Tribunal decisions are cited using the 'neutral citation' (e.g. *[2011] UKUT 136 AAC* – see also para. 19.68); the file reference (e.g. *CH/3853/2001*) is used for older decisions.

Judgment and discretion

1.48   Sometimes a decision about HB or CTR requires the authority to use its judgment. The law uses terms like 'reasonable', 'appropriate', 'good cause' or 'special circumstances' to show that the authority has a judgment to make. Examples of judgments are:

+ whether it is 'reasonable' for the authority to award benefit on two homes in the case of person who has fled violence (para. 3.12);

1.47   www.osscsc.gov.uk/aspx/default.aspx (Great Britain)
       www.dsdni.gov.uk/index/law_and_legislation/ni_digest_of_case_law/nidoc_database.htm
       (Northern Ireland)

- how much it is 'appropriate' to restrict the rent in exempt accommodation (para. 9.24);
- whether a claimant has 'good cause' for a late claim (para. 5.58);
- whether a claimant has 'special circumstances' for their delay in notifying an advantageous change in circumstances relating to HB (para. 17.14).

1.49   And sometimes a decision about HB or CTR allows the authority to use its discretion. A discretion differs from a judgment in the sense that an authority may choose what to do. The law usually says that an authority 'may' do something to show that it has a discretion. Examples of discretion are:

- whether to award discretionary HB or CTR (paras. 23.2 and 10.40);
- whether to recover a recoverable overpayment of HB (para. 18.26);
- the appropriate assessment period for estimating earnings (para. 14.7).

Judicial review

1.50   When using judgment or discretion, authorities are bound by the principles of administrative law evolved by the courts. If they ignore these they can be challenged by applying to the High Court (or in Scotland the Court of Session) for 'judicial review'. Examples of when a challenge may be successful are if the authority:

- fails to consider each case on its merits, instead applying predetermined rules;
- takes into account matters which it ought not to consider;
- does not consider matters which it ought to take into account; or
- reaches a conclusion that no reasonable authority could have come to (what is reasonable here means rational rather than what is the best decision).

1.51   For more on judicial review, see *Judicial Review Proceedings,* Jonathan Manning, Legal Action Group; or *Judicial Review in Scotland,* Tom Mullen and Tony Prosser, Wiley.

HB guidance: DWP

1.52   The DWP (Department for Work and Pensions) is the central government department responsible for HB policy. It publishes guidance on the schemes which is often very useful and is referred to throughout this guide. But (like this guide itself) it is guidance not law: *CH/3853/2001.*

1.53   DWP guidance includes the following:

- *Housing Benefit and Council Tax Benefit Guidance Manual* (GM);
- *Subsidy Guidance Manual;*
- *HB/CTB Overpayments Guide* (OG);
- *Guidance on Discretionary Housing Payments;*
- circulars in the 'A' series (about adjudication and operations);

- circulars in the 'F' series (about fraud);
- circulars in the 'S' series (about statistics and subsidy);
- circulars in the 'G' series (about general matters); and
- circulars in the 'U' series (about urgent matters).

1.54 The manuals are available online [www] as are the 'A', 'S', 'G' and 'U' circulars. The 'F' circulars are not available to the public. Strictly speaking, DWP circulars do not apply to Northern Ireland although the authorities there generally accept the validity of 'A' circulars (unless the law in Northern Ireland is different).

CTR guidance

1.55 Government guidance on CTR is the responsibility of the DCLG (Department of Communities and Local Government) in England, of the Welsh Government and Scottish Government in Wales and Scotland respectively.

1.54   www.dwp.gov.uk/local-authority-staff/housing-benefit/claims-processing/operational-manuals/
www.dwp.gov.uk/local-authority-staff/housing benefit/user-communications/

2 Who is eligible for HB/CTR?

2.1   This chapter explains who can get HB and/or CTR. It describes:

♦   the basic conditions for getting HB/CTR;

♦   who is eligible for HB/CTR;

♦   who is excluded from HB/CTR;

♦   what payments HB can meet;

♦   liability for rent; and

♦   non-commercial, 'contrived', and other lettings where HB cannot be paid.

Basic conditions for getting HB/CTR

2.2   To get HB, the claimant must satisfy all the conditions in paragraph 2.3. To get CTR the claimant must satisfy all the conditions in paragraph 2.4. Once an award of HB/CTR is made, it continues until the claimant no longer satisfies all those conditions, at which point it ends (para. 17.37).

Housing benefit

2.3   The basic conditions for HB are:

♦   the claimant is liable (or treated as liable) to pay rent for a dwelling in the UK (paras. 2.14, 2.27 and 2.33), and/or in Northern Ireland rates (chapter 11);

♦   the claimant occupies that dwelling as their normal home (chapter 3);

♦   the claimant (or someone on their behalf) makes a valid claim and provides relevant information and evidence (chapter 5);

♦   the claimant is not a member of an excluded group (para. 2.8);

♦   the claimant's capital does not exceed £16,000 (para. 13.13) – but this does not apply if the claimant is on guarantee credit;

♦   any deductions for non-dependants (para. 6.16) do not exceed the claimant's eligible rent (and/or in Northern Ireland rates);

♦   the claimant's income is not too high (para. 2.5); and

♦   the result of the calculation of HB is at least 50p per week (para. 6.13) – but in Northern Ireland this does not apply to HB for rates.

There are also rules about when a person is treated as not being liable to make payments even though they have a legal liability to do so (para. 2.35).

2.3   AA 1(1),(1A),(1B); CBA 130(1),(4),134(1)(4); NIAA 1(1),(1A),(1B); NICBA 129(1), 130(1),(3)

Council tax rebate

2.4   The basic conditions for CTR are:

- the claimant is liable to pay council tax in respect of a dwelling (para. 10.8);
- the claimant has their sole or main residence in that dwelling (para. 10.8) – and in Scotland they must also occupy it as their normal home (chapter 3);
- the claimant (or someone on their behalf) makes a valid claim and provides relevant information and evidence (chapter 5);
- the claimant is not a member of an excluded group (para. 2.7);
- the claimant's capital does not exceed £16,000 (para. 13.13) – but this does not apply if the claimant is on guarantee credit, and nor does it apply to second adult rebate;
- any deductions for non-dependants (para. 6.16) do not exceed the claimant's eligible council tax; and
- the claimant's income is not too high (para. 2.5) – but this does not apply to second adult rebate.

However, in England (and to a lesser extent in Wales) the details of the CTR scheme can vary locally (para. 10.22) – for example, the £16,000 capital limit is lower in the areas of some English authorities

How low must the claimant's income be?

2.5   A claimant's income is low enough for them to get HB/CTR if any of the following applies:

- they are in receipt of JSA(IB), ESA(IR), income support or guarantee credit, or treated as being in receipt of those benefits (para. 6.6 and table 6.1);
- they have no income (para. 6.10);
- their income is less than or equal to their applicable amount (para. 6.10); or
- their income is greater than their applicable amount but the 'taper' calculation (para. 6.11) still leaves an entitlement to HB/CTR.

Examples and types of HB and CTR

2.6   Examples of the cases in which a claimant can get HB or CTR or both are in table 2.1. HB is awarded as a rent rebate (para. 16.16) to people renting from a council or the Northern Ireland Housing Executive. HB is awarded as a rent allowance (para. 16.19) to people renting from other landlords. CTR (and in Northern Ireland HB for rates) is awarded as a rebate (paras. 16.13-14 and 11.18-19).

2.4   LGFA 13A, sch 1A, sch 1B

Table 2.1: Examples of who can get HB/CTR

People who own their home	Not eligible for HB (because not liable for rent) Eligible for CTR
People in shared ownership schemes	Eligible for HB (on their rent) Eligible for CTR
People renting self-contained accommodation	Eligible for HB Eligible for CTR
People renting non-self-contained accommodation	Eligible for HB Not eligible for CTR (because not liable for council tax)

Exclusions from HB/CTR

Exclusions from CTR

2.7 The following people cannot get CTR:

◆ full-time students who are not liable for council tax (paras. 10.11-12);

◆ most other full-time students (para. 22.23 – but the rules for second adult rebate are different: paras. 6.35-44);

◆ some migrants and recent arrivals to the UK (chapter 20);

◆ all under-18-year-olds (because they cannot be liable for council tax: para. 10.12);

◆ people who are severely mentally impaired (unless they are liable for council tax, which is unusual: paras. 10.11-12);

◆ owners and other landlords of unoccupied dwellings (para. 10.9);

◆ owners and other landlords of houses in multiple occupation (para. 10.9).

Exclusions from HB

2.8 The following people cannot get HB:

◆ most full-time students (para. 22.23);

◆ some migrants and recent arrivals to the UK (chapter 20);

◆ many under-18-year-old care leavers (para. 2.9);

◆ members of religious orders (para. 2.13); and

◆ people on universal credit (paras. 1.8-9 and 23.33) – unless they are in 'exempt accommodation' (paras. 9.4-6).

Care leavers aged under 18

2.9   Certain 16-year-olds and 17-year-olds who have left local authority care are not entitled to HB (paras. 2.10-12); instead responsibility for providing support falls on the social services authority.

2.10   Except as described below (para. 2.12) a 16 or 17-year-old is not entitled to HB if he or she:

* has been looked after (in Scotland, looked after and 'accommodated') by social services for a period or periods amounting to at least 13 weeks in total which began after he or she reached the age of 14 and which ended after reaching the age of 16; or
* in England, Wales or Northern Ireland, would have satisfied the first condition but for the fact that at the time they reached the age of 16 they were in hospital or detained in an institution as the result of a court order.

2.11   In calculating the 13 weeks, any periods of four weeks or less spent in respite care are ignored provided that at the end of each period the child or young person was returned to the care of their parent (or the person with parental responsibility). In Scotland 'accommodated' includes instances where the child was placed under a supervision requirement following a children's hearing.

2.12   The exclusion from HB does not apply:

* in England, Wales and Northern Ireland to a child/young person who was placed with a family for a continuous period of six months or more unless that placement broke down and the child ceased to live with the person concerned. This rule applies whether the six month period started before or after social services finished looking after the child;
* in Scotland if the child/young person was placed by social services with a member of their family aged at least 18 or with the person who was looking after them before they went into care.

Members of certain religious orders

2.13   Members of a religious order who are fully maintained by it, including monks and nuns in enclosed orders, are not eligible for HB (or CTR because the owner is liable). The DWP (GM A3.257) points out that members of religious communities (as opposed to religious orders) are often eligible for HB since they frequently do paid work or retain their own possessions.

2.9   Children Act 1989 sch 2 para 19B; Children (Leaving Care) Act 2000 s6;
        Children (Leaving Care) Act (Northern Ireland) 2002 s6;
        SI 2001 No 2189; SI 2001 No 2874; SI 2004 No 747; SI 2004 No 1732; NISR 2005 No 221

2.12   SI 2004 No 747 Reg (2)(2)(c); NISR 2005 No 324 Reg 2(2)

2.13   HB 9(1)(j); HB60+ 9(1)(j); NIHB 9(1)(j); NIHB60+ 9(1)(j)

Which housing costs can HB meet?

2.14 HB is available towards a claimant's 'eligible rent'. As explained in chapter 7, this typically includes all or part of what the claimant is charged. This section describes the special rules for certain types of accommodation. (For night shelters, see para. 3.6.)

Owner-occupiers and long leaseholders

2.15 A person who owns their home, or whose partner does, is not eligible for HB. The same applies to someone with the right to sell the freehold only with the consent of other joint owners. It also applies to a long leaseholder. A long lease is one which was for more than 21 years when it was first granted, and complies with the legal formalities of being a lease: *R(H) 3/07*. However, owners and leaseholders may get help through their passport benefits (chapter 25).

Shared owners

2.16 A shared ownership scheme (also called equity sharing) means that the person is part-buying and part-renting their home – which can be from a social landlord or from a private firm. In Great Britain a shared owner is eligible for HB on their rent (paras. 9.90-91, and for mortgage interest see chapter 25).

Co-owners

2.17 Payments under a co-ownership scheme are not eligible for HB. A co-ownership scheme is one in which the tenant is a member who will be entitled to a payment related to the value of the home when their membership ends.

Co-op tenants

2.18 Co-operative tenants are eligible for HB for their rent provided they have no more than a nominal equity share in the property.

Hire purchase and credit sale agreements

2.19 Payments under a hire purchase (for example to buy a mobile home) or credit sale agreement are not eligible for help under the HB scheme.

Rental purchase and conditional sale agreements

2.20 Payments under a rental purchase or conditional sale agreement are eligible for HB, except any element that relates to furniture or other moveable goods.

2.15   HB 2(1), 12(2)(a),(c),(f); HB60+ 2(1), 12(2)(a),(c),(f); NIHB 2(1), 13(2)(a); NIHB60+ 2(1), 13(2)(a)

2.16   HB 2(1), 12(2)(a); HB60+ 2(1), 12(2)(a)

2.17   HB 2(1), 12(2)(b); HB60+ 2(1), 12(2)(b)

2.18   HB 12(1); HB60+ 12(1); NIHB 13(1); NIHB60+ 13(1)

2.19   HB 12(2)(d); HB60+ 12(2)(d); NIHB 13(2)(b); NIHB60+ 13(2)(b)

2.20   HB 12(1)(i),(2)(d); HB60+ 12(1)(i),(2)(d); NIHB 13(1)(h),(2)(h); NIHB60+ 13(1)(h),(2)(b)

These agreements are ones in which the whole or part of the purchase price is paid in instalments over a specified period of time and completion of the sale is deferred until the final instalment has been paid (GM A4.140).

Houseboats, mobile homes and caravans

2.21   Houseboat mooring charges and berthing fees, and caravan and mobile home site charges are eligible for HB and so is the rent if it is rented out. 'Houseboat' can include a canal narrow boat *(CH/4250/2007)*. 'Caravan and mobile home' includes those of people with a nomadic or travelling cultural tradition (regardless of their race or origin) – including travellers, travelling show people, and those who no longer travel for reasons of health or age – for whom there are also rules about their eligible rent (para. 9.36) and how HB is paid (para. 16.17).

Other miscellaneous housing costs met by IS/JSA/ESA

2.22   For working age claims certain other miscellaneous housing costs that are met through IS/JSA(IB)/ESA(IR) (chapter 25) such as payments for a tent and its pitch are excluded from HB. If an HB claimant receives help with housing costs through IS/JSA/ESA for the first time (including homeowners: para. 2.15) HB can continue for a further four weeks.

Care homes and independent hospitals

2.23   Residents of 'care homes' and 'independent hospitals' are not eligible for HB. In Scotland the equivalent institutions are known as the 'care home service' and 'independent healthcare service' and in Northern Ireland 'residential care homes', 'nursing homes' and 'independent hospitals'. If the residence is temporary see paragraphs 3.22-23, 3.33-35 and table 3.1.

Bail and probation hostels

2.24   Payments on a bail or probation hostel are not eligible for HB. See table 3.1 for HB towards the normal home while absent.

Crown tenants and former Crown tenants

2.25   In Great Britain, all Crown or tenants of a government department are excluded from HB, except homes managed by the Crown Estate Commissioners or tenants of the Duchy of Cornwall or Duchy of Lancaster. In Northern Ireland, only tenants of the Ministry of Defence are excluded from HB. Tenants excluded by this rule can get help towards their rent on a passport benefit (chapter 25) or from a voluntary scheme run by their landlord.

2.21   HB sch 2 para 3; HB60+ sch 2 para 3

2.22   HB 11(2),(4); NIHB 11(2),(4)

2.23   HB 2(1), 9(1)(k),(4); HB60+ 9(1)(k),(4); NIHB 2(1), 9(1)(k),(4); NIHB60+ 9(1)(k),(4); CPR sch 3 para 9; NICPR sch 3 para 9

2.24   HB 7(5); HB60+ 7(5); NIHB 7(5); NIHB60+ 7(5)

2.25   HB 2(1) 12(2)(e); HB60+ 2(1) 12(2)(e); NIHB 2(1) 13(2)(c); NIHB60+ 2(1) 13(2)(c)

2.26 Former Crown tenants (and licensees) are eligible for HB. This applies when their agreement has been terminated but they are continuing to occupy and liable to pay mesne or violent profits. (See GM A3.213.)

Liability to pay rent

2.27 The general rule is that a claimant is eligible for HB only if he or she is liable (has a legal obligation or duty) to pay rent for the home.

The meaning of 'rent'

2.28 The term 'rent' has various meanings in different branches of the law. As far as HB is concerned, all of the types of payment shown in table 2.2 count as rent. In chapters 7- 9, the term 'actual rent' is used to mean the total of all the payments in table 2.2 which the claimant is liable to pay on his or her home.

Table 2.2: Payments counted as rent for HB purposes

- Rent in its ordinary sense, whether under a tenancy or licence, including board and lodging payments and payments for 'use and occupation'.
- 'Mesne profits' in England, Wales and Northern Ireland or 'violent profits' in Scotland (paid after a tenancy or right to occupy is terminated).
- Houseboat mooring charges and berthing fees and caravan and mobile home site charges (even if owned by the claimant, and in addition to rental if not owned).
- Payments made by residents of charitable almshouses.
- Payments under rental purchase agreements.
- Payments for crofts and croft land in Scotland.

The nature of liability for rent

2.29 Liability for rent arises under a tenancy, but for HB includes any kind of 'periodical payments' made in return for the right to occupy (para. 2.28). There is no requirement for a written agreement (GM A3.50): word of mouth alone may be sufficient: *R v Poole BC ex p Ross*. The landlord must normally have a sufficient legal interest in the dwelling to grant the letting, but exceptions can arise: *CH/2959/2006*.

2.30 Most landlords would expect to end the agreement if the tenant does not pay and large arrears may indicate that there is no further liability:

2.27   CBA 130(1)(a); NICBA 129(1)(a); HB 8(1)(a); NIHB 8(1)(a); NIHB60 I 8(1)(a)

T2.2   HB 12(1); HB60+ 12(1); NIHB 13(1); NIHB60+ 13(1)

CH/1849/2007. However, the fact that there has been no payment of the rent 'even for an extensive period, does not of itself mean there is no legal liability' and nor is this necessarily implied by the fact that the rent actually changing hands is less than the rent on the tenancy agreement: *[2010] UKUT 43 AAC.*

2.31 It is not possible in law to grant a tenancy to oneself, nor can liability arise under a tenancy 'granted' to someone who already has the right to occupy that dwelling. For example, if a couple are joint owners of a property and one leaves, the absent member cannot 'grant' a tenancy to the remaining occupier.

2.32 A claimant who is unable to act, or is aged under 18, may have someone appointed to act for them (paras. 5.5-7). If they do not and are incapable of understanding the agreement they are entering, this can make the agreement void under Scottish law: *[2011] UKUT 354 AAC;* but does not do so in the rest of the UK: *CH/2121/2006* and *[2012] UKUT 12 (AAC).*

Treating a claimant as liable even when he or she is not

2.33 Any of the following, even if not liable to pay rent, are treated by law as liable, and are therefore eligible for HB:

(a) the partner of the liable person (including the partner of a full-time student who is not eligible for HB: para. 22.24);

(b) a former partner of the liable person who has to make the payments in order to continue to live in the home because the liable person is not doing so;

(c) anyone who has to make the payments to continue to live in the home because the liable person is not making them and the authority considers it reasonable to treat him or her as liable to make them;

(d) a person whose liability is waived by the landlord as reasonable compensation for repairs or redecoration work actually carried out by the tenant – but only up to eight benefit weeks in respect of any one waiver;

(e) someone who has actually met his or her liability before claiming.

If the rent is varied, the claimant is treated as liable for the revised amount due.

Examples: Treated as liable to pay rent

A claimant has been deserted by her partner. Although she is not the tenant, the landlord will allow her to remain in the property if she continues to pay the rent. She should be treated as liable if her former partner is not paying.

A claimant is the son of a council tenant. He takes over responsibility for paying rent while his father is working abroad for two years. The son should be treated as liable if it is reasonable to do so.

2.33 HB 8(1)(b)-(e),(2); HB60+ 8(1)(b)-(e),(2); NIHB 8(1)(b)-(e),(2); NIHB60+ 8(1)(b)-(e),(2)

Table 2.3: Non-commercial agreements

◆ *General principles in reaching a decision on commerciality:* Each case must be decided on its facts and is a matter of judgment *(R(H) 1/03)* but the concept is 'notoriously imprecise and difficult' *(CH/2491/2007)*. A letting will be non-commercial if the main basis on which it is made is not commercial even if the original purpose was commercial, so long as the reasons for the change can be identified: *CH/3497/2005*.

◆ *Relevant matters to be taken into account:* These are not limited to the financial relationship: all the terms of the agreement should be considered *(R v Sutton LBC ex parte Partridge)*. The important factor is whether the arrangements are 'arms length' or more akin to arrangements between close relatives contributing towards their keep or household expenses: *R v Sheffield HBRB ex parte Smith*.

◆ *Sham legal agreements:* The true factual basis of the arrangements is what matters: if they indicate that the letting is a 'truly personal arrangement' then it will be non-commercial even though the written documents give the appearance of legal liability: *CH/3282/2006*.

◆ *Lettings to family members and/or people with disabilities:* A letting by a parent to a disabled child could be commercial. Whilst a family arrangement may indicate that the letting is non-commercial it is one factor and not decisive. The fact that the landlord might not evict but accept a lower rent if HB was not awarded is not evidence that it is non-commercial but bowing to the inevitable. Proper weight should be given to all factors and focussing on one aspect only (such as care and support) is grounds for appeal *(CH/296/2004)*. However, more recent decisions have found that the legislation is 'ill-suited to providing humane outcomes in these cases' and have sometimes found these arrangements to be non-commercial *(CH/1096/2008 and CH/2491/2007)*.

◆ *Lettings to former foster children:* An old DWP circular (HB/CTB A30/95) advised that arrangements for paying rent (e.g. when the child reaches age 18) should not be treated as non-commercial.

◆ *Personal friendship between the parties:* Of itself this cannot turn a commercial arrangement into a non commercial one *(R v Poole BC ex parte Ross* and *CH/4854/2003)*. Nor can the fact that the claimant cared for the landlord after an accident: *[2009] UKUT 13 AAC*.

◆ *Arrangements that take into account the claimant's religion:* If an arrangement has all the characteristics of something that is non-commercial, the fact it takes into account the religious beliefs of the claimant cannot make it commercial. Nor does this fact infringe their right to freedom of religion *(R(H) 8/04)*.

2.34   The rule in paragraph 2.33(b) and (c) is designed to help someone who could arrange to become the tenant but who has not (yet) done so remain in their home. It can be used if the tenant has been absent for too long to get HB (para. 3.32), or has left permanently, and a partner or other person remains. The liable person need not be an individual; they could be a company or other body *(R(H) 5/05)* – including, presumably, the executors of a deceased tenant. As regards what is reasonable (in relation to (c)), if the only reason the liable person is not paying is because they are excluded from HB (paras. 2.35-56) then, it may not be reasonable to award HB to someone else *(CH/606/2005)*.

Table 2.4: Case law on contrived liabilities

- *Liability for rent and taking advantage of the HB scheme:* These are separate considerations should not be confused: *CSHB/718/2002.*

- *The circumstances and intentions of both parties are relevant:* The authority must consider these before reaching a conclusion that the tenancy is contrived. Particular consideration should be to the consequences if HB is not paid. If it seems unlikely that the landlord will ask the claimant to leave so that the dwelling can be re-let then this is evidence that the letting is contrived: *R v Sutton HBRB ex parte Keegan.*

- *Letting to relatives:* Except where the letting is excluded from HB by one of the other provisions in this section (paras. 2.38-55) accommodation provided by a parent to their children is not of itself evidence of a contrived letting: *R v Solihull HBRB ex parte Simpson.*

- *Letting to people on low incomes generally:* The mere fact that the claimant could not afford the rent cannot be taken as evidence that the letting is contrived although in extreme cases a high rent may support that contention. Before the authority can reach a conclusion that the tenancy is contrived there must be clear evidence that this is so, it cannot merely be inferred (*Solihull* case).

- *Letting to people on low incomes to make a profit:* There is no objection to landlords doing this and landlords may even organise their affairs to 'maximise the amounts payable by HB'. In doing so 'the size of the charges and the profit [that results] are relevant [...] only in so far as they show abuse' (see next bullet): *CH/39/2007.*

- *Charging higher rents to groups outside the normal rent restriction rules:* These types of arrangement will usually be contrived. For example lettings to vulnerable tenants (para. 9.21); or complex arrangements designed to take advantage of specific rules such as 'exempt accommodation' (paras. 9.22-30). *(R v Manchester CC ex parte Baragrove Properties; CH/3933/2006 and CH/136/2007).*

'Contrived' lettings and other exclusions from HB

2.35 The remainder of this chapter describes the circumstances in which a claimant cannot get HB, even though he or she is in fact liable for rent. The law does this by saying the claimant is treated as not liable to make the payments.

Non-commercial agreements

2.36 The claimant is not eligible for HB if the agreement under which he or she occupies is not on a commercial basis. In reaching its decision the authority must consider whether the agreement contains terms which are not legally enforceable. The regulations do not define what constitutes a commercial basis and how each should be decided but this has been explained by the courts and tribunals. Table 2.3 provides a summary of the case law and guidance.

Contrived liability for rent

2.37 The claimant is not eligible for HB if the authority is satisfied that his or her liability 'was created to take advantage of the HB scheme' (usually called a 'contrived' tenancy). The regulations do not describe what constitutes a contrived tenancy but this has been explained by the courts and tribunals. Table 2.4 provides a summary of the case law and further guidance can be found in GM paragraphs A3.310-319.

Landlord a close relative residing in the dwelling

2.38 If the claimant's landlord is a 'close relative' (para. 2.39) of the claimant, or of the claimant's partner, and the landlord also resides in the dwelling (para. 2.40), the claimant is not eligible for HB.

2.39 A 'close relative' is:

* a parent, step-parent or parent-in-law; or
* brother or sister; or
* son, son-in-law, daughter, daughter-in-law, step-son, step-daughter; or
* the partner of any of the above.

2.40 The terms 'brother' and 'sister' include 'half-brothers' and 'half-sisters' (GM paras. A3.240-241 and *R(SB) 22/87*), but not 'step-brothers' or 'step-sisters'.

2.41 For the landlord to count as 'residing in' the same dwelling as the claimant (para. 2.38), it is not necessary to share all the accommodation, merely some essential living accommodation: *CH/542/2006*. Similarly, if the tenant has exclusive possession of one room in a house, this does not mean that the

---

2.36   HB 3(4),9(1)(a),(2); HB60+ 3(4),9(1)(a),(2); NIHB 3(4),9(1)(a),(2); NIHB60+ 3(4),9(1)(a),(2)

2.37   HB 9(1)(l); HB60 + 9(1)(l); NIHB 9(1)(l); NIHB60+ 9(1)(l)

2.38   HB 9(1)(b); HB60+ 9(1)(b); NIHB 9(1)(b); NIHB60 + 9(1)(b)

2.39   HB 2(1); HB60+ 2(1); NIHB 2(1); NIHB60 + 2(1)

landlord is not residing with him or her: *CH/3656/204*. Despite the slight difference of wording, the definition of 'residing with' (para. 4.43) also applies here (GM A3.238).

Renting a former joint home from an ex-partner

2.42   If a couple separate and the one remaining in the home, or a new partner, makes payments to the one who has left, they are not eligible for HB.

2.43   The rule would apply if the informal shared living arrangements changed but the dwelling overall did not, for example, if a lodger formed a relationship with their landlord but then reverted to being a tenant. This exclusion does not constitute discrimination under the Human Rights Act: *R (Painter) v Carmarthenshire County Council HBRB* and *[2011] UKUT 301 AAC*.

Responsibility for the landlord's child

2.44   A claimant is not eligible for HB if they or their partner are responsible for the landlord's child (i.e. someone under the age of 16). The DWP (GM A3.269) emphasises that 'responsibility for a child' means more than 'cares for'.

2.45   This can be a difficult rule to interpret as it blurs certain established concepts so far as means-tested benefits are concerned. It would appear to apply where the 'landlord' is the parent, or has adopted a child, but where the child is nevertheless considered to be part of the claimant's family for JSA(IB), IS or HB purposes. This rule has been found not to be contrary to the Human Rights Act: *R v Secretary of State for Social Security, ex parte Tucker*.

Certain trusts for the benefit of the landlord's close relative

2.46   A trust is an arrangement whereby the legal ownership (title) of property is separated from its benefits (such as the right to live in it or receive income). The title is held by the trustees who ensure that its benefits are delivered for use by someone else, 'the beneficiary'.

2.47   A claimant is not eligible for HB if his or her landlord is a trustee of a trust of which one of the following is a trustee or a beneficiary:

+ the claimant or partner; or
+ the claimant's or partner's close relative (para. 2.39) if the close relative 'resides with' (para. 4.43) the claimant; or
+ the claimant's, or partner's, former partner;

unless in each case the authority is satisfied that the liability was not intended to take advantage of the HB scheme. 'Beneficiary' here means someone who could benefit from the trust by occupying the property in question: *CH/4/2008*.

2.42   HB 9(1)(c); HB60+ 9(1)(c); NIHB 9(1)(c); NIHB60+ 9(1)(c)

2.47   HB 9(1)(e),(3); HB60+ 9(1)(e),(3); NIHB 9(1)(e),(3); NIHB60+ 9(1)(e),(3)

2.48   A claimant is not eligible for HB if his or her landlord is a trustee of a trust of which the claimant's or partner's child is a beneficiary. Unlike in the previous paragraph, this rule has no exception.

Renting from a company of which one is a director or an employee

2.49   A claimant is not eligible for HB if his or her landlord is a company of which one of the following is a director or an employee:

* the claimant or partner; or
* the claimant's or partner's close relative (para. 2.39) if the close relative 'resides with' (para. 4.43) the claimant; or
* the claimant's, or partner's, former partner;

unless in each case the claimant satisfies the authority that the liability was not intended to take advantage of the HB scheme. Note also that this rule does not apply if a claimant is employed by a company and rents from a director of the company (since a director is not the company itself).

2.50   The DWP advises (GM para. A3.271) that a 'company' means a registered company. This can be checked with Companies House for any part of the UK and can be done online [www] for a small fee (normally £1.00).

Former non-dependants

2.51   A claimant is not eligible for HB if:

* he or she was, at any time prior to the creation of the rent liability, a non-dependant of someone who resided in the dwelling; and
* that person continues to reside in the dwelling,

unless the authority is satisfied that the liability was not intended to take advantage of the HB scheme.

Former owners (sale and rent back or mortgage rescue)

2.52   A claimant is not eligible for HB if:

* he or she, or a partner, previously owned the dwelling (including owning it on a long lease: para. 2.15); and
* owned it within the last five years (even if the claimant subsequently moved out and then back in: *CH/3698/2008*),

unless the claimant is able to satisfy the authority that he or she or a partner could not have continued to live in the dwelling without letting go of ownership.

2.48   HB 9(1)(f); HB60+ 9(1)(f); NIHB 9(1)(f); NIHB60+ 9(1)(f)

2.49   HB 9(1)(e),(3); HB60+ 9(1)(e),(3); NIHB 9(1)(e),(3); NIHB60+ 9(1)(e),(3)

2.50   www.companies-house.gov.uk

2.51   HB 9(1)(g),(3); HB60+ 9(1)(g),(3); NIHB 9(1)(g),(3); NIHB60+ 9(1)(g),(3)

2.52   HB 9(1)(h),(ha); HB60+ 9(1)(h),(ha); NIHB 9(1)(h),(ha); NIHB60+ 9(1)(h),(ha)

Good advice on this is given in DWP circular HB/CTB A5/2009 in the light of the increasing number of these cases, also known as 'sale and rent back' cases.

2.53 Whether the claimant could have remained in the dwelling is a practical test based on fact – and in exceptional cases this can include the claimant's perceptions if the stress of the situation they were in forced a quick sale: *R(H) 6/07*. Authorities are entitled to examine why the claimant gave up ownership and what other options they might have had, such as getting work to finance the mortgage, taking in a tenant, etc: *CH/1586/2004*. The claimant is not expected to act irresponsibly (e.g. using a credit card to pay mortgage arrears): *CH/2340/2008*. The claimant may have had no real choice if a mortgage lender would have sought possession and a housing association used a mortgage rescue scheme to buy the property and rent it back to them (GM A3.282-286).

Tied accommodation

2.54 A claimant is not eligible for HB if his or her, or a partner's, occupation of the dwelling is a condition of employment by the landlord. The DWP advises (GM A3.291) that this test should not be taken to mean 'as a result of the employment'. A retired employee, for example, may continue to live in previously tied accommodation but this would no longer be as a condition of employment by the landlord, and so this rule would not prevent eligibility for HB.

Illegal and unlawful tenancies and sub-tenancies

2.55 Sub-tenancies which are created in breach of a clause in the head lease not to sublet or assign the tenancy do not prevent the assignment or sub-letting from being valid between the head tenant and sub-tenant: *Governors of Peabody Donation Fund v Higgins* (not a HB case). Such lettings are unlawful rather than illegal and expose the head tenant to eviction for breach of the agreement. Given that there is a legal liability for rent it seems that these lettings are eligible for HB, unless it is also a letting to which paragraphs 2.35-54 above apply.

2.56 An illegal letting is one in which its creation would necessarily involve committing a criminal offence. An example would be where a landlord lets a dwelling which he or she knows is in contravention of a Housing Act prohibition order. In contrast to unlawful contracts, illegal contracts are generally not binding and so would not be eligible for HB. Where a letting was not illegal at the time it was created (e.g. prior to a prohibition order) it seems likely it would remain binding until the end of the next rental period.

2.56   HB 9(1)(i); HB60+ 9(1)(i); NIHB 9(1)(i); NIHB60+ 9(1)(i)

3 Occupying the home

3.1 This chapter explains:

* what it means to occupy somewhere as a home;
* when a claimant can get HB, and in Scotland CTR, before moving into their home, after moving out, and on two homes;
* the HB/CTR rules about temporary absences from home; and
* the Scottish CTR rules about absences from Great Britain.

Overview

3.2 HB/CTR can only be awarded on a dwelling if:

* in HB, the claimant occupies it as their home;
* in CTR in England and Wales, the claimant is resident in it;
* in CTR in Scotland, the claimant meets both of the above conditions.

Residence is described in paragraphs 10.8-9. Occupation as a home is described below (and see also paras. 3.7-45).

Occupation as a home

3.3 HB, and in Scotland CTR, is awarded on accommodation the claimant occupies as a home. This means the dwelling which is 'normally occupied as a home' by:

* the claimant; or
* if they have a family (para. 4.8), the claimant and their family *(CH/2521/2002)*.

Except as described later (paras. 3.7-19, 3.25-26 and 3.29), it means only one home.

Normally occupied as a home

3.4 Whether a dwelling is 'normally occupied as a home' is a question of fact to be decided in each case, and is not restricted to considering where someone's 'centre of interests' is *(CH/1786/2005)*. It usually means more than simply being liable for rent/council tax: it means being physically present – but exceptions can arise. For example, a claimant aged 87 who had terminated her former tenancy, whose family had moved her furniture and possessions into her new home, but who was unable to move because she was taken ill at the last minute, was held to be 'normally occupying her new home *(R(H) 9/05)*. However,

---

3.3   CDA 130(1)(a), NICBA 129(1)(a); HB 7(1); HB60+ 7(1); NIHB 7(1); NIHB60+ 7(1); CTS 5(1); CTS60+ 5(1)

accommodation occupied only for a holiday or business purposes is not a home and therefore is not eligible.

3.5 In considering which home the claimant normally occupies, the authority must have regard to any other dwelling occupied by the claimant or family, no matter whether it is here or abroad. The DWP advises (GM para. A3.356) that this requirement is not intended to exclude from eligibility someone who has set up home in this country but whose family, no longer being part of his or her household, remain abroad.

Night shelters

3.5 A night shelter may or may not meet the definition of a 'dwelling [...] occupied as [the claimant's] home.' If it does not, the claimant is not eligible for HB (paras. 2.2-2.3). This is the effect of *[2013] UKUT 65 (AAC)* which held that 'a person who is allowed to stay overnight (for a charge) at a night shelter but is not allowed to remain there during the day and so has to leave in the morning taking all of his belongings with him, and has no right to stay in any part of the night shelter or indeed right generally to stay there (in the sense that if he turns up late and the shelter is full he will be turned away), is not occupying a dwelling as his home.' This case depends on its particular facts and states that it is not 'intended to prescribe how HB claims for rough sleepers should be decided.'

Moving home and benefit on two homes

3.7 This section applies to HB and, in Scotland only, CTR. In Scotland the rules apply independently for the two benefits, so for any particular rule the claimant may meet the conditions for HB and CTR, or just HB or just CTR.

Remaining liable for rent/council tax on a former home

3.8 A claimant who has moved home, but remains liable for rent/Scottish council tax on their old home, is eligible for HB/Scottish CTR on

a) both old and new homes, if they are liable on both and liability on both 'could not reasonably have been avoided'; or

b) their old home, if they are liable only there and that liability 'could not reasonably have been avoided'.

But in each case this applies only for the period after they have moved into their new home, and only for up to four weeks from the date of the move. (See also para. 3.10, and for calculation rules para. 3.30.)

3.9 In HB, the 'two homes' version of the rule (para. 3.8(a)) is also called 'the overlapping HB rule'. It often applies when someone in privately rented accommodation is offered social housing at short notice, and has to take up the new letting

---

3.5   HB 7(2); HB60+ 7(2); NIHB 7(2); HB60+ 7(2); CTS 5(2); CTS60+ 5(2)

3.8   HB 7(6)(d),(7); HB60+ 7(6)(d),(7); NIHB 7(6)(d),(7); NIHB60+ 7(6)(d),(7); CTS 5(6)(d),(7); CTS60+ 5(6)(d),(7)

(and moves in) before notice on the old one has run out (see example 1).

3.10   In HB, the 'one home' version of the rule (para. 3.7(b)) can apply when someone moves from a rented home:

* to live with relatives (see example 2); or
* to a care home – in which case it can follow on from an award of HB during a trial period *(R(H) 4/06)* (see para. 3.33(a), and the example there);
* to prison following sentencing – in which case it can follow on from an award of HB during a period on remand (para. 3.33(b), table 3.1, and the example there); or
* other accommodation where no rent is payable (or if it is of the kind that is not eligible for HB as described in chapter 2).

3.11   Further considerations for both versions of the rule are as follows:

* the claimant must have moved into the new home. If they have a family they must have moved in too, and must be occupying it as a home rather than preparing it for occupation *(CH/1911/2006* para. 19);
* in considering whether liability could reasonably have been avoided, the authority may look at what alternatives were open to the claimant *(CH/4546/2002);*
* DWP advice that the claimant's circumstances should be exceptional (GM A3.682) can mislead authorities, since the only legal test is one of reasonableness;
* The rule does not apply when a claimant moves out for repairs to be done (para. 3.24).

3.12   The authority may request the claimant to provide evidence that the conditions for the rule are met (e.g. about liability and reasonableness). But unless the claimant is moving from one authority area to another, there is no legal requirement for them to make a separate claim for the period in question.

Examples: Liable for rent on a former home

1. HB on both old and new homes ('overlapping HB')

A claimant (already on HB) has been living in privately rented accommodation where the rent is due monthly on the 15th of the month and notice of one month is due if the claimant wishes to leave.

On Thursday 1st August 2013, the claimant is invited to view a housing association property (in the same local authority area) which he is then offered and accepts. The housing association insists that the tenancy must begin on Monday 5th August. On Friday 2nd August the claimant writes to his old landlord giving notice. The landlord insists that the claimant must pay to the end of August. The claimant moves in to his housing association home on Monday 5th August.

The authority accepts that the claimant meets all the conditions for HB on both homes (para. 3.8(a)) and awards HB from Monday 5th August for the new address and until Friday 30th August at the old address; so HB is awarded for both homes for three weeks and four days.

2. HB on a former home

A claimant (already on HB) has been living in housing association accommodation where the rent is due on Mondays and notice of four weeks is due if the claimant wishes to leave.

On Thursday 1st August 2013 the claimant's brother is found to be seriously ill and the claimant decides to go as soon as possible and live in his house to care for him. She decides to give up her housing association tenancy and gives her notice in on Monday 5th August to expire on Sunday 1st September 2013. She moves out of her housing association tenancy on Wednesday 7th August, handing the keys back the same day.

The authority accepts that the claimant meets all the conditions for HB on the address she has left (para. 3.8(b)) and awards HB on the housing association tenancy up till the end of the tenancy (covering three weeks and five days from the day she left till the end of her liability).

Fleeing violence or fear of violence

3.13   A claimant is eligible for HB/Scottish CTR on two rented homes for up to 52 weeks if he or she:

* has left and remains absent from the former home through fear of violence
  * in the home, or
  * by a person who was formerly a member of the claimant's family; and
* has an intention to return to it; and
* is liable for rent/Scottish council tax on both that home and where he or she is now living; and
* it is reasonable to award HB/Scottish CTR on both homes.

(For calculation rules see paras. 3.30 and 13.74. If the claimant is liable for rent/Scottish council tax only on the homes they have left, see para. 3.33(b) and table 3.1.)

3.14   Actual violence need not have occurred for the rule to apply. The claimant has only to be afraid of violence occurring. If the authority considers, however, that the fear of violence is one that is not reasonably held (*CH/1237/2004* para. 18) or that the claimant brought it upon himself or herself, it may consider it unreasonable that benefit should be paid in respect of both homes.

3.13   HB 7(6)(a); HB60+ 7(6)(a); NIHB 7(6)(a); NIHB60+ 7(6)(a); CTS 5(6)(a); CTS60+ 5(6)(a)

3.14   HB 7(10); HB60+ 7(10); NIHB 7(10); NIHB60+ 7(10); CTS 5(10); CTS60+ 5(10)

3.15 If the fear is of violence in the home, it need not be related to a family or former family member. It could be related to anyone, so long as it is feared that violence could occur in the home. If the fear is of violence outside the home, it must be a former member of the claimant's family who poses the threat of violence. This includes not only an ex-partner but also an adult child. On the other hand, it is of course the case that someone who is afraid of violence outside the home may well be afraid of it coming into the home.

3.16 The rule applies only if the claimant intends to return to the home they have left. This can include an intention to return when it becomes safe to do so – for example, if the claimant is taking steps to exclude the former partner and intends to return when that has happened. If, from the outset, the claimant does not intend to return, HB/Scottish CTR can be paid for up to four weeks (para. 3.8).

3.17 Authorities are advised to check regularly that the claimant intends to return to the previous home (GM A3.631). If the claimant subsequently decides not to return, HB/Scottish CTR on the former home stops. The benefit paid on the former home while the claimant had the intention to return will have been properly paid and is not an overpayment (GM A3.632).

Waiting for adaptations for a disability

3.18 If a claimant becomes liable for rent/Scottish council tax on a new dwelling, but does not move into it straight away because they are necessarily waiting for it to be adapted to meet their disablement needs or those of a family member (para. 4.8), the claimant is eligible for HB/Scottish CTR for up to four weeks before moving in, so long as the delay in moving is reasonable. To qualify under this rule, the adaptation must involve a change to the fabric or structure of the dwelling; furnishing, carpeting or decorating are not enough (*R(H)4/07* paras. 6-11).

3.19 In this case, if the claimant is also liable for rent on their old home, they are eligible for HB on both homes during those four weeks. (For calculation rules, see para. 3.30.) Whether in the case of HB for one home or two, HB can be awarded only after the claimant has moved in and the claim, or notice of the move, must be made promptly (para. 3.31).

Waiting for a social fund payment, etc

3.20 A claimant who is liable for rent/Scottish council tax on a new dwelling but does not move into it straight away is eligible for HB/Scottish CTR on that dwelling for up to four weeks before moving in so long as:

* the move was delayed pending the outcome of an application for a social fund payment or similar local authority provisions (paras. 13-44-45) to help with the move or with setting up home;

3.18   HB 7(6)(e); HB60+ 7(6)(e); NIHB 7(6)(e); NIHB60+ 7(6)(e); CTS 5(6)(e); CTS60+ 5(6)(e)

3.19   HB 7(8)(b)(ii),(c)(i); HB60+ 7(8)(b)(ii),(c)(i); NIHB 7(8)(c)(i); NIHB60+ 7(8)(c)(i); CTS 5(8)(b)(ii),(c)(i); CTS60+ 5(8)(b)(ii),(c)(i)

3.20   HB 7(8)(c)(ii); HB60+ 7(8)(c)(ii); NIHB 7(8)(c)(ii); NIHB60+ 7(8)(c)(ii); CTS 5(8)(c)(ii); CTS60+ 5(8)(c)(ii)

- the delay in moving is reasonable; and
- they have reached pension credit age (paras. 1.20-22), or have a child aged under 6, or someone in the family is disabled in one of the ways relevant to a disability premium or disabled child premium.

3.21   In this case, the claimant is not eligible for HB/Scottish CTR on his or her old home as well – a feature of the rule that has been criticised as discriminating against someone moving from a furnished rented home to his or her first unfurnished rented home. Benefit can be awarded only after the claimant has moved in and the claim must be made promptly (para. 3.31).

Waiting to leave hospital or a care home

3.22   If a claimant becomes liable for rent on a new dwelling, but does not move into it straight away because they are waiting to leave a hospital, care home or independent hospital (para. 2.23), they are eligible for HB/Scottish CTR for up to four weeks before moving in, so long as the delay in moving is reasonable.

3.23   This might arise if someone's departure from hospital or a care home is delayed. Benefit can be awarded only after the claimant has moved in and the claim must be made promptly (para. 3.31).

Moving out for repairs to be done

3.24   A claimant who has had to leave the normal home while it is having essential repairs, and who has to make payments (e.g. rent or mortgage payments) on one but not both the normal home and the temporary accommodation, is treated as occupying the home for which payments are made. They are then eligible for HB/Scottish CTR only on that home (if they are liable for rent/council tax there).

Large families

3.25   Where the claimant's family (para. 4.8) is so large they have been housed by a housing authority (in Northern Ireland, the NIHE) in two separate dwellings, the claimant is eligible for HB/Scottish CTR on both homes. The DWP (GM para. A3.660) advises that both homes should be provided, but not necessarily owned, by the local authority. There is no time limit in this case.

What is 'one' home?

3.26   It is possible for two buildings to be one 'home' for HB purposes, for example if statutory overcrowding would otherwise arise (*R(H) 5/09* para. 22 and *CH/4018/2007*). Similar situations have arisen in relation to JSA(IB) and have been approved by the Court of Appeal: (*Secretary of State for Work and Pensions*

3.22   HB 7(8)(c)(iii); HB60+ 7(8)(c)(iii); NIHB 7(8)(c)(iii); NIHB60+ 7(8)(c)(iii); CTS 5(8)(c)(iii); CTS60+ 5(8)(c)(iii)

3.24   HB 7(4); HB60+ 7(4); NIHB 7(4); NIHB60+ 7(4); CTS 5(4); CTS60+ 5(4)

3.25   HB 7(6)(c); HB60+ 7(6)(c); NIHB 7(6)(c); NIHB60+ 7(6)(c); CTS 5(6)(c); CTS60+ 5(6)(c)

v Miah, R(JSA)9/03). Also, two flats knocked together, though rented from two landlords, might constitute 'one home' *(CH/1895/2008).* In the former CTB scheme, two nearby flats in a block, used by a single family as one home (with bedrooms in one flat and living areas in the other), could be a single residence. Arguably, CTR should therefore be awarded on the combined amount of council tax in similar situations.

Single and lone parent students and trainees

3.27   A single claimant or lone parent who is:

* a student who is in the 'eligible student groups' (table 22.1); or
* on a government training course (para. 3.28),

and who has two homes but is liable to make payments (e.g. rent) on only one, is treated as normally occupying that one (and is thus eligible for HB/Scottish CTR on it), even if he or she in fact normally lives in the other one.

3.28   The training courses referred to are those provided by or via the Secretary of State, a government department, Skills Development Scotland, Scottish Enterprise, or Highlands and Islands Enterprise; or by a local authority on behalf of one of those bodies, either direct or via another organisation.

Student couples

3.29   A couple (para. 4.10) are eligible for HB/Scottish CTR on two homes if one is a student in the eligible groups and the other is not a student, or if both are students each of whom is a student in the eligible groups (table 22.1). But occupying two homes must be unavoidable and it must be reasonable to pay benefit on two homes (table 22.2). There is no time limit in this case.

Calculation of benefit on two homes

3.30   In the cases above in which HB is awarded on two homes (paras. 3.8, 3.13, 3.19, 3.25 and 3.29), HB is calculated as follows: add together the two eligible rents, then make any non-dependant deduction(s) only once, then subtract 65% of any excess income (para. 6.11) only once *([2011] UKUT 5 (AAC)* para. 23). If the two homes are in different authority areas, the two authorities must work together to achieve this – making sure in particular that no part of the claimant's income is taken into account by both of them at the same time *([2011] UKUT 5 (AAC)* para. 33). The law makes no provision for calculating Scottish CTR on two homes, but a similar approach could be adopted.

3.27   HB 7(3); HB60+ 7(3); NIHB 7(3); NIHB60+ 7(3); CTS 5(3); CTS60+ 5(3)

3.28   HB 7(18); HB60+ 7(18); NIHB 7(18); NIHB60+ 7(18); CTS 2(1); CTS60+ 2(1)

3.29   HB 7(6)(b); HB60+ 7(6)(b); NIHB 7(6)(b); NIHB60+ 7(6)(b); CTS 5(6)(b); CTS60+ 5(6)(b)

3.30   HB 80(9); HB60+ 61(11); NIHB 78(10); NIHB 60+ 59(10)

Entitlement prior to moving in: prompt claims

3.31   In the cases above in which HB/Scottish CTR is awarded before someone moves in (paras. 3.18, 3.20 and 3.22), it is necessary to claim (or notify the move) promptly (in HB before or in the first week of the new liability for rent) – unless benefit is backdated (para. 5.51). If the claim is then refused (perhaps because at that time the authority is not sure that the claimant will in fact move in), and the claimant reapplies within four weeks, the reapplication should be treated as having been made at the same time as the refused claim. And the payment of benefit cannot start until the claimant actually does move in.

Temporary absences from home

3.32   This section applies to HB and CTR throughout the UK. It describes when claimants can get HB/CTR during a temporary absence from their home.

3.33   The law gives three rules about temporary absences. During an absence from their home, a claimant is eligible for HB/CTR:

(a) or up to 13 weeks during any trial period in a care home (or immediately following that: *R(H) 4/06*) – so long as the claimant intends to return to their normal home if the care home is unsuitable (but the total absence from home must not exceed 52 weeks); or

(b) for up to 52 weeks if they are absent (in the UK or abroad) for one of the reasons in table 3.1 – so long as the claimant intends to return to their normal home within 52 weeks or, in exceptional circumstances, not substantially later; or

(c) for up to 13 weeks during an absence (in the UK or abroad) for any other reason – so long as the claimant intends to return to their normal home within a strict 13 weeks.

However, for Scottish CTR (only), different rules apply to absences from Great Britain (paras. 3.47-52).

The intention to return

3.34   Each of the above rules requires the claimant to intend to return to their normal home. It is the claimant's intention which is relevant (not, say, the intention of a relative or official) but that intention must be capable of being realised. In one case a claimant desired to return from his nursing home to his housing association property, but the commissioner held that to desire is not the same as to intend (*CSHB/405/2005* para. 30). It had been found as a fact that it was objectively impossible for the claimant to return, so the absence from home provisions could not apply to him.

3.31   HB 7(9); HB60+ 7(9); NIHB 7(9); NIHB60+ 7(9); CTS 5(9); CTS60+ 5(9)

3.33   HB 7(11)-(18); HB60+ 7(11)-(18); NIHB 7(11)-(18); NIHB60+ 7(11)-(18); CTP sch 1 para 5; CTR 19

Example: Trying out a care home and then deciding to stay there

A woman who rents her home has been on HB and CTR for a while. She goes into a care home for a six-week trial period to see if it suits her.

+ She remains eligible for HB and CTR.

In the fourth week of her trial, she decides that this is the care home for her and gives four weeks' notice to her former landlord. The authority is satisfied that she could not reasonably have avoided the liability at her old address.

+ She remains eligible for HB and CTR for the additional four-week period.

Table 3.1: People who can get HB/CTR during an absence of up to 52 weeks

Claimants in prison etc, who have not yet been sentenced (para. 3.40).

Claimants in a probation hostel, or a bail hostel, or bailed to live away from their normal home.

Claimants in a care home or independent hospital (para. 2.23) who are not trying it out (e.g. during periods of respite care).

Claimants who are patients in hospital, or receiving medically approved* care.

Claimants undergoing medical treatment or medically approved* convalescence or who are absent because their partner or child is undergoing this.

Claimants undertaking medically approved* care of someone else.

Claimants caring for a child whose parent or guardian is absent from home in order to receive medical treatment or medically approved* care.

Claimants following a training course (as defined in para. 3.28).

Students who are eligible for HB/CTR (e.g. if they have to study away from home for part of their course).

Claimants absent because of fear of violence in their normal home (regardless of who it would be from) or fear of violence from a former member of their family (whether this would occur in the normal home or elsewhere). This applies to people other than those mentioned in paragraph 3.13 because, for example, they are staying with relatives and are not liable to pay rent on two homes but intend to return to occupy their original home.

* Note: 'medically approved' means approved in writing by a GP, nurse or similar but this need not be in a formal certificate (GM A3.541).

T 3.1 HB 7(16)(c); HB60+ 7(16)(c); NIHB 7(16)(c); NIHB60+ 7(16)(c); CTP sch 1 para 5(3),(6); CTR 19(3),(6)

Additional conditions

3.35　　In each of the above cases (para. 3.33), the claimant must still be liable for rent/council tax on their normal home and the part of the home the claimant normally occupies must not be let or sub-let.

Counting the length of the absence

3.36　　The 13-week and 52-week time limits refer to absences which are continuous: *R v Penwith DC HBRB ex parte Burt.* So if the claimant (with the exception of prisoners on temporary release: para. 3.42) returns to, and occupies the dwelling as a home, even for a short time, the allowable period of temporary absence starts again. The DWP suggests (GM A3.460) that a stay at home lasting, for example, only a few hours may not break the absence but one that lasts at least 24 hours may do so.

3.37　　Depending upon the facts of the case, however, the authority may decide that the claimant's normal home is elsewhere for HB purposes (paras. 3.3-5). If another person occupying the dwelling starts paying rent in the absence of the claimant, the authority should consider treating that other person as liable and therefore eligible for HB (para. 2.33).

3.38　　The assessment of whether or not the period of temporary absence is likely to exceed 13/52 weeks has to be made by reference to the date at which the claimant left the dwelling in question (*CH/1237/2004* para. 12). Continued entitlement has to be judged on a week by week basis. If at any date it becomes likely that the 13/52 weeks will be exceeded, then that is a relevant change of circumstances, allowing a re-consideration of the entitlement (*CH/1237/2004* para. 12). Once it becomes clear that the claimant is going to be away for more than 13 or 52 weeks, entitlement ends under the temporary absence rule (but see para. 3.8(b) for the circumstances in which the claimant may be entitled to up to four weeks additional entitlement).

3.39　　In the case of the absences in table 3.1, if the absence is unlikely to substantially exceed the 52-week period, and if there are exceptional circumstances, the authority must pay up to the end of the 52nd week of absence. DWP guidance (GM A3.532) suggests that the term 'substantially exceed' relates to periods of absence greater than 15 months. It is, however, for the individual authority to interpret the term. The GM illustrates the concept of exceptional circumstances with the examples of someone prevented from returning home by an unanticipated event, and a discharge from hospital being delayed by a relapse. Other circumstances may also be considered.

Absences in prison, etc

3.40　　A claimant in prison, etc, can get HB/CTR for up to 52 weeks on their

---

3.35　　HB 7(11)-(17); HB60+ 7(11)-(17); NIHB 7(11)-(17); NIHB60+ 7(11)-(17); CTP sch 1 para 5(2); CTR 19(2)

normal home until they are sentenced (table 3.1). This means that almost all prisoners on remand can get HB/CTR.

3.41 If and when the claimant is sentenced to prison, etc, this counts as a change of circumstances. The relevant question is then: 'Will they return home within 13 weeks of when they left home?' Only if the answer is 'yes' can the claimant continue to get HB under the temporary absence rule *(CH/499/2006)* – and this time limit is strict *(CH/1986/2009)*. However, in deciding this, it should be borne in mind that most fixed-term sentences qualify for remission, so claimants with a sentence of up to six months (or up to ten months if they are eligible for Home Detention Curfew) are likely to be entitled. The claimant's own prediction of their release date is irrelevant if release could be considered earlier *(CH/2638/2006,* in which a parole hearing should have occurred earlier than it did). For further guidance see GM A3.512-518.

Prisoners on temporary release

3.42 Prisoners on temporary release ('home leave' or 'ROTL' – release on temporary licence) are counted as still being in prison, unless they were already eligible for HB immediately beforehand under the above rules (paras. 3.40-41).

Absences on bail

3.43 As indicated in table 3.1, a person on bail can get HB/Scottish CTR on his normal home for up to 52 weeks. This applies whether the person is in a bail hostel or bailed to live anywhere other than the normal home (e.g. at a relative's).

Example: Remand and conviction

A man has been receiving HB for a while. He is then arrested and detained on remand pending his trial.

+ The authority should assume that he will be absent for no more than 52 weeks. He therefore remains eligible for HB.

Fifteen weeks later he is tried, found guilty, and sentenced to a term of one year's imprisonment.

+ Although he will serve only six months in prison (after remission), and although the 15 weeks he has been on remand count towards this, his total absence from home now exceeds 13 weeks. His eligibility for HB under the temporary absence rule ends. The fact that he has been sentenced is a change in his circumstances (chapter 17). (But the HB he was awarded for his 15 weeks on remand was nonetheless correctly paid.) If, however, the necessary conditions are met (para. 3.8(b)) the claimant may be entitled to a further four weeks of HB.

3.42 HB 7(14)-(15); HB60+ 7(14)-(15); NIHB 7(14)-(15); CTP sch 1 para 5(4)-(5); CTR 19(4)-(5)

3.43 HB 7(16)(c); HB60+ 7(16)(c); NIHB 7(16)(c); NIHB60+ 7(16)(c); CTP sch 1 para 5(3)(a); CTR 19(3)(a)

Death of claimant

3.44   There is no provision to award HB/CTR following the death of the claimant (see the reasoning in *R(IS) 3/04* para. 18). HB must cease at the end of the benefit week containing the date of the death under the normal rule about changes of circumstances (paras. 17.21 and 17.37); and CTR ceases on the day before the date of the death (because there is no liability for council tax from the date of death onwards). If the claimant has a surviving partner, he or she may make their own claim. They are not 'covered' by their deceased partner's claim (but see paras. 5.33-34). Also, the fact that the estate of the deceased may be required to pay for a notice period on the property does not mean that the deceased (or the estate) is still entitled to HB.

Notifying a temporary absence

3.45   In CTR a claimant on pension credit – or in HB any pension age claimant (table. 1.4) – has a duty to notify the authority of an absence exceeding or likely to exceed 13 weeks. Apart from that, there is no requirement to notify the authority in advance of a temporary absence *(CH/996/2004)*.

Claiming during a temporary absence

3.46   It is also possible for someone not on HB/CTR to become eligible during a temporary absence (e.g. because their income goes down), and in such cases a claim is required in the normal way (chapter 5).

Scottish CTR: absences from GB

3.46   Presence in Great Britain is one of the conditions for getting CTR in Scotland. This section describes when a claimant is treated as being present, and can get Scottish CTR, despite being absent from Great Britain. It does not apply to HB, or to CTR in England and Wales.

First month: all temporary absences

3.48   A claimant who is entitled to Scottish CTR remains eligible for it during the first month of temporary absence from GB, whatever the reason, so long as they were not absent from GB on more than two occasions during the 52 weeks before it began.

3.45   HB60+ 69(6)(c); NIHB60+ 65(4)(c); CTP sch 8 para 9(7); CTR 115(7)

3.47   LGFA 80, 113, sch 2 para 1

3.48   CTS 18(1)(a),(2); CTS60+ 18(1)(a),(2)

Second month: a death in the family

3.49   The claimant is then eligible for Scottish CTR during the second month's temporary absence from GB, but only if the absence is in connection with the death of:

- a member of their family (para. 4.8); or
- a close relative (para. 2.38) of the claimant or a family member,

and the authority is satisfied that it would be unreasonable to expect the claimant to return to GB.

First six months: illness, disability, etc.

3.50   A claimant who is entitled to Scottish CTR remains eligible for it during the first six months of a temporary absence from GB if the absence is solely in connection with:

- the claimant or a member of their family (para. 4.8) being treated for an illness or physical or mental disability, by a person qualified to provide medical treatment, physiotherapy, or similar or related treatment; or
- the claimant undergoing convalescence or care, which results from treatment for an illness or physical or mental disability they had before they left GB, and which is medically approved (as described in the note to table 3.1).

'Temporary'

3.51   In the above cases (paras. 3.46-48) the absence must be 'temporary'. So the claimant must have an intention to return; and if the claimant subsequently decides not to return to GB, Scottish CTR stops.

No time limit: certain occupations

3.52   A claimant is treated as being in GB (and eligible for Scottish CTR) during an absence of any length from GB, if it is in their capacity as:

- a member of HM forces;
- an aircraft worker or mariner with a UK contract of employment;
- a continental shelf worker in EU or Norwegian waters; or
- a Crown servant.

Their partner is treated as being in GB if the only reason they are outside GB is that they are living with the claimant.

3.49   CTS 18(4),(5); CTS60+ 18(4),(5)

3.50   CTS 2(1), 18(1)(b),(3),(5),(6); CTS60+ 2(1), 18(1)(b),(3),(5),(6)

3.52   CTS 17; CTS60+ 17

4 The claimant's household

4.1 This chapter explains how people who live in the claimant's dwelling are categorised, since different categories of people affect the assessment of HB/CTR in different ways. It describes:

* what a household is;
* who counts as a member of the claimant's family (partners and dependent children);
* who counts as a couple;
* who is responsible for a dependent child;
* fostering and adoption;
* temporary absences of partners and children;
* who counts as a non-dependant; and
* others in the claimant's dwelling.

Table 4.1 summarises the categories.

Table 4.1: Occupants of a dwelling

The members of a claimant's household include:

* family members:
  * the claimant (para. 4.7)
  * their partner(s) (para. 4.9)
  * dependent children or young persons (para. 4.23)
* foster children (para. 4.35)
* non-dependants (para. 4.39)

Others in the dwelling may include:

* lodgers (with or without board) (para. 4.48)
* joint occupiers, whether joint owners or joint tenants (para. 4.52)
* certain carers (para. 4.54)

4.2 Many terms in this chapter have special meanings. For example, 'family' is very precise (para.4.8), unlike in day-to-day life. Others have their ordinary meaning, for example 'household' (paras. 4.3-6). These, and other terms, are shared with the passport benefits; important case law from other benefits is therefore included.

Membership of a household

4.3   What constitutes a 'household' is not defined in the law. The term should therefore be given its common sense meaning as being a domestic arrangement involving two or more people who live together as a unit *(R(IS) 1/99)*; and this implies that its members have a reasonable level of independence and self-sufficiency *(R(SB) 8/85)*. It includes both members of the 'family' (para. 4.8) and others such as non-dependants (table 4.1).

4.4   Whether someone is part of the claimant's household depends upon the particular facts in each case. However, it requires more than their transitory presence: it requires a settled course of daily living *(R(F) 2/81)*. Someone making a short visit is not a member of the household; they can only be a household member if that is where they spend the major part of their time.

4.5   A person cannot be a member of more than one household at once *(R(SB) 8/85)*. Two people maintaining separate homes cannot be part of the same household *(R(SB) 4/83)*.

4.6   A house may contain one household or a number of households. Two or more people living in the same dwelling are likely to constitute separate households if:

- they have independent arrangements for cooking and storage of food;
- they have separate eating arrangements;
- there is no evidence of family life;
- they arrange their financial affairs independently;
- they have exclusive use of separate accommodation and/or their own obligations for housing costs (even if their liability is to someone at the same address).

Example: Occupiers of a dwelling

A claimant has the following people in his (large) home.

- His partner and dependent children. They are his benefit family (para. 4.8).
- A foster child. This child is disregarded in assessing HB/CTR (para. 4.35), and so is the income from fostering (para. 13.65). When the foster child grows up, see table 2.3.
- His parents and his sister. They are his non-dependants (para. 4.39).
- His sister has a partner who lives abroad. Because the partner does not live there, the partner is disregarded in assessing HB/CTR.
- The sister's baby. The baby is disregarded in assessing HB/CTR (para. 4.47).
- A lodger who rents a room from him. Part of the income from the lodger is counted (table 13.3).

Claimant and family

4.7   The law divides claimants into the following kinds:

- a single claimant – i.e. a claimant who does not have a partner and is not responsible for a child or young person;

- a lone parent – i.e. a claimant who does not have a partner and is responsible for a child or young person; or

- a member of a couple or polygamous marriage – whether or not responsible for a child or young person. Only one member of a couple or polygamous marriage may claim (para. 5.4).

4.8   The claimant's 'family' for benefit purposes means:

- the claimant's partner(s); and

- any child(ren) or young person(s) the claimant is responsible for (not just sons and daughters);

so long as, in each case, they are members of the claimant's household (paras. 4.3-6 and 4.34).

Partners

4.9   A partner means the other member of a couple or the other members of a polygamous marriage.

4.10   The term 'couple' refers to:

- a man and woman who are married to each other and are members of the same household;

- a man and woman who are not married to each other but are living together as husband and wife;

- two people of the same sex who are civil partners of each other and are members of the same household; or

- two people of the same sex who are not civil partners of each other but are living together as if they were civil partners.

Married couples and civil partners

4.11   Married couples and civil partners are a couple only if they are members of the same household (paras. 4.3-6). A married couple or civil partners who live in different dwellings are not a couple – nor are they if they live in the same dwelling but live separate lives and do not constitute a household *(CIS/072/1994)*. In such a case one would not be the partner of the other.

4.7   HB 2(1); HB60+ 2(1); NIHB 2(1); NIHB60+ 2(1); CTP 2(1),4; CTR 2(1),4

4.8   CBA 137(1); NICBA 133(1); CTP 6; CTR 6

4.9   CBA 137(1); NICBA 133(1); HB 2(1); HB60+ 2(1); NIHB 2(1); NIHB60+ 2(1), CTP 2(1); CTR 2(1)

4.11   HB 2(1); HB60+ 2(1); NIHB 2(1); NIHB60+ 2(1); CTP 2(1),4; CTR 2(1),4

Living together as husband and wife or as civil partners

4.12   A man and woman who are not married to each other but are 'living together as husband and wife' are a couple for benefit purposes. So are two people of the same sex who are not civil partners but who are living together as if they were.

4.13   The law does not define the phrase 'living together as husband and wife'. DWP guidance on the matter notes that it is important to consider the changing nature of modern-day relationships (GM C1 annex A para. A1.03).

4.14   The first consideration is the purpose of the parties in living together *(Crake and Butterworth v the Supplementary Benefit Commission)*. The HB/CTR schemes recognise many different ways in which two people could live together in the same dwelling, e.g. joint occupiers, landlady/lodger, etc.

4.15   If the purpose of the parties is unclear, the question of whether a couple are living together can only be decided by looking at their relationship and living arrangements and asking whether they can reasonably be said to be those of a married couple. A body of case law developed. This is considered in detail in vol. 3, chapter 11, paras. 1104-11061 of the DWP *Decision Maker's Guide* [www].

4.16   The case law *(Crake* para. 4.14) suggests that the following factors need to be considered before deciding that two people are a couple:

- whether or not they share the same household;
- the stability of the relationship;
- the financial arrangements;
- the presence or absence of a sexual relationship;
- shared responsibility for a child;
- public acknowledgment that they are a couple.

4.17   While all the above factors should be considered, none individually is conclusive (GM C1 Annex A para. A1.02). What matters is the general relationship as a whole *(R(SB)17/81)*. The GM *(C1, Annex A paras. A1.07-10)* provides authorities with advice regarding the information they should gather and the questions they should ask when considering whether two people are living together as husband and wife or as civil partners.

4.18   Even when two people are part of the same household they may not be a couple: what matters is the reason why they live together. For example, two people who lived together for reasons of 'care, companionship and mutual convenience' were held not to be a couple *(R(SB) 35/85)*. A couple whose relationship has ended should not be treated as partners if they maintain

---

4.12   HB 2(1); HB60+ 2(1); NIHB 2(1); NIHB60+ 2(1); CTP 2(1); CTR 2(1)

4.15   www.dwp.gov.uk/publications/specialist-guides/decision-makers-guide/

separate households (paras. 4.5-6). When a relationship comes to an end, a shared understanding that it has ended and the actual living arrangements are more important than shared responsibilities and financial arrangements *(CIS/72/1994)*. But a shared understanding may not be sufficient to show that they form separate households in the case of a married couple *(CIS/2900/1998)*.

4.19   If the DWP has treated two people as a couple for JSA(IB), ESA(IR), IS or pension credit awards it does not mean that the authority must do so *(R(H)9/04)*. Although the authority may regard the DWP decision as satisfactory in the absence of any contrary evidence, if the claimant asserts that the DWP's decision is wrong the authority has to reach its own conclusion *(R(H)9/04 para. 37)*. Conversely, if the DWP has awarded a passport benefit on the basis that someone is not part of a couple then the authority is not normally entitled to take a different view. The exception would be if the authority has evidence of fraud which the DWP is unaware of and has not considered *(CH/4014/2007)*.

Polygamous marriage

4.20   A polygamous marriage is one in which a party to it is married to more than one person. The ceremony of marriage must have taken place under the law of a country which permits polygamy. No marriage that takes place in the UK is valid if one of the partners is already married. When a polygamous marriage is formed in the UK, a second or subsequent partner should be treated as a non-dependant (GM C1.42).

Absence of partner

4.21   A partner is normally treated as a member of the household even if temporarily absent. (For absences of the claimant, see chapter 3.) Temporary absence is not defined for CTR; but for HB a partner stops counting as a member of the household if they are living away from the other family members and:

- they do not intend to resume living with them; or
- the absence is likely to exceed 52 weeks, unless there are exceptional circumstances where the person has no control over the length of the absence (e.g. in hospital) and the absence is unlikely to be substantially more than 52 weeks.

4.22   When a partner does not count as a member of the household, their needs, income and capital should not be taken into account when calculating HB/CTR. Any money received from an absent partner should be treated as maintenance (paras. 13.125-126).

4.20   HB 2(1); HB60+ 2(1); NIHB 2(1); NIHB60+ 2(1); CTP 5; CTR 5

4.21   HB 21(1),(2); HB60+ 21(1),(2); NIHB 19(1),(2); NIHB60+ 19(1),(2); CTP 8(1); CTR 8(1)

Children and young persons

4.23   Children and young persons are members of the claimant's family for HB/CTR purposes if they meet the following conditions. In particular, the claimant must be responsible for them (para. 4.31), and (which usually follows from that) they must be a member of the claimant's household (para. 4.34).

4.24   A 'child' means someone under the age of 16.

4.25   A 'young person' means someone aged 16 or over who:

+ is a qualifying person for child benefit purposes (paras. 4.26-30); and
+ is not on JSA(IB), ESA(IR) or IS; and
+ is not a care leaver under 18 (paras. 2.9-12).

When a young person ceases to meet these conditions, they stop being included in the claimant's applicable amount (chapter 12) and become a non-dependant (but see table 6.3 for the cases in which no non-dependant deduction applies).

A qualifying young person for child benefit purposes

4.26   A qualifying young person for child benefit purposes is:

+ a person aged 16, from the date they reach that age up to and including the following 31st August; or
+ a person aged 16 years and over but under 20, who is undertaking a course of full-time non-advanced education (para. 4.27), or undertaking approved training (para. 4.28), which they started before reaching the age of 19; or
+ in certain circumstances, a person who has left such education or training (paras. 4.29-30).

4.27   An education course counts as full-time if the average time spent during term-time in tuition, practical work, supervised study, or taking examinations exceeds 12 hours per week. And a person is treated as undertaking a course during the period between the end of one course and the start of another, so long as they are enrolled on and start the latter course. Non-advanced education is education up to and including GCE (A Level), advanced GNVQ or equivalent, Scottish certificate of education (higher level), Scottish certificate of sixth year studies, and equivalents.

4.28   Approved training means training provided under the following programmes (so long as it is not provided through a contract of employment):

+ in England – 'Entry to Employment' or 'Programme Led Pathways';
+ in Wales – 'Skillbuild', 'Skillbuild Plus' or 'Foundation Modern Apprenticeships';

4.24   HB 2(1); HB60+ 2(1); NIHB 2(1); NIHB60+ 2(1); CTP 2(1); CTR 2(1)

4.25   HB 2(1),19; HB60+ 2(1),19; NIHB 2(1),17; NIHB60+ 2(1),17; CTP 2(1),6; CTR 2(1),6

4.26   HB 2(1),19; HB60+ 2(1),19; NIHB 2(1),17; NIHB60+ 2(1),17; CTP 2(1),6; CTR 2(1),(6)

- in Scotland – 'Get Ready for Work', 'Skillseekers' or 'Modern Apprenticeships'; or
- in Northern Ireland – 'Access' or 'Jobskills Traineeships'.

4.29   Someone who has left education or training continues to be a qualifying young person for child benefit purposes up to and including the week including the terminal date; or if they attain the age of 20 on or before that date, the week including the last Monday before they were 20. The terminal date is whichever of the following dates occurs first after they have ceased education or training:

- the last day in February;
- the last day in May;
- the last day in August;
- the last day in November.

4.30   In addition to the above, child benefit is extended for 16 and 17 year olds who have left education or training if:

- they are registered for work, education or training with the Careers or Connexions Service; and
- they are not engaged in remunerative work; and
- an application for payment of child benefit during the extension period is made within three months of the date education or training ended.

The child benefit extension period begins on the first day of the week after the week in which education or training stopped and ends 20 weeks later.

Responsibility for a child or young person

4.31   The claimant is considered responsible for any child or young person they normally live with. This is usually straightforward; and when it is, receipt (or not) of child benefit is irrelevant. But if a child or young person spends equal amounts of time in different households (e.g. when parents have separated), or if there is doubt over which household they are living in, they are treated as normally living with the person who gets the child benefit. And if no-one gets child benefit, the child or young person is considered the responsibility of:

- the person who has claimed child benefit; or
- the person the authority considers has 'primary responsibility' if more than one person has made a claim for the child benefit or no claim has been made.

A child or young person can only be the responsibility of one person in any one benefit week (GM C1.91).

4.32   A child or young person for whom the claimant is not responsible (because of spending more time in another household) is excluded from the claimant's applicable amount (chapter 12), and excluded when deciding the size

---

4.31   HB 20; HB60+ 20; NIHB 18; NIHB60+ 18; CTP 7; CTR 7

of accommodation the claimant needs (chapters 7-9): *R v Swale HBRB ex p Marchant* and *[2010] UKUT 208 ACC.*

4.33　　　Grandchildren (and the like) in a claimant's home can be dealt with in different ways, depending on the facts, as illustrated in the examples (which reflect DWP advice: GM C1.70).

Example: Three generations living together

+ A claimant's daughter aged 15 lives with her, as does the daughter's baby. The claimant gets child benefit for them both. The authority decides that the claimant is responsible for them both, and includes both in the claimant's family (and thus in her applicable amount).

+ Later, (after leaving school) the daughter claims income support for herself. The authority decides that the daughter and baby now form a separate family, and so excludes them from the claimant's family (and applicable amount).

In both cases, the daughter and baby are included in deciding the size of accommodation the claimant needs. Although in the second situation they form two separate families, they are nevertheless part of the same household.

4.34　　　A child or young person for whom the claimant is responsible (paras. 4.31-33) is always a member of the claimant's household, with exceptions only in the cases of fostering, pre-adoption and longer absences (paras. 4.35-38).

Fostering, adoption, etc

4.35　　　A child or young person is not counted as a member of the claimant's household if they are:

+ absent from the claimant's home and being looked after by a local authority, or in Scotland or Northern Ireland are in the care of a local authority or the Department;

+ a foster child placed with the claimant or partner by a local authority or voluntary organisation, or in Scotland and Northern Ireland boarded out with the claimant or partner; or

+ placed for adoption or custodianship with the claimant or partner or elsewhere (though once adopted, they become a member of the household).

Such a child or young person is excluded from the claimant's applicable amount, and excluded when deciding the size of accommodation the claimant needs (chapters 7-9).

4.34　　HB 21(1),(2); HB60+ 21(1),(2); NIHB 19(1),(2); NIHB60+ 19(1),(2); CTP 8(1); CTR 8(1)

4.35　　HB 21(3),(4); HB60+ 21(3),(4); NIHB 19(3),(4); NIHB60+ 19(3),(4); CTP 8(2),(3); CTR 8(2),(3)

4.36 A child or young person in local authority care who lives with the claimant under supervision must be treated as a member of the household (GM C1.120). So must a child or young person in care who returns to live with the claimant for part or all of a benefit week if, given the nature and frequency of the visits, it is reasonable to do so (GM C1.150).

Absence of child or young person

4.37 A child or young person is normally treated as a member of the household even if temporarily absent. Temporary absence is not defined for CTR; but for HB a child or young person stops counting as a member of the household if they are living away from the other family members and:

- they do not intend to resume living with them; or
- the absence is likely to exceed 52 weeks, unless there are exceptional circumstances where the person has no control over the length of the absence (e.g. in hospital) and the absence is unlikely to be substantially more than 52 weeks.

4.38 A child or young person who is absent in any other circumstance, e.g. attending boarding school, should be regarded as temporarily absent and treated as a member of the family (GM C1.140).

Non-dependants

4.39 In broad terms, a non-dependant is someone who normally resides with the claimant on a non-commercial basis (the full definition is in paras. 4.41-47). Typical examples are adult daughters, sons, other relatives and friends.

4.40 Non-dependants cannot get HB/CTR for any payments they make for their keep. The one exception is that a non-dependant who takes over paying the claimant's rent (because the claimant is not paying it) may be able to get HB (para. 2.33(c)).

Definition

4.41 HB/CTR law defines everyone who 'normally resides' with the claimant (or with whom the claimant 'normally resides') as a non-dependant, unless they fall within any of the categories in table 4.2.

4.42 Additionally, if the claimant (or partner) has a lodger who is not eligible for HB in their own right (because they have a contrived or similar letting: paras. 2.35-54), that person is a non-dependant (GM C1.184).

4.36   HB 21(5); HB60+ 21(5); NIHB 19(5); NIHB60+ 19(5); CTP 8(4); CTR 8(4)

4.37   HB 21(1),(2); HB60+ 21(1),(2); NIHB 19(1),(2); NIHB60+ 19(1),(2); CTP 8(1); CTR 8(1)

4.41   HB 3(1),(2); HB60+ 3(1),(2); NIHB 3(1),(2); NIHB60+ 3(1),(2); CTP 9(1),(2); CTR 9(1),(2)

4.42   HB 3(3); HB60+ 3(3); NIHB 3(3); NIHB60+ 3(3); CTP 9(3); CTR 9(3)

Table 4.2: People who are not non-dependants

- Members of the claimant's family (para. 4.8)
- Foster children etc, who are not counted as the claimant's household (paras. 4.35 and 4.47)
- Lodgers (para. 4.48) and members of their household (but see para. 4.42)
- Joint occupiers (para. 4.52)
- Certain paid carers (para. 4.58)
- A resident landlord and members of their household (e.g. a landlady's adult daughter)

Residing with

4.43   To count as a non-dependant, a person must 'normally reside' with the claimant (or the claimant must 'normally reside' with them). So someone who is staying with the claimant but normally resides elsewhere is not a non-dependant (para. 4.46).

4.44   For HB purposes a person does not count as normally residing with the claimant if they share only a bathroom, toilet or communal area (halls, passageways and rooms in common use in sheltered accommodation). So someone in self-contained accommodation, within the same building as the claimant, does not count as a non-dependant even if they share a bathroom and toilet with the claimant.

4.45   Sharing more of the accommodation than a bathroom, toilet or communal area with the claimant is a necessary but not a sufficient condition for deciding that they reside with the claimant *(Kadhim v Brent LBC)*. The person must also have the sort of relationship that could be described as 'residing with' in an ordinary sense. This is more than simply sharing parts of the accommodation.

4.46   Case law has also examined what it means to 'normally' reside with the claimant. In one case the claimant's cousin came to live with her for ten weeks after being deported from the USA. She took him in rather than see him living on the streets as he had no source of income while waiting for his JSA claim. He slept on the sofa. The commissioner decided he was not normally residing with the claimant, so a non-dependant deduction did not apply *(CH/4004/2004)*. In another case, the claimant's mentally ill daughter had been evicted and moved in with her. The tribunal decided that she was not normally residing with the claimant during the first six months of her stay, but that there was sufficient evidence to show that she was after that, so a non-dependant deduction applied only after the six months *(CH/3935/2007)*.

4.44   HB 3(4) sch 1 para 8; HB60+ 3(4) sch 1 para 8; NIHB 3(4) sch 1 para 8; NIHB60+ 3(4) sch 1 para 8

Non-dependants' families

4.47 The partner of a non-dependant is also a non-dependant (but there is only one non-dependant deduction, if any: para. 6.28). For children of non-dependants there is usually no non-dependant deduction (table 6.3).

Others who may live in the claimant's dwelling

Lodgers

4.48 A lodger is someone who lives with the claimant on a commercial basis and pays the claimant or claimant's partner 'rent'. HB/CTR rules divide lodgers into two kinds:

(a) lodgers who pay an inclusive charge for accommodation and at least some cooked or prepared meals (sometimes called 'boarders');

(b) lodgers who pay a rent which does not include meals (sometimes called 'sub-tenants').

4.49 In the first case above (para. 4.48(a)), 'meals' must be provided – for example, breakfast every day is enough. They must be cooked or prepared, and consumed, in the accommodation or associated premises; and the cooking or preparation of the meal must be done by someone other than the boarder or a member of their family.

4.50 Income from a lodger is taken into account in the assessment of the claimant's HB/CTR (table 13.3). The method is more favourable for a claimant who provides meals. A lodger may claim HB in their own right subject to the normal rules.

Lodger vs. non-dependant

4.51 Both lodgers and non-dependants may make payments to the claimant and have exclusive occupation of, say, a bedroom. But there are 'many examples... of family arrangements and acts of friendship or generosity not... giving rise to a tenancy even where exclusive occupation is given' ([2012] UKUT 114 (AAC)). The distinction between a lodger and a non-dependant therefore hinges more on whether there is a tenancy or similar commercial arrangement between the parties.

Joint occupiers

4.52 A joint occupier is someone other than the claimant's partner who is jointly liable with the claimant to make payments in order to occupy the dwelling. Joint occupiers include both joint owners and joint tenants. They might

---

4.48   HB 3(2)(e); HB60+ 3(2)(e); NIHB 3(2)(e); NIHB60+ 3(2)(e); CTP 9(2)(e); CTR 9(2)(e)

4.49   HB sch 5 para 42; HB60+ 2(1); NIHB sch 6 para 44; NIHB60+ 2(1); CTP 2(1); CTR 2(1)

4.52   HB 3(2)(d),(3); HB60+ 3(2)(d),(3); NIHB 3(2)(d),(3); NIHB60+ 3(2)(d),(3); CTP 9(2)(e),(3); CTR 9(2)(e),(3)

be three friends or two brothers or mother and daughter (and so on). They may refer to themselves as house-sharers or flatsharers. They are not the same as tenants in a 'house in multiple occupation' (para. 10.9).

4.53 Each joint occupier is eligible for HB/CTR in their own right (so long as they meet the conditions in the ordinary way); and this often means apportioning the rent, council tax or rates (chapters 7-11).

Carers

4.54 If a claimant receives care from their partner, a dependent child, a non-dependant, a lodger or a joint occupier, that person is taken into account in HB/CTR according to the category just mentioned. For example, if the claimant's nephew comes to care for her, the nephew is taken into account as a non-dependant and there are no further rules.

4.55 Other resident carers are included in deciding the size of accommodation the claimant needs (chapters 7-9) – and this can also apply to non-resident carers.

4.56 But resident carers are excluded from counting as a non-dependant (so there is no non-dependant deduction for them) if:

- the carer lives with the claimant to look after them or a partner; and
- the carer is engaged by a charitable or voluntary organisation (not a public or local authority); and
- that organisation makes a charge to the claimant or partner for the services provided.

Domestic staff

4.57 It is not unheard-of for claimants to have staff, such as nannies, au pairs and so on. Staff have no effect on the claimant's HB/CTR (but the claimant may require space for them in their home).

Second adults

4.58 The term 'second adult' is relevant only to second adult rebate and includes non-dependants and probably carers and staff (para. 6.37).

4.58   HB 3(2)(f); HB60+ 3(2)(f); NIHB 3(2)(f); NIHB60+ 3(2)(f); CTP 9(2)(f); CTR 9(2)(f)

5   Making a claim

5.1   This chapter describes how to claim HB and CTR and when awards start. It explains:

- who makes the claim and how claims are made;
- the information and evidence needed;
- how complete and incomplete claims are dealt with;
- when awards start (date of claim and first day of entitlement); and
- backdating.

This chapter does not apply when someone already on HB/CTR moves from one address to another within an authority's area, as this is a change in circumstances (para. 17.16) and does not require a claim for HB/CTR.

Who makes the claim

5.2   HB and CTR can only be awarded if a claim is made. This is the responsibility of the claimant (or 'applicant' as CTR law calls them) – and the claimant can ask anyone they like to help with filling in the application form.

Claims by people who were on CTB

5.3   People who were on CTB on 31st March 2013, or made a CTB claim which was not decided by that date, are treated as having claimed CTR with effect from 1st April 2013.

Couples

5.4   In the case of a couple or polygamous marriage (paras. 4.10, 4.20) one partner makes the claim (though in practice both may be asked to sign the claim form). They may choose between them which partner this is to be. If they cannot agree, the authority must choose. In some cases a couple are better off if one partner rather than the other is the claimant. These are identified in this guide as they arise (e.g. paras. 5.52, 10.30, 12.23, 12.36, 20.12).

People unable to act

5.5   A claim may be made by a third party if the claimant is unable, for the time being, to act. In such cases, that person takes over all rights and responsibilities

5.2   AA 1,5; NIAA 1,5; LGFA sch 1 para 2(5)

5.3   LGFA sch 1A para 9

5.4   HB 82(1); HB60+ 63(1); NIHB 80(1); NIHB60+ 61(1); CTP sch 7 para 4(1); CTR 109(1)

5.5   HB 82(6); HB60+ 63(6); NIHB 80(6); NIHB60+ 61(6); CTP sch 7 para 4(2)-(7); CTR 109(2) (6)

in relation to the HB/CTR claim. (The rules in paras. 5.6-7 apply to HB and to CTR in England and Wales. Though they are not contained in CTR law in Scotland, similar principles apply.)

5.6   Where one of the following has been appointed to act for the claimant, the authority must accept a claim from him or her:

* a receiver or deputy appointed by the Court of Protection;
* an attorney;
* in Scotland, a judicial factor or other guardian;
* in Northern Ireland, a controller appointed by the High Court; or
* a person appointed by the DWP to act on the claimant's behalf in connection with some other benefit.

5.7   In any other case, the authority may accept a written request from an individual over 18, or a firm or organisation, to be the claimant's 'appointee' – for example, a friend or relative, a social worker or solicitor. In doing this the authority should take account of any conflict of interests. Once appointed, an appointee has all the rights and responsibilities that would normally belong to the claimant. Either the authority or the appointee can terminate the appointment by giving four weeks' written notice.

How to claim

Claims made to the authority

5.8   Claims for HB and CTR are made to the authority – or to someone acting on its behalf (paras. 1.26-27). (For claims made via the DWP, see para. 5.9 for HB and para. 5.11 for CTR.) Many authorities accept HB/CTR claims by telephone or online; and can require claimants to approve a written statement of a telephone claim, or keep written or electronic records of an online claim. In all other cases, HB/CTR claims must be in writing to a 'designated office', which can be the authority's benefit office, a county council office, a social landlord's address, etc. Application forms must be provided free of charge and give the address of every designated office and optionally an online address.

Claims via the DWP

5.9   Claims for HB can be made via the DWP as follows (for CTR, see para. 5.11). Most claims for JSA, ESA, IS or pension credit (or IB when it is linked to a former claim) are made by telephone to a DWP 0800 number (para. 25.16). During the call, the claimant is asked whether they wish to claim HB and if they do information relevant to HB is collected. The information is verified by the DWP

5.8   HB 2(1), 83; HB60+ 2(10, 64; NIHB 2(1), 81; NIHB60+ 2(1), 62; CTP 2(1), sch 7 paras 2,3,11-13; CTR 2(1), sch 1 paras 2,3,13-14

5.9   HB 2(1),83(4),111; HB60+ 2(1),64(5),(5B),92; NIHB 2(1),81(4), NIHB60+ 2(1),62(5).(5B)

if possible at an interview (which can be fast tracked if there is the threat of an eviction) or by post. The DWP then sends the authority an electronic 'LAID' (local authority input document, known as 'LACI' in ESA cases), even if the claimant does not qualify for the DWP benefit or withdraws their claim for it. The LAID/LACI is a computer generated claim form with the claimant's answers filled in. The DWP also sends the authority a 'customer statement'.

5.10   The following are the main exceptions to the above procedure. People who opt to make a 'fast track' telephone claim to the DWP (e.g. because they know they wish to claim JSA(C) only) are not invited to claim HB during the call: they should claim HB direct from the authority. People telephoning to make a 'rapid reclaim' for JSA or ESA (i.e. within 12 weeks of a previous award ending) are posted an HB form (HBRR1) by the DWP and advised to send it to the authority. People claiming a DWP benefit other than by telephone (e.g. ESA or pension credit) are posted an HB form (HCTB1) by the DWP and advised to send it to the authority. The DWP also uses form HCTB1 in this way (marked 'CMS contingency') when their computer is unable to accept telephone claims.

5.11   From 1st April 2013, people making a claim to the DWP for the benefits mentioned (para. 5.9) are asked whether they wish to claim CTR, and if they do relevant information is forwarded to the authority. But this does not constitute a claim for CTR: the claim for CTR should be made direct to the authority.

Amending or withdrawing a claim

5.12   Before a decision is made on a claim, the claimant may:

- amend it: the amendment is treated as having been made from the outset;
- withdraw it: the authority is then under no duty to decide it.

A telephone claim (paras. 5.8-10) may be amended or withdrawn by telephone or in writing. Amendments and withdrawals of other claims must be in writing. If the telephone claim was to the authority, any amendment must be to them; if it was to the DWP, it could be to either.

Information and evidence

5.13   The claimant is responsible for providing 'certificates, documents, information and evidence' which are 'reasonably required by the authority in order to determine... entitlement' to HB or CTR. This applies when they make a claim (para. 5.20), and also during the course of an award (para. 17.37). The authority may also ask the claimant to attend an interview, but may not insist on this: *R v Liverpool CC ex parte Johnson No. 2*. Evidence should be obtained direct from a third party only with the claimant's written agreement (GM para. D3.400), but this is usually given in the declaration made in connection with a claim.

5.12   HB 87; HB60+ 68; NIHB 83; NIHB60+ 64; CTP sch 8 para 8; CTR 114

5.13   AA 5(1); NIAA 5(1); HB 83(1),86(1),(1A); HB60+ 64(2),67(1),(1A); NIHB 81(1),82(1),(1A); NIHB60+ 62(2),63(1),(1A); CTP sch 8 para 7(1),(4),(6); CTR 113(1),(4),(6)

5.14   The law does not specify (except as described in paras. 5.15-16) what information and evidence is required in relation to particular matters. In practice authorities require evidence about household members and their status, income and capital (for claimants not on a passport benefit), occupation of the dwelling (when appropriate), rent (in rent allowance cases), and other matters; and expect claimants to provide original documents rather than copies. In written claims, a signature by the claimant is a reasonable requirement, and many authorities also require a signature by a partner.

Information the claimant need not disclose

5.15   An authority cannot require any information or evidence whatsoever about the following types of payment, whether they are made to a claimant, partner, non-dependant or second adult:

* payments from the Macfarlane Trusts, the Eileen Trust, MFET Ltd, the Skipton Fund, the Caxton Fund, the Fund or the London Bombing Charitable Relief Fund, and in certain cases payments derived from those sources (para. 13.118);
* payments in kind of capital from a charity or from the above sources;
* payments in kind of income (para. 13.130) from any source.

National Insurance numbers

5.16   In HB and CTR the claimant must either provide their National Insurance (NI) number and the NI number of their partner, along with information or evidence establishing this; or provide information or evidence enabling it to be ascertained; or make an application for an NI number and give information or evidence to assist with this – even if it is highly improbable that one will be granted: *CH/4085/2007.* There are three exceptions:

* the rule does not apply (to claimant or partner) for claims for HB made in respect of a hostel (para. 9.45);
* the rule does not apply in certain cases where the claimant's partner is a foreign national (para. 20.14);
* in Scotland the rule is not included in CTR law.

Matters relating to the provision of an NI number are appealable, including the evidence needed to ascertain one: *CH/1231/2004*; and the consequences in an HB/CTR decision of a refusal to allocate one: *2009 UKUT 74 (ACC).*

Claimants on a passport benefit, etc

5.17   If a claimant has been lawfully awarded a passport benefit (table 6.1) by the DWP, this is binding on the authority as proof that (at the relevant dates) the

---

5.15   HB 86(2),(4); HB60+ 67(2),(4); NIHB 82(2),(4); NIHB60+ 63(2),(4); CTP sch 8 para 7(5),(7); CTR 113(5),(7)

5.16   AA1(1A); NIAA 1(1A); HB 4; HB60+ 4; NIHB 4; NIHB 60+ 4; CTP sch 8 para 7(2),(3); CTR 113(2),(3)

claimant fulfils the income-related conditions for receiving maximum HB/CTR (paras. 6.4 and 13.3): *R v Penwith District Council ex parte Menear and R v South Ribble Council Housing Benefit Review Board.* If a claimant has been lawfully awarded savings credit or universal credit, certain figures also are binding on the authority (paras. 13.162 and 13.170).

Information gathered by the DWP

5.18   In HB (only), the law requires the authority to use information relevant to HB, without verifying its accuracy, if it is supplied by the DWP and relates to a claim for or an award of: attendance allowance, bereavement allowance, bereavement payment, carer's allowance, disability living allowance, employment and support allowance, incapacity benefit, income support, jobseeker's allowance, retirement pension, state pension credit, universal credit, widowed parent's allowance or winter fuel payment. But the authority need not use information which is more than 12 months old, nor if the authority has reason to believe that the information has changed since the DWP obtained it.

In practice, the DWP verifies the evidence relevant to a claim for HB made via them (paras. 5.9-10) – but there are exceptions (for example, the DWP does not verify capital if the claimant says it is below £6,000). The DWP advises that authorities 'should accept' that it has 'taken the appropriate action' in relation to such evidence (CMS Guide for local authorities, March 2010).

Nil income claims, etc

5.19   No-one is required to claim HB via the DWP (even if that is the normal procedure: para. 5.9); some claimants may need to claim HB from the authority while waiting for a DWP benefit to be assessed. The DWP recommends authorities 'do not ask the [claimant] to provide information and evidence that you know will be collected by [the DWP] unless the claim is urgent, (CMS Guide for local authorities, March 2010). However, if there is evidence of the claimant's actual circumstances, it is not reasonable (para. 5.13) to delay assessing HB to wait for a DWP decision. If the claimant has no income, they qualify for maximum HB/CTR (para. 6.10) regardless of what the DWP decides: including a claimant living off voluntary payments from friends or relatives, or payments in kind, or their own savings.

Similarly, no claimant can be compelled to claim a DWP benefit; some claimants prefer to claim HB/CTR without doing so (perhaps because they are living off savings or the kinds of payment mentioned above). There is no power to refuse a claim for HB/CTR because it is thought the claimant 'ought' (in some sense) to be on a DWP benefit.

5.18   SI 2007/2911; NISR 2007/467

Complete and incomplete claims

What is a complete claim

5.20   A claim is complete if it is made:

* in writing or online (para. 5.8) and is on an application form approved by the authority and completed in accordance with the instructions on the form – including any instructions to provide information and evidence;

* in some other written form which the authority accepts as sufficient in the circumstances of a particular case or class of cases, having regard to whether the information and evidence provided with it is sufficient;

* by telephone (paras. 5.8-9) and the claimant provides the information and evidence required to decide the claim.

Dealing with complete claims

5.21   A complete claim (also sometimes called an 'effective' or 'valid' claim) must be decided by the authority, as described in paragraphs 16.2 onwards.

Dealing with incomplete claims

5.22   An incomplete claim (also sometimes called a 'defective' claim) is one which is received by the authority (or DWP if appropriate) but which does not meet the conditions given above (para. 5.20). The authority should give the claimant the opportunity of doing whatever is needed to make it complete. In the case of a claim via the DWP, however, the DWP may do this (but if it does not, the authority must). Depending on the circumstances, this could mean:

* the authority sending the claimant a claim form;

* the authority returning a form to the claimant for completion; or

* the authority or the DWP requesting information and evidence (or further information and evidence) from the claimant.

In all cases, the authority must also inform the claimant of the duty to notify relevant changes of circumstances which occur, and say what these are likely to be.

5.23   The claimant must be allowed at least one month to provide what is required (para. 5.28), and must be allowed longer if it is reasonable to do so. In the case of telephone claims, the law specifically permits more than one reminder, and the month is counted from the last such reminder. In the case of written and online claims, some authorities send a reminder, allowing a further period for the reply. In all these cases, if the claimant does what is required within the time limit, the claim is treated as having been complete from the outset.

5.20   AA 1,5,6; NIAA 1,5; HB 83(1),(4C),(9); HB60+ 64(2),(5D),(10); NIHB 81(1),(4C),(9); NIHB60+ 62(2),(5D),(10); CTP sch 7 paras 2,3,11; CTR sch 1 paras 2,3,13

5.22   HB 83(4D)-(4E); (6)-(9), 86(1)(2); HB60+ 64(5E)-(5F) (7)-(9), 67(1),(2); NIHB 81(4D)-(4E), (6)-(9), 82(1),(2); NIHB60+ 62(4D)-(4E), (7)-(9),63(1),(2); CTP sch 7 paras 4-7, sch 8 paras 5(3)-(5),7(4),(6); CTR 110(3)-(5), 113(4),(6), sch 1 paras 4-7

Deciding incomplete claims

5.24   Even if a claim is incomplete it must be decided by the authority (but see para. 5.20). In such cases, the authority may:

- decide that the claimant is not entitled to HB/CTR because they do not satisfy the conditions of entitlement, as they have not provided the necessary information or evidence; or

- make a negative inference (which means 'assume the worst') in order to make its decision. For example, if a claimant's bank statement shows that he withdrew £20,000 three weeks ago, and he refuses to explain this, it might be reasonable to decide that his capital remains £20,000.

In each case, the claimant may appeal to a tribunal (para. 19.24).

Claims not received

5.25   The authority has no duty to decide a claim that was not received – for example an application form which is lost in the post. An (attempted) telephone claim in which the claimant does not answer all the questions, or fails to approve a written statement if requested to do so (para. 5.8), is treated as 'not received' – but in this case the authority may nonetheless decide it. An (attempted) online claim which the authority's computer does not accept or which is not in the form approved (para. 5.8) is treated as 'not received'. In all these cases, if the claimant claims HB/CTR again, authorities should consider whether the conditions for backdating are met (para. 5.51).

When HB/CTR starts

Overview

5.26   HB and CTR start on the Monday following the claimant's 'date of claim' (or for CTR in Wales only, on the date of claim). But if the 'week-one-yes rule' applies, they can start earlier. The details are in the remainder of this chapter. The main rules are:

- the 'date of claim' usually means the date the claimant first notified their intention (to one of the relevant offices) to claim HB/CTR – but it can be earlier (para. 5.30);

- the 'week-one-yes rule' applies if the claimant becomes liable for rent/council tax/rates on their new home (paras. 5.47-48).

5.24   HB 83(4F),89; HB60+ 64(5G),70; NIHB 85; NIHB60+ 66; CTP sch 8 para 5(3)-(5); CTR 110(3)-(5)

5.25   HB 83(4),(4B),(4C) sch 11 paras 2(7),4; HB60+ 64(5),(5C),(5D) sch 10 paras 2(7),4;
        NIHB 81(4),(4B),(4C) sch 11 paras 2(7),4; NIHB60+ 62(5),(5C),(5D) sch 10 paras 2(7),4;
        CTP sch 7 paras 3,11(7); CTR sch 1 paras 3,13(7)

5.26   HB 76(1),(2); HB60+ 57(1),(2); NIHB 74(1),(2); NIHB60+ 55(1),(2); CTP 45(1),(2); CTR 106(1),(2)

Duration of award

5.27   There is no fixed limit to an award of HB/CTR. Entitlement may change if there is a change in circumstances (para. 17.19). Otherwise it simply continues until the claimant:

- stops being entitled – for example, gains too much capital or income, dies or becomes an ineligible student (para. 17.37); or

- in the case of HB only, fails to respond to a request for information or evidence and then the award is terminated (para. 17.73).

Definition of 'month'

5.28   Many of the rules in this guide refer to allowing someone a 'month' to do something in connection with a claim, etc. This means a calendar month, and the month is counted as follows *(R(IB) 4/02)*:

- if the authority issues a letter on 26th June inviting the claimant to provide something, the claimant has provided it within a month if he or she gets it to the authority by the end of 26th July;

- if the authority issues a letter on 31st January inviting a claimant to provide something, the claimant has provided it within a month if he or she gets it to the authority by the end of 28th (or 29th) February.

Things sent out by the authority (such as requests for information or evidence, decision letters) are counted in the law as being sent out on the date of posting. Things received by the authority (such as claims, information and evidence) are counted in the law as being received on the date of receipt. In the case of online communications, this means the date recorded by the computer as the date of sending or receipt unless the authority reasonably directs otherwise.

Definition of 'benefit week'

5.29   Many of the rules in this guide refer to a 'benefit week' (or 'reduction week' as it is known in CTR law). A benefit week (for HB/CTR) begins on a Monday and ends on the following Sunday.

Date of claim

5.30   The rules about what counts as the claimant's 'date of claim' are summarised in table 5.1 (and were confirmed in *R(H) 9/07*). Further details follow.

5.28   HB sch 11 para 4; HB60+ sch 10 para 4; NIHB sch 11 para 4; NIHB60 sch 10 para 4; DAR 2; NIDAR 2; CTP sch 7 para 13; CTR sch 1 para 15

5.29   HB 2(1); HB60+ 2(1); NIHB 2(1); NIHB60+ 2(1); CTP 2(1); CTR 2(1)

5.30   HB 83(5); HB60+ 64(6); NIHB 81(5); NIHB60+ 62(6); CTP sch 8 para 5; CTR 110

Table 5.1: Date of claim for HB/CTR: summary

Situation	Date of claim
The claimant asked for a form (or notified an intention to claim) and returns it, properly completed, within one month of when it was sent out (or longer if reasonable)	The day the claimant asked for it (or notified the intention to claim)
The claim is made within one month of the claimant's partner's death or the claimant's and partner's separation, and the partner was on HB/CTR at the time	The day of the death or separation
The claimant or a partner was awarded JSA(IB), ESA(IR), IS, guarantee credit or universal credit and the claim for HB/CTR is received within one month of when the claim for that benefit was received	The first day of their entitlement to JSA(IB), ESA(IR), IS, guarantee credit or universal credit
The claimant or a partner is on JSA(IB), ESA(IR), IS or guarantee credit, and the claim for HB/CTR is received within a month of them first becoming liable for rent/council tax	The first day of their liability for rent/council tax
In any other case	The day the HB/CTR claim is received

♦ Detailed rules are in para. 5.31 onwards. See also para. 5.51 for backdating.

Notifying an intention to claim

5.31 This rule applies if:

* the claimant notified their intention to claim HB/CTR to the authority or DWP;
* it sent the claimant an application form; and
* the claimant returned the form within one month of when it was sent out, or longer if reasonable.

5.32 In this case, the date of claim is the day the claimant notified their intention to claim to the office in question. The claimant can do this 'by any means' (which includes telephoning, emailing, writing, texting, visiting or sending a friend: *CIS/2726/2005*).

5.31   HB 83(5)(d); HB60+ 64(6)(d); NIHB 81(5)(d); NIHB60+ 62(6)(d); CTP sch 8 para 5(f); CTR 110 (1)(f)

Example: Date of claim following notice of an intention to claim

On Thursday 24th October 2013, a claimant realises she might qualify for HB and telephones the authority to ask to claim. The authority sends an application form out that very day. She posts it back and it reaches the authority on Friday 8th November 2013.

Her date of claim is Thursday 24th October 2013 and (unless the week-one-yes rule applies: para. 5.47) the first day of her entitlement to HB is the following Monday, 28th October 2013.

Claims following death or separation

5.33   This rule applies if:

 • the claimant claims HB/CTR within one month of their partner's death or of their separation from their partner; and

 • that partner was on HB/CTR at the time of the death or separation.

5.34   In this case, the date of claim is the date of the separation or death in question, the intention being that there should be no gap in entitlement to HB/CTR. The one month time limit cannot be extended, but in some cases backdating should be considered (para. 5.1).

Passport benefit and universal credit claimants generally

5.35   This rule applies if:

 • the claimant or a partner claims and is awarded a passport benefit (JSA(IB), ESA(IR), IS or guarantee credit) or universal credit; and

 • the claimant's HB/CTR claim is received by the authority or the DWP no more than one month after the passport benefit or universal credit claim was received by the DWP.

5.36   In this case, the date of claim for HB/CTR is the date of first entitlement to the passport benefit (and in the case of JSA(IB) and ESA(IR) this means the first 'waiting day') or to universal credit. The one month time limit cannot be extended.

Passport benefit claimants who become liable for rent, rates or council tax

5.37   This rule applies if:

 • the claimant or their partner is receiving a passport benefit (table 6.1); and

 • they become liable for rent, rates or council tax for the first time; and

---

5.33   HB 83(5)(c); HB60+ 64(6)(c); NIHB 81(5)(c); NIHB60+ 62(6)(c); CTP sch 8 para 5(e); CTR 110(1)(e)

5.35   HB 83(5)(a); HB60+ 64(6)(a); NIHB 81(5)(a); NIHB60+ 62(6)(c); CTP sch 8 para 5(a),(c),(2),(8); CTR 110(1)(a),(c),(2),(8)

5.37   HB 83(5)(b); HB60+ 64(6)(b); NIHB 81(5)(b); NIHB60+ 62(6)(b); CTP sch 8 para 5(b),(d); CTR 110(1),(b),(d)

* the HB/CTR claim is received by the authority or the DWP no more than one month after the new liability begins.

5.38 In this case, the date of claim for HB is the first day of their new liability for rent or rates; the date of claim for CTR is the first day of their new liability for council tax. The one month time limit cannot be extended.

Other claims

5.39 This rule applies if none of the earlier rules applies (but see also para. 5.51).

5.40 In this case, the date of claim is the day the claim is received by the benefit authority or the county council (if authorised) or the DWP (paras. 5.9-10).

Advance claims

5.41 The following rule (para. 5.42) applies if a claimant claims:

* HB/CTR up to 17 weeks before they reach pension credit age (para. 1.20); or
* HB/CTR up to 17 weeks before an event which makes them entitled to HB/CTR (pension age claimants); or
* HB/CTR up to 13 weeks before an event which makes them entitled to HB/CTR (working age claimants); or
* CTR, or HB for rates, up to eight weeks before they become liable for council tax/rates;
* HB for a period of up to four weeks before moving into their home if they meet the conditions in paragraph 3.31.

The third and fourth rules do not, however, apply to someone who counts as a migrant or new arrival (chapter 20).

5.42 In these cases, the date of claim is:

* in the first three cases above, any date in the week before the benefit week (para. 5.29) containing the birthday or event in question;
* in the fourth case above, the date of first liability for council tax/rates;
* in the fifth case above, the day the claim was received (para. 5.40), or if later, the date the claimant actually moves in.

Delays in setting council taxes

5.43 This rule applies, in Scotland only, when:

* an authority delays setting its council tax until after 31st March; and
* a CTR claim is made within four weeks after the council tax is set.

5.39 HB 83(5)(e); HB60+ 64(6)(e); NIHB 81(5)(e); NIHB 62(6)(e); CTP sch 8 para 5(g); CTR 110(1)(g)

5.41 HB 7(7),83(10),(11); HB60+ 7(7); 64(11),(12); NIHB 7(7); 81(10),(11); NIHB60+ 7(7); 62(11),(12); CTP sch 8 para 5(6),(7); CTR 110(6),(7)

5.43 CTS 85(4); CTS60+ 65(4)

5.44 In this case, the date of claim for CTR is set so that entitlement begins on 1st April in that year (or the benefit week in which the person's entitlement begins if this falls between 1st April and the date the claim is received).

First day of entitlement

The general rule

5.45 The general rule is that the claimant's first day of entitlement to HB/CTR is the Monday following their 'date of claim' (paras. 5.30-44). Even if their date of claim is a Monday, their first day of entitlement is the following Monday. The exceptions follow.

CTR in Wales

5.46 For CTR only, and only in Wales, the general rule is that the claimant's first day of entitlement to CTR is their exact 'date of claim' (paras. 5.30-44), whichever day of the week it falls on; and (for CTR only) the 'week-one-yes rule' does not apply.

The week-one-yes rule

5.47 The week-one-yes rule applies only if the claimant or partner becomes liable for rent/council tax/rates in the benefit week (para. 5.29) containing their 'date of claim', and moves in during or before that week. In such cases, their entitlement begins on the day their liability for rent/council tax/rates begins, whichever day of the week that falls on. (It does not apply to CTR in Wales: para. 5.46.)

5.48 What if a claimant does not 'move in' until a day or so after their liability begins (but within the week in question)? The law appears clear that HB begins on the first day of their liability (within the week in question). The fourth example illustrates this. But many authorities instead pay from the day they move in, causing a day or two of rent arrears in the claimant's new home. This may be because of the DWP's choice of words when it advises that the week-one-yes rule 'enables HB awards to match a period of occupancy' (GM para. A6.81), or due to older DWP guidance which has been withdrawn (circular HB/CTB A8/2006).

The rule for certain dwellings with daily rents

5.49 This rule applies in HB only, and only to residents who are liable to pay their rent on a daily basis to:

  ◆ a hostel (para. 9.45); or

  ◆ any other accommodation in which they have been placed as a homeless

---

5.45　HB 76(1); HB60+ 57(1); NIHB 74(1); NIHB60+ 55(1); CTP 45(1); CTR 106(1)

5.46　CTPW sch 1 para 39; CTRW 104

5.47　HB 76(2),80(3)(a); HB60+ 57(2); 61(4)(a); NIHB 74(2),78(4)(a); NIHB60+ 55(2); 59(4)(a);
　　　 CTP 45(2); CTR 106(2)

person and which is board and lodging accommodation, accommodation licensed to the authority, or short-term leased accommodation (with a lease of no more than 10 years) outside the authority's housing revenue account.

Examples: First day of entitlement

The general rule

A man claims HB/CTR because his income has reduced. His date of claim is Thursday 18th July 2013.

His first day of entitlement to HB/CTR is the Monday following his date of claim, which is Monday 22nd July 2013.

The week-one-yes rule: whole weeks

A woman moves into her flat on Monday 1st July 2013, and is liable for rent and council tax from that very day. Her date of claim is Thursday 4th July 2013.

Her first day of entitlement to HB/CTR is the day her liability for rent/council tax begins, which is Monday 1st July 2013. (The answer is the same whether the rent is due weekly, monthly or on any other basis.)

The week-one-yes rule: part weeks

A woman moves into her flat on Saturday 8th June 2013, and is liable for rent and council tax from that very day. Her date of claim is Friday 7th June 2013.

Her first day of entitlement to HB/CTR is the day her liability for rent/council tax begins, which is Saturday 8th June 2013. In her first week she gets two-sevenths of a week's HB and CTR (for the Saturday and the Sunday). (The answer is the same whether the rent is due weekly, monthly or on any other basis.)

The week-one-yes rule: claimant does not move in immediately

A man has been living with relatives (and not liable for rent or council tax there). He obtains a housing association tenancy which starts on Monday 3rd June 2013. He does not fully move in until Wednesday 5th June 2013, and that is the night he starts sleeping there. His date of claim for HB/CTR is Thursday 6th June 2013.

His first day of entitlement to HB is Monday 3rd June 2013 (but see para. 5.48). His first day of entitlement to CTR depends on when he is regarded for council tax purposes as becoming liable for council tax. Practice varies, but it is likely to be Monday 3rd June 2013 or Wednesday 5th June 2013.

Note: The examples differ for CTR in Wales (para. 5.46).

5.49   HB 76(3)-(5); HB60+ 57(2)-(4); NIHB 74(3)-(5); NIHB60+ 55(2)-(4)

5.50   In such cases, there is no time limit on when the residents may claim, and their HB is always awarded back to when they moved into the accommodation. In other words, their first day of entitlement to HB is always the day they moved in. In practice, this rule is likely to be needed only for short periods (as leaving it any longer may mean the claimant is no longer available to provide the information and evidence necessary for their claim).

Backdating

5.51   The remainder of this chapter explains how HB and CTR can be backdated to cover periods in the past. The main rules are as follows:

+ for pension age HB and CTR claims, backdating for up to three months is automatic (para. 5.54);

+ for working age HB claims, backdating requires the claimant to have good cause and can be for up to six months (para. 5.56);

+ for working age CTR claims, backdating varies across Great Britain (para. 5.57).

'Pension age' vs 'working age' claims

5.52   Pension age and working age claims are defined in paragraphs 1.20-22 and table 1.4. In CTR only, some couples meet both definitions, so whether (or for how long) they qualify for backdated CTR can depend on which of them is the claimant (para. 10.30).

5.53   The following points apply to both age groups:

+ It is the date of claim which is backdated. So even if the claimant is not currently entitled to HB/CTR a backdated award can still be made.

+ When HB/CTR are backdated they are calculated using the rules which applied at the relevant times. Entitlement during the backdated period need not have been continuous or at the same address (or even, arguably, in the same authority's area).

+ Basing a claim for HB/CTR on an application which was (on the balance of probability) received by the authority or DWP (paras. 5.8-9), but was then mislaid or not acted on, is not backdating (because in fact a claim was made).

Backdating HB/CTR for pension age claims

5.54   For all pension age claims (para. 5.52), a claim for HB/CTR covers any period in the three months before the day the claim is actually received (or the day they notified their intention to claim, so long as they followed that up within the relevant time limits: paras. 5.31-32) – but only back to the day they reached pension credit age, or the day they became liable for rent or council tax, if these are later.

5.54   HB60+ 64(1),(1A); NIHB60+ 62(1),(1A); CTP sch 8 para 6; CTR 111

5.55 The claimant does not have to ask for this rule to apply, and does not have to have 'good cause' (or any reason whatsoever): the rule applies automatically in all cases.

> ### Example: Backdating for pension age claimants
>
> A claimant aged 73 sends in his first ever claim for HB/CTR. It reaches the authority on Friday 13th September 2013. He would have qualified for several years for a small amount of HB/CTR had he applied.
>
> His date of claim is Friday 14th June 2013, which is three months earlier, and (unless the week-one-yes rule applies: para. 5.47) the first day of his entitlement to HB/CTR is the following Monday, 17th June 2013 (but see para. 5.46 for Wales).

Backdating HB for working age claims

5.56 For working age claims (para. 5.52), HB must be backdated if the claimant:

- requests this in writing (whether on the authority's application form or separately later); and
- 'had continuous good cause for [his or her] failure to make a claim' (as described in paras. 5.58 onwards).

HB cannot be backdated more than six months before the written request (even if it was received later than the claim for HB).

Backdating CTR for working age claims

5.57 For working age CTR claims (para. 5.52), the rules about backdating vary:

- In Scotland, the CTR backdating rules are always the same as for HB (para. 5.56).
- In Wales, the CTR backdating rules are usually the same as for HB but with a time limit of three months. However authorities may extend (or reduce) this time limit and vary the backdating rules in other ways (para. 10.28).
- In England, it is up to each authority to decide what provisions, if any, to make about backdating CTR (para. 10.25). For example, some authorities allow backdating for 'good cause' for up to six months, and some have no backdating (but may consider making a discretionary council tax reduction instead: para. 10.40).

5.56   HB 83(12),(12A); NIHB 81(12),(12A); CTR 112

'Good cause'

5.58   Good cause has been explained by tribunals and courts right back to
the late 1940s, and this case law is binding: *CH/5221/2001*. Recent cases are
summarised in table 5.2. The following are the main principles.

5.59   Good cause includes 'any fact that would probably have caused a
reasonable person to act as the claimant did', but they are expected to take
reasonable steps to ascertain what their rights may be. However, 'claimants
cannot always be assumed to have an understanding of public administration'
(CS/371/1949, quoted with approval in *CH/450/2004).* However, this 'traditional
formulation' has more recently been criticised *([2010] UKUT 64 (ACC))* because:

* it does not reflect the language of the regulations;

* it introduces subjective elements while what is 'reasonable' is objective;

* though ignorance *of itself* is not good cause, it may be a factor to be taken
  into account. The law does not 'require a person to be acquainted with the
  "rules and regulations".'

Table 5.2: Backdating for working age HB claims: case law

This table summarises case law about backdating HB since 2002. See also
paragraphs 5.53 and 5.56. Considerations relating to 'good cause' may also
apply to CTR (para. 5.57).

* *Case law on other benefits:* Case law about other DWP benefits is
  binding on HB *(CH/5135/2001, CH/5221/2001).*

* *What constitutes a request:* A request for backdating does not have to
  be expressed as such: it needs merely to be a claim for a past period. For
  example, it could be a late claim following the end of an earlier award
  (CH/3402/2005).

* *Backdating if claimant does not qualify during the period:* The question
  of backdating does not arise if the other conditions of entitlement are
  not satisfied in the backdated period *(CH/996/2004).*

* *Backdating if claimant qualifies for only part of the period:* So long as
  there is good cause, there is nothing to stop HB from being backdated
  for a period in the past (within the time limit) but then to cease in the
  past because entitlement ceased *(CH/1237/2004).*

* *Good cause and illness:* If a claimant was ill, the test of good cause is
  related not to the severity or seriousness of the illness but to the
  resulting incapability of the claimant to claim *(CH/5135/2001).*

* *Good cause and mental incapacity:* In deciding good cause, a mentally

disabled person is treated as having their mental age not their chronological age *(CH/393/2003)*.

* *Inability to speak English:* Not speaking English is not in itself good cause, particularly if there is evidence of a growing community with good facilities speaking the claimant's language *(CH/3579/2003)*.

* *Good cause in the case of a couple:* In the case of a couple, it is only the claimant's circumstances that are relevant and the other partner does not have to show good cause *(CH/3817/2004)*.

* *Good cause and a mistaken belief reasonably held:* The claimant (who had mental health problems) had believed he did not have to pay council tax because he was on income support. He had good cause because he had not been careless or sought to obtain something to which he was not entitled. He had a firmly held misunderstanding which amounted to a mistaken belief reasonably held *(CH/450/2004* and see para. 5.60). Similarly, a reasonably held belief that one cannot get HB if one has not paid national insurance contributions might amount to good cause *(CH/2198/2008)*.

* *Good cause and ignorance:* Though ignorance is not in itself good cause, it may be a factor to be taken into account. The law does not 'require a person to be acquainted with the rules and regulations' *([2010] UKUT 64 (ACC))*.

* *Good cause and imprisonment:* The claimant had thought he could not qualify for HB because delays with his parole hearing made his absence greater than 13 weeks. Due to the particular complications in this case, the claimant had good cause *(CH/2639/2006)*.

* *Good cause and failure to receive documents from the authority:* A failure to receive a document from the authority is not to be dismissed as possible good cause. In all three cases cited here, the document was a renewal claim form *(CSHC/352/2002, CH/3009/2004, CI 1/3402/2005)*.

Example: Backdating HB for good cause

A claimant aged 53 sends in his first ever claim for HB. It reaches the authority on Friday 13th September 2013. He would have qualified for several years for a small amount of HB had he applied. His claim includes a request to backdate his award to Monday 1st July 2013 when he was admitted to hospital. He was so ill that it was impossible for him to communicate throughout his time in hospital. He came home from hospital on Tuesday 3rd September 2013, but took a few days to start thinking about his finances. He has a grown-up daughter living with him throughout.

Although his daughter could have made a claim for him, this has no effect on his backdating: *CH/3817/2004.* While in hospital and unable to communicate he could not claim or ask someone to claim for him, so he had good cause.

Taking eight days to claim after such a bad illness is reasonable, so during those eight days he also had good cause.

Because he had continuous good cause, his HB must be backdated to Monday 1st July 2013, the day he went into hospital. His HB therefore starts on Monday 8th July 2013.

Note that in any backdating case, it is often possible to think of some other fact that might alter the outcome. In this case for example, was he so ill before he went into hospital that his HB should be backdated further.

5.60   The case law establishes that good cause usually falls into four categories:

+ the claimant was so ill (physically or mentally) or otherwise unable to act that they could not claim and could not ask someone to claim for them;

+ someone the claimant should have been able to rely on (such as the authority, the DWP, an advice agency and possibly others) advised them they could not get HB (or where appropriate CTR) when in fact they could;

+ there were good reasons for the claimant not believing they could claim, amounting to more than just not thinking or not caring;

+ some external factor prevented the claimant from making a claim (e.g. failure of the postal services, imprisonment).

5.61   The above are the commonest categories, and have been relevant to people who have lost earnings or jobs during the recession. Other situations may also amount to good cause. Disputes about good cause are appealable to a First-tier Tribunal (para. 19.18) – and also to an Upper Tribunal (para. 19.90) because they are regarded as questions of law *(R(SB) 39/91)* as well as fact.

6   Calculating HB and CTR

6.1   This chapter explains:

+ how to calculate HB and CTR;
+ non-dependant deductions;
+ the HB benefit cap;
+ how to calculate second adult rebate; and
+ converting figures to weekly amounts.

6.2   The CTR rules in this chapter vary across Great Britain (paras. 6.5, 6.8, 6.12, 6.14, 6.17 and 6.36). There are also differences between 'working age' and 'pension age' claims (as defined in table 1.4 and paras. 1.20-22).

Calculating HB and CTR

6.3   The following steps (paras. 6.4-15) give the calculation of HB and CTR. Table 6.2 summarises the rules.

Maximum benefit

6.4   The starting point for all HB and CTR calculations is the claimant's weekly 'maximum benefit'. This is:

+ in HB, the claimant's weekly maximum eligible rent and/or rates in Northern Ireland;
+ in CTR, the claimant's weekly eligible council tax;
+ minus (in each of those cases) any non-dependant deductions which apply.

Chapters 7-11 define maximum eligible rent, eligible council tax and rates, and explain when they are split between joint occupiers.

6.5   For working age claims in England, maximum CTR can be lower (para. 10.25); for example, it can be limited to a percentage of council tax (usually between 70% and 90%) or to a particular band. For pension age claims in England and all claims in Scotland and Wales, there are no limitations to maximum CTR.

On a passport benefit

6.6   A claimant on a passport benefit qualifies for maximum benefit (para. 6.4). Table 6.1 lists who is on a passport benefit.

6.4   CBA 130(1),(3)(a),130A; NICBA 129(1),(3)(a),129A; HB 70; HB60+ 50; NIHB 68; NIHB 60+ 48; CTP sch 1 para 7(1); CTR 29(1)

6.6   CBA 130(1),(3)(a),130A; NICBA 129(1),(3)(a),129A; HB 2(3), sch 5 paras 4,5, sch 6 paras 5,6; HB60+ 2(3),26; NIHB 2(3) sch 6 paras 4,5, sch 7 paras 5,6; NIHB60+ 2(3),24; CTP sch 1 paras 2, 10(2); CTR 13, 16, 32(2)

Table 6.1: Passport benefits

In calculating HB and CTR, a person counts as being 'on a passport benefit' if they are:

- on guarantee credit
- on income support – IS
- on income-based jobseeker's allowance – JSA(IB)
- on income-related employment and support allowance – ESA(IR)
- entitled to JSA(IB) or ESA(IR) but not receiving it because of a sanction
- in the 'waiting days' before JSA(IB) or ESA(IR) start – or would start apart from a sanction
- subject to a restriction in their JSA(IB) or IS as a result of breaching a community order.

Capital

6.7   A claimant with capital over £16,000 (assessed as in chapters 13 to 15) does not qualify for any HB or CTR. (But being on a passport benefit over-rides this; and see para. 6.31 for whether they qualify for second adult rebate.)

6.8   For working age CTR claims in England, this capital limit can be lower (para. 10.25): in some areas it is as low as £6,000. It is always £16,000 for pension age CTR claims in England, all CTR claims in Wales and Scotland, and all HB claims.

Income and excess income

6.9   In all other cases, the claimant's weekly income (chapters 13-15) is compared with their applicable amount (chapter 12).

6.10   A claimant with no income, or whose income is less than their applicable amount, qualifies for maximum benefit (para. 6.4).

6.11   If the claimant's income is more than their applicable amount, the difference between the two is called 'excess income'. The claimant qualifies for maximum benefit (para. 6.4) minus a percentage of this excess income. The percentage – also called a 'taper' – is:

- 65% in calculating HB (for rent);
- 20% in calculating CTR;
- 20% in calculating HB for rates in Northern Ireland.

6.7   CBA 130(1),(3)(a),130A; NICBA 129(1),(3)(a),129A; CTP 11(2); CTR 23

6.9   CBA 130(1),(3),130A; NICBA 129(1),(3),129A; CTP sch 1 para 3(f); CTR 14(f),17(f)

6.11   CBA 130(1),(3),130A,131(5),(8); NICBA 129(1),(3),129A; CTP sch 1 paras 3, 10(3); CTR 14, 17, 32(3)

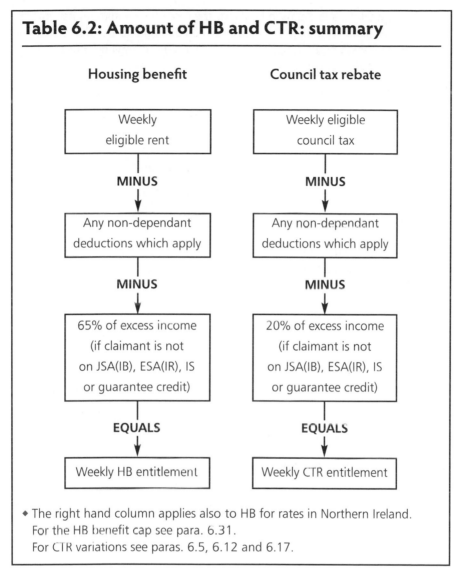

Table 6.2: Amount of HB and CTR: summary

Housing benefit	Council tax rebate
Weekly eligible rent	Weekly eligible council tax
MINUS	**MINUS**
Any non-dependant deductions which apply	Any non-dependant deductions which apply
MINUS	**MINUS**
65% of excess income (if claimant is not on JSA(IB), ESA(IR), IS or guarantee credit)	20% of excess income (if claimant is not on JSA(IB), ESA(IR), IS or guarantee credit)
EQUALS	**EQUALS**
Weekly HB entitlement	Weekly CTR entitlement

- The right hand column applies also to HB for rates in Northern Ireland. For the HB benefit cap see para. 6.31.
  For CTR variations see paras. 6.5, 6.12 and 6.17.

6.12 For working age CTR claims in England, the CTR taper can be higher (para. 10.25): in some authorities it is as high as 35%. It is always 20% for pension age CTR claims in England and all CTR claims in Wales and Scotland.

Minimum benefit

6.13 If the amount of HB calculated as above is less than the 'minimum benefit' figure, then it is not awarded. For HB for rent the figure is 50p per week. There is no minimum figure for HB for rates in Northern Ireland.

6.13   CBA 131(9);HB 75; HB60+ 56, NIHB 73; NIHB60+ 54

6.14   For working age claims in England, there can be a minimum benefit figure for CTR (para. 10.25): it is usually between 50p and £5 per week. There is no minimum benefit figure for pension age CTR claims in England, nor for any CTR claims in Wales and Scotland.

Other calculation rules

6.15   The amount of HB can be reduced to recover an overpayment (para. 18.11-12) or administrative penalty (para. 18.64). For working age claims, HB is also subject to a benefit cap (para. 6.31). In CTR there is an alternative calculation called second adult rebate (para. 6.35), and if the claimant qualifies the 'better buy' must be considered (para. 6.40).

Non-dependant deductions

6.16   A non-dependant is, in broad terms, a grown-up son, daughter, friend or relative who lives in the claimant's home (para. 4.39). The calculation of HB and CTR assumes they will contribute to the claimant's rent, rates, and/or council tax. This contribution is called a 'non-dependant deduction' – because it is deducted from the eligible rent in the calculation of maximum benefit (para. 6.4). It is sometimes also called a non-dependant 'charge' or 'contribution'. This section explains when non-dependant deductions apply, and how much they are. Appendix 5 gives the rules in more detail.

6.17   For working age CTR claims in England, the rules in this section can vary (para. 10.25): in particular, non-dependant deductions can be higher. The rules cannot be varied for pension age CTR claims in England, nor for any CTR claims in Wales and Scotland, nor for HB.

When no deduction is made

6.18   There is no deduction for any non-dependant listed in table 6.3. And there is no non-dependant deduction for a member of the 'family' (para. 4.8), or lodger – because those are not non-dependants.

6.19   Also, there are no deductions for any non-dependant at all, if the claimant or any partner:

- ◆ is blind or has recently regained their sight (paras. 12.49-51); or
- ◆ receives the care component of disability living allowance payable at any rate; or
- ◆ receives attendance allowance payable at any rate (or any of the related benefits in para. 12.48).

6.16   HB 3; HB60+ 3; NIHB 3; NIHB60+ 3; CTP 9; CTR 9

6.18   HB 3(2),74(7),(8),(10); HB60+ 3(2),55(7)-(9); NIHB 3(2),72(7),(8),(10); NIHB60+ 3(2),53(7)-(9);
       CTP 9(2), sch 1 para 8(7),(8); CTR 9(2),30(7),(8)

6.19   HB 2(1),74(6), HB60+ 2(1),55(6); NIHB 2(1),72(6); NIHB60+ 2(1),53(6); CTP sch 1 para 8(6),(11),(12);
       CTR 2(1),30(6)

The last two cases do not apply if the benefits mentioned cease – for example, when the claimant or partner has been in hospital for four weeks. (For CTR variations, see para. 6.17.)

Examples: Calculating HB and CTR

(For variations which can apply in CTR, see paras. 6.5 and 6.12.)

Claimant on a passport benefit

A claimant has no non-dependants: she lives alone. Her eligible rent is £105.00 per week. The council tax on her home would be £20.00 per week apart from the fact that she qualifies for a 25% council tax discount, which reduces her liability to £15.00 per week.

Claimants on JSA(IB), ESA(IR), IS or guarantee credit get maximum benefit – which equals their eligible rent and eligible council tax.

HB:	Eligible rent equals weekly HB	£105.00
CTR:	Eligible council tax equals weekly CTR	£15.00

Claimant not on a passport benefit

A couple have no non-dependants. They are not on JSA(IB), ESA(IR), IS or guarantee credit. Their joint weekly income exceeds their applicable amount by £20.00. Their eligible rent is £130.00 per week. Their eligible council tax liability is £22.56 per week.

Claimants with excess income get maximum benefit minus a percentage of their excess income.

HB:	Eligible rent	£130.00
	minus 65% of excess income (65% x £20.00)	£13.00
	equals weekly HB	£117.00
CTR:	Eligible council tax	£22.56
	minus 20% of excess income (20% x £20.00)	£4.00
	equals weekly CTR	£18.56

When a deduction is made

6.20   In all cases not mentioned above (paras. 6.18-19) there is one non-dependant deduction per non-dependant (or per non-dependant couple: para. 6.28), as follows:

6.20   HB 74(1),(2),(9); HB60+ 55(1),(2),(10); NIHB 72(1),(2),(9); NIHB60+ 53(1),(2),(10); CTP sch 1 para 8(1),(2); CTR 30(1),(2)

- if the non-dependant is in 'remunerative work' (para. 6.22), the amount of the deduction depends on the level of their gross income (para. 6.24);
- if the non-dependant is not in remunerative work, the amount of the deduction is always the lowest amount.

The details and the figures are in table 6.4. (For CTR variations, see para. 6.17.)

Assuming the amount of a non-dependant deduction

6.21   It is common practice for authorities to assume the amount of a non-dependant deduction until they know what the non-dependant's actual circumstances are; and the law specifically permits the use of the highest deduction for anyone in remunerative work (but not if this is unlikely to reflect the non-dependant's likely circumstances: *CH/48/2006*). In all such cases, once the authority has evidence showing what the true deduction should be, it should award any arrears of HB/CTR that are due as a result (but for HB see paras. 17.11-12 if the claimant takes more than a month to provide this evidence).

Table 6.3: Non-dependants with no deduction

A non-dependant who is:

- aged under 18
- in certain circumstances, in receipt of a passport benefit or savings credit – see table 6.4 for details
- a youth trainee
- in prison or similar forms of detention
- a patient who has been in hospital for 52 weeks or more
- a temporary resident or visitor or any other person whose normal home is elsewhere
- for HB only, a member of the armed forces (regular or reserve) away on operations
- for HB only, a full-time student during the period of study (para. 22.20)
- for HB only, a full-time student during the summer vacation (para. 22.20) and he/she is not in remunerative work
- for HB only, a full-time student and the claimant or their partner is aged 65 or over
- for CTR only, a person who falls within any of the groups who are 'disregarded persons' for council tax purposes

Note: Appendix 5 gives further information. For CTR variations, see para. 6.17.

6.21   HB 74(1)(a); HB60+ 55(1)(a); NIHB 72(1)(a); NIHB60+ 53(1)(a); CTP sch 1 para 8(1)(a); CTR 30(1)(a)

T6.3   HB 74(7),(8); HB60+ 55(7),(8); NIHB 72(7),(8); NIHB60+ 53(7),(8); CTP sch 1 para 8(7),(8); CTR 30(7),(8)

Table 6.4: Weekly non-dependant deductions

	HB	CTR
If non-dependant is on certain benefits:		
• on JSA(IB)/ESA(IR)/IS aged 25+	£13.60	£0.00
• on JSA(IB)/IS aged under 25	£0.00	£0.00
• on ESA(IR) aged under 25: main phase	£13.60	£0.00
• on ESA(IR) aged under 25: assessment phase	£0.00	£0.00
• on JSA(C)/ESA(C) any age	£13.60	£3.65
• on pension credit (either kind)	£0.00	£0.00
If non-dependant works less than 16 hours/week, or is on maternity, paternity, adoption or sick leave	£13.60	£3.65

If non-dependant works 16+ hours/week (and is not on leave as described above) and has gross income of:

HB

• £394.00 or more per week	£87.75
• £316.00 to £393.99 per week	£79.95
• £238.00 to £315.99 per week	£70.20
• £183.00 to £237.99 per week	£42.90
• £124.00 to £182.99 per week	£31.25
• under £124.00 per week	£13.60

CTR

• £401.00 or more per week	£10.95
• £322.00 to £400.99 per week	£9.15
• £186.00 to £321.99 per week	£7.25
• under £186.00 per week	£3.65

| **Any other non-dependant not in work:** | £13.60 | £3.65 |

Notes:

See also table 6.3 and paragraphs 6.18-19 for when there is no deduction.

For references to 16 hours/week or more, see paras. 6.22-23.

Figures in the right-hand column also apply to HB for rates in Northern Ireland. For working age CTR claims in England, figures in the right-hand column can vary (para. 6.17).

Remunerative work

6.22   'Remunerative work' is work for which payment is made, or expected, and which averages 16 hours or more per week. Once a person is in remunerative work, it includes recognised, customary or other holidays, and also periods of absence without good cause.

6.23   Remunerative work does not include:

+ maternity, paternity or adoption leave (with the right to return to work under a contract or under employment law);

+ absences due to illness (whether or not wages or sick pay are being paid);

+ periods the person is laid off;

+ voluntary work;

+ work where the person's only income is from a Sports Council Award; or

+ any benefit week in which the non-dependant receives a passport benefit (table 6.1) for four days or more.

Gross income

6.24   It is gross income, not net income, which is used in the case of a non-dependant (para. 6.20, and for CTR variations see para. 6.17). This means income from all sources before the deduction of tax and national insurance (except those in para. 6.27). Although the law does not give a list of what income to include, authorities are likely to include the following in full:

+ earnings (before tax, national insurance, etc have been deducted);

+ self-employed net profit (after the deduction of reasonable expenses but before tax, national insurance, etc have been deducted);

+ social security benefits, pensions and tax credits (except those in para. 6.27);

+ state, occupational and private pensions;

+ rental income;

+ maintenance;

+ charitable and voluntary income;

+ interest on savings.

6.25   Gross income of a non-dependant in remunerative work is averaged over any recognisable cycle. If there is none, the authority should take into account the expected hours of work and (unless the non-dependant is just starting work) the average in the period before the claim for HB/CTR – which should be five weeks unless some other period would give a more accurate estimation.

6.22   HB 6(1),(5); HB60+ 6(1),(5); NIHB 6(1),(5); NIHB60+ 6(1),(5); CTP 10(1),(5); CTR 10(1),(5)

6.23   HB 2(1),6(6)-(8); HB60+ 2(1),6(6)-(8); NIHB 2(1),6(6)-(8); NIHB60+ 2(1),6(6)-(8); CTP 10(6)-(8); CTR 10(6)-(8)

6.24   HB 74(1),(2); HB60+ 55(1),(2); NIHB 72(1),(2); NIHB60+ 53(1),(2); CTP sch 1 para 8(1),(2); CTR 30(1),(2)

6.26 If the recognisable cycle of work is one year (e.g. in a school), weekly hours are averaged only during the periods the non-dependant works (e.g. term-times). The result applies during both those periods and the periods they do not work (e.g. holidays). But changes in income are taken into account. So a non-dependant who is a school assistant could count as being in remunerative work throughout the year, but changes in their income may mean different levels of non-dependant deduction in term-times and holidays.

Examples: Calculating HB and CTR

(For variations which can apply in CTR, see paras. 6.5, 6.12 and 6.17.)

Claimant on ESA(IR) with working non-dependant

A claimant is on ESA(IR). Her eligible rent is £100.00 per week. Her eligible council tax liability is £19.00 per week. Her 26-year-old son lives with her. He earns £450 per week gross for a 35-hour week.

Claimants on ESA(IR) get maximum benefit, which in this case involves a non-dependant deduction. The son is in remunerative work and the level of his gross income means the highest level of deduction applies in both HB and CTR (table 6.4).

HB:	Eligible rent	£100.00
	minus non-dependant deduction	£87.75
	equals weekly HB	£12.25
CTR:	Eligible council tax	£19.00
	minus non-dependant deduction	£10.95
	equals weekly CTR	£8.05

Claimant on ESA(IR) with non-dependant on JSA(IB)

The son in the previous example loses his job and starts receiving JSA(IB).

The calculation is as above, except that now there is no non-dependant deduction in CTR and the lowest deduction applies in HB (table 6.4).

HB:	Eligible rent	£100.00
	minus non-dependant deduction	£13.60
	equals weekly HB	£86.40
CTR:	Eligible council tax	£19.00
	no non-dependant deduction applies	
	equals weekly CTR	£19.00

6.25   HB 6(7),(4),(5); HB60+ 6(2),(4),(5); NIHB 6(2),(4)-(5); NIHB60+ 6(2),(4),(5); CTP 10(4),(5); CTR 10(4),(5)

6.26   HB 6(3); HB60+ 6(3); NIHB 6(3); NIHB60+ 6(3); CTP 10(3); CTR 10(3)

6.27 The following items are disregarded in full in assessing a non-dependant's gross income:

- disability living allowance (either or both components);
- attendance allowance (or any of the related benefits in para. 12.48);
- payments from (or originally derived from) the Macfarlane Trusts, the Eileen Trust, MFET Ltd, the Skipton Fund, the Caxton Fund, the Fund, the Independent Living Funds and the London Bombing Charitable Relief Fund (paras. 13.118, 13.120).

Non-dependant couples

6.28 In the case of a non-dependant couple (or a polygamous marriage), only one deduction applies, being the higher (or highest) of any that would have applied to the individuals if they were single claimants. In appropriate cases, there is no deduction (e.g. if they are both under 18). For the purpose of the various gross income limits in table 6.4, each non-dependant partner is treated as possessing the gross income of both of them. (For CTR variations, see para. 6.17.)

Non-dependants of joint occupiers

6.29 The following rules apply when a claimant is jointly liable for the rent or council tax on his or her home with one or more other persons who are not his or her partner, and there is also a non-dependant living there (but for CTR variations see para. 6.17):

(a) If the non-dependant is part of the household (para. 4.3) of only one of them, then the whole non-dependant deduction is made in any claim for benefit made by that one, and no deduction is made in any claim for benefit made by the others.

(b) If the non-dependant is part of the household of more than one of them, the amount of the non-dependant deduction is shared between them. Any of them claiming benefit gets his or her resulting share of the non-dependant deduction.

- In CTR, the share must be equal between the joint occupiers (but only between the ones who are jointly liable for the council tax on the home; and then only if they are jointly liable as joint owners or joint tenants, and not merely as partners in a couple or polygamous marriage: para. 10.10(a)).

- In HB, the share need not be equal: the authority should take into account the number of joint occupiers concerned and the proportion of rent each pays (para. 7.21).

6.27   HB 74(1),(2),(9); HB60+ 55(1),(2),(10); NIHB 72(1),(2),(9); NIHB60+ 53(1),(2),(10); CTP sch 1 para 8(9),(10),(13); CTR 2(1),30(9)

6.28   HB 74(3),(4); HB60+ 55(3),(4); NIHB 72(3),(4); NIHB60+ 53(3),(4); CTP sch 1 para 8(3),(4); CTR 30(3),(4)

6.29   HB 74(5); HB60+ 55(5); NIHB 72(5); NIHB60+ 53(5); CTP sch 1 para 8(5); CTR 30(5)

Delayed non-dependant deductions for people aged 65+

6.30   The following rule applies when:

+ the claimant or any partner is aged 65 or more; and

+ a non-dependant moves in, or there is any change in a non-dependant's circumstances which causes an increase in the amount of the deduction.

In such cases the change in entitlement to HB or CTR is not implemented until the day 26 weeks after the change actually occurred. But (except for CTR in Wales) if that is not a Monday, it is implemented from the following Monday.

The HB Benefit Cap

6.31   This section and chapter 23 describe how the benefit cap can reduce the claimant's HB. The purpose of the benefit cap is to ensure that the total amount of support received from HB and certain other benefits by the claimant and their family while out of work does not exceed a fixed weekly figure. The benefit cap only applies to HB for working age claimants (paras. 1.20-22). Exceptions and detailed rules about how it is calculated can be found in chapter 23.

Introduction of the benefit cap and its phased roll-out

6.32   The benefit cap is fully in force for all authorities in Great Britain from 15th April 2013. However, no authority is required to apply the cap and reduce benefit until it receives notice from the DWP (although an authority could apply the cap if it had the evidence and information to determine it). The benefit cap is not law in Northern Ireland at the time of writing but it is included in the Welfare Reform Bill being debated by the Assembly.

6.33   Since the authority does not have to apply the cap until the DWP gives notice (para. 6.32), the DWP can control its roll-out – which it is expected to do. From the start date (para. 6.32) it applies to just four authorities (Bromley, Croydon, Enfield and Haringey). The roll-out to other authorities is expected to take place on a phased basis between July and September 2013.

Calculating the reduction and its effect on HB

6.34   If the cap applies HB (as calculated in paras. 6.3-30) is reduced. How to calculate the amount of the reduction is described in chapter 23. If applying the full reduction reduces HB to nil or less than the minimum (para. 6.13) then the minimum award is made: this so that the claimant can apply for a DHP (para. 23.6).

6.30   HB60+ 59(10)-(13); NIHB60+ 57(12)-(15); CTP sch 1 para 46(10)-(13); CTR 107(10) (13)

6.32   HB 75B

6.34   HB 75D(2)

Second adult rebate

6.35   This section explains the type of CTR known as second adult rebate (SAR). It applies only in England and Scotland (and is called 'alternative maximum CTR' in the law). SAR is awarded to the claimant (the council tax payer) but based on the circumstances of a 'second adult' (para. 6.37). Because of the 'better buy' comparison (para. 6.44), it is awarded only if the claimant is better off on it than on CTR using the rules described earlier.

6.36   For working age claims in England, the rules in this section can vary (para. 10.25): in some areas there is no entitlement to SAR, in others entitlement is lower. The rules cannot be varied for pension age claims in England, nor for any claims in Scotland. (There is no SAR in Wales: para. 10.28.)

Who is a 'second adult'?

6.37   A second adult is:

- a non-dependant (para. 6.16);
- who is not a 'disregarded person' (para. 6.38).

People who live with the claimant on a commercial basis but without paying rent (e.g. a live-in carer or employee) are also second adults, so long as they are not disregarded persons.

Who are 'disregarded persons'?

6.38   A disregarded person is anyone who is disregarded for council tax discount purposes. Typical examples are young people, people who are severely mentally impaired, and certain students, youth trainees, apprentices and carers. Appendix 5 gives the full rules.

Eligibility for SAR

6.39   A claimant is eligible for SAR if:

- all, or all but one, of the people liable for council tax on their home (claimant/partner/joint occupiers: para. 10.10) are disregarded persons;
- there is at least one second adult in their home;
- the claimant does not receive rent from anyone aged 18 or more in their home; and
- the additional condition (in para. 6.40 or 6.41 as appropriate) is met.

6.37   CTP sch 1 para 4(3), sch 3 para 1(1); CTR 15(3),18(3), sch 4 para 1(1)

6.38   CTP sch 1 para 4(3)(a); CTR 15(3)(a),18(3)(a)

6.39-41 CTP sch 1 paras 4(1),(2),9(1),10(4), sch 3 para 1; CTR 15(1),(2),18(1),(2),31(1),32(4), sch 4 para 1

The student type of SAR

6.40 The additional condition for this type of SAR is that everyone in the claimant's home is either:

* a student who is not in the 'eligible student groups' listed in table 22.1; or
* a second adult on JSA(IB), ESA(IR), IS or pension credit.

In this case, the amount of SAR equals 100% of the claimant's liability for council tax (but for variations see para. 6.36).

The general type of SAR

6.41 The additional condition for this type of SAR is that the gross income of the second adult(s) is low enough. The amount of SAR can be up to 25% of the claimant's liability for council tax. The details are in table 6.5 (but for variations see para. 6.36).

Table 6.5: Amount of second adult rebate

Student type of SAR

All cases	100%

General type of SAR

Second adult is on JSA(IB)/ESA(IR)/IS/pension credit	25%
(or, if there are two or more second adults, all of them are)	
Second adult is not on JSA(IB)/ESA(IR)/IS/pension credit	
(or, if there are two or more second adults, at least one is not):	
with gross income:	
under £183.00 pw	15%
£183.00–£238.99 pw	7½%
£239 or more pw	nil

Gross income includes the income of a partner. If there are two or more second adults it means the combined gross income of all of them (and their partners).

Second adults' gross income

6.42 It is gross income, not net income, which is used for a second adult. This is assessed in precisely the same way as the gross income of a non-dependant (paras. 6.24-27). The income of a partner of a second adult is included as theirs (even if the partner is a disregarded person and so could not personally be a

---

T6.5   CTP sch 3 para 1(2); CTR sch 4 para 1(2)
6.42   CTP sch 3 paras 2,3; CTR sch 4 paras 2,3

second adult). And if the claimant has more than one second adult, the authority uses the combined income of all of them (and of their partners) to assess second adult rebate. Table 6.5 gives the figures.

SAR for joint occupiers

6.43 In the case of joint occupiers, each joint occupier who makes a claim qualifies for his or her share of the total amount of SAR. This share must always be equal between all the joint occupiers.

The 'better buy'

6.44 A claimant cannot get the main type of CTR (para. 6.3 onwards) and SAR at the same time. If they qualify for both, they are awarded whichever of the two is higher (or, if the two are the same, the main type of CTR). This is called a 'better buy' comparison. In the case of joint occupiers, this comparison is carried out separately for each of them.

Example: Better buy

Lone parent with one non-dependant/second adult

A lone parent is liable for council tax of £16 per week on her home. She has excess income of £25. The only people living with her are her daughter of 15 and her son of 21. The son's gross income is £200 per week. Only the daughter (because of being under 18) is a 'disregarded person'.

Main CTR calculation

Weekly eligible council tax	£16.00
minus non-dependant deduction for son (he works under	
16 hours a week, so the lowest deduction applies: table 6.4)	£3.65
minus 20% of excess income (20% x £25.00)	£5.00
equals CTR	£7.35

SAR calculation

The level of the son's gross income means that the claimant qualifies for a 7½% second adult rebate:

weekly second adult rebate (7½% x £16.00)	£1.20

Better buy comparison

The claimant's CTR is the higher of the two amounts, which is £7.35.

(For variations which could affect this example, see paras. 6.5, 6.12, 6.17 and 6.32.)

6.43   CTP sch 1 para 9(2),(3); CTR 31 (2),(3)

6.44   CTP sch 1 para 10(5)-(6); CTR 32 (5),(6)

Conversion to weekly amounts, etc

Rent and rates

6.45   Whenever a weekly figure is needed for rent (and any rates payable with it), the following rules apply (and the same rules apply to service charges):

* for rent due in multiples of weeks, divide the rent (and any rates) by the number of weeks it covers;

* for rent due calendar monthly (or in multiples of calendar months), divide by the number of months (if necessary) to find the monthly figure, then multiply by 12 to find the annual figure, then divide by 52 to find the weekly figure;

* for rent due daily (or, in any case other than above, in multiples of days), divide by the number of days (if necessary) to find the daily figure, then multiply by seven to find the weekly figure.

Rent-free periods

6.46   No HB is awarded during rent-free periods, including in Northern Ireland rate-free periods where rates are paid with the rent. HB is awarded only for periods in which rent is due (and if a rent-free or rate-free period begins or ends part way through a benefit week, the eligible rent and rates that week are calculated on a daily basis: para. 6.45).

6.47   During the periods in which rent is due, the calculation factors (i.e. applicable amount, income and any non-dependant deductions) are adjusted as follows:

* if rent is expressed on a weekly basis: multiply the calculation factors by 52 or 53, then divide by the number of weeks when rent is due in that year;

* if rent is not expressed on a weekly basis: multiply the calculation factors by 365 or 366, then divide by the number of days when rent is due in that year.

Council tax

6.48   Whenever a weekly figure is needed for council tax liability, the following rules apply:

* for annual figures, divide the council tax by 365 (366 in financial years ending in a leap year) to find the daily figure, and then multiply the daily figure by seven;

* for figures which do not relate to a whole year, divide the council tax by the number of days it covers to find the daily figure, and then multiply the daily figure by seven.

6.45   HB 80; HB60+ 61; NIHB 78; NIHB60+ 59

6.46   HB 81(1),(2),(3); HB60+ 62(1),(2),(3); NIHB 79(1),(2),(3); NIHB60+ 60(1),(2),(3)

6.48   CTP sch 1 para 7(1)(b); CTR 29(1)(b)

Income

6.49   Whenever a weekly income figure is needed, the following rules apply:

* for an amount relating to a whole multiple of weeks, divide the amount by the number of weeks it covers;

* for an amount relating to a calendar month, multiply the amount by 12 to find the annual figure, then divide the annual figure by 52;

* for an amount relating to a year, there are two rules. For working age claims, divide the annual amount by 365 or 366 as appropriate to find the daily figure, and then multiply the daily figure by seven. For pension age claims, simply divide the annual amount by 52;

* for an amount relating to any other period longer than a week, divide the amount by the number of days it covers to find the daily figure, then multiply the daily figure by seven;

* for an amount relating to a period less than a week, that is the weekly amount (see examples).

Examples: Extra income for a few days

A claimant on HB has fixed earnings from a job, which are correctly taken into account in his claim; but he gets an extra source of income from an extra job for three days.

* If he earns £450 (net of tax and NI) from an extra job for the three days, Tuesday 24th to Thursday 26th July 2012 (helping to prepare for a sporting event), this £450 is taken into account as his weekly income from that extra source. It appears to be used as income in week commencing Monday 23rd July 2012 (though the law is vague on this point).

* If he earns £750 (net of tax and NI) from an extra job for the three days, Saturday 28th to Monday 30th July 2012 (helping to run a sporting event), this £750 is taken into account as his weekly income from that extra source. It is used as income in week commencing Monday 30th July 2012 (and the law appears clear on this point).

Rounding

6.50   In HB, the authority may 'if appropriate' round any amount involved in the calculation to the nearest penny, halfpennies being rounded upwards. In CTR, there is no similar rule: indeed, calculating entitlement to at least six decimal places avoids reconciliation errors at the end of the financial year. Decision notices sent to claimants about their HB/CTR entitlement may be rounded to the nearest penny.

6.49   HB 33(1); HB60+ 33(1); NIHB 30(1); NIHB60+ 31(1); CTP sch 1 para 17(1); CTR 40(1),50(1).

6.50   HB 80(8); HB60+ 61(7); NIHB 78(8); NIHB60+ 59(7)

7   Eligible rent: social sector

7.1   HB is worked out by reference to the claimant's eligible rent. This chapter explains how the eligible rent is assessed for tenants of a social landlord. Different rules apply to private sector tenants (chapter 8) and certain special cases (both private and social sector: chapter 9).

7.2   This chapter covers:

- who counts as a social sector tenant in this chapter;
- how the eligible rent of a social tenant is assessed and when it can be restricted;
- the new 'social sector size criteria' rules from 1st April 2013, whereby HB is paid at a reduced rate for social tenants who are deemed to be under-occupying their home;
- the rules about which service charges are eligible for HB (this also applies to the cases described in chapter 9).

Who counts as a social sector tenant?

Meaning of 'landlord' and managing agent

7.3   The method of assessing a claimant's eligible rent is usually determined by the status of their landlord (e.g. public, private or not-for-profit). The details are in paragraphs 7.4-16. 'Landlord' means immediate landlord but does not include a managing agent. So, for example, properties owned by a private landlord but managed by a housing association are treated as private, but properties leased by a housing association from a private landlord are assessed as housing association lettings.

Tenants of 'social' landlords treated as special cases

7.4   The following lettings are treated as special cases and are described in chapter 9:

- if the tenant occupies 'exempt accommodation' (paras. 9.4-6) their eligible rent is always assessed as in paragraph 9.8,
- a shared ownership tenant has their eligible rent assessed as in paragraph 9.91 whoever their landlord is;
- if the tenant is housed by the authority in temporary accommodation (other

---

7.3   HB 13C(5),14(1),(2), sch 2; HB60+ 13C(5),14(1),(2), sch 2; NIHB 14C(5),15(1), sch 3;
NIHB60+ 14C(5),15(1), sch 3

than its own housing stock) to meet a homelessness duty their eligible rent is assessed as in paragraphs 9.92-98;

◆ if the letting is a stock transfer tenancy the eligible rent is usually assessed in the same way as for a council tenant – see paragraph 7.6;

◆ if the tenant has a protected tenancy (paras. 9.85-88) that does not fall in any of the above categories, their eligible rent is assessed as in paragraph 9.89.

For any other tenant whose landlord is not the authority or a registered housing association (para. 7.8) see paragraphs 7.14-16.

Council/NIHE tenants

7.5   A tenant of the HB authority (i.e. in Great Britain a council tenant or council ALMO tenant, or in Northern Ireland a NIHE tenant) has their eligible rent assessed as a social sector tenant (paras. 7.17-38). There are no exceptions to this rule – tenants of the authority cannot be in exempt accommodation. (But see para. 7.15 for tenants of an English county council).

Former public sector tenancies (stock transfer tenancies)

7.6   The eligible rent of a former council/NIHE tenancy that was part of a stock transfer to a housing association (or other body) is also assessed as a social tenant (paras. 7.17-38). The only exceptions are as follows:

◆ if the letting qualifies as 'exempt accommodation', the eligible rent is always assessed as in paragraph 9.8);

◆ if the above does not apply and the letting is a protected tenancy (paras. 9.85-88), the eligible rent is assessed as in paragraph 9.89;

◆ if neither of the above apply and authority considers the rent is unreasonably high, the eligible rent is usually assessed as a rent referral case: see table 7.1 for details.

Tenants of registered housing associations: the general rule

7.7   A tenant of a registered housing association (paras. 7.8-10) has their rent assessed as a social tenant – except in stock transfer cases (para. 7.6) and in the cases described in paragraph 7.11.

7.5   HB 11(1),12B(2),12C(2),12D(2); HB60+ 11(1),12B(2),12C(2),12D(2); CPR sch 3 para 5(1);
        NIHB 11(1),13A(2),13B(2),13C(2); NIHB60+ 11(1),13A(2),13B(2),13C(2); NICPR sch 3 para 5(1)

7.7   HB 13C(5)(a)-(c),14(1),(2), sch 2 para 3; HB60+ 13C(5)(a)-(c),14(1),(2), sch 2 para 3;
        NIHB 14C(5)(a)-(c),14(1),(3), sch 3 para 3; NIHB60+ 14C(5)(a)-(c),14(1),(3), sch 3 para 3

Table 7.1: Assessing the eligible rent for stock transfer tenancies

Former public sector stock transferred on or after 7th October 2002

If a letting is a former local authority, new town or NIHE property, and was transferred to the new owner on or after 7th October 2002, it is a rent referral case (para. 9.31) only if:

- there has been a rent increase since the transfer took place; and
- the authority considers that the rent is unreasonably high.

Otherwise the claim is assessed as a social tenant (paras. 7.17-18).

Former public sector stock transferred before 7th October 2002

If a letting is a former local authority, new town or NIHE property, and was transferred to the new owner before 7th October 2002, it is a rent referral case (para. 9.31) only if:

- there has been a rent increase since the transfer took place; and
- the authority considers that either
  - the rent is unreasonably high; or
  - the accommodation is unreasonably large.

Otherwise the claim is assessed as a social tenant (paras. 7.17-18).

'Registered housing association' and 'housing association'

7.8   'Registered housing association' means a housing association (para. 7.10) that is:

- in England, registered with the Homes and Communities Agency;
- in Scotland, registered with the Scottish Government;
- in Wales, registered with the Welsh Government; or
- in Northern Ireland, registered with the DSD.

7.9   In Scotland and Wales, registered housing associations are known as 'registered social landlords'. In England they are known as 'private registered providers of social housing' (often shortened to 'registered providers'). 'Private' here simply means non-council (because councils are also registered providers).

T7.1   HB 13C(5)(a), sch 2 para 11; HB60+ 13C(5)(a), sch 2 para 11
        NIHB 14C(5)(a), sch 2 para 5; NIHB60+ 14C(5)(a), sch 2 para 5

7.8   HB 2(1); HB60 2(1); NIHB 2(1); NIHB60+ 2(1)

7.10 'Housing association' means a society, body of trustees, or company:

+ whose objects or powers include the power to provide, manage, construct or improve housing; and

+ which does not trade for profit or, if it does, is limited by its constitution not to pay interest or dividends above five per cent.

A 'housing association' may (or may not) also be a charity registered with the Charity Commissioners.

Tenants of registered housing associations: exceptions to the general rule

7.11 The exceptions to the general rule (para. 7.7) for a tenant of a registered housing association are as follows:

+ the letting qualifies as 'exempt accommodation'; the eligible rent is assessed as in paragraph 9.8 (but see para. 7.13 if the authority considers the rent to be reasonable);

+ if the letting is not exempt accommodation, and the authority considers the rent is unreasonably high, the eligible rent is assessed as a rent referral case (para. 9.31) (including in England, if the landlord is profit-making and the dwelling is 'social housing': para. 7.12);

+ in England only, if neither of the above apply, and the landlord is profit making and the dwelling is let at a market rent (i.e. is not 'social housing': para 7.12), the eligible rent is assessed under the LHA rules (chapter 8).

7.12 For the above purposes (para. 7.11), a dwelling is 'social housing' if it is 'made available to people whose needs are not adequately served by the commercial [...] market' and either it is let below a market rent (such as part of the Affordable Rent Programme) or it is a shared ownership tenancy (para. 9.90).

7.13 If a letting is exempt accommodation and the authority considers the rent to be reasonable, the eligible rent is assessed in the same way as for a council tenant (but the source of the law is different: 'old' regulation 13 applies). The crucial difference from other social sector cases is that social sector size criteria do not apply to exempt accommodation (para. 7.26).

Tenants of charities and other not-for-profit landlords

7.14 A tenant of any other 'social landlord' (para. 7.15) that is not a registered housing association is treated in exactly the same way as any other private tenant: their eligible rent is assessed under the local housing allowance rules (chapter 8). The only exceptions are in paragraph 7.16.

7.10   HB 2(1); HB60+ 2(1); NIHB 2(1); NIHB60+ 2(1)

7.11   HB sch 2 para 3; HB60+ sch 2 para 3; CPR sch 3 para 4(1)(b); NIHB sch 3 para 3; NIHB60+ sch 3 para 3; NICPR sch 3 para 4(1)(b)

7.12   Housing and Regeneration Act 2008, s68-70

7.15 For the above purpose (para. 7.14) 'social landlord' includes all (or a combination of) the following: a housing association that is not registered (para. 7.10), a registered charity, an English county council (i.e. not the HB authority) or any other not-for-profit body.

7.16 The exceptions to the general rule (paras. 7.14-15) are:

* if the letting qualifies as 'exempt accommodation' (para. 9.4) the eligible rent is always assessed as in paragraph 9.8;

* if the above exception does not apply and the letting is a protected tenancy (paras. 9.85-88), the eligible rent is assessed as in paragraph 9.89;

* if the previous two exceptions do not apply and the letting qualifies as a hostel (para. 9.45), the eligible rent is assessed as a rent referral case with the special rules that apply to hostels (paras. 9.41 and 9.46)

* if none of the above apply but there has been a continuous claim at the same address since before 7th April 2008, the eligible rent is assessed as a rent referral case (paras. 9.40-41).

In any other case (assuming the tenant is not a boarder or the dwelling a caravan or mobile home, etc) the eligible rent is assessed under LHA rules (chapter 8).

Eligible rent

7.17 The eligible rent of a local authority tenant or registered housing association tenant where the general rule applies (paras. 7.7 and 7.11) is worked out as follows:

* the actual rent payable on their dwelling (subject to limits and any apportionment: paras. 7.19-22);

* minus an amount for service charges which are ineligible for HB (para. 7.39 onwards) and in Northern Ireland the amount for rates except where the tenant is billed separately.

But in many cases a deduction is made from the eligible rent and this lower figure, 'the maximum eligible rent', is used to calculate HB (para. 7.18).

Example: Eligible rent for a council tenant

A claimant rents a council flat. His actual rent is £65 per week. This figure includes £5 per week for the cleaning and lighting of communal areas and £12 per week for the use of an emergency alarm service.

His eligible rent is calculated as follows. The charge for the communal areas is eligible for HB. However, the charge for the emergency alarm service is not eligible, so this has to be deducted from his actual rent to find his eligible rent. His eligible rent is therefore £53 per week.

7.17   HB 12B(2); HB60+ 12B(2); NIHB 13A(2); NIHB60+ 13A(2)

7.18 A maximum eligible rent is calculated for certain working age claims where the claimant's home is considered to be too large: the rules are described in paragraphs 7.23-38.

Restrictions on unreasonably high rents

7.19 In all social sector cases the authority possesses an 'over-riding power to reduce the eligible rent' (para. 7.17) if it considers it to be too high. In practice it is hardly ever used, though it is a possibility even for council tenant cases *(Burton v Camden London Borough Council)*.

7.20 The power exists when 'it appears... that in the particular circumstances of the case the eligible rent... is greater than it is reasonable to meet by way of HB'. If it is, the eligible rent is reduced to 'such lesser sum as seems... to be an appropriate rent in that particular case'. This requires the authority to use its judgment (para. 1.48), and to take the personal circumstances of the claimant into account *(R v HBRB of the City of Westminster ex parte Laali)*.

Joint tenants

7.21 If the claimant is a joint tenant (para. 4.52), the eligible rent figure is apportioned between each of the joint tenants. To do this, the authority must decide how much of the actual rent is fairly attributable to each joint tenant, taking into account the number of people paying towards the rent, the proportion of rent paid by each and any other relevant circumstances – such as the size and number of rooms each occupies, whether there is any written or other agreement between them – and also the presence or absence of the joint occupiers concerned *(CH/3376/2002)*. The rent is apportioned among all the joint occupiers including those who are students (or otherwise ineligible for HB) *(Nagshabandi v LB Camden and Another)*.

Example: Joint tenants

Tom, Dick and Harry

Three unrelated friends in their thirties, Tom, Dick and Harry, jointly rent a three-bedroom housing association house, where the rent for the whole house is £150 per week (and this does not include any service charges). They have a bedroom each and share the kitchen and all other facilities. They have each contributed one-third of the rent in the past. Harry loses his job and claims HB, saying that his share remains one-third.

Harry's eligible rent is very likely to be regarded as £50 per week. It is possible that a fairer split would be something other than one-third each, but unlikely based on the information given.

7.19 HB 12B(6); HB60+ 12B(6); NIHB 13A(7); NIHB60+ 13A(7)

7.20 HB 12B(6); HB60+ 12B(6); NIHB 13A(7); NIHB60+ 13A(7)

7.21 HB 12B(4),12C(2); HB60+ 12B(4),12C(2); NIHB 13A(4),13B(2); HB60+ 13A(4),13B(2)

> **Tom moves out**
>
> Tom moves out. He is not replaced. Dick and Harry agree between them that they should contribute equally to the rent.
>
> Harry's eligible rent is now very likely to be regarded as £75 per week – unless the authority considers that the new rent is unreasonable and has the power to restrict it (paras. 7.19-20).

Business premises

7.22   Rent on any part of a property which is used for business, commercial or other non-residential purposes is not eligible for HB. For example, if a claimant rents both a shop and the flat above it, only the rent relating to the flat is eligible for HB. If the rent on the business premises is not specified separately from the rent on the home, it is necessary for the authority to decide how much relates to each. For self-employed claimants who work from home, see paragraph 15.24.

The social sector size criteria

What are the social sector size criteria?

7.23   In Great Britain new rules introduce the social sector size criteria from 1st April 2013. These rules apply to working age tenants (para. 7.26) whose eligible rent is assessed as for a social sector tenant (paras. 7.5-13). These rules have been dubbed the 'bedroom tax' by tenants and landlords opposed to the changes.

At the time of writing, these rules do not apply to Northern Ireland because the Welfare Reform Bill is still making its way through the Assembly. It is expected that similar rules will be introduced later in the year.

7.24   If the tenant's home is larger than required according to the size criteria (table 7.2) then the eligible rent is reduced. In law this reduced figure is known as the 'maximum rent social sector' and it is this figure that is used to calculate the maximum HB (para. 6.4). The reduced rent is calculated as a fixed percentage deduction from the full eligible rent according to the degree by which the tenant is considered to be under-occupying (para. 7.35).

7.25   The reduced rent figure represents a notional rent for a dwelling that would be the right size for that household. The policy intention is to broadly mirror the size criteria for private tenants (paras. 8.14-35) – although there are a number of differences in the way the rules work.

7.22   HB 12B(3),12C(2); HB60+ 12B(3),12C(2); NIHB 12(4),13A(3),13B(2); NIHB60+ 12(4),13A(3),13B(2)

Exemptions: pensioners and supported housing

7.26   These rules affect claims where the rent is assessed as a social tenant (paras. 7.5-13) except they do not apply where either the claimant or their partner has attained state pension credit age or the claimant occupies exempt accommodation. Note that the exemption for pension credit age claimants includes any working age claim (para. 1.21) where the claimant has opted to claim a working age passport benefit instead of pension credit.

Protected groups: when the size-related reduction is delayed

7.27   If the claimant is not exempt (para. 7.26) the deduction is delayed for up to 13 or 52 weeks (as appropriate) if the claimant is in a protected group (para. 7.28).

7.28   The protected groups are the same as for LHA claims and other special cases (para. 8.52): they apply when the tenant could previously afford the rent (i.e. was not claiming HB) or when a former household member has died within the last 12 months. The protection periods are 13 and 52 weeks respectively. The rules are fully described in paragraphs 8.52-59 (but all the relevant law is in the regulations in the footnote).

Table 7.2: The social sector size criteria

For who counts as an occupier for these purposes, see paragraph 7.30.

- ◆ One bedroom is allowed for each of the following occupiers, each occupier coming only within the first category which applies to him or her:
  - a couple (para. 4.10);
  - a single person aged 16 or more;
  - two children of the same sex under the age of 16;
  - two children (of the same or opposite sexes) under the age of 10;
  - any other child.
- ◆ Plus one (or two if both apply) additional bedroom in any case where:
  - the claimant or the claimant's partner (or both of them) requires overnight care (paras. 8.27-32);
  - the claimant or the claimant's partner (or both of them) is a qualifying foster parent (para. 8.24).

7.26   HB A13(2)(d); CPR sch 3 para 5(1),(2)

7.28   HB 12BA

T7.2   HB B13(5),(6)

When is a social tenant under-occupying?

7.29 Table 7.2 shows how to work out how many bedrooms the claimant and their household require. If they occupy accommodation with more bedrooms, a deduction is made from their eligible rent (para. 7.18).

Examples: Social sector size criteria

Tenant is under-occupying: deduction applies

A tenant lives with his partner in a four bedroom council house. The weekly rent is £80.00. They have four children, two boys aged 15 and 5 and two girls, both aged 12.

The size criteria apply as follows: one bedroom is allocated for the tenant and his partner, one for the two girls and one for the two boys. They are deemed to be under-occupying by one bedroom so their eligible rent is reduced by £11.20 (14% of £80.00). The maximum HB used to calculate their HB entitlement is £68.80 (£80.00 − £11.20). If the tenant is on JSA(IB) his weekly HB would be £68.80. If the tenant has an excess income then the tapered excess would be deducted from this figure to arrive at his weekly HB.

Tenant is not under-occupying

A lone parent lives in a four bedroomed house which she rents from a registered housing association. The weekly rent is £120.00. She has four children: three girls aged 12, 12 and 5 and one boy aged 15. Under the size criteria she is entitled to four bedrooms: one for her, one for the two older girls, one for the boy (no other boy aged under 16 to share with) and one for the remaining girl. She is not under-occupying and so her maximum weekly HB is £120.00.

7.30 In deciding the size of accommodation the claimant qualifies for (table 17.2), the following occupiers are taken into account:

- the claimant and any family member (partner, children, young persons: para. 4.8) but excludes any child for which the claimant does not have primary responsibility (para. 4.31)
- non-dependants (para. 4.39);
- any lodgers in the claimant's home (paras. 4.48-51);
- a son/daughter (etc) of the claimant or their partner who is a member of the armed forces away on operations (para. 8.22);
- any other people who 'occupy the claimant's dwelling as their home'.

7.29   HB B13(7)(b),(8)

7.31   The considerations which apply in LHA cases also apply here in the same way, including: who is a member of the claimants' family (chapter 4) or another occupier (paras. 8.21-23 and 8.25); people who qualify for an additional bedroom as a foster parent (para. 8.24) or an overnight carer (paras. 8.26-31); resident carers (para. 8.33); and who needs an additional room for disablement needs (paras. 8.34-35).

What counts as a bedroom?

7.32   There is no definition in the regulations of what counts as a bedroom. Therefore it is up to the authority to decide on a case by case basis. In the vast majority of cases the authority will use the category that the landlord has provided (Circular HB/CTB A4/2012), but the authority is not bound by the landlord's classification.

7.33   Because there is no set definition, the term 'bedroom' must be given its ordinary everyday meaning (para. 1.44); thus the authority is entitled to use its judgment (para. 1.48). In most cases this will mean that if the room is furnished as a bedroom or was used as a bedroom when the tenant first moved in, then it is reasonable for the authority to rely on this.

7.34   The authority is not bound by the definition of what can be counted as a bedroom from the overcrowding legislation. However, where in a particular case the outcome is that the tenant is under-occupying for HB but in breach of the overcrowding legislation then it is reasonable to assume the claim is assessed in such a way as to resolve that conflict. Such instances will be rare because the overcrowding legislation counts living rooms (not just bedrooms) as being suitable for sleeping in.

How much is the deduction?

7.35   The amount of the deduction is calculated as follows:

- ◆ if the dwelling has one bedroom more than the appropriate size for that household (as judged by the social sector size criteria) then a deduction of 14% of the eligible rent is made;

- ◆ if the dwelling has two or more bedrooms more than the household requires then a deduction of 25% of the eligible rent is made.

In cases where the eligible rent has been restricted (paras. 7.19-20), the deduction is calculated using the unrestricted rent. To calculate the deduction for a joint tenancy, see paragraph 7.38.

7.36   Where it appears to the authority that the resulting figure after the standard deduction (para. 7.35) 'is greater than is reasonable to meet by way of HB' then the authority has the power to reduce that figure to an amount it

---

7.34   Housing Act 1985 s326, Housing (Scotland) Act 1987 s137

7.35   HB B13(2)(a),(3)

7.36   HB B13(4)

considers to be reasonable. The power mirrors the power to reduce the eligible rent and all the considerations in paragraph 7.20 apply.

7.37 The reduced eligible rent figure is the figure that is used to calculate the tenant's maximum housing benefit (para. 6.4). If a non-dependant deduction applies (para. 6.16 onwards), or the tenant has an 'excess income' (paras. 6.11-12 and table 6.2), or both, any resulting deduction(s) is made from this reduced eligible rent.

Joint tenants

7.38 For joint tenants the standard deduction (para. 7.35) is calculated using the full eligible rent (i.e. before any restriction and without any apportionment: paras. 7.20-1) and it it this figure that is then apportioned between the joint tenants in the same way as in paragraph 7.21.

Service charges

7.39 The remainder of this chapter deals with service charges (and related charges) which may be included in a claimant's actual rent, or payable as well as the rent. It applies to the social sector cases described in this chapter, and the exempt accommodation and rent referral cases (chapter 9) but not to LHA cases (paras. 8.5-6). It explains which charges are eligible for HB and which are not. It covers:

* general information about service charges (including their definition);
* who is responsible for valuing services (the rent officer or the authority);
* which service charges are eligible or ineligible for HB;
* how service charges are valued;
* the rules about specific types of service charge.

For a comparison between service charges and other charges that may be included in someone's rent, see paragraphs 7.43, 7.67 and 7.69.

The importance of service charges

7.40 Many tenants pay for services either in with their rent (whether or not they are mentioned in their letting agreement) or separately. As illustrated in the examples, there are two main methods of showing service charges in letting agreements:

* a claimant's rent may be shown as so much per week (or month, etc) including certain services; or
* it may be shown as so much per week (or month, etc) with an amount for service charges being due on top of the rent.

7.38   HB B13(2)(a),(c)
7.39   HB 12(8),12B(2),(5),13(2),(5),(7); HB60+ 12(8),12B(2),(5),13(2),(5),(7); ROO sch 1 paras 7,9;
          NIHB 12(8),13A(2),(6),14(2),(5),(7), sch 2 paras 7,9;
          NIHB60+ 12(8),13A(2),(6),14(2),(5),(7), sch 2 paras 7,9

7.41   Whether a service charge is eligible for HB affects the amount of a claimant's eligible rent (para. 7.17), which in turn affects the amount of his or her HB.

+ If a charge is 'eligible for HB', this means that it is a charge which can be included in a claimant's eligible rent. It does not need to be valued; and no deduction is made for it at any stage in deciding the amount of a claimant's eligible rent unless the charge for it is excessive (para. 7.50).

+ If a charge is 'ineligible for HB', this means that it is a charge which cannot be included in a claimant's eligible rent. With certain exceptions, it needs to be valued and deducted at some point in deciding the amount of a claimant's eligible rent (para. 7.42).

The above points have become important in exempt accommodation cases (para. 9.2), where providers of exempt accommodation have found it essential to detail the charges for the services they provide, and authorities have found it essential to look carefully at each individual service, to decide which are ineligible and, for those which are eligible, whether the charge is reasonable.

Examples: Service charges

1. A council tenant weekly claimant's rent is expressed as being £100 including £20 for fuel for the claimant's own room and £10 per fortnight for heating, lighting, cleaning and maintaining communal areas. In this case the eligible rent is £80 per week. The ineligible charge for fuel for the claimant's own room is deducted.

2. A housing association claimant's rent is expressed as being £70 plus £20 for fuel for the claimant's own room and £10 for heating, lighting, cleaning and maintaining communal areas. In this case the eligible rent is £80 per week. The eligible charge for the communal areas is added.

Notes

+ The facts in the two examples are the same but are expressed differently.

+ Information about the service charges illustrated is given later in this chapter.

+ The terms 'net rent' and 'gross rent' are sometimes used to distinguish between different methods of expressing a rent figure. But they are used in different ways nationally and are best avoided for HB purposes.

Who deals with service charges

7.42   In Great Britain, service charges may be dealt with by the authority or the rent officer (or both of them) in assessing a claimant's eligible rent. In Northern Ireland, service charges are always dealt with by the NIHE. Fuller details are given in the remainder of this chapter, but in general terms:

- in social sector and exempt accommodation cases, it is the authority which assesses all matters relating to service charges;
- in rent referral cases, the council decides which charges are ineligible but the rent officer (or NIHE) values them (paras. 9.55-57). (However, for meals see para. 7.60.)

Definition of 'services'

7.43   The law defines 'services' as 'services performed or facilities... provided for, or rights made available to, the occupier...' and 'service charge' as any periodical charge for any such service.

Which service charges are eligible?

7.44   Service charges are eligible for HB, so long as they:

- have to be paid as a condition of occupying the dwelling as a home; and
- are not listed in the regulations as ineligible (as described in the following paragraphs); and
- are not excessive in relation to the service provided (para. 7.48).

The rules about specific types of service charge, and whether they are eligible for HB, are in paragraphs 7.50 onwards.

7.45   The first of the above conditions need not have applied from the date the letting agreement began. A service charge is eligible for HB (subject to the other conditions) whenever the claimant agreed to pay it, if the only alternative would have been to lose his or her home. (Note also that a different rule applies in the case of charges for garages, land, etc: paras. 7.22 and 7.72.)

7.46   Details of which service charges are eligible for HB (subject to the above points) follow, and are summarised in table 7.3. Helpful advice on services is given by the DWP (GM paras. A4.700-950).

7.47   Sometimes services are provided 'free' to a claimant but this is often because the charge is wholly funded from elsewhere. The DWP points out in relation to hostel residents (though the point is relevant to all claims) that 'HB should be based only on items included in the resident's charge. [Authorities] must confirm which services are included in the hostel charge' (GM para. A4.1950).

Valuing ineligible service charges

7.48   When the authority has the duty of valuing ineligible service charges (para. 8.15), this is done as follows:

7.43   HB 12(8); HB60+ 12(8); CPR sch 3 para 5; NIHB 13(8); NIHB60+ 13(8); NICPR sch 3 para 5

7.44   HB 12(1),(8),12B(2), 13(2); HB60+ 12(1),(8),12B(2),13(2); CPR sch 3 para 5(1); ROO sch 1 para 7; NIHB 13(1),(8),13A(2),14(2), sch 2 para 7; NIHB60+ 13(1),(8),13A(2),14(2), sch 2 para 7; NICPR sch 3 para 5(1)

7.48   HB 12B(2),13(1), sch 1 para 3; HB60+ 12B(2),13(1), sch 1 para 3; ROO sch 1 para 7, NIHB 13A(2),14(2) sch 1 para 3, sch 2 para 7; NIHB60+ 13A(2),14(2), sch 1 para 3, sch 2 para 7

- if the amount can be identified from the letting agreement or in some other way, the authority uses the amount so identified as the value;

- but if this identified amount is unrealistically low for the service provided, or if the amount cannot be identified, the authority must decide what amount is fairly attributable to the value;

- however, different rules can apply for water charges, fuel and meals (paras. 7.51-60).

Table 7.3: Service charges summary

As described throughout this chapter, further details apply in many of the following cases.

Type of service charge	Eligible for HB?
Water charges	NO
Provision of a heating system	YES
Fuel for communal areas	YES
Other fuel	NO
Meals	NO
Furniture/household equipment	YES
Communal window cleaning	YES
Other exterior window cleaning which the occupier(s) cannot do	YES
Other window cleaning	NO
Communal cleaning	YES
Other cleaning	NO
Emergency alarm systems	NO
Counselling and support	NO
Medical/nursing/personal care	NO
Day-to-day living expenses	NO
Most communal services relating to the provision of adequate accommodation	YES

T 7.3   HB sch 1 paras 1,5; HB60+ sch 1 paras 1,5; NIHB sch 1 paras 1,5; NIHB60+ sch 1 paras 1,5

Valuing eligible service charges

7.49 If it is necessary to value eligible service charges (for example, in exempt accommodation cases), the authority values them as follows:

+ if the amount can be identified from the letting agreement or in some other way, the authority uses the amount so identified as the value;

+ but if this identified amount is excessive, or if the amount cannot be identified, the authority must decide what amount is fairly attributable to the value.

Excessive eligible service charges

7.50 The authority must take account of the cost of comparable services to decide whether the charge is excessive and if it is the authority must decide how much would be reasonable and disallow the excess.

Water charges

7.51 In Great Britain, water charges (including any sewerage or environmental charges) are not eligible for HB so any charges included in the rent must be deducted. (But no deduction is made if the claimant pays water charges direct to the water company, since they are not part of the rent.) The same applies in Northern Ireland, though for the time being, until a separate system for water charging is in place, water charges remain eligible for HB in respect of rates (although the rates element is deducted from the rent).

7.52 As regards water charges (etc) for communal areas (e.g. a garden tap for residents to water their various gardens), the law is not entirely clear, but on balance it appears that, if they are separately identified, they are eligible for HB.

7.53 In social sector and exempt accommodation cases, the authority decides the value of water charges as follows:

+ if the charge is based on consumption, either the actual amount or an estimate;

+ otherwise, if the claimant's accommodation is a self-contained unit, the actual amount of the charge;

+ otherwise, a proportion of the water charge for the self-contained unit equal to the floor area of the claimant's accommodation divided by the floor area of the self-contained unit (but in practice authorities sometimes use simpler methods).

In rent referral cases, the rent officer (or NIHE) values water charges (para. 9.56).

7.49   HB 12B(2),13(2), sch 1; HB60+ 12B(2),13(2), sch 1; ROO sch 1 para 7;
        NIHB 13A(2),14(2), sch 1, sch 2 para 7; NIHB60+ 13A(2),14(2), sch 1, sch 2 para 7

7.50   HB 12B(6),12C(2), sch 1 para 4; HB60+ 12B(6),12C(2), sch 1 para 4; NIHB 13A(7),13B(2), sch 1 para 4;
        NIHB60+ 13A(7),13B(2), sch 1 para 4

7.51   HB 2(1),12B(2),(5),13(2); HB60+ 2(1),12B(2),(5), 13(2); ROO sch 1 para 7;
        NIHB 13A(2),(6),14(2), sch 2 para 7; NIHB60+ 13A(2),(6),14(2), sch 2 para 7

Fuel

7.54   Charges for fuel (such as gas, electricity, etc, and also any standing charges or other supply costs) are not eligible for HB so any charges included in the rent must be deducted. (No deduction is made if the claimant pays fuel charges direct to the fuel company, since they are not part of the rent.)

7.55   There are two exceptions to the above:

◆ a charge for the provision of a heating system is eligible for HB, but only if it is separate from the fuel charge;

◆ a fuel charge for communal areas is eligible for HB, but only if it is separate from the fuel charge for the claimant's own accommodation. Communal areas are areas of common access (e.g. hall, stairway) including, in sheltered accommodation only (para. 7.68), common rooms (e.g. dining room, lounge).

7.56   In social sector and exempt accommodation cases, the rules depend on whether the amount of the charge is known (paras. 7.57-58). In rent referral cases (chapter 9) the rent officer (or NIHE) values fuel charges (para. 9.56).

Table 7.4: Standard weekly fuel deductions

If the claimant and any family occupy more than one room

Fuel for heating	£25.60
Fuel for hot water	£2.95
Fuel for lighting	£2.05
Fuel for cooking	£2.95
Fuel for any other purpose	NIL
Fuel for all the above	£33.55

If the claimant and any family occupy one room only

Fuel for heating and any hot water and/or lighting	£15.30
Fuel for cooking	£2.95
Fuel for any other purpose	NIL
Fuel for all the above	£18.25

7.54   HB 12B(2),13(2), sch 1 paras 5-8; HB60+ 12B(2),13(2), sch 1 paras 5-8; ROO sch 1 para 7;
          NIHB 13A(2),14(2), sch 1 paras 5-8, sch 2 para 7; NIHB60+ 13A(2),14(2), sch 1 paras 5-8, sch 2 para 7

T7.4   HB sch 1 para 8; HB60+ sch 1 para 8; NIHB sch 1 para 8; NIHB60+ sch 1 para 8

7.57 If the charge is identifiable, the authority uses this figure as the fuel charge. However, if this is unrealistically low or includes an element for communal areas which cannot be separated out, the charge is treated as unidentifiable.

7.58 If the amount of a charge is not identifiable, the authority deducts the standard amounts, as shown in table 7.4 (a lower deduction applies for claimants who only occupy one room). If the standard amounts are applied, the authority must invite the claimant to provide evidence from which the 'actual or approximate' amount of the charge can be estimated; and, if the evidence is reasonable, the authority must estimate the value of the fuel charge.

Meals

7.59 Charges for meals are not eligible for HB so any charges included in the rent must be deducted. For these purposes, 'a meal' includes preparation (e.g. where it is prepared somewhere else and then delivered) and also the provision of unprepared food (e.g. cereal, bread still in its wrappings).

7.60 In social sector cases, exempt accommodation and rent referral cases (chapter 9) the authority (not the rent officer) makes the deduction for meals. The authority deducts the standard amounts shown in table 7.5 in all cases; the actual amount the landlord charges for meals is never used. A deduction is made for each person whose meals are included in the rent (whether this is the claimant, a member of the family or some other person such as a non-dependant). No deduction applies for anyone whose meals are not included (for example, a baby). When appropriate, deductions are calculated separately (for example fewer meals may be provided for someone who goes out to work than for someone who does not).

Table 7.5: Standard weekly meals deductions

A separate amount is assessed and deducted for each person whose meals are provided.

If at least three meals are provided every day

For the claimant, and each other person from the first Monday in September following his or her 16th birthday	£25.85
For each child	£13.10

If breakfast only is provided

For the claimant, and each other person of any age	£3.15

7.59   HB 12B(2),13(2), sch 1 paras 1(a)(i),2; HB60+ 12B(2),13(2), sch 1 paras 1(a)(i),(2); ROO sch 1 para 7; NIHB 13A(2),14(2), sch 1 paras 1(a)(i),(2), sch 2 para 7; NIHB60+ 13A(2),14(2), sch 1 paras 1(a)(i),(2), sch 2 para 7

T7.5   HB sch 1 para 2; HB60+ sch 1 para 2; NIHB sch 1 para 2; NIHB60+ sch 1 para 2

All other cases

For the claimant, and each other person from the first
Monday in September following his or her 16th birthday   £17.20

For each child   £8.65

Furniture and household equipment

7.61   Charges for the use of these are eligible for HB; unless there is an intention that they will become part of the claimant's personal property, in which case they are ineligible.

Cleaning and window cleaning

7.62   Except where the cost is met by Supporting People (para. 7.66) charges for the following are eligible for HB:

- cleaning rooms and windows in communal areas (using the same definition of 'communal areas' as in para. 7.55); and

- cleaning the outsides of windows which no-one in the household can do.

Any other cleaning and window cleaning (such as cleaning the claimant's own accommodation) is not eligible for HB (but may be met by Supporting People).

Other communal services, etc

7.63   Charges for the following communal services are eligible for HB:

- children's play areas;

- equipment for receiving free-to-view broadcasts ('Freeview' channels) and its relay into the home through the communal areas, including any charges for the installation, upgrade and maintenance of that equipment (less any element included for subscription channels) (but see also paragraph 7.64);

- communal laundry facilities;

- other services which are related to the provision of adequate accommodation.

7.64   The DWP advises (GM para. A4.730, and see chapter A4 generally) that the last item includes:

- portering and refuse removal;

7.61   HB 12B(2),13(2), sch 1 para 1(b); HB60+ 12B(2),13(2) sch 1 para 1(b); ROO sch 1 para 7;
         NIHB 13A(2),14(2), sch 1 para 1(b), sch 2 para 7; NIHB60+ 13A(2),14(2), sch 1 para 1(b), sch 2 para 7

7.62   HB 12B(2), 13(2), sch 1 paras 1(a)(iv),8; HB60+ 12B(2), 13(2), sch 1 paras 1(a)(iv),8; ROO sch 1 para. 7;
         NIHB 13A(2), 14(4), sch 1 paras 1(a)(iv),8, sch 2 para 7;
         NIHB60+ 13A(2), 14(4), sch 1 paras 1(a)(iv),8, sch 2 para 7

7.63   HB 12B(2),13(2), sch 1 para 1(a); HB60+ 12B(2),13(2), sch 1 para 1(a); ROO sch 1 para 7;
         NIHB 13A(2),14(2), sch 1 para 1(a), sch 2 para 7; NIHB60+ 13A(2),14(2), sch 1 para 1(a), sch 2 para 7

- lifts, communal telephones and entry phones; and
- the time people such as scheme managers or caretakers spend on eligible services.

It is usually assumed that gardening charges are eligible for HB, on the basis that they (like general maintenance) are related to the provision of adequate accommodation – but not if they are excessive (or indeed optional): *CH/755/2008.*

Other day-to-day living expenses, etc

7.65 Charges for the following are not eligible for HB so any charges included in the rent must be deducted:

- laundry (e.g. washing sheets, etc, for the claimant);
- transport;
- sports facilities;
- TV (and radio) rental, licence and subscription fees and any other charges for providing equipment to the individual home (e.g. a TV, individual satellite dish, set-top box);
- any other leisure items or day-to-day living expenses; or
- any other services which 'are not related to the provision of adequate accommodation'.

Support charges

7.66 Support charges are never eligible for HB. This includes charges for:

- cleaning and window cleaning over and above that mentioned in paragraph 7.62;
- emergency alarm systems (to summon assistance in the event of a fall, an accident, etc);
- counselling and support; and
- medical, nursing and personal care.

Claimants who need such services may be able to have the cost met by Supporting People, a government programme for funding support services administered by local authorities (in Northern Ireland by the NIHE) and independent of HB. For a detailed explanation of care, support and supervision in 'exempt accommodation' please see paragraph 9.6 and table 9.1.

7.65 HB 12B(2),13(2), sch 1 para 1(a),(g); HB60+ 12B(2),14(2), sch 1 para 1(a),(g); ROO sch 1 para 7;
NIHB 13A(2),14(2), sch 1 para 1(a),(g), sch 2 para 7; NIHB60+ 13A(2),14(2), sch 1 para 1(a),(g), sch 2 para 7

7.66 HB 12B(2),13(2), sch 1 para 1(c)-(f); HB60+ 12B(2),13(2), sch 1 para 1(c)-(f); ROO sch 1 para 7;
NIHB 13A(2),14(2), sch 1 para 1(c)-(f), sch 2 para 7; NIHB 13A(2),14(2), sch 1 para 1(c)-(f), sch 2 para 7

7.67   In some situations it is difficult to distinguish what constitutes a support charge and what is merely part of the rent as any landlord would charge it (and therefore eligible for HB: para. 7.70). Chasing rent arrears would usually be an example of the latter: most landlords would regard it as part and parcel of their day-to-day work. But it might be regarded as support if it formed a substantial part of the work of staff e.g. advice and counselling for hostel residents with difficulty budgeting.

'Sheltered accommodation'

7.68   Whether accommodation counts as 'sheltered accommodation' is relevant to the eligibility of certain fuel and cleaning charges for HB (paras. 7.55 and 7.62). The term is not defined in the regulations, but has been explained by an Upper Tribunal as 'something more than ordinary accommodation or shelter… [in other words] accommodation provided for people who are in some way (and probably for some defined reason) more vulnerable than most people are, or are vulnerable in a particular kind of way […] if there are resident staff at hand, there need not be a warden/manager or an alarm system': *[2011] UKUT 136 AAC*. This description was approved in the Court of Appeal: *[2011] AACR 38*, which also described the definition of sheltered accommodation as being wide enough to include 'extra care' and 'very sheltered' (but not care homes).

Other items included in setting rents

7.69   Authorities and tribunals pay more attention nowadays to the distinction between services (as described above) and other costs included when the landlord sets the rent. For example, overheads, management costs, maintenance, and passing on costs like council tax, are usually regarded as rent rather than a service. The mere fact that a landlord categorises something wrongly (such as showing a charge for voids as a service) should not be held against it, particularly if the landlord is 'finding its way' in rent setting: *CH/3528/2006*. The tenancy agreement does not determine whether an item is rent or a service charge: it is the law which does so: *[2009] UKUT 28 AAC* (a case where a space for a carer was called a 'support' charge but was in fact rent: see also para. 7.73).

Overheads, management costs, council tax, etc

7.70   A landlord's normal overheads (such as maintenance, insurance, management costs, charges for voids in certain types of accommodation, and so on) count as rent, not services. The rent (including these items) is eligible for HB (subject to the overall reasonableness of the rent: paras. 7.19-20). In particular, this includes any part of the rent towards the landlord's liability for council tax (e.g. if the claimant has a resident landlord or lives in a house made up of bedsits).

7.70   HB 11(3); HB60+ 11(3); NIHB 11(3); NIHB60+ 11(3)

7.71   HB 2(4)(a); HB60+ 2(4)(a); NIHB 2(4)(a); NIHB60+ 2(4)(a)

Increases to cover arrears of rent

7.71 If a claimant's rent has been increased in order to recover arrears of rent or other charges, that part of the rent is ineligible for HB. This rule applies only if an individual claimant's rent is increased to cover his or her own arrears on a current or former home. It does not apply when landlords increase rents on all their properties as a result of arrears generally.

Garages, land, etc

7.72 The rent on a garage, mobility scooter shed, or any other buildings, gardens or land included in the claimant's letting agreement, is eligible for HB if:

- they are used for occupying the dwelling as a home; and
- the claimant acquired them at the same time as the dwelling; and
- the claimant has no option but to rent them at the same time.

They are also eligible for HB if the claimant has made or is making reasonable efforts to end liability for them.

Space for a carer

7.73 In social sector and exempt accommodation cases, if the claimant has a carer, space for the carer is taken into account in the normal way in assessing the eligible rent: *[2009] UKUT 28 AAC* (a case where the space for a live-in carer was included in the claimant's eligible rent). This can be the case even if the live-in carer occupies a room down the corridor from the claimant: *[2009] UKUT 116 AAC*. In the latter case, the claimant was a disabled student who had a carer. The carer had exclusive use of their own room. The judge held that the carer's room was capable of being part of the claimant's accommodation, saying that 'functionally and purposively, the claimant needed two rooms to live – one for himself and one for his carer. Commonsense dictates that it should not matter whether there is a connecting door between the two.' The situation is different if a claimant's carer(s) do not live in the claimant's home (for example where a claimant has a rota of carers); or if a claimant wishes her parents to be able to stay to care for her, but they live elsewhere: *[2009] UKUT 79 AAC*. For the rules for LHA and rent referral cases, see paragraphs 8.26-35 and 9.75.

8 Eligible rent: private sector (LHAs)

8.1 This chapter explains how to work out the claimant's eligible rent in private sector cases. With exceptions (para. 8.3 and table 8.1) these fall within the local housing allowance (LHA) scheme. The chapter covers:

- which claims fall within the LHA scheme;
- how to assess eligible rent in LHA cases;
- which size or category of dwelling applies to each claimant;
- which occupiers are included;
- the restrictions for under-35 year olds;
- when an extra bedroom is included for a foster parent or carer or for disability needs;
- how the LHA figures are set; and
- the protections for certain groups of claimants.

8.2 The LHA scheme was introduced nationally on 7th April 2008 and has since been amended several times. (The transitional protection relating to changes in 2011 and 2012 has ceased.) LHA rates now always apply annually – this year, from 1st April 2013 (para. 8.10); though they can change during the year if the claimant's household size alters and in certain other circumstances (para. 8.11).

Who falls within the LHA scheme?

8.3 All private sector HB cases are LHA cases unless they fall within any of the exceptions in table 8.1. As that table shows, to be an LHA case, the claimant's date of claim must fall on or after 7th April 2008, or the claimant must have moved home on or after that date.

Overview of the LHA scheme

8.4 The key features of the LHA scheme are:

- a claimant's eligible rent simply equals the LHA figure that applies to them;
- however no claimant can get more than their actual rent;
- the LHA figures are set in Great Britain by the rent officer and in Northern Ireland by the NIHE;
- the LHA figures depend on the size or category of accommodation applicable to the claimant, and on the area they live in;
- the LHA figures are publicly available.

8.3   HB 2(1), 13C(1),(2)(a)-(c); HB60+ 2(1), 13C(1),(2)(a)-(c)

Table 8.1: Exceptions to the LHA scheme

The following are never LHA cases:

- ◆ council and NIHE lettings (i.e. all lettings where HB is awarded as a rebate: paras. 7.5 and 16.16);

- ◆ council and NIHE stock transfer tenancies (para. 7.6 and table 7.1);

- ◆ lettings from registered housing associations – except, in England, profit-making registered providers (paras. 7.11-13);

- ◆ mobile homes, caravans and houseboats (para. 9.44);

- ◆ hostel lettings (para. 9.45);

- ◆ any letting where the rent officer/NIHE has decided that the claim is treated as a boarder case (para. 9.79);

- ◆ protected tenancies (paras. 9.84-88);

- ◆ shared ownership cases (para. 9.90);

- ◆ any letting which is exempt accommodation (social accommodation where care, support or supervision is provided: para. 9.4);

- ◆ any other case where the date of claim (para. 5.30) fell before 7th April 2008, and the claimant has not moved home on or since that date (para. 9.38).

Eligible rent in LHA cases

8.5   In LHA cases, the claimant's eligible rent (also called 'maximum rent (LHA)' in the law) is simply the LHA figure applying in their area to the size or category of dwelling appropriate for their household (paras. 8.36 onwards), but there are protections for certain groups of claimants (paras. 8.52-59).

8.6   However, if the claimant's actual rent is lower than the LHA figure, their eligible rent equals their actual weekly rent. This is the case even when their actual rent includes services which – in other HB cases – would be ineligible for HB (paras. 7.39 onwards).

8.7   Also, the 'overriding power to reduce eligible rent' applies in LHA cases (as well as other cases) – enabling the authority to restrict the eligible rent to below the LHA figure. The power exists when 'it appears… that in the particular circumstances of the case the eligible rent… is greater than it is reasonable to meet' by way of HB. If it is, the eligible rent is reduced to 'such lesser sum as

---

T8.1   HB 2(1),13C(5)-(6); HB60+ 2(1),13C(5)-(6)

8.5   HB 13D(1); HB60+ 13D(1); NIHB 14D(1)

8.6   HB 13D(4),(5),(12); HB60+ 13D(4),(5),(12); NIHB 14D(4),(5),(12)

8.7   HB 12B(1),(6), 13D(4)(b),(12); HB60+ 12B(1)(6), 13D(4)(b),(12)

seems… to be an appropriate rent in that particular case'. This requires the authority to use its judgment (para. 1.40), and to take the personal circumstances of the claimant into account *(R v HBRB of the City of Westminster ex parte Laali).*

When LHAs start to apply to a case

8.8 When a claim for HB is an LHA case, the authority uses the LHA figure which applies on the date of the claim. When a non-LHA case becomes an LHA case as a result of the claimant moving home, the authority uses the LHA figure applying on the date of the move. In each of these circumstances, the figure then lasts until it has to be changed (paras. 8.10-13).

Awards for past periods

8.9 If HB is backdated (para. 5.51), the LHA figure which applies is the one relating to the beginning of that past period (and this figure is used until it has to be changed: paras. 8.10-13).

April changes to LHAs

8.10 When the rent officer or NIHE issues new LHA figures for the beginning of April each year (para. 8.39) these apply automatically in all LHA cases. In 2013 they always apply from 1st April. In future years they apply from the first Monday in April for claimants whose rent is due weekly or in multiples of weeks, and on 1st April for all other cases.

Other changes to LHAs

8.11 The claimant's LHA figure is also reviewed, and changed if appropriate, whenever:

(a) the size or category of dwelling applying to them changes (typically because someone has moved in or out: table 8.2); or

(b) a member of the family or a relative (para. 8.59) with no separate right of occupation dies (referred to in the law as a 'linked person') even if this would not change the size or category of dwelling applying to the claimant; or

(c) the claimant moves (within the area of the authority or outside it); or

(d) the claimant's actual weekly rent changes, and the authority is notified of that fact. This rule, introduced on 1st April 2013, enables the authority to reconsider the comparison described earlier (para. 8.6).

8.8   HB 2(1),12D(1),(2),13C(1),(2)(a)-(c),13D(12); HB60+ 2(1),12D(1),(2),13C(1),(2)(a)-(c),13D(12);
      NIHB 2(1),13(1),(2),14C(1),(2)(a)-(c),14D(10); NIHB60+ 2(1),13C(1),(2),14C(1),(2)(a)-(c),14D(10)

8.9   HB 13C(2)(a); HB60+ 13C(2)(a); NIHB 14C(2)(a),114A(10); NIHB60+ 14C(2)(a),95A(10)

8.10 HB 13C(3); HB60+ 13C(3); NIHB 14C(3); NIHB60+ 14C(3); DAR 8(15)

8.11 HB 2(1),12D(1),(2),13C(2)(d),(3),(4),(6); HB60+ 2(1),12D(1),(2),13C(2)(d),(3),(4),(6);
      NIHB 2(1),13C(1),(2),14C(2)(d),(3),(4),(6); NIHB60+ 2(1),13C(1),(2),14C(2)(d),(3),(4),(6)

8.12 In each of the above events (para. 8.11), the new LHA figure applies from the same day the change of circumstances applies from (paras. 17.18 onwards).

8.13 Event (a) (in para. 8.11) nearly always means that the claimant's HB will change. In event (b) the claimant's HB is unlikely to change (because of the protection for bereavement: para 8.56). In event (c), the claimant's HB changes only if a different LHA figure now applies to them. Event (d) is uncommon, but can result in either an increase or a decrease in the claimant's HB. No other changes in the claimant's circumstances trigger a change to their LHA figure.

Examples: Eligible rent and LHA figures

A new claim

A claimant has lived in her home since 2011. She decides to claim HB.

Her date of claim falls on Thursday 4th July 2013.

So she falls within the LHA scheme from Thursday 4th July 2013.

(Her HB will probably start the following Monday: para. 5.45.)

A move

A claimant has lived in her home since 2006, and has been on HB since 2007.

She moves home on Monday 16th September 2013.

So she falls within the LHA scheme from Monday 16th September 2013.

A change of circumstances

A claimant has been on HB within the LHA scheme since May 2013.'

A non-dependant then moves in – so she requires an extra bedroom.

The non-dependant moves in on Wednesday 11th September 2013.

And the new LHA applies from Monday 16th September 2013.

Sizes and categories of dwelling

8.14 In LHA cases, a claimant's eligible rent depends on the size and category of dwelling appropriate for them (para. 8.5). Table 8.2 shows which category applies to which groups of claimant; and further details follow (paras. 8.15-35).

8.12   DAR 7A,8(15); NIDAR 7A

8.14   HB 13D(2),(3); HB60+ 13D(2),(3); NIHB 14D(2),(3); NIHB60+ 14D(2),(3)

Table 8.2: Categories of accommodation

Details of the occupiers	LHA category
Single claimants and couples (with no children and no-one else in the household):	

- if the claimant, or in the case of a couple either of them, falls within any of the excepted groups in para. 8.16 — One-bedroom self-contained accommodation

- other single claimants aged under 35 (i.e. 'young individuals') — One-bedroom shared accommodation

- other single claimants (i.e. aged 35+) and couples (regardless of age), who have in their accommodation: — One-bedroom self-contained accommodation

    - exclusive use of at least two rooms (counting only bedrooms and living rooms, but regardless of whether they share other facilities); or

    - exclusive use of one room and of a bathroom, a toilet and a kitchen or cooking facilities

- other single claimants (i.e. aged 35+) and couples (regardless of age) — One-bedroom shared accommodation

All lone parents and couples with children, plus all cases where there are other occupiers in the household (para. 8.15) — Accommodation with the number of bedrooms indicated below

Counting up bedrooms

A bedroom is allocated for each of the following only up to a maximum of four bedrooms:

- each lone parent or couple;
- each other person aged 16+;
- two children under 16 of the same sex;
- two children under 10 of the same or opposite sex;
- any other child;
- an overnight carer or foster parent if appropriate (paras. 8.24 and 8.27).

However, the rules can be more generous in the case of couples and children who need their own bedrooms because of severe disabilities (paras. 8.33-35).

Which occupiers are included?

8.15   In deciding the size of accommodation the claimant qualifies for (table 8.2), the following occupiers are taken into account:

- ◆ the claimant and any members of their family (para. 4.8)
- ◆ non-dependants (para. 4.39) and lodgers (paras. 4.48-51); and
- ◆ other people who 'occupy as their home the dwelling to which the claim or award [of HB] relates' – but this excludes joint tenants who are not a member of the claimant's household (para. 8.19).

However, the maximum size of accommodation in an LHA case is a four-bedroom dwelling, regardless of the number of occupiers.

Examples: What size dwelling?

1. A single claimant

A single claimant aged 37 is renting a bedsit in a house in multiple occupation.

So she qualifies for the LHA for one-bedroom shared accommodation.

2. The claimant moves

The same claimant as above moves to a one-bedroom self-contained flat.

So she qualifies for the LHA for one-bedroom self-contained accommodation.

3. A younger single claimant

A single claimant aged 23 is renting a bedsit in a house in multiple occupation.

He qualifies for the LHA for one-bedroom shared accommodation.

4. A couple with two children

A couple have two children, a boy aged 7 and a girl aged 9.

The children are under 10, so are expected to share a bedroom, so the couple qualify for the LHA for two-bedroom accommodation.

5. The older child reaches 10

The same couple as above, but the daughter reaches 10.

Now one of the children is aged 10 or more, and they are of opposite sexes, so they are no longer expected to share a bedroom, and the couple qualify for the LHA for three-bedroom accommodation.

6. A couple with a lodger

A couple without children have a lodger in their home.

They qualify for two-bedroom accommodation.

8.15   HB 13D(12); HB60+ 13D(12); NIHB 14D(10); NIHB60+ 14D(10)

Definition of 'young individual'

8.16 For LHA claims, every claimant who is a 'young individual' only qualifies for the shared accommodation rate (table 8.2). A 'single claimant' (para. 4.7) who is under the age of 35 is a 'young individual' unless he or she:

(a) is under the age of 22 and was formerly in social services care under a court order (under section 31(1)(a) of the Children Act 1989 in England and Wales, or equivalent provisions in Scotland and Northern Ireland) which applied (or continued to apply) after his or her 16th birthday;

(b) is under the age of 22 and was formerly provided with accommodation by social services (under section 20 of the Children Act 1989 in England and Wales, or equivalent provisions in Scotland and Northern Ireland) but is no longer in that accommodation or remains in it but the accommodation is no longer provided by social services;

(c) qualifies for a severe disability premium in the assessment of his or her HB (para. 12.35), income support or JSA(IB);

(d) is aged 25 or over (but under 35) and has been in a homeless hostel for three months (the full details are in para. 8.17);

(e) is aged 25 or over (but under 35) and is an ex-offender who poses a serious risk of harm to the public and who is managed under a multi-agency ('MAPPA') agreement (e.g. police, social services) at management level 2 or 3 (see circular HB/CTB A14/2011 for details);

(f) has one or more non-dependants; or

(g) requires an overnight carer (para. 8.27).

Former residents of homeless hostels

8.17 A person aged 25 or over does not count as a young individual if he or she:

- has occupied a hostel for homeless people for at least three months, which does not need to have been continuous, and does not appear to need to have been recent (for example it could have been when they were under 25); and

- during that time was offered, and accepted, support with rehabilitation or resettlement within the community.

For these purposes, 'hostel' has its normal HB meaning (para. 9.45), and a hostel counts as being for homeless people if its 'main purpose... is to provide accommodation together with care, support or supervision for homeless people with a view to assisting [them] to be rehabilitated or settled within the community'.

8.16   HB 2(1),(1A),(1C); HB60+ 2(1); NIHB 2(1),(1A),(1C); NIHB60+ 2(1)

8.17   HB 2(1),(1A),(1B); NIHB 2(1),(1A),(1B)

Joint tenants

8.18   Joint tenants who are a member of the claimant's household are included as an occupier: *[2011] UKUT 156 (AAC)* (where the claimant's father was included).

8.19   For joint tenants who are not members of the same household, each joint tenant is allocated the category applying to himself or herself. For single joint tenants, this is likely to be one-bedroom shared accommodation in the majority of cases. This is because it is unlikely that they will meet the conditions in table 8.2 required to qualify for one-bedroom self-contained accommodation: 'exclusive' use of two rooms requires there to be a legal entitlement to the exclusive use, not just exclusive use in practice: *[2011] UKUT 156 (AAC)*.

Examples: Joint occupiers

1. Three friends

Three friends jointly rent a three-bedroom house. They maintain separate households.

They each qualify for the LHA for one-bedroom shared accommodation.

2. Two sisters, one with a non-dependant

Two sisters jointly rent a three-bedroom house They maintain separate households. One has a grown-up son living with her.

The son is the non-dependant of his mother.

So his mother qualifies for the LHA for two-bedroom accommodation – and there is a non-dependant deduction in her case only.

Joint tenants with non-dependants

8.20   If amongst joint tenants, one has a non-dependant (for example three friends live together and the mother of one of them lives with them), that joint tenant qualifies for two-bedroom accommodation (and any non-dependant deduction applies to that joint tenant alone).

General considerations about who is an 'occupier'

8.21   A number of questions have arisen about which occupiers are included in deciding what size of accommodation the claimant needs. These apply to LHA cases, social sector cases (para. 7.30) and rent referral cases (para. 9.75), as do the following paragraphs.

Determining who is an occupier is for the authority not the rent officer: *R v Swale BC HBRB ex p Marchant*. In doing this the authority should have regard to the general HB rules about who is an occupier (chapter 3); and even though some of the law was originally written only to apply to the claimant or partner,

---

8.19   HB 13D(12); HB60+ 13D(12); NIHB 14D(10); NIHB60+ 14D(10)

it should be adapted to apply to non-dependants (for example): *[2010] UKUT 129 AAC.* An appeal can be made to a tribunal about which occupiers are included: *[2010] UKUT 79 AAC* – even though the tribunal cannot alter LHA figures or rent officer rents (paras. 8.49-50 and table 19.2).

Armed forces absences

8.22   Since 1st April 2013 if a son, daughter, step-son or step-daughter of the claimant is in the armed forces (regular or reserve), he or she continues to count as an occupier of the home during an absence on operations, so long as he or she:

* was a non-dependant (paras. 4.39-46) before that absence (regardless of whether a non-dependant deduction then applied); and
* intends to return to reside in the dwelling when that absence ends.

Shared children

8.23   Generally speaking a child who spends time in the homes of each of his or her parents (who live apart) is included as an occupier only in the home of the parent who is 'responsible' for him or her, typically the one who receives child benefit (para. 4.31, and see the *Marchant* case (paras. 4.32 and 9.75)).

Fostering/kinship and pre-adoption

8.24   Since 1st April 2013 if the claimant or partner is a qualifying parent or carer, they are entitled to one further bedroom, but the total number of bedrooms (even in these cases) cannot exceed four. The claimant or partner is a qualifying parent if they:

* have a child or young person placed with them as a foster parent or kinship carer or prior to adoption (in any of the circumstances described in para. 4.35); or
* have been approved as a foster parent or kinship carer but have not yet had a placement – but in this case only for 52 weeks.

If this applies, and the rule relating to overnight carers (para. 8.27) also applies, the claimant is entitled to two extra bedrooms (up to the maximum of four).

Students and others gradually leaving home

8.25   When a student starts at a university and lives in a hall of residence, coming home frequently, it is correct to include them as an occupier of the parent's home: *[2009] UKUT 67 (AAC), [2010] UKUT 129 (AAC).* By perhaps the second year, especially if the student has taken on the rent of a flat or house, this is less likely to be the case. There is no fixed rule, each case depending on the facts.

8.22   HB 2(1), 13D(12); HB60+ 2(1), 13D(2)

8.24   HB 2(1), 13D(3A),(3B); HB60+ 2(1), 13D(3A),(3B)

Carers and disablement needs

8.26   This section explains when an additional bedroom can be added for:

 * an overnight non-residential carer (paras. 8.27-32);
 * a resident carer (para. 8.33); and
 * when a disabled child or a partner needs their own room (paras. 8.34-35).

Overnight carers

8.27   If the claimant or partner is a 'person who requires overnight care' (or if both of them are) they are entitled to one further bedroom. This means one bedroom, not two, even if both require overnight care; and the total number of bedrooms cannot (even in these cases) exceed four. A 'person who requires overnight care' is defined as someone who meets both the following conditions. This can apply only to the claimant or a partner; not a child, non-dependant or anyone else in the household.

The first condition

8.28   The first condition is that the person:

 * is in receipt of the highest or middle rate of the care component of disability living allowance; or
 * is in receipt of attendance allowance; or
 * provides the authority with 'sufficient [evidence] to satisfy the authority that [the person] requires overnight care'.

The last point means, for example, that someone who ought perhaps to be on one of the benefits in question, but hasn't claimed it, meets the first condition.

The second condition

8.29   The second condition is that the authority is satisfied that the person reasonably requires, and has in fact arranged, that one or more people who do not occupy the dwelling as their home:

 * is engaged in providing overnight care for the person; and
 * regularly stays overnight in the dwelling for that purpose; and
 * is provided with the use of a bedroom for that purpose which is additional to those occupied by the people who occupy the dwelling as their home.

8.30   The second condition is met whether the person always has the same overnight carer, or a rota of overnight carers. It is not enough to require a carer only by day. The carer must stay overnight 'regularly' – not so much as regularly as clockwork, but more that there is a general pattern of overnight care.

8.27   HB 13D(3); HB60+ 13D(3); NIHB 14D(3); NIHB60+ 14D(3)

8.28   HB 2(1); HB60+ 2(1); NIHB 2(1); NIHB60+ 2(1)

8.29   HB 2(1); HB60+ 2(1); NIHB 2(1); NIHB60+ 2(1)

8.31 There must be an actual bedroom provided for the carer, and it must be additional to the bedrooms occupied by the person cared for and other members of the household. It appears that a person who sleeps downstairs in their living room because they cannot get upstairs has, however, effectively converted their living room into a bedroom, so a bedroom upstairs can be said to be 'additional'.

Temporary absence or waiting to move in

8.32 The second condition is also met if the person requiring the care does not currently occupy the dwelling, but the authority is satisfied that:

* the dwelling has the additional bedroom; and
* the person will in due course arrange for it to be used as described above.

This could apply to someone who is temporarily absent (para. 3.32), or someone who is waiting to leave hospital or a care home (para. 3.22).

Resident carers

8.33 A live-in carer is included as an occupier if they occupy the accommodation as their home (regardless of who they care for). This applies whether they are a relative or someone else, and whether or not they are paid.

Additional bedroom for disablement needs

8.34 If two children need a bedroom each because of severe disabilities, then each is allocated a bedroom even if the normal rules (table 8.2) would not permit this. This is the effect of the Court of Appeal's decision in *Burnip v Birmingham CC and others: [2012] EWCA Civ 629,* and has applied since 15th May 2012 (the date of that decision).

8.35 The situation is slightly less clear in the case of a couple who require two bedrooms because of severe disabilities (rather than one: table 8.2). Although the *Burnip* case (para. 8.34) was about disabled children, it seems very likely that it applies equally to such couples.

How the LHA figures are set

8.36 It is the rent officer/NIHE (paras. 9.33-34) who determines:

* all LHA figures (paras. 8.38-44); and
* the 'broad rental market areas' they apply to (paras. 8.45-46).

Publicity

8.37 LHA figures and broad rental market areas are public information, and the authority must 'take such steps as appear to it appropriate' to bring them to the attention of people who may be entitled to HB. Most authorities have published

---

8.32   HB 2(1); HB60+ 2(1); NIHB 2(1); NIHB60+ 2(1)

8.33   HB 13D(12); HB60+ 13D(12); NIHB 14D(10); NIHB60+ 14D(10)

them on their websites and elsewhere. They are also available for the whole of Great Britain and for Northern Ireland online [www].

Determining the LHA figures

8.38   The rent officer sets LHA figures for the following categories of dwelling:

* one-bedroom shared accommodation;
* one-bedroom self-contained accommodation;
* two-bedroom dwellings;
* three-bedroom dwellings; and
* four-bedroom dwellings.

In each case the rent officer must give a weekly figure and an approximate monthly equivalent: it is the weekly figure which is used in assessing HB.

8.39   The rent officer determines the LHA figures annually to apply from the beginning of each April (para. 8.10). This is done within 20 working days after the publication of the preceding September's Consumer Price Index (CPI).

Data and assumptions

8.40   The rent officer sets the LHA figures by taking account of the range of rents which a landlord 'might reasonably have been expected to obtain' on dwellings which:

* are let on assured tenancies;
* have the relevant number of rooms for the category in question;
* are in a reasonable state of repair; and
* are in the relevant broad market area (paras. 8.45-46).

But if within a broad rental market area, there are insufficient rents to enable the rent officer to provide a representative LHA figure for a particular category of dwelling, the rent officer may add 'rents for dwellings in the same category in other areas in which a comparable market exists.'

8.41   When setting LHA figures, the rent officer must:

* 'assume that no-one who would have been entitled to [HB] had sought or is seeking the tenancy': in practice they do this simply by ignoring any rent payable by a person on HB; and
* exclude the value of all ineligible service charges.

8.37   HB 13E; HB60+ 13E; NIHB 14E; NIHB60+ 14E
        Great Britain: https://lha-direct.voa.gov.uk/search.aspx
        Northern Ireland: www.nihe.gov.uk/index/benefits/lha/current_lha_rates.htm

8.38   ROO 4B(6), sch 3B para 1; NIED 3(6), sch para 1

8.39   ROO 2,4B(2A),(3A); SI 2012 No 646; NISR 2012/157; NIHB sch 2 para 15; NIHB60+ sch 2 para 15;
        NIED 3(2),(3)

8.40   ROO sch 3B para 2(1),(5); NIED sch para 2(1),(5)

8.41   ROO sch 3B para 2(7); NIED sch para 2(7)

8.42 Each year's LHA figure is set at the lower of:

- the rent at the 30th percentile of the data described above; or
- the previous year's LHA figure uprated by the Consumer Price Index (CPI) for the preceding September.

8.43 If the result of the above calculations results (most unusually) in the LHA figure for a larger category of dwelling being lower than the LHA figure for a smaller category, the figure for the larger is increased to equal that for the smaller.

National LHA caps

8.44 Finally, if the result of the above calculation (paras. 8.40-43) exceeds the national LHA cap, the rent officer instead fixes the LHA as equal to the national cap. The national cap is as follows:

- £250 pw for one-bedroom (shared or self-contained) accommodation;
- £290 pw for two-bedroom accommodation;
- £340 pw for three-bedroom accommodation;
- £400 pw for four-bedroom accommodation.

Determining broad rental market areas

8.45 The rent officer determines each broad rental market area in the same way for both LHA cases and rent referral cases (para. 9.72) (except that in Northern Ireland it applies to LHA cases only: para. 9.73), and this is defined in the law as follows:

- The area must be one where a person 'could reasonably be expected to live having regard to facilities and services for the purposes of health, education, recreation, personal banking and shopping, taking account of the distance of travel, by public and private transport, to and from those facilities and services'.
- It must contain 'residential premises of a variety of types' held on a 'variety of tenancies'.
- It must contain 'sufficient privately rented premises' to ensure that the rent officer's figures 'are representative of the rents that a landlord might reasonably be expected to obtain in that area'.

The areas are then normally defined by reference to postcodes.

8.46 In practice, some council areas contain more than one broad rental market area, some are made up of just one, and some broad rental market areas are made up of more than one council area. The DWP takes the view that the areas can be fairly large, and that *R (Heffernan) v the Rent Service* (in which the House of Lords criticised this in relation to rent referral cases) no longer applies.

8.42   ROO sch 3B para 2(2)-(4),(6),(9)-(11); NIED sch para 2(2)-(4),(6),(9)-(11)

8.43   ROO sch 3B para 3; SI 2012 No 646; NISR 2012/157; NIED sch para 3

8.44   ROO sch. 3B para. 2(12); NIED sch para 2(12)

8.45   ROO sch 3B paras 4,5; NIED sch paras 4,5

Amending areas or figures

8.47 Rent officers can amend individual LHA figures. They can also amend broad rental market areas but only where the Secretary of State agrees this should be done. In either case, they must notify authorities of this.

8.48 The above amendments are taken into account in HB as follows:

* if a claimant's LHA goes down as a result, this is implemented as a change of circumstances from the Monday following the date the rent officer makes their amendment (so this should not result in the claimant being overpaid);

* if a claimant's LHA goes up as a result, this is implemented back to the date the LHA in question applied from (so the claimant gets his or her arrears).

Appeals about the areas or figures

8.49 Unlike the law on rent officer referrals, there is no right of appeal to another rent officer about a broad rental market area or about the amount of an LHA figure. Nor is there a right of appeal to a tribunal (though an appeal to a tribunal can be about the number of occupiers and therefore which particular LHA figure is to be applied). This means that any challenge would have to be by judicial review in the High Court (Sheriff Court in Scotland).

8.50 Some judicial reviews were begun (e.g. in relation to the London broad rental market areas) before LHAs came in, but all were settled by negotiation. Those judicial reviews were begun by authorities, but it would seem that an individual claimant might also be able to do this.

Statistics provided to the rent officer

8.51 In order to assist the rent officer in excluding the effect of HB on market rents (para. 8.41), each authority sends the rent officer statistics. This is done between the first and fifth working day of every month, and contains details of rents, facilities, letting dates and dates of HB entitlement for everyone who was receiving HB in the private sector at any time in the previous month.

Eligible rent: protected groups

8.52 The HB rules described in this chapter, and in chapters 7 and 9, can mean that a claimant's eligible rent is lower than their actual rent, leaving them to pay the shortfall or get into rent arrears. This arises:

* **in private sector cases** – when the LHA figure is lower than the claimant's rent (para. 8.5);

8.47   ROO 4B(1A); NIED 3(1)

8.48   HB 18A; HB60+ 18A; ROO 7A(4); NIHB 14F; NIHB60+ 14F

8.51   HB 114A(1),(2); HB60+ 95A(1),(2)

- **in social sector cases** – when the claimant occupies accommodation larger than appropriate (paras. 7.23-38);
- **in exempt accommodation cases** – when the claimant occupies unreasonably large or expensive accommodation (paras. 9.13-14);
- **in rent referral cases** – when the rent officer's or NIHE's rent determination is lower than the claimant's rent (paras. 9.41).

8.53   However, certain groups of claimant are wholly or partly protected against these eligible rent restrictions. The two protections described below (paras. 8.54-59) apply to all the above types of HB case (para. 8.52). One further protection applies only to exempt accommodation cases and is described in paragraphs 9.21-23.

People who could formerly afford their accommodation

8.54   A claimant falls within this protected group if:

- they or any combination of the occupiers of their home (para. 8.58) could afford the financial commitments there when the liability to pay rent was entered into (no matter how long ago that was); and
- neither the claimant nor any partner has received HB for any period in the 52 weeks prior to their current claim.

The protection in such cases lasts for the first 13 weeks of the award of HB. It gives the claimant time to move without the additional pressure of having insufficient HB.

8.55   While the protection lasts, the claimant's eligible rent is:

- the full actual rent payable on their dwelling;
- minus amounts for services which are ineligible for HB (worked out in the same way as for social sector rents: paras. 7.39-68);
- minus, in Northern Ireland, the amount for rates, except where the tenant is billed separately.

People who have had a bereavement

8.56   A claimant falls within this protected group if:

- any of the occupiers of their home (para. 8.58) has died within the last 12 months (including occupiers who were temporarily absent); and
- the claimant has not moved home since the date of that death.

8.57   The protection in such cases lasts until 12 months after that death. During that period it works as follows. If the claimant was on HB at the date of the death, their eligible rent must not be reduced to below whatever was their eligible rent immediately before that date (it is, however, increased if any rule requires this). If the claimant was not on HB at the date of the death, their eligible rent is worked out in the same way as in paragraph 8.55.

8.54   HB 12D(5); HB60+ 12D(5); NIHB 13C(5); NIHB60+ 13C(5)
8.56   HB 12D(3); HB60+ 12D(3); NIHB 13C(3); NIHB60+ 13C(3)

Who is an 'occupier'?

8.58 For the purposes of the above protected groups, the only 'occupiers' taken into account are:

- the claimant and any family (partner, children, young persons: para. 4.8); and
- any 'relative' of the claimant or partner (including non-dependants, lodgers, sub-tenants and joint occupiers) who has no separate right to occupy the dwelling.

In the law, the term 'linked persons' is also used to refer to the above occupiers.

Who is a 'relative'?

8.59 A 'relative' is defined as:

- a parent, daughter, son, sister or brother;
- a parent-in-law, daughter-in-law, son-in-law, step-daughter or step-son, including equivalent relations arising through civil partnership;
- a partner of any of the above (i.e. by marriage or civil partnership, or by living together as husband and wife or civil partners); or
- a grandparent, grandchild, aunt, uncle, niece or nephew.

Examples: The protected groups

Redundancy

A claimant makes a claim for HB after he is made redundant. His actual rent is high. He moved to this address when he was in a well-paid job and could easily afford the rent and outgoings. He has not been on HB in the last 52 weeks.

Because of the protection for people who could formerly afford their accommodation, his eligible rent must not be restricted in any way for the first 13 weeks of his award of HB. During those weeks, his eligible rent is his actual rent minus amounts for any ineligible services.

Bereavement

A claimant makes a claim for HB after the death of her husband. She has not moved since her husband's death. Her actual rent is high.

Because of the protection for people who have had a bereavement, her eligible rent must not be restricted in any way until the first anniversary of her husband's death. Until then, her eligible rent is her actual rent minus amounts for any ineligible services.

8.58   HB 2(1),12D,13ZA; HB60+ 2(1),12D,13ZA; CPR sch 3 para 5; NIHB 2(1),13C,14A; NIHB60+ 2(1),13C,14A; NICPR sch 3 para 5

8.59   HB 2(1); HB60+2(1); NIHB 2(1); NIHB60+2(1)

9 Eligible rent: special cases

9.1   This chapter explains how to work out the claimant's eligible rent in the following special cases. These can arise with both social and private lettings:

- exempt accommodation (also called 'old cases');
- rent referral cases – including the further rules for boarders, caravans, mobile homes, houseboats and hostels;
- protected tenancies (and similar lettings);
- shared ownership cases; and
- certain temporary accommodation for homeless households.

Exempt accommodation

9.2   This section gives the rules about exempt accommodation. This means certain accommodation with care, support or supervision rented from certain social landlords (paras. 9.4 6).

Overview of exempt accommodation

9.3   The key features of the exempt accommodation rules are as follows:

- a claimant's eligible rent is the full rent on their dwelling minus amounts for ineligible services and (in Northern Ireland) rates;
- the eligible rent can be lower in certain circumstances;
- there are protections for certain groups of claimant;
- rent determinations made by the rent officer/NIHE are not binding on the authority.

Definition of exempt accommodation

9.4   A dwelling is 'exempt accommodation' if:

(a) the accommodation is 'provided by':
- a housing association, whether registered or unregistered,
- a registered charity,
- a non-profit-making voluntary organisation, or
- in England only, a non-metropolitan county council;

(b) but only if (in each of the cases) 'that body or a person acting on its behalf also provides the claimant with care, support or supervision'.

9.4   CPR sch 3 para 4(1)(b),(10); NICPR sch 3 para 4(1)(b),(9)

9.5   The above two conditions (para. 9.4), must both be satisfied for a home to be exempt accommodation. Within a group of dwellings, each individual home must satisfy both conditions. Just because one does, does not automatically mean another will – e.g. if support is in fact provided only to some residents (CH/1289/2007):

  ◆   As regards the first condition (para. 9.4(a)), what it means for accommodation to be 'provided by' the organisation concerned is clearly limited to cases in which the tenant's immediate landlord is one of the relevant bodies (*CH/3900/2005* and *[2009] UKUT 12 (AAC)*).

  ◆   As regards the second condition (para. 9.4(b)), the care, support or supervision must be provided either by the landlord itself or by someone else on its behalf – and there are many other considerations to take into account, as shown in table 9.1. Many of the cases quoted there, though lengthy, are worth reading through for further guidance. The DWP gives a very helpful summary of the older cases in circular HB/CTB A22/2008.

9.6   In Great Britain only, a dwelling is also 'exempt accommodation' if it is a resettlement place for which the provider previously received grant funding from the DWP under section 30 of the Jobseekers Act 1995 (sometimes referred to as resettlement grant).

9.7   Exempt accommodation is so called because it has been exempt over the years from several of the HB changes restricting claimants' eligible rent. The cases are sometimes also called 'old cases' because, regardless of the actual age of the case, the rules for assessing eligible rent are based on those in force before January 1996. Most 'supported accommodation' (to use a loose term) is 'exempt accom-modation' but only the above definition is relevant in HB. A former separate category known as 'exempt claimants' no longer exists. Since 6th April 2009, a case only falls within the rules in this section if it meets the above definition of exempt accommodation.

Eligible rent in exempt accommodation

9.8   In exempt accommodation the claimant's eligible rent is:

  ◆   the actual rent payable on their dwelling (but this is subject to limits: paras. 9.13-30; and see also para. 9.89 for protected tenancies);

  ◆   minus amounts for service charges which are ineligible for HB. These are worked out in the same way as for social sector rents (paras. 7.17-22);

  ◆   minus, in Northern Ireland, the amount for rates, except where the tenant is billed separately.

The resulting figure is adjusted when necessary (para. 9.9).

9.7   CPR sch 3 para 4(1)(a),(2); NICPR sch 3 para 4(1)(a),(2); SI 2007/2868

9.8   HB 12B(2); HB60+ 12B(2); NIHB 13A(2); NIHB60+ 13A(2)

Table 9.1: Exempt accommodation: care, support or supervision (CSS): case law

* **Provision of CSS 'on behalf of' the landlord:** For CSS to be provided 'on behalf of' the landlord, there must be 'a sense of agency between the [CSS provider and the landlord], or to put it another way, a contract, or something akin to it'. An arrangement that is merely a joint venture is not enough; nor is it enough that there is a contract between the CSS provider and e.g. social services *(R(S) v Walsall MBC, confirming R(H) 2/07)*.

* **CSS provided by landlord as well as care provider:** The landlord may provide 'care, support, or supervision' without being the principal provider of it to that particular tenant *([2010] AACR 2 para. 188)*.

* **Meaning of CSS:** the phrase 'care, support or supervision' has its ordinary English meaning *(R(S) v Walsall MBC, confirming R(H) 2/07)*.

* **Availability of CSS:** The CSS must be available in reality to the tenant, and there must be a real prospect that they will find the service of use *(R(H) 4/09 and [2009] UKUT 109 (AAC) para. 44)*.

* **Who pays for the CSS?** It is irrelevant that the landlord is (or is not) paid to provide the CSS by someone else *([2009] UKUT 107 (AAC) para. 71)*.

* **How does the landlord provide the CSS?** CSS can be provided by making arrangements for it, or by paying for someone to do it *([2009] UKUT 107 (AAC) para. 71)*.

* **Need for and provision of 'support':** 'What matters is simply whether support is provided to more than a minimal extent, and it is... implicit that support is not "provided" unless there is in fact some need for it' *([2009] UKUT 150 (AAC) para. 73)*.

* **Meaning of 'support':** 'Support' means that the landlord does more than an ordinary landlord would do *(R(H) 4/09)*. It might well be characterised as 'the giving of advice and assistance to a claimant in coping with the practicalities of [their] life, and in particular [their] occupation of the property' *([2010] AACR 2 para. 129)*.

* **Continuity of support:** There must be a degree of continuity in the provision of the support *(R(H) 4/09)*. For example, help with gaining exemption from council tax because the tenant is severely mentally impaired is more like a setting up cost and is not enough *([2010] AACR 2 para. 120)*.

- **Examples of 'support':** Support is in general more than ordinary housing management; and carrying out repairs and maintenance do not generally amount to support. But if the tenancy agreement 'imposes unusually onerous repairing and maintenance obligations on the landlord', this can amount to support; as can the fact that a claimant's disabilities impose a 'materially greater burden on the landlord' *([2009] UKUT 107 (AAC) para. 71).*

- **Minimal CSS:** For accommodation to be exempt accommodation the CSS must be more than minimal. On the facts of the cases in question an average of ten minutes per tenant per week was not enough *(R(H) 7/07),* but three hours per tenant per week might be enough *(CH/1289/2007).*

- **Examples of minimal support:** Just helping with HB claims and reviews, and carrying out safety and security inspections, was not enough to be more than minimal *([2010] AACR 2 para. 188).*

- **Examples of more than minimal support:** 'Proactively considering what physical improvements or alterations to the properties could usefully be made' in the case of adaptations desirable in the light of the tenant's disability, could be enough *([2010] AACR 2 para. 188).*

- **Availability of CSS from elsewhere:** 'The likely nature, extent and frequency of [the CSS, in this case repair and maintenance works], and the extent of support available to the claimant from elsewhere' are to be taken into account in considering whether the CSS was more than minimal *([2009] UKUT 107 (AAC) para. 71).*

- **When there is no relevant history:** Where there is no history of the support being provided (because it is a new development), it is necessary to look at what is contemplated *([2009] UKUT 109 (AAC)).*

- **Note on carers:** While the presence of a live-in carer may or may not amount to CSS (depending on who provides the carer), the case law on carers in exempt accommodation is more relevant to the question of whether the eligible rent should be restricted (para. 9.13).

9.9   Adjustments to the eligible rent are made in the same way as in social sector cases for:

- joint tenants (para. 7.21);
- business premises (para. 7.22);
- overheads, management costs and council tax (para. 7.70);
- garages and land (para. 7.72); and
- space for a carer or for disablement needs (para. 7.73).

9.9   HB 11(3), 12B(3)-(4), 12C(2); HB60+ 11(3), 12B(3)-(4), 12C(2); NIHB 11(3), 12(4)-(6), 13A(3)-(4), 13B(2); NIHB60+ 11(3), 12(4)-(6), 13A(3)-(4), 13B(2)

Exempt accommodation and rent determinations

9.10   Exempt accommodation cases require a rent determination – made by the rent officer in Great Britain and by the NIHE in Northern Ireland – as follows:

+ for the types of dwelling described in paragraph 9.36 (e.g. rented from a registered housing association), no rent determination is required (or permitted) unless the rent or size is unreasonable (para. 9.37);

+ for any other exempt accommodation a rent determination is always required.

9.11   When a rent determination is required for exempt accommodation, the same procedures apply as in rent referral cases (paras. 9.50-52).

9.12   However, a crucial difference exists from all other rent referral cases. In exempt accommodation cases, rent determinations are not binding (though they may affect subsidy: paras. 24.33-34): they merely play an advisory role in the authority's consideration of whether to restrict the claimant's eligible rent (paras. 9.13-30).

Rent restrictions in exempt accommodation

Eligible rent restrictions

9.13   In exempt accommodation, the authority may restrict the claimant's eligible rent if the rent, the size of the accommodation, or a rent increase is unreasonable; but in many cases claimants are also protected against this (para. 9.20). This section gives the detail about these rent restrictions, and table 9.2 provides a summary.

9.14   In applying these rules, the authority:

+ must not take a blanket approach (GM para. A4.962): each step must be considered in the individual circumstances of each case and in the light of the case law (described below), and is open to appeal;

+ must not restrict a claimant's eligible rent just because of the subsidy rules (paras. 24.33-34). The requirements of the HB regulations (given below) are the only test that is relevant in deciding whether or not benefit should be restricted.

Deciding what is 'unreasonable' by finding comparables

9.15   The first question is whether:

+ the rent is unreasonably high; or

+ the accommodation is unreasonably large for all the occupiers; or

+ a rent increase is unreasonably high; or

9.10   HB 14(1)-(2), sch 2; HB60+ 14(1)-(2), sch 2; NIHB 15(1),(3), sch 3; NIHB60+ 15(1),(3), sch 3

9.13   HB 13ZA; HB60+ 13ZA; NIHB 14A; NIHB60+ 14A; CPR sch 3 para 5(1),(2); NICPR sch 3 para 5(1),(2)

9.15   CPR sch 3 para 5(1),(2); NICPR sch 3 para 5(1),(2)

◆　a rent increase is unreasonably soon after another increase during the previous year.

9.16　　As regards size, the question of who counts as an occupier is open to interpretation (since 'occupier' is not further defined for these purposes) and appeal (chapter 19), but it is not limited to the groups listed in paragraph 8.58 (and the social sector size criteria do not apply (para. 7.13). Though the *Swale and Marchant* case (para. 8.22) may affect how some authorities interpret 'occupier' for these purposes, there is an argument that that case was about the definition of 'occupier' in a different context and so is not binding here.

9.17　　In all the above cases, authorities:

◆　must make a comparison (as regards the rent, size or rent increase, as appropriate) with suitable alternative accommodation (paras. 9.18-19);

◆　may additionally take account of any rent determination provided by the rent officer/NIHE (paras. 9.10-12) – and the DWP advises that they 'must' do this (GM para. A4.1122), bearing in mind that the rent officer's function is different;

◆　must not, at this stage, take into account the impact of the subsidy rules on their own finances (paras. 24.33-34).

Table 9.2: HB restrictions: a summary

Step one: Is the rent or size unreasonable?

The claimant's HB can be restricted only if, compared with suitable alternative accommodation:

◆　the rent is unreasonably high; or

◆　the dwelling is unreasonably large; or

◆　a rent increase is unreasonable.

Step two: Is the claimant in a protected group?

Protections against HB restrictions can apply for claimants:

◆　who could afford their accommodation when their letting began; or

◆　who have had a death in their home; or

◆　who have one or more children or young persons, or have reached pension credit age (para. 1.21), or are sick or disabled.

Step three: How much should the eligible rent be restricted?

If the rent is unreasonable (step one) and none of the protections applies (step two), the authority decides how much to reduce the claimant's eligible rent.

9.18　　Authorities should make the comparison by working through the following questions *(R v Beverley BC HBRB ex p Hare)*:

(a) what is the actual rent (including all eligible and ineligible services) for the claimant's dwelling?

(b) what type of alternative accommodation is suitable for the claimant? and, in order to determine this, what services are needed to make the alternative accommodation suitable and what other factors need to be taken into account (para. 9.19)?

(c) what rent (including all eligible and ineligible services) would be payable for such accommodation?

(d) is the rent in (a) unreasonably high by comparison with the rent in (c)?

'Unreasonably high' means more than just 'higher' *(Malcolm v Tweeddale DC HBRB* and *CH/4306/2003)*. This rule also applies to unreasonable rent increases *(CH/2214/2003)*: para. 9.32.

9.19   In deciding what alternative accommodation would be suitable for the claimant (para. 9.18(b)), authorities:

♦ must take account of the nature of the alternative accommodation and the exclusive and shared facilities provided, having regard to the age and state of health of all the occupiers (as defined in para. 8.58). 'For example, a disabled or elderly person might have special needs and require more expensive or larger accommodation' (GM para. A4.1171);

♦ must only take into account alternative accommodation with security of tenure which is reasonably equivalent to what the claimant currently has (GM para. A4.1170);

♦ must have 'sufficient information to ensure that like is being compared with like... Unless that can be done, no safe assessment can be made of the reasonableness of the rent in question or the proper level of value' *(Malcolm v Tweeddale DC HBRB)*;

♦ may take account of alternative accommodation outside the authority's own area if there is no comparable accommodation within it. But if this is necessary, it is unreasonable to make 'comparisons with other parts of the country where accommodation costs differ widely from those which apply locally' (GM para. A4.1172).

Protected groups

9.20   Three groups of claimants are protected against the effect of the above rules about HB restrictions. The first two groups (people who could formerly afford their accommodation, and people who have had a bereavement), and the rules applying to them, are the same as those described in paragraphs 8.54-57; the details of the third group, and the rules applying to it, are described below.

9.19   CPR sch 3 para 5(1),(2); NICPR sch 3 para 5(1),(2)

9.20   CPR sch 3 para 5(1),(2); NICPR sch 3 para 5(1),(2)

Vulnerable people

9.21   A claimant falls within this protected group if any of the occupiers of his or her home (as defined in paras. 8.58-59):

+ has reached state pension credit age (para. 1.21); or

+ is responsible for a child or young person in the household (paras. 4.3 and 4.23-38); or

+ is incapable of work for social security purposes (para. 12.23) including those with limited capability for work. This is decided by the DWP, not the authority; and is decided by reference to the present-day definition of 'incapable of work' *(CH/4424/2004)*.

In such a case, the authority must not reduce the claimant's eligible rent unless there is suitable alternative accommodation available (para. 9.22) and it is reasonable to expect the claimant to move (para. 9.23).

9.22   What counts as suitable alternative accommodation was described earlier (para. 9.19). The point here is that it must be available. For example, accommodation the claimant has recently left, or an offer of accommodation the claimant has refused, may be available – but only while it actually remains available to the claimant, and not after it has been let to someone else. However, the authority is not an accommodation agency, and 'it is… quite sufficient if an active market rent is shown to exist in houses in an appropriate place at the appropriate level [to which the] rent is restricted'. Provided the authority has at least evidence of that, it is sufficient 'to point to a range of properties, or a bloc of property, which is available without specific identification of particular dwelling houses' *(R v East Devon DC HBRB ex p Gibson)*. The DWP follows this and emphasises that 'authorities should regard accommodation as not available if, in practice, there is little or no possibility of the claimant being able to obtain it, for example because it could only be obtained on payment of a large deposit which the claimant does not have' (GM para. A4.1222).

9.23   In deciding whether it is reasonable to expect the claimant to move, authorities must take into account:

+ the claimant's prospects of retaining employment; and

+ the effect on the education of a child or young person who would have to change school (this means any child or young person mentioned in para. 8.58).

The authority must take individual circumstances into account when considering 'suitability', 'availability' and 'reasonableness' and its decision could be overturned if, for example, there was no evidence that it had considered the effect of a move on a child's education: *R v Sefton MBC ex p Cunningham*.

9.21   CPR sch 3 para 5(1),(2); NICPR sch 3 para 5(1),(2)

9.23   CPR sch 3 para 5(1),(2); NICPR sch 3 para 5(1),(2)

Restricting the eligible rent

9.24   The final question (if it applies at all, considering the above points) is how much to restrict the eligible rent. If the authority has decided that the claim is unreasonable and the claimant is not entitled to one of the protections described above then it must make a restriction. However, in deciding what level to apply it must use its judgment and discretion as to how much and, according to the circumstances of the case, it may be as little as a penny a week. In considering the level of the restriction, the authority must work through the following questions:

(a) are there any circumstances which may make a small reduction appropriate?

(b) what is the appropriate amount for the reduction? and

(c) how was that appropriate amount arrived at?

The above is based on the judgments in *Mehanne v Westminster CC HBRB* and *R v Beverley BC HBRB ex p Hare.* As regards (b) above, the authority must not reduce the claimant's eligible rent below the cost of comparable alternative accommodation: *R v Brent LBC ex p Connery.*

9.25   As regards all the above questions, authorities must consider what is appropriate in the individual circumstances of each case. There may be cases in which the minimum reduction is appropriate. There are also cases in which the minimum reduction is appropriate for the time being but may be increased later on. In practice, authorities sometimes restrict the rents to the rent determination made by the rent officer/NIHE (paras. 9.10-12). However, such a determination does not take into account the claimant's personal circumstances, as the authority is required to do (para. 9.23).

The impact of subsidy

9.26   The authority cannot take into account the impact of the subsidy rules (paras. 24.33-34) when deciding whether the rent/size is unreasonable or whether a member of the household is in a protected group (i.e. steps one and two in table 9.2) or in any case at all where the claimant is protected (paras. 9.20-21).

9.27   However, it may consider the subsidy implications in deciding the amount of the restriction to be applied (i.e. step three in table 9.2): *R v Brent LBC ex p Connery.* In reaching its decision on this final step the authority must properly exercise its judgment and discretion (paras. 1.48-49) and in doing so the DWP's opinion is that the authority 'cannot restrict on financial grounds alone' (GM para. A4.1173).

9.24   CPR sch 3 para 5(1),(2); NICPR sch 3 para 5(1),(2)

Restrictions on rent increases

9.28   When the rent is increased during an existing HB award the authority must restrict all or part of the increase if it considers that the level of increase is:

* unreasonable in comparison with suitable alternative accommodation; or
* unreasonable because it is less than a year since the last increase.

9.29   In deciding whether a rent increase is unreasonable as above, the test is whether the rent increase was unreasonably high by comparison with 'more suitable' rather than 'less suitable' accommodation: *[2009] UKUT AAC*. If a tribunal has to consider this it must make its decisions relevant to the period in the past when the authority should have been making its decision about the rent increase; and insofar as evidence was unavailable or unclear, it is required to make findings about what was likely to have been the case: *[2009] UKUT AAC*. Otherwise, in deciding the level of the restriction the same considerations as in paragraphs 9.24-25 apply.

9.30   The claimant is protected from having an increase to their eligible rent restricted, if any of the occupiers in their home have recently died and they have not moved since the death. This protection lasts for 12 months from the date of the death and is described in detail in paragraphs 8.56-57.

Rent referral cases

9.31   This section gives the rules about rent referral cases. These include certain unreasonably large or expensive social sector lettings (paras. 9.35-37), and older or special types of private sector lettings (para. 9.38).

Overview of the rent referral scheme

9.32   The key features of the rent referral scheme are as follows:

* a claimant's eligible rent is set by reference to various rent determinations;
* these are made in Great Britain by the rent officer and in Northern Ireland by the NIHE;
* they are binding on the authority (except in exempt accommodation: paras. 9.10-12);
* there are protections for certain groups of claimant.

The rent officer

9.33   Rent officers are independent of the authority. In England, they are employed by the Rent Service, which comes under the Valuation Office Agency; in Wales by the Rent Officer Service (part of the Welsh Government); and in Scotland by the Rent Registration Service (part of the Scottish Government).

9.28   CPR sch 3 para 5(1),(2); NICPR sch 3 para 5(1),(2)

The Northern Ireland Housing Executive

9.34   In Northern Ireland, the NIHE has the same HB functions as the rent officer does in Great Britain and in this chapter any reference to the rent officer should, in Northern Ireland, be taken to mean the NIHE carrying out those HB functions.

Social sector rent referral cases

9.35   For a social sector case to be a rent referral case, both the conditions in the next two paragraphs must be met (but see para. 9.39 for exceptions).

9.36   The first condition is that the dwelling must be:

+ rented from a registered housing association (paras. 7.8-9 and 7.11); or

+ a caravan, mobile home or houseboat on land belonging to the authority itself (see also para. 16.17); or

+ a gypsies' or travellers' caravan or mobile home (para. 2.21) where the payments are to a county council.

However, for stock transfer lettings (para. 7.6 and table 7.1) no rent determination is required before the first rent increase after the date of the transfer.

9.37   The second condition is that the authority considers:

+ that the rent is unreasonably high; or

+ for pension age claimants only (paras. 1.20-22) that the dwelling is unreasonably large for the occupiers.

Private sector rent referral cases

9.38   The following private sector cases are rent referral cases (but see para. 9.39 for exceptions):

+ a boarder (para. 9.43);

+ a caravan, mobile home or houseboat (para. 9.44);

+ a hostel (para. 9.45); and

+ any other private sector letting in which the claimant has been continuously entitled to HB at the same address since before 7th April 2008.

This includes profit-making lettings of registered providers of housing as well as commercial lettings.

Exceptions

9.39   Protected tenancies (para. 9.84) and shared ownership cases (para. 9.90) are never rent referral cases. There are also further rules for exempt accommodation (paras. 9.10-12).

9.35   HB 14(1),(2)(b), sch 2; HB60+ 14(1),(2)(b), sch 2; NIHB 15(1),(3)(b), sch 3; NIHB60+ 15(1),(3)(b), sch 3

9.38   HB 12D(1),12M(2),(3)(a); HB60+ 12D(1),12M(2),(3)(a); NIHB 13C(1),13D(2),(3),(a); NIHB60+ 13C(1),13D(2),(3),(a)

Eligible rent in rent referral cases

9.40 In rent referral cases, the claimant's eligible rent (also called 'maximum rent' in the law) is set by reference to rental valuations provided by the rent officer/NIHE. These are called 'rent determinations' and are summarised in table 9.3.

The general rule

9.41 The eligible rent in a rent referral case is either the figure returned to the authority net of any service charge determination (para. 9.56) or, if it results in a lower figure, the lowest of the following figures:

* the claim-related rent determination (para. 9.58);
* the local reference rent determination (para. 9.62);
* the single room rent determination if applicable (para. 9.66).

Exceptions to this rule and other special cases are described in paragraphs 9.42-49.

Joint tenants

9.42 The same rules apply where the claimant is a joint tenant except that before deciding which of the figures is the lowest, the claim-related rent determination and any local reference rent determination (but not a single room rent determination) have to be apportioned between the joint tenants. The apportionment is done as described in paragraph 7.21.

Boarders

9.43 The eligible rent of a boarder is the same as in the general rule except that before deciding which of the figures is the lowest, the standard amount for meals (table 7.5) is always deducted from the claim-related rent determination and also any local reference rent determination (but never from a single room rent determination). In Great Britain there are additional procedures for boarders (paras. 9.79-83).

Caravans, mobile homes and houseboats

9.44 Where a claim relates to charges for a stand on a caravan or mobile home site or for mooring charges the eligible rent is the lowest of:

* the referred rent less any service charge determination (para. 9.56);
* any significantly high rent determination or exceptionally high rent determination;
* any local reference rent or (if the claimant is a young individual) single room rent determination.

9.41   HB 12C(2),(3),13(1)-(3),(5); HB60+ 12C(2),(3),13(1)-(3),(5); ROO 2(1)(a);
        NIHB 2(1)(a),13B(2),(3),14(1)-(3),(5); NIHB60+ 2(1)(a),13B(2),(3),14(1)-(3),(5)

9.42   HB 12C(2); HB60+ 12C(2); NIHB 13B(2); NIHB60+ 13B(2)

9.43   HB 13(4)-(7); HB60+ 13(4)-(7); NIHB 14(4)-(7); NIHB60+ 14(4)-(7)

Table 9.3: Rent determinations: key terms

Referred rent (para. 9.54)

This equals the claimant's actual rent. In Great Britain it is the figure the authority refers to the rent officer (RO). In Great Britain and Northern Ireland the RO/NIHE uses it in considering all rent determinations.

Service charge determination (para. 9.55)

This is the RO's/NIHE's valuation of ineligible services.

Claim-related rent determinations (para. 9.58)

This is the RO's/NIHE's valuation of an appropriate rent for the case. It is the lowest of:

◆ the referred rent;

◆ a significantly high rent determination (para. 9.59);

◆ a size-related rent determination (para. 9.60);

◆ an exceptionally high rent determination (para. 9.61).

Local reference rent determination (para. 9.62)

This is the RO's/NIHE's valuation of a mid-point rent appropriate for dwellings of an appropriate size.

Single room rent determination (para. 9.66)

This is the RO's/NIHE's valuation of an appropriate rent for single room shared accommodation. It is used only if the claimant is a 'young individual' (i.e. for many single claimants under 35: para. 9.67).

◆ These are simplified descriptions. For full details, see paras. 9.53-78.

Hostels

9.45 For HB purposes a 'hostel' is any building:

◆ that provides domestic accommodation which is not self-contained together with meals or adequate facilities for preparing food; and

◆ which is:

• managed or run by a registered housing association or registered provider of housing, or

• run on a non-commercial basis, and wholly or partly funded by a government department or agency or local authority, or

• managed by a registered charity or non-profit-making voluntary organisation which provides care, support or supervision with a view to assisting the rehabilitation of the residents or their resettlement into the community.

9.46   The eligible rent for a dwelling in a hostel is the lowest of:

◆ the referred rent less any service charge determination (para. 9.56); or

◆ any significantly high rent determination or size-related rent determination: none of the other determinations apply.

Once a determination has been made for one dwelling it applies to all similar dwellings in the hostel for 12 months.

Examples: Eligible rent in rent referral cases

1. Sole tenant

A claimant under the age of 25 is a sole tenant of her home. Her actual rent is £80 per week The rent officer has provided the following figures:

◆ a claim-related rent determination of £70 per week;

◆ a local reference rent determination of £65 per week;

◆ a single room rent determination of £60 per week

So her eligible rent is simply the lowest of the above figures, which is £60 per week.

2. Joint tenants

Three claimants in their 30s jointly rent a house for £180 per week. They have identical rooms. The rent officer has provided the following figures:

◆ a claim-related rent determination of £150 per week;

◆ a local reference rent determination of £135 per week;

◆ no single room rent determination (because none of them are under 25).

The two figures given have are divided between the three joint tenants, giving £50 per week and £45 per week.

So the eligible rent of each of them is the lower of those two figures, which is £45 per week.

Protected groups

9.47   In rent referral cases the same protections apply as in LHA cases:

◆ the 13-week protection applies for people who could afford the accommodation when they first took it on (para. 8.54); and

---

9.45   HB 2(1); HB60+2(1); NIHB 2(1); NIHB60+2(1); ROO 6(2); NIED

9.46   HB 14; HB60+ 14; NIHB 15; NIHB60+ 15

9.47   HB 13ZA; HB60+ 13ZA; CPR sch 3 para 5; NIHB 14ZA; NIHB60+ 14ZA; NICPR sch 3 para 5

◆ the 12-month protection applies for people who have had a bereavement in the household (para. 8.56).

The law is identical to LHA cases but the source is different (for which see footnotes to this paragraph).

Can the eligible rent be even lower?

9.48 In certain circumstances the authority may decide to use its 'over-riding power to reduce the eligible rent' (described in paragraph 8.7) to a level below the rent officer's lowest figure.

9.49 Also if, during an award of HB, the claimant's actual rent reduces to below the eligible rent calculated as above (which would be rare), the eligible rent is reduced to match the actual rent minus any ineligible service charges included in it. For these purposes ineligible service charges are assessed as in paragraphs 7.39 onwards.

When rent determinations are made

9.50 A rent determination is made on each of the following occasions:

◆ whenever the authority receives a new claim which is a rent referral case (paras. 9.35 and 9.38);

◆ whenever it is notified of a 'relevant change of circumstances'. These are all listed in table 9.5;

◆ whenever 52 weeks have passed since the authority last had the duty to make a determination.

However, there are further rules for hostel cases (para. 9.45) and 'pre-tenancy determinations' (para. 9.76).

9.51 In Great Britain, the authority should refer the case to the rent officer within three working days of the above events. The rent officer should provide the necessary determinations within five working days after receiving the referral or any further information needed (26 working days if they intend the visit the dwelling). In Northern Ireland the Executive should make its determinations within three working days.

When determinations take effect

9.52 Table 9.4 shows what date a rent determination takes effect in a particular case.

9.48 HB 12B(1)(6),12C(2),(3); HB60+ 12B(1)(6),12C(2),(3)

9.49 HB 13ZB; HB60+ 13ZB; NIHB 14B; NIHB60+ 14B

9.50 HB 14(1)-(3),(6)-(8) sch 2 para 2; HB60+14(1)-(3),(6),(7),(9) sch 2 para 2; NIHB 15,16,sch 3 para 2; NIHB60 I 15,16,sch 3 para 2

Table 9.4: When determinations are implemented

Reason triggering the determination	Date rent officer or NIHE determination is implemented from
A claim	The start of the award of HB
A 'relevant change of circumstances'	The date the change itself takes effect (typically the following Monday: chapter 17)
52 weeks have passed	If the new determination means that the claimant qualifies for:
	more HB or the same amount, and the claimant's rent is payable weekly or in multiples of weeks: the day the referral was due, unless that is not a Monday, in which case from the Monday immediately before that day
	more HB or the same amount, and the claimant's rent is payable otherwise than above: the day the referral was due (which could be any day of the week)
	less HB (regardless of when rent is payable): the Monday following the date the rent officer determination 'was received' by the authority.

Examples: Rent determinations and implementation dates

The claimant's first ever claim for HB was received by the authority on Tuesday 8th March 2011 and the authority referred the details to the rent officer that very day. The authority awarded HB from Monday 14th March 2011.

* The rent officer's figures therefore applied from Monday 14th March 2011.

There are no changes in the claimant's circumstances, so the next rent referral is made 52 weeks after the last one, which is Tuesday 6th March 2012. The rent officer's reply is received by the authority on Thursday 15th March 2012.

* If the rent officer's new figures mean the claimant is entitled to more HB (or the same amount) and the claimant's rent is due weekly or in multiples of weeks, then they apply to her case from Monday 5th March 2012.

* If the rent officer's new figures mean the claimant is entitled to more HB (or the same amount) and the claimant's rent is due calendar

T 9.4   DAR 7A(3),8(6A),(6B); NIDAR 7A(3),8(6A),(6B)

monthly or daily, then they apply to her case from Tuesday 6th March 2012 (on a daily basis).

♦ If the rent officer's new figures mean the claimant is entitled to less HB, then they apply to her case from Monday 19th March 2012 (the Monday after the authority received them).

The claimant's non-dependant (who has been there all along so far) moves out on Saturday 2nd June 2012. Because this is a relevant change of circumstances, a further referral is required on Saturday 2nd June 2012 and can be made up to three days after that date. It is in fact made on Tuesday 5th June 2012.

♦ The resulting new figures (whether higher, lower or the same) apply to the claimant's case from the Monday after the change of circumstances, namely Monday 4th June 2012.

Unless there are further changes in the claimant's circumstances, the next rent referral is due 52 weeks after the last one, which is Wednesday 5th June 2013.

How rent determinations are made

9.53 The following paragraphs define the various determinations used in rent referral cases. In Great Britain the rent officer bases the determinations on the date the authority made the referral. In Northern Ireland they are based on the date the authority requires a determination. In either case, if the claimant has left the dwelling, determinations are based on the circumstances at the end of the letting.

The referred rent

9.54 This is simply the claimant's actual rent. In Great Britain it is the figure the authority refers to the rent officer. In Great Britain and Northern Ireland it is the figure used in making all the following determinations.

Service charge determinations

9.55 In a rent referral case the authority refers the claimant's actual rent to the rent officer. The authority will identify in the referral which (if any) service charges are ineligible for HB (paras. 7.48-68). The authority (not the rent officer) must decide which services are ineligible and therefore this decision is appealable.

9.56 The rent officer provides a valuation of any ineligible charges identified by the authority. This is a service charge determination and any further rent determinations (paras. 9.58-70) are compared to this figure (e.g. in deciding whether the rent is significantly high). Unless one of the other determinations (paras. 9.58-70) results in a lower figure, the claimant's eligible rent equals the actual rent referred to the rent officer (para. 9.55) minus this service charge determination.

9.55   ROO sch 1 paras 4(2)(b), 6(3),7; NIHB sch 2 paras 6(3),7; NIHB60+ sch 2 paras 6(3),7

Table 9.5: 'Relevant changes of circumstances'

◆ Except in hostel cases (para. 9.45), there has been a change in the number of occupiers (excluding the beginning or end of an absence on operations as described in para. 8.22).

◆ Any child or young person in the household has reached the age of 10 or 16 – but only if, at the last referral, the rent officer or NIHE made a size-related rent determination (para. 9.60).

◆ The claimant or partner has started or ceased being eligible for an extra bedroom – as a foster parent or for an overnight carer (table 9.6).

◆ There has been a change in the composition of the household – but only if, at the last referral, the rent officer or NIHE made a size-related rent determination (para. 9.60). (One example is when two people have ceased to be a couple.)

◆ There has been a substantial change or improvement in the condition of the dwelling – regardless of whether there has been an associated change in the rent. (For example, central heating has been installed.)

◆ The claimant has moved to a new dwelling.

◆ There has been a substantial change in the terms of the letting agreement (excluding a change in a term relating to rent alone) – regardless of whether there has been an associated change in the rent. (For example, the landlord has taken over the responsibility for internal decorations from the tenant or vice versa.)

◆ There has been a rent increase and:

  • the rent increase was made under a term of the letting agreement (which need not be in writing but must be a term of the letting in question, not merely a provision of law: *CH/3590/2007*) and that term is the same (or substantially the same) as when the previous rent determination was made; and

  • at the previous referral, the rent officer or NIHE did not make any of the following determinations: a 'significantly high rent determination', a 'size-related rent determination' or an 'exceptionally high rent determination' (paras. 9.59-61).

◆ When the previous rent determination was made, the claimant was not a 'young individual' (para. 9.67), but the claimant in the current case is a 'young individual'.

T 9.5   HB 14(1),(8), sch 2 para 2; HB60+14(1),(8), sch 2 para 2; NIHB 15(1), sch 3 para 2; NIHB60+15(1),(8), sch 3 para 2

9.57 If the authority has provided evidence of service charge costs, the rent officer will normally accept these unless they are very high or if he/she believes the landlord is delivering the service inefficiently. If the authority has provided no evidence of costs then the rent officer will normally use a standard deduction from their own evidence base as a starting point.

Claim-related rent determinations

9.58 This determination is made in all cases. It is not a separate valuation in its own right but only:

* the lowest of the following three determinations (paras. 9.59 61); or
* if none of those exist, the referred rent (para. 9.54).

Significantly high rent determinations

9.59 This determination is made if the claimant's actual rent is above a reasonable market rent level and the difference is 'significant' rather than substantial. It is the highest market rent the landlord might reasonably have been expected to obtain for the claimant's dwelling that is not significantly high, having regard to similar dwellings in the vicinity (Great Britain) or locality (Northern Ireland) (paras. 9.71-72).

Size-related rent determinations

9.60 This determination is made if the claimant's dwelling exceeds the size criteria (table 9.6). It is the notional market rent the landlord might reasonably expect to obtain on a hypothetical property that has the number of rooms that match the size criteria but otherwise resembles the claimant's dwelling or corresponds to it as closely as possible. The rental evidence from which this valuation is made is normally drawn from the vicinity (Great Britain) or locality (Northern Ireland) (paras. 9.72-73). But where there is no evidence of dwellings that are the right size, the rent officer must use the nearest vicinity/locality to the dwelling where it does exist.

Exceptionally high rent determinations

9.61 This determination is not property specific: it is made if any of the above determinations (paras. 9.58-61) is 'exceptionally high' compared with other rents in the neighbourhood or in Northern Ireland the locality (paras.9.72 73). Because it is set by reference to the neighbourhood (rather than the broad rental market area) it is not necessarily the same rent as the highest rent used to calculate the mid-point in a local reference rent determination (para. 9.64).

9.58   ROO sch 1 para 6; NIHB sch 2 para 6; NIHB60+ sch 2 para 6

9.59   ROO sch 1 para 1; NIHB sch 2 para 1; NIHB60+ sch 2 para 1

9.60   ROO sch 1 para 2; NIHB sch 2 para 2; NIHB60+ sch 2 para 2

9.61   ROO 6(2) sch 1 para 3; NIHB sch 2 para 3; NIHB60+ sch 2 para 3

Local reference rent determinations

9.62　　This determination is made if any of the above determinations (paras. 9.58-61) exceeds the local reference rent (para. 9.63) for the appropriate category of dwelling.

9.63　　The 'local reference rent' is the mid-point between the highest and lowest rents for dwellings in the broad rental market area (in Northern Ireland the locality) that have the same number of rooms that the claimant occupies or that match the size criteria if the claimant's household exceeds it.

9.64　　To decide what is the highest and lowest rent, the rent officer or NIHE must exclude any rents that are exceptionally high or low. This is usually done by plotting a graph of all the rents in ascending order. The highest and lowest rents are found at the points on the line at which the curve starts to rise/fall steeply at either end (so that the remaining rents in the middle broadly form a straight line): *Heffernan (No.2) v the Rent Service.*

9.65　　The rental evidence used to calculate the local reference rent must match the size criteria – or the size of the claimant's dwelling if smaller. And in the case of one-room dwellings they must be in the same category as the claimant's dwelling. The categories are:

◆　one-room dwellings where the claimant is a boarder;

◆　other one-room dwellings where the tenant shares a kitchen, toilet, bathroom and living room with someone who is not a member of their household (paras. 4.3-6 and 9.74);

◆　any other one-room dwellings.

Single room rent determinations

9.66　　This determination is made only if the claimant is a 'young individual' (and in Great Britain the authority notifies the rent officer of that fact).

9.67　　In rent referral cases, every claimant who is single (para. 4.7) and is under the age of 35 is a 'young individual' unless he or she:

◆　falls within any of exceptions (a) to (g) in paragraph 8.16; or

◆　rents their home from a registered housing association (paras. 7.8-10) or lives in a hostel (para. 9.45).

9.68　　The single room rent determination is the mid-point between the highest and lowest rents for a bedroom:

◆　with the use of a shared living room;

◆　with shared use of a toilet and bathroom; and

◆　with shared use of a kitchen, and no exclusive use of facilities for cooking or preparing food.

9.62　　ROO 6(2) sch 1 para 4; NIHB sch 2 para 4; NIHB60+ sch 2 para 4

9.68　　ROO 6(2) sch 1 para 5; NIHB 15(3)(a), sch 2 para 5; NIHB60+ 15(3)(a), sch 2 para 5

9.69 Rent Service guidance states that the evidence must match the criteria above exactly, so for example if there is no shared living room or more than one shared living room it should be excluded.

9.70 It is calculated in the same way as the local reference rent. The highest and lowest rent should not include ineligible service charges (apart from meals). The rent officer or NIHE must deduct the ineligible charges at the start of the process, not from the single room rent at the end.

General rules

9.71 All rent determinations 'assume that no one who would have been entitled to housing benefit had sought or is seeking the tenancy' (this is designed to prevent 'feedback' whereby HB levels start to influence and distort market rents). Rents used to make determinations are what 'a landlord might reasonably have been expected to obtain'. Lettings used as comparables are assumed to be in a reasonable state of repair and let on an assured tenancy (uncontrolled tenancy in Northern Ireland). Comparables exclude rents payable to housing associations and registered charities.

The areas used for comparison

9.72 As described above (paras. 9.59-61), the following terms are used in Great Britain in setting rent determinations:

* a 'broad market area' has the same meaning as in LHA cases (paras. 8.45-47);
* a 'neighbourhood' means 'a distinct area of residential accommodation';
* a 'vicinity' is 'the area immediately surrounding the dwelling' (or, for size-related rent determinations only, if that area does not contain any comparable dwellings, the nearest area which does).

9.73 In Northern Ireland, a single term 'locality' is used in place of all the above. This is not defined, but it seems reasonable that its meaning varies so that where in Great Britain the term 'neighbourhood' is used, 'locality' has an approximately similar meaning to neighbourhood; and so on.

The size criteria

9.74 The size criteria are shown in table 9.6. They are used for size-related, exceptionally high and local reference rent determinations. They allow for every 'occupier' (para. 9.75).

9.71   ROO sch 1 paras 1-5,7,8; NIHB sch 2 paras 1-5,7,8; NIHB60+ sch 2 paras 1-5,7,8

9.72   ROO sch 1 paras 1(4), 3(5), 4(6),(7)

9.73   NIHB sch 2 paras. 1-5; NIHB60+ sch 2 paras. 1-5

9.74   ROO 2(1), sch 2 para. 1A

9.75　　For these purposes an 'occupier' is:

- the claimant and members of their family (para. 4.8);
- non-dependants (para. 4.39) and lodgers (paras. 4.48-51);
- joint occupiers; and
- other people who 'occupy the dwelling as their home'.

Questions about who is included as an occupier are the same as in considering the number of rooms required in LHA cases (and paras. 8.21-35 apply equally to rent referral cases).

Table 9.6: The size criteria for rent referral cases

These are relevant for size-related rent determinations (para. 9.60), exceptionally high rent determinations (para. 9.61) and local reference rent determinations (para. 9.62). For who counts as an occupier for these purposes, see paragraph 9.75.

- One room is allowed as a bedroom for each of the following occupiers, each occupier coming only within the first category which applies to him or her:
  - a couple (para. 4.10);
  - a single person aged 16 or more;
  - two children of the same sex under the age of 16;
  - two children (of the same or opposite sexes) under the age of 10;
  - a child under the age of 16.

  An additional bedroom can be allocated for a foster parent (para. 8.24) and/or for an overnight carer (para. 8.27).
- One, two or three living rooms are allowed as follows:
  - one if there are one to three occupiers;
  - two if there are four to six occupiers;
  - three if there are seven or more occupiers.
- The size criteria relate to the total number of bedrooms or living rooms allowed (under either of the above headings). It is irrelevant whether the claimant actually uses those as bedrooms or living rooms.

T 9.6　　ROO sch 2; NIHB sch 2 para 10; NIHB60+ sch 2 para 10

Pre-tenancy determinations

9.76 In rent referral cases, the claimant can request a rent determination to be made before they move into a new home – or before they enter a new letting agreement on their current home (so long as it is at least 11 months since their last agreement began). This is called a pre-tenancy determination (PTD). It can help them decide whether they will be able to afford the letting or the new rent. To get a PTD, the claimant must complete and sign an application requesting the authority to do this, and the landlord must sign to show their consent.

9.77 In Great Britain the authority forwards this to the rent officer within two working days – unless it is invalid or there is already a valid determination for the case, in which case the authority notifies the claimant of that. The rent service should provide a rent determination within five working days. In Northern Ireland, the Executive should make a rent determination within seven working days.

9.78 When an authority receives an HB claim on a dwelling to which a PTD applies, it uses the PTD as though it was an ordinary rent determination. This lasts until there is a relevant change of circumstances (table 9.5) or 52 weeks have passed.

Boarder cases in GB

9.79 In Great Britain when the authority receives a claim where part of the rent includes an amount for meals together with an amount for other services it refers the details of the case to the rent officer first to decide whether the claim should be treated as a boarder case.

9.80 In this first stage the authority applies to the rent officer for a 'board and attendance determination', and supplies only the following information:

(a) the address of the dwelling including the postcode and any room number;

(b) the length of the tenancy and when it began;

(c) whether the rent includes charges for any ineligible fuel, meals or water;

(d) whether the rent includes charges for any ineligible cleaning, window cleaning, emergency alarm systems, medical, nursing or personal care, or general counselling and support; and

(e) the total rent payable, after deducting (only) the authority's valuation of the charges mentioned in (d).

9.81 The rent officer then determines whether a 'substantial' amount of the rent under the tenancy is attributable to board and attendance (and thus whether

---

9.76   HB 14; HB60+14; ROO 3(1); NIHB 16; NIHB60+16

9.79   HB 13D(10),(11); HB60+ 13D(10),(11)

9.80   HB 12D(3),(5),13ZA; 114A(3),(4); HB60+ 12D(3),(5),13ZA; 95A(3),(4); CPR sch 3 para 5; NIHB 13C(3),(5),14A

the claim is treated as a boarder case), and informs the authority of the outcome. Anecdotal evidence consistently suggests that rent officers do not consider breakfast alone to be 'substantial'.

9.82   If the rent officer notifies the authority that it is a boarder case, the authority provides all the information it normally provides in a rent officer referral (apart from the information it has already provided) and this counts as the date of the referral. The rent officer then makes a determination on the same basis as any other rent officer referral (paras. 9.55-70, but see para. 9.43), and all the rules about rent officer referrals apply, including the rules about redeterminations (appeals to the rent officer).

9.83   If the rent officer notifies the authority that the claim is not a boarder case, the authority simply treats the case as an ordinary LHA case and all the rules in chapter 8 apply.

Protected tenancies

9.84   This section describes how to calculate eligible rent for protected tenancies and similar lettings. These are sometimes called 'registered rent cases'.

9.85   The terms 'protected tenant' and 'protected tenancy' are not terms used in the law or guidance. In ordinary usage these terms are used to describe certain tenancies in which the security and rent levels are regulated by the 'Rent Acts' which govern the law for certain types of tenancy started before 1989. In this guide the terms include all pre-January 1989 tenancies in Great Britain, and certain older tenancies in Northern Ireland (para. 9.88), whether or not the tenancy is protected by the Rent Acts or the rent has been registered (i.e. fixed) by the rent officer.

9.86   In England and Wales a letting is a protected tenancy if it is:

◆   any kind of letting that was entered into before 15th January 1989; or

◆   a housing association secure tenancy; or

◆   any other type of housing association or private sector letting where the rent officer is entitled to register a rent.

9.87   In Scotland a letting is a protected tenancy if it is:

◆   any kind of letting that was entered into before 2nd January 1989; or

◆   a housing association or any other kind of private sector letting where the rent officer is entitled to register a rent.

9.81   ROO 4C(1)

9.82   HB 14(4A), 114A(5); HB60+ 14(4A), 95A(5); ROO 4C(2); NIHB 16(3A); NIHB60+ 16(3A)

9.85   HB sch 2 paras 4-8; HB60+ sch 2 paras 4-8; NIHB sch 3 para 4; NIHB60+ sch 3 para 4

9.88   In Northern Ireland a letting is a protected tenancy if it is one to which article 3 of the Housing (Northern Ireland) Order 1978 applies, i.e. either the rent is controlled (tied to a historic rateable value) or is fixed by a rent officer. In broad terms this includes:

* certain tenancies that began before 1st October 1978;
* any tenancy that began on or after 14th June 2006 where the dwelling was built or converted before 6th November 1956 and does not meet the fitness standard.

Eligible rent

9.89   For protected tenancies, the claimant's eligible rent is worked out in the same way as for a social tenant (paras. 7.17-22) – except that:

* the social sector size criteria do not apply, unless the landlord is a registered housing association (paras. 7.8-10);
* where the rent has been registered by the rent officer, the eligible rent cannot exceed this;
* where (in the case of an assured tenant) the rent has been fixed by a rent assessment committee, the eligible rent cannot exceed that figure – but this lasts only for one year from the date the rent was fixed (and is rare).

Shared ownership

9.90   This section describes how to calculate eligible rent in shared ownership cases. A shared ownership scheme (also called 'equity sharing') means that the person is part-buying and part-renting their home – which can be from a social or private landlord.

Eligible rent

9.91   In shared ownership cases, the claimant's eligible rent is worked out in the same way as for a council tenant (paras. 7.5 and 7.17-22), except that the social sector size criteria (paras. 7.23-38) do not apply (para. 7.4). HB cannot cover the claimant's mortgage payments – but mortgage interest payments may be met by other benefits (chapter 25).

9.89   HB 12B(2); A13(2)(a); HB60+12B(2); NIHB 13A(2); NIHB60+ 13A(2); CPR sch 3 para 5(1),(2); NICPR sch 3 para 5(1),(2)

9.90   HB 12B(2); A13(2)(b), 14(2)(b), sch 2 para 12; HB60+ 12B(2) 14(2)(b), sch 2 para 12; NIHB 13A(2); NIHB60+ 13A(2)

9.91   HB A13(2)(b)

Homeless households in temporary accommodation

9.92 This section applies in Great Britain to households housed in 'temporary accommodation' (paras. 9.94-96) provided by the authority to discharge a homelessness duty (but if the accommodation provided is part of the authority's own stock, see para. 9.98).

9.93 Where the claimant is housed in temporary accommodation (paras. 9.94-96) the eligible rent is assessed as described in paragraph 9.97 but the authority may not receive full subsidy to cover the cost (paras. 24.37-42 and table 24.1).

What is temporary accommodation?

9.94 A letting only counts as 'temporary accommodation' if it meets both the first and second conditions in paragraphs 9.95-96 below.

9.95 The first condition is that the accommodation must have been made available by the authority or a registered housing association (para. 7.8) to that household in order to discharge the authority's homelessness duty.

9.96 The second condition is that the accommodation is:

* 'board and lodging' (as defined in paragraph 24.41);
* held by the local authority or registered housing association on a short-term lease (as defined in table 24.1); or
* any other accommodation provided by another body which the authority or registered housing association has a right to use under an agreement (other than a leasehold agreement).

Eligible rent in temporary accommodation

9.97 In temporary accommodation cases (paras. 9.94-96) the eligible rent is assessed as for a social sector tenant but the social sector size criteria (paras. 7.23-38) do not apply. In theory, the assessment method depends on whether the landlord (para. 7.3) is the authority or a registered housing association, but in practice if the rent is reasonable it makes no difference (paras. 7.7, 7.13).

Eligible rent: households housed in authority's own stock

9.98 If the dwelling counts as part of the authority's own stock then the eligible rent is assessed as for a council tenant in the normal way (chapter 7). Note that certain short-term leased properties do not count as the authority's stock and so will qualify as 'temporary accommodation'.

9.92   HB A13(2)(e),(3),(4)

9.95   HB A13 (3)

9.96   HB A13(4)

9.97   HB A13(2)(e)

10 Council tax rebate

10.1   This chapter applies only in Great Britain (England, Wales and Scotland), where council tax is the form of local taxation. It covers:

- an overview of the council tax itself, and who has to pay it;
- the exemptions, disability reductions and discounts which can reduce or eliminate council tax liability;
- a summary of the CTR schemes in England, Wales and Scotland;
- how to calculate the eligible council tax for CTR and second adult rebate purposes; and
- discretionary council tax reductions.

Council tax overview

10.2   The council tax is the means by which local people help meet the cost of local public services in Great Britain. It is a tax on residential properties known as dwellings. In England, Scotland and Wales the same authorities that are responsible for administering HB/CTR (para. 1.25) are also responsible for the billing and collection of the tax. Table 10.1 lists the key considerations that arise when considering council tax liability, etc. Fuller details of the council tax are in CPAG's regularly revised *Council Tax Handbook* (Alan Murdie and Martin Ward, Child Poverty Action Group), which covers many matters not included in this guide (such as billing, payment, penalties, and so on).

Table 10.1: Council tax: key considerations

- Which dwelling is being considered?
- What valuation band does it fall into?
- How much is the council tax for that band?
- Who is liable to pay the council tax there?
- Is the dwelling exempt from council tax altogether?
- Do they qualify for a disability reduction?
- Do they qualify for a discount?
- Do they qualify for CTR, including second adult rebate?
- Should the council award a discretionary council tax reduction?

Dwellings and valuation bands

10.3   One council tax bill is issued per dwelling, unless the dwelling is exempt (para. 10.12). A dwelling means a house, a flat, etc, whether lived in or not, and also houseboats and mobile homes that are used for domestic purposes.

10.4   The amount of tax depends first on which valuation band a dwelling has been allocated to, and this is shown on the bill. The lower the valuation band, the lower the tax. An amount for each band is fixed each year by the billing or local authority, and often includes amounts for other bodies (such as a county council, a parish council, the police, etc).

10.5   In England and Scotland, dwellings are valued as at 1st April 1991 (taking effect from 1st April 1993) and there are eight valuation bands – band A to band H. In Wales, dwellings are valued as at 1st April 2003 and there are nine valuation bands – band A to band I. In each case, band A is the lowest.

10.6   The valuation list holds current details of which band dwellings are in. The full valuation list can be viewed on-line [www].

Increased council tax

10.7   In England and Wales, council tax liability can be increased for dwellings which have been unoccupied and substantially unfurnished for two years or more. The increase (depending on the individual authority) can be up to 50%.

Who is liable to pay council tax?

10.8   Council tax is normally payable by someone resident in the dwelling (but there are also exceptions described in the next paragraph). A 'resident' is someone aged 18 or over, solely or mainly resident in the dwelling. Where there is more than one resident the liable person is the one with the greatest legal interest in the dwelling. So if a resident home-owner has a lodger, the home-owner is liable, not the lodger. If a resident council, housing association or private tenant has a lodger, the tenant is liable, not the lodger.

10.9   The most common exceptions to the above rule are that the owner (or other landlord) is liable for council tax on:

* a 'house in multiple occupation'. This means a dwelling occupied by separate households with separate lettings but some shared facilities;
* many hostels and care homes; and
* unoccupied dwellings (unless they are exempt).

In other words, the residents (in the first two cases) are not liable, but many owners pass on the cost of paying the council tax (along with any other overheads) when fixing the rent.

10.6   England and Wales: www.voa.gov.uk; Scotland: www.saa.gov.uk

Joint liability

10.10   There are two ways in which joint liability (or 'joint and several liability') arises:

(a) if there is more than one resident with the greatest (or only) legal interest in the dwelling they are jointly liable for the council tax. For example two sisters who jointly own their home, or three friends who jointly rent their home, are jointly liable;

(b) if the liable person has a partner living with him or her, then the partner is jointly liable (even if he or she has no legal interest in the property). This applies to couples and polygamous arrangements.

For exceptions see the next paragraph. For how jointly liable residents are dealt with in CTR, see paragraphs 10.34-38. There are further rules (not in this guide) about joint liability for unoccupied properties.

Students and people with severe mental impairment

10.11   The exceptions to the above rules on joint liability relate to students and people who are severely mentally impaired. A person counts as 'severely mentally impaired' as described in category 13 in appendix 5; and as a student (for these purposes) as described in category 6 of that appendix. Such a person is not jointly liable if there is another resident with the same legal interest in the dwelling who is neither severely mentally impaired nor a student. See the next paragraph if they are all severely mentally impaired, or all students.

Exemptions

10.12   Only dwellings, rather than people, can be exempt from the council tax. The following occupied dwellings are exempt from council tax:

◆ dwellings where all the residents are students;

◆ in England and Wales only, dwellings where all the occupants (though their normal residence is elsewhere) are students;

◆ halls of residence mainly occupied by students;

◆ dwellings where all the occupiers are severely mentally impaired, including cases where the only other occupiers are students (but this does not apply to dwellings where the owner rather than the occupier is liable: para. 10.9);

◆ dwellings occupied only by people under 18;

◆ armed forces accommodation;

◆ in England and Wales only, annexes or similar self-contained parts of a property which are occupied by an elderly or disabled relative of the residents living in the rest of it; and

◆ in Scotland only, certain dwellings used as trial flats by registered housing associations for pensioners and disabled people.

10.13 Various unoccupied dwellings are also exempt. For example, an unoccupied dwelling which is substantially unfurnished is exempt for six months (but see para. 10.7) – and there are many other categories.

Disability reductions

10.14 The council tax bill is reduced if a dwelling has at least one disabled resident and provides:

+ an additional bathroom or kitchen for the use of the disabled person;
+ an additional room, other than a bathroom, kitchen or toilet, used predominantly to meet the disabled person's special needs – such as a downstairs room in a two storey house which has to be used as a bedroom by the disabled person because of the nature of the disability; or
+ sufficient floor space to enable the use of a wheelchair required by the disabled person within the dwelling.

10.15 In each case the authority must be satisfied that the facility in question is either essential, or of major importance, for the disabled person (who may be an adult or a child) in view of the nature and extent of the disability. Disability reductions are not limited to specially adapted properties.

10.16 The effect of the reduction is that the person is liable for the amount that would be due if his or her dwelling was in the next lowest valuation band (or in the case of a band A dwelling, one-sixth less than normal).

Discounts

10.17 The council tax bill can be reduced if:

+ there is only one resident in the dwelling. In this case there is always a discount of 25 per cent; or
+ there are no residents in the dwelling (unless the dwelling is exempt). In this case, there can be a discount of up to 50% (depending on the individual authority) or in some cases an increase rather than a discount (para. 10.7).

10.18 When considering the number of people in the dwelling, certain people including students, apprentices, carers, severely mentally impaired people and under-18-year-olds are disregarded. Appendix 5 describes the categories of person who are disregarded. A person can be disregarded for the purpose of awarding a discount but still liable to pay the tax.

Obtaining an exemption, disability reduction or discount

10.19 An authority is expected to take reasonable steps to ascertain whether exemptions, disability reductions and discounts apply to the dwellings in its area. These can be awarded on the basis of information available to it, or someone can write requesting this. There is no time limit on obtaining exemptions, disability reductions or discounts, though the authority is entitled to seek appropriate evidence. Appeals about all these things go first to the authority and then to a Valuation Tribunal: the procedures are the same as for CTR appeals (paras. 19.111).

Examples: Council tax liability, exemptions and discounts

Unless stated below, none of the following are students, severely mentally impaired, or under 18.

A couple with a lodger

A couple live in a house which the man owns in his name only. They have children in their 20s living at home, and a lodger who rents a room and shares facilities.

The couple are jointly liable for the council tax, because the man is the resident with the greatest legal interest in the dwelling and the woman is jointly liable with him by being his partner. There is no reason to suppose they qualify for exemption, or a disability reduction or a discount.

A lone parent

A lone parent owns her home and lives there with her three children, all under 18.

The lone parent is solely liable for the council tax, because she is the resident with the greatest legal interest in the dwelling. She is the only (adult) resident so she qualifies for a 25% discount.

Three sharers

Three friends jointly rent a house (in other words all their names are on the tenancy agreement). No-one else lives with them.

They are all jointly liable for the council tax, because they are all residents with the greatest legal interest in the dwelling. There is no reason to suppose they qualify for exemption, or a disability reduction or a discount.

The sharers' circumstances change

One of the sharers leaves and is not replaced. One of the others becomes a full-time university student.

The remaining non-student resident is now the only liable person (para. 10.11), and qualifies for a 25% discount because the student is disregarded when counting the residents (para. 10.18).

Other reasons why liability may be lower

10.20 In addition to the disability reductions and discounts mentioned above, authorities can offer a discount for prompt payment of the tax or the adoption of certain payment methods. In some areas council tax may be 'capped' by the government to a lower figure, and in a few areas there may be a 'transitional reduction' in liability because of recent re-organisation of authority boundaries.

Council tax rebate

10.21   Council tax rebate (CTR) begins on 1st April 2013. It is referred to in the law as a 'council tax reduction'. CTR replaces the former council tax benefit (CTB) which ceased on 31st March 2013; but claimants on CTB at the point of change are transferred onto CTR without having to make a separate claim (para. 5.3).

10.22   As described below (paras. 10.24-30), details of the CTR schemes vary:

- ◆ between England, Wales and Scotland;
- ◆ in England and (to a lesser extent) in Wales from one authority to another; and
- ◆ between pension age and working age claims (para. 10.30).

Table 10.2 summarises the main differences along with other key points.

10.23   CTR rules about many procedural matters are the same across Great Britain, including in particular most of the rules about how to claim (chapter 5).

Table 10.2: CTR national variations, 2013-14

	England	Wales	Scotland
Eligibility for CTR (paras. 10.24-29)	P: Eligible W: Varies locally – usually eligible	Eligible	Eligible (extra rules for two homes and absences: paras. 3.6, 3.45)
Upper capital limit (paras. 6.7-8)	P: £16,000 W: Varies locally up to £16,000	£16,000	£16,000
Maximum CTR (paras. 6.4-5)	P: 100% of council tax W: Varies locally up to 100%	100% of council tax	100% of council tax
Excess income taper (paras. 6.11-12)	P: 20% W: Varies locally	20%	20%
Second adult rebate (paras. 6.31-32)	P: Included in CTR W: Varies locally	Not included in CTR	Included in CTR
Minimum CTR (para. 6.14)	P: No minimum W: Varies locally	No minimum	No minimum
Start date of CTR (paras. 5.45-46)	Monday following date of claim	Exact date of claim	Monday following date of claim

Backdating limit (paras. 5.54, 5.57)	P: 3 months W: Varies locally up to 6 months	P: 3 months W: 3 months – can be improved locally	P: 3 months W: 6 months
Extended payments (para. 17.43)	P: Included in CTR W: Varies locally	Included in CTR – can be improved locally	Included in CTR
Overpayments (para. 18.2)	Recoverable via council tax account	Recoverable via council tax account	Recoverable via council tax account
Appeals (para. 19.111)	To authority then Valuation Tribunal	To authority then Valuation Tribunal	To authority and see para. 19.112
Migrant eligibility (table 20.1)	Excluded as for HB	Excluded as for HB	Excluded as for HB
Student eligibility (para. 22.1)	P: Included W: Varies locally	P: Excluded W: Excluded as for HB	P: Included W: Excluded as for HB

* Entries are simplified. 'P' refers to pension age and 'W' to working age claims (para. 10.30). Other entries refer to both groups.

CTR in England

10.24 Authorities in England may make and run their own local CTR schemes. These must obey certain 'prescribed requirements' set by the government. The key requirement is that pension age claimants (para. 10.30) must be eligible for CTR (including second adult rebate) in almost the same way as they were for CTB.

10.25 However, there is no similar requirement for working age claimants (para. 10.30), so English local CTR schemes can vary substantially. For example, some authorities have:

* set limits on the amount of eligible council tax;
* reduced the upper capital limit to below £16,000;
* increased non-dependant deductions;
* varied the assessment of some types of income;
* increased the excess income taper above 20%;
* limited or removed entitlement to backdated CTR;
* limited or removed entitlement to second adult rebate;

10.23 CTP schs 7,8; CTPW schs 12-14; CTS 81-91; CTS60+ 59-71; SI 1993 No. 355

10.24 LGFA 13A, sch 1A para 2; CTP 11(1), 14

10.25 LGFA 13A, sch 1A para 2

or done several of those things (see table 10.2). Other authorities have preferred to settle for the 'default' CTR scheme (para. 10.26).

10.26   English authorities which failed to make a local CTR scheme by 31st January 2013 must instead operate a 'default' CTR scheme set by the government. For the 2013-14 financial year the key feature of the default scheme is that all claimants (of working or pension age) are eligible for CTR (including second adult rebate) in almost the same way as they were for CTB.

CTR in Wales

10.27   Authorities in Wales may make and run their own local CTR schemes, which must obey certain 'prescribed requirements' set by the Welsh Ministers. Welsh authorities which failed to do this by 31st January 2013 must instead operate a 'default' CTR scheme set by the Welsh Ministers. For the 2013-14 financial year the prescribed requirements and the default scheme are substantially the same (para. 10.28).

10.28   In Wales in 2013-14, all claimants (of working or pension age) are eligible for CTR – but with the following main differences from CTB (see also table 10.2):

+ backdating in working age claims need not exceed three months, though individual authorities may choose to extend this;
+ there is no provision for second adult rebate.

CTR in Scotland

10.29   In Scotland, the CTR scheme is the same for all authorities, with no local variations, and is almost identical to CTB. However, the Scottish Ministers have added rules relating to CTR on two homes and to absences from Great Britain (paras. 3.6 and 3.45).

Pension age vs working age claims

10.30   The distinction between 'pension age' and 'working age' claims is usually clear-cut (paras. 1.20-22). The exception applies in CTR to couples on JSA(IB), ESA(IR), IS or UC, when one (or both) have reached state pension credit age. Such couples (regardless of which partner is the CTR claimant) meet the definition for either age group (table 1.4). When this affects eligibility for CTR or the amount of CTR (see table 10.2 for examples), it seems reasonable to apply whichever of the rules (pension age or working age) is most favourable.

10.26   LGFA 13A, sch 1A para 4; CTR 1
10.27   LGFA 13A, sch 1B paras 2-7
10.28   CTPW 1,12,13,19; CTRW 1,3,13,19
10.29   LGFA 80,113, sch 2 para 1; CTS 12-14; CTS60+ 12-14
10.30   CTP 3; CTR 3; CTPW 3; CTRW 3; CTS 12; CTS60+ 12

Eligible council tax

10.31   A claimant's 'eligible council tax' is the figure used in calculating his or her entitlement to the main type of CTR (para. 6.3) and/or second adult rebate (para. 6.35). It can differ in those two cases, as mentioned in the appropriate places below. An example is at the end of this chapter.

10.32   A claimant's weekly eligible council tax is calculated by working through the following steps:

1. Start with the council tax due on his or her home.
2. If the claimant is entitled to a disability reduction, use the council tax figure after that reduction has been made.
3. If the claimant is entitled to a discount, use the council tax figure after that discount has been made.
4. Apportion the result if the claimant is a joint occupier (see below).
5. Convert it to a weekly figure (as described in para. 6.55).

10.33   All the above steps apply when calculating eligible council tax for the main type of CTR and the student type of second adult rebate (para. 6.40). But steps 3 and 4 are omitted when calculating eligible council tax for the general type of second adult rebate (para. 6.41 – and see para. 10.38). See also paragraph 10.39 about other items which can affect a council tax bill.

Apportionment for joint occupiers

10.34   A joint occupier is one of two or more people who are jointly liable to pay the council tax on a dwelling (para. 10.10), other than just a couple or polygamous arrangement. In such cases, the figures used in calculating eligible council tax are apportioned between the joint occupiers for CTR purposes (but not second adult rebate: para. 10.38).

10.35   This apportionment is found by dividing the total council tax liability by the number of people who are jointly liable.

10.36   If among several jointly liable people some are a couple or polygamous marriage, the law is unclear. It is possible authorities will follow former practice (based on DWP advice about CTB: GM para. A2.91: example) so that if there are three jointly liable people, two of whom are a couple, then the couple are eligible for CTR on two-thirds of the council tax liability and the other person on one-third.

10.37   In most cases, students and people who are severely mentally impaired are not jointly liable for council tax (para. 10.11) so the apportionment ignores them.

10.32   CTP sch 1 para 7(1),(6); CTR 29(1),(6); CTPW sch 1 para 2(1),(6); CTRW 27(1),(6); CTS 66(1); CTS60+ 47(1)

10.34   CTP sch 1 para 7(3)-(5); CTR 29(3)-(5); CTPW sch 1 para 2(3)-(5); CTRW 27(3)-(5); CTS 66(2),(3); CTS60+ 47(2),(3)

Variations when calculating general second adult rebate

10.38   As mentioned in paragraph 10.33, there are two differences in the rules for calculating eligible council tax for the general type of second adult rebate:

- Step 3 in paragraph 10.32 does not apply. In other words, a claimant's eligible council tax is calculated as though he or she did not qualify for any council tax discount. This is for mathematical reasons. As illustrated in the following example, a claimant who qualifies for a discount does not lose it.

- Step 4 in paragraph 10.32 does not apply. In other words, there is no apportionment between joint occupiers. Instead, the apportionment will be done after the calculation of second adult rebate is otherwise complete (as described in para. 6.39).

Other items affecting eligible council tax

10.39   The following additional rules apply to CTR (including second adult rebate):

- if the authority grants a discretionary council tax reduction, CTR is calculated on liability after that reduction is made;

- in the case of an authority which offers discounts against its council taxes for people who pay in a lump sum or by a method other than cash (e.g. direct debit), CTR is calculated on liability before those discounts are subtracted;

- if lower council taxes are set as a result of council tax 'capping' procedures, these apply from the beginning of the financial year, and CTR is calculated (throughout the financial year) on the lower amount;

- if a penalty is added to a council tax bill, CTR is calculated as if that penalty was not included.

Discretionary council tax reductions

10.40   In England and Wales only, an authority may reduce any liability for council tax (whether or not the person qualifies for CTR). This is a wide discretion, which permits the authority to reduce liability 'to such extent as it thinks fit' and 'includes power to reduce an amount to nil'. This can be done 'in relation to particular cases or by determining a class of case in which liability is to be reduced to an extent provided by the determination.'

10.41   A claim for such a reduction may be made in writing or (if the authority permits it) by telephone or online. Authorities which provide reductions for a class of cases (para. 10.40) may treat an application for CTR as being also for a discretionary reduction.

10.38   CTP sch 1 para 9, sch 3 para 1(2); CTR 9, sch 4 para 1(2); CTS 78, sch 2 paras 1,4; CTS60+ 56, sch 5 paras 1,4

10.39   CTP sch 1 para 7(2); CTR 29(2); CTPW sch 1 para 2(2); CTRW 27(2); CTS 66(1)(a)(ii); CTS60+ 47(1)(a)(ii)

10.40   LGFA 13A(1)(c),(6),(7)

10.41   CTP sch 7 para 9; CTPW sch 12 para 11

Example: Eligible council tax

The claimant and his household

A claimant's dwelling falls in band D, which in his area is £1,350 per year. With him lives only his niece (as his non-dependant). The claimant is a full-time student with income from several sources, including a grant towards his disablement needs. His niece is on JSA(IB). The claimant qualifies for:

◆ a disability reduction, because he has a large enough house to use his wheelchair indoors (para. 10.14). This is worth £150 per year; and

◆ a 25% council tax discount, because he is a full-time student, so there is only one countable resident in his home, his niece (para. 10.18). This is worth £300 per year.

Eligible council tax for CTR

In calculating CTR his eligible council tax is the figure obtained by deducting both the disability reduction and the discount from the amount for the dwelling. This is (£1,350 – £150 – £300 =) £900, the weekly equivalent of which is (to the nearest penny) £17.26 (para. 10.32).

It turns out, though, when the authority assesses his entitlement to CTR, that he does not qualify because he has too much capital.

Eligible council tax for second adult rebate

In calculating second adult rebate his eligible council tax is the figure obtained by deducting the disability reduction from the amount for the dwelling but not the discount (para. 10.38). This is (£1,350 – £150 =) £1,200, the weekly equivalent of which is (to the nearest penny) £23.01.

Because his niece is on JSA(IB), he qualifies for second adult rebate equal to 25% of the last figure (table 6.6). This is (to the nearest penny) £5.75. On an annual basis this is £300.

His resulting liability for council tax

The following are the annual figures:

The council tax for the dwelling is	£1,350
He is granted his disability reduction of	– £150
He is granted his discount of	– £300
He is granted second adult rebate of	– £300
So his resulting liability is	= £600

Note: The amount of CTR could be lower or nil (paras. 10.22-29).

11 Eligible rates

11.1   This chapter applies only in Northern Ireland, where domestic rates are the form of local taxation. It covers:

- an overview of domestic rates, and who has to pay them;
- the exemptions and disability reductions which can reduce or eliminate the amount of rates payable;
- how to calculate the eligible rates for HB purposes; and
- how to calculate any rate relief and lone pensioner allowance which may be payable in addition to, or without any HB for rates.

Rates overview

11.2   Domestic rates are the means by which local people help meet the cost of local public services in Northern Ireland. Rates are a tax on residential properties known as dwellings. They are made up of local rates which help fund district councils, and regional rates which help fund centrally delivered services. Land and Property Services are responsible for the billing and collection of the tax.

Table 11.1: Domestic rates: key considerations

- Which dwelling is being considered?
- What is the capital value (or social sector value) for that dwelling?
- What is the aggregate rate poundage in that district?
- Who is liable for the rates?
- Is the dwelling exempt from rates altogether?
- Do they qualify for a disability reduction?
- Do they qualify for full or partial HB on their rates?
- Do they qualify for rate relief on any remaining rates?
- Do they qualify for lone pensioner allowance on any remaining rates?

Dwellings and annual rates

11.3   The domestic rate is an annual bill. One rates bill is issued per dwelling; unless the dwelling is exempt (para. 11.8). A 'dwelling' means any house, flat, etc, whether lived in or not, and also a houseboat or mobile home that is used for domestic purposes.

11.4   The amount of rates depends first on the capital value which the dwelling has been allocated, and this is shown on the bill. The lower the capital value the lower the annual rates bill. An annual rate in the pound ('rate poundage') is fixed each year by the district council and levied together with the regional rate poundage. The amount of annual rates charged is calculated by multiplying the capital value by the aggregate rate poundage; however, the amount may be lower than this due to capping (para. 11.5).

11.5   The capital value of the dwelling is set as the assessed sale value of the dwelling as at 1st January 2005, capped to a maximum value of £400,000. However, for NIHE and registered housing association tenants the capital value is substituted by a 'social sector value' which is calculated by the DSD based on the rent paid for the property.

11.6   Capital values, social sector values and the rate poundage can be viewed on-line at the Land and Property Services website [www].

Liability for rates

11.7   One rates bill goes to the owner or occupier of each dwelling. For example:

* the rates bill for NIHE and housing association tenants goes to the NIHE or housing association – and so increases the overall amount payable by the tenant;
* the rates bill for some private sector tenants goes to the landlord – who may include this amount in setting the amount of rent due;
* the rates bill for some private sector tenants goes to the tenant;
* the rates bill for an owner-occupied dwelling goes to the owner-occupier.

Exemptions

11.8   Certain dwellings are exempt from rates. This is not automatic – an application must be made to Land and Property Services. An occupied dwelling is exempt if the landlord is a registered charity. The first residents of newly built owner-occupied homes that are 'low carbon' are exempt from rates for two years, or five years in the case of zero carbon homes. Prior to 1st December 2009, certain dwellings occupied by persons aged under 18, certain care leavers and students were exempt from rates and this continues provided the application was made before that date.

Disability reductions

11.9   The rates bill is reduced by 25% for dwellings which have been adapted or extended because of the occupant's disability. Reductions are not automatic: an application must be made to Land and Property Services.

11.6   www.dfpni.gov.uk/lps/

11.8   NISR 2010/66

Rate rebates, rate relief and lone pensioner allowance

11.10 Anyone who is liable to pay rates on their normal home (including tenants whose rent includes an amount towards their landlord's rates) can get any or all of rate rebate, rate relief or lone pensioner allowance. There are two groups who cannot get rate rebate or rate relief but can get lone pensioner allowance. These are:

- certain people who are migrants or recent arrivals in the UK (chapter 20);
- most full-time students (for exceptions see table 22.1).

11.11 A person is eligible for all three of these schemes whether they pay rates direct to Land and Property Services, or via the rent they pay their landlord. Unless a tenant receives a rate bill in their own name, it is always assumed that the rent they pay their landlord includes an element for rates.

11.12 However, in the case of a tenanted dwelling, a rate rebate, rate relief or lone pensioner allowance cannot be awarded until a rates bill is issued. Once it is issued, a rate rebate and rate relief are awarded retrospectively if the claimant notifies the NIHE within one month of receiving it, a time limit which can be extended in special circumstances. Otherwise benefit is awarded according to the usual HB rules (paras. 5.45-50). In the case of lone pensioner allowance, the award starts from the date rates liability commenced, or the date the person qualifies if later.

Rate rebates and eligible rates

What are rate rebates?

11.13 A rate rebate (HB for rates) reduces a claimant's rates. It is worked out in a similar way to HB for rent. It is funded by subsidy payable to Land and Property Services or NIHE. For where to apply for a rate rebate, see paragraph 1.25 and table 1.5.

Eligible rates

11.14 A claimant's eligible rates is the figure used in calculating his or her entitlement to rate rebate (HB for rates). It is calculated by working through the following steps:

1. Start with the annual rates due on his or her home (paras. 11.4-5) after any capping that may apply.
2. If the claimant is entitled to a disability reduction (para. 11.9), use the rates figure after that has been made.

11.10 NICBA 129(1)(a); NIHB 8(1)(a),9(1); 10(1),53(1); NIHB60+ 8(1)(a); 9(1),10(1)

11.11 NIHB 12(2), 13(3)(b),(6); NIHB60+ 12(2), 13(3)(b),(6)

11.14 NIHB 11(1)(a), 12(3), 78(3); NIHB60+ 11(1)(a), 12(3), 59(3)

3. Apportion the result if the claimant is a joint occupier (para. 11.16).

4. Convert it to a weekly figure (as described in para. 6.45).

Note that unlike HB for rent, there is no power to restrict the eligible rates if the dwelling is too expensive or too large.

Impact of rates changes on eligible rent

11.15   When a tenant's rent includes an amount for rates (para. 11.11), a change in the rates (such as the new amount applying from each April, or following the award of a disability reduction) means the person's eligible rent changes too. Since there is no duty on the tenant or landlord to advise of changes to rates, the NIHE alters the tenant's HB for rent and HB for rates automatically when advised by Land and Property Services.

Apportionment of eligible rates

11.16   The eligible rates figure is apportioned if:

* someone occupies only part of a rateable unit – for example a lodger or someone living in a multi-occupied property. In this case only the proportion of the rates payable for their accommodation is eligible for a rate rebate;

* two or more people are jointly liability to pay rates – for example in a joint tenancy (see para. 7.21);

* part of the rateable unit is in business use – such as a shop with a flat above. This is done in the same way as for eligible rent (para. 7.22).

Calculating rate rebate

11.17   The method of calculating rate rebates (HB for rates) is given in paragraphs 6.4-11 and 6.45-46. As with HB for rent, non-dependant charges may apply: see paragraphs 6.16-30 for details. Examples of the calculation are at the end of this chapter.

Awarding rate rebate as a credit or as a payment

11.18   A rate rebate is awarded as a credit to the rates account for the dwelling in question, but there is one exception. The NIHE may choose (at its discretion) to pay HB for rates as an allowance (along with any HB for rent) if:

* the claimant's rent includes an amount for rates (para. 11.11); and

* the claimant qualifies for HB for rent (or would do but for any non-dependant deduction or the application of the taper percentage).

11.15   NIHB 12(1),(2); 84(2)(a),(b); NIHB60+; 12(1),(2),65(2)(a),(b)

11.16   NIHB 12(2),(4)-(6); NIHB60+; 12(2),(4)-(6)

11.18   NIHB 87(2),88,89(5); NIHB60+ 68(2),69,70(5)

11.19 When HB is paid as an allowance, it is paid to either the claimant or landlord, following the same rules as HB for rent (paras. 16.15-30 and 16.53-61). In addition to those rules, if the total HB (for rent and rates) is £2 per week or less it can be paid four-weekly; and if it is less than £1 per week it can be paid every six months.

> ### Example: Calculation of eligible rates
>
> A dwelling has a capital value of £135,000 in an area where the rate poundage is £0.0057777 per £1 of capital value. Capping does not apply so the annual rates payable are:
>
> $$£135,000 \times 0.0057777 = £780.00$$
>
> The weekly eligible rates (to the nearest 1p) are therefore:
>
> $£780.00 \div 365 \times 7 =$ £14.96 if paid separately from rent or
>
> $£780.00 \div 52 =$ £15.00 if paid along with rent

Rate relief

What is rate relief?

11.20 The rate relief scheme was introduced in Northern Ireland on 1st April 2007 following changes in the assessment of domestic rates from being a theoretical rental value to the open market capital value. Because of the way rate rebates are calculated, people receiving a rate rebate get no financial benefit from a change in their rates. The rate relief scheme gives them an extra reduction to compensate for this.

11.21 Rate relief is not part of the HB scheme, and is funded from the rates themselves rather than from government subsidy. Some people may not be eligible for HB but will qualify for rate relief and as the same information is required from the claimant a full HB assessment is always carried out.

Who gets rate relief?

11.22 Rate relief is considered automatically (so no claim is needed) for everyone who:

- ◆ qualifies for a rate rebate; but
- ◆ still has rates to pay – other than any non-dependant deduction or repayment of an overpayment.

So people who get maximum HB (para. 6.4) for rates, including where they are repaying an overpayment, cannot get rate relief. Everyone else who claims a rate rebate can get rate relief. A person who does not qualify for a rate rebate can claim rate relief separately if he/she has rates to pay.

11.22 NISR 2007/203; NISR 2007/204; NISR 2007/244; NISR 2011/43

Calculating rate relief

11.23   Rate relief is calculated in the same way as a rate rebate – except that:

* rate relief is worked out on the amount of rates remaining after rate rebate has been granted – ignoring any non-dependant deduction;

* the rate of the carer premium (all claims) and the personal allowance in pension age claims is higher (para. 11.24);

* for pension age claims there is a higher capital limit of £50,000 (tariff income applies as in HB);

* the taper percentage used in the calculation is 12% of excess income.

Examples of the calculation are given at the end of this chapter.

11.24   The applicable amount is calculated the same way as for HB except:

* for both working age and pension age claims the rate of the carer premium is £39.96;

* for claims where the claimant or their partner have attained state pension credit age (para. 1.21) but are aged under 65 the personal allowance is: £167.21 for a single claimant or lone parent, £244.26 for a couple;

* for claims where the claimant or their partner are aged 65+ the personal allowance is: £188.03 for a single claimant or lone parent, £269.45 for a couple.

Awarding rate relief

11.25   Rate relief is used to reduce the amount of rates payable on the dwelling. For owner-occupiers and private tenants, it is credited to the rates account by Land and Property Services. For NIHE and housing association tenants, it is awarded to the landlord and so reduces the overall rent and rates payable by the claimant.

Reconsiderations and appeals

11.26   The rules about getting a written statement of reasons, requesting a reconsideration, and requesting an appeal, are the same as those relating to HB for rent (chapter 19). Although rate relief is not a social security benefit, an appeal tribunal nonetheless deals with appeals and, whenever practicable, deals with the rate relief appeal at the same time as any HB appeal.

Overpayments of rate relief

11.27   The conditions for recovering overpaid rate relief are the same as those for recovering overpaid HB for rent (paras. 18.10-14).

11.24 NISR 2007/203, Reg 17(2)(c); NISR 2007/244; NISR 2011/43

11.25 NISR 2007/203; NISR 2007/204

11.26 NISR 2007/203; NISR 2007/204

11.27 NISR 2007/203; NISR 2007/204

11.28 Recoverable overpayments of rate relief can be recovered by any lawful method, but the main methods used are:

- ◆ charging them back to the rates account;
- ◆ deducting them from the claimant's future rate relief.

11.29 A recoverable overpayment of rate relief can be charged back to the rates account. But this method is not normally used in the case of NIHE or housing association tenants, unless the person has died or left and there remains sufficient credit on their account to make recovery from it.

11.30 A recoverable overpayment of rate relief may be deducted from the claimant's future award of rate relief. The level of deduction is limited to the amounts in table 18.3. But this limit does not apply to deductions from lump sum arrears of rate relief. Deductions to recover rate relief overpayments are additional to those to recover HB overpayments.

Lone pensioner allowance

What is lone pensioner allowance?

11.31 Lone pensioner allowance was introduced in Northern Ireland on 1st April 2008 following a review of domestic rating policy by the Northern Ireland Executive, which concluded that single people over 70 required further assistance to help with rates charges. In some respects it is similar to the single person discount within council tax but applies only to people aged 70 or above. People may qualify for lone pensioner allowance whether or not they qualify for HB or rate relief.

11.32 Lone pensioner allowance is not part of either the HB or rate relief schemes and is funded by the Northern Ireland Executive.

Who gets lone pensioner allowance?

11.33 Anyone aged 70 or over who lives alone (but see para. 11.34 for details of limited exceptions) and has to pay rates on their normal or only home will receive lone pensioner allowance. The allowance is not means tested; however, it is not awarded automatically, but must be claimed either along with a claim for HB and/or rate relief or separately. If a person qualifies for full HB and/or rate relief they cannot also get lone pensioner allowance as this is based on the rates still left to pay.

Living alone

11.34 In limited circumstances a person can still be classed as living alone and thus qualify for lone pensioner allowance even though someone else lives in their household. This applies if:

- ◆ the person living with the claimant is a resident carer (conditions apply);
- ◆ the person living with the claimant is aged less than 18;

- the claimant is receiving child benefit for the person;
- the person living with the claimant is severely mentally impaired (conditions apply).

Calculating lone pensioner allowance

11.35   As lone pensioner allowance is not means tested, anyone who qualifies will receive a 20% reduction on the rates charge they have to pay. Where the person also receives any or all of HB, rate relief or a disability reduction the allowance is applied to the amount of rates left to pay. If the person does not receive HB, rate relief or a disability reduction the allowance will be applied to the full rates charge. Examples of lone pensioner allowance calculations are at the end of this chapter.

Awarding lone pensioner allowance

11.36   Like rate relief, lone pensioner allowance is used to reduce the amount of rates payable on the dwelling. For owner-occupiers and private tenants, it is credited to the rate account by Land and Property Services. For NIHE and housing association tenants, it is awarded to the landlord and so reduces the overall rent and rates payable by the claimant.

Overpayments of lone pensioner allowance

11.37   Overpayments of lone pensioner allowance are only likely to occur when the claimant ceases to live alone or no longer has rates to pay. Overpayments of lone pensioner allowance cannot be recovered from either HB or rate relief unless the claimant agrees to this but can be recovered by any other lawful method. In the case of owner-occupiers or private tenants this will most likely be by charging them back to the rates account. In the case of NIHE or housing association tenants, if the tenant has died or left there may be sufficient credit on their account or assets in an estate to make recovery. In the unlikely event that a person again qualifies for lone pensioner allowance recovery may be effected by deduction from lump sum arrears of the new award.

Appeals

11.38   Appeals relating to lone pensioner allowance will be considered by the Valuation Tribunal and must be made within 28 days of being notified of the decision. This differs from the usual time limit of one month within both the HB and rate relief schemes.

Examples: Rate rebate, rate relief and lone pensioner allowance

A claimant without a non-dependant

A couple in their 40s have no non-dependants. They are not on JSA(IB), ESA(IR) or income support. Their income exceeds their applicable amount by £20 per week. Their eligible rates are £15 per week.

Rate rebate (HB for rates) £

Eligible rates	15.00
minus 20% of excess income (20% of £20.00)	– 4.00
equals weekly rate rebate	11.00

Rate relief

Rates due after rate rebate	4.00
minus 12% of excess income (12% of £20.00)	2.40
equals weekly rate relief	1.60

A claimant with a non-dependant

A single claimant in her 50s has a non-dependant son living with her. The claimant is not on JSA(IB), ESA(IR) or income support. Her income exceeds her applicable amount by £10 per week. Her eligible rates are £18.00 per week. Her son works full-time with gross income of £400 per week.

Rate rebate (HB for rates) £

Eligible rates	18.00
minus non-dependant deduction	– 9.90
minus 20% of excess income (20% of £10.00)	– 2.00
equals weekly rate rebate	6.10

Rate relief

Rates due after rate rebate – ignoring non-dependant deduction	2.00
minus 12% of excess income (12% of £10.00)	– 1.20
equals weekly rate relief	0.80

Lone pensioner allowance

A person aged 72 lives alone and has a weekly rates charge of £18.
She does not receive either HB or rate relief.

	£
Weekly rates to pay	18.00
Minus lone pensioner allowance (20% of £18)	3.60
Net amount to pay	14.40

If the same person receives £10 per week HB and £2 per week rate relief.

	£
Weekly rates to pay	18.00
Minus HB	10.00
Minus rate relief	2.00
Rates left to pay	6.00
Minus lone pensioner allowance (20% of £6)	1.20
Net amount to pay	4.80

12 Applicable amounts

12.1   This chapter describes how applicable amounts are assessed in HB and CTR. It covers:

* basic rules about applicable amounts;
* the detailed conditions for personal allowances, premiums and components; and
* further rules and special cases.

12.2   The terms 'family', 'single claimant', 'lone parent', 'couple', 'partner', 'child' and 'young person' are defined in paragraphs 4.7-38. For 'pension age' and 'working age' see paragraph 1.21.

Basic rules

What is an applicable amount?

12.3   An applicable amount reflects the basic living needs of the claimant and family. It is compared with the claimant's (and any partner's) income when calculating how much HB or CTR he or she is entitled to (paras. 6.9-11).

How much is the applicable amount?

12.4   A claimant's applicable amount is the total of:

* a personal allowance for the claimant (and any partner);
* a personal allowance for each child or young person in the family; and
* any additional amounts (known as premiums and components) they qualify for.

The figures for 2013-14 are given in table 12.1. Detailed conditions are in the rest of this chapter.

12.5   Authorities in England have the power to vary applicable amounts for working age CTR claims (paras. 10.24-26). In practice they have not done this.

CTR claimants on universal credit

12.6   If the claimant is on UC, the authority does not calculate an applicable amount itself. Instead it uses the claimant's maximum award of UC calculated by the DWP (para. 23.xx) as his or her applicable amount. This is a monthly figure, and the authority converts it to a weekly one by multiplying by 12 and dividing the result by 52.

12.4   CBA 135; NICBA 131; HB 22,23; HB60+ 22; NIHB 20,21; NIHB60+ 20; CTP 6; CTR 25-27

12.6   CTR 28

Table 12.1: Weekly HB/CTR applicable amounts

Personal allowances

Single claimant	aged under 25 – on main phase ESA	£71.70
	aged under 25 – other	£56.80
	aged 25+ but under pension age	£71.70
	over pension age but under 65	£145.40
	aged 65+	£163.50
Lone parent	aged under 18 – on main phase ESA	£71.70
	aged under 18 – other	£56.80
	aged 18+ but under pension age	£71.70
	over pension age but under 65	£145.40
	aged 65+	£163.50
Couple	both under 18 – claimant on main phase ESA	£112.55
	both under 18 – other	£85.80
	at least one aged 18+ both under pension age	£112.55
	at least one pension age, both under 65	£222.05
	at least one aged 65+	£244.95
Plus for each dependent child		£65.62

Additional amounts

Family premium	at least one dependent child	£17.40
Disability premium	single claimant/lone parent	£31.00 *
	couple (one/both qualifying)	£44.20 *
Disabled child premium	each dependent child	£57.89
Enhanced disability premium	single claimant/lone parent	£15.15 *
	couple (one/both qualifying)	£21.75 *
	each dependent child	£23.45
Work related activity component	single claimant/lone parent/couple	£28.45 *
Support component	single claimant/lone parent/couple	£34.80 *
Carer premium	claimant or partner or each	£33.30
Severe disability premium	single rate	£59.50
	double rate	£119.00

* Only awarded with working age claims (para. 1.21).

Examples: Applicable amounts

Except for the lone parent in the fourth example, none of the following qualifies for any of the premiums for disability or for carers.

Single claimant aged 23

Personal allowance:

Single claimant aged under 25	£56.80
No additional amounts apply	
Applicable amount	£56.80

Couple with two children aged 13 and 17

The older child is still at school so still counts as a dependant of the couple.

Personal allowances:

Couple, at least one over 18, both under pension age	£112.55
Child aged 13	£65.62
Child aged 17	£65.62
Additional amount: family premium	£17.40
Applicable amount	£261.19

Couple aged 38 and 65

Personal allowance:

Couple at least one aged 65	£244.95
Applicable amount	£244.95

Disabled lone parent with a child aged 6

The lone parent is in receipt of the highest rate of the care component of disability living allowance and so qualifies for a disability premium and enhanced disability premium. She has one child aged 6. Her mother (who lives elsewhere) receives carer's allowance to care for her. So she does not qualify for the severe disability premium.

Personal allowances:

Lone parent aged over 18 (and under pension age)	£71.70
Child	£65.62
Additional amounts:	
Family premium	£17.40
Disability premium (single rate)	£31.00
Enhanced disability premium (single rate)	£15.15
Applicable amount	£200.87

Better off problems for people on ESA

12.7 Employment and support allowance is summarised in table 12.2. Its interaction with HB/CTR applicable amounts causes better off problems for couples – the sense that they can be better or worse off depending on which of them is the claimant for HB/CTR purposes and which is the partner (para. 5.4).

12.8 These better off problems arise in relation to:

◆ the personal allowance for couples under 18 (para. 12.12);

◆ the disability premium for couples (para. 12.20 and the example there); and

◆ the enhanced disability premium for couples (para. 12.33).

12.9 Authorities should alert couples when they would be better off if they swapped the claimant role (DWP circular A11/2008).

Table 12.2: Employment and support allowance: summary

ESA is for people with a 'limited capacity for work' due to sickness or disability. They can get ESA(C) or ESA(IR) (appendix 3).

Awards of ESA(C) and ESA(IR) are divided into:

◆ an 'assessment phase': weeks 1 to 13;

◆ a 'main phase': weeks 14 onwards.

Main phase ESA is higher because it includes:

◆ a 'work-related component'; or

◆ a 'support component'.

HB/CTR applicable amounts also include these components from week 14 of a claimant's award of ESA(C)* (para. 12.17).

Until March 2014, some people on IB/SDA/IS are still being transferred onto ESA.

HB/CTR applicable amounts can include transitional protection for those onto ESA(C)* (para. 12.27).

* These rules do not apply to people on ESA(IR), because they get maximum HB/CTR (para. 6.4).

Detailed conditions

12.10 This section gives the detailed conditions for the personal allowances, premiums, components and transitional additions that make up an applicable amount (para. 12.4). General rules and special cases are in paragraphs 12.44-54.

Personal allowances: claimant and partner

12.11 A personal allowance is always awarded for the claimant (if they are single or a lone parent), or both if they are a couple. (For polygamous marriages see para. 12.53.)

12.12 As table 12.1 shows, couples who are both under 18, and only one of whom is on main phase ESA, are better off if the one on main phase ESA is the HB/CTR claimant (paras. 12.7-9).

Personal allowances: children and young persons

12.13 A personal allowance is awarded for each child or young person in the claimant's family (paras. 4.23-38).

How many premiums and components at once

12.14 Except as described in the remainder of this chapter, there are no limitations on how many premiums and components can be awarded at a time.

Family premium

12.15 The condition for this premium is that there is at least one child or young person in the claimant's family (paras. 4.23-38) – whether the claimant is in a couple or is a lone parent.

12.16 A higher 'protected rate' of family premium applies to certain lone parents who have been on HB, or CTB followed by CTR, since 5th April 1998. The protected rate is £22.20. The conditions are in the 2011-12 guide.

Work-related activity component and support component

12.17 A work-related activity component or support component is awarded only to working age claimants (para. 1.21) who are on main phase ESA(C) (table 12.2).

12.11   HB 22, sch 3 para 1; HB60+ 22, sch 3 para 1; NIHB 20, sch 4 para 1; NIHB60+ 20, sch 4 para 1;
          CTP 6, sch 2 para 1; CTR 25,26, sch 2 para 1, sch 3 para 1

12.13   HB sch 3 para 2; HB60+ sch 3 para 2; NIHB sch 4 para 2; NIHB60+ sch 4 para 2; CTP sch 2 para 2;
          CTR sch 2 para 2, sch 3 para 3

12.14   HB sch 3 paras 4-6; HB60+ sch 3 para 4; NIHB sch 4 paras 4-6; NIHB60+ sch 3 para 4;
          CTP sch 2 para 4; CTR sch 2 para 4, sch 3 paras 5-7

12.15-16 HB sch 3 para 3; HB60+ sch 3 para 3; NIHB sch 4 para 3; NIHB60+ sch 4 para 3; CTP sch 2 para 3;
          CTR sch 2 para 3, sch 3 para 4

12.17-19 HB sch 3 paras 21-24; NIHB sch 4 paras 21-24; CTR sch 3 paras 18-22

12.18   Only one component at a time can be awarded in HB/CTR:

- if a single claimant or lone parent gets a component in their ESA(C), they get that component in their HB/CTR applicable amount;
- if only one partner in a couple gets a component in their ESA(C), they get (one lot of) that component in their HB/CTR applicable amount;
- if both partners in a couple qualify for the same component in their ESA(C), they get (one lot of) that component in their HB/CTR applicable amount;
- if in a couple one partner qualifies for one component in their ESA(C) and the other partner qualifies for the other component in their ESA(C), they get (one lot of) the claimant's component in their HB/CTR applicable amount.

In the last case, the couple are better off if the one on ESA(C) support component is the HB/CTR claimant (paras. 12.7-9)

12.19   If a person's ESA assessment is delayed with the effect that their ESA component is awarded retrospectively, their HB/CTR component is also awarded retrospectively to the start of the claimant's 14th week on ESA. This does not normally lead to an over- or under-payment of HB/CTR.

Disability premium

12.20   A disability premium is awarded only to working age claimants (para. 1.21). The conditions are as follows – and in the case of a couple, the couple rate is awarded even if only one partner fulfils the conditions:

- the claimant (or in the case of a couple, either partner) must count as 'disabled or long-term sick' in one of the ways described in paragraphs 12.21-23 – but note that it must be the claimant, not the partner, in the cases described in para. 12.23; and
- the claimant must not be on ESA(C), nor during a period of disqualification from ESA(C) – but note that it does not matter if the partner is on ESA(C).

So if in a couple one partner is on ESA(C) and the other is not, they can be better off if the one who is not on ESA(C) is the HB/CTR claimant (paras. 12.7-9). This is illustrated in the example.

'Disabled or long-term sick'

12.21   The claimant or their partner counts as 'disabled or long-term sick' (para. 12.20) if they:

- are blind or have recently regained their sight (paras. 12.49-51); or
- are in receipt of any of the qualifying disability benefits in paragraph 12.22; or
- are treated as long-term sick in the way described in paragraph 12.23; or
- have an invalid vehicle supplied by the NHS or get DWP payments for car running costs.

12.20   HB sch 3 para 12; NIHB sch 4 para 12; CTR sch 3 para 9

Example: A 'better off' problem for couples

Information

A working age couple meet the condition for a disability premium which relates to being disabled or long-term sick (e.g. one of them is on DLA or is registered blind), but one partner in the couple is on ESA(C).

Entitlement to additions in the HB/CTR applicable amount

This depends on which partner is the HB/CTR claimant.

(a) If the HB/CTR claimant is on ESA(C):

their HB/CTR applicable amount does not include a disability premium (at any point), but it does include a work-related activity or support component from the claimant's 14th week on ESA(C).

(b) If the HB/CTR partner is on ESA(C):

their HB/CTR applicable amount includes a couple-rate disability premium (from the beginning), but it never includes a work-related activity or support component.

Conclusion

So they are better off if (b) applies to them – by over £25 per week in HB and over £5 per week in CTR, during the first 13 weeks on ESA(C) (and by a lower amount after that).

12.22 The qualifying disability benefits (para. 12.21) for the disability premium are:

(a) disability living allowance; or

(b) any benefit which is treated as attendance allowance (para. 12.48); or

(c) war pensioner's mobility supplement; or

(d) the disability element or severe disability element of working tax credit; or

(e) severe disablement allowance; or

(f) incapacity benefit payable at the long-term rate, or if they are terminally ill the short-term higher rate.

In the case of items (e) and (f) the claimant or any partner must be 'in receipt' (para. 12.44) of that benefit and not merely entitled to it. In certain circumstances the premium can continue if one of the qualifying benefits in (a) or (b) is lost due to a period in hospital: see paragraph 12.54 and table 12.4 for details.

12.21-26 HB sch 3 para 13; NIHB sch 4 para 13; CTR sch 3 para 10

Who counts as 'long-term sick'?

12.23   As an alternative to paragraph 12.22, the claimant (but not the claimant's partner) counts as long-term sick and qualifies for the disability premium if he or she:

- ◆   is incapable of work; and
- ◆   has been incapable of work (para. 12.24) for a 'qualifying period' (paras. 12.25-26) of:
  - •   28 weeks (196 days) if they are terminally ill, or
  - •   52 weeks (364 days) in any other case.

This route helps people qualify for the disability premium who are incapable of work but who do not get incapacity benefit. For couples, it must be the claimant – not their partner – who qualifies. It is therefore important which partner makes the claim (para. 5.4).

12.24   'Incapable of work' means the same here as it does for incapacity benefit – and this decision is always made by the Jobcentre Plus office (*R(H)3/06* and GM para. BW3.148). Broadly, during the first 28 weeks the person must demonstrate that they are incapable of following their normal job and thereafter (or from the outset if they have no normal occupation) any work. Broadly, a person is 'terminally ill' if their death can be expected within six months.

'Qualifying period'

12.25   The qualifying period (para. 12.23) need not be continuous. Any number of periods can be added together so long as the gap between each is eight weeks or less (104 weeks or less, in the case of a 'welfare to work beneficiary': table 12.3). A 'gap' means a period during which the person either is capable of work or is disqualified from incapacity benefit. After the qualifying period is completed, there are further 'linking rules' (described below). See paragraph 12.52 where the qualifying person starts on a government training scheme.

'Linking rules'

12.26   Once a person has completed the qualifying period, there are linking rules as follows:

- ◆   the claimant does not qualify for a disability premium during a gap;
- ◆   after a gap of eight weeks or less (104 weeks or less, in the case of a 'welfare to work' beneficiary: table 12.3), the person qualifies for a disability premium straight away;
- ◆   after a gap of more than eight weeks (104 weeks in the case of a 'welfare to work' beneficiary), the person does not qualify for a disability premium until they have completed a fresh qualifying period.

Breaks in HB/CTR during the qualifying period or after it do not affect this rule.

Table 12.3: Definition of 'welfare to work beneficiary'

For all HB/CTR purposes, this means a person who:

*   has been incapable of work for at least 28 weeks (196 days); and
*   has stopped receiving one of the benefits or advantages which is described in paragraph 12.25 and is dependent on that person being incapable of work; and
*   has – within seven days of ceasing to be incapable of work – started:
    *   remunerative work (paras. 6.22-23), or
    *   Work Based Training for Adults (in England and Wales), or
    *   Training for Work (in Scotland); and
*   has notified the DWP of the fact that he or she has started work, and has done so within one month of the date on which he or she ceased to claim that he or she is incapable of work (or, in certain cases, has won a social security appeal relating to this).

Such a person counts as a welfare to work beneficiary for 104 weeks only. The DWP is responsible for informing the claimant that protection applies (GM para. BW3.159).

Transitional protection for IB and SDA claims converted to ESA

12.27   When a person transfers from IB or SDA to ESA(C) (table 12.2) they face a drop in income if they previously qualified for a disability premium in HB/CTR. To prevent this, they are awarded a transitional addition in their HB/CTR applicable amount.

12.28   The amount of the transitional addition equals:

*   their HB/CTR applicable amount immediately before they transferred onto ESA(C); minus
*   their HB/CTR applicable amount immediately after that transfer.

In most cases transferred during 2013-14 this is £2.55 for single claimants and lone parents, and £15.75 for couples.

12.29   After that the transitional addition is reduced by an amount equal to any increase in their applicable amount (whether due to annual up rating or a change of circumstances). Other changes of circumstances (e.g. in income) have no effect on it.

12.28 30 HN sch 3 paras 27-31; NIHB sch 4 paras 27-31; CTR sch 3 paras 25-29

12.30   The transitional addition ends when:

+ it reduces to nil because of the above rules (para. 12.29); or

+ the claimant moves off ESA (e.g. receives JSA instead); or

+ the claimant's HB/CTR ends (but if they go back onto HB/CTR it starts again so long as the gap in entitlement is no longer than 12 weeks – or 104 weeks for a welfare to work beneficiary: table 12.3); or

+ on 5th April 2020 (if it lasts that long).

Disabled child premium

12.31   The condition for this premium is that a child or young person in the family:

+ is blind or has recently regained their sight (paras. 12.49-51); or

+ receives disability living allowance (either component payable at any rate).

A disabled child premium is awarded for each child or young person who qualifies. If the child/young person dies the premium continues for eight weeks following the death. Special rules apply if the child is in hospital – see paragraph 12.54 and table 12.4 for details.

Enhanced disability premium

12.32   This premium can be awarded in respect of a child or young person in the family, and/or in respect of the claimant or partner for working age claims (para. 1.21). Two or more of these premiums are awarded if appropriate – for example, if a claimant or partner qualifies and also one or more children or young persons qualify. Special rules apply where disability living allowance is lost following a period in hospital (para. 12.54 and table 12.4).

12.33   The conditions for an enhanced disability premium in the case of the claimant or partner are as follows – and in the case of a couple who meet the conditions, it is always the couple rate which is awarded (never the single rate):

+ it can be awarded only in working age HB/CTR claims (para. 1.21); and either

+ the claimant (or, in the case of a couple, either partner) receives the highest rate of the care component of disability living allowance; or

+ the claimant qualifies for an ESA(C) support component (table 12.2).

So if in a couple only one partner gets a support component in their ESA(C), they are better off if that one is the HB/CTR claimant (paras. 12.7-9).

12.31   HB sch 3 para 16; HB60+ sch 3 para 8; NIHB sch 4 para 16; NIHB60+ sch 4 para 8;
         CTP sch 2 para 8; CTR sch 2 para 8, sch 3 para 13

12.32-34 HB sch 3 para 15; HB60+ sch 3 para 7; NIHB sch 4 para 15; NIHB60+ sch 4 para 7;
         CTP sch 2 para 7; CTR sch 2 para 7, sch 3 para 12

12.34 The condition for an enhanced disability premium in the case of a child or young person is that they receive the highest rate of the care component of disability living allowance. It continues for eight weeks following the child's death.

Severe disability premium

12.35 There are three conditions for this premium:

- the claimant must be receiving one of the following qualifying benefits:
  - the middle or highest rate of the care component of disability living allowance, or
  - attendance allowance at either rate, or
  - a benefit which is treated as attendance allowance (para. 12.48); and
- they must have no non-dependants (but see paragraph 12.37 below for exceptions); and
- no-one must be receiving carer's allowance in respect of them (but see paragraphs 12.38 and 12.44 for circumstances where the carer will be treated as either in receipt or not in receipt of carer's allowance).

In the case of a couple, except where one member is blind (para. 12.49), both members must be in receipt of a qualifying benefit. Special rules apply where a qualifying benefit is lost following a period in hospital (paras. 12.36, 12.38, 12.54 and table 12.4).

12.36 A single claimant or lone parent who satisfies all three conditions gets the single rate of severe disability premium. In the case of a couple or a polygamous marriage, a severe disability premium is awarded as follows:

- if both members of a couple satisfy all three conditions, they get the double rate;
- if both members of a couple satisfy the first two conditions but only one satisfies the third condition, they get the single rate;
- if, in a couple, the claimant satisfies all three conditions, and their partner is blind or recently regained their sight (paras. 12.49-51), they get the single rate. In this case, if the 'wrong' partner makes the claim, they should be advised to 'swap the claimant role';
- if a couple have been getting the double rate, but one partner then ceases to satisfy the first condition because of having been in hospital for four weeks, they get the single rate from that point;
- in the case of a polygamous marriage, they get the double rate of severe disability premium if all members of the marriage satisfy all three conditions in paragraph 12.35; the single rate if all members of the marriage satisfy the first two of those conditions but someone receives a carer's allowance

12.35-38 HB sch 3 para 14; HB60+ sch 3 para 6; NIHB sch 4 para 14; NIHB60+ sch 4 para 6;
CTP sch 2 para 6, sch 3 para 11

in respect of caring for one of them; and the single rate if the claimant satisfies all three conditions and all the other members of the marriage are blind or recently regained their sight (paras. 12.49-51).

12.37   For the purposes of determining the second condition (para. 12.35), the following persons do not prevent the award of a severe disability premium:

* any person aged under 18 or who is excluded from the definition of a non-dependant (table 4.2);
* non-dependants who are blind or recently regained their sight (paras. 12.51-53);
* non-dependants receiving:
  * the middle or highest rate of the care component of disability living allowance, or
  * attendance allowance, or
  * a benefit which is treated as attendance allowance (para. 12.48).

12.38   For the purpose of determining whether the severely disabled person has a carer receiving carer's allowance in respect of them (para. 12.35) the following considerations apply:

* the carer is not treated as in receipt of carer's allowance if it is overlapped by other benefits (paras 12.44 and 12.47);
* a backdated award of carer's allowance is ignored as regards any period before the first payment is made: in other words the backdated part does not cause an overpayment;
* in the case of couples or polygamous marriages, the carer is treated as in receipt of a carer's allowance if they have lost it because the claimant or the partner they are caring for has been in hospital for four weeks or more. This will ensure that a couple in receipt of the single rate will continue to receive it at the same rate when one member goes into hospital (paras 12.35-36);
* the carer is treated as if they are in receipt of carer's allowance if it is not awarded because of the loss of benefit rules following certain benefit fraud convictions.

Example: Severe disability premium, etc

A husband and wife are both under pension age and both receive the middle rate of the care component of disability living allowance. Neither of them is or has recently been registered or certified blind. Their daughter of 17 is in full-time employment and lives with them. Their son lives elsewhere and receives carer's allowance for caring for the husband. No-one receives carer's allowance for the wife.

Disability premium: Because of receiving disability living allowance, they are awarded the couple rate of disability premium.

> **Enhanced disability premium:** Because they get the middle (not the highest) rate of the care component of disability living allowance, this cannot be awarded.
>
> **Severe disability premium:**
> + Both receive the appropriate type of disability living allowance.
> + Although their daughter is a non-dependant, she is under 18.
> + Someone receives carer's allowance for caring for only one of them.
>
> So they are awarded the single rate of severe disability premium (for the second reason in para. 12.36).

Carer premium

12.39   The condition for this premium is that the claimant (or, in the case of a couple, either partner) is entitled to (paras. 12.41, 12.44) carer's allowance or was entitled to carer's allowance within the past eight weeks.

12.40   A single claimant who satisfies the condition gets one carer premium. A couple can get one or two carer premiums, one if one of them fulfils the condition, two if both do. In the case of a polygamous marriage a carer premium is awarded for each partner that satisfies the conditions.

12.41   A claimant only has to be 'entitled' and not 'in receipt', so where carer's allowance is overlapped by another benefit (see examples) that is sufficient. Once a claim for carer's allowance has been made and entitlement established, it will continue indefinitely until they no longer satisfy the conditions for it (e.g. the person being cared for dies). It does not matter that the original claim for carer's allowance was made before the HB/CTR claim: they will continue to be 'entitled' to carer's allowance without the need to make a further claim for it *(CIS/367/2003)*. Note that certain carers entitled to carer's allowance before 28th October 2002 and who reached the age of 65 before that date remain entitled to it, even if they cease to care for the disabled person.

12.42   A person will be treated as in receipt of carer's allowance if they lose it as a result of taking part in a government training scheme (para. 12.52).

Interaction of carer and severe disability premium

12.43   Although entitlement to carer's allowance results in the award of a carer premium for the carer, the person cared for may lose a severe disability premium (though not retrospectively: para. 12.38). However this happens only if the carer's

---

12.39-40 HB sch 3 paras 7(2),17; HB60+ sch 3 paras 5(2),9; NIHB sch 4 paras 7(2),17; NIHB60+ sch 4 paras 5(2),9; CTP sch 2 paras 5(2),9; CTR sch 2 paras 5(2),9, sch 3 paras 8(2),14

12.41   SI 2002 No. 1457; NISR 2002 No. 321

12.43   HB sch 3 para 19; HB60+ sch 3 para 11; NIHB sch 4 para 19; NIHB60+ sch 4 para 11; CTP sch 2 para 11; CTR sch 2 para 11, sch 3 para 16

allowance (or part of it) is actually being paid to the carer (para. 12.44) – and not in the situation illustrated in the second example. It is therefore possible for a couple who care for each other to qualify for a severe disability premium (at the single or double rate) and two carer premiums.

Examples: Carer premium and overlapping benefits

Claimant over 65

A claimant and her partner are both aged over 80 and in receipt of retirement pension. She looks after her partner who has been in receipt of attendance allowance since 1st February 2013. On 8th February 2013 she made a claim for carer's allowance and was notified by the DWP that she was entitled to carer's allowance but it could not be paid because it was overlapped by her retirement pension (in other words, payment of the latter prevents payment of the former).

On 6th May 2013 she makes a claim for HB/CTR for the first time and is awarded HB/CTB from 11th February 2013 (para. 5.54). The award includes the carer premium. If her partner subsequently dies, she would no longer be entitled to carer's allowance, but the premium would continue for a further eight weeks.

Claimant under 65

A claimant aged 33 is in receipt of ESA(C). He cares for his severely disabled sister who receives the highest rate of disability living allowance care component. He lives alone in his own flat. He claims carer's allowance and is entitled to it but it cannot be paid because it is overlapped by his ESA(C). Once having claimed carer's allowance he remains 'entitled' to it indefinitely until such time as he no longer meets the conditions for it (e.g. he starts work, becomes a student or his sister dies or no longer qualifies for disability living allowance). While he remains entitled to carer's allowance he should be awarded the carer premium in his HB/CTR without the need for a further claim for carer's allowance even if there are breaks in his HB/CTR award. Note that his sister would also be entitled to the severe disability premium, because although he is 'entitled' to carer's allowance he is not 'in receipt' of it (para 12.44).

General rules and special cases

Being 'in receipt' of a benefit including 'main phase ESA'

12.44   Receipt of a state benefit forms part of the condition for many of the rules in this chapter. For these purposes, a person is 'in receipt' of a benefit only if it is paid in respect of himself or herself, and only during the period for which it is awarded. Except as described in paragraph 12.47 below, a person is not 'in receipt' if they are entitled to that benefit but it cannot be paid due to the overlapping benefit rules.

12.45   A further rule applies for 'main phase ESA' (table 12.2). For the purposes of qualifying for the personal allowances (table 12.1), a claimant counts as being 'on main phase ESA', in the 14th and subsequent weeks of ESA, even if they are being awarded only national insurance credits (but no payments of ESA itself) as a result of their ESA claim.

DWP concessionary payments

12.46   For the purpose of entitlement to any premium, a DWP concessionary payment compensating for non-payment of any qualifying benefit is treated as if it were that benefit.

Overlapping social security benefits

12.47   Where a claimant is entitled to a qualifying benefit but does not receive it because of the rules about overlapping social security benefits (for example if widow's pension is payable instead of incapacity benefit) then the claimant will not normally be treated as being in receipt of the qualifying benefit except in the following circumstances:

*   if they qualify for the carer's premium (para. 12.39);
*   if they qualified for that premium before the relevant qualifying benefit was overlapped. In such cases they will continue to be treated as in receipt of the qualifying benefit during any period in which they would be in receipt of that benefit but for the overlapping benefit rules. This rule protects claimants from a reduction in their benefit merely because they became entitled to an overlapping benefit at some later date;
*   if the qualifying benefit is only partially overlapped (i.e. the overlapping benefit is paid at a rate which is less than the qualifying benefit).

12.44   HB sch 3 para 19; HB60+ sch 3 para 11; NIHB sch 4 para 19; NIHB60+ sch 4 para 11; CTP sch 2 para 11; CTR sch 2 para 11, sch 3 para 16

12.46   HB sch 3 para 18; HB60+ sch 3 para 10; NIHB sch 4 para 18; NIHB60+ sch 4 para 10; CTP sch 2 para 10; CTR sch 2 para 10, sch 3 para 15

12.47   HB sch 3 paras 7,19; HB60+ sch 3 paras 5,11; NIHB sch 4 paras 7,19; NIHB60+ sch 4 paras 5,11; CTP sch 2 paras 5,11; CTR sch 2 paras 5,11, sch 3 paras 8,16

Benefits treated as attendance allowance

12.48		A person is treated as in receipt of attendance allowance (paras. 6.19, 12.22, 12.35, 12.37, 13.52 and 13.62) if they receive any type of increase for attendance paid with an industrial injuries benefit or war disablement pension. Qualifying payments include constant attendance allowance, 'old cases' attendance payments, severe disablement occupational allowance and exceptionally severe disablement allowance (GM BW2 annex B para. 7).

Meaning of blind or recently regained sight

12.49		For the purpose of determining whether a non-dependant deduction applies (para. 6.19) or entitlement to certain premiums in this chapter (paras. 12.21, 12.31, 12.35-36) a person is 'blind' if they satisfy the appropriate condition in paragraph 12.50, and is treated as blind if they have recently regained their sight (para. 12.51).

12.50		A person is blind if:

- ◆	in England or Wales, they are blind and are registered as such with the local authority social services department; or

- ◆	in Scotland, they are certified blind and are registered as such with the local authority social services department; or

- ◆	in Northern Ireland, they are blind and are registered as such with the Health and Social Services Board.

12.51		A person who has ceased to be registered as blind (para. 12.50) as a result of having recently regained their sight will continue to be treated as blind for a further 28 weeks following the date on which they were removed from the register.

People on training courses or in receipt of a training allowance

12.52		Once a person qualifies for the disability premium by virtue of being incapable of work (paras. 12.23-24) or the carer premium by virtue of being in receipt of carer's allowance (para. 12.39), if they go on a government-run or approved training course (para. 13.127) or receive a training allowance, they are treated as if they continue to satisfy the relevant condition. This rule avoids creating a disincentive to training.

12.48		HB 2(1); HB60+ 2(1); NIHB 2(1); NIHB60+ 2(1); CTP 2(1); CTR 2(1)

12.49-51	HB sch 3 para 13; HB60+ sch 3 para 13; NIHB sch 4 para 13; NIHB60+ sch 4 para 13; CTR sch 3 para 10

12.52		HB 2(1), sch 3 para 7(1), 13(5); HB60+ 2(1), sch 3 para 5(1); NIHB 2(1), sch 4 para 7(1), 13(5); NIHB60+ 2(1), sch 4 para 5(1); CTP 2(1), sch 2 para 5(1); CTR 2(1), sch 2 para 5(1), sch 3 para 8(1)

Polygamous marriages

12.53   The personal allowance for a claimant in a polygamous marriage (para. 4.20) is the appropriate amount in table 12.1 for a couple according to the age of the oldest member in the marriage plus the appropriate amount below for each additional spouse in excess of a couple:

- where all of the partners in the marriage are under pension age (para. 1.21): £40.85;
- where at least one of the partners is pension age or over but none of them are aged 65 or over: £76.65;
- where at least one of the members of the marriage is aged 65 or over: £81.45.

Premiums and components are awarded in a similar way as for a couple.

People in hospital

12.54   Certain premiums (e.g. severe disability and carer) may be lost as a result of losing a qualifying benefit after a period in hospital – see table 12.4 for details. In addition, after a continuous period in hospital of 52 weeks the claimant's right to benefit will be lost altogether (paras. 3.3, 3.33), or in the case of any dependants (adults or children) they are likely to cease to be treated as a member of the family (paras. 4.21, 4.37). In both cases this will override any special rules in table 12.4.

12.53   HB 23; HB60+ sch 3 para 1; NIHB 21; NIHB60+ sch 4 para 1; CTP sch 2 para 1; CTR 27 sch 2 para 1

Table 12.4: Loss of certain premiums after a period in hospital

Disability, disabled child and enhanced disability premium (paras. 12.20 and 12.31-34)

+ Where the claimant/partner/child loses their disability living allowance (including in the case of the disability premium one of the benefits in paragraph 12.48) solely because they have been in hospital for four weeks* (12 weeks in the case of a child) or more the relevant premium will continue or, in the case of a new claim, is still awarded.

Severe disability premium (para. 12.35)

+ In the case of a single claimant or a lone parent where payment of a qualifying benefit is lost because they have been in hospital for four weeks* then the premium will be lost.

+ In the case of couples or polygamous marriages where one or more members would be in receipt of a qualifying benefit but for the fact they have been in hospital for four weeks* they will continue to be treated as in receipt of that benefit and the premium will continue to be awarded – see also paragraph 12.38.

Carer premium (para. 12.39)

+ Where a carer goes into hospital, entitlement to carer's allowance is not normally lost until after 12 weeks, after which the carer premium will continue for a further eight weeks (making 20 in total).

+ Where a disabled person has been in hospital for four weeks* (12 in the case of a child) they will lose their disability living allowance/attendance allowance or equivalent benefit with the result that their carer will lose entitlement to carer's allowance. The carer premium will continue for a further eight weeks (para. 12.39).

* The four/twelve week period may not be continuous but may be made up of two or more distinct periods which are less than 29 days apart.

T12.4　　HB sch 3 paras 13(1)(a)(iii), 14(5)(a), 15(1),16(a),17(2); HB60+ sch 3 paras 6(7)(a),7,8(a),9(2); NIHB sch 4; paras 13(1)(a)(iii),14(5)(a),15(1),16(a),17(2); NIHB60+ sch 4 paras 6(7)(a),7,8(a),9(2); CTP 6(2), sch 2 paras 6-9; CTR 25(2),26(2), sch 2 paras 6-9, sch 3 paras 10-14

13 Income and capital

13.1 This and the following two chapters describe how income and capital are assessed in HB and CTR. Chapters 14 and 15 give additional information about employed earners and the self-employed. This chapter covers:

- how different rules apply for different groups of claimants;
- general matters;
- benefits, pensions, and other state help;
- local schemes for war pensions, etc;
- the home, property and possessions;
- savings and investments;
- trust funds and awards for personal injury;
- other items of income and capital;
- notional income and capital; and
- the separate rules used for claimants on savings credit or universal credit.

13.2 All references in this chapter to the income or capital of a claimant should be read as also referring to the income or capital of a partner (para. 13.5).

Claimants on JSA(IB), ESA(IR), IS or guarantee credit

13.3 If a claimant is on JSA(IB), ESA(IR), IS or guarantee credit (or his or her partner is), the whole of his or her (and any partner's) income and capital is fully disregarded. There are no exceptions whatsoever. The remainder of this chapter therefore does not apply in such cases. (Paragraphs 6.4-6 explain how their entitlement to HB/CTR is assessed.) If the claimant or partner receives arrears of these benefits, all their income and capital is disregarded for the period the arrears cover, and thereafter the arrears are treated as capital (table 13.2) which is usually disregarded for one year (para. 13.38).

Claimants on savings credit or universal credit

13.4 Special rules apply for assessing the income and capital of a claimant who is (or whose partner is) on savings credit (paras. 13.161-168) or universal credit (paras. 13.169-171).

13.3   HB sch 4 para 12, sch 5 paras 4,5, sch 6 paras 5,6; HB60+ 26;
       NIHB sch 5 para 12, sch 6 paras 4,5, sch 7 paras 5,6; NIHB60+ 24;
       CTP sch 1 para 13, sch 5 para 24;
       CTR 35, sch 6 para 24, sch 7 para 14, sch 8 paras 9,10, sch 10 paras 8,9

Other cases: whose income and capital counts

13.5 In all cases other than the above (paras. 13.3-4), for the purposes of assessing HB and CTR, a claimant is treated as possessing any income and capital belonging to:

* the claimant themself; and

* any partner.

13.6 The income and capital of a child or young person is always disregarded. Income and capital is assessed differently for non-dependants (paras. 6.24-27) and second adult rebate (para. 6.42).

13.7 However, if it appears that a claimant (not on JSA(IB), ESA(IR), IS or guarantee credit) and non-dependant have entered into arrangements to take advantage of the HB or CTR scheme, the authority may treat the claimant as possessing the non-dependant's income and capital (instead of, not as well as, their own). This is very rare.

Working age vs. pension age claims

13.8 Many of the rules for assessing income and capital differ between 'working age' and 'pension age' claimants (as defined in para. 1.21 and appendix 7). One key difference is in the way the HB/CTR regulations deal with income:

* for pension age claims, nothing counts as income unless the law says it does;

* for working age claims, everything counts as income unless the law says it does not.

This and other differences are described whenever relevant throughout this chapter.

CTR variations

13.9 For working age CTR claims in England, the assessment of income and capital can vary from authority to authority (para. 10.25). No variations apply to any other CTR claims.

HB variations

13.10 For HB in Great Britain, the only variation is in the assessment of certain war pensions (para. 13.59). No similar variations apply to HB (for rent or rates) in Northern Ireland.

13.5   HB 25,45; HB60+ 25; NIHB 22,42; NIHB60+ 23; CTP sch 1 para 11; CTR 27,33,63

13.7   HB 26; HB60+ 24; NIHB 23; NIHB60+ 22; CTP sch 1 para 12; CTR 34

13.8   HB 27,33(1),36,38, 40; HB60+ 29, 33; NIHB 24,28(1),33,35,37; NIHB60+ 27,31; CTP sch 1 paras 16,17; CTR 40,49,52,54,57,61

Definitions and general matters

Which types of income and capital count

13.11   Some types of income and capital are wholly disregarded; some are partly disregarded; and some are counted in full (table 13.1). Also, in some cases claimants can be treated as having income or capital they do not in fact possess: this is known as 'notional' income or capital (para. 13.146).

Distinguishing capital from income

13.12   The distinction between income and capital is usually straightforward (as illustrated in table 13.1). If a difficulty arises, the DWP advises (GM paras. BW1.70-71): 'As a general rule, capital includes all categories of holdings which have a clear monetary value... A payment of capital can normally be distinguished from income because it is (i) made without being tied to a period, and (ii) made without being tied to any past payment, and (iii) not intended to form part of a series of payments.' Selected cases are summarised in table 13.2.

Why capital is assessed

13.13   A claimant's capital is first assessed under the rules in this chapter, then taken into account as follows:

- if it amounts to more than £16,000, the claimant is not entitled to HB/CTR at all (except second adult rebate, para. 6.31); otherwise
- for working age claims, the first £6,000 is completely ignored;
- for pension age claims, the first £10,000 is completely ignored;
- the remainder up to £16,000 is treated as generating 'tariff income' (para. 13.14).

The £6,000/£10,000 figure is called the 'lower capital limit'. The £16,000 figure is called the 'upper capital limit': it can be less than £16,000 for working age CTR claims in England (para. 6.8).

Tariff income

13.14   'Tariff income' is assessed as follows (and illustrated in the examples):

- from the total amount of assessed capital deduct £6,000 for working age claims but £10,000 for pension age claims;
- then divide the remainder by 250 for working age claims but 500 for pension age claims;
- then, if the result is not an exact multiple of £1, round the result up to the next whole £1. This is the claimant's weekly tariff income.

13.13   HB 43,52; HB60+ 29(2),43; NIHB 40,49; NIHB60+ 27(2),41; CTP 11(2),sch 1 para 16; CTR 23,71,72

Table 13.1: Examples of capital and income

Capital which is (wholly or partly) taken into account

- Savings in a bank, etc
- National Savings Certificates, stocks and shares
- Property (unless it falls within one of the numerous disregards)
- Redundancy pay (with some exceptions)
- Tax refunds

Capital which is disregarded

- The home a claimant owns and lives in
- A self-employed claimant's business assets
- Arrears of certain state benefits
- Certain compensation payments
- A life insurance policy which has not been cashed in

Income which is (wholly or partly) taken into account

- Earnings from a job or from self-employment
- Pensions
- Certain state benefits (e.g. contribution-based jobseeker's allowance, retirement pension)
- Rent received from a lodger in the claimant's home
- Tariff income from capital

Income which is disregarded

- Reimbursement of expenses wholly incurred in the course of a job
- Certain state benefits (e.g. disability living allowance, attendance allowance)
- Charitable or voluntary payments
- Maintenance received for a child
- Fostering payments

These are just some examples, and are simplified. The detailed rules are given later in this chapter. For working age CTR claims in England, see also paragraph 13.9.

Table 13.2: Capital vs. income: case law

* *Income and capital not defined:* The HB/CTR regulations do not (except in the case of income for pension age claims: para. 13.8) provide a definition of income or capital. Instead they 'operate at stage after the money has been classified' *(CH/1561/2005).*

* *Determining income vs. capital:* The first task is to 'determine the true characteristics of the payment in the hands of the recipient' *(Minter v Hull City Council,* para. 19).

* *The views of the parties:* The label ('income' or 'capital') attached to the payment by the payer and/or the recipient is irrelevant *(Minter v Hull CC,* para. 21).

* *Payment in settlement of a claim:* If a payment is in settlement of a claim, how it is paid – as a lump sum or periodically – does not matter *(Minter v Hull CC,* para. 22)

* *Lump sum payments under equal pay, sex discrimination etc. legislation:* In the facts of this case, such payments were properly characterised as being in respect of wages, so they were income in the past, not capital. The 'contrast between the size of the payment and the employees' level of wages' did not matter *(Minter v Hull CC,* para. 23). An earlier case *([2009] UKUT (AAC)),* which held that a pay settlement for a part-time worker was capital, may now be wrong.

* *Income can turn into capital:* 'A payment of income is treated as income when received. It remains income for the period in which it is paid. Any surplus at the end of that period metamorphoses into capital' *(CH/1561/2005).* (See para. 13.96.)

How capital is assessed

13.15 The whole of a claimant's capital (including that of any partner) is taken into account from the date it is received (but see para. 13.17), unless it is disregarded as described in this chapter. Capital the claimant has in fact given away is not included: *[2012] UKUT 127 (AAC)* (but see para. 13.147).

If a claimant says that capital in their name is in fact held for someone else, the burden of proof (para. 1.41) is on the claimant to show this, but they need not prove it is held on trust for that person *[2010] UKUT 437 (AAC)* (which was about a joint bank account but appears to apply equally in other instances). For the treatment of trusts, see paragraphs 13.107 onwards.

13.15   HB 44; HB60+ 44; NIHB 41; NIHB60+ 42; CTP sch 1 para 31; CTR 63

Valuing capital in general

13.16   The following rule applies whenever a property, shares, or anything else has to be valued for HB/CTR purposes. Other parts of this chapter also have to be taken into account for specific items. The rule has three steps:

◆   take the current market or surrender value of the capital item;

◆   then disregard 10% if selling it would involve costs;

◆   then disregard any debt or charge secured against it.

Other than secured debts, a claimant's debts (e.g. rent arrears) cannot be set off against their capital *(CH/3729/2007).*

13.17   In practice, a claimant's capital is usually valued at his or her date of claim and revalued only if there is a reasonably large change. But it should be revalued whenever there is a change which affects entitlement to HB/CTR.

13.18   Authorities may seek the assistance of the Valuation Office Agency in London in valuing capital items such as dwellings or other property. Forms authorities may use for this purpose appear in the Guidance Manual (BW1 annex E), and for further guidance see DWP circular HB/CTB A25/2009.

Examples: Calculating tariff income

Pension age claim

A single pension age claimant has capital, assessed under the rules in this chapter, of £12,085.93.

The first £10,000 is disregarded, leaving £2,085.93. Divide this by 500 and round up to the next whole £1. The tariff income is £5.

Working age claim

A single working age claimant has capital, assessed under the rules in this chapter, of £12,085.93.

The first £6,000 is disregarded, leaving £6,085.93. Divide this by 250 and round up to the next whole £1. The tariff income is £25.

(For CTR in England, see also para. 6.8.)

13.16   HB 47; HB60+ 45; NIHB 44; NIHB60+ 43; CTP sch 1 para 32; CTR 65

Valuing jointly held capital

13.19   The following rule applies when a capital item (e.g. a property) is held jointly by two or more people. An example is given below:

+ first assume that all the joint owners own an equal share in the capital item;
+ then value the person's resulting assumed share (as in para. 13.16) and count that as his or her capital.

13.20   But if an item is held in distinct, known shares (e.g. one person holds a one-third share and the other a two-thirds share), the actual share should be valued (as in para. 13.16) and counted as the person's capital *(R(IS) 4/03)*. That actual share may itself have minimal value *(CH/1953/2003)*.

Examples: Valuing capital

Company shares

A claimant owns 1,000 shares in a company. The sell price is currently £0.50 each.

From the current market value (1,000 x £0.50 = £500) deduct 10% (£50) giving £450. Assuming no debt or charge is secured on the shares, the value for HB/CTR purposes is therefore £450.

A jointly owned property

A claimant and her sister jointly own some land. The authority accepts Valuation Office Agency valuations that:

+ if the whole of the land was sold, it would fetch £10,000;
+ if a half-share in the land was sold, the half-share would fetch £4,000.

The claimant has recently taken out a loan for £2,000 using the land as security (and none of the loan has yet been repaid).

The claimant's share of the capital in the land is valued as follows:

+ first the claimant is treated as owning half of the land;
+ then this half share is valued. The authority values it at £4,000;
+ then 10% is deducted for sales costs: £4,000 minus £400 leaves £3,600;
+ then the loan is deducted: £3,600 minus £2,000 leaves £1,600.

The value for HB/CTR purposes is therefore £1,600.

Why income is assessed

13.21   A claimant's earned and unearned income, assessed as described in this and the next two chapters, is compared with his or her applicable amount in calculating how much HB or CTR he or she is entitled to (paras. 6.9-11).

13.19   HB 51; HB60+ 49; NIHB 48; NIHB60 + 47; CTP sch 1 para 36; CTR 70

How income is assessed

13.22   The whole of a claimant's income (including that of any partner) is taken into account, unless it is disregarded as described in this chapter (though for pension age claims what counts as income is limited: para. 13.8. For working age CTR claims in England, see also para. 13.9.)

13.23   The HB and CTR rules distinguish earned income (i.e. earnings received by employed earners or by the self-employed) from unearned income (e.g. pensions, benefits, rent received by the claimant, and so on). Chapter 14 deals with earnings from a job, chapter 15 with self-employed earnings. The rules about unearned income are in this chapter.

Deciding which weeks income belongs to

13.24   The general objective for HB/CTR purposes is '[calculating or] estimating the amount which is likely to be [the claimant's or partner's] average weekly income'. However, there are many specific rules and these are given in this and the next two chapters as they arise. Where there is no specific rule, it is usually straightforward to decide according to the facts of the case which week or weeks a claimant's income belongs to for HB/CTR purposes.

Arrears of income

13.25   In broad terms, it is usually the case that if a claimant receives arrears of income, then those arrears are treated as being income belonging to the week or weeks to which they relate (except to the extent that they are income which is disregarded). It is because of this that certain arrears of income are disregarded as capital (*CH/1561/2005,* and see table 13.2). Exceptions to this and further specific rules are given in this and the next chapter as they arise.

Income tax

13.26   The income tax payable on any kind of income, even income not listed elsewhere in this guide, is disregarded in the assessment of that income.

Converting income to a weekly figure

13.27   For HB/CTR purposes, income must be converted (if necessary) to a weekly figure. The details are given in paragraph 6.49.

13.22   HB 27,31,40; HB60+ 30; NIHB 24,28,37; NIHB60+ 28; CTP sch 1 para 24; CTR 49,54,57

13.24   HB 27(1); HB60+ 30(1); NIHB 24(1); NIHB60+ 28(1); CTP sch 1 para 24(1); CTR 57(1)

13.25   HB 31(2),79(6),(7); NIHB 28(2),77(8),(9); CTR 49(2),107(8),(9)

13.26   HB sch 5 para 1; HB60+ 33(12); NIHB sch 6 para 1; NIHB60+ 31(11); CTP sch 1 para 17; CTR 40(13), sch 8 para 4

Social security benefits, tax credits and war pensions

13.28   This section gives the rules about the assessment for HB/CTR purposes of social security benefits and pensions, tax credits, and war pensions. Paragraphs 13.29-36 give general rules, paragraphs 13.37-63 give rules for individual benefits.

State benefits and tax credits: general rule for current payments

13.29   Except where otherwise indicated (paras. 13.37-63), social security benefits, tax credits and war pensions are counted in full as unearned income. All the following social security benefits and tax credits are counted in full:

+ bereavement allowance;
+ carer's allowance;
+ child tax credit (but see also paras. 13.35 and 13.46-48);
+ employment and support allowance (contribution-based);
+ incapacity benefit and severe disablement allowance;
+ industrial injury disablement benefit (except certain increases, para. 13.52);
+ jobseeker's allowance (contribution-based);
+ maternity allowance;
+ retirement pensions;
+ working tax credit (but see also paras. 13.35 and 13.46-48).

13.30   Except in the case of working tax credit and child tax credit (para. 13.46), the period over which these are taken into account is 'the period in which that benefit is payable'.

Social security benefits: general rule for arrears

13.31   Except when indicated in the following paragraphs (see in particular para. 13.32), arrears of social security benefits and pensions are counted as unearned income for the period they cover.

Social security benefits: large arrears due to official error

13.32   In the case of several benefits (e.g. DLA: para 13.53), arrears are disregarded as capital for 52 weeks from the date of payment. In those cases (identified in this section as they arise), there is a lengthened disregard if:

+ the underpayment was due to official error; and
+ the amount of the arrears is £5,000 or more.

13.29   HB 31(1); HB60+ 29(1); NIHB 28(1); NIHB60+ 27(1); CTP sch 1 paras 16,25; CTR 39(1),58(1)

13.30   HB 31(2); HB60+ 33(6); NIHB 28(2); NIHB60+ 31(6); CTP sch 1 para 17(7); CTR 40(7),49(2)

13.31   HB 79(7); HB60+ 33(6); NIHB 77(9); NIHB60+ 31(6); CTP sch 1 paras 17(7),46(9); CTR 40(7),107(9)

13.32   HB sch 6 para 9; HB60+ sch 6 paras 18,21,22; NIHB sch 7 para 9; NIHB60+ sch 7 paras 18,21,22; CTP sch 6 paras 18,21,22; CTR sch 10 para 12, sch 9 paras 18,21,22

In such cases, the arrears are then disregarded (if this would be longer than the 52 weeks) for as long as the claimant or any partner remain continuously entitled to HB/CTR (including periods for which the partner remains continuously entitled after the claimant's death).

> ### Example: Arrears of employment and support allowance
>
> A claimant, who has been receiving HB for many years, has been receiving contribution-based ESA since January 2012. It has been taken into account as her income for HB purposes from that date. In June 2013, following a successful appeal, she is paid arrears of contribution-based ESA for the period from October 2011 to January 2012.
>
> The arrears are her income for the period from October 2011 to January 2012. The authority may therefore reassess her entitlement to HB for that period, which may result in an overpayment (chapter 18).

Reduced social security benefits

13.33　If the amount of a social security benefit is reduced (for example, in order to recover a previous overpayment), the gross amount (i.e. before the reduction) is counted as unearned income. (But there are exceptions: paras. 13.34-35.)

13.34　However, if the amount of a state benefit is reduced due to the overlapping social security benefit rules, or (for pension age claims) due to hospitalisation, the net amount (i.e. after the reduction) is counted as unearned income. The net amount is also used when IB is reduced for a person in receipt of an occupational pension: *CH/51/2008*.

Reduced tax credits

13.35　If the amount of WTC or CTC (para. 13.46) has been reduced to recover an overpayment which arose in a previous tax year, the net amount of WTC or CTC (i.e. after the deduction) is counted as income.

Increases in social security benefits for dependants

13.36　With some social security benefits, an increase can be added for a dependent partner, or other dependent adult(s) or child(ren). For working age claims, an increase for any member of the family (para. 4.8) counts as unearned income if the benefit it is paid with counts as unearned income. The same applies for pension age claims, but only to increases for a partner.

13.33　HB 40(5); HB60+ 29(3),(4); NIHB 37(3); NIHB60+ 27(3),(4); CTP sch 1 para 16(2),(3); CTR 39(2),(3),54(3)

13.34　HB 40(5); HB60+ 29(3),(4); NIHB 37(3); NIHB60+ 27(3),(4); CTP sch 1 para 16(2),(3); CTR 39(2),(3),54(3)

13.35　HB 2(1),40(6); NIHB 2(1),37(4); CTR 2(1),54(5)

13.36　HB sch 5 para 52; HB60+ 29(1)(j); NIHB sch 6 para 54; NIHB60+ 27(1)(h); CTP sch 1 para 16(1)(j); CTR 39(1)(j), sch 8 para 53

JSA(IB), ESA(IR), IS, state pension credit and universal credit

13.37 Current payments of:

◆ savings credit and universal credit count in full as unearned income – but there are special rules for assessing HB/CTR for anyone on these (paras. 13.161-171);

◆ guarantee credit, JSA(IB), ESA(IR) and IS are disregarded in full as income (together with any other income or capital: para. 13.3).

13.38 Except for universal credit, arrears of all of the above benefits, including payments compensating for non-payment of them, are disregarded as income; and are disregarded as capital for 52 weeks from the date of payment, or longer for some large underpayments (para. 13.32).

13.39 Note that the rules about changes to pension credit awards can also operate in a way that effectively causes them to be disregarded as income (para. 17.27 and table 17.4).

Certain former JSA(IB) or IS claimants

13.40 The whole of a claimant's unearned income is disregarded if he or she lost entitlement to JSA(IB) or IS on 1st April 2003, and the only reason for this was that the assessment of his or her JSA(IB) or IS no longer included support charges because they became payable by Supporting People (para. 13.68). This applies only to CTR and HB for rates in Northern Ireland (but not to HB for rent anywhere in the UK). It mainly affects long leaseholders and is rare.

HB, CTR and discretionary housing payments and reductions

13.41 Current payments of HB/CTR are disregarded as income. Arrears of HB/CTR, including payments compensating for non-payment of them, are disregarded as income; and are disregarded as capital for 52 weeks from the date of payment, or longer for some large underpayments (para. 13.32).

13.42 Discretionary housing payments (para. 23.2) are disregarded in full as income; and are disregarded as capital for 52 weeks from the date of payment, or longer for some large underpayments (para. 13.32). Discretionary council tax reductions (para. 10.40) are disregarded as capital for 52 weeks for pension age claimants only.

13.37　HB sch 5 paras 4, 5, 7, sch 6 para 9; HB60+ 26, 27,44(3), sch 6 paras 21,22;
　　　　NIHB sch 6 paras 4, 5,8, sch 7 para 9; NIHB60+ 24, 25,42(3), sch 7 paras 21, 22;
　　　　CTP sch 1 paras 13,14,31(3); CTR 35,36,63(3), sch 8 paras 8,9,12, sch 10 para 12

13.40　CTP sch 5 para 24; CTR sch 6 para 24, sch 8 para 10; NIHB sch 6 para 6

13.41　HB sch 5 para 51 sch 6 para 9; HB60+ 29(1)(j), sch 6 paras 21,22;
　　　　NIHB sch 6 para 53, sch 7 para 9; NIHB60+ 27(1)(h), sch 7 paras 21,22;
　　　　CTR sch 1 para 16(1)(j), sch 8 paras 42,57, sch 9 paras 21,22,sch 10 para 12

In work credit

13.43   Payments of in work credit are disregarded in full as income.

Social fund payments and loans

13.44   Disregard in full as income and capital payments and loans from the social fund – including winter fuel payments, funeral payments and maternity grants.

'Local welfare provision' or 'occasional assistance'

13.45   Disregard in full, as income and capital, any payments made by English local authorities or the equivalent provision made in Scotland or Wales which:

◆   meet or help meet an immediate short-term need arising from an exceptional event or exceptional circumstances that would otherwise risk a person's well being; or

◆   enable a person to establish or maintain a settled home if he or she has been (or without the payment might be) in prison, hospital, a residential care establishment or other institution, or homeless or otherwise living an unsettled way of life.

Working tax credit and child tax credit

13.46   Working tax credit (WTC) and child tax credit (CTC) are assessed as follows for HB/CTR purposes. For pension age claims, CTC is disregarded, but WTC is counted, as unearned income. For working age claims, both are counted as unearned income. In each case, the period over which they are taken into account is the period they cover, as follows:

(a) in the case of a daily instalment, the one day in respect of which it is paid;

(b) in the case of a weekly instalment, the period of seven days ending on the day on which it is due to be paid;

(c) in the case of a two-weekly instalment, the period of 14 days commencing six days before the day on which the instalment is due to be paid (because two-weekly instalments of WTC/CTC are due at the end of the first week of the two weeks they cover);

(d) in the case of a four-weekly instalment, the period of 28 days ending on the day on which it is due to be paid (though there may be exceptions due to the way the Inland Revenue pays these).

13.43   HB sch 5 para 62; NIHB sch 6 para 62; CTR sch 8 para 64

13.45   HB sch 5 para 31 sch 6 para 20; HB60+ 29(1); NIHB sch 6 para 32 sch 7 para 21; NIHB60+ 27(1); CTI sch 1 para 16(1); CTR sch 8 para 38, sch 10 para 25

13.46   HB 32; HB60+ 29(1)(b),32; NIHB 29; NIHB 27(1)(b),30; CTP sch 1 paras 16(1)(b), 27; CTR 59

13.47   HB 27(1),(2),34(e), sch 4 para 17; sch 5 para 56; HB60+ sch 4 para 9, sch 5 para 21; NIHB 24(1),(2),31(e), sch 5 para 17, sch 6 para 58; NIHB60+ sch 5 para 9, sch 6 para 22; CTP sch 4 para 10, sch 5 para 21; CTR 75(1),(2),60(e), sch 5 para 10, sch 6 para 21, sch 7 para 18, sch 8 para 58

13.47 There are two further rules for special circumstances:

- Certain recipients of WTC qualify for a disregard from their earnings of £17.10 per week (para. 14.30). If (uncommonly) their earnings are insufficient for this £17.10 disregard to be made in full from them (as described in para. 14.31), £17.10 is instead disregarded from their WTC.

- Certain claimants with child care costs qualify for a disregard from their earnings (para. 14.17). If (uncommonly) their earnings are insufficient for this disregard to be made in full from them, any balance of the disregard is made from their WTC (para. 14.19).

13.48 Arrears of WTC and CTC are never counted as income; and are disregarded as capital for 52 weeks (one year for pension age claims) from the date of payment, or longer for some large underpayments (para. 13.32). (The effect of this rule is that the arrears themselves cannot create an overpayment of HB/CTR.) The same rule applies to payments compensating for non-payment of WTC/CTC.

Child benefit and guardian's allowance

13.49 Child benefit and guardian's allowance are both disregarded in full as income.

Maternity, paternity and adoption benefits

13.50 Statutory maternity, paternity and adoption pay count as earnings (as described in para. 14.50). For Sure Start maternity grant see paragraph 13.44, for adoption allowances see paragraph 13.66.

Benefits for sickness, incapacity and disability

13.51 Most benefits for sickness and/or disability are treated under the general rule (13.29-30) and so count in full as income (but see para. 13.33), including carer's allowance, ESA(C), incapacity benefit, severe disablement allowance and industrial injuries disablement benefit (except certain increases). The only exceptions are:

- ESA(IR) (paras. 13.3 and 13.37);
- war disablement pensions (paras. 13.58-62);
- disability living allowance, attendance allowance, personal independence payments and AFIPs (para. 13.52-53);

13.48 HB 46(9), sch 6 para 9; HB60+ 44(3), sch 6 paras 18,21; NIHB 43(8), sch 7 para 9; NIHB60+ 42(3), sch 7 para 18,21;
CTP sch 1 para 31(3); CTR 63(3),64(10), sch 9 paras 18,21, sch 10 para 12

13.49 HB sch 5 para 50,65; HB60+ 29(1)(j); NIHB sch 6 par 52,64; NIHB60+ 27(1)(h);
CTP sch 1 para 16(1)(j); CTR 39(1)(j), sch 8 paras 52,66

13.50 HB 35(1)(i); HB60+ 29(1)(j); NIHB 32(1)(i); NIHB60+ 27(1)(h); CTP sch 1 para 16(1)(j); CTR 39(1)(j),51(1)(j)

- those benefits treated as attendance allowance (para. 12.48) which are paid as increases to industrial and war disablement pensions (paras. 13.52-53);
- statutory sick pay (which counts as earnings as described in para. 14.50).

Benefits for attendance and mobility

13.52 Current payments of the following are disregarded in full as income:

- disability living allowance;
- attendance allowance;
- personal independence payments;
- armed forces personal independence payments (AFIPs);
- any benefit treated as attendance allowance (para. 12.48);
- war pensioners mobility supplement; and
- payments compensating for non-receipt of the above.

13.53 Arrears of the above are disregarded in full as income. They are also disregarded as capital for 52 weeks from the date of payment, or longer for some large awards of arrears (para. 13.32).

State retirement pension: payments and deferral

13.54 State retirement pension counts in full as unearned income. A person who chooses to defer their state retirement pension can choose between a lump sum now, or increased payments later, and can change their mind about this (subject to conditions). Except for CTR in Scotland, the amount of a lump sum is disregarded as capital (until and unless the person opts to have increased payments rather than a lump sum). Increased payments count in full as income. For treatment of occupational and personal pensions see paras. 13.93-94. For winter fuel payments see para. 13.44.

Christmas bonus

13.55 The 'Christmas bonus' of £10, which is awarded each year to certain claimants on long-term benefits (e.g. retirement pension and disability living allowance) is disregarded as income.

13.52   HB sch 5 paras 6-9; HB60+ 29(1)(j), sch 6 para 21; NIHB sch 6 paras 7-10; NIHB60+ 27(1)(h);
        CTP sch 1 para 16(1)(j), sch 6 para 21; CTR sch 8 paras 11-14, sch 9 para 21

13.53   HB sch 6 para 9; NIHB sch 7 para 9; CTR sch 10 para 12

13.54   HB 60+ sch 6 para 26A; SI 2005/2677 Reg 11,12, CPR 2; NIHB60+ sch 7 para 28;
        CTP sch 6 28A, sch 6 para 28; CTR sch 9 para 28

13.55   HB sch 5 para 32; HB60+ 29(1)(j); NIHB sch 6 para 33; NIHB60+ 27(1)(h); CTP sch 1 para 16(1)(j);
        CTR 39(1)(j), sch 8 para 38

Widowed parent's allowance

13.56 Disregard £15 per week from current payments (subject to the overriding £20 disregard: para. 13.160). Arrears are counted as unearned income for the period they cover apart from the £15 per week disregard.

Bereavement payment

13.57 Bereavement payment is a lump-sum, one-off payment and so counts as capital (not income). For funeral payments see paragraph 13.44.

War pensions for bereavement and disablement

13.58 The following rules apply to:

- war widow's, war widower's and war disablement pensions, war pensions for surviving civil partners, and also guaranteed income payments under the Armed Forces and Reserve Forces Compensation Scheme;
- payments to compensate for non-payment of any of the above;
- payments analogous to any of the above from governments outside the UK.

See also the rules for gallantry awards (para. 13.134) and Second World War payments etc (paras. 13.122-124).

13.59 In England, Wales and Scotland £10 per week is disregarded as income from the above payments for the period they cover (subject to the over-riding £20 disregard, para. 13.160), plus any additional amount from a 'local scheme'. Many councils operate a 'local scheme' whereby a larger amount (usually 100%) of any current payments or arrears of the first item (in para. 13.58) are disregarded as income (para. 23.17).

13.60 In Northern Ireland all of the above payments (including any amounts for attendance or mobility: para. 13.52) are disregarded in full as income.

13.61 In England, Wales, Scotland and Northern Ireland there is no disregard of the capital value of arrears of any of these payments apart from any amounts for attendance or mobility (para. 13.52).

13.62 Arrears of amounts granted for attendance or mobility (para. 13.52) are disregarded as capital for 52 weeks from the date of payment, or longer for some large underpayments (para. 13.32). The same applies to payments compensating for non-receipt of such amounts.

13.56 HB sch 5 para 16; HB60+ sch 5 paras 7,8; NIHB sch 6 para 17; NIHB60+ sch 6 paras 8,9;
CTP sch 5 paras 7,8; CTR sch 6 paras 7,8, sch 8 para 21

13.57 HB60+ 29(1)(j); NIHB60+ 27(1)(h); CTP sch 1 para 16(1)(j); CTR 39(1)(j)

13.58 HB sch 5 paras 7-9,15,52-54; HB60+ 29(1), sch 5 paras 1-6, sch 6 paras 21,22;
NIHB sch 6 paras 8-10,15,16,54-56; NIHB60+ 27(1), sch 6 paras 1-7, sch 7 paras 21,22;
CTP sch 1 paras 16(1)(j), sch 5 paras 1-6, sch 6 paras 21,22;
CTR sch 6 paras 1-6, sch 8 paras 8,12-14,20,53-55, sch 9 paras 21,22

'Pre-1973' war widows and widowers special payment

13.63   Special payments paid to 'pre-1973' war widows, widowers and surviving civil partners (from April 2013 paid at £86.99 per week) are disregarded as income. For working age claims any arrears are also disregarded as capital for up to 52 weeks.

Social services payments for care and support

13.64   This section gives the rules about the treatment of certain payments for childcare, community care and other support services. In Great Britain these payments are usually made by the local authority social services department or by a voluntary body on their behalf. In Northern Ireland these payments are made by the Health and Social Services Board, a Health and Social Services Trust, a Juvenile Justice Centre, or by a voluntary body on their behalf.

Note, however, that money held by the Court of Protection (i.e. by social services on behalf of an incapacitated claimant) counts in full as capital: *[2011] UKUT 157 (AAC)*.

Fostering (kinship), boarding out and respite care payments

13.65   For pension age claims all such payments are disregarded in full (as income): there are no further conditions. For working age claims disregard these payments in full as income if they are received from a local authority or voluntary organisation or (in the case of respite care payments) a primary care trust; and also disregard (in the case of respite care payments), contributions required from the person cared for. Any sum accumulated from allowances paid counts as capital and cannot be disregarded as an implied trust *(CIS/3101/2007)*. (In Scotland, foster care payments are known as kinship care payments.)

Adoption allowances and special guardianship payments

13.66   Both are paid by local authorities, special guardianship payments being for support services. Disregard all such payments in full (as income): there are no further conditions.

13.63   HB sch 5 paras 53-55, sch 6 para 39; HB60+; sch 5 para 23;
           NIHB sch 6 paras 55-57, sch 7 para 40; NIHB60+ sch 6 para 24; CTP sch 6 para 25;
           CTR sch 8 paras 54-56, sch 10 para 42, sch 9 para 25, sch 10 para 42

13.65   HB sch 5 paras 26,27; HB60+ 29(1); NIHB sch 6 paras 27,28; NIHB60+ 27(1); CTP sch 1 para 16(1);
           CTR 39(1) sch 8 paras 31,32

13.66   HB 2(1), sch 5 para 25; HB60+ 29(1); NIHB 2(1), sch 6 para 26; NIHB60+ 27(1);
           CTP sch 1 para 16(1); CTR sch 8 para 30)

Community care, direct care and other social services payments

13.67   For pension age claims disregard all such payments in full (as income); and also disregard 'direct care' payments as capital: in each case there are no further conditions. For working age claims disregard in full (both as income and capital):

♦   any social services payment made for the purposes of avoiding taking children into care or to children and young persons who are leaving or have left care;

♦   any payment made by social services to a young person formerly in their care which is passed on to the claimant. To qualify, the young person must be aged 18 or over and continue to live with the claimant;

♦   any social services community care payment.

Supporting people payments

13.68   Supporting people payments (usually administered by social services to assist people with certain support costs in their home) are disregarded in full as income.

The home, property and possessions

13.69   This section is about how things the claimant owns affect HB/CTR, including the home, a former or future home, other property and rent received by the claimant (and for property held in a trust, see para. 13.111).

Homes and other property

13.70   The claimant's current, former or future home can be disregarded and so can a home or other property (including non-domestic property) which the claimant has never occupied, if the conditions in the following paragraphs apply. The disregards described below can apply one after another, so long as the relevant conditions are met (as illustrated in the example).

The claimant's home

13.71   Disregard the capital value of the dwelling normally occupied as the claimant's home, and any land or buildings (including in Scotland croft land) which are part of it or are impracticable to sell separately. There is no time limit. This disregard is limited to one home per claim but see the other headings below.

13.67   HB sch 5 paras 26,28,28A,57, sch 6 paras 19,19A,58-60; HB60+ 29(1) sch 6 para 26D;
NIHB sch 6 paras 27,29,29A,61, sch 7 paras 20,20A,55-57; NIHB60+ 27(1) sch 7 para 28C;
CTP sch 1 para 16(1), sch 6 para 29; CTR sch 8 paras 31,33,34,57, sch 10 paras 23,62-64

13.68   HB sch 5 para 63, sch 6 para 57; HB60+ 29(1); NIHB sch 6 para 63, sch 7 para 54; NIHB60+ 27(1);
CTP sch 1 para 16(1); CTR 64(7), sch 8 para 19, sch 10 para 38

13.71   HB sch 6 para 1; HB60+ 2(1), sch 6 para 26; NIHB sch 7 para 1; NIHB60+ 2(1), sch 7 para 26;
CTP sch 6 para 26, CTR sch 9 para 26, sch 10 para 4

A relative's home

13.72   Disregard the capital value of the home of a partner or relative of anyone in the claimant's family (para. 4.8), if that partner or relative has attained the qualifying age for state pension credit (appendix 7) or is incapacitated. There is no time limit. The property may be occupied by others as well as the partner or relative. Any number of properties may be disregarded under this rule. 'Relative' is defined in paragraph 8.59. 'Incapacitated' is not defined for this purpose and so has its ordinary English meaning; in particular, it is not linked to state benefits or to the claimant's applicable amount.

An intended home

13.73   Disregard the capital value of a property which the claimant intends to occupy as a home as follows:

* in all cases, for 26 weeks from the date of acquisition or such longer period as is reasonable; and/or

* if the claimant is taking steps to obtain possession (e.g. if there are squatters or tenants), for 26 weeks from the date the claimant first seeks legal advice or begins legal proceedings, or such longer period as is reasonable; and/or

* if the property requires essential repairs or alterations, for 26 weeks from the date the claimant first takes steps to render it fit for occupation or reoccupation as his or her home, or such longer period as is reasonable. This could apply for example to the normal home of a claimant in temporary accommodation.

A former home

13.74   There is no disregard of the capital value of a claimant's former home as such. However, a former home may well fall within one of the following headings (paras. 13.75-81) (which also apply to other property): if it does not, then it is taken into account as capital.

Property for sale

13.75   Disregard the capital value of any property the claimant intends to dispose of (e.g. sell or transfer), for 26 weeks from the date when the claimant first takes steps to dispose of it, or for such longer period as is reasonable. This can apply to a former or second home or any other property. It can apply to more than one property.

13.72   HB sch 6 para 4(a); HB60+ sch 6 para 4(a); NIHB sch 7 para 4(a); NIHB60+ sch 7 para 4(a);
           CTP sch 6 para 4(a); CTR sch 9 para 4(a), sch 10 para 7(a)

13.73   HB sch 6 paras 2,27,28; HB60+ sch 6 paras 1-3; NIHB sch 7 paras 2,28,29; NIHB60+ sch 7 paras 1-3;
           CTP sch 6 paras 1-3; CTR sch 9; paras 1-3, sch 10 paras 10,32-33

13.75   HB sch 6 para 26; HB60+ sch 6 para 7; NIHB sch 7 para 27; NIHB60+ sch 7 para 7;
           CTP sch 6 para 7; CTR sch 9 para 7, sch 10 para 31

Couples and divorce, dissolution and estrangement

13.76   If a claimant has divorced their partner or dissolved their civil partnership with them or become estranged from them, disregard the whole capital value of the claimant's former home (and any land or buildings which are part of it or are impracticable to sell separately) as follows:

- for any period when it is occupied by the former partner if he or she is now a lone parent. This could begin straight after the divorce/estrangement, or later on, and there is no time limit in this case; and/or

- for 26 weeks from the date it ceased to be occupied. The time limit in this case cannot be extended, but the property may fall within one of the other disregards afterwards.

Note that (unlike in the next paragraph) the claimant must have formerly lived there as his or her home for this disregard to apply. 'Divorce' (in the case of married couples) and 'dissolution' (in the case of civil partners) have their ordinary meaning. 'Estrangement' (in all cases) means more than just physical separation, namely that the couple in question consider their relationship to be over *(CH/117/2005)*; it need not be an acrimonious split and the fact that one party might want them to get back together is irrelevant *(CH/3777/2007)*.

Couples and separation

13.77   If a claimant has not divorced their partner, dissolved their civil partnership with them, or become estranged from them, but the HB/CTR rules treat him or her as no longer being in a couple or polygamous marriage (because of the rules about absence of a partner: para. 4.21), disregard the whole capital value of any property currently occupied as a home by the former partner. There is no time limit. Note that (unlike in the previous paragraph) it is irrelevant who used to live there. This rule does not apply if the reason the two people do not live in the same household as a couple is that the relationship has broken down even if the two remain on civil terms *(CH/3777/2007)*.

Disputed assets when a relationship ends

13.78   When a relationship ends, ownership of a property may be in dispute. This can sometimes mean the current market value of the property (paras. 13.16-20) is nil until ownership of the property is settled.

13.76   HB sch 6 para 25; HB60+ sch 6 para 6; NIHB sch 7 para 26; NIHB60+ sch 7 para 6; CTP sch 6 para 6; CTR sch 9 para 6, sch 10 para 30

13.77   HB sch 6 para 4(b); HB60+ sch 6 para 4(b); NIHB sch 7 para 4(b); NIHB60+ sch 7 para 4(b); CTP sch 6 para 4(b); CTR sch 9 para 4(b), sch 10 para 4(b)

Example: The capital value of a property following relationship breakdown

- A married couple in their forties jointly own the house they live in. They do not own any other property. They have one child at school. They claim CTR. The man is the claimant.

  The value of the house is disregarded as capital: it is their normal home (para. 13.71). However, they turn out not to qualify for CTR because they have too much income.

- The couple separate (but are not estranged).The man leaves and rents a room in a shared house. He does not intend to return (and so they no longer count as a couple: para. 4.21). He claims HB and CTR for the flat.

  In the man's claim, his share of the house is disregarded: it is the home of his former partner from whom he is separated (para. 13.77).

- They divorce. The terms of the divorce are that the man retains a one-third share in the house; but that the house cannot be sold until their child is 18.

  In his claim, his share of the house is disregarded: it is his former home and is occupied by his former partner from whom he is divorced and who is a lone parent (para. 13.76).

- More than 26 weeks after their divorce, their child leaves school. The house is not put up for sale and the man does not seek his share of its value.

  In his claim, his one-third share in the house must now be taken into account (paras. 13.76 and 13.19).

- The house is put up for sale.

  In the man's claim, his share in the house is now disregarded as capital for 26 weeks (or longer if reasonable: para. 13.75).

- The house is sold, and the man puts his share into a bank account and starts trying to raise a mortgage using the money. It seems likely that he will be able to buy somewhere within the next two or three months.

  In his claim, this money is disregarded: it is the proceeds of the sale of his former home and he plans to use it to buy another property within 26 weeks (para. 13.80).

Housing association deposits

13.79   For working age claims, disregard in full as capital any amount deposited with a housing association (para. 7.10) in order to secure accommodation. There is no such disregard for pension age claims.

13.79   HB sch 6 para 11(a); NIHB sch 7 para 11(a); CTR sch 10 para 14(a)

Money from selling a home

13.80 For working age claims, disregard in full as capital:

* money from the sale of the claimant's former home – this could include, for example, any compensation paid resulting from compulsory purchase (specific provision is made in the Northern Ireland regulations) or money held by the claimant or a solicitor following a sale; and

* any refund of a deposit with a housing association (para. 13.79),

but only if it is intended for purchasing another home within 26 weeks, or such longer period as is reasonable. (However, interest accrued on the money is counted as capital in the normal way: para. 13.97.) If the money is available but is subject to a dispute as to the claimant's share, then the claimant cannot benefit from the extended disregard by taking a hard line in negotiations even if it compromises their position. Neither can they benefit from the disregard if they have not yet decided what they will do with the money when they receive it (both points: *CH/2255/2006*). For pension age claims a different rule applies (para. 13.81).

Money for buying a home

13.81 For pension age claims, payments (or amounts deposited in the claimant's name) for the sole purpose of buying a home are disregarded for one year from the date of receipt. Apart from lasting longer, this is wider than the rule for working age claims (para. 13.80). It includes home sale proceeds and money refunded by a housing association, but also (for example) money given or loaned by a relative for that purpose.

Valuing property generally

13.82 The general rules about valuing capital apply to a property which has to be taken into account as capital for HB/CTR purposes (paras. 13.16-20). In such cases, an authority can get a free valuation of property from the Valuation Office Agency (a model form which can be used for this purpose is in GM chapter BW1 annex D).

Valuing property which is rented out

13.83 Unless it forms part of the capital assets of a business (or in certain circumstances a former business: para. 15.7), property a claimant owns and has rented out is valued as described earlier (paras. 13.16-20). However, the fact that it is rented out will affect its market value; for example, the presence of a sitting tenant can reduce it: *CH/1953/2003*. For information about rental income see paragraphs 13.84-85 and tables 13.3-4.

13.80 HB sch 6 paras 3,11(b); NIHB sch 7 paras 3,11(b); CTR sch 10 paras 6,14(b)

13.81 HB60+ sch 6 paras 18,20(a); NIHB60+ sch 7 paras 18,20(a); CTP sch 6 paras 18,20(a); CTR sch 9 paras 18,20(a)

13.83 HB sch 6 para 7; HB60+ sch 6 para 5; NIHB sch 7 para 7; NIHB60+ sch 7 para 5; CTP sch 6 para 5; CTR sch 9 para 5, sch 10 para 10

Receiving rent

13.84   Table 13.3 shows how rent received by the claimant from people living in their home is taken into account. See also the example. Table 13.4 shows how rent received from property other than the claimant's home is taken into account.

13.85   The value of the right to receive rent is disregarded as capital.

Payments for work on the home

13.86   The following disregard applies to such payments:

♦ For working age claims, payments (from anyone) solely for essential repairs or improvements to the home, and grants from a local authority to purchase, alter or repair an intended home, are disregarded as capital for 26 weeks from the date of payment, or such longer period as is reasonable.

♦ For pension age claims, payments, or amounts deposited in the claimant's name, (from anyone) solely for essential repairs or improvements to the home or an intended home are disregarded for one year from the date of receipt.

Table 13.3: Rent received from people in the claimant's home

Household members

♦ Disregard the whole of any rent, 'keep', etc, received from a child or young person in the family (paras. 4.23-38) or from a non-dependant (para. 4.39).

Lodgers whose rent includes meals (para. 4.48(a))

♦ Disregard the first £20.00 pw of that rent.

♦ Count only half the rest as unearned income.

♦ A separate £20.00 pw is disregarded for each individual boarder who is charged for – even a child – regardless of whether they have separate agreements.

Lodgers whose rent does not include meals (para. 4.48(b))

♦ Disregard the first £20.00 pw of that rent (including any payments within the gross charge for services such as heating).

♦ Count all the rest as unearned income.

♦ A separate £20.00 pw is disregarded for each letting.

13.84   HB sch 6 para 33; HB60+ sch 6 para 28; NIHB sch 7 para 34; NIHB60+ sch 7 para 30; CTP sch 6 para 31; CTR sch 9 para 31, sch 10 para 37

Table 13.4: Rent received on property other than the claimant's home

Pension age claims

Rent received on property (other than the claimant's home) is disregarded in full as income in all circumstances.

Working age claims in which the property's value is disregarded as capital

This applies to rent received on one of the types of property (other than the claimant's home) whose capital value is disregarded (as described in paras. 13.71-77 and 15.7):

- Take the amount of the rental income for an appropriate period (e.g. six months, a year).
- Disregard any payment towards mortgage repayments (both interest and capital repayments) or any council tax (in Northern Ireland domestic rates) or water charges the claimant is liable to pay during that period on the property (note that other outgoings cannot be disregarded).
- Count the balance (converted to a weekly figure) as the claimant's unearned income.

Working age claims in which the property's value counts as capital

This applies to rent received on one of the types of property whose value is taken into account as his or her capital (even if for some reason the capital value is nil for HB/CTR purposes):

- Take the amount of the rental income for an appropriate period (e.g. six months, a year).
- Deduct any outgoings incurred in respect of the letting (e.g. agents' fees, tax due on the income, repairs, cleaning, council tax, water charges, repayments of mortgages/loans, etc).
- The balance (if any) is capital (not income) for HB/CTR purposes.

13.86   HB sch 6 paras 10,38; HB60+ sch 6 paras 18,20(b); NIHB sch 7 paras 10,39;
NIHB60+ sch 7 paras 18,20(b); CTP sch 6 paras 18,20(b); CTR sch 9 paras 18,20(b), sch 10 paras 14,41

T 13.3   HB sch 5 paras 21,22,41; HB60+ 29(1), sch 5 paras 9,10; NIHB sch 6 paras 23,44;
NIHB60+ 27(1), sch 6 paras 10,11; CTP sch 5 paras 9,10; CTR 39(1), sch 6 paras 9,10, sch 8 paras 26,27

T 13.4   HB 46(4), sch 5 para 17(1),(2); HB60+ 29(1), sch 5 para 22; NIHB 43(4), sch 6 para 18(1),(2);
NIHB60+ 27(1), sch 6 para 23; CTP sch 1 para 16(1) ,sch 5 para 23;
CTR 39(1),64(5), sch 6 paras 22,23, sch 8 para 22

Example: Letting out a room

A couple in their 20s are on HB and CTR. They have a spare room and they let it out to a lodger for £80.00 per week inclusive of fuel for heating etc, and water charges (but not meals).

Because they do not provide meals, their income from this lodger is £80.00 minus £20.00, which is £60.00 per week.

Later, the same couple agree with the lodger that if he increases what he pays to £100.00 per week, they will feed him.

Because they provide meals, their income from this lodger is £100.00 minus £20.00, which is £80.00, the result being divided in two, which is £40.00 per week.

Tax refunds for mortgage interest

13.87   For working age claims, tax refunds for interest on a mortgage taken out for purchasing a home, or for carrying out home repairs or improvements, are disregarded in full as capital. There is no such disregard for pension age claims.

Mortgage and loan protection policies

13.88   The following applies if a claimant has taken out insurance against being unable (perhaps because of unemployment or sickness) to pay his or her mortgage or any other loan (for example a car loan), and is now receiving payments under that insurance policy. For pension age claims all payments received under that insurance policy are disregarded (as unearned income). For working age claims they are disregarded only insofar as they cover the cost of:

- ◆ the repayments on the mortgage or other loan; and
- ◆ any premiums due on the policy in question; and
- ◆ (only in the case of a mortgage protection policy) any premiums on another insurance policy which was taken out to insure against loss or damage to the home and which was required as a condition of the mortgage.

Compensation and insurance payments for the home or possessions

13.89   Such payments are disregarded (as capital) if they are for repair or replacement following loss of, or damage to, the claimant's home or personal possessions. For working age claims they are disregarded for 26 weeks from the date of payment, or such longer period as is reasonable. For pension age claims they are disregarded for one year from the date of receipt.

13.87   HB sch 6 para 21; HB60+ 29(1); NIHB sch 7 para 22; NIHB60+ 27(1); CTP sch 1 para 16(1); CTR 39(1), sch 10 para 26

13.88   HB sch 5 para 29; HB60+ 29(1); NIHB sch 6 para 30; NIHB60+ 27(1); CTP sch 1 para 16(1); CTR 39(1), sch 8 para 35

Compensation for compulsory purchase

13.90 The treatment of compensation for compulsory purchase of the claimant's home depends on the type of payment being made. The rules are:

- compensation for the market value of the home (but not other property) is disregarded for 26 weeks or longer (one year for pension age claims) (paras. 13.80-81);
- elements of disturbance payments for the replacement of fixtures and fittings are disregarded for 26 weeks or longer (one year for pension age claims) (para. 13.89);
- there is no specific rule to deal with other elements of the disturbance payments (such as the cost of a removal van) – this is probably unintended. However, where the service provider is paid directly then it can be disregarded (paras. 13.130 and 13.155).
- Home loss payments count in full as capital except where they are intended to be used to buy a new home (para. 13.81).

Personal possessions

13.91 Disregard in full (as capital) the value of the claimant's personal possessions. A personal possession is any physical asset other than land and assets used for business purposes *(R(H)7/08)*. For working age claims, the law specifically mentions that if they were purchased for the purpose of obtaining or increasing entitlement to HB/CTR, their capital value should be taken into account.

Savings, investments and private income

13.92 This section is about savings, investments, insurance policies, etc. When these are taken into account, they are valued as described in paragraphs 13.16-20. (But for national savings certificates, see para. 13.98.) The following terms are used below:

- the 'surrender value' (of an insurance policy, for instance) means what the claimant would be paid if he or she cashed it in now rather than waiting for it to mature;
- the 'value of the right to receive income' (from an annuity, for instance) means what the claimant would be paid in return for transferring the right to receive the income to someone else.

13.89 HB sch 6 para 10; HB60+ sch 6 paras 18,19; NIHB sch 7 para 10; NIHB60+ sch 7 paras 18,19; CTP sch 6 paras 18,19; CTR sch 9 paras 18,19, sch 10 para 13

13.91 HB sch 6 para 12; HB60+ sch 6 para 8; NIHB sch 7 para 12; NIHB60+ sch 7 para 8, CTP sch 6 para 8; CTR sch 9 para 8, sch 10 para 15

Occupational and personal pensions

13.93 Pension payments received by the claimant count in full as unearned income, after deducting tax and disregarding any amount required to be paid by a court pension-splitting order *(CH/1672/2007)*. This includes occupational and personal pensions. It also includes payments by the Pension Protection Fund: these are government payments to people who have lost out on their occupational pension scheme because it was under-funded when it began to be wound up and because the employer is now insolvent or has ceased to exist (and so cannot make up the shortfall).

13.94 The value of the right to receive money from an occupational or personal pension scheme (para. 13.92) is disregarded as capital. So is the actual capital held in a pension scheme (because while it is held there it does not belong to the claimant).

Savings and cash

13.95 These count in full as capital. For example, money in a bank account (or under the mattress) is counted as capital (but see the next paragraph). However, if a claimant has two or more accounts at the same bank, and the bank has the power to use credits on one to pay off an overdraft on another, then it is the net amount of capital (across those accounts) that is taken into account: *[2011] UKUT 63 AAC.*

Income paid regularly into an account

13.96 Regular payments of income (e.g. earnings, benefits, pensions) into a claimant's bank or similar account should not be counted as capital for the period they cover (table 13.2). For example, if earnings are paid in monthly, only what is left at the end of the month is capital. In practice, authorities often do not do this unless claimants ask them to.

Interest

13.97 Except where other rules in this chapter state otherwise, interest or other income derived from capital (on a bank account, etc) is counted not as income but as capital. For working age claims the law spells out that this is done from

---

13.93   HB 2(1),35(2),40(10), sch 5 para 1; HB60+ 29(1)(x),33(12); NIHB 32(2),37(8), sch 6 para 1; NIHB60+ 27(1)(v),31(11); CTP sch 1 paras 16(1)(x),17(13), sch 6 para 24; CTR 39(1)(x),40(13), sch 9 para 24, sch 10 para 35

13.94   HB sch 6 para 31; HB60+ sch 6 para 24; NIHB sch 7 para 32; NIHB60+ sch 7 para 24; CTP sch 6 para 33; CTR sch 9 para 33

13.95   HB 44(1); HB60+ 44(1); NIHB 41(1); NIHB60+ 42(1); CTP sch 1 para 31(1); CTR 63(1)

13.97   HB 46(4); HB60+ 29(1), sch 5 paras 22,24; NIHB 43(4); NIHB60+ 27(1), sch 6 paras 23,25; CTP sch 5 paras 22,23; CTR 64(5), sch 6 paras 23,24

the date it is due to be credited to the claimant, and it seems logical that this would also apply to pension age claims.

National Savings and Ulster savings certificates

13.98 These count as capital and are valued as in paragraph 13.16 (i.e. their market value). The DWP advises authorities (GM BW1.440) to use the online valuation calculator [www]. For further guidance on valuing, see GM BW1.441-451.

Shares and other investments

13.99 These count as capital. They are valued as described in the general rules (paras. 13.16 20), with the effect that:

* shares are valued at their 'sell' price. Then disregard 10% towards the cost of their sale;
* unit trusts are valued at their 'sell' price. Normally this already allows for notional sales costs. If it does not, disregard 10% for this;
* income bonds count in full.

Life insurance policies

13.100 Disregard (as capital) the surrender value of a life insurance policy (para. 13.92). (This includes instruments, such as bonds, which have a life insurance element: *R(IS)7/98.*) But count as capital any money actually received from it (e.g. if the claimant actually cashes in all or part of it).

Funeral plan contracts

13.101 For pension age claims, disregard the value of a funeral plan contract. To qualify, the contract provider (which would normally be a firm or company but need not be so) must contract to provide or secure the provision of a funeral for the claimant or partner in the UK, and that must be the sole purpose of the contract. There is no such disregard for working age claims.

Annuities

13.102 If the claimant has an annuity, it means he or she has invested an initial lump sum with an insurance company which, in return, pays the claimant a regular income. Count this in full as unearned income. Disregard (as capital) the surrender value of the annuity, and also the value of the right to receive income from it (para. 13.92). Unless the claimant is legally required to do so (para. 13.93)

13.98   www.nsandi.com

13.100   HB sch 6 para 17; HB60+ sch 6 para 11; NIHB sch 7 para 18; NIHB60+ sch 7 para 11;
         CTP sch 6 para 11; CTR sch 9 para 11, sch 10 para 21

13.101   HB60+ sch 6 para 12; NIHB60+ sch 7 para 12; CTP sch 6 para 8, sch 9 para 8

13.102   HB sch 6 para 13; HB60+ 29(1), sch 6 para 25; NIHB sch 7 para 13; NIHB60+ 27(1), sch 7 para 25;
         CTP sch 1 para 6(1); CTR 39(1), sch 9 para 32, sch 10 para 16

money paid over from an annuity to a former spouse cannot be disregarded as an implied trust and in any case an annuity paid by a former employer cannot normally be assigned *(CH/1076/2008).*

Home income plans

13.103　If the claimant has a home income plan, it means he or she raised a loan using his or her home as security, has invested the loan as an annuity and, in return, gets a regular income. Part of this income is used to repay the loan, part may be used to repay the claimant's mortgage, and part may be left over for the claimant to use. Count the income received by the claimant as unearned income, but only after deducting (if they have not been deducted at source):

- ◆ any tax payable on that income;
- ◆ any repayments on the loan which was raised to obtain the annuity; and
- ◆ any mortgage repayments made using the income (using the figures for the repayments which apply after tax has been deducted from them).

Disregard (as capital) the surrender value of the annuity, and the value of the right to receive income from it (para. 13.92).

Equity release schemes

13.104　If the claimant is in an equity release scheme, it means that he or she receives (loaned) payments which are advanced by a lender at regular intervals and are secured on his or her home. For pension age claims, such payments count in full as income (even though they are a loan). For working age claims there is no specific rule in the law (but see para. 13.140).

Life interest and liferent

13.105　If a claimant has a life interest or (in Scotland) liferent, it means he or she has the right to use a property or other asset during his or her or someone else's lifetime, after which it will pass to someone else. The actual value to the claimant (if any) of the life interest or liferent is counted as capital; and any actual income the claimant receives from it is counted as earned or unearned income as appropriate. Disregard as capital the value of the right to receive income from it (para. 13.92).

Reversionary interest

13.103　HB 41(2), sch 5 para 18, sch 6 para 13; HB60+ 29(1), sch 5 para 11, sch 6 para 29;
　　　　NIHB 38(2), sch 6 para 19, sch 7 para 13; NIHB60+ 27(1), sch 6 para 12, sch 7 para 31;
　　　　CTP sch 1 para 16(1), sch 6 paras 11,32; CTR 39(1), sch 5 para 11, sch 9 para 32, sch 10 para 16

13.104　HB60+ 29(1)(w),(8); NIHB60+ 27(1)(u),(8); CTP 16(1)(w),(5); CTR 39(1)(w),(5)

13.105　HB sch 6 para 15; HB60+ sch 6 para 27; NIHB sch 7 para 16; NIHB60+ sch 7 para 29;
　　　　CTP sch 6 para 30; CTR sch 9 para 30, sch 10 para 19

13.106　HB sch 6 para 7; HB60+ sch 6 para 5; NIHB sch 7 para 7; NIHB60+ sch 7 para 5;
　　　　CTP sch 6 para 5; CTR sch 9 para 5, sch 10 para 10

13.106 If a claimant has a reversionary interest, it means he or she will not possess a property or other asset until some future event (for example, the death of a relative). Disregard in full the capital value of a reversionary interest. (Different rules apply to a property the claimant has rented out: table 13.4).

Trust funds and compensation payments

13.107 This section is about the assessment of:

* trusts in general;
* personal injury payments and trusts; and
* special (i.e. set up and/or funded by the Government) trusts and compensation payments.

Trusts in general

13.108 A trust is a way of holding an asset, whether money, shares, property, etc.

* The 'trustee' (or trustees) have legal ownership of the asset: they hold it and have the right and responsibility to dispose of it within the terms of the trust.
* The 'beneficiary' (or beneficiaries) have beneficial ownership: it is held for their (current or future) use.

Claimants who are trustees

13.109 If a claimant holds an asset as a trustee (para. 13.108), its value is disregarded. For a claimant to count as a trustee, it is not enough merely to plan to give the asset away. They must have received the asset on clearly stated terms requiring them to hold it for someone else; or they must have clearly and consistently expressed that they hold an asset for someone else and given up all intentions of using it for themselves: *R(IS) 1/90*. A recent case *([2012] UKUT 115 (AAC))* confirms that trusts do not arise only from legal documents, In that case, a woman inherited money from her aunt. She said this was on the understanding from her aunt that she share it with her five children. Though this was not recorded in writing, it was held to be capable of being what English law calls a 'secret trust'.

Claimants who are beneficiaries

13.110 If a claimant is a beneficiary of a trust (para. 13.108), two matters arise: the capital value of the assets held in the trust (para. 13.111), and any payments received from the trust (para. 13.112).

13.111 The capital value of a trust (of which the claimant is a beneficiary) is disregarded if the trust is discretionary (i.e. the payments are at the trustee's

---

13.111 HB60+ sch 6 para 30; NIHB60+ sch 7 para 32; CTP sch 6 para 33

discretion) or reversionary (e.g. if the claimant cannot obtain the assets until they reach 21: para. 13.106). For pension age claims only, property held in a trust (e.g. a house) is also disregarded – but only if the trust makes payments or has the discretion to make payments to the claimant or partner. In all other cases, the value of the trust counts in full as the claimant's capital.

13.112 Payments a claimant receives from a trust are counted in full as their capital or income as appropriate (para. 13.12), with one exception. The exception only applies for pension age claims in which the claimant receives payments of income from a discretionary trust:

- £20 is disregarded if the payments are for food, ordinary clothing or footwear or household fuel; rent, council tax, water charges or in Northern Ireland rates for which the claimant is liable; or housing costs (such as mortgage interest payments: chapter 25) that could be met by guarantee credit (but this is subject to the over-riding £20 disregard: para. 13.160);
- the whole amount is disregarded if the payments are for anything else.

Personal injury payments of income

13.113 Payments of income for a personal injury (of the claimant or any partner), including payments from a trust, are disregarded in full as income.

Personal injury payments of capital

13.114 Payments of capital for a personal injury (of the claimant or any partner), including payments from a trust, are disregarded in full. (The same applies to compensation from a solicitor for professional negligence, up to the amount that would otherwise have been paid: *[2011] UKUT 102 (AAC).*) There is no time or other limit for pension age claims and in these cases the disregard equals the amount of the personal injury payment: the particular money need not be kept track of. For working age claims there are two limits:

- the disregard lasts only for 52 weeks from the payment date (sometimes called a 'grace period' since within this period the money is likely to be spent or, if not, it should be possible to form a trust to hold the money); and
- there is only one 52-week disregard per personal injury. If someone gets two or more payments for the same personal injury, the 52 weeks runs only from the first such payment.

13.112 HB60+ sch 5 para 12; NIHB60+ sch 6 para 13; CTP sch 5 para 12; CTR sch 6 para 12

13.113 HB sch 5 para 14; HB60+ sch 5 para 12; NIHB sch 6 para 14; NIHB60+ sch 6 para 13; CTP sch 3 para 12; CTR sch 6 para 12, sch 8 para 19

13.114 HB sch 5 para 14A; HB60+ sch 6 para 17; NIHB sch 7 para 14A; NIHB60+ sch 7 para 17; CTP sch 6 para 18; CTR sch 9 para 17, sch 10 para 18

13.115 HB sch 6 para 14; HB60+ sch 6 para 17; NIHB sch 7 para 14; NIHB60+ sch 7 para 17; CTP sch 6 para 17; CTR sch 9 para 17, sch 10 para 17

Personal injury payments held in a trust

13.115 Any payments for personal injury (of the claimant or any partner) which are held in a trust are disregarded in full (as capital) without time limit (and for working age claims so is the value of the right to receive income from them: para. 13.92). For pension age claims the disregard equals the amount of the personal injury payment: the particular money need not be kept track of. If the trust pays the money out to the claimant it is then also disregarded for the reasons in the previous two paragraphs.

Personal injury payments administered by a court

13.116 Compensation for personal injury (of claimant or partner), if paid into a court and administered by the court on the compensated person's behalf, is disregarded in full (as capital) without time limit. The same applies to money which is held by someone other than a court but is administered subject to the order or direction of a court. If the compensated person is under 18, the same points apply to compensation for the death of a parent.

Personal injury payments under a court order or out-of-court settlement

13.117 For working age claims, periodic payments under a court order for personal injury (of claimant or partner) are counted as unearned income. For pension age claims, the following periodic payments are disregarded (as income):

- payments under a court order for accident, injury or disease of the claimant, partner or child;
- payments in an out-of-court settlement for injury of the claimant or partner.

Macfarlane, Independent Living and similar trusts

13.118 Payments from any of the following trusts are usually disregarded in full (as described in para. 13.119):

- The Independent Living Fund (2006) (to help severely disabled people to live independently);
- The Macfarlane Trust, the Macfarlane (Special Payments) Trust, the Macfarlane (Special Payments) (No. 2) Trust (for people with haemophilia infected with HIV through blood products);
- 'The Fund', and the Eileen Trust (for people who contracted HIV through NHS products);

13.116 HB sch 6 paras 45,46; HB60+ sch 6 para 17; NIHB sch 7 para 45; NIHB60+ sch 7 para 17; CTP sch 6 para 17; CTR sch 9 para 17, sch 10 paras 50,51

13.117 HB 41(5); HB60+ sch 5 paras 14,15; NIHB 38(4); NIHB60+ sch 6 paras 15,16; CTP sch 5 paras 14,15; CTR 55(5), sch 6 paras 14,15

13.118 HB 2(1), sch 5 para 35, sch 6 paras 24,34,55; HB60+ 29(1), sch 6 para 14; NIHB 2(1), sch 6 para 37, sch 7 paras 25,35,52; NIHB60+ 27(1), sch 7 para 14; CTP sch 1 para 16(1), sch 6 para 4; CTR 39(1), sch 8 para 41, sch 9 para 14, sch 10 paras 29,38,59

- MFET Ltd (a successor trust to the Macfarlane and Eileen trusts);
- The Skipton Fund and the Caxton Fund (for people infected with hepatitis C through blood products);
- The Variant Creutzfeldt-Jacob Disease Trust (for people who have contracted variant CJD and their families).

13.119 Any payments made from the first five trusts are disregarded in full as income and capital. Also disregarded are payments from the Skipton Fund (which are made as lump sum capital payments) and Caxton Fund. Payments from the second to fourth of these trusts can still be disregarded if they are passed on to certain relatives as a gift or an inheritance (and are always disregarded if received by the claimant or the partner of a pension age claimant). For further details see GM para. BW2.620. Payments from the sixth trust are made as a lump sum capital payment (as an interim and final award). They are disregarded indefinitely if they are made to the person who has contracted vCJD, or to their partner or surviving partner. They are disregarded for two years if made to the parent or guardian of a child who has vCJD.

The London Bombing Charitable Relief Fund

13.120 Payments from the London Bombing Charitable Relief Fund (set up to assist victims of the bombings on 7th July 2005) are disregarded, without time limit, as both income and capital.

Compensation for families of the disappeared

13.121 In Northern Ireland only, compensation payments by the Secretary of State to the families of the disappeared are disregarded (as capital) for 52 weeks from the date of receipt.

Second World War payments

13.122 Disregard in full (as capital), without time limit, the *ex gratia* payments of £10,000 made by the Secretary of State to people who were imprisoned or interned by the Japanese during the Second World War. Authorities should not attempt to identify the particular £10,000: £10,000 should simply be disregarded from the capital the claimant has.

13.123 Also disregard in full as capital, without time limit, any payment (apart

---

13.120 HB 2(1), sch 5 para 35, sch 6 para 25; HB60+ 29(1), sch 6 para 16;
         NIHB 2(1), sch 6 para 37, sch 7 para 25; NIHB60+ 27(1), sch 7 para 16;
         CTP 2(1), sch 1 para 16(1), sch 6 para 16; CTR 39(1), sch 9 para 16, sch 10 para 29

13.121 NIHB sch 7 para 58; NIHB60+ sch 7 para 27

13.122 HB sch 6 paras 54,56; HB60+ sch 6 paras 13,15;
         NIHB sch 7 paras 51,53; NIHB60+ sch 7 paras 13,15;
         CTP sch 1 para 16(1), sch 6 paras 13,15; CTR sch 9 paras 13,15, sch 10 paras 58,60

from a war pension) made to compensate for the fact that, during the Second World War, the claimant or partner or either's deceased spouse or civil partner:

+ was a slave labourer or a forced labourer; or
+ had suffered property loss or personal injury; or
+ was a parent of a child who had died.

13.124 Subject to the over-riding £20 disregard (para. 13.160), £10.00 per week is disregarded as income from any pension paid by the German or Austrian Government to the victims of Nazi persecution for the period it covers. There is no disregard of the capital value of arrears.

Other items of income and capital

Maintenance received for a child

13.125 Disregard in full as income any payments received towards the maintenance of a child for all pension age claims, and also in the case of a working age claim if it is paid (whether voluntarily or under an order or agreement) by any 'liable relative'. Liable relative means.

+ a spouse or civil partner from whom the claimant or partner is separated or divorced;
+ a parent (including step-parent) of a dependent child or young person (paras. 4.24-25), or of a child or young person who does not count as a member of the claimant's family because they are claiming IS, JSA(IB) or ESA(IR) themselves;
+ a person who is making payments of maintenance and who for that reason may reasonably be treated as the father (regardless of whether fatherhood has been settled by, say, a court).

Maintenance received for an adult

13.126 If maintenance is received by the claimant or their partner that is not child maintenance (para. 13.125), then disregard £15 as unearned income – but only if there is at least one child or young person in the family (i.e. they receive the family premium) and:

+ in the case of working age claims the payment is made by the claimant's former partner or the claimant's partner's former partner;

13.124 HB sch 5 para 15(g); HB60+ sch 5 para 1(g); NIHB sch 6 para 15(f); NIHB60+ sch 6 para 2;
CTP sch 5 para 1(g); CTR sch 6 para 1(g)

13.125 HB sch 5 para 47A; HB60+ 29(1)(o); NIHB sch 6 para 49A; NIHB60+ 27(1)(m); CTP sch 1 para 16(1)(o);
CTR 39(1)(o), sch 8 para 50

13.126 HB sch 5 para 47; HB60+ sch 5 para 20; NIHB sch 6 para 49; NIHB60+ sch 6 para 21;
CTP sch 5 para 20; CTR sch 6 para 20, sch 8 para 49

◆ in the case of pension age claims the payment is made by the spouse, civil partner, former spouse or former civil partner of either the claimant or the claimant's partner.

If two or more maintenance payments are received in any week the maximum disregard is £15.

Government work programme training schemes

13.127 People on government work programme training schemes are normally also on JSA(IB), ESA(IR) or IS (paras. 13.3 and 13.37-38). The rules for people on a training scheme but who are not on JSA(IB), ESA(IR) or IS are so rarely needed that they are not given in full here but there are two possibilities:

◆ for pension age claims, all such payments are disregarded as income: there are no further conditions;

◆ for working age claims, expenses payments for travel etc are disregarded as income and capital. The treatment of other payments depends on the particular type of training scheme (e.g. Access to Work, Lone Parent Work Search, Better Off In Work Credit). For details see GM BW2.597-611.

Sports awards

13.128 For pension age claims, these are disregarded if paid as income but counted if paid as capital. For working age claims, they are dealt with as follows:

◆ Any amounts awarded in respect of the claimant's or a member of the family's food (excluding vitamins, minerals or other special performance-enhancing dietary supplements), ordinary clothing or footwear (excluding school uniform and sportswear), household fuel, rent, council tax, water charges or in Northern Ireland eligible rates, are counted in full as income or capital as appropriate.

◆ Any other amounts are disregarded as unearned income, and as capital for 26 weeks from the date of payment.

Charitable and/or voluntary payments

13.129 Payments which are charitable and/or voluntary (such as payments from family, friends or charities) are assessed as follows:

◆ payments of income are disregarded in all circumstances;

◆ lump sum payments in kind (i.e. payments of goods rather than money) are disregarded (as capital);

13.127 HB 2(1),46(7), sch 5 paras A2,A3,13,49,58,60,61; sch 6 paras A2,A3,8,35, 43,44,49; NIHB 2(1),43(7), sch 6 paras 12,51,60, sch 7 paras 8,36,44; CTR 2(1),64(8), sch 8 paras 2,3,18,51,60,62,63, sch 10 paras 11,39,47,48,53

13.128 HB 2(1), sch 5 para 59, sch 6 para 50; HB60+ 29(1); NIHB 2(1), sch 6 para 61, sch 7 para 49; NIHB60+ 27(1); CTP sch 1 para 16(1); CTR 2(1),39(1), sch 8 para 61, sch 10 para 54

13.129 HB 46(6), sch 5 para 14, sch 6 para 34; HB60+29(1); NIHB 43(6), sch 6 para 14, sch 7 para 35; NIHB60+ 27(1); CTP sch 1 para 16(1); CTB 39(1),64(7), sch 8 para 9, sch 10 para 38

* other payments of capital are disregarded for pension age claims but count as capital for working age claims.

These rules are of particular importance when a claimant has no income other than the above (e.g. during a period when he or she fails to 'sign on') and thus qualifies for maximum HB/CTR (paras. 5.19 and 6.10).

Payments in kind

13.130 A 'payment in kind' is a payment made in goods (e.g. fuel, food) rather than in money (e.g. cheques, cash). Payments in kind of unearned income are always disregarded (and see para. 13.129). Payments in kind of earned income are usually disregarded (para. 14.40). But payments in kind of self-employed income count in full in the assessment of that income (because there is no specific disregard in such a case).

Concessionary coal and cash in lieu

13.131 Concessionary coal is disregarded as income, being a payment in kind. Cash in lieu of concessionary coal counts as income for working age claims *(R v Doncaster Metropolitan Borough Council and Another ex p Doulton)*, but is disregarded as income for pension age claims.

Health benefits and prison visits payments

13.132 All the following payments are disregarded in full as unearned income (and for working age claims are also disregarded as capital for 52 weeks from the date of payment):

* payments for travel for hospital visits;
* health service supplies or payments in lieu of free milk and vitamins;
* healthy start vouchers;
* Home Office payments for travel for prison visits.

Jurors' allowances

13.133 These are disregarded for pension age claims. For working age claims, they are disregarded except insofar as they compensate for loss of earnings or loss of a social security benefit. The exception is that neither disregard applies to CTR in Scotland.

13.130 HB 40(1), sch 5 para 23; HB60+ 29(1); NIHB 37(1), sch 6 para 24; NIHB60+ 27(1); CTP sch 1 para 16(1); CTR 39(1),54(1), sch 8 para 28

13.131 HB 40(1), sch 5 para 23; HB60+ 29(1); NIHB 37(1), sch 6 para 24; NIHB60+ 27(1); CTP sch 1 para 16(1); CTR 39(1),54(1), sch 8 para 28

13.132 HB sch 5 paras 44-46, sch 6 paras 40-42; HB60+ 29(1), sch 6 para 26C; NIHB sch 6 paras 46-48, sch 7 paras 41-43; NIHB60+ 27(1), sch 9 para 38A; CTP sch 1 para 16(1); CTR 39(1), sch 8 paras 46-48, sch 10 paras 43-46

13.133 HB sch 5 para 39; HB60+ 29(1); NIHB sch 6 para 41; NIHB60+ 27(1); CTP sch 1 para 16(1); CTR 39(1), sch 8 para 4

Gallantry awards

13.134   For working age claims, the following are disregarded (as both income and capital without time limit); but for pension age claims, surprisingly, they count in full as capital (apart from any amounts paid as income, which are disregarded): Victoria Cross and George Cross payments; the lump sum payments of up to £6,000 for those who have agreed not to receive any further payments of income from those; and analogous awards for gallantry from this country or another country.

Parental contributions to students

13.135   The following rules apply to contributions made by claimants to a student son or daughter ('student' is defined in paras. 22.5-18):

◆   If a claimant has been assessed as being able to make a contribution to the student's grant (other than a discretionary grant) or loan, the whole of the assessed contribution is disregarded from the claimant's income.

◆   If a claimant contributes towards the maintenance of a student under the age of 25, who has a discretionary grant or no grant, the amount of the contribution is disregarded in the assessment of the claimant's income – but only up to a maximum weekly figure. The maximum weekly figure is £56.80 minus the weekly amount of any discretionary grant.

So far as possible the above are disregarded from unearned income, then any balance is disregarded from earned income.

Education Maintenance Allowances, etc

13.136   Disregard (as income) Education Maintenance Allowances or Awards (EMAs), including Assisted Places Allowances and, in England only, similar payments under section 14 of the Finance Act 2002 (which are gradually replacing EMAs). These payments are usually for 16 to 18-year-olds in non-advanced education or towards a child's travel to school. For working age claims only, disregard EMA bonuses as capital for 52 weeks from the date of payment.

Service user group members' expenses

13.137   Expenses paid to members of service user groups (for health authorities, social landlords, etc) are disregarded as income.

13.134   HB sch 5 para 10, sch 6 para 47; HB60+ 29(1); NIHB sch 6 para 11, sch 7 para 46; NIHB60+ 27(1); CTP sch 1 para 16(1); CTR 39(1), sch 8 para 15, sch 10 para 52

13.135   HB sch 4 para 11, sch 5 paras 19,20; HB60+ sch 4 para 6, sch 5 paras 18,19; NIHB sch 5 para 11, sch 6 paras 20,21; NIHB60+ sch 5 para 6, sch 6 paras 19,20; CTP sch 4 para 7, sch 5 paras 18,19; CTR sch 5 para 7, sch 7 para 13, sch 8 paras 23,24

13.136   HB sch 5 para 11, sch 6 para 51; HB60+ 29(1); NIHB sch 6 para 12, sch 7 para 49; NIHB60+ 27(1); CTP sch 1 para 16(1), sch 5 para 53; CTR 39(1), sch 8 para 16, sch 10 para 55

13.137   HB 35(2)(d), sch 5 para 2A; HB60+ 35(2)(f); NIHB 32(2)(d), sch 6 para 2A; NIHB60+ 33(2)(e); CTP sch 1 para 18(2)(f); CTR 41(2)(t), 51(2)(d), sch 8 para 6

Career development loans

13.138 In Great Britain only, career development loans are paid under arrangements between the Learning and Skills Council and certain national banks. For pension age claims, they are disregarded as income. For working age claims, only the element of the loan which relates to living expenses is taken into account, and even this is disregarded if the course which the loan supports has been completed. Note that this rule does not apply to other types of loan for living expenses for people who are undertaking education or training.

Assistance with repaying student loans

13.139 Disregard (as unearned income) any payment made to a former student to help with repaying his or her student loan. This applies whether the payer pays it direct or via the ex-student. It includes Government payments under the Teacher Repayment Loan Scheme, but also includes any other case.

Loans

13.140 A genuine loan increases a person's capital (until and to the extent that he or she spends it). However, it is at least possible for a loan to be income (*Morrell v Secretary of State for Work and Pensions* reported as *R(IS) 6/03,* and see para. 13.12) depending on the circumstances of the case, but the burden of proof that it should be lies with the authority *(CH/2675/2007).* Note that the law expressly requires this in the case of student loans (paras. 22.30-35), career development loans for working age claims (para. 13.138) and equity release schemes for pension age claims (para. 13.104).

Outstanding instalments of capital

13.141 For pension age claims, outstanding instalments of capital count as capital when received (para. 13.15).

13.142 For working age claims, if at the claimant's date of claim for HB/CTR (or the date of any reconsideration), he or she is entitled to outstanding instalments of capital (i.e. instalments due after that date), the authority must consider whether the sum of the outstanding instalments and the claimant's other capital exceeds £16,000. If it does, the outstanding instalments are disregarded as capital but are counted as income. The law does not set out a way of doing this. If it does not, the outstanding instalments are counted as capital from the date of claim (or reconsideration).

13.138 HB 41(4), sch 5 para 13; HB60+ 29(1); CTP sch 1 para 16(1); CTR 39(1),55(4), sch 8 para 18

13.139 HB sch 5 para 12; HB60+ 29(1); CTP sch 1 para 16(1); CTP 39(1), sch 8 para 17

13.142 HB 41(1), sch 6 para 18, NIHB 38(1), sch 7 para 19; CTR 55(1), sch 10 para 22

Capital outside the UK

13.143 The following rules apply if a claimant possesses capital in a country outside the UK.

* If there is no prohibition in that country against bringing the money to the UK, value it at its market or surrender value in that country; then disregard 10% if selling it would incur costs; then disregard any mortgage or other 'encumbrance' (e.g. a loan) secured on it; then disregard any charge for converting it into sterling; and count the remainder as capital.

* If there is such a prohibition, value it at what a willing buyer in the UK would give for it; then disregard 10% if selling it would incur costs; then disregard any mortgage or other 'encumbrance' (e.g. a loan) secured on it; and count the remainder as capital.

Income outside the UK

13.144 The following rules apply if a claimant is entitled to income (including earnings as well as unearned income) payable in a country outside the UK.

* If there is no prohibition in that country against bringing the money to the UK, treat it as income in the normal way, allowing any disregard which may apply (including any earnings disregard in the case of earned income); also disregard any charge for converting it into sterling.

* If there is such a prohibition, disregard it. For working age claims, also disregard as capital the value of the right to receive income from it (para. 13.92).

Expenses for unpaid work

13.145 Expenses for unpaid work (whether for a charity, voluntary organisation, friend or neighbour) are disregarded. (For expenses for paid work, see para. 14.43.)

Notional income and capital

13.146 In the situations described below a claimant is treated as possessing income and/or capital he or she does not in fact possess – known as 'notional' income and/or capital. The notional income or capital is assessed as if it was actual income or capital and any relevant disregards must be applied.

13.143 HB 48, sch 6 para 23; HB60+ 46, sch 6 para 23; NIHB 45, sch 7 para 24; NIHB60+ 44, sch 7 para 23; CTP sch 1 para 33, sch 6 para 23; CTR 66, sch 9 para 23, sch 10 para 28

13.144 HB sch 5 paras 24,33, sch 6 para 16; HB60+ sch 5 paras 16,17; NIHB sch 6 paras 25,34, sch 7 para 17; NIHB60+ sch 6 paras 17,18; CTP sch 5 paras 16,17; CTR sch 6 paras 16,17, sch 8 paras 29,39

13.145 HB sch 5 para 2; HB60+ 29(1); NIHB sch 6 para 2; NIHB60+ 27(1); CTP sch 1 para 16(1); CTR 39(1), sch 8 para 5

13.146 HB 42(11),(12),49(7); HB60+ 47(5); NIHB 39(11),(12),46(7); NIHB60+ 45(5); CTP sch 1 para 34(5); CTR 56(9),(10),67(9)

Deprivation

13.147   A claimant who deliberately deprives himself or herself of capital or income with the purpose of qualifying for HB (or for more HB) is treated as still having it for HB purposes. The same applies independently for CTR. It is the claimant's 'purpose' which must be taken into account (not the item they spent the money on). Whether the claimant seeks to recover the money they have deprived themselves of, appears irrelevant (and this was confirmed in the case of a bankrupt claimant whose receiver did not seek to do so: *[2009] UKUT 96 AAC*.)

13.148   Authorities sometimes (wrongly) confuse what the money was spent on with what the claimant's purpose was. This is emphasised in the case law: 'the test is one of purpose, and the obtaining of benefit should form a positive part of [the claimant's] planning'; and a claimant who had not thought about consequences could not have acted with the purpose of obtaining benefit: *[2011] UKUT 500 (AAC)*. Another case illustrates this *(R(H) 1/06)*. In that case, the claimant was a schizophrenic man without an appointee who lived in 'an intolerable level of chaos'. He had a big windfall and telephoned the authority to arrange for his HB to be stopped. When he re-claimed four months later, he had almost none of this capital left: it had gone on 'alcohol and high living'. The authority said he had deprived himself of this money. The commissioner was satisfied that it had not been shown that the claimant appreciated what he was doing, or the consequences of it; the test whether someone spent capital 'for the purpose of' getting (more) HB is subjective, and should take account of the claimant's mental state and capabilities. For a useful discussion of the case law in deprivation cases see *CH/1367/2008*.

13.149   For pension age claims one special rule applies. It is that repaying or reducing a debt, or purchasing goods or services reasonable in the claimant's circumstances is never deprivation. The rule is automatic, and applies regardless of the claimant's purpose. For any other question of deprivation in the case of this age group, and for all questions of deprivation in the case of working age claims, the claimant's purpose is the only determining factor.

Diminishing notional capital

13.150   If a claimant is treated as having notional capital for the above reason (paras 13.147-149), the amount of notional capital taken into account is reduced each week, broadly speaking, by the amount of any HB, CTR, JSA(IB), ESA(IR) or IS (but not WTC or CTC), lost as a result of the claimant being treated as having notional capital. For further details, see GM paras. BW1.760-807.

13.147   HB 42(1),49(1); HB60+ 41(8),47(1); NIHB 39(1),46(1); NIHB60+ 39(8),45(1);
CTP sch 1 paras 22(9),34(1); CTR 45(9),56(1),67(1)

13.149   HB60+ 47(2); NIHB60+ 45(2); CTP sch 1 para 34(2); CTR 67(2)

13.150   HB 50; HB60+ 48; NIHB 47; NIHB60+ 46; CTP sch 1 para 35; CTR 68,69

Money available on application

13.151 The claimant can be treated as having money which he or she has not applied for but could. The details follow.

13.152 For pension age claims, the rule is limited to the following two items, and does not apply to any other kind of income, or any kind of capital at all:

+ state retirement pension (but not an amount a person does not get because they have chosen a lump sum instead: para. 13.54); and

+ private or occupational pensions.

13.153 For working age claims, any income or capital which the claimant could have on application (in other words, simply by applying for it) is treated as possessed by him or her from the date it could be obtained. For example, this rule is sometimes used in the case of unclaimed child benefit.

13.154 The rule (para. 13.153) does not apply to:

+ working tax credit or child tax credit;

+ income from a DWP rehabilitation allowance;

+ payments under government work programme training schemes (including payments to a scheme provider);

+ income or capital from a discretionary trust or a trust for personal injury (paras. 13.111-117); or

+ any kind of disregarded capital.

Also the DWP advises that this rule should not be applied in the case of income from any other social security benefit unless the authority is sure about the amount the person could receive (GM para. BW2.682).

Payments given to one person but used by another

13.155 If income (including payments in kind: para. 13.130) is paid in A's name but used by B for food, household fuel, clothing or footwear (other than school uniform and sportswear), eligible rent (apart from any non-dependant deduction), council tax, water charges or in Northern Ireland eligible rates, it is treated as belonging to B. For working age claims only, the rule applies also to capital.

13.156 This rule must not be used in relation to the trusts in paragraph 13.118 or income from a service user group (para. 13.137). Nor must it be used in relation to occupational or personal pensions (including payments from the Pension Protection Fund: para. 13.93) if the intended beneficiary is bankrupt or sequestered, and payment is made to a trustee (or similar) for him or her, and any family have no other income.

13.152 HB60+ 2(1),41; NIHB60+ 2(1),39; CTP 2(1), sch 1 para 22; CTR 45

13.153 HB 42; NIHB 39; CTP sch 1 para 23; CTR 46

13.155 HB 42(6)(a),(13),49(3),(8); HB60+ 42; NIHB 39(6)(a),(14),46(3),(8); NIHB60+ 40; CTP sch 1 para 23; CTR 46,56(3),(11),67(5)

Up-ratings

13.157 If the April up-rating date for social security benefits or tax credits is different from that for HB/CTR (table 1.3), they are generally treated as up-rated on the same date as HB/CTR (paras. 17.39-40). The same applies if the 'Assessed Income Figure' (used when the claimant or partner is on savings credit: para. 13.164) changes at that time.

Work paid at less than the going rate

13.158 This rule applies only for working age claims. If the claimant is paid less than the going rate for a job, he or she is treated as having whatever additional pay is reasonable in the circumstances. The means of the employer must be taken into account, as should other relevant factors (for example, at the present time people may have few choices in the labour market). This rule does not apply to voluntary work or to claimants on a government training programme or DWP-approved work placement. When this rule is used, disregard notional tax and national insurance contributions and apply the earnings disregards (paras. 14.14-33).

Relationship to a company

13.159 This rule applies only for working age claims. It applies to a claimant who is not the sole owner of, or a partner in, a company, but whose relationship to that company is analogous to someone who is. In such cases, the claimant's share of the capital of that company is assessed as though he or she was the sole owner or partner (chapter 15) and any actual share of the company he or she possesses is disregarded.

The over-riding £20 disregard from certain income

13.160 In any particular claim for HB/CTR, the maximum weekly disregard per claim is £20 from any or all of the following:

* in Great Britain, certain war pensions for bereavement or disablement (para. 13.59) (but this does not stop an authority from running a local scheme: paras. 13.59);

* widowed parent's allowance (para. 13.56);

* for working age claims, student loan and access fund income (table 22.4 and para. 22.40);

* for pension age claims, certain payments made by trusts (para. 13.112).

13.157 HB 42(8); HB60+ 41(9),(10); NIHB 39(8); NIHB60+ 39(11),(12); CTP sch 1 para 22(13),(14); CTR 45(13),(14),56(5)

13.158 HB 42(9),(10); NIHB 39(9),(10); CTR 56(6),(7)

13.159 HB 49(5),(6); NIHB 46(5),(6); CTR 67(7),(8)

13.160 HB sch 5 para 34; HB60+ sch 5 para 12(3); NIHB sch 6 para 35; NIHB60+ sch 6 para 13(3); CTP sch 5 para 12(3); CTR sch 6 para 12(3), sch 8 para 40

Assessing people on savings credit

13.161 This section explains how income and capital are assessed for HB/CTR if the claimant or any partner is on savings credit (so long as they are not also on guarantee credit). It over-rides the rules described earlier in this chapter.

Income and capital are assessed by the DWP

13.162 A claimant on savings credit has had their income and capital assessed by the DWP (i.e. the pension, disability and carers service). With the exceptions mentioned below, the authority must use the DWP's assessment of income and capital in assessing the claimant's HB/CTR. Table 17.4 gives more information about the date these figures take effect.

The DWP must notify the authority

13.163 The DWP must notify the authority of its assessment of income and capital within two working days of the following (or in either case as soon as reasonably practicable thereafter):

♦ the date the DWP did the assessment, if the person has already claimed or is already on HB/CTR by that time; or

♦ the date the authority informs the DWP that the claimant or partner has claimed HB/CTR, in all other cases.

13.164 In particular, the DWP must include in the decision notice its 'assessed income figure' ('AIF'). This is the DWP's assessment of the person's net weekly income (including tariff income).

13.165 If the DWP notifies the authority of new figures at any time, this is implemented as a change of circumstances in the HB/CTR claim (table 17.4).

When the authority adjusts the DWP's assessed income figure

13.166 Once the DWP has notified the authority of the claimant's assessed income figure, it is adjusted by the authority – but only if one (or more) of the things in table 13.5 applies. This is simply to reflect differences in assessing income for pension credit purposes as opposed to HB/CTR purposes. An example is at the end of this chapter.

When the authority adjusts the DWP's capital figure

13.167 The capital figure notified by the DWP is never (apart from the one exception below) adjusted. In particular, if the DWP notifies a figure above £16,000, the claimant is not entitled to HB/CTR at that time.

13.162 HB60+ 27(1); NIHB60+ 25(1); CTP sch 1 para 14(1); CTR 36(1)

13.163 HB60+ 27(2),(3); NIHB60+ 25(2),(3)

13.166 HB60+ 27(4),(5); NIHB60+ 25(4),(5); CTP sch 1 para 14(2),(3); CTR (2),(3)

13.167 HB60+ 27(6),(7); NIHB60+ 25(6),(7); CTP sch 1 para 14(5); CTR 36(5)

Table 13.5: Claimants on savings credit: adjustments to the DWP's assessed income figure (AIF)

All the amounts mentioned in this table are weekly.

(a) Start with the DWP's assessed income figure

(b) Add the amount of savings credit payable

(c) If the claimant receives the following, deduct the amount shown*:

• earned income if the claimant is a lone parent	£5 (table 14.1)
• earned income if the claimant is doing exempt work	£99.50 or £20 as appropriate (table 14.1)
• earned income if the claimant meets the conditions for the additional earnings disregard	£17.10 (para. 14.30)
• earned income if the claimant meets the conditions for the child care disregard	the whole amount, up to the appropriate limit (para. 14.17)
• maintenance received from a current or former spouse or civil partner	the full HB/CTR disregard (paras. 13.125-126)
• pensions for war bereavement or disablement	any amount disregarded under a local scheme (i.e. any amount over £10: para. 13.59)

(d) Make the following (very rare) adjustments if appropriate:

- add the income of any partner who was ignored in assessing pension credit but has to be taken into account in HB/CTR

- if the authority determines that a non-dependant's income and capital should be used instead of the claimant's (para 13.7), use this income instead of the DWP's assessment

* Each deduction equals the difference between what is disregarded in the assessment of pension credit and what is disregarded in HB and CTR (but in CTR in England can be subject to the details of any local variations for working age claims).

13.168 The one exception works as follows. If the DWP notified the authority that the claimant's capital was £16,000 or lower and then the claimant's capital rises above £16,000 during the course of the DWP's 'assessed income period' (the period during which the DWP does not reconsider the amount of a claimant's income or capital) then entitlement to HB/CTR ends.

Example: A war widow on savings credit

Information

A war widow aged 81 gets savings credit of £12.00 per week. She also gets a war widow's pension of £57.60 per week and retirement pension and an occupational pension, and has some capital.

The DWP notifies the authority of its assessed income figure (AIF) of £155.05 and notifies her capital as being £12,000. The authority dealing with her claim has a local scheme whereby it disregards the whole of a war widow's pension.

Assessment (table 13.5)

The authority starts with the DWP's assessed income figure (£155.05) and adds her savings credit (£12.00), giving a total of £167.05.

It then disregards all but £10.00 of the war widow's pension of £57.60 (in other words, it disregards £47.60). This gives her net income for HB/CTR purposes of £119.45 per week. It must use this figure in calculating her entitlement to HB/CTR.

In this case, this is less than her applicable amount (only £10 of her war pension is disregarded for state pension credit) and she is entitled to maximum HB/CTR.

The authority must accept that her capital is £12,000 at the outset (and must not calculate tariff income because the DWP has already included this in the AIF).

If evidence later arises of an increase in her capital, perhaps taking it above £16,000, the authority must re-assess her capital; but no action is taken upon this re-assessment unless the amount is greater than £16,000.

13.168 HB60+ 27(8); NIHB60+ 25(8); CTP sch 1 para 14(4),(5); CTR 36(4),(5)

Assessing people on universal credit

13.169 This section explains how income and capital are assessed for CTR if the claimant or any partner is on universal credit. It overrides the rules described earlier in the chapter. However, the rules for CTR in Scotland may differ when UC cases are introduced there.

For HB, it is expected that rules similar to the following may apply in exempt accommodation cases (but in all other cases claimants on UC cannot get HB: para. 23.xx).

Income and capital are assessed by the DWP

13.170 A claimant on universal credit has their income and capital as assessed by the DWP. With the adjustments mentioned below, the authority must use the DWP's income and capital figures in assessing HB/CTR.

When the authority adjusts the DWP's figures

13.171 The authority adjusts the DWP's income figure as shown in table 13.6. The DWP's capital figure is not adjusted.

Table 13.6: Claimants on universal credit: adjustments to the DWP's income figure

---

(a) Start with the DWP's monthly income figure.

(b) Add the monthly amount of universal credit payable.

(c) Multiply the above by 12 and divide by 52 to obtain a weekly figure.

(d) Make the following (very rare) adjustment if appropriate:

- If the authority determines that a non-dependant's income and capital should be used instead of the claimant's (para. 13.7), use this income instead of the DWP's assessment.

Notes:

Discretionary council tax reductions (para. 10.40) can apply in these cases, as they apply in all CTR cases.

See para. 13.169 for possible exceptions to the rules in this table.

---

14 Employed earners

14.1 This chapter explains how employed earners' income from employment is assessed. It covers:

- deciding who is an employed earner;
- assessing gross earnings over an appropriate period (the assessment period);
- making deductions to arrive at the figure used in calculating HB/CTR;
- the earned income disregards;
- the disregard for child care costs;
- the additional disregard for people working at least 16/30 hours per week;
- particular kinds of earnings and expenses; and
- starting work, absences from work and ending work

This chapter applies only if the claimant and any partner are not on JSA(IB), ESA(IR), IS, pension credit or universal credit (paras. 13.3-4). Apart from that, it applies to the assessment of a claimant's earnings and to those of any partner.

14.2 This chapter does not apply to the earnings of a non-dependant or second adult. The law does not say how this should be done, although it must be gross (not net) of tax and national insurance. In practice, most authorities assess a non-dependant or second adult's income under the rules in this chapter, but using the total (gross) earnings figure rather than the net earnings figure.

CTR variations

14.3 For working age CTR claims in England, the assessment of earnings can vary from authority to authority (para. 10.25), although in practice most authorities have adopted the rules described in this chapter. No variations apply to any other CTR claims.

Who is an 'employed earner'?

14.4 A person is an 'employed earner' if they are employed in Great Britain (or in Northern Ireland employed in NI or the Republic) either under a contract of service, or in an office, with earnings. Employed earners who are employed under a contract of service include employees who work for a wage or salary. The employed earners who work 'in an office' include directors of limited companies (para. 14.42), local authority councillors (para. 14.41) and clergy.

14.3 CTP 14(2),15(2)
14.4 CBA 2(1)(a); IIB 2(1), HB60+ 2(1); NIHB 2(1); NIHB60 + 2(1); CTP 2(1); CTR 2(1)

The assessment of earnings

14.5   The authority needs to work out a net weekly earnings figure after appropriate disregards to use in the benefit calculation. To do this it must:

- identify that there are earnings derived or likely to be derived from employment as an employed earner;
- establish the gross earnings over an appropriate assessment period;
- deduct amounts attributable to income tax and Class 1 national insurance contributions;
- deduct half of any approved pension contribution;
- convert the net amount if necessary to a weekly figure;
- deduct a fixed earned income disregard and, if appropriate, amounts for child care and for certain people working at least 16/30 hours per week.

In certain circumstances notional (rather than actual) earnings are used (para. 13.158) but this does not apply to pension age claims (para. 1.21).

Gross earnings

14.6   Gross earnings means the total amount of earnings after certain work expenses (para. 14.44) have been deducted but before any deductions by the employer for tax, national insurance or anything else.

The assessment period

14.7   The authority must identify an appropriate assessment period that can be used as the basis for calculating or estimating the average weekly earnings figure. Its aim should be to identify the period that provides the most accurate basis on which to do this. The law gives the following guidelines for this:

- (a) if the earnings relate to a period of one week or less, then weekly gross earnings equal the amount for that period;
- (b) if the earnings are regular and do not fluctuate, then weekly gross earnings are found by taking an average over the period running up to the date of claim or any reconsideration (see para. 14.8);
- (c) if the claimant has not been employed long enough for (b) to apply, then weekly gross earnings are based on what the claimant has been paid, so long as this is representative;
- (d) if the claimant's hours vary over a recognisable cycle, then weekly gross earnings are averaged over the period of the complete cycle (including any periods where the claimant does no work, but excluding other absences). This is specified in the law only for pension age claims but would equally be reasonable for working age claims;

14.7   HB 2(1),29; HB 60+ 2(1),33; NIHB 2(1),26; NIHB60+ 2(1) 31; CTP 2(1), sch 1 para 17; CTR 2(1),40,47,50

(e) if it would be fairer to do so, or there is as yet no evidence of earnings, then weekly gross earnings should be assessed from a certificate of (actual or estimated) earnings. Authorities usually include these with their application forms for claimants to give to their employers to complete;

(f) if some other method would produce a fairer estimate of weekly gross earnings, then that method is used.

When earnings begin or change during an award, the above points apply again.

14.8 When applying method (b) above, there are small differences depending on age:

◆ for working age claims (para. 1.21), they are averaged over:
  • the previous five weeks if the claimant is paid weekly, or
  • the previous two months if the claimant is paid monthly, or
  • any period which would produce a fairer result;
◆ for pension age claims (para. 1.21) they are averaged over:
  • the previous four payments if the last two are less than one month apart, or
  • the previous two payments if those are one month or more apart, or
  • any period which would produce a fairer result.

Examples: Weekly net earnings

The 'net earnings' figures below meet the definition in paragraph 14.9.

1. Straightforward weekly earnings

A claimant's net earnings have been £224.48 pw over each of the past five weeks, and there is nothing to suggest that they vary in any way.

So the claimant's net earnings are £224.48 pw.

2. Straightforward monthly earnings

A claimant's net earnings have been £1,122.44 pcm over each of the past two months, and there is nothing to suggest that they vary in any way.

So the claimant's net earnings are £1,122.44 pcm, which converts (multiply by 12 and divide by 52) to £259.02 pw.

3. Variable weekly earnings

A claimant's basic net earnings have been £123.45 pw over each of the past five weeks, and there is nothing to suggest that this basic rate of pay varies. But the claimant gets a variable bonus, which everyone agrees has averaged £23.45 net pw over the recent months and will continue to do so.

So the claimant's net earnings are the sum of those two figures, £146.90 pw.

14.8   HB 29; HB60 + 33; NIHB 26; NIHB60 + 31; CTP sch 1 para 17; CTR 40,47,50

4. One-off bonus

A claimant's net earnings have been £960.73 pcm over each of the past two months, and there is nothing to suggest that they vary in any way – except that last month the claimant got a bonus of £250 net. Everyone confirms that this was a one-off bonus when ownership of her place of work changed hands, and is unlikely ever to occur again.

So the claimant's net earnings are £960.73 pcm, which converts (multiply by 12 and divide by 52: para. 6.49) to £221.71 pw. It would be unreasonable to include the bonus in the circumstances given.

5. A variation to earnings

A claimant's net earnings were £250.01 pw over each of the past three weeks, and £265.02 for the two weeks preceding them. The claimant explains that they have taken a small pay cut at his factory, and this is confirmed by the employer.

So the claimant's net earnings are £250.01 pw. After all, based on the information, this is likely to be his earnings in the future.

Calculating net earnings

14.9   Net earnings are the gross earnings over the assessment period less:

* income tax;
* Class 1 national insurance contributions;
* half of any sum paid by the employee towards an occupational or personal pension scheme.

Deducting income tax and national insurance contributions

14.10   When the claimant's actual gross earnings are used (as opposed to an estimate), any income tax or Class 1 national insurance contributions deducted (or paid from them) must be deducted from those earnings. But when the claimant's gross earnings are estimated, notional amounts for the income tax payable (using the basic rate of tax applicable to the assessment period and less only the personal allowance for a person aged under 65, whatever the claimant's actual circumstances) and Class 1 national insurance contributions must be deducted from those estimated earnings on a pro-rata basis.

14.11   If a claimant in Northern Ireland works in the Republic, the amounts deducted are those which the NIHE estimates would have been deducted if they worked in Northern Ireland.

Deducting half of pension contributions

14.12   Whether the claimant's actual or estimated gross earnings are used, half of any contributions they make (or which would be payable on the estimated earnings) to an occupational or personal pension scheme, must be deducted from the gross earnings figure.

Conversion to a weekly figure

14.13   If a claimant's earnings are paid other than weekly, they must be converted to a weekly figure as described in paragraph 6.49.

Earned income disregards

14.14   An earned income disregard is deducted from the claimant's earnings. The amount depends on the type of case (table 14.1). The highest disregard that applies is deducted once only from the total earnings. For example, if the claimant has more than one job, or if the claimant has a partner and they both work, the disregard is made to the combined earnings.

14.15   If the earnings are paid in a foreign currency (including, in Northern Ireland, earnings from employment in the Republic paid in euros), any banking charge or commission that is paid to convert the earnings into sterling is deducted in addition to any earned income disregard.

14.16   In addition to any disregard applied above (paras. 14.14-15) further disregards may also apply where the claimant or their partner:

+ contributes towards the maintenance of a student (para. 13.135);
+ pays child care expenses (para. 14.17);
+ meets the conditions for the additional earnings disregard (para. 14.30) (broadly they work for at least 16/30 hours per week as appropriate).

14.11   NIHB 33; NIHB60 I 34

14.12   HB 36; HB60+ 36; NIHB 33; NIHB60+ 34; CTP sch 1 para 19; CTR 42,52

14.14   HB 36(2), sch 4; HB60+ 36(1), sch 4; NIHB 33(2), sch 5; NIHB60+ 34(1), sch 5; CTP sch 1 para 19(1), sch 4; CTR 42(2),52(2), sch 5, sch 7

14.15   HB sch 4 para 14; HB60+ sch 4 para 10; NIHB sch 5 para 14; NIHB60+ sch 5 para 10; CTP sch 4 para 11; CTR sch 5 para 11, sch 7 para 16

Table 14.1: Weekly earned income disregards

£99.50 – certain permitted work

This weekly disregard applies (per single claimant or couple) to people on ESA(C) (or national insurance credits instead of ESA(C)), incapacity benefit or severe disablement allowance, who have been allowed to earn up to £99.50 pw from 'permitted work' without it affecting those benefits. The disregard in HB/CTR equals the amount received from this permitted work, up to £99.50 pw. The £99.50 upper limit is set at 16 times the national minimum wage so it increases whenever the minimum wage is raised.

£25 – lone parents

Except where the preceding £99.50 disregard applies, this weekly disregard is for anyone who counts as a lone parent for HB/CTR purposes (para. 4.7).

£20 – working age claims:
certain disabled people, carers or special occupations

For working age claims (para. 1.21), except where the £99.50 or £25 disregard applies, this weekly disregard applies to earned income (per single claimant or per couple) in the following cases:

(a) the claimant's applicable amount includes a disability premium (para. 12.20) or severe disability premium (para. 12.35); or a work related activity component or support component (para. 12.17);

(b) if (a) does not apply: the claimant or their partner are in receipt of ESA(C), incapacity benefit or severe disablement allowance (or national insurance credits instead of one of these benefits) and they are allowed by the DWP to earn up £20 in 'permitted work' because they have limited work capability;

(c) if (a) or (b) do not apply: a carer premium has been awarded in the claimant's applicable amount (but in the case of a couple the disregard can only be made from the earnings of the carer); or the claimant or their partner are employed in one of the special occupations listed in paragraph 14.38.

£20 – pension age claims:
certain disabled people, carers or special occupations

For pension age claims (para. 1.21), except where the £99.50 or £25 disregard applies, this weekly disregard applies to earned income (per single claimant or per couple) in the following cases:

(a) the claimant or their partner:

> - are in receipt of any of the qualifying benefits (a) to (f) in paragraph 12.22 or attendance allowance or main phase ESA (para. 12.17);
> - treated as long term sick (para. 12.23) (but unlike the rules for the disability premium it can be either the claimant or their partner);
> - receiving national insurance credits as a result of their ESA claim on the basis that they would have been awarded the work-related component or the support component (paras. 12.17 and 12.45) if ESA had been in payment; or
> - previously qualified for the £20 disregard at least eight weeks before reaching pension credit age (para.1.21) and there have been no breaks of more than eight weeks in either their HB/CTR award or their employment since they attained pension credit age.
>
> (b) if (a) does not apply, rules (b) and (c) for working age claims above apply in the same way to pension age claims.
>
> **£10 or £5 – any other couples or single claimants**
>
> In any case not mentioned above, the weekly disregard is:
>
> - £10 per couple;
> - £5 per single claimant.

The child care disregard

14.17   In addition to the disregards in table 14.1, certain child care costs up to the maximum limit (para. 14.18) are disregarded where both the following conditions are met:

- the claimant is:
  - a lone parent who works 16 hours or more each week (para. 14.21), or
  - part of a couple where both members work 16 hours or more each week (para. 14.21), or
  - part of a couple where one member (claimant or partner) works 16 hours per week and the other is incapacitated (para. 14.26), or in hospital or prison (serving a sentence or on remand), or aged 80 or over; and
- the claimant or their partner pays 'relevant child care costs' (para. 14.27) in respect of a child that satisfies the age condition (para. 14.29).

T14.1   HB 36(2) sch 4 paras 3-11; HB60+ sch 4 paras 1-7; NIHB sch 5 paras ; NIHB60+ sch 5 paras 1 7; CTP sch 4 paras 1-8; CTR sch 5 paras 1-8, sch 7 paras 4-12

14.17   HB 28; HB60+ 31; NIHB 25; NIHB60+ 29; CTP sch 1 para 25; CTR 58

The amount of the child care disregard

14.18 The amount of the disregard equals the amount of the child care costs that the claimant/partner pays up to a maximum of:

+ £175.00 per week if the claimant has one child; or

+ £300.00 per week if the claimant has two or more children.

The child care costs must be 'relevant child care costs' that are paid in respect of a child that satisfies the age condition (paras. 14.27-29).

14.19 The disregard is made as far as possible from earnings (from employment or self-employment). If the disregard is greater than the claimant's and any partner's earnings, the balance is deducted from any working tax credit or child tax credit the claimant or partner receives (para. 13.47). Apart from that, it cannot be disregarded from unearned income.

14.20 The amount the claimant or partner pays is averaged over whichever period, up to a year, gives the most accurate estimate of the charges, taking account of information given by the person providing the care.

Working 16 hours a week

14.21 A person counts as working 16 hours a week if they are in 'remunerative work'. Remunerative work means the same here as in paragraphs 6.22-23, but also (for the purposes of the child care disregard) includes when the person is on sick leave or maternity/paternity/adoption leave: the precise circumstances are described in the following paragraphs.

14.22 A claimant/partner who is on sick leave is treated as being in remunerative work for up to 28 weeks, if they are in receipt of one of the sickness benefits in the next paragraph and they were in work the day before that benefit is first paid. For those paid income support or credited with national insurance contributions the 28 week period begins on the day the person is first paid income support or the first day of the period that the contributions are credited.

14.23 The qualifying sickness benefits (para. 14.22) are: statutory sick pay, short-term incapacity benefit at the lower rate, employment and support allowance, income support awarded on the grounds of incapacity for work, or national insurance contribution credits awarded on the grounds of incapacity for work or limited work capability (para. 12.45).

14.18 HB 27(3); HB60+ 30(3); NIHB 24(3); NIHB60+ 28(3); CTP sch 1 para 24(3); CTR 57(3)

14.19 HB 27(1)(c); HB60+ 30(1)(c); NIHB 24(1)(c); NIHB60+ 28(1)(c); CTP sch 1 para 24(1)(c); CTR 57(1)(c)

14.20 HB 28(10); HB60+ 31(10); NIHB 25(10); NIHB60+ 29(10); CTP sch 1 para 25(q); CTR 58(10)

14.21 HB 28(2)-(4),(14)-(15); HB60+ 31(2)-(4), (14)-(15); NIHB 25(2)-(4), (14)-(15);
NIHB60+ 29(2)-(4), (14)-(15); CTP sch 1 para 25(2)-(4),(15),(16); (14)-(16); CTR 58(2)-(4),(16),(17)

14.24 A claimant/partner who is on maternity, paternity or adoption leave is treated as being in remunerative work if they:

- were in remunerative work in the week before the leave started;
- are continuing to pay relevant child care charges (para. 14.27); and
- are entitled to statutory maternity, paternity or adoption pay, maternity allowance, or income support because of paternity leave.

14.25 Statutory maternity pay, statutory adoption pay and maternity allowance can be paid for a maximum of 39 weeks. A person on maternity, paternity or adoption leave should be treated as in remunerative work from the day the leave starts until the first of the following events occurs:

- the day the leave ends;
- the day entitlement to the statutory pay or allowance ends – if no child care element of working tax credit is in payment on that date; or
- the day that entitlement to the child care element of working tax credit ends.

'Incapacitated'

14.26 The other member of a couple who is not working (para.14.17) counts as 'incapacitated' if:

- the applicable amount includes the support component or the work-related activity component or the disability premium because of that member's limited work capability/disability (paras. 12.17, 12.23);
- they receive:
  - disability living allowance, or attendance allowance or any similar benefit (para. 12.48), or would receive one of these benefits but for the fact that they are in hospital (table 12.4),
  - incapacity benefit paid at the short-term higher rate or long-term rate,
  - severe disablement allowance, or
  - ESA which includes a work-related or support component;
- they are the claimant and have been accepted by the DWP as having limited work capability (para. 12.17) or as being incapable of work (para. 12.23) for a continuous period of 196 days (ignoring any breaks of up to 12 or eight weeks respectively); or
- they have an NHS invalid carriage or other similar vehicle.

Relevant child care costs

14.27 To qualify for the child care disregard (para. 14.17), the claimant or partner must be paying one or more of the following to care for at least one child in their family (so long as that child satisfies the age condition: para. 14.29):

14.26 HB 28(11); HB60+ 31(11); NIHB 25(11), NIHB60+ 29(11); CTP sch 1 para 25(10); CTP 58(11)

- a registered child-minder, nursery or play scheme;
- a child-minding scheme for which registration is not required (e.g. run by a school, local authority or, in Northern Ireland, Crown property);
- child care approved for working tax credit purposes;
- any other out-of-school-hours scheme provided by a school on school premises or by a local authority (in Northern Ireland an education and library board or HSS trust) – but, in this case only, the child must be aged 8 or more;
- a foster parent/kinship carer (so long as they are not the foster parent/kinship carer of the child in question) – under the Fostering Services Regulations 2002 (or equivalent provisions in Wales), or Looked After Children (Scotland) Regulations 2009;
- a domiciliary care worker – under the Domiciliary Care Agencies Regulations 2002 (or equivalent provisions in Wales); or
- anyone else who is not a relative of the child, where the care is provided wholly or mainly in the child's home. For this purpose, 'relative' has the meaning given in paragraph 8.59.

14.28   The last item includes care provided by a friend who comes in to look after the claimant's children in the claimant's home, but not care provided by (say) the child's grandparent (because a grandparent is a 'relative'). And the disregard does not apply to payments in respect of compulsory education, nor to payments made by a claimant to his or her partner (or vice versa) if the child is the responsibility of at least one of them (para. 4.31).

The age condition

14.29   A child satisfies the age condition until:

- the first Monday in September after their 15th birthday; or
- if the child meets the conditions for a disabled child premium (para. 12.31), or would do so except for having regained sight, the first Monday in September after their 16th birthday.

14.27   HB 28(7),(8); HB60+ 31(7),(8); NIHB 25(7),(8); NIHB60+ 29(7),(8); CTP sch 1 para 25(7),(8); CTR 58(7),(8)

14.29   HB 28(6),(13); HB60+ 31(6),(13); NIHB 25(6),(13); NIHB60+ 29(6),(13); CTP sch 1 para 25(6),(13); CTR 58(6),(14)

The additional earnings disregard

14.30   In addition to the disregards in table 14.1 (and para. 14.17 if applicable), the additional earnings disregard is made if:

- the claimant or any partner receives the 30 hour element in their working tax credit (which means that HMRC considers they meet the conditions); or
- they meet one of the conditions in paragraph 14.32 (which means the authority considers they meet the conditions regardless of any working tax credit award).

The amount of the disregard and how it is applied

14.31   The additional earnings disregard is £17.10 per week. It is deducted from earned income except if (along with the other earned income disregard(s) which apply: paras. 14.15-17) it would result in a negative earned income figure, in which case the deduction is made in assessing income from working tax credit (para. 13.47).

Qualifying when there is no 30 hour tax credit award

14.32   If the claimant/partner does not receive the 30 hour element of working tax credit (para. 14.30) they nonetheless qualify for the disregard if they meet one of the following conditions:

- the claimant or any partner is aged at least 25 and that person works on average for at least 30 hours per week;
- the claimant (or their partner if they have one) works on average for at least 16 hours per week and they are responsible for a dependent child or young person;
- in the case of working age claims (para. 1.21), the claimant (or their partner if they have one) works on average for at least 16 hours per week and their applicable amount includes a disability premium or the work related activity component or the support component; or
- in the case of pension age claims (para. 1.21), the claimant (or their partner if they have one) works on average for 16 hours per week and that person (i.e. in the case of a couple the one that works) meets the conditions for the disabled/long-term sick earned income disregard (table 14.1).

14.33   For the above purposes, the question of whether anyone works 16 hours or more per week on average is decided as in paragraphs 6.22-23; and the question of whether anyone works 30 hours or more per week on average is decided in the same way (apart from the different number of hours).

14.30   HB sch 4 para 17; HB60+ sch 4 para 9; NIHB sch 5 para 17; NIHB60+ sch 5 para 9; CTP sch 4 para 10; CTR sch 5 para 10, sch 7 para 18

14.31   HB sch 5 para. 56; HB60+ sch 5 para. 21; CTP sch 5, para 21; CTR sch 6 para 21, sch 8 para 58

Particular kinds of earnings and expenses

Bonuses, tips and commission

14.34   All forms of bonuses, tips and commission derived from the employment are included in the assessment of gross earnings.

Arrears of earnings

14.35   Any arrears of pay count as earnings for the period they relate to.

Tax refunds

14.36   For working age claims (para. 1.21) tax refunds on earnings count as capital (not earnings), including in Northern Ireland any similar payments from the Irish Republic.

Earnings paid in a lump sum

14.37   For working age claims (para. 1.21), if the claimant or partner have earnings that are paid in a lump sum (or in any other form which could in broad terms be characterised as capital), they are however counted as earnings. They are averaged over the period they cover. This applies to lump sum payments in settlement of claims under equal pay, sex discrimination and similar legislation (table 13.2).

Special occupations annual bounty

14.38   For working age claims (para. 1.21), any bounty paid by the special occupations counts as capital (not earnings) if it is paid annually or at longer intervals. For these purposes the 'special occupations' means part-time fire-fighters, auxiliary coast guards, part-time life-boat workers, and members of the Territorial Army or similar reserve forces.

Non-cash vouchers

14.39   If an employee receives non-cash vouchers that are taken into account in the calculation of national insurance contributions, their value is counted as earnings and should appear on pay slips (circular HB/CTB A17/1999). Non-cash vouchers that are not taken into account in the calculation of national insurance contributions are disregarded as a payment in kind (para. 14.40).

14.34   HB 35(1); HB60+ 35(1); NIHB 32(1); NIHB60+ 33(1); CTP sch 1 para 18(1); CTR 41(1),51(1)

14.35   HB 79(7); HB60+ 59(7); NIHB 77(9); NIHB60+ 57(9); CTP sch 1 para 46(9); CTR 107(9),50(9)

14.36   HB 46(2); NIHB 43(2); CTR 64(2),(3)

14.37   HB 41(3); NIHB 38(3); CTR 55(3)

14.38   HB 46(1); NIHB 43(1); CTR 64(2)

14.39   HB 35(1)(k); HB60+ 35(1)(g); NIHB 32(1)(l); NIHB60+ 33(1)(g); CTP sch 1 para 18(1)(g); CTR 41(1)(g) 51(1)(l)

Payments in kind

14.40　With the exception of certain non-cash vouchers (para. 14.39), payments in kind (i.e. payments of goods rather than money) do not count as earnings and are completely disregarded (para. 13.130). The DWP advises (GM paras. BW2.99-101) that credits received by way of Local Exchange Trading Schemes ('LETS') do not count as payments in kind, but should be given a cash value as earnings.

Councillors' allowances

14.41　Councillors' allowances, except for expenses payments, count as employed earnings *(R(IS) 6/92)*. (For further advice on these, see GM paras. BW2.83-95.)

Company directors

14.42　Company directors (registered with Companies House) are 'office holders' (para. 14.4) and are therefore employed earners:

- the income paid by the company to the director is assessed as earned income under the usual rules;
- their interest (or share of it) in the company is assessed as capital (and see also para. 13.159).

Work expenses

14.43　The treatment of work expenses met by an employer is as follows:

- if they are for travel to work, or for the cost of caring for a child or other dependant, these must be added in as part of the employee's earnings;
- if they are for other items wholly, exclusively and necessarily incurred in the performance of the job, these are disregarded in full.

14.44　Work expenses met by an employee and not paid back by the employer may not be disregarded against the employee's earnings (but see paragraph 14.17 as regards child care expenses). But if they are wholly and exclusively (see para. 15.22) and necessarily incurred in the performance of the employment (e.g. travel costs between work places as opposed to travel to the claimant's place of employment) they should be deducted to arrive at the gross earnings figure that is used as the starting point for the calculation of net earnings *(R(IS) 16/93* and *CIS 507/94)*. Some employed earners may not have a 'place of employment', for example, a care worker who could be asked to work anywhere in a particular authority's area, in which case all of the travel expenses paid by the employer should be disregarded *(CH/1330/2008)*.

14.43　HB 35(1)(f),(2)(b), sch 5 para 3; HB60+ 29(1)(f),(2)(b); NIHB 32(1)(f),(2)(b), sch 6 para 3; NIHB60+ 33(1)(f),(2)(b); CTP sch 1 para 18(1)(f),(2)(b); CIR 41(1)(f),51(1)(f), sch 8 para 7

Expenses in unpaid work

14.45　Expenses received by a person doing unpaid work are disregarded in full if they are paid by a charitable organisation or non-profit-making voluntary organisation, or if the person does any kind of work voluntarily. Expenses paid to members of service user groups (para. 13.133) are also disregarded.

Starting work

14.46　When a claimant starts work, earnings should be taken into account from the beginning of the job – not (if different) the first pay day (but note the rules on 'extended payments' – paras. 17.42-49; and for changes of circumstances see chapter 17).

Advances or loans from an employer

14.47　An advance of earnings or employer loan counts as capital, not earnings. (This is to stop them being counted twice: after all, no deduction can be made from gross earnings when the person repays them.)

Absences from work and ending work

14.48　The general rules are described below. More details are in tables 14.2 and 14.3 (and for changes of circumstances see chapter 17).

Holiday pay

14.49　Holiday pay counts as earnings (see tables 14.2 and 14.3) but:

- any holiday pay from employment which ended before the first day of HB/CTR entitlement is disregarded; and

- for pension age claims, any holiday pay payable more than four weeks after an absence, break or ending work (tables 14.2 and 14.3), counts as capital.

Sick pay, maternity pay, paternity pay and adoption pay

14.50　Statutory sick pay, maternity pay, ordinary and additional paternity pay and adoption pay, and employer's sick, maternity, paternity and adoption pay, and corresponding Northern Ireland payments (or in Northern Ireland, corresponding Great Britain payments or payments from the Republic), count as earnings (but see table 14.2).

14.45　HB sch 5 para 2; HB60+ 29(1); NIHB sch 6 para 2; NIHB60+ 27(1); CTR sch 1 para 16(1); CTR sch 8 para 5

14.47　HB 46(5); NIHB 43(5); CTR 64(6)

14.48　HB 35; HB60+ 35; NIHB 32; NIHB60+ 33; CTP sch 1 para 18; CTR 41,51

14.49　HB 35(1)(d),46(3); HB60+ 35(1)(d), sch 4 para 8; NIHB 32(1)(d),43(3); NIHB60+ 33(1)(d), sch 5 para 8; CTP sch 1 para 18(1)(d), sch 4 para 9; CTR 64(4), sch 7 para 2, sch 5 para 9

14.50　HB 2(1), 35(1)(i),36(3); HB60+ 35(1)(h)-(j); NIHB 2(1), 32(1)(i)(j),33(3); NIHB60+ 33(1)(h)-(j),(l); CTP 2(1), sch 1 paras 18(1)(h)-(l),19(2); CTR 42(2),52(3)

Retainers

14.51   Retainers are payments made for a period when no actual work is done, for example to employees of school meals services during the school holidays. These count as earnings (but see tables 14.2 and 14.3).

Strike pay

14.52   Strike pay does not count as earned income (since it is not paid by an employer). For working age claims (para. 1.21) it counts as unearned income (but see tables 14.2 and 14.3) and for pension age claims it is disregarded (para. 13.8).

Table 14.2: Absences from work

Periods while someone receives a retainer

+ Reassess earnings if they change (for example, if the person is paid less during the summer holidays). (See also para. 14.7(d).)

Holidays, absences without good cause, and strikes

+ Reassess earnings if they change (for example, if the person is paid less during holidays, or nothing during a strike). (See also para. 14.49.)

Sick leave, maternity leave, paternity leave, adoption leave, lay off, suspension and other absences with good cause

The following rules apply so long as the employment has not terminated.

+ If the absence for any of these reasons began before the first day of entitlement to HB/CTR count only the following as earnings (and only if they are received during the absence):
    • retainers;
    • statutory or employer's sick, maternity, paternity or adoption pay;
+ If the absence for any of these reasons begins on or after the first day of entitlement to HB/CTR reassess earnings if they change (e.g. their pay is lower). See also para. 14.49.

14.51   HB 35(1)(e); HB60+ 35(1)(e); NIHB 32(1)(e); NIHB60+ 33(1)(e); CTP sch 1 para 18(1)(e); CTR 41(1)(e),51(1)(e)

14.52   HB60+ 29(1); NIHB60+ 27(1); CTP sch 1 para 16(1); CTR 39(1)

T 14.2   HB sch 4 paras 1(c), 2; CTP sch 4 para 9; CTR sch 5 para 9, sch 7 paras 1,2

Redundancy payments

14.53   Redundancy payments (including those paid periodically rather than in a lump sum) do not count as earnings. They count as capital (but see table 14.3 for the treatment of other payments which may be made on redundancy – such as payments in lieu of notice (i.e. instead of notice) and compensation payments).

Table 14.3: Ending work

Pension age claims (para. 1.21) – ending work

Disregard any earnings (except royalties etc, paras. 15.41-43) from employment which ended before the first day of entitlement to HB/CTR.

Working age claims (para. 1.21) – ending remunerative work

(16 or more hours per week: para 6.22)

If remunerative work ends before the first day of entitlement to HB/CTR for any reason other than retirement disregard all earnings except:

* a retainer;

* any employment tribunal award including any 'out of court' settlement.

Working age claims (para. 1.21) – ending part-time work

(Under 16 hours per week: para 6.22)

If employment ends before the first day of entitlement to HB/CTR disregard all earnings except for retainers.

Other circumstances

In all cases (remunerative/non-remunerative work and regardless of age) if employment ends on or after the first day of entitlement the authority should reassess to take changes and ending of earnings into account under the general rules about changes of circumstance (chapter 17).

14.53   HB 35(1)(b),(g); HB60+ 35(1)(b); NIHB 32(1)(b),(g); NIHB60+ 33(1)(b); CTP sch 1 para 18(1)(b);
        CTR 41(1)(b),51(1)(b),(g)

T 14.3 HB sch 4 paras 1(b), 2; HB 60+ sch 2 para 8; CTP sch 4 para 9; CTBR sch 5 para 9, sch 7 paras 1,2;
        HB 35(1)(e); HB60+ 35(1)(e); NIHB 32(1)(e); NIHB60+ 33(1)(e); CTP sch 1 para 18(1); CTR 41,25(1)(e)

15 The self-employed

15.1 This chapter gives the rules for assessing income and capital from self-employment. It covers:

- deciding who is self-employed;
- deciding what assessment period to use;
- establishing the gross income derived from the business during that period;
- establishing the allowable expenditure during that period;
- calculating pre-tax profit (chargeable income) for that period;
- allowing for tax and national insurance;
- allowing for half of any pension contributions; and
- calculating net profit.

15.2 This chapter applies only if the claimant and any partner are not on JSA(IB), ESA(IR), income support, pension credit or, for CTR assessment, universal credit. Apart from that, it applies to the self-employed capital and income of a claimant and any partner. In some cases the rules are different depending on whether it is a working age or pension age claim or application. For more information on these points, and other general considerations, see paragraphs 13.2-10. Also note that in England the ability of authorities to create their own CTR schemes for working age claims for pensioners) means that different rules as described in this chapter may apply (para. 10.25). For example, for working age self-employed applicants some authorities have proposed assuming that the minimum amount of income to be taken into account for each hour of self-employment is the relevant minimum wage figure (or some variant on this theme). Read the specific wording of the relevant CTR scheme – usually to be found on the authority's website.

15.3 This chapter does not apply to the self-employed income of a non-dependant or second adult: the law does not lay down any particular way of assessing income from self-employment in such cases. In practice most authorities assess their income under the rules in this chapter, but using the pre-tax profit figure rather than the net income figure.

Who is 'self-employed'?

15.4 A person is self-employed if they are gainfully employed in Great Britain (or in Northern Ireland gainfully employed in NI or the Republic) in employment that does not count as 'employed earner' employment (para. 14.4). Sometimes a person may also be employed as an employed earner – in which case there is income from both self-employment and 'employed earner' employment to be assessed.

15.5	A person may be a sole trader or in a business partnership, and therefore be a self-employed earner. But someone who is a director of a limited company is an office holder in the company and any monies received in that capacity should be treated as employed earner's earnings (para. 14.42).

15.6	The following do not count as self-employed income:

+	new enterprise allowance (para. 15.20);
+	fostering and respite care payments (para. 13.65);
+	Sports Council awards (para. 13.128);
+	rent received by the claimant on their home (table 13.3);
+	rent received by the claimant on property other than their home (table 13.4) *(R(FC) 2/92)*, unless the renting of property constitutes gainful self-employment (perhaps because of the number of properties rented out).

Capital, etc

15.7	Assets of a business wholly or partly owned by a claimant are disregarded as capital when he or she:

+	is self-employed in that business – so long as the assets are held in the course of self-employment *(CH/4258/2004)*;
+	has ceased to be self-employed – for as long as is reasonably needed for disposal. In these circumstances, income from (the former) self-employment is also disregarded (apart from royalties and similar payments: para. 15.41); or
+	is not self-employed because of sickness or disability, but intends to be as soon as able to. In this case, the assets are disregarded for 26 weeks from the date of any claim for HB/CTR, and then for whatever period is reasonable to enable the return to self-employment.

15.8	It is sometimes necessary to decide whether capital is personal or part of the business. In general, the test depends on whether the capital is 'part of the fund employed and risked in the business' *(R(SB) 4/85* para 11). For example, an amount in a self-employed claimant's personal bank account is not disregarded as a business asset if it is neither employed nor risked in the business.

15.4	CBA 2(1)(b); HB 2(1); HB60+ 2(1); NIHB 2(1); NIHB 60+ 2(1); CTP 2(1); CTR 2(1)

15.6	HB 37(1)-(2); HB60+ 38(1)-(2); NIHB 34(1)-(2); NIH60+ 36(1)-(2); CTP sch 1 para 21(1),(2); CTR 44(1),(2),53(1),(2)

15.7	HB sch 4 para 2A sch 6 para 8; HB60+ sch 4 para 8 sch 6 paras 9,10; NIHB sch 7 para 8; NIHB60+ sch 7 paras 9,10; CTP sch 6 paras 9,10; CTR sch 7 para 3, sch 9 paras 9,10 sch 10 para 11

Income: the assessment period

15.9   The income and expenses of a self-employed person are estimated by reference to an 'assessment period'. This should be whatever period is appropriate to enable the most accurate estimation of average weekly earnings *(CH/329/2003)*. For working age claims the period must not be longer than one year. For pension age claims it must be a year (so long as the claimant has been self-employed for at least a year). The year does not need to be the year immediately before the claim or the date the claim is looked at – and could in appropriate cases be an estimated future period (para. 15.13). In all cases, the general principle is that income and expenses in the assessment period are used to calculate HB and CTR.

People who have been self-employed for at least a year

15.10   For people who have been self-employed for some time, the DWP advises that the assessment period should normally be that of the last year's trading accounts, but that a shorter or different period may be used if that period is more representative of the current trading position (GM para. BW2.330).

15.11   A person who claims HB/CTR during the course of self-employment should usually have evidence of his or her recent actual income and expenses from that self-employment. It would usually be reasonable in such cases for the authority to ask for the claimant's most recent accounts showing business-related income and expenditure (regardless of whether these are prepared by the claimant, an accountant or someone else) but the supplied figures may need adjustment because the way certain items are treated for accounting purposes is different from the way they are treated for HB/CTR purposes (table 15.2).

People who have been self-employed for less than a year

15.12   If someone has been self-employed for less than a year, the assessment period is whatever period (during which they have been self-employed) will give the most accurate assessment.

People setting up in business

15.13   A person who claims HB/CTR when he or she is just setting up in self-employment cannot possibly have evidence of his or her actual income and expenses from that self-employment. In such cases, the DWP recommends that the claimant's income and expenses should be estimated (GM para. BW2.333). Most authorities have forms claimants can fill in giving their estimates. These estimates (unless they are unreasonable) are typically used to assess the claimant's HB/CTR for a short period, say 13 weeks. The claimant should then be advised to keep proper records of income and expenses during that period, so that he or she can send them in to be used as evidence for the following period.

15.9   HB 2(1), 30; HB60+ 2(1), 37; NIHB 2(1), 27; NIHB60+ 2(1), 35; CIP 2(1), sch 1 para 20; CTR 2(1), 43,48

If the nature of a business changes

15.14   If the nature of a claimant's business changes in such a way as to affect the normal pattern of business, e.g. the loss of a major customer or changing from full-time to part-time self-employment, the authority should again identify an assessment period that allows it to calculate the earnings with the greatest accuracy, e.g. starting with the date the change occurred and ending on the date for which the most recent figures regarding earnings and expenditure are available *(CH/329/2003)*.

Can the figures be altered later?

15.15   Once the various figures have been assessed as described above, they can be altered later only if they were based on a mistake of fact or law or there was an official error, or if there has subsequently been a relevant change of circumstances (e.g. as in para. 15.14).

Accounting methods

15.16   Self-employed people usually account for their income and expenditure using one of the following methods:

- ◆ a 'cash' basis – counting income as being received on the day they receive the money and counting expenses as being incurred on the day they pay the money out; or

- ◆ an 'on paper' basis – counting income as being received on the day they issue their bill or invoice for it and counting expenses as being incurred on the day they receive a bill or invoice for them; or

- ◆ the basis required (roughly speaking) for income tax purposes – counting income as being received on the day they issue their bill or invoice or the day they receive the money, whichever happens first, and counting expenses as being incurred on the day they receive a bill or invoice or the day they pay the money out, whichever happens first.

15.17   For HB/CTR purposes, it doesn't matter which of the above methods the claimant uses, so long as it is reasonable and representative of their income and expenses, and consistent during their period of trading.

Gross income derived from the business

15.18   Having selected an assessment period, the next step is to establish the gross income derived from the business during that period. For this purpose:

- ◆ only payments of income are taken into account. A payment of capital into a business (e.g. an investment in the business by a relative or bank) is disregarded (para. 15.7); and

---

15.18   HB 37(1), 38(1),(3); HB60+38(1); NIHB 34(1), 35(1),(3); NIHB60+ 36(1); CTP sch 1 para 21(1),29(1);
            CTR 44(1); 53(1), 61(1), (3)

+ income from some other source, i.e. not 'derived from' the business, falls under whatever rules apply to that kind of income (para. 15.19 and chapter 13).

There are also special rules for deciding what period royalties and other similar payments belong to (paras. 15.41-43).

Grants, loans and the access to work scheme

15.19 These are assessed as follows:

+ grants are not usually 'derived from' self-employment. Usually they are a separate source of income or capital – typically voluntary or charitable (para. 13.129);

+ genuine loans are not income (para. 13.140). Money from a loan forms part of the claimant's capital. If it is a loan to the business it is therefore disregarded (para. 15.7);

+ disabled people setting up in self-employment can get payments under the government's Access to Work scheme: these are disregarded as income (para. 13.127).

New enterprise allowance

15.20 The new enterprise allowance provides help and support for people who claim JSA and who want to start their own business. It consists of a weekly allowance payable for up to 26 weeks and a low cost loan. The allowance is disregarded as unearned income. The loan is disregarded as a business asset (DWP A8/2011 paras. 1-8). The weekly allowance should also not be included in the earnings from self-employment for HB/CTR assessments (DWP A11/2011 paras. 12-13).

Allowable expenditure

15.21 Having worked out the gross income in the assessment period, the next step is to allow for the expenses incurred in running the business during the assessment period. The two general principles are:

+ expenses are allowed for if they are 'wholly and exclusively incurred' for the purpose of the business; but

+ the authority cannot allow an expense if it is not satisfied, given the nature and the amount, that it has been 'reasonably incurred'.

Examples of expenses that are usually allowable (subject to the above points) are in table 15.1. The law also contains rules about particular kinds of expenditure and these are summarised in table 15.2.

15.20 HB 37(1); HB60+38(1); CTP sch 1 para 21(1); CTR 44(1); 53(1)

15.21 HB 38(3)(a),(7); HB60+ 39(2)(a),(6); NIHB 35(3)(a),(7); NIHB60+ 37(2)(a),(6); CTP sch 1 para 29(2)(a),(3),(b); CTR 61(3)(a),(4),(7)

Table 15.1: Typically allowable types of expenditure

The items in this table do not appear in the law, but are typically allowable in the assessment of self-employed income for HB/CTR purposes (subject to the tests in para 15.21 and the points in paras 15.22-27 and table 15.2). The table does not list every possible allowable expense.

transport	vehicle costs
protective clothing	advertising
postage, carriage and delivery	telephone
legal and accountancy fees	staff costs
subscriptions to professional/trade bodies	fuel costs
rent, rates and other premises costs	cleaning
buying in stocks and supplies	bank charges
hire and leasing charges	stationery
insurance costs	repair costs

The law also contains rules about particular kinds of expenditure and these are summarised in table 15.2.

'Wholly and exclusively incurred' and 'reasonably incurred'

15.22   With many small businesses, particularly when someone is working from home, or only has the use of one car, certain items of expenditure (such as the cost of gas and electricity for heating and lighting including any standing charges, petrol, road fund licence, insurance premiums, etc) may relate to both business and private use. Where such expenses can be apportioned on for example a time basis this can be used to identify the amount wholly and exclusively used for business purposes. This process of apportionment should be used not just for items like heating, lighting and petrol but also for items such as the standing charge, road fund licence and insurance even if it might otherwise be argued that no proportion could be said to relate exclusively to business use (*R(FC) 1/91* followed in *R(H) 5/07*). Such apportionment is also appropriate in relation to the loan interest and capital repayments for a replacement car used partly for non-business purposes even though the car would have been replaced if the person were not in business *(R(H) 5/07)*. In this case the apportionment of both the loan interest and capital repayments should be in accordance with the amount of business mileage as a percentage of total mileage in the assessment period. As in tax law and practice, however, there is no need for this to be the result of a detailed calculation, so long as any estimate is obtained reasonably.

T 15.1   HB 38(3)(a),(7); HB60+ 39(2)(a),(6); NIHB 35(3)(a),(7); NIHB60+ 37(2)(a),(6);
         CTP sch 1 para 29(2)(a),(3),(b); CTR 61(3)(a),(4),(7)

Table 15.2: Particular types of expenditure

		Allowable?
(a)	Interest payments on any business loan	Yes
(b)	Sums (except interest payments) employed or intended to be employed in setting up or expanding the business	No
(c)	Income spent on repairing an existing business asset (except to the extent that any sum is payable under an insurance policy for this)	Yes
(d)	Capital repayments on loans for repairing an existing business asset (except to the extent that any sum is payable under an insurance policy for this)	Yes
(e)	Capital repayments on loans for replacing business equipment or machinery (the term includes a car: para. 15.22 *(R(H) 5/07)*)	Yes
(f)	Capital repayments on any other business loans	No
(g)	Any other capital expenditure	No
(h)	Depreciation of any capital asset (also called a capital allowance)	No
(i)	Losses incurred before the beginning of the assessment period	No
(j)	Excess of VAT paid over VAT received in the assessment period	Yes
(k)	Proven bad debts	Yes*
(l)	Other debts	No*
(m)	Expenses incurred in the recovery of any debt	Yes
(n)	Business entertainment	No
(o)	Any sum for a domestic or private purpose	No
*	*The regulations state this for working age claims, but it is equally reasonable in the case of pension age claims.*	

15.23 To decide whether expenditure is 'reasonably incurred' the authority must consider the circumstances of the individual case *(R(P)2/54)* including the person's earnings from the business *(R(G) 1/56)*. Where an item of expenditure is appropriate and necessary it should always be considered reasonably incurred unless excessive *(R(G) 7/62)*. If it is excessive, only that part considered reasonable should be allowed as a deduction.

Rent – working from home

15.24 An appropriate proportion of the rent paid by someone working from home should also be deducted as a business expense. Relevant factors in arriving at a figure to use would include the size of the working area in relation to the rest of the home and the proportion of time that area is utilised for business as opposed to domestic purposes. A tribunal was found not to have erred where it decided that an appropriate amount to allow for the rent payable in respect of a second bedroom used for business purposes was the difference between the actual rent for the two-bedroomed property and the rent officer's valuation for a one bedroom flat (*R(H) 5/07* para. 12). Where part of someone's rent is identified as a deductible business expense and the claimant's HB is based on the actual rent rather than a local housing allowance the allowed expense should also be deducted from the claimant's eligible rent (paras. 7.17 and 7.22).

Drawings taken by the claimant from the business

15.25 Claimants may take 'drawings' from their business as a kind of wages or salary for themselves. These must not be allowed as a business expense (GM. paras. BW2.390-396) nor should they be taken into account as income *(R(H) 6/09)*.

Couples where one employs the other

15.26 If the claimant pays their partner to work for the business, this is allowable as a business expense. It counts as the partner's earnings. The rules are different if the couple are in a business partnership (para. 15.29).

Self-employed child minders

15.27 For claimants who are self-employed child minders, instead of working out what their actual expenses are, two-thirds of their total earnings are disregarded in lieu of expenses. No actual expenses can be allowed for.

Example: A self-employed window cleaner

Dennie Wroclaw, a self-employed window cleaner, provides accounts for his most recent year's trading, showing annual income (with tips) of £10,268 and the following expenses:

- petrol and other costs for van (attributable to business use) £2,356
- telephone costs (attributable to business use) £270
- advertising £507

15.27 HB 38(9); HB60+ 39(8); NIHB 35(9); NIHB60+ 37(8); CTP sch 1 para 29(8); CTR 61(9)

- meals (while working) £613
- postage and stationery £63
- equipment and overalls £187
- sundry £21
- total £4,017

In assessing his HB/CTR, the following points apply:

- the figures all appear reasonable and believable;
- 'sundry' (miscellaneous) is an allowable expense if it is reasonable;
- meals in this instance are not an allowable expense, so his expenses are reduced from £4,017 by £613 (for the meals) to an allowable figure of £3,404.
- his pre-tax profit for the year is £10,268 (total earnings) minus £3,404 (allowable expenses), which is £6,864;
- deductions are then made for notional tax and national insurance (table 15.3) to give his annual net profit (he does not contribute to a pension scheme);
- his annual net profit is converted to a weekly figure (para. 6.49) and the relevant earned income disregards are then made (para. 14.14).

Example: A self-employed childminder

Hendl Drimic, a self-employed childminder, provides evidence that her total earnings are £180 per week.

In assessing her HB/CTR, the following points apply :

- it is reasonable to assess her total earnings as £180 per week;
- of this, two-thirds (£120) is disregarded, leaving £60 per week as her pre-tax profit;
- the annual equivalent of her pre-tax profit is too low for deductions to be made for notional tax and national insurance (table 15.3) and she does not contribute to a pension scheme, so her weekly net profit is simply £60;
- the relevant earned income disregards are then made (para. 14.14).

Pre-tax profit (chargeable income)

15.28   The next step is to work out the claimant's 'pre-tax profit' (referred to in the law as 'chargeable income'):

* the income derived from the business during the assessment period (paras. 15.18-20)

* minus allowable expenditure over the assessment period (paras. 15.21-27)

* equals pre-tax profit.

Business partnerships

15.29   If the claimant is self-employed in a partnership, the pre-tax profit (as defined above) should be assessed for the partnership and then split between the business partners. This split should reflect how the business partners actually share their income. This split is required even if the business partners are a couple because it will ensure the correct calculation of notional tax and national insurance (para. 15.35). The rules are different if one partner in a couple employs the other (para. 15.26).

15.30   The rules regarding the business partner's share of the net profit also apply to 'share fishermen'.

Nil income from self-employment

15.31   If the claimant's allowable expenses exceed his or her total income, then pre-tax profit is nil *(R(H) 5/08)*. So income from self-employment is nil.

More than one employment

15.32   If a self-employed claimant is engaged in any other employment or self-employment, the losses from one cannot be set against the income from the other; nor can any loss by one member of a family be set against the earnings of another *(R(H) 5/08)*.

If the pre-tax profit appears unrepresentative

15.33   If the pre-tax profit appears unlikely to represent the claimant's income, the authority should consider whether selecting a different assessment period would produce a more accurate estimate (para. 15.9).

15.28   HB 38(1)(a),(3); HB60+ 39(1)(a),(3); NIHB 35(1)(a),(3); NIHB60+ 37(1)(a),(3); CTP sch 1 para 29(1)-(3); CTR 61(1),(3),(4)

15.29   HB 38(1)(b),(4); HB60+ 39(1)(b); NIHB 35(1)(b),(4); NIHB60+ 37(1)(b); CTP sch 1 para 29(1)(b),(3); CTR 61(1)(b),(c),(4)

15.32   HB 38(10); HB60+ 39(9); NIHB 35(10); NIHB60+ 37(9); CTP sch 1 para 29(9); CTR 61(10)

Notional income tax and notional NICs

15.34 Allowances are made for income tax and national insurance contributions ('NICs'). However, the authority must work these out itself, based on the claimant's pre-tax profit. The figures calculated by the authority are known as 'notional income tax' and 'notional NICs'. They usually differ from the actual income tax and NICs paid by the claimant. In Northern Ireland, if the claimant is employed in the Republic the authority deducts what it considers would have been deducted had they worked in Northern Ireland.

The calculations

15.35 The calculations are given in table 15.3. An example is given at the end of this chapter. The tables apply to annual amounts of pre-tax profit. If a claimant's assessment period was a different length (e.g. 13 weeks), convert pre-tax profit into an annual figure before doing the calculations (para. 6.49). In the case of a couple, work through the calculations separately for each one who has self-employed income.

15.36 Table 15.3 gives the figures for the tax year from 6th April 2013 to 5th April 2014. The law says authorities should use the tax rate and national insurance figures 'applicable to the assessment period'. Interpreting this phrase is difficult when accounts span two tax years (as is common). Some authorities split the pre-tax profit and work out two part-year amounts of notional tax/NI. Others take the full annual pre-tax profit, and either use the tax/NI figures which apply at the end date of the assessment period, or use the tax/NI figures which apply at the date of claim for (or supersession of) HB/CTR.

Pension contributions

15.37 An allowance is made for half of any pension contributions payable by self-employed claimants. This applies to periodical (e.g. monthly – but not lump sum) contributions to personal pension schemes (so long as they are tax-deductible), and to (nowadays uncommon) annuities for a retirement pension for the claimant or a dependant.

15.38 If a claimant starts or stops making such payments, or changes their amount, this is a change of circumstances and HB/CTR are reassessed.

15.39 To find the annual equivalent of a pension contribution, multiply a calendar monthly contribution by 12 – or in any other case, divide the contribution by the number of days it covers and multiply by 365.

15.34   HB 39; HB60+ 40; NIHB 35(12),36; NIHB60+ 37(11),38; CTP sch 1 para 30; CTR 62

15.35   HB 39; HB60+ 40; NIHB 36; NIHB60+ 38; CTP sch 1 para 30; CTR 62

15.36   HB 39; HB60+ 40; NIHB 36; NIHB60+ 38; CTP sch 1 para 30; CTR 62

15.37   HB 38(11),(12); HB60+ 36(11),(12); NIHB 35(11),(13); NIHB60+ 37(10),(12); CTP sch 1 para 29(10),(11); CTR 61(11),(12)

Table 15.3: Calculating notional income tax and national insurance contributions: 2013-14 tax year

Income tax

(a) Start with the annual pre-tax profit figure.

(b) Subtract the appropriate age related personal allowance, e.g. £9,440 for people born after 5/4/1948.[1]

(c) If there is a remainder multiply it by 20%[2]

(d) The result is the amount of notional tax.

Class 2 NICs

If the annual pre-tax profit figure is £5,725[3] or more, then the amount of notional class 2 NICs is £140.40.[4]

Class 4 NICs

(a) Start with the annual pre-tax profit figure (unless this is greater than £41,450[5], in which case start with £41,450).

(b) Subtract £7,755.[5]

(c) If there is a remainder, multiply it by 9%. The result is the amount of notional class 4 NICs.

The person may have class 2 alone, or both class 2 and class 4.

Notes

1   £9,440 is the basic personal allowance for people born after 5th April 1948. Higher allowances apply to people born before 6th April 1948 but these reduce by £1 for every £2 of income above £26,100 until the basic personal allowance is reached.

2   The 40% tax rate is not used in assessing notional income tax, nor are any allowances taken into account other than as above.

3   £5,725 is the lower threshold for class 2 NICs. If the person's pre-tax profit is lower, then the notional class 2 NICs figure is nil (regardless of whether the claimant has applied to HMRC for exemption).

4   £140.40 is 52 times £2.70 (the weekly rate of class 2 NICs), there being 52 Sundays in the 2013-14 tax year.

5   £7,755 is the lower threshold, and £41,450 the upper threshold, for class 4 NICs. The 2% class 4 NIC rate for income above £41,450 is not used in assessing notional NICs. (The regulations have not been amended to keep them up-to-date with NIC rules, but this appears to be their intention.)

Net profit

15.40 The final step is to work out the claimant's 'net profit'. It is always advisable to work this out at first on an annual basis:

- pre-tax profit (paras. 15.28-33)
- minus notional income tax and NI contributions, and half of pension contributions (paras. 15.34-39)
- equals net profit.

The law does not say how to convert the result to a weekly figure, but the best way is to divide the annual figure by 365 (366 in a leap tax year) and multiply the result by 7. Note that 2011-12 was a leap tax year and 2015-16 is a leap year.

Royalties, etc

15.41 The following are treated as gross income from self-employment (para. 15.18):

- royalties or other payments received for the use of, or the right to use, any copyright, design, patent or trademark; and
- payments received by authors under the Public Lending Right Scheme or a similar international scheme,

but only if the claimant is the first owner of the copyright etc (i.e. not producing the work as an employee) or an original contributor to the book etc.

15.42 For pension age claims (para. 1.21), the above payments – along with any other 'occasional payments' – are treated as though they are paid in respect of a year.

15.43 For working age claims (para. 1.21), work through the following (separately for HB and for CTR):

(a) Add together the weekly HB or CTR the claimant would be entitled to had they not received the payment, and the earned income disregard(s) applying in the claimant's case.

(b) The result of (a) is the claimant's weekly gross income from the payment.

(c) It is taken into account for the number weeks (including part weeks) found by dividing the payment by the result of (a).

(So if the result of (a) was £50 and the claimant received £2,000, it would be a gross income of £50 for 40 weeks.)

15.40 HB 38(1)-(3); HB60+ 39(1)-(3); NIHB 35(1)-(3); NIHB60+ 37(1)-(3); CTP sch 1 para 29(1)-(3); CTR 61(1),(3)

15.41 HB 37(3), HB60+ 29(1)(q) (r), NIHB 34(3), NIHB60+ 27(1)(o)(p), CTP sch 1 para 16(1)(q),(r),17(5),(6); CTR 39(1)(q),(r),40(5),(6),53(3),(4)

15.42 HB60+ 33(4),(5),(8); NIHB60+ 31(4),(5),(8); CTP sch 1 para 17(5); CTR 40(5)

15.43 HB 37(4); NIHB 34(4); CTR 53(4)

Example: Notional tax and NI contributions and net profit: 2013-14

A 52-year-old's annual pre-tax profit is £10,000. She contributes £460 per year to a personal pension scheme.

Notional income tax (table 15.3)

(a)	Start with the annual pre-tax profit figure. This is	£10,000
(b)	Subtract the personal allowance of £9,440. This leaves	£560
(c)	Multiply £560 by 20%. This gives	£112
(d)	So her notional tax is:	£112

Notional class 2 NICS (table 15.3)

The annual pre-tax profit figure (£10,000) is greater than £5,725, so the amount of her notional class 2 NICs is £140.40.

Notional class 4 NICS (table 15.3)

(a) Start with the annual pre-tax profit figure (which is not greater than £41.450). This is £10,000.

(b) Subtract £7,755.

(c) Multiply the remainder (which is £2,245) by 9%.

This is £202.05 – which is the amount of her notional class 4 NICs.

Net profit

Annual pre-tax profit	£10,000.00
minus notional income tax	£112.00
minus notional class 2 NICs	£140.40
minus notional class 4 NICs	£202.05
minus half of annual contributions to pension scheme	£230.00
Equals annual net profit:	£9,315.55
On a weekly basis this is (£9,315.55 ÷ 365* x 7 =)	£178.65

Don't forget to apply the earned income disregards (paras. 14.14, 14.17 and 14.30).

* 2013-14 is not a leap year.

16 Decisions, notices and payment

16.1 This chapter explains:
- how quickly a claim should be dealt with and benefit paid;
- who must be notified of the authority's decisions;
- the information that must be given to the claimant and others;
- how and when HB/CTR should be paid;
- the requirement to make a payment of HB in 14 days (or a payment on account) for rent allowance claimants;
- when HB should be paid to the claimant and when to the landlord or agent; and
- who else may receive payment of a rent allowance.

Dealing with claims and changes

How quickly should claims be dealt with and benefit paid?

16.2 Once the authority has received a claim, and all the information and evidence it reasonably requires from the claimant, it has the following duties:
- it must reach a decision on the claim within 14 days or as soon as reasonably practicable after that;
- it must notify persons affected (para. 16.10) as soon as the claim is decided or as soon as reasonably practicable after that;
- in HB cases, it should make a payment within 14 days of the receipt of the claim or as soon as reasonably practicable after that;
- in rent allowance cases, if it cannot meet the 14 day decision-making timetable it should consider making a payment on account (para. 16.23).

All the above duties apply to HB. There are variations for CTR (para. 16.5).

Exceptions to the requirement to decide a claim

16.3 The authority does not have to meet the above time limits if a claim is not made in the proper time and manner (para. 5.8), or is not supported by reasonably required information or evidence from the claimant (para. 5.13), or has been withdrawn (para. 5.12).

16.2   HB 89(2),90(1)(a),91(3); HB60+ 70(2),71(1)(a),72(3); NIHB 85(2),86(1)(a),87(3); NIHB60+ 66(2),67(1)(a),68(3); CTP sch 8 paras 11,12(1)(a); CTR 116,117(1)(a)

16.3   HB 89(2); HB60+ 70(2); NIHB 85(2); NIHB60+ 66(2); CTP sch 8 para 11; CTR 116

How quickly should other decisions be made?

16.4   The authority also has to make a decision when:

+ it changes (or ends) an award of HB or CTR due to a change of circumstances (para. 17.16) or following a review (para. 17.52);

+ it changes (or ends) an award of HB due to a reconsideration (para. 19.10), mistake (para. 17.56) or termination (para. 17.73);

+ there is a recoverable overpayment (chapter 18).

In these cases the authority must notify persons affected within 14 days of making the decision or as soon as possible after that (but for CTR see also para. 16.5).

CTR variations

16.5   All the above rules and time limits (paras. 16.2-4) apply to CTR in England and Wales, but the contents of notices vary (paras. 16.11-12). In Scotland, CTR law gives the exceptions to the requirement to decide a claim (para. 16.3), but does not require authorities to make decisions within a particular time limit (paras. 16.2, 16.4) or to issue notifications (para. 16.9).

Performance

16.6   Authorities have a duty to allocate sufficient resources according to their caseload such that the vast majority of claims can be processed within the 14 day time limit. The fact that many authorities fail to meet this standard is not an excuse but makes the need for judicial intervention 'all the greater': *R v Liverpool CC ex parte Johnson No. 1*. Authorities in Great Britain are expected to report to the DWP on their average processing times for new claims and change events (the 'right time performance indicator': para. 1.29). The DWP also collects other processing data from authorities. Information on each authority's performance is available on the DWP's Housing Benefits Operational Database (HoBod) [www].

Remedies for delays

16.7   Authorities are expected to meet the time limits in most cases. Delays are normally only justifiable, for example, in periods of peak pressure such as the annual up-rating. When authorities fail to meet the time limits, remedies to ensure that they meet their obligations in the future include:

+ complaints to the appropriate ombudsman (para. 1.30);

+ action in the High Court or Court of Session in Scotland for judicial review to require authorities to make a decision; and

+ action in the County Court or Sheriff Court to require authorities to make a payment if they have agreed that the claimant is entitled: *Waveney DC v Jones*.

16.4   HB 90(1)(b); HB60+ 71(1)(b); NIHB 86(1)(b); NIHB60+ 67(1)(b); CTP sch 8 para 12(1)(b); CTR 117(1)(b)

16.6   www.dwp.gov.uk/asd/hobod/

16.8 In England and Wales, local authorities and registered social landlords are expected to comply with the Civil Procedure Rules pre-action protocol before seeking possession for rent arrears [www]. Its terms require that possession proceedings should not start against a tenant who has provided the authority with all the evidence required to process their claim, provided that there is a reasonable expectation of entitlement and they have paid any other sums to the landlord not covered by HB. Under the Civil Procedure Rules, the court has the power to summon the authority to explain any delays or problems with a claim, and costs may be sought from the authority where it can be shown that HB problems have caused the litigation.

Who should be notified and how?

16.9 The authority must issue a written notice about each decision it makes in relation to HB (throughout the UK) and, in England and Wales, CTR. These notices must be issued to each 'person affected' by the decision (para. 16.10) and must contain the matters described below (paras. 16.11-12). Authorities in Scotland are not required to issue notices about CTR.

Persons affected

16.10 A 'person affected' means any of the following whose rights, duties or obligations are affected by the decision in question:

+ the claimant;
+ where a claimant is unable for the time being to act on his or her own behalf (para. 5.5):
  - a deputy (or in Northern Ireland controller) appointed by the Court of Protection with power to claim or receive benefit;
  - in Scotland, a tutor, curator, judicial factor or other guardian acting or appointed in terms of law administering the claimant's estate;
  - an attorney appointed with a general power or with a power to receive benefit;
  - a person appointed by the authority to act for the claimant;
  - a person appointed by the Secretary of State (in practice a manager at the DWP office) to act on the claimant's behalf and treated as an appointee by the authority;
+ in HB only, the landlord or agent — in relation to a decision about whether to pay a rent allowance to them rather than the claimant (paras. 16.31-56); or

---

16.7 www.justice.gov.uk/civil/procrules_fin/contents/protocols/prot_rent.htm

16.9 HB 90; HB60+ 71; NIHB 86; NIHB60+ 67; CTP sch 8 para 12(1); CTR 117(1)

16.10 HB 2(1); HB60+ 2(1); NIHB 2(1); NIHB60+ 2(1); CTB 2(1); CTB60+ 2(1); DAR 3; NIDAR 3; CTP sch 8 para 12(7),(8); CTR 117(7),(8)

- ◆ in HB only, anyone – including the landlord or agent – from whom the authority has decided that an overpayment is recoverable (paras. 18.29-30).

No-one else is a 'person affected' (para. 19.6) but, so long as they fall within the above list, the term includes corporate bodies such as housing associations and letting companies. More than one person may be affected by a decision. For example, if the authority decides to recover an overpayment of HB from the landlord, both the landlord and the claimant are a 'person affected'.

Contents of notices

16.11 Every notice (whatever the decision and whether or not the person is entitled) must state:

- ◆ the right of the person affected to ask for a written statement of reasons (para. 19.8) and how and when to do this (HB and, in England only, CTR);
- ◆ their right to appeal if that right applies to the decision (para. 19.24) and how and when to do this (HB and, in England and Wales, CTR);
- ◆ their right to ask the authority to reconsider (para. 19.10) and how and when to do this (HB only); and
- ◆ their duty to notify relevant changes of circumstances (para. 17.3) and what these might be (HB and, in England and Wales, CTR). CTR notices must also state what the consequences of not doing so might be.

16.12 The following further rules apply:

- ◆ notices about a decision on a claim for HB or, in Wales only, CTR must also contain the information in table 16.1, along with any other matter the authority considers relevant;
- ◆ notices about a decision on a claim for CTR in England need not contain the information in table 16.1; except that when CTR is awarded, they must state how it will be paid (paras. 16.13-14);
- ◆ for notices about changes to HB/CTR entitlement, see paragraphs 17.17, 17.68 and 19.17;
- ◆ for HB notices issued to landlords or agents, see paragraphs 16.66-67.

Payments of CTR

16.13 Payment of CTR is normally in the form of a rebate (credit) to the claimant's council tax account, so reducing their overall liability for the tax. Any resulting credit on a council tax account may be refundable: the DCLG advises this can be done 'where, for example, [the claimant] is no longer liable for council tax' (*Localising council tax support,* November 2012, para 23).

16.11 HB 90 sch 9 paras 2-6; HB60+ 71 sch 8 paras 2-6; NIHB 86 sch 10 paras 2-6;
    NIHB60+ 67, sch 9 paras 2-6; CTP sch 8 para 12(2),(4); CTR 117(2),(4)

16.12 HB sch 9; HB60+ sch 8; NIHB sch 10; NIHB60+ sch 9; CTP sch 8 para 12(3); CTR 117(3)

16.13 LGFA 10(1)

Table 16.1: Decisions on claims: information notified to the claimant

This table applies to HB and, in Wales only, CTR (para. 16.12).

Claimants entitled to HB/CTR

+ Their first day of entitlement to HB/CTR.
+ Their normal weekly amount of HB/CTR.
+ If HB is to be paid as a rent allowance, the date and period of payment (and for payment to a landlord/agent, see para. 16.67).
+ How CTR will be paid (paras. 16.13-14).
+ Their duty to notify changes, and what these might be (para.17.3).

Claimants not entitled to HB/CTR

+ The reason why they are not entitled to HB/CTR.
+ If HB is not awarded because it is less than 50p (para. 6.13), that fact and the amount not awarded.

All claimants (whether or not entitled to HB/CTR)

+ Their rights to a written statement, and to appeal, etc (para. 16.11).
+ Their weekly eligible rent/rates/council tax.
+ The amount and category of any non-dependant deductions.
+ Unless they are on a passport benefit (table 6.1), their applicable amount and how it was worked out.
+ Unless they are on a passport benefit, universal credit or savings credit, their weekly earned income and weekly unearned income.
+ If they are on universal credit, their weekly income (paras. 13.169-171).
+ If they are on savings credit, the DWP's figures for income and capital, any adjustment made to them, and the amount of their savings credit (paras. 13.161-168).
+ In HB, if standard deductions were made for fuel, that fact and how they can be varied (para. 7.58).

T 16.1 HB sch 9 paras 1-10,14; HB60+ sch 8 paras 1-10,14; NIHB sch 10 paras 1-10,14;
NIHB60+ sch 9 paras 1-10,14

16.14　However, in England and Wales only, the authority may pay CTR direct to the claimant if:

* they are jointly liable for council tax (para. 10.10); and
* awarding CTR as a rebate 'would be inappropriate'.

If the claimant is unable to act, this payment can be made to an appointee (para. 16.10; and for the similar HB rule see para. 16.72).

Payments of HB

16.15　The rest of this chapter is about HB only. HB is paid as follows:

* HB for a council or NIHE tenant is awarded as a rebate to the claimant's rent account (para. 16.16);
* HB for any other tenant (e.g. a private or housing association tenant) is awarded as an allowance (i.e. a payment) either to the claimant or to their landlord/agent (paras. 16.19 onwards);
* HB for rates in Northern Ireland is normally awarded as a rebate (para. 11.18).

Payment of HB for tenants of a housing authority or NIHE

16.16　Payment of HB is called a 'rent rebate' when the landlord is a housing authority or the NIHE. In such cases payment of HB is normally in the form of a rebate (credit) to the claimant's rent account, so reducing their overall liability for rent. But there are two exceptions, as follows (and different rules apply for cases involved in HB payment demonstration projects: para. 23.20).

16.17　The first exception applies only to caravans, mobile homes and houseboats where the occupier is:

* liable to pay site rent or mooring charges to the housing authority; but
* payments of rent itself (for the caravan, etc) to someone other than the housing authority – for example, to a private landlord.

In such cases HB for the site rent or mooring charges, even though payable to the housing authority, is awarded as a rent allowance together with the HB for the rent (paras. 16.19 onwards).

16.18　The other exception applies when the authority has made the claimant's dwelling the subject of (in England and Wales) an interim or final management order, or an interim or final empty dwelling order (under section 102, 113, 133 or 136 of the Housing Act 2004); or (in Scotland) a management control order (under section 74 of the Antisocial Behaviour etc (Scotland) Act 2004).

16.14　CTP sch 8 para 14; CTR 18

16.16　AA 134(1A); NIAA 126(1)(b);

16.17　HB 91A(1),(2); HB60+ 72A(1),(2)

16.18　HB 91A(3); HB60+ 72A(3)

In such cases, the authority takes over responsibility for managing the property and the rent becomes payable to it instead of the landlord. The HB payments, however, are awarded as a rent allowance (paras. 16.19 onwards).

Payment of HB for all other cases

16.19   Payment of HB is called a 'rent allowance' when the landlord is anyone other than a housing authority or the NIHE. This includes HB for tenants of private landlords, housing associations (para. 7.8), stock transfer landlords (table 7.1) and other types of landlord (para. 7.14). The HB is paid by cheque, credit transfer, etc (para. 16.20). A later part of this chapter explains who the payment is made to (whether the claimant, someone acting for them, landlord or agent: paras. 16.31 onwards).

16.20   In deciding how and when to pay HB, authorities must take into account the time and frequency of the claimant's rent payments, and the payee's reasonable needs and convenience. Insisting on payment by crossed cheques or credit transfer arrangements is not reasonable if the payee does not have a bank account: *R (Spiropoulos) v Brighton and Hove CC* (GM para. A6.120, GLHA para. 5.87). Such decisions are not appealable to a tribunal, but a person affected can request a reconsideration at any time (para. 19.10).

First payments of HB

16.21   By the 14th day after the authority receives a claim for HB for a rent allowance, it should issue:

+ a payment of actual entitlement to HB or, if it cannot
+ a 'payment on account' of HB.

Payments on account

16.22   A 'payment on account' is an estimated amount of HB, awarded in rent allowance cases only, to prevent the claimant suffering from delays. (It used also to be called an 'interim payment', though this term does not appear in the law.)

16.23   A claimant has a right to a payment on account if:

+ it is a rent allowance case (para. 16.19); and
+ the authority is unable to decide on the amount of benefit payable within 14 days of receipt of the claim; and
+ that inability has not arisen out of the claimant's failure, without good cause, to provide necessary information or evidence.

16.19   AA 134(1B); NIAA 126(1)(c); HB 91(1),94(1); HB60+ 87(1),75(1); NIHB 87(1),91(1); NIHB60+ 68(1),72(1)

16.20   HB 91(1); HB60+ 72(1); NIHB 87(1); NIHB60+ 68(1); DAR sch para 1; NIDAR sch para 1

16.23   HB 93(1); HB60+ 74(1); NIHB 90(1); NIHB60+ 71(1)

The payment on account should be what the authority considers reasonable based on whatever information is available to it about the individual claimant's circumstances.

16.24　Payments on account are not discretionary and (provided that the claimant has done all that is required of them) a payment must be made within 14 days. This was confirmed in the case *R v Haringey LBC ex parte Ayub,* where it was also held that no separate claim or request for a payment on account is required. The fact that no request is necessary is reinforced in DWP guidance (GM A6.158).

16.25　There is no duty to make a payment on account if the claimant has failed, without good cause, to provide necessary information and evidence. The following (the first three of which are confirmed by the DWP: GM para. A6.161) do not prevent a payment on account:

* delays by the rent officer in rent referral cases (para. 9.31);
* delays by the DWP in confirming entitlement to IS, JSA(IB), ESA(IR) or pension credit;
* delays by the Home Office in confirming conditions of entry or stay;
* delays by some other party in providing evidence – such as by a landlord to provide evidence of rent;
* failure by the claimant to supply information which they have not been asked specifically to provide.

16.26　When the authority makes a payment on account, it must notify the claimant that if it turns out to be more than their actual entitlement, it will be recoverable from the person to whom it was paid (para. 18.37). And when the authority decides the claimant's actual entitlement, it must adjust this – up or down – to take account of any under- or over-payment caused by the payment on account. Decisions about such adjustments are appealable, but other decisions relating to payments on account (such as whether to make one and how much it is to be) are not (table 19.2).

Frequency of rent allowance payments

16.27　The following rules apply in rent allowance cases, once the authority has issued its first payment or payment on account (para. 16.21). (Different rules apply for cases involved in HB payment demonstration projects: para. 23.20.)

16.28　When HB is payable to the claimant or someone acting for them (rather than the landlord or agent), the authority may pay it at one of the following intervals, and should normally do so at the end of the period in question:

* two weeks – and if the claimant's weekly HB entitlement is more than £2, the claimant can insist on two-weekly payments; or
* four weeks; or

16.26　HB 93(2),(3); HB60+ 74(2),(3); NIHB 90(2),(3); NIHB60+ 71(2),(3); DAR sch para 1(b); NIDAR sch para 1(b)

16.27　HB 92(1),(2),(5)-(7); HB60+ 73(1),(2),(5)-(7); NIHB 89(1),(2),(5)-(7); NIHB60+ 70(1),(2),(5)-(7)

- one calendar month; or
- at intervals greater than one month – but in this case only with the consent of the person entitled;
- once a term – but only for students (and in reality this never happens); or
- weekly – but only if the authority considers that:
    - (a) paying HB over a longer period would lead to an overpayment, or
    - (b) the claimant is liable to pay rent weekly and it is in his or her interests (or that of the family) to receive weekly payments.

Point (b) above can be helpful in cases where claimants have difficulty in budgeting over a longer period. DWP guidance suggests that 'authorities are not expected to make special enquiries as to whether this applies' but if, for example, social services advise that the claimant has difficulties then weekly payment can be made (GM A6.143).

16.29 When HB is payable to a landlord or agent, the authority may pay it at the following intervals, and should normally do so at the end of the period in question:

- four weeks; or
- at the authority's discretion, one calendar month – but only if the claimant's rent liability is calendar monthly.

16.30 However, if the authority is paying HB direct to a landlord for more than one claimant, the first payment for a new claimant may be made at a shorter interval than four weeks 'in the interest of efficient administration'. This allows the authority to align the payment cycles of all claimants who have the same landlord.

Who should HB rent allowances be paid to?

16.31 HB for anyone other than a council tenant or NIHE tenant is awarded as a rent allowance. This section describes who payments of HB are made to in such cases. It covers:

- when HB is paid to the claimant and when to their landlord or agent – and related considerations (paras. 16.32-71); and
- when HB is paid to an appointee, nominee or next of kin (paras. 16.72-75).

LHA rules vs non-LHA rules

16.32 There are two sets of payment rules:

- the 'LHA payment rules' (table 16.2) apply to LHA and boarder cases (chapter 8 and para. 9.79) (in other words, everyone who falls within the LHA scheme or who the rent officer has decided is a boarder) in England, Wales and Scotland;

16.29 HB 92(3),(4)(a); HB60+ 73(3),(4)(a); NIHB 89(3),(4)(a); NIHB60+ 70(3),(4)(a)
16.30 HB 92(4)(b); HB60+ 73(4)(b); NIHB 89(4)(b); NIHB60+ 70(4)(b)

- the 'non-LHA payment rules' (table 16.3) apply to all other rent allowance cases – including housing association cases, other non-LHA cases (such as exempt accommodation rent referral cases, and so on) – and also to LHA cases in Northern Ireland.

16.33 For both sets of rules, the starting point is that HB is paid to the claimant. But each set of rules then goes on to say when HB must or may be paid to the landlord/agent.

Table 16.2: LHA payment rules

These rules apply to all claims which fall within the LHA scheme in Great Britain.

The authority *must* pay HB to a landlord/agent if any of the following apply:

- there are arrears of rent of eight weeks or more – unless it is in the overriding interests of the claimant not to pay the landlord/agent;
- part of the claimant's JSA, ESA, income support, or pension credit is being paid direct to the landlord/agent; or
- the claimant has died and before the death the authority decided to pay the landlord/agent.

Additionally, the authority *may* pay HB to a landlord/agent if any of the following apply:

- the authority previously had to pay the landlord/agent for one of the above reasons;
- the authority considers that paying the landlord will assist the claimant in securing or retaining their letting;
- the claimant is likely to have difficulty managing their finances;
- it is improbable that the claimant will pay their rent;
- for a period not greater than eight weeks while the authority is considering whether any of the last three points applies;
- the claimant has not paid part or all of the rent, and the authority considers paying the landlord would be in the interests of efficient administration; or
- the claimant has left the accommodation with arrears owing to the landlord/agent (in which case payment to the landlord/agent is limited to those arrears).

In all other cases, the authority *must* pay HB to the claimant.

T16.2 HB 95,96; HB60+ 76,77; NIHB 92,93; NIHB60+ 73,74

'Landlord' and 'agent '

16.34 When HB is payable to a landlord/agent under any of the rules in this chapter, this means it is payable to the landlord if the landlord collects the rent, but to the agent if the agent collects the rent.

LHA payment rules

16.35 In LHA and boarder cases (para. 16.32) in Great Britain, HB is paid to the claimant unless one of the following rules applies (paras. 16.36-52). The rules are summarised in table 16.2. Further considerations are in paragraphs 16.57 onwards.

HB must be paid to landlord: eight weeks' rent arrears

16.36 Under the LHA payment rules (and also the non-LHA rules), the authority must pay the HB to the landlord/agent if the claimant has rent arrears equal to eight weeks or more, except where the authority considers it to be in the overriding interest of the claimant not to pay the landlord/agent.

16.37 For the above purposes, the term 'rent' includes ineligible service charges that must be paid if the claimant is to occupy the home. The authority should estimate the time it will take to clear the arrears and review the case at that point (GLHA 5.86) – but see also paragraph 16.43.

16.38 This duty to pay a landlord/agent only arises if the landlord/agent (or someone else) informs the authority that there are eight weeks' or more arrears. It is not up to the authority to find this out for itself: *R v Haringey LBC ex parte Ayub*.

16.39 Whether or not there are eight weeks' rent arrears is a question of fact (paras. 1.39-42), which begs the question of when rent becomes due and when it is in arrears. Although First-tier Tribunal decisions are not binding (para. 19.67), one well argued decision has influenced the DWP (*Doncaster v Coventry City Council*, 032/09/00932, 5th October 2009: see circular HB/CTB A26/2009). The chairman in that case held that:

> 'Rent is in arrears once the contractual date for payment has passed irrespective of whether rent is due in advance or in arrear.'

Example: Eight weeks' rent arrears

A private landlord lets a calendar-monthly tenancy from 1st July 2013, with the rent due in advance on the 1st of each month.

So by 2nd August 2013, there are two calendar months of rent arrears, which is more than eight weeks of arrears, so the landlord is entitled to require the authority to pay HB direct to the landlord.

16.36 HB 95(1)(b); HB60+ 76(1)(b); NIHB 92(1)(b); NIHB60+73(1)(b)

16.37 HB 2(1); HB60+ 2(1); NIHB 2(1); NIHB60+2(1)

16.40   If there are eight weeks' rent arrears, and the claimant does not want payment to be made to the landlord, it is for the claimant to show that it is in their overriding interest for this not to be done: *CH/3244/2007* paras. 9-10. This must be more specific than an unparticularised assertion of a dispute with the landlord. For example, in a dispute over the need for essential repairs to be carried out, the Commissioner indicated her expectation that the claimant's evidence would include a solicitor's letter setting out the alleged essential repairs and a schedule of disrepair provided by a builder or surveyor: *CH/3244/2007* para. 9.

HB must be paid to landlord: deductions from DWP benefits

16.41   Under the LHA payment rules (and also the non-LHA rules), the authority must pay the HB to the landlord/agent if part of the claimant's (or partner's) entitlement to one of the following benefits is being paid to the landlord/agent to meet arrears (or to meet the cost of ineligible services of a hostel resident) as described in appendix 6:

- ◆   income support;
- ◆   JSA (income-based or contribution-based);
- ◆   ESA (income-related or contribution-based); or
- ◆   pension credit (guarantee or savings credit).

This should continue until the DWP stops making the relevant (rent arrears or service charges) deductions. DWP local offices should inform authorities of appropriate cases (GM A6.188).

HB must be paid to landlord: following a death

16.42   Under the LHA payment rules (and also the non-LHA rules), the authority must pay the HB to the landlord/agent if the claimant has died, and before the death the authority had already decided to pay the landlord/agent – but only up to the amount of any rent remaining unpaid at the date of the death. Although this sounds obvious, it means that an executor cannot argue that the money should instead be paid to them (but see also para. 16.75).

HB may be paid to landlord: following one of the above situations

16.43   Under the LHA payment rules (but not the non-LHA rules), the authority may pay HB to the landlord/agent if it previously had to do so (under the rules in paras. 16.36-41) during the current award of HB. For example, although rent arrears may have reduced below eight weeks (para. 16.37), the authority may continue to pay the landlord nonetheless.

16.41   HB 95(1)(a); HB60+ 76(1)(a); NIHB 92(1)(a); NIHB60+73(1)(a)

16.42   HB 97(5); HB60+ 78(5); NIHB 94(5); NIHB60+75(5)

16.43   HB 96(3A)(a),(b)(iii); HB60+ 77(3A)(a),(b)(iii)

HB may be paid to landlord: to secure or retain a letting

16.44   Under the LHA rules (and also the non-HA rules) the authority may pay HB to the landlord/agent if it 'considers that it will assist the claimant in securing or retaining' a letting. This is a wide-ranging discretion, and may sugar the pill for landlords who might otherwise not wish to carry on taking HB claimants

HB may be paid to landlord: difficulty managing finances

16.45   Under the LHA payment rules (but not the non-LHA rules), the authority may pay the HB to the landlord/agent if:

* it 'considers that the claimant is likely to have difficulty in relation to the management of [their] financial affairs'.

16.46   The DWP suggests this might apply if a claimant has difficulty managing a budget, and that other possible indicators are a medical condition, illiteracy, an inability to speak English, fleeing domestic violence, leaving care or leaving prison, debt problems, undischarged bankruptcy, an inability to obtain a bank account, or receipt of supporting people payments or charitable help (GLHA 5.61-5.71).

HB may be paid to landlord: improbable claimant will pay rent

16.47   Under the LHA payment rules (but not the non-LHA rules), the authority may pay the HB to the landlord/agent if:

* it 'considers that it is improbable that the claimant will pay [their] rent'.

16.48   The DWP suggests this might apply if the claimant has consistently failed to pay the rent on past occasions without good reason (GLHA 4.10). The terms of the tests are however predictive – what is likely to happen, not what has happened *(CH/2986/2005).*

16.49   The DWP has emphasised to authorities that a number of bodies are likely to be able to offer guidance on whether a claimant is or is not likely to pay their rent, mentioning bodies such as Community Health Teams and Leaving Care Teams (Circular HB/CTB A26/2009). However, this can clearly be extended to any responsible person with knowledge of the claimant – such as (chosen at random), a doctor, a substance misuse key worker, a hostel landlord, a reliable friend – or indeed the claimant themselves. In particular, if the authority itself has assisted a claimant to obtain a private tenancy, 'this will often be reliable evidence that a person has had difficulties managing their rent in the past and in many cases [payment to the landlord] is likely to be appropriate' (Circular HB/CTB A26/2009).

16.44   HB96(3A)(b)(iv); HB60+ 77(3A)(b)(iv).

16.45   HB 96(3A)(a),(b)(i); HB60+ 77(3A)(a),(b)(i)

HB may be paid to landlord: while considering who to pay

16.50   Under the LHA payments rules (but not the non-LHA rules), the authority may pay the HB to the landlord/agent if it 'suspects' that any of the above may apply (paras. 16.44-49), and is therefore considering who to pay. Payments to the landlord/agent under this rule are limited to eight weeks. Not all authorities use this rule. Some prefer to make payments to the claimant (perhaps following the DWP's idea that they can then see how the claimant handles those payments: GLHA 5.71). Others suspend HB payments (para. 16.65).

HB may be paid to landlord: discretion and guidance

16.51   The above rules (paras. 16.43-50 – and also the other 'may' rules in table 16.2) are discretionary. The DWP has given extensive guidance to authorities on them (GLHA 4.00-6.102), but as with all discretions (para. 1.49), authorities must apply the law. Any attempt to impose rules upon themselves or to accept guidance without question may fetter that discretion and render the decision wrong in law: *CH/2986/2005.* In particular, the guidance has at various times referred to 'vulnerability' or 'safeguarding', terms which do not appear in the law and which have sometimes misled authorities.

16.52   Anyone with a proper interest may make representations to the authority regarding the problems the claimant is having in managing their financial affairs or the likelihood of them paying the rent – such as the claimant themselves, a relative, a friend, someone acting on the claimant's behalf, a welfare organisation, the landlord/agent or others. The authority may also take account of information that it already holds or obtains from a home visit without the need for representations (GLHA 5.40-42, 6.40-41).

Non-LHA payment rules

16.53   In non-LHA cases in Great Britain, and all cases in Northern Ireland (whether LHA or not), HB is paid to the claimant unless one of the following rules applies (paras. 16.54-56). The rules are summarised in table 16.3. Further considerations are in paragraphs 16.57 onwards.

When HB must be paid to landlord

16.54   Under the non-LHA payment rules, the authority must pay the HB to the landlord/agent in the same circumstances as apply under the LHA payment rules (paras. 16.36-42).

16.50   HB 96(3B); HB60+ 77(3B)

16.54   HB 95; HB60+76; NIHB 92; NIHB60+ 73

When HB may be paid to landlord

16.55   Under the non-LHA payment rules (but not the LHA rules) the authority may pay the HB to the landlord/agent in the circumstances shown in the second part of table 16.3.

16.56   The above rules mean in practice that the majority of housing association tenants, and many private tenants, have their HB paid to their landlord/agent. What constitutes the 'interests of the claimant and family' is not necessarily the same as the tests used in LHA cases (paras. 16.44-49) but may well come to be regarded as similar.

Table 16.3: Non-LHA payment rules

These rules apply to housing association cases, rent referral cases, all other cases which do not fall within the LHA scheme, plus, in Northern Ireland, cases which fall within the LHA scheme.

The authority *must* pay HB to a landlord/agent if any of the following apply:

+ there are arrears of rent of eight weeks or more – unless it is in the overriding interests of the claimant not to pay the landlord/agent;
+ part of the claimant's JSA, ESA, income support or pension credit is being paid direct to the landlord/agent; or
+ the claimant has died and before the death the authority decided to pay the landlord/agent.

Additionally, the authority *may* pay HB to a landlord/agent if any of the following apply:

+ the claimant asks for this or agrees to it;
+ the authority considers it is in the best interests of the claimant or family to do so; or
+ the authority considers that paying the landlord will assist the claimant in securing or retaining their letting;
+ the claimant has not paid part or all of the rent, and the authority considers paying the landlord would be in the interests of efficient administration;
+ the claimant has left the accommodation with arrears owing to the landlord/agent (in which case payment to the landlord/agent is limited to those arrears).

In all other cases, the authority *must* pay HB to the claimant.

16.55   HB 96; HB60+ 77; NIHB 93; NIHB60+ 74

T16.3   HB 95,96; HB60+ 76,77; NIHB 92,93, NIHB60+ 73,74

Other considerations about paying HB

Is the landlord/agent 'a fit and proper person'?

16.57   Under both the LHA and non-LHA payment rules, HB must not be paid to the landlord/agent if they are not a 'fit and proper person' – unless it is in the overriding interests of the claimant for payments to be made to the landlord/agent.

16.58   This rule can be used if the landlord/agent is involved in fraudulent acts related to HB. The DWP suggests (GM A6.200) that the authority might also consider whether the landlord/agent has regularly failed to report changes in tenants' circumstances which he or she might reasonably be expected to know might affect entitlement; or repay an overpayment which the authority has decided is recoverable.

16.59   In deciding whether the landlord/agent is 'fit and proper', the authority should not base its judgment on:

- the landlord/agent's undesirable activity in non-HB matters – such as contravention of the Housing Acts (GM A6.197); or
- the fact that the landlord/agent makes use of the right to request a reconsideration or appeal before repaying any recoverable overpayment; or
- the fact that the landlord/agent has made complaints of maladministration to the local government ombudsman.

16.60   The DWP advises that the 'fit and proper' test should only be applied where the authority is 'doubtful about the landlord/agent's honesty in connection with HB' (GM A6.198).

16.61   Even if a landlord/agent is not a 'fit and proper person', HB may be paid to them if it is in the overriding interest of the claimant to do so (GM A6.204).

Assisting claimants to manage payments of HB

16.62   As a matter of good practice authorities are expected to provide claimants with details of banks and building societies in their area that offer basic bank accounts. Where necessary – so that claimants can open such accounts – authorities are encouraged to provide a verification letter that financial institutions may be prepared to accept as confirmation of the claimant's identity.

16.63   Claimants who have bank accounts with overdrafts may face problems getting HB payments. A bank customer can choose how any further money paid into an account is used (this is called the 'first right of appropriation'), but banks can take a great deal of persuasion to recognise this.

Payment of HB discharges liability for rent

16.64   When rent allowance is paid to a landlord/agent this discharges the

---

16.57   HB 95(3),96(3); HB60+ 76(3),77(3); NIHB 92(4),93(3); NIHB 73(4),74(3)

16.61   HB 96(3)(b); HB60+ 77(3)(b); NIHB 93(3)(b); NIHB60+ 74(3)(b)

claimant's liability to pay that amount of rent unless the authority recovers it as an overpayment from that landlord/agent (table 18.5).

Suspending HB while considering who to pay

16.65   When considering whether HB should be paid to the claimant or someone else the authority has the power to suspend payment (para. 17.70 and see CH/1821/2006), though the DWP encourages authorities not to delay payment when considering the issue (GLHA 5.81).

Information provided to claimants and landlords/agents

16.66   Once the question arises of whether to pay a claimant or landlord/agent, and once a decision is then made, both parties (as a 'person affected') should be notified of that decision within 14 days (para. 16.2) – and this has been confirmed as applying in LHA cases as well as others: *CH/180/2006*.

16.67   When HB is paid to the landlord/agent the notice must inform them of:

*   the amount payable and the date from which payments will start;
*   their duty to report any change of circumstances which might affect the award and the kind of change which should be notified;
*   that if overpayment occurs which is recovered from payments made to other blameless tenants (para. 18.46), then those tenants must be treated as having paid their rent to the value of the amount recovered.

Appeals about who to pay HB to

16.68   Both the landlord/agent and claimant have appeal rights in relation to the decision: *CH/180/2006*. If one of them appeals the decision both are parties to the appeal. Both should be given notice of the appeal, the opportunity to request an oral hearing; and both are entitled to be present and heard: *CH 2986/2005*.

16.69   The authority should make sure that HMCTS is informed of the landlord/agent's address and any submission put to the tribunal by one of the parties must be copied to the others. The appeal itself is a full rehearing and is not limited to scrutiny of the authority's decision on judicial review grounds: *R(H) 6/06*.

When the wrong person has been paid

16.70   If the authority decided to pay the landlord/agent but paid the claimant instead, the law offers two approaches. Either, the landlord/agent is not entitled to HB for the same period and should seek compensation from the authority instead *(R(H) 2/08, [2010] UKUT 254 (AAC))*; or, if the payment was unlawful (paras. 16.36-42), the authority must pay the landlord/agent and recover the overpayment from the claimant: *[2008] UKUT 31 (AAC)*.

16.64   HB 95(2); HB60+ 76(2); NIHB 92(2); NIHB60+ 73(2)

16.66   HB sch 9 para 11; HB60+ sch 8 para 11; NIHB sch 10 para 11; NIHB60+ sch 9 para 11

16.67   HB sch 9 paras 11-12; HB60+ sch 8 paras 11-12; NIHB sch 10 paras 11-12; NIHB60+ sch 9 paras 11-12

Can a landlord/agent refuse to accept HB?

16.71   A landlord has the right to refuse to accept payments of rent (e.g. via HB) from anyone who is not a party to the tenancy agreement *(Bessa Plus Plc v Lancaster),* typically, for example, the tenant's partner. This may cause problems particularly where the non-tenant member of a couple should be the claimant (e.g. paras. 12.18, 22.24). In such cases the authority should pay the claimant, or the claimant's nominee (para. 16.73), or the authority may identify the payments made to the landlord as made on behalf of the liable person.

Other people who may receive a rent allowance

Appointee

16.72   When an appointee acts for a claimant who is currently incapable of managing his or her own finances (paras. 5.5 and 16.10), payment may be made to the appointee. (For the similar CTR rule see para. 16.14.)

Nominee

16.73   If the claimant requests in writing that the authority makes payment to another person (i.e. a corporate body or an individual aged 18 or more), the authority may make payments to that person. The DWP incorrectly refers to this person as an 'agent' and advises that the claimant must be unable to collect the money himself or herself (GM para. A6.181). This is not the case, however, as the law states that the claimant may be able to act on their own behalf.

16.74   The DWP (GLHA paras. 5.100-101) indicates that this power is subject to the rules governing direct payments to landlords. The DWP contends that as a result where a claim has been decided under the LHA rules the authority must not use its power to pay a person nominated by the claimant if that person is the claimant's landlord. The law does not appear to support this, though the existence of the separate rules regarding direct payments to landlords is something the authority may take account of when considering paying a nominee who is the landlord.

A dead claimant's personal representative or next of kin

16.75   When a claimant dies any rent allowance must be paid to their personal representative or, if there is none, next of kin, provided a written request is made within one year of the death (or longer if the authority allows). The next of kin must be aged 16 or over and take priority in the following order: spouse, children and grandchildren, other relatives (parents, brothers, sisters or their children). But see paragraph 16.42 if the claimant dies with rent arrears.

16.72   HB 94(2); HB60+ 75(2); NIHB 91(2); NIHB60+ 72(2)

16.73   HB 94(3); HB60+ 75(3); NIHB 91(3); NIHB60+ 72(3)

16.75   HB 97(1)-(3); HB60+ 78(1)-(3); NIHB 94(1)-(3); NIHB60+ 75(1)-(3)

17 Changes to entitlement

17.1 This chapter explains how a claimant's entitlement to HB or CTR can change or end. It covers:

- the duty to notify changes of circumstances to the authority;
- how changes are dealt with;
- when changes take effect;
- 'extended payments' and 'continuing payments';
- reviewing awards of HB/CTR; and
- additional HB rules about 'revisions' and 'supersessions', correcting decisions, and suspending, restoring and terminating an award.

Why decisions can change

17.2 Decisions can change because there has been a change in the circumstances of the claimant, or someone else relevant to the claim such as a household member or (in HB) a landlord, or in the law itself (paras. 17.18-51). They can also change when the authority reviews entitlement (paras. 17.52-53) or as a result of the disputes and appeals procedures (chapter 19).

Duty to notify changes

Relevant changes

17.3 The claimant has a duty to notify any 'relevant' change of circumstances. The same duty applies to anyone acting for the claimant (paras. 5.5-7), and in HB to anyone who receives payments (such as a landlord: para. 16.31). This means any change which the claimant (or other person) could reasonably be expected to know might affect:

- entitlement to HB/CTR; or
- the amount of HB/CTR; or
- the method of payment (including who should be paid).

The duty to notify begins on the date the claim is made, and continues for as long as the person is in receipt of HB/CTR. (For time limits etc, see paras. 17.7-13.).

17.4 The law lists changes that must be notified and changes that need not be notified (summarised in tables 17.1 and 17.2). These are not exhaustive. For example, a claimant should also notify the authority of changes in:

17.3 HB 88(1),(6); HB60+ 69(1),(9); NIHB 84(1); NIHB60+ 65(1); CTP sch 8 para 9(1),(6); CTR 115(1),(6)

- personal details (name, address, etc);
- rent (unless the claimant is a council or NIHE tenant) and in Northern Ireland rates (unless collected by Land and Property Services);
- family and household details (which could affect the applicable amount or non-dependant deductions);
- capital and income; and
- any matter which affects whether HB is payable to the landlord.

Table 17.1: Changes the claimant must notify

The following is a list of the items specifically mentioned in the law. The claimant's duty is wider (paras. 17.3-4).

Working age claims (para. 1.20)

- The end of the claimant's (or partner's) entitlement to JSA(IB), ESA(IR) or IS
- Changes where a child or young person ceases to be a member of the family: e.g. when child benefit stops or he or she leaves the household

Pension age claims (para. 1.20)

- Changes in the details of the claimant's letting (HB rent allowances only)
- Changes affecting the residence or income of any non-dependant
- Absences exceeding or likely to exceed 13 weeks

Additional matters for claimants on savings credit

- Changes affecting any child living with the claimant (other than age) which might affect the amount of HB/CTR
- Changes to capital which take it (or may take it) above £16,000
- Changes to a non-dependant if the non-dependant's income and capital was treated as being the claimant's (para. (d) of table 13.5)
- Changes to a partner who was ignored in assessing savings credit but is taken into account for HB/CTR (para. (d) of table 13.5)

Additional matters for claimants on second adult rebate

- Changes in the number of adults in the home
- Changes in the total gross incomes of the adults in the home
- The date any adult in the home ceases to receive JSA(IB), ESA(IR) or IS

T17.1 HB 88; HB60+ 69; NIHB 84; NIHB60+ 65; CTP sch 8 para 9; CTR 115

Table 17.2: Changes the claimant need not notify

- ◆ Beginnings or ends of awards of pension credit (either kind) or changes in the amount – because it is the DWP's duty to notify the authority
- ◆ Changes which affect JSA(IB), ESA(IR) or IS but do not affect HB/CTR
- ◆ Changes in council tax
- ◆ Changes in rent if the claimant is a council or NIHE tenant
- ◆ Changes in rates in Northern Ireland if collected by the Rating Service
- ◆ Changes in the age of any member of the family or non-dependant
- ◆ Changes in the HB or CTR regulations

How to notify changes

17.5   A change must be notified to the authority – or to someone acting on its behalf (paras. 1.26-27). (For notifications to the DWP, see para. 17.6.) Some authorities accept notification by telephone or online, though they can require written rather than telephone notifications, or require written or electronic records to be kept by those making online notifications. In Scotland, for CTR only, authorities can specify an address which claimants can attend to notify births and deaths. In all other cases, changes must be notified in writing to a 'designated office' (para. 5.8). However HB law adds that an authority may accept notification by any other method it agrees to in a particular case.

17.6   If the claimant (or partner) is on JSA or IS and is starting work, and this will mean that JSA/IS will cease (or JSA(C) will change), the claimant may notify this by telephone to the DWP. This applies only for HB purposes and is part of the DWP's 'in and out of work' process.

CTR time limits, etc

17.7   For CTR in England and Wales the claimant has a duty to notify relevant changes within 21 days of when they occur or as soon as reasonably practicable thereafter. There is no equivalent time limit for CTR in Scotland.

17.8   CTR law does not say what should happen if the claimant fails to notify a relevant change or (in England and Wales) exceeds the above time limits. In practice, if the change would:

T17.2   HB 88(3)(4); HB60+ 69(3),(4); NIHB 84(2),(3); NIHB60+ 65(2),(3); CTP sch 8 para 9(3),(4); CTR 115(3),(4)

17.5   HB 88(1),(4),(6), 88A, sch 11; HB60+ 69(1),(4),(9), 69A, sch 10; NIHB 84(1),(3), 84A, sch 11; NIHB60+ 65(1),(2), 65A, sch 10; CTP sch 7 para 11, sch 8 para 9(2); CTR 115(2), sch 1 para 11

17.7   CTP sch 8 para 9(2); CTR 115(2)

- reduce or end entitlement to CTR – authorities are likely to regard an overpayment as having occurred and recover it (para. 18.2);
- increase entitlement to CTR – it is arguable that authorities should award the arrears (since council tax law does not generally contain time limits for adjusting liability: para 10.19), but claimants should not rely on this and it is likely to be a matter for Valuation Tribunals and the courts to decide (chapter 19).

HB time limits, etc

17.9 For HB, there is a one month time limit for notifying changes, which can be extended to 13 months in special circumstances (para. 17.14). Rather than placing a duty on the claimant to meet these time limits, HB law spells out the consequences of not doing so – which in practice amounts to the same thing.

17.10 If the claimant fails to notify a relevant change, or exceeds the above time limits, and the change would:

- reduce or end entitlement to HB – an overpayment has occurred: this may or may not be recoverable (chapter 18);
- increase entitlement to HB – special rules apply (paras. 17.11-15).

HB: late notification of beneficial changes

17.11 The following rule (para. 17.12) applies when the claimant:

- has a duty to notify a relevant change (para. 17.3), and the change would increase entitlement to HB (a 'beneficial change'); but
- takes longer than one month to do so (or longer in special circumstances: paras. 17.14-15).

17.12 In such cases the change is treated (for HB purposes) as occurring on the date the authority received the notification. In other words the claimant loses money, as illustrated in the example.

17.13 The rule does not apply to changes in pension credit or in social security benefits (in such cases the rules in paras. 17.27-28 and 17.30-33 apply instead).

HB: extending the time limit for notifying a beneficial change

17.14 In the case of a change of circumstances which increases entitlement to HB, the one month time limit for notifying it is extended (and the claimant does not lose money) if:

- the notification is received by the authority within 13 months of the date on which the change occurred; and

---

17.10 DAR 8(2); NIDAR 8(2)

17.11 DAR 7(2)(a),(3), 8(3),(5); NIDAR 7(2)(a), 8(3),(5)

17.14 DAR 9; NIDAR 9

- the claimant also notifies the authority of his or her reasons for failing to notify the change earlier; and
- the authority is satisfied that there are or were 'special circumstances' as a result of which it was not practicable to notify the change within the one month time limit. The longer the delay (beyond the normal one month), the more compelling those special circumstances need to be; and
- the authority is satisfied that it is reasonable to allow the claimant's late notification of the change. In determining this, the authority may not take account of ignorance of the law (not even ignorance of the time limits) nor of the fact that an Upper Tribunal or court has taken a different view of the law from that previously understood and applied.

17.15   If the authority refuses the claimant's late notification, the claimant has the right to ask the authority to reconsider or to appeal (chapter 19).

Example: HB: late notified beneficial change

A claimant's wages went down four months ago, but the claimant did not inform the authority until today. The authority asks why she delayed, but she has no special circumstances.

The change is implemented from the Monday following the day the claimant's written notification of the change was received by the authority. The claimant does not get her arrears. (However, if the claimant has 'special circumstances', she may get her arrears: para. 17.14.)

Dealing with changes

Decisions, information and evidence

17.16   The authority must decide whether to alter (or end) entitlement to HB/CTR as a result of the change, and may request the claimant to provide information and evidence it requires in connection with this. The claimant is responsible for providing this in the same way as when they made their claim (para. 5.13). In HB the law adds that the authority must take it into account if they provide it within one month, or longer if reasonable.

Notifications

17.17   When the authority alters (or ends) entitlement to HB/CTR, it must notify the claimant (and any other person affected: para. 16.10) within 14 days or as soon as reasonably practicable. The notification must include:

17.16   AA 5(1)(hh); NIAA 5(1)(hh); HB 86(1); HB60+ 67(1); NIHB 82(1); NIHB60+ 63(1); DAR 4(5), 7(5); NIDAR 4(4), 7(5); CTP sch 8 para 7(1); CTR 113(1)

17.17   HB 90(1)(b), sch 9; HB60+ 71(1)(b), sch 8; NIHB 86(1)(b), sch 10; NIHB60+ 67(1)(b), sch 9; CTP sch 8 para 1(b),(2)-(4); CTR 117(1)(b),(2)-(4)

- its new decision (CTR cases) or a statement of what it has altered (HB cases); and

- their rights to obtain a written statement of reasons and to appeal, etc (para. 16.11).

The exception to the above is that in Scotland CTR law contains no duty to notify.

When changes take effect

17.18   This section describes when a change takes effect in the claimant's entitlement to HB/CTR. There are two steps involved:

- determining the date the change actually occurred; and

- working out (from that) what date it takes effect in HB/CTR.

The date a change occurs: the general rule

17.19   The starting point is that the date a change actually occurs is the date something new happens (for example, a new baby, a birthday, a change in pay, a rent increase). This is a question of fact (paras. 1.39-43).

17.20   In HB only, late-notified beneficial changes can be treated as occurring on the date the notification was received (paras. 17.11-12). Other special cases in HB and CTR are described below (paras. 17.23-51).

The date a change takes effect: the general rule

17.21   The date a change takes effect is:

- in CTR in Wales, the exact date the change occurs (whatever day of the week this is);

- in HB (throughout the UK), and in CTR in England and Scotland, the Monday after the date the change occurs. Even if the change occurs on a Monday, HB/CTR change on the following Monday.

17.22   There are different rules in HB for moves, changes in rent, and changes in social security benefits; and in HB and CTR for changes in pension credit. These and other special cases are described below (paras. 17.23-51).

Moves and changes in rent, rates or council tax liability

17.23   This rule applies when:

- the claimant moves home; or

- the claimant's liability for rent or council tax (or in Northern Ireland rates) changes.

17.21   HB 79(1); HB60+ 59(1); NIHB 77(1); NIHB60+ 57(1); DAR 7(2)(a)(i), 8(2); NIDAR 7(2)(a)(i), 8(2); CTP sch 1 para 46(1),(5),(6); CTR 107(1),(5),(6)

17.24 The date a claimant's rent, council tax or rates go up (or down) is usually clear. The date a move occurs can be less straightforward. However, it is the date the claimant changes their normal home, rather than a date on a letting agreement, etc (*R(H) 9/05* para. 3.4). The date these changes take effect is shown in table 17.3.

Table 17.3: Moves and changes in rent, council tax and rates

What the change is	When it takes effect in HB/CTR
CTR	
All moves and all changes in council tax liability	CTR changes on the exact day
HB for hostels with a daily rent liability (para. 5.49)	
All moves and all changes in rent liability	HB changes on the exact day
HB in all other cases	
If HB continues after the move or change in rent/rates	HB changes on the exact day
If HB ends as a result of the move or change in rent/rates	HB continues until the end of the benefit week containing the move or change in rent/rates

---

17.25 The following changes also take effect on a daily basis:

- the beginning or end of a rent-free period;
- starting or stopping being eligible for HB on a former home, or on two homes, including stopping being eligible because the (4 weeks or 52 weeks) time limit runs out (paras. 3.8 and 3.13). This also applies in Scotland to CTR on two homes.

17.24 HB 79(2),(2A)(a),(8), 80(4)(b),(c),(10); HB60+ 59(2),(2A)(a),(8), 61(4)(b),(c),(11); NIHB 77(2),(3)(a),(10), 78(4)(b),(c),(9); NIHB60+ 57(2),(3)(a),(14), 59(4)(b),(c),(9); CTP sch 1 para 46(3),(4); CTR 107(3),(4)

T17.3 As para. 17.24

17.25 HB 79(2A)(b),(2B), 80(11), 81(2); HB60+ 59(2A)(b),(2B), 61(12), 62(2); NIHB 77(3),(4),(11), 78(10), 79(3); NIHB60+ 57(3),(4),(15), 59(10), 60(2)

17.26   Whenever a claimant is eligible for HB on two homes, eligible rent in each benefit week is calculated by adding together the daily eligible rent for the two addresses for the appropriate number of days (as illustrated in the last of the examples).

Examples: Moves and changes in liability

Moving within an authority's area

A woman moves from one address to another within an authority's area on Friday 1st November 2013. She is liable for rent and council tax at her old address up to and including Thursday 31st October and at her new address from Friday 1st November.

- ◆   Her HB and CTR change on and from Friday 1st November (on a daily basis) to take account of her new eligible rent and eligible council tax.

Moving out of an authority's area

A man moves out of an authority's area on Saturday 18th May 2013. He is liable for rent and council tax at his old address (which is not a hostel) up to and including Friday 17th May.

- ◆   His HB ends at the end of the benefit week containing his last day of liability for rent, in other words his last day of HB is Sunday 19th May.
- ◆   His CTR ends on the last day of his liability for council tax. In other words his last day of CTR is Friday 17th May.

A rent increase

A woman's rent goes up on Saturday 15th June 2013.

- ◆   If her entitlement to HB changes as a result, it changes on and from Saturday 15th June (on a daily basis).

HB on two homes

A woman flees violence on Wednesday 3rd July 2013. She leaves a council tenancy at which the eligible rent is £70 pw. She goes to a hostel where the eligible rent is £140 pw, payable on a daily basis. Her intention to return to the council tenancy means that she is eligible for HB on both homes.

- ◆   In benefit week commencing Monday 1st July her eligible rent is a full week's eligible rent at the council tenancy (£70.00) plus five-sevenths of a week's eligible rent at the hostel (£120), totalling £190.

Changes to pension credit

17.27 If a change in either guarantee credit or savings credit, whether due to a change in the claimant's circumstances or due to official error (para. 17.57), affects the claimant's entitlement to HB/CTR, this takes effect from the date shown in table 17.4.

Table 17.4: When pension credit starts, changes or ends

What the change is	When it takes effect in HB/CTR*
Pension credit starts, increasing entitlement to HB/CTR	The Monday following the first day of entitlement to pension credit
Pension credit starts, reducing entitlement to HB/CTR	The Monday following the date the authority receives notification from the DWP about this (or, if later, the Monday following the first day of entitlement to pension credit)
Pension credit changes or ends, increasing entitlement to HB/CTR	The Monday of the benefit week in which pension credit changes or ends
Pension credit changes or ends, reducing entitlement to HB/CTR:	
• if this is due to a delay by the claimant in notifying a change in circumstances to the DWP	The Monday of the benefit week in which pension credit changes or ends
• in any other case	The Monday following the date the authority received notification from the DWP about this (or, if later, the Monday following the pension credit change or end)

* If any of the above would take effect during a claimant's 'continuing payment' period (para. 17.50), the change is instead deferred until afterwards.

Changes to universal credit

17.28 When a claimant's entitlement to universal credit starts, changes or ends, the general rules apply (paras. 17.19-22). (For the assessment of universal credit as income, see paras. 13.169-171.)

Changes to tax credits

17.29 When a claimant's entitlement to working tax credit or child tax credit starts, changes or ends, the general rule applies (paras. 17.19-22). But because of the way tax credits are paid (para. 13.46) it can involve counting backwards or forwards from the pay date to work out when the change actually occurs. Table 17.5 explains this and includes examples.

Table 17.5: When a tax credit starts, changes or ends

Four-weekly instalments

The pay date is the last day of the 28 days covered by the tax credit instalment.

So if a four-weekly instalment is due on the 30th of the month, it covers the period from 3rd to 30th of that month (both dates included).

For example:

* if that is the first instalment ever of a claimant's tax credit, their HB/CTR changes on the Monday following the 3rd of the month;
* if that is the first instalment of a new rate of a claimant's tax credit, their HB/CTR changes on the Monday following the 3rd of the month;
* if that is the last instalment of a claimant's tax credit, the date the change occurs is the 31st of the month, and their HB/CTR changes on the Monday following the 31st of the month.

Weekly instalments

The pay date is the last day of the 7 days covered by the tax credit instalment.

So if a weekly instalment is due on the 15th of the month, it covers the period from 9th to 15th of that month (both dates included).

For example:

* if that is the first instalment ever of a claimant's tax credit, their HB/CTR changes on the Monday following the 9th of the month;
* if that is the first instalment of a new rate of a claimant's tax credit, their HB/CTR changes on the Monday following the 9th of the month;
* if that is the last instalment of a claimant's tax credit, the date the change occurs is the 16th of the month, and their HB/CTB changes on the Monday following the 16th of the month.

Different rules apply for CTR in Wales: para. 17.21.

Changes relating to social security benefits

17.30 The following rules apply when entitlement to a social security benefit starts, changes, ends or is reinstated. They apply to all social security benefits (apart from the credits described in paras. 17.27-29) received by the claimant, a partner, or a child or young person.

17.31 The date such a change actually occurs is the first day of the person's new, different, nil or re-instated entitlement.

17.32 The date the change takes effect:

- in HB, is shown in table 17.6. This is also called the 'relevant benefit rule';
- in CTR, follows the general rules in paragraph 17.21.

(Sometimes this can result in different dates for the two benefits.)

Table 17.6: HB: changes in social security benefits

What the change is	When it takes effect in HB
A social security benefit reduces or ends:	
All cases (whether HB increases, reduces or ends as a result)	HB changes on the Monday following the change (see also paras. 17.42 and 17.50)
A social security benefit starts, increases or is re-instated:	
If HB increases as a result	HB increases on the exact day (or from the start of the HB award if later)
If HB reduces or ends as a result	HB reduces or ends on the Monday following the change
If HB ended as above, but the social security benefit is then reinstated	HB is reinstated on the exact day
Exception for ESA:	
If a person converts onto ESA or converts from one ESA component to another (para. 12.2)	HB changes on the exact day

(This table does not apply to credits: paras. 17.27-29.)

17.30   HB 79(1); HB60 I 59(1); NIHB 77(1); NIHB60+ 57(1); DAR 4(7B),(7C), 7(2)(i),(p),(q), 8(14), (14D),(14E); NIDAR 4(6B),(6C), 7(2)(h), 8(11); CTP sch 1 para 46(1),(2); CTR 107(1),(2)

T17.6   As para. 17.30

17.33   When a social security benefit is found to have been awarded from a date in the past, any resulting increase in HB/CTR is awarded for the past period (so the claimant gets their arrears: see the second example). In HB, this is because the 'relevant benefit rule' over-rides the rule about late notification of beneficial changes (para. 17.13). In CTR it is the effect of the general rules (para. 17.21).

Changes in income, capital, household membership, etc

17.34   The general rules (paras. 17.19-22) apply to all other changes – including changes in income, capital, membership of the family or household, and so on. But see also paragraph 6.30 for when non-dependant deductions are delayed, and paragraph 13.25 for when arrears of income are (or are not) taken into account.

17.35   Authorities also have a discretion to disregard, for up to 30 weeks, changes in tax, national insurance and the maximum rate of tax credits when these result from a change in the law (e.g. the Budget). This discretion does not apply to CTR in Scotland (and is in any case rarely used).

Examples: Changes to social security benefits

Going on to disability living allowance (DLA)

A claimant on HB/CTR is awarded DLA from Thursday 16th May 2013. The date of change is Thursday 16th May. So her entitlement to HB/CTR goes up on Thursday 16th May.

A claimant is found to have been awarded DLA from a date in the past.

No matter how far the DLA goes back, the authority must award the claimant any as-yet-unawarded premium that flows from being on DLA (and remove any non-dependant deductions if appropriate) all the way back to the start of his award of DLA (or the start of his award of HB/CTR if later).

Starting work

17.36   The general rules (paras. 17.19-22) apply when someone starts work. Their effect is that a claimant who starts work on a Monday gets a whole week of HB and (except in Wales) CTR as though they had not started work. They may – after that – also qualify for an extended payment (para. 17.42).

Changes ending HB/CTR

17.37   The general rules (paras. 17.19-22) apply to any change of circumstances which means that the claimant no longer satisfies all the basic conditions for benefit (paras. 2.3-4) – for example if their capital now exceeds the upper limit or income is now too high to qualify.

17.35   HB 34; HB60+ 34; NIHB 31; NIHB60+ 32; CTP sch 1 para 28; CTR 60

Changes in the law: case law (the anti-test-case rule)

17.38   In HB only, the 'anti-test case rule' applies when an Upper Tribunal or court decides a case (a 'lead case') by interpreting the law in a new way. It requires all similar cases ('look-alike cases') to be amended to follow the new interpretation from the date of the decision on the lead case (not earlier). This does not apply to cases an authority should have decided before the decision on the lead case; nor to appeals which a First-tier Tribunal 'stayed' to await the decision on the lead case; nor to decisions by Upper Tribunals: *CH/532/2006*.

Changes in the law: regulations and up-ratings

17.39   When regulations relevant to HB/CTR are amended, the authority alters the claimant's entitlement to HB/CTR from the date on which the amendment takes effect (unless entitlement reduces to nil, in which case para. 17.37 applies). (For up-rating dates, see table 1.3 and para. 13.157.)

More than one change

17.40   If more than one change occurs in a case, each is dealt with in turn. But the following rules apply when changes which actually occur in the same benefit week would have an effect (under the earlier rules in this chapter) in different benefit weeks:

* In HB only, if one of the changes is in:
  * the annual up-rating (but only in the case of claimants whose rent is due weekly or in multiples of weeks);
  * the amount of liability for rent on a dwelling;
  * moving into a new dwelling; or
  * starting or stopping being eligible for HB on a former home or on two homes, including when the (4 weeks or 52 weeks) time limit runs out,

  the other changes in entitlement instead apply when that applies. And for this rule, the first item in the above list takes priority over the other three.
* For HB in all other cases, all the changes take effect from the Monday of the benefit week in which the changes actually occur.
* In all CTR cases, work out the various days on which the changes have an effect (under the earlier rules): all the changes instead apply from the earliest of these dates.

17.41   A further variation to the above applies when a person converts onto ESA (table 12.2) during the period from 1st to 16th April (both dates inclusive). In 2013, such a change takes effect on 1st April.

17.38 CPSA sch 7 paras 4(5),(6),18; NICPSA sch 7 paras 4(4),(5); DAR 7(2)(b); NIDAR 7(2)(b)

17.39 HB 79(3); HB60+ 60(3); NIHB 77(3); NIHB60+ 58(3); DAR 8(10); NIDAR 8(12)

17.40 HB 79(4),(5); HB60+ 59(4),(5); NIHB 77(6),(7); NIHB60+ 57(6),(7); DAR 7(2)(q), 8(14E); NIDAR 7(2)(h), 8(11); CTP sch 1 para 46(7); CTR 107(7)

Extended payments

17.42   Extended payments (EPs) help long-term unemployed people who find work, by giving them four weeks extra HB/CTR. They are also known as 'extended reductions' (in CTR law) or HB/CTR 'run-on'. They are like the extended payments some people get in JSA or ESA (and people often get both at the same time).

Entitlement

17.43   A claimant is entitled to an EP if they meet the conditions in table 17.7. Authorities in England and Wales can vary those conditions for CTR EPs (paras. 10.25 and 10.28), and in Wales the law specifies that this can include making EPs more generous.

17.44   No claim is required for an EP. All the matters referred to in table 17.7 are for the authority to determine (not the DWP). The claimant must be notified about their entitlement to an EP (or not).

Period and amount

17.45   An EP is awarded from the date the change (getting a job, etc) takes effect, and it lasts for four weeks (as illustrated in the example). In each of those four weeks, the amount of the EP is the greater of:

(a) the amount awarded in the last full benefit week before the EP started. For HB, this means the amount that would have been awarded if there was no benefit cap (para. 6.31);

(b) the amount which would be the claimant's entitlement in that particular week if there were no such thing as EPs. For example, a claimant whose non-dependant left home might qualify for more HB/CTR this way.

17.46   Throughout the EP, all changes in the claimant's circumstances are ignored. But if a claimant's entitlement to HB on two homes ceases during the EP, the amount of EP is reduced by the amount of the eligible rent on the home they no longer qualify for HB for. And no EP is awarded for rent/rates/council tax during any period during which the claimant is not liable for rent/rates/council tax.

17.47   If the claimant or a partner reaches pension age during the EP, the figure used for (b) throughout the EP is whichever would have been higher using their entitlement before and after that age. (This rule applies in HB, and in Scotland to CTR, but not to CTR in England or Wales.)

17.42   HB 2(1),72,73; HB60+ 2(1),53; NIHB 2(1),70,71; NIHB60+ 2(1),51; CTP 2(1), sch 1 para 38; CTR 2(1), 87,88,94,95,100

17.43   CTPW 31(3)

17.45   HB 72A,72B,72E,73A,73B,73E; HB60+ 53A,53B; NIHB 70A,70B,71A,71B; NIHB60+51A,51B; CTP sch 1 paras 39,40; CTR 89,90,96,97,101,102

17.47   HB60+ 52; NIHB60+ 50

Table 17.7: Entitlement to an extended payment

Claimants who have been on a 'qualifying income-related benefit'

The claimant is entitled to an extended payment if:

+ the claimant or any partner starts employment or self-employment, or increases his or her hours or earnings;
+ this is expected to last for at least five weeks;
+ the claimant or partner has been entitled to ESA(IR), JSA(IB), JSA(C) or IS continuously for at least 26 weeks (or any combination of those benefits in that period);
+ immediately before starting the job, etc, the claimant or partner was on ESA(IR), JSA(IB) or IS. At this point being on JSA(C) is not enough; and
+ entitlement to ESA(IR), JSA(IB) or IS ceases as a result of starting the job, etc.

Claimants who have been on a 'qualifying contributory benefit'

The claimant is entitled to extended payment if:

+ the claimant or any partner starts employment or self-employment, or increases his or her hours or earnings;
+ this is expected to last for at least five weeks;
+ the claimant or partner has been entitled to ESA(C), IB or SDA continuously for at least 26 weeks (or any combination of those benefits in that period);
+ immediately before starting the job, etc, the claimant or partner was on ESA(C), IB or SDA. And neither of them must be on ESA(IR), JSA(IB) or IS; and
+ entitlement to ESA(C), IB or SDA ceases as a result of starting the job, etc.

Example: Extended payments

A claimant who meets all the conditions for an extended payment starts work on Monday 8th July 2013.

His award of HB/CTR continues up to and including Sunday 14th July 2013. His extended payment covers the period from Monday 15th July 2013 to Sunday 11th August 2013. If he then continues to qualify for HB/CTR after that, the new amount of HB/CTR is awarded from Monday 12th August 2013.

117.7 As para. 17.42

HB/CTR after an extended payment

17.48   If the claimant qualifies for HB/CTR based on their new income after the end of the EP, this is awarded in the normal way – and there is no requirement for the claimant to make a fresh claim for this.

Variations for movers

17.49   Claimants who are entitled to an EP are entitled to it even if they move home during the EP. In Great Britain, if the move is to another authority's area, the determination, notification and award of the EP is done by the authority whose area the claimant is moving out of. That authority may liaise with the authority whose area the claimant is moving into; and may pay the EP to them or to the claimant.

Continuing payments

Entitlement

17.50   Continuing payments are awarded in HB/CTR whenever the DWP informs the authority that a claimant on JSA(IB), ESA(IR) or income support has reached pension credit age (para. 1.20) (or 65 if they stayed on JSA(IB) beyond that age), or has a partner and the partner has claimed pension credit. Continuing payments enable the award of HB/CTR to continue without a break while their new entitlement to pension credit (if any) is determined.

Period and amount

17.51   The continuing payment starts immediately after the last day of entitlement to JSA(IB)/ESA(IR)/IS, and lasts for four weeks plus any extra days to make it end on a Sunday. The amount during that period is calculated by treating the claimant as having no income or capital. And if they move home, the claimant's eligible rent or council tax or rates are the higher of the amounts at the old and new addresses; and any non-dependant deductions are based on the circumstances at the new address.

17.48   HB 72D,73D; HB60+ 53D; NIHB 70C,71C; NIHB60+ 51C; CTP sch 1 para 42; CTR 92,99,104

17.49   HB 72C,73C,115,116; HB60+ 53C,96,97; CTP sch 1 paras 41,44, sch 6 paras 1,2; CTR 91,98,103,105

17.50   HB60+ 54; NIHB60+ 52; CTP sch 1 para 43; CTR 93

> ### Example: Continuing payments
>
> A man is on HB/CTR and JSA(IB) when he reaches 65, on Thursday 12th September 2013. The DWP informs the authority that his entitlement to pension credit is being considered.
>
> His continuing payment of HB/CTR is awarded from Thursday 12th September 2013 to Sunday 13th October 2013 – a total of four weeks and four days.
>
> By then the authority knows the claimant's entitlement to HB/CTB based on his new circumstances, and awards this from Monday 14th October 2013.

Reviewing awards of HB/CTR

17.52 The authority may reconsider any decision it has made about HB or CTR, and in doing so may request the claimant to provide information and evidence it reasonably requires (para. 5.13). In HB the law adds that it must take this into account if it is provided within one month, or longer if reasonable.

17.53 A review may show that:

* there has been an unreported change of circumstances, in which case the earlier rules apply (paras. 17.18-51);

* a decision was wrong from the outset. HB law has special rules for this (paras. 17.56-68). CTR does not, but in practice the considerations in paragraph 17.8 are also likely to apply here.

In both the above situations the authority must notify what it has done (para. 16.4).

Terminology peculiar to HB

Revisions and supersessions

17.54 In HB law, a changed decision is also known as a revision or a supersession:

* a 'revision' is required when a decision was wrong from the outset. When a decision is revised, the revision goes back to the beginning (to the date of the decision in question);

* a 'supersession' is required when there has been a change of circumstances. When a decision is superseded, the supersession does not go right back: there is always a 'before' and an 'after'.

Some examples are given in table 17.8. Each of the above results in a new decision, which can itself be revised or superseded or appealed.

17.52 AA 5(1); NIAA 5(1); HB 86(1),(3); HB60+ 67(1),(3); NIHB 82(1),(3); NIHB60+ 63(1),(3); DAR 4(5), 7(5); NIDAR 4(5), 7(5); CTP sch 8 para 7(4),(6); CTR 113(4),(6)

17.54 CPSA sch 7; NICPSA sch 7; DAR 4,7,8; NIDAR 4,7,8

Closed period supersessions

17.55 A 'closed period supersession' is done when someone's entitlement to
HB is discovered to have reduced to nil for a fixed period in the past (and
recommenced at the same or a different rate after that). For example, a claimant
has been on JSA(IB) (and HB) for many years but worked last Christmas for a
fixed contract of three weeks for a very high income. He did not declare that fact
then, but it is discovered now. A 'closed period supersession' means that the
authority (now) reduces his entitlement to nil for that past period (and recovers
the overpayment: chapter 18). The advantage (administratively and to the
claimant) is that the claimant remains currently entitled to HB (based on his
original claim) without needing to reclaim. There have been doubts about this
rule, but it is correct in income support *(CIS/2595/2003),* and the DWP considers
it to be correct in HB (circular HB/CTB A6/2009).

Table 17.8: Revisions and supersessions: examples

Situation	How it is dealt with in HB
Changes of circumstances	
A change notified more than one month after it occurred (this time limit can be extended) if the claimant qualifies for more HB	**Supersession:** Typically, from the Monday following the day the authority receives the notification (paras. 17.11-13)
Any other change of circumstances	**Supersession:** Typically, from the Monday following the day the change occurs (paras. 17.21-22)
Overpayments and official errors	
Overpayments, whatever the cause; and underpayments caused by official error	**Revision or supersession:** From when the overpayment or underpayment began
Successful requests for a reconsideration, etc	
Reconsiderations requested within one month (which can be extended)	**Revision:** From the date the decision took effect or should have
Reconsiderations requested outside that time limit (sometimes called an 'any time review')	**Supersession:** From the Monday of the week in which the authority received the request
Appeals if the authority is able to revise in the claimant's favour instead	**Revision:** From the date the decision took effect or should have

Correcting HB decisions

17.56 This section describes how the authority can correct mistakes in an HB decision – either because it has noticed the mistake itself, or because someone has pointed the mistake out. (These rules do not apply to CTR.)

17.57 The law uses four different terms for this:

* a 'mistake of fact' means that the decision was based on an incorrect fact (without at this stage saying that it was necessarily anybody's fault);

* an 'error of law' means that the decision was based on an incorrect understanding of the law;

* an 'accidental error' is something on the lines of a slip of the pen – a failure by the authority to put into action (or to record) its true intentions;

* an 'official error' is defined independently (para.17.59) and can include one or a combination of the above *(CH/943/2003)*.

Example: 'Mistake of fact' and 'error of law'

In deciding a claim for HB, an authority determined that a man and a woman were not a couple.

This would be a mistake of fact if the authority made its decision not knowing that they were actually married (e.g. because the claimant had lied or the authority misread the application form).

It would be an error of law if the authority wrongly believed that two unmarried people could never be a couple for HB purposes.

Correcting accidental errors

17.58 The authority may correct an accidental error in any decision (including a revised or superseding decision), or the record of any decision, at any time. The correction is deemed to be part of the decision or record, and the authority must give written notice of the correction as soon as practicable to the claimant and any other person affected.

Correcting other official errors

17.59 The authority may revise (or supersede if it cannot revise) a decision at any time if the decision arose from an 'official error'. An 'official error' means an error by an authority, the DWP or HM Revenue and Customs – or someone acting on their behalf (such as a contractor or a housing association which verifies HB claims). However, something does not count as an 'official error' if it was caused wholly or partly by any person or body other than the above, nor if it is an error of

---

17.58 DAR 10A(1),(2); NIDAR 10A(1),(2)

17.59 DAR 1(2),4(2); NIDAR 1(2),4(2)

law which is shown to have been an error only by a subsequent decision of the Upper Tribunal, the NI Commissioners or a court.

17.60   The effect may be that there has been an underpayment of HB (in which case the arrears must be awarded – no matter how far back they go) or an overpayment (which may or may not be recoverable: chapter 18).

When an appeal decision applies to a case

17.61   The authority may revise a decision at any time to take account of an appeal decision in the same case (made by a tribunal, the Upper Tribunal, the NI Commissioners or a court) which the authority was not aware of at the time it made the decision.

Mistakes of fact resulting in an overpayment

17.62   The authority may revise or supersede a decision at any time if the decision was made in ignorance of, or was based on a mistake as to, some material fact – and the decision was, as a result, more favourable than it would otherwise have been. This creates an overpayment (which may or may not be recoverable: chapter 18).

Mistakes of fact discovered within one month

17.63   The authority may revise a decision if, within one month of the date of notifying it, or longer if reasonable, the authority has sufficient information to show that it was made in ignorance of, or was based on a mistake as to, some material fact. This could arise only in the case of increases to entitlement (for decreases see para. 17.62).

Other mistakes of fact

17.64   If none of the previous rules in this section apply, the authority may supersede a decision at any time if the decision was made in ignorance of, or was based on a mistake as to, some material fact. It could arise only in the case of increases to entitlement (for decreases see para. 17.62).

17.65   The supersession in such a case takes effect from the Monday at the beginning of the benefit week in which:

 ◆ the request was received from the claimant or other person affected (if a request was indeed made); or

 ◆ the authority first had information to show that the original decision was made in ignorance or mistake of fact (in any other case).

17.61   DAR 4(7); NIDAR 4(6)

17.62   DAR 4(2); NIDAR 4(2)

17.63   DAR 4(1),8(4),(5); NIDAR 4(1),8(4),(5)

17.64   CPSA sch 7 para 4(5),(6); NICPSA sch 7 para 4(4),(5); DAR 7(2)(b),8(4)(5); NIDAR 7(2)(b),8(4),(5)

17.65   DAR 8(4)-(5); NIDAR 8(4)-5)

Other errors of law

17.66 A final rule applies if a decision was based on an error of law but was not due to 'official error' (para. 17.59). (This could arise if the Upper Tribunal, NI Commissioners or a court interpret the law in an unexpected way: para. 17.38.) The authority may supersede the decision at any time. The supersession takes effect from the date on which it is made (or, if earlier, from the date the person's request was received).

Information and evidence

17.67 When reconsidering a decision for the above reasons (paras. 17.56-66), the authority may request the claimant to provide information it requires – and must take it into account if they provide it within one month, or longer if reasonable.

Notifying the outcome

17.68 Whenever the authority alters a decision under the above rules (paras. 17.59-66), it must write notifying the claimant and any other person affected, of:

♦ the decision it has altered; and

♦ the person's right to request a written statement of reasons, to request a reconsideration, and to appeal to a tribunal, and how and when to do these things.

Suspending, restoring and terminating HB

17.69 This section describes how an authority may suspend, restore and terminate HB. (There are no similar provisions in CTR.) To suspend means stopping making payments for the time being, usually in order to avoid an overpayment or to seek information or evidence. To restore means starting payments again – either at the same amount as before or at a different amount, depending on the circumstances. To terminate means ending an award of HB altogether.

Suspending HB

17.70 The authority may suspend HB if any of the following circumstances apply:

(a) the authority doubts whether the conditions of entitlement to HB are fulfilled;

(b) the authority is considering whether to change a decision about HB;

(c) the authority considers there may be a recoverable overpayment of HB;

17.66 CPSA sch 7 para 4(5),(6); NICPSA sch 7 para 4(4),(5); DAR 7(2)(b); NIDAR 7(2)(b)

17.67 DAR 4(5), 7(5); NIDAR 4(4)

17.68 DAR 10; NIDAR 10; HB sch 9; HB60+ sch 8; NIHB sch 10; NIHB60+ sch 9; CTB sch 8; CTB60+ sch 7

(d) a First-tier or Upper Tribunal has made a decision (in this or another case) and the authority is awaiting the decision or a statement of reasons, or is considering making a further appeal;

(e) an appeal has been made, or leave to appeal has been sought, against a decision of a First-tier or Upper Tribunal or court in the case to be suspended;

(f) an appeal has been made, or leave to appeal has been sought, against a decision of an Upper Tribunal or court in a different HB case, and this may affect the case to be suspended;

(g) the claimant (or another person affected) has failed to provide information or evidence needed by the authority to consider changing a decision about HB.

In such cases, HB is usually suspended in full (though the law permits an authority to suspend only part).

Restoring HB

17.71　　When payments of HB have been suspended, the authority must restore them (to the extent that the claimant remains entitled) within 14 days of the following or as soon as reasonably practicable:

- in cases (a) to (c) (para. 17.70), the authority is satisfied that HB is properly payable and no outstanding matters remain to be resolved;
- in case (d), the authority decides not to make the further appeal (if it decides to make the further appeal case (e) then applies);
- in cases (e) and (f), the appeal or request for leave has been determined;
- in case (g), the claimant has responded as required (para. 17.72).

Information and evidence

17.72　　When payments of HB have been suspended for failure to provide information or evidence (para. 17.70(g)), the authority must notify the claimant of the suspension and of what information and evidence is required. The claimant must then, within one month or such longer period as the authority considers necessary:

- provide the information or evidence required; or
- satisfy the authority that the information or evidence does not exist, or is impossible for them to obtain.

17.70　DAR 11,13(1),(2); NIDAR 11,13(1),(2)

17.71　DAR 13(3),(4); NIDAR 13(3),(4)

17.72　CPSA sch 7 para 15; NICPSA sch 7 para 15; DAR 14; NIDAR 14

Terminating HB

17.73 When payments of HB have been suspended for failure to provide information or evidence (para. 17.70(g)) and the claimant fails to respond as required (para. 17.72) HB entitlement is terminated from the date on which the payments were suspended (i.e. no further payments are made). In some cases, termination should not be done unless a reminder request has been sent: *[2008] UKUT 13 (ACC)*. Terminating benefit under this rule is a kind of supersession: *CH/2555/2007*. The rule cannot be used to end HB from an earlier date: *CH/3736/2006,* so if entitlement did end earlier, this is done as an (ordinary) supersession from that earlier date. The second of the examples illustrates this. As may be observed, the two concepts (termination as a type of supersession, and ordinary supersession at nil) each have the same effect of stopping someone's HB (though the case law generally disapproves of this being described as 'cancelling' HB, because that word does not appear in the law: *CH/2555/2007*). If in the above or other circumstances HB was wrongly terminated, it must be reinstated: *CH/2995/2006*.

17.74 A decision to terminate HB must be notified to the claimant and any other person affected

Appeals

17.75 The claimant has a right of appeal to a First-tier Tribunal (table 19.2) about a decision to terminate HB *(CH/402/2007)*, or to restore HB at a different amount or for a different reason; but not about a determination to suspend HB, or to restore HB at the same amount for the same reasons. A decision to suspend HB may, however, be challenged by judicial review if it is irrational: *[2012] EWHC 1840 (Admin)*.

Examples: Suspending, restoring and terminating HB

A change of circumstances

The authority obtains information that a claimant on HB has changed jobs. It suspends his award immediately, and writes to him allowing him one month to respond.

After two weeks, he sends in the necessary information and evidence, and he remains entitled to HB.

The authority restores his HB from the date payments were suspended, making any change in his entitlement from the Monday after the day he got the new job.

Another change of circumstances

A claimant has been on HB for some years. On Wednesday 19th June 2013 the authority obtains information that he has been doing undeclared work. It suspends his award from the earliest possible date so that the last payment of HB is for week ending Sunday 23rd June 2013, and writes to him allowing him one month to respond.

Shortly afterwards he writes in to admit that he has been working since Monday 8th April 2013 and knows that he does not qualify for HB based on those earnings.

The authority terminates his HB on Sunday 23rd June 2013. It also supersedes his HB (at nil) from Monday 15th April 2013. This creates an overpayment of HB from Monday 15th April to Sunday 23rd June inclusive. The overpayment is not due to official error and so is recoverable.

A review

The authority decides to review a claimant's award of HB and sends her a short form asking her to confirm her circumstances, allowing her one month to reply. Because the claimant does not reply within the month, the authority suspends her HB and writes to her requesting her to say what her circumstances are, allowing her one further month to respond.

Because the claimant again does not reply within a month, the authority terminates her award of HB and notifies her of this.

Two weeks later she returns the original short form, declaring that her circumstances have not changed. The authority is satisfied with this and restores her HB from the date payments were suspended.

18 Overpayments

18.1   This chapter explains:

- what an overpayment is;
- how overpayments are caused;
- which overpayments are recoverable;
- the amount of an overpayment;
- the discretion to recover an overpayment;
- who to recover from;
- the methods of recovery;
- information that must be included in overpayment notices;
- court action to recover an overpayment; and
- administrative and civil penalties.

Excess CTR

18.2   Unlike the HB and the former CTB scheme there are no nationally prescribed rules about excess CTR. The DCLG has reframed excess CTR as an underpayment of council tax (*Localising council tax support: administrative matters – guidance note,* paras. 28-35 <www>). Where someone has paid too little council tax because of excess CTR the authority is able to recover any such excess as unpaid council tax (in the absence of limitations in its local scheme). The council tax billing, collection and enforcement rules have been amended to allow for these 'adjustments' to CTR. Rules for dealing with excess CTR (as opposed to the billing for, or enforcement of, unpaid council tax) may be found in an authority's local scheme. There is significant variation between authorities ranging from 'an overpayment is rectified by the amount being clawed back by an adjustment to the council tax bill' to 'the treatment of overpayments of council tax support reflects the former CTB regulations'. The power to devise local schemes has also allowed authorities to make more subtle changes to the considerations previously applicable to excess CTB, e.g. 'no underlying entitlement for periods of overpayment are to be calculated'. To the extent that a local scheme refers to the previous rules for recovery of excess CTB, guidance may be found in the previous edition of this guide or the description of the analogous HB provisions set out in the following paragraphs.

18.2   http://tinyurl.com/DCLGNote
           Council Tax (Administration and Enforcement) Regulations 1992 (SI 1992/613)
           Council Tax (Administration and Enforcement) (Scotland) Regulations 1992 (SI 1992/1332)

What is an overpayment?

18.3 When more HB is awarded than someone is entitled to, this is an 'overpayment'. It may have been paid (e.g. to a claimant or landlord) or rebated (e.g. to a rent or in Northern Ireland a rates account).

18.4 Overpayments arise when the authority revises or supersedes an award of HB (table 17.8). Tribunals dealing with appeals about overpayments expect the authority to be able to show which revisions or supersessions established the overpayment *(CH/3439/2004* and *C3/07-08(IS))*.

18.5 For every HB overpayment the authority must:

- establish its cause;
- determine whether or not it is recoverable; – and if it is
- calculate the correct period and the correct amount;
- consider whether or not to recover it;
- determine who to recover it from; and
- notify the claimant and any other person affected, within 14 days or as soon as reasonably practicable thereafter.

Example: An overpayment

A claimant under 65 is on HB. On 5th May 2012 her adult son comes to live with her. The claimant has a duty to inform the authority of this but does not do so until 3rd August 2012. The authority determines that a non-dependant deduction should have been made for the son from Monday 7th May 2012: this is a supersession. The claimant has received HB up to and including Sunday 5th August 2012. An overpayment of HB has occurred for 13 weeks.

The cause of an overpayment

18.6 The authority must establish the cause of an HB overpayment in order to:

- decide whether or not it is recoverable;
- notify the right people of the right things;
- claim the correct amount of subsidy; and
- in some cases, determine the method of recovery.

18.7 The main ways in which an overpayment can arise are:

- local authority error, e.g. the authority fails to act on notice of a change of circumstances provided by the claimant;
- DWP error, e.g. a jobcentre plus or pension, disability and carers service makes a mistaken award of JSA(IB)/ESA(IR), income support or pension credit;

18.3 AA 75(1),76(1); NIAA 73(1); HB 99; HB60+ 80; NIHB 96; NIHB60+ 77

- claimant error, e.g. the claimant fails to inform the authority of a change of circumstances which he or she has a duty to report, such as the end of entitlement to JSA(IB)/ESA(IR) or income support; or
- third party error, e.g. a landlord in receipt of HB notifies an incorrect rent increase;
- no-one's fault, e.g. the claimant wins a backdated pay award and this affects entitlement to HB in the past;
- a payment on account turns out to be too great;
- technicalities to do with payment of HB, e.g. a claimant is awarded a rebate for a future period, and then entitlement changes *([2011] UKUT 7 (AAC))*; or
- other reasons.

How is an overpayment 'caused'?

18.8   In identifying the cause of the overpayment the appropriate consideration is what is the substantial cause of the overpayment viewed in a commonsense way *(R (Sier) v Cambridge CC HB Review Board [2001]; [2010] UKUT 57 (AAC)* at [19]) or who really caused the overpayment *([2011] UKUT 266 (AAC)* at [68].) The claimant or a third party can only 'cause' an overpayment if they intentionally or unintentionally misrepresent, or fail to disclose a material fact. However, someone may not be expected to disclose a fact if they were given clear advice to the contrary by an official of the authority or the DWP *(R(SB) 3/89)*. For how the authority, the DWP or HMRC can cause an overpayment, see paragraph 18.13.

More than one cause of an overpayment

18.9   If there is more than one cause of an overpayment, these must be separated out *(CH/2409/2005, CH/858/2006)*. For example, a claimant may fail to notify the authority that their earnings have increased. The authority may then not act on that information quickly enough once it is informed. In such a case the two causes, periods and amounts of the overpayment must be separately identified, and separate decisions must be made about whether the two amounts are recoverable.

Which overpayments are recoverable

Overpayments which cannot be recovered

18.10   An HB overpayment is not recoverable if:

- it arose because of 'official error' by a relevant authority (para. 18.13); and
- the claimant, someone acting on their behalf, or the payee, could not reasonably have been expected to realise it was an overpayment (para. 18.14).

18.10 HR 100(2); HB60+ 81(2); NIHB 97(2); NIHB60+ 78(2)

Overpayments which can be recovered

18.11   An overpayment is recoverable if:

- it arose because of 'official error' (para. 18.13) and the claimant, someone acting on his or her behalf, or the payee, could reasonably have been expected to realise it was an overpayment (para. 18.14); or
- it is due to an error (or fraud) of the claimant or a third party; or
- it is no-one's fault.

18.12   The following overpayments are also recoverable:

- an overpayment of HB to a council or NIHE tenant, which was caused by an 'official error' (para. 18.13) but which relates to a period in the future (*[2011] UKUT 7 (AAC)* at [14, 27-31]);
- an overpayment of a payment on account of HB (para. 16.22) which is being recovered by deductions from ongoing HB;
- an overpayment of HB for rates in Northern Ireland caused by a retrospective reduction in regional rates.

Meaning of 'official error'

18.13   An official error is a mistake, whether in the form of an act or omission, made by the authority, the DWP or HMRC – or someone on their behalf (such as a contractor or a housing association which verifies HB claims). It does not include cases when the claimant, someone acting on their behalf, or the payee, caused or materially contributed to that error. The test is whether the claimant contributed towards the error, not whether they contributed towards the over-payment (*CH/215/2008*). Exactly what is and is not an official error has often been considered on appeal. The main cases are summarised in table 18.1.

Table 18.1: Overpayments case law: meaning of 'official error'

- *Terminology:* A 'mistake' is not different from an 'official error' and it is artificial to try and read different meanings into these two terms (*CH/943/2003*).
- *Relevant authority:* In this context includes any part of the authority and is not confined to any department within it (*CH/3586/2007*).
- *Designated office:* The claimant's circumstances had been repeatedly notified to the housing department. Not to pass the information on to

---

18.11   HB 100(1); HB60+ 81(1); NIHB 97(1); NIHB60+ 78(1)

18.12   HB 93(3),100(4); HB60+ 74(3),81(4); NIHB 90(3),97(4); NIHB60+ 71(3),78(4)

18.13   HB 100(3); HB60+ 81(3); NIHB 97(3); NIHB60+ 78(3)

the benefits service or advise the claimant to do so was an official error which the claimant had not contributed to *(CH/2567/2007)*.

+ *Whether official bodies talk to each other:* The House of Lords in an income support case established an important principle for DWP benefits, which has a bearing on HB. The Court of Appeal in the same case had held that one department of the DWP was to be presumed to know what another department of the DWP knows. The House of Lords overruled this as unrealistic: 'the claimant's duty is to tell whom she is told to tell' *(Hinchy v Secretary of State for Work and Pensions,* reported as *R(IS)7/05)*.

+ *Previous tribunal decisions:* Official error includes where an earlier tribunal has decided that a DWP/Revenue decision is wrong *(CH/943/2003)*.

+ *Overpayment caused by DWP benefit being reinstated on appeal:* Where the overpayment is caused by the reinstatement of a DWP benefit following an appeal this does not amount to an official error *(CH/38/2008)*.

+ *Failure by DWP to pass on information:* The failure of the DWP to notify the authority that JSA(IB) or income support has ceased is not an official error because the claimant has a duty to notify the authority of this *(R v Cambridge CC ex parte Sier)*. But this does not apply to pension credit (and some other) cases in which it is the pension, disability and carers service's duty to notify the authority of changes.

+ *Failure by DWP to act on a promise:* If the DWP undertook to forward a notice of a change to the authority and then failed to do so, that might amount to official error *(CH/939/2004, CH/3761/2005)*.

+ *Failure by the authority to cross-check:* The fact that the claimant disclosed income (etc) in a previous claim (which they did not disclose in their current claim) does not mean that the authority's failure to cross-check is official error *(R(H) 1/04, CH/2794/2004)*.

+ *Failure to recognise relevant information on document provided for a different purpose:* There is no general rule that the failure to recognise information as relevant which was provided for a different purpose cannot be official error: it depends on the particular circumstances *(CH/3925/2006)*.

+ *Failure by authority to check potential changes:* Failure by the authority to check up on potential changes in entitlement to a tax credit is not official error *(R(H) 2/04)*, nor is failure to check up on a potential increase in incapacity benefit *(CH/687/2006)* or earnings *(CH/3/2008)*.

+ *Delay by authority in dealing with a notified change:* In a case in which the claimant notified her increased earnings on 19th April, but the authority did not take them into account until 13th May (24 days later), this was quick enough not to constitute official error. In reaching this decision, the commissioner compared the authority's duty to act on a change of circumstances with its duty to act on a claim, where there is a time limit of 14 days (para. 16.2). The 24 days the commissioner allowed in this case was based on its individual circumstances *(CH/858/2006)*.

◆ *Delay in applying to the rent officer:* A delay in applying to the rent officer can be an official error *(CH/361/2006)*.

◆ *Claimant reports wrong amount of benefit due to overpayment deductions:* If the claimant reports the incorrect amount of incapacity benefit because the DWP is making deductions, the fact that the authority does not realise the mistake does not amount to an official error *(CH/56/08)*.

◆ *Claimant's method of notifying changes:* Where a claimant had notified a change by telephone but not in writing, and the council had failed to act on it, this did not necessarily mean that the claimant had materially contributed to the official error *(CH/2409/2005)*.

Awareness of being overpaid

18.14   An overpayment which arose due to official error is recoverable only if the claimant, a person acting on their behalf, or the payee, could reasonably have been expected to realise that it was an overpayment – either at the time the payment was received, or at the time of any decision notice relating to it. Exactly how this rule should be applied has often been considered on appeal. The main cases are summarised in table 18.2.

Table 18.2: Overpayments case law: awareness of being overpaid in official error cases

◆ *Purpose of the rule:* The purpose of the rule is to protect a claimant who has relied on being entitled to the payment so that, having innocently spent it, they do not have to repay money they cannot afford *(CH/1176/2003)*.

◆ *'Was' or 'might be' an overpayment?* The test is whether there was a reasonable expectation that there was an overpayment not whether there might be one *(R v Liverpool CC ex parte Griffiths, CH/2935/2005, CH/858/2006)*.

18.14 HB 100(2); HB60+ 81(2); NIHB 97(2); NIHB60+ 78(2)

- *Burden of proof:* The burden of proof is on the person stating that they could not reasonably have been expected to realise – not on the authority stating that they could *(CH/4918/2003).* But the question of 'burden of proof' only arises in borderline cases (paras. 1.41-43).

- *What can a person reasonably be expected to realise?* The test of what someone could reasonably have been expected to realise varies according to the person's knowledge, experience and capacity *(R v Liverpool CC ex parte Griffiths).* For example, someone who had needed the authority's help to fill in his application form may be less likely to realise he was overpaid *(CH/2935/2005);* someone from a country where (the equivalent of) tax credits are taken into account in a different way (in the assessment of the equivalent of HB) might not realise that they are taken into account as income in the UK *(CH/858/2006).*

- *An ordinary reasonable claimant:* An 'ordinary reasonable claimant' cannot be expected to go and find out more about the HB scheme than they are informed of by the authority in the notice of their award *(CH/2554/2002).*

- *Receipt of a notice:* Whether a person could reasonably have been expected to realise at the time of any notice, refers to a notice about the award of HB, not the overpayment notice – otherwise the rule would be meaningless *(CH/1176/2003).*

- *Comprehensible notice:* If a notice of an award contains the basis of the calculation in a reasonably clear manner, and it is clear that there has been a mistake in the claimant's favour, then the overpayment is recoverable – because the claimant could reasonably have been expected to realise *(CH/2409/2005).*

- *Claimant queries notice but authority continues to pay wrong amount:* Where the claimant queries the decision notice but the authority continues to pay, there comes a point where the claimant is entitled to rely on the notice and accept the authority knows best *(CH/3240/2007).*

- *Reference to wages omitted in notice:* If there was no reference at all to the claimant's wages in the notice, whereas their other income was listed, a 'claimant of normal intelligence' could reasonably be expected to deduce that there had been a mistake and that they were overpaid *(CH/2554/2002).*

- *Reference to state retirement pension omitted in the decision notice:* If there was no reference at all to the claimant's state retirement pension in the notice, the claimant might have concluded that the pension was being ignored (perhaps because it was disregarded or because everybody of his age received one); and 'a typical claimant cannot reasonably be expected to read or understand the calculations' so they could not reasonably be expected to deduce that they were overpaid *(CH/2554/2002)*.

♦ *A disparity between the claimant's declared earnings and the notified assessment:* Where there is a large disparity between the claimant's declared earnings and the authority's assessment as set out in the decision notice (in this case earnings of £210 assessed and notified as less than £50) then it would be reasonable to expect the claimant to realise that they must be being overpaid *(CH/2943/2007)*. For a similar case relating to an incorrect eligible rent, see *[2008] UKUT 6 AAC*.

♦ *The claimant must have some reason to believe the authority's figures are wrong:* A claimant cannot be expected to seek advice unless they have some reason to believe the figures are wrong. A tribunal should ask the claimant how they reconciled their own knowledge of their earnings with the figures in the notice, to give them the opportunity to explain why they could not be expected to realise there was an over-payment *(CH/2943/2007)*.

♦ *Claimant telephoned to say they thought there was a mistake:* If there has been an official error, and the claimant alleges they telephoned to say they thought there had been, then the authority should determine whether they in fact did so before going on to consider if this affects whether the overpayment is recoverable *(CH/4065/2001)*.

♦ *Claimant's other actions in relation to the award:* The authority in this case had asked for evidence of earnings for the wrong period. The claimant provided what they asked for, but not other evidence that would have shown his income was higher. His other actions (including telephoning to check things) suggested he was not trying to mislead and there was no reason to suppose he could reasonably have been expected to realise there was an overpayment *(CH/1780/2005)*.

♦ *Time of receipt of a payment:* The 'time' of a payment by cheque is fairly narrow, but a telephone call from the authority a couple of hours after the claimant received a large HB cheque, advising her it was incorrect, may be soon enough to mean that the claimant was aware at the 'time of receipt' that it was an overpayment *(CH/1176/2003)*.

♦ *When the overpayment is a rebate:* If the overpayment is of a rebate, the authority may need to consider whether the claimant could reasonably have been expected to realise that there was an overpayment 'at the times when credits were applied to his rent account' *(CH/1675/2005)*.

♦ *What a landlord could have realised:* When the question arises of what a landlord company or housing association could have realised, it is what the whole organisation might reasonably have been expected to have realised that is relevant *(CH/4918/2003)*.

The amount of a recoverable overpayment

18.15 The amount of a recoverable overpayment is the difference between what was paid or awarded and what the person was entitled to. The following rules can reduce the amount of the HB overpayment.

Underlying entitlement

18.16 When calculating the amount of a recoverable overpayment, any amount 'which should have been determined to be payable' in respect of the period of overpayment must be deducted. This means whatever would have been awarded (to the claimant, or to any partner had they claimed) if the authority had known the true facts of the case throughout, and all changes of circumstances had been notified on time. HB not recovered from the claimant under this rule is called 'underlying entitlement' to distinguish it from an actual award of HB. The application of the underlying entitlement rule is mandatory but the DWP has expressed concern that some authorities are not considering it when there has been an overpayment (DWP G2/2013, para. 16).

Why underlying entitlement can occur

18.17 In the past there were many situations in which underlying entitlement could occur, but nowadays there are two:

- ◆ underlying entitlement overrides the rule about late notice of beneficial changes (para. 17.11). See example 1; and
- ◆ underlying entitlement overrides the rule about late requests for a reconsideration (paras. 17.64 and 19.15).

Underlying entitlement is not needed when a closed period supersession is used to deal with a break in entitlement (para. 17.55).

The stage at which the authority allows underlying entitlement

18.18 When a recoverable overpayment arises, the authority may already have information enabling it to allow underlying entitlement (as in example 1). And in all cases, unless there is no possibility of underlying entitlement (e.g. the claimant had more than £16,000 throughout the overpayment period), the authority should invite the claimant to provide information and evidence to establish underlying entitlement (OG paras. 3.50-3.80) (using the usual rules about obtaining information and evidence: para. 5.13) and the onus is on the claimant to do this *(R(H) 1/05)*.

18.19 If underlying entitlement has not been identified when the authority determines and notifies the overpayment, the claimant (or other overpaid person) may ask the authority to reconsider or appeal to a tribunal (chapter 19) – and in doing so may include information which establishes underlying entitlement. Once the time limit for appeal has expired (one month which can be increased to 13 months in special circumstances), it is not possible to allow underlying entitlement (OG para. 3.57) – unless there has been an official error (para. 17.59).

Calculation rules for underlying entitlement

18.20   There are two calculation rules:

- ◆ only underlying entitlement falling within the overpayment period is used to reduce the overpayment;
- ◆ underlying entitlement may reduce an overpayment to nil, but it can never be used to actually pay money out.

Examples: Underlying entitlement

1. When there has been late notice of a change

Information: A claimant's non-dependant moved out six months ago, but the claimant did not tell the authority until three months ago (and had no special circumstances for lateness) so the authority removed the non-dependant deduction from three months ago. Today it is discovered that the claimant has been doing undeclared work since nine months ago.

Assessment: Underlying entitlement means the authority must reduce the amount of the overpayment due to the undeclared work by the amount it could not award in relation to the non-dependant moving out. This results in a lower recoverable overpayment; it may even reduce the overpayment to nil; but in no circumstances can it result in the claimant being awarded more benefit.

2. Calculation rules

Information: In a particular case, there is a recoverable overpayment of £5 per week for weeks 1 to 20 inclusive (20 x £5 = £100), and underlying entitlement (because the claimant did not notify a beneficial change on time) in weeks 11 to 20 inclusive of £15 per week.

Assessment: The underlying entitlement in weeks 11 to 20 inclusive (10 x £15 = £150) is used to reduce the overpayment (£100). It is enough to reduce the recoverable overpayment to nil. The remainder of the underlying entitlement cannot be awarded.

If a claimant still paid rent to the authority

18.21   During the overpayment period a council tenant claimant may have paid rent above their erroneous liability. Those payments may be deducted from the recoverable overpayment. The rule applies equally to payments of rates in Northern Ireland.

18.21 HB 104(2); HB60+ 85(2); NIHB 101(2); NIHB60+ 82(2)

Where a claimant moves home within the same authority

18.22 When calculating a recoverable overpayment caused by a claimant changing address the authority has the discretion to offset the HB entitlement at the new address against the overpayment on the previous property. This rule can only be used however where:

- the claimant was awarded a rent allowance on the old address; and
- the HB on the old and new home is paid to the same person (i.e. the same claimant or same landlord, etc) by the same authority.

Where this amount is deducted an equivalent amount is treated as having been paid in respect of the claimant's new home.

Example: Calculating a recoverable overpayment where the claimant moves home

The claimant receives a rent allowance of £100 a week. The claimant moves to a new home where they receive HB of £110 a week. The claimant doesn't tell the authority about the move for three weeks after leaving the earlier address leading to an overpayment of £300 on the old address.

The claimant is entitled to £330 a week on the new address for the same period. The authority may reduce the amount of the recoverable overpayment on the claimant's old home by £300 reducing it to nil and paying the claimant the residual £30 in relation to the new home.

The diminution of capital rule

18.23 This rule applies if a recoverable overpayment:

- arose due to capital being wrongly taken into account (for any reason); and
- lasted for more than 13 weeks.

18.24 In such cases, the following steps apply:

- at the end of the first 13 weeks of the overpayment period, the claimant's capital is treated as reduced by the amount overpaid during those 13 weeks. This gives an imaginary capital figure which is used to assess the overpayment after that;
- the same is done again at the end of each 13 weeks until the end of the overpayment period;
- but for calculating HB after the end of the overpayment period, the claimant's actual capital is used (not the imaginary amount).

This reflects the fact that if the claimant had been awarded less HB due to the capital being taken into account, they might have used some of their capital to pay their rent or, in Northern Ireland, rates.

18.22 HB 104A, HB60+ 85A; NIHB 101A; NIHB60+ 82A

18.23 HB 103; HB60+ 84; NIHB 100; NIHB60+ 81

18.25   The above is complicated enough, but the law has a further cruel twist: the above 'diminution of capital rule' is not the same as the 'diminishing notional capital rule' (para. 13.150), and the two are calculated in different ways.

Example: The diminishing capital rule

A claimant failed to declare capital of £16,033. When this is discovered, there has been a recoverable overpayment for 30 weeks. Throughout that time she got HB of £9 per week, she had no other capital at all, and the figure of £16,033 remained the same.

- In the first 13 weeks, she is not entitled to HB:

  Overpayment: 13 x £9   = £117

- Her capital is then treated as reduced by this amount:

  £16,033 – £117   = £15,916

- In the second 13 weeks, based on this reduced capital,

  she is entitled to HB of £5 per week,

  so the overpayment is £4 per week:

  Overpayment: 13 x £4   = £52

- Her capital is then treated as further reduced by
  this amount: £15,916 – £52   = £15,864

- In the remaining 4 weeks, based on this further

  reduced capital, she is still entitled to HB of

  £5 per week,so the overpayment is still £4 per week:

  Overpayment: 4 x £4   = £16

- So the total overpayment of HB for the 30 weeks is   £185

The discretion to recover

18.26   If an overpayment is 'recoverable' (paras. 18.11-12), this means the authority has the discretion to recover it or not recover it (para. 1.49). The question of whether an overpayment is recoverable is therefore separate from the question of whether to recover it. Cases must be looked at on their merits, and the DWP advises that 'due regard' should be had to individual circumstances (OG paras. 2.230-233).

18.27   A claimant can ask the authority not to recover a recoverable overpayment but has no right of appeal to a tribunal about this (*[2011] UKUT 266 (AAC)* at [71]). In unreasonable or irrational cases the claimant could instead seek judicial review. This was done in a case where an authority sought to recover an overpayment caused by a war pension awarded for a past period – though the outcome was that the court required the authority to think again and did not ban recovery *(R v South Hams District Council ex p Ash)*.

Who to recover from

18.28 The HB rules about who to recover overpayments from have changed, and are much clearer, with effect from 6th April 2009. The previous rules apply to overpayments from before that date: *CH/4213/2007* (and may be found in the 2008-09 edition of this guide).

Recovery of overpaid HB

18.29 A recoverable overpayment of HB may be recovered as follows:

- if the overpayment was caused by the claimant or payee, or someone on their behalf (para. 18.8), it is recoverable only from that person (and if there is more than one such person, it is recoverable from any of them); but

- if the overpayment was due to official error and the claimant or payee, or someone on their behalf, could reasonably have been expected to realise it was an overpayment (para. 18.14), it is recoverable only from that person (and if there is more than one such person, it is recoverable from any of them); but

- in any other case (e.g. if the overpayment was no-one's fault) it is recoverable from the claimant and (if different) the payee (in other words from either of them).

18.30 If, for any of the above reasons, the overpayment is recoverable from the claimant, it is also recoverable from their partner if specific conditions are met (para. 18.32). In some cases, the effect of the above rules is that there can be a choice about who to recover from (para. 18.35).

Recovery of HB from claimants

18.31 Most recoverable overpayments of HB can be recovered from the claimant; and if the claimant has died it can be recovered from their estate. In fact, the only cases in which a recoverable overpayment of HB cannot be recovered from the claimant (and can only be recovered from the payee, typically a landlord or agent) are:

- when the payee was the cause of the overpayment (and the claimant played no part in causing it); or

- when the payee could reasonably have been expected to realise there was an official error overpayment (and the claimant could not have done so).

18.28 SI 2008/2824 regs 4-7; NISR 2008/504 Regs 2,3

18.29 AA 75(3); NIAA 73(3); HB 101(2),(3A); HB60+ 82(2),(3A); NIHB 98(2),(3A); NIHB60+ 79(2),(2A)

18.31 HB 101(2),(3A); HB60+ 82(2),(3A); NIHB 98(2),(3A); NIHB60+ 79(2),(3A)

Recovery of HB from partners

18.32 Whenever a recoverable overpayment of HB can be recovered from the claimant (for any of the reasons in para. 18.29), it can also be recovered from their partner – if they were a couple when the overpayment was made and at the time of recovery. A former partner (following the end of a relationship or death) or a new partner after the period of the overpayment does not meet this rule so a recoverable overpayment cannot be recovered from them. When recovery is to be made from a partner they should be separately notified. They have the same rights of appeal as the claimant: *CH/3622l2006* (para. 18.36). The rules limit the methods of recovery from a partner to:

- making deductions from the partner's future HB (para. 18.42); or
- making deductions from the partner's future DWP benefits (para. 18.45)

Recovery of HB from landlords and agents

18.33 The effect of the above rules (para. 18.29) is that a recoverable overpayment of HB can only be recovered from a landlord/agent if it was them (rather than the claimant) who was paid the HB; and one of the following must also apply:

- either the landlord/agent caused the overpayment;
- or (in the case of an official error overpayment) the landlord/agent could reasonably have been expected to realise there was an overpayment;
- or the overpayment was no-one's fault – in which case it is recoverable from either the claimant or the landlord/agent; and the mere fact that the landlord/agent knew nothing of the overpayment does not prevent recovery from them: *Warwick DC v Freeman*.

In such cases, HB may be recovered from the landlord if the landlord was paid the HB, but from the agent if the agent was paid the HB (even if the agent has paid it to the landlord: *R(H)10/07* and *CH/761/2007*). When recovery is to be made from a landlord/agent they must be separately notified and have the same rights of appeal as the claimant: *CH/3622/2006* (para. 18.36).

18.34 However, an authority must not recover HB from a landlord/agent if:

- the landlord/agent notifies the authority or the DWP in writing that they suspect there has been an overpayment; and
- it appears to the authority that there are grounds for instituting proceedings for an offence in relation to the overpayment, or that a deliberate failure to report a relevant change of circumstances (other than moving home) caused the overpayment; and

---

18.32 HB 102(1ZA); HB60+ 83(1ZA); NIHB 99(1A); NIHB60+ 80(1A)

18.33 AA 75(3); NIAA 73(3); HB 101(2),(3A); HB60+ 82(2),(3A); NIHB 98(2),(3A); NIHB60+ 79(2),(3A)

18.34 AA 75(3); NIAA 73(3); HB 101(1); HB60+ 82(1); NIHB 98(1); NIHB60+ 79(1)

- the authority is satisfied that the landlord/agent did not collude in the over-payment, nor contribute (through action or inaction) to its period or amount.

For example, if a landlord/agent in receipt of HB notifies the authority that the claimant is doing undeclared work, and does so promptly, this prevents the authority from recovering the resulting overpaid HB from the landlord/agent provided that the landlord's warning notice reaches the authority before it discovers the overpayment *(CH/2411/2006)*.

A choice about who to recover HB from

18.35 When the above rules (para. 18.29) allow an authority to recover an HB overpayment from more than one party (e.g. landlord/agent and claimant), the parties have a joint and several liability to repay *(R(H) 6/06)*. The authority may choose which to recover from. In one case an authority billed two parties at the same time, and a commissioner said this was 'unfortunate' but had no lasting effect on the appeal *(CH/2583/2007)*.

Appeals about who to recover HB from

18.36 Once the authority has identified which party or parties it may recover an overpayment from, and notified them (all) of this, each of them is a 'person affected' (para. 16.10) and so may ask the authority to reconsider or appeal to a tribunal (chapter 19).

18.37 A tribunal's jurisdiction is limited to deciding first, the true entitlement for the period in question and second, whether the resultant overpayment is legally recoverable from more than one person. But it does not have the power to decide the third and final stage: how the recovery should be enforced *(CH/2298/2007)*. A tribunal has a duty to decide whether the authority's selection of the party or parties was correctly drawn up – but not whether it is fair or appropriate to recover from one party rather than another *(R(H) 6/06 and CH/4213/2007)*. This applies whether the appellant is the landlord/agent or the claimant *(CH/1129/2004)*. In unreasonable or irrational cases the appellant could instead seek judicial review.

Methods of recovery

18.38 Authorities may recover a recoverable overpayment of HB by any lawful method. The following methods, laid down in the law, are described in this section:

- deducting overpaid HB from the claimant's or partner's future HB;
- deducting overpaid HB from the claimant's or partner's DWP benefits;
- deducting overpaid HB from a blameless tenant's HB;
- deducting overpaid HB from a guilty landlord/agent's payments;
- deducting overpaid HB from a landlord/agent's own HB or DWP benefits;
- deducting overpaid HB from earnings (direct earnings attachment – DEA);
- pursuit through the courts or as if under a court order.

Charging overpaid HB to a rent account

18.39   Any excess CTR may be recovered by charging the applicant's council tax account – in other words adding the overpayment to that account – and issuing a new bill. This means the excess CTR simply becomes council tax arrears recoverable under council tax law.

18.40   There is no equivalent rule for HB for a council or NIHE tenant. Although their rent account can include a record of overpaid HB, the overpayments do not normally constitute rent arrears – and should not, for example, lead to eviction (unlike the arrears in para. 18.43).

18.41   Table 18.5 identifies when overpaid HB recovered through the rent account results in rent arrears for the tenant.

Deducting overpaid HB from future awards of HB

18.42   A recoverable overpayment of HB may be deducted from the claimant's or partner's future award of HB, but this deduction is limited in three ways:

◆ the award of HB must not be reduced below 50p a week;

◆ the amount deducted in 2013-14 must not be greater than shown in table 18.3; and

◆ the authority should consider deducting a lower amount in cases where hardship might otherwise arise.

The first two limits do not apply to deductions from lump sum arrears of HB.

Table 18.3: Maximum weekly deductions from HB (2013-14)

◆ If the claimant has been found guilty of fraud, or admitted fraud after caution, or agreed to pay an administrative penalty (para. 18.69)   £18.00

◆ In any other case   £10.80

Plus, in each of the above cases, 50% of:

◆ any £5, £10, £20 or £25 earned income disregard (table 14.1)

◆ any disregard of regular charitable or voluntary payments (para. 13.129)

◆ the £10 disregard of war disablement or war widow's or widower's pension (para. 13.59)

18.42   AA 75(4),(5); NIAA 73(4),(5); HB 102; HB60+ 83; NIHB 99; NIHB60+ 80

T18.3   AA 75(4),(5); NIAA 73(4),(5); HB 102; HB60+ 83; NIHB 99; NIHB60+ 80

18.43 The deductions leave the claimant with more rent to pay – or rent arrears if they do not (table 18.5). These rent arrears do not have to be separately identified – and can, for example, lead to eviction (unlike the arrears in para. 18.40).

18.44 The deductions count as recovery from the claimant, not the landlord/agent. This is true even when HB is paid to the landlord/agent, and in such cases the landlord/agent has no right to appeal to a tribunal (chapter 19) about the deductions *(R(H) 7/04)*.

Deducting overpaid HB from DWP benefits

18.45 A recoverable overpayment of HB may be deducted from the claimant's or partner's DWP benefits (table 18.4) – but only if the HB overpayment was due to misrepresentation of, or failure to disclose, a material fact (para. 18.8); and only if the authority is unable to recover overpaid HB from future awards of HB.

Table 18.4: Recovering HB overpayments from DWP benefits

A recoverable overpayment of HB may be deducted from:

• income support	• retirement pension
• jobseeker's allowance	• incapacity benefit
• employment and support allowance	• state pension credit
• personal independence payment	• universal credit
• maternity allowance	• carer's allowance
• industrial injuries benefits	• disability living allowance
• widow(er)'s benefits	• attendance allowance
• bereavement benefits	• equivalent EU and Swiss benefits

but not from:

• child benefit	• working tax credit
• guardian's allowance	• child tax credit
• war pensions	• statutory sick, maternity, paternity or adoption pay

---

Deducting overpaid HB from a blameless tenant's HB

18.46 If a recoverable overpayment of HB was paid to a landlord/agent, it may be deducted from payments to that landlord/agent of another tenant's HB. This is

---

18.45 HB 102(1),105,106; HB60+ 83(1),86,87; NIHB 99(1),102,103; NIHB60+ 80(1),83,84

18.46 AA 75(5),(6); NIAA 73(5),(6); HB sch 9 para 15(2); HB60+ sch 8 para 15(2); NIHB sch 10 para 15(2); NIHB60+ sch 9 para 15(2)

often called 'recovery by schedule' (because it is usually only done in the case of landlords/agents with several tenants on HB) or recovery from a 'blameless tenant' (because the other tenant had nothing to do with the overpayment).

Table 18.5: When recovered HB overpayments create rent arrears

This table is about whether recovered overpayments of HB turn into rent arrears for the claimant.

Rent rebate (local authority/NIHE tenants)

* *Recovery by deductions from ongoing benefit or arrears of HB* (para. 18.42): Assuming the tenant does not pay any shortfall then this always creates rent arrears (because at no point has the rent due been paid).

* *Recovery by charging the tenant's rent account or by sending the tenant a bill* (paras. 18.40 and 18.50): Recovery by this method does not create rent arrears *(R v Haringey ex p Ayub)* except if:

    (a) the tenancy agreement expressly allows for recovered overpayments of HB to be charged as additional rent; or

    (b) following the recovery the tenant fails to say which debt (rent or overpayment) any payments should be attributed to – in which case any payment will go against the earliest debt first.

Rent allowance

* *Recovery by deductions from ongoing benefit or arrears of HB* (para. 18.42): As for rent rebates above.

* *Recovery from the blameless tenant's HB* (paras. 18.46-47): This never results in rent arrears for the blameless tenant; and does not result in rent arrears for the tenant to whom the overpayment relates except in the same circumstances as in (a) and (b) above.

* *Recovery from the landlord by deductions from the landlord's own benefits or by sending the landlord a bill* (paras 18.49-50): The tenant to whom the overpayment relates is treated as not having paid the amount of rent which has been repaid (as a recoverable overpayment) so this creates rent arrears.

* *Recovery by deductions from a guilty landlord's payments* (18.48): The tenant to whom the overpayment relates is treated as having paid the rent to the value of the deduction.

T 18.5   AA 75(5),(6); NIAA 73(5),(6); HB 95(2),107(1),(2); HB60+ 76(2),88(1),(2); NIHB 92(2),104(1),(2); NIHB60+ 73(2),85(1),(2)

18.47   The authority must notify the landlord/agent which tenant's HB was overpaid and who the blameless tenant is. The blameless tenant is not notified, but the landlord/agent must treat them as having paid rent equal to the amount deducted.

Deducting overpaid HB from a guilty landlord/agent's payments

18.48   Special rules apply to the recovery of rent by a landlord/agent ('the landlord') and to the information on the authority's decision notice where:

- the overpayment is one for which the landlord has agreed to pay a penalty (para. 18.34) or been convicted of fraud; and
- recovery is to be from the landlord; and
- recovery is by deduction from the HB paid by the authority to the landlord for the tenant to whom the overpayment relates.

In these circumstance the landlord has no right in relation to the recovered amount against the tenant and must treat the tenant's rent as paid by the same amount. The authority must notify the landlord and tenant of these matters.

Deducting overpaid HB from a landlord's own benefits

18.49   If a recoverable overpayment of HB was paid to a landlord/agent, it may (though this is rare) be recovered from the landlord's personal entitlement to:

- HB (in which case the limits in table 18.3 do not apply); or
- DWP benefits (table 18.4) – but only if the overpayment was due to misrepresentation of, or failure to disclose, a material fact.

Recovering HB by sending a bill

18.50   Any recoverable overpayment of HB may be recovered by sending a bill to any person it can be recovered from (paras. 18.28-34). This can be followed up by court action (paras. 18.58-62).

The effect of insolvency on recovery

18.51   The DWP's *Overpayments Guide* (OG paras. 7.166-260) provides detailed information on the recovery of overpayments where a person's insolvency has led to formal measures such as bankruptcy, the making of a debt relief order (DRO) (in England and Wales) or sequestration (in Scotland) [www]. For England and Wales, however, this guidance now needs to be read in the light of the Supreme Court's judgment in *SSWP v Payne & Cooper.* Where bankruptcy has started or an overpayment has been included in a DRO the authority cannot recover an

---

18.47   AA 75(5),(6); NIAA 73(5),(6); HB 106(2); HB60+ 87(2); NIHB 103(2); NIHB60+ 84(2)

18.48   AA 75(5)(b); NIAA 73(5)(b); HB 107; HB60+ 88; NIHB 104; NIHB60+ 85

18.49   AA 75(5); NIAA 73(5); HB 106(2); HB60+ 87(2); NIHB 103(2); NIHB60+ 84(2)

18.50   HB 102(1); HB60+ 83(1); NIHB 99(1); NIHB60+ 80(1)

18.51   www.dwp.gov.uk/docs/hbopg-courts.pdf

overpayment that was decided before the order was granted. The Supreme Court has confirmed that the authority cannot recover such overpayments even by making deductions from on-going benefit entitlement. Authorities are told in DWP circular U6/2011 that they should stop such recoveries if they are making them. The circular also tells authorities that the DWP is considering what effect the Supreme Court's judgment has on recovery for other forms of insolvency such as individual voluntary arrangements and how recovery during types of insolvency unique to Scotland such as sequestration and trust deeds is dealt with. Once the bankruptcy or DRO is discharged the liability to repay is also discharged except for fraudulent overpayments.

Note, however, that an overpayment that was determined after a bankruptcy order (even if it relates to a period before that order) or not included in the DRO may be recovered both during and after the order is discharged using any recovery method *(R(H)9/09)*.

Direct earnings attachment (DEA)

18.52   Authorities may recover recoverable overpayments by requiring an employer to make deductions from a liable person's earnings without the need for court action. But this requirement cannot be placed on new businesses (which start between 8th April 2013 and 31st March 2014) or micro-businesses (those with less than ten employees immediately before 8th April 2013). DWP's Impact Assessment (2011) [www] suggests that this method of recovery is useful for those who are no longer in receipt of benefit and who will not come to a voluntary agreement to repay the debt.

18.53   The authority must send a notice to both the liable person and the employer before deductions can be made. The employer should tell the authority if they are not the employer of the liable person or if they think the new business or micro-business exemption applies. This should be done within ten days of the day after the notice was sent.

18.54   The authority may vary the notice to decrease or increase amounts or to substitute a new employer for a previous one. Where an employer is required to make deductions under more than one notice they should deal with them in date order.

18.55   The DEA notice has effect from the next pay-day which falls a minimum of 22 days after the date on which it is given or sent. The amounts to be deducted are prescribed in legislation (schedule 2 of SI 2013 No 384). The employer may deduct up to £1 for administrative costs. The liable person's net earnings should not be reduced below 60% of protected net earnings.

18.52 HB 106A; HB60+ 87A, Reg 18 and sch 1 of SI 2013 No 384
       www.legislation.gov.uk/uksi/2013/384/pdfs/uksifia_20130384_en.pdf
18.53 Regs 19,24 of SI 2013 No 384
18.54 Regs 25-26,29 of SI 2013 No 384
18.55 Regs 17,19,20(9) of SI 2013 No 384

18.56 The employer must notify the liable person of the amount of the deductions and pay the amount deducted (excluding that for administrative costs) to the authority. The employer must also keep records of the amounts deducted and of people in respect of whom such deductions have been made.

18.57 The liable person must tell the authority within seven days if they leave the employment or when they become employed or re-employed. The employer should also tell the authority if the liable person is no longer employed by them. It is a criminal offence to fail to make or pay deductions or to provide information.

Court action

18.58 Although the DWP advises that 'it is for authorities to decide how far to pursue recovery', it expects a serious attempt at recovery and encourages court action in appropriate cases (OG paras. 7.40, 7.42). This court action can be civil proceedings for debt, but the following procedure is more appropriate.

The simplified debt recovery procedure

18.59 Authorities have the power to recover HB overpayments by execution in the County Court in England and Wales as if under a court order; and in Scotland as if it were an extract registered decree arbitral.

England and Wales

18.60 In England and Wales, this procedure allows an HB overpayment determination to be registered directly as an order of the County Court without the need to bring a separate action. The DWP has provided some much needed guidance on this procedure (OG paras 7.50-7.71). The authority applies to the court on a standard form (form N 322A) [www], enclosing a copy of the overpayment notice and the relevant fee. The notice must include all the matters in paragraph 18.66 (OG para. 5.07). An officer of the court then makes an order and a copy is sent to the authority and the debtor. Once an order has been made, the normal methods of enforcement are available to the authority – a garnishee order allowing the authority to obtain money owed to the debtor by a third party; a warrant of execution against goods executed by the county court bailiff; or a charging order, normally against land.

18.61 There is no appeal against the above order, but the claimant or landlord/agent may apply to the court to set it aside if the overpayment notice

---

18.56   Reg 21-22 of SI 2013 No 384

18.57   Regs 23,30 of SI 2013 No 384

18.59   AA 75(7),76(6); NIAA 73(7)

18.60   www.dwp.gov.uk/docs/hbopg-courts.pdf
         http://hmctscourtfinder.justice.gov.uk/courtfinder/forms/n322a-enq.pdf

was defective or the authority has ignored their HB appeal rights. In the case of other disputes, they should ask the authority to reconsider or appeal to a tribunal (chapter 19) *(Ghassemian v Borough of Kensington and Chelsea)*.

Scotland

18.62   In Scotland, an HB overpayment determination is immediately enforceable as if it were an extract registered decree arbitral (OG paras. 7.140-7.143). It does not need to be registered with the Sheriff Court. The usual methods of enforcement are available – arrestment of earnings; poinding and warrant sale; arrestment of moveable property and inhibition of heritable property.

Time limits

18.63   The above procedures must be started within six years in England and Wales (s.9 The Limitation Act 1980). This limitation does not apply to any other method of recovery – such as by deductions from future HB (OG paras. 7.00-05). In Scotland overpayments cannot be recovered by any method after 20 years (s.7 of The Prescription and Limitation (Scotland) Act 1973) (OG paras. 7.10-13).

18.64   This time limit does not affect how far back an overpayment can go. For example, it may be discovered today that someone has been overpaid since the beginning of the HB scheme, and the authority may make a determination to recover it. But the further the overpayment goes back, the more difficult it may be for the authority to obtain the evidence needed to prove the overpayment to the court (OG para. 7.00).

Overpayment decision notices

18.65   For every recoverable overpayment, a decision notice must be sent to every person it can be recovered from (paras. 18.28-34), because each of these is a 'person affected' (para. 16.10) – regardless of which party the authority will actually recover it from *(R(H) 6/06)*. This should be done within 14 days of the determination being made or as soon as reasonably practicable thereafter.

18.66   Overpayment notices must contain the following information:

+ the fact that there is a recoverable overpayment;
+ the reason why there is a recoverable overpayment;
+ the amount of the recoverable overpayment;
+ how that amount was calculated;
+ the benefit weeks to which the recoverable overpayment relates;
+ if overpaid HB is to be deducted from future HB, the amount of the deduction;

18.63   s38 Limitation Act 1980 as amended by s108 Welfare Reform Act 2012

18.65   HB 90(1)(b); HB60+ 71(1)(b); NIHB 86(1)(b); NIHB60+ 67(1)(b)

18.66   HB sch 9 para 15; HB60+ sch 8 para 15; NIHB sch 10 para 15; NIHB60+ sch 9 para 15

* any other relevant matters;
* the person's right to request a written statement, to request the authority to reconsider, and to appeal to a tribunal, and the manner and time in which to do these things.

Table 18.6: Overpayments case law: notices and effect on recovery

---

* *Failure to give a reason why there is a recoverable overpayment:* To say it was due to a 'change of circumstances' is not itself an adequate explanation as it covers a multitude of possibilities and so does not give the person affected sufficient information to be able to judge whether they have grounds for an appeal *(R v Thanet DC ex parte Warren Court Hotels Ltd)*.

* *Failure to identify the parties the overpayment is recoverable from:* A notice naming only a landlord as the person from whom the overpayment could be recovered was quashed (and so had no effect), because it should have named both the claimant and the landlord *(CH/3622/2005,* in which the commissioner followed *R(H) 6/06)*.

* *Failure to issue a complete overpayment notice:* An authority that issues an incomplete notice may undermine the legal basis of its debt recovery action *(Warwick DC v Freeman)*.

* *Impact on power to recover:* There is no legally recoverable debt until the authority makes the appropriate decision and issues the required notice *(R (Godwin) v Rossendale BC)*. Decisions must be clear and unambiguous with proper use of statutory language and dates *(C3/07-08(IS))*. But if the defect in a notice is only trivial and no substantial harm is caused as a result, the authority may be entitled to recover the overpaid benefit *(Haringey LBC v Awaritefe)*.

* *Recovery taken before notice issued:* If, in a 'blameless tenant' case, an authority recovers HB before issuing a valid notice, the landlord/agent can apply to the court for repayment of the recovered HB *(Waveney DC v Jones)*.

* *Recovery volunteered before notice issued:* If a landlord/agent voluntarily pays a bill for overpaid HB before the authority has issued a valid notice, they cannot obtain repayment because (unlike in Jones, above) they could have resisted recovery by requesting the authority to reconsider or appealing to a tribunal *(Norwich CC v Stringer)*.

18.67 Sometimes overpayment notices are poor or incomplete. How this affects recovering the overpayment has often been considered on appeal and in the courts. The main cases are summarised in table 18.6.

The DWP advises authorities that recovery of HB overpayments by deduction from future HB should not begin until one month after notice (unless the overpayment is small) to allow time for an appeal to be made (but advises that it may issue an invoice); or sending a bill for HB (OG paras. 4.390 and 4.400).

HB overpayments, excess CTR and fraud

18.68 The Social Security Administration Act 1992 creates several offences related to HB fraud. It allows English and Welsh authorities to investigate and prosecute for these offences. These powers are however being restricted following the introduction of the Single Fraud Investigation Service (SFIS). This is a single service with powers to investigate and sanction all benefit and tax credit offences. It combines resources across authorities, HMRC, and DWP. Officers working for authorities should see the DWP's Fraud Circulars and the SFIS knowledge hub [www]. SFIS however has no powers in relation to CTR fraud. Powers to allow authorities to investigate and prosecute such fraud are set out in the amended Local Government Finance Act 1992. Regulations made under those powers provide English and Welsh authorities with investigatory powers, and create offences and administrative penalties in relation to local CTR schemes. These resemble the rules relating to HB found in the Social Security Administration Act 1992.

Administrative penalties

18.69 An authority may offer an individual the chance to pay an 'administrative penalty' rather than face prosecution, if:

◆ a recoverable HB overpayment or excess CTR was caused by an 'act or omission' on that person's part; and

◆ there are grounds for bringing a prosecution against them for an offence relating to that HB overpayment or excess CTR.

The person does not have to agree to a penalty. They can opt for the possibility of prosecution instead.

18.70 The offer of a penalty must be in writing, explain that it is a way of avoiding prosecution, and give other information – including the fact that the person can change their mind within 14 days (including the date of the

---

18.68 AA Part VI
www.dwp.gov.uk/docs/eia-single-fraud-investigation-service-wr2011.pdf
https://knowledgehub.local.gov.uk/web/singlefraudinvestigationservicesfiscommunicationshub
LGFA ss 14A-14C,

18.69 AA 115A; NIAA 109A; SI 1997/2813; NISR 1997/514 LGFA s.14C, SI 2013/501

agreement), and that the penalty will be repaid if the claimant successfully challenges it by asking for a reconsideration or appeal (OG para. 4.672). Authorities do not normally offer a penalty (but prosecute instead) if an overpayment is substantial or there are other aggravating factors (such as being in a position of trust).

18.71 For HB the amount of the penalty is 50% of the recoverable overpayment (subject to a minimum of £350 and a maximum of £2,000). For offences that were committed before 8th May 2012 or span that date the penalty is 30% of the recoverable overpayment (DWP F6/2012, para 4.2). For excess CTR the penalty is 50% of the excess (subject to a minimum of £100 and a maximum of £1,000).

18.72 An offer of a penalty may also be made where an act or omission could have resulted in a recoverable HB overpayment or excess CTR and there are grounds for bringing a prosecution for a related offence. In these cases for HB the penalty is the fixed amount of £350 and for CTR the fixed amount of £100.

Civil penalties

18.73 From 1st October 2012 an authority may impose a civil penalty of £50 on someone who makes incorrect statements in a benefit claim without taking reasonable steps to correct them or has been awarded benefit but who fails to disclose information or report changes in their circumstances without reasonable excuse. In each case, the action or inaction has to result in an overpayment wholly after 1st October 2012 before a civil penalty can be considered. If the claimant is successfully prosecuted for a fraud or offered an administrative penalty or caution they cannot be issued with a civil penalty for the same offence. The amount of the civil penalty is added to the amount of the overpayment.

18.73 AA 115C-115D; SI 2012 No 1990

19 Disputes and appeals

19.1   This chapter is about resolving disputed HB or CTR decisions and the related appeal procedures. The process of resolving disputed HB decisions is more highly regulated than that applicable to CTR decisions. The issues covered in this chapter include:

◆ getting more information about a HB decision;

◆ asking the authority to reconsider a decision;

◆ HB appeals to an independent tribunal;

◆ further appeals on HB decisions to the Upper Tribunal (in Great Britain) or the Social Security Commissioners (in Northern Ireland);

◆ the separate system of appeals to a rent officer regarding determinations they have made in non-LHA cases; and

◆ the separate system for resolving CTR disputes and appeals

CTR appeals

19.2   A separate system of CTR appeals applies and is described at the end of this chapter (paras. 19.111-125).

HB disputes and appeals

19.3   An outline of the HB dispute and appeal procedure and the related time limits are set out in table 19.1. This chapter describes the rules in Great Britain and the main variations in Northern Ireland (NI). Please refer to the legislation in the footnotes for further NI details.

19.4   In Great Britain HB appeals go to the First-tier Tribunal [www]. Further appeals (on a point of law and if given permission) then go to the Upper Tribunal [www]. Administrative arrangements are the responsibility of Her Majesty's Courts and Tribunal Service (HMCTS).

19.5   In Northern Ireland HB appeals are considered by an independent Appeal Tribunal. Further appeals (on a point of law and if given permission) then go to the NI Social Security Commissioners [www]. Administrative arrangements are the responsibility of the Appeals Service (NI) and the NI Court Service [www].

19.3   www.justice.gov.uk/guidance/courts-and-tribunals/tribunals/sscs/index.htm
www.justice.gov.uk/guidance/courts-and-tribunals/tribunals/aa/index.htm

19.4   www.courtsni.gov.uk/en-GB/Tribunals/OSSC/Pages/OSSC.aspx
www.dsdni.gov.uk/index/taser appeals_service.htm

Table 19.1: The HB disputes and appeals procedure

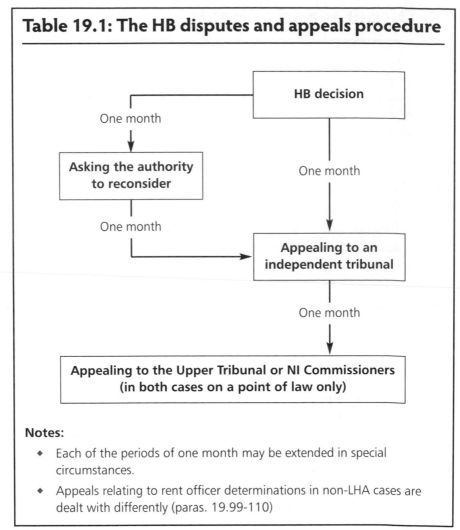

Notes:

- Each of the periods of one month may be extended in special circumstances.
- Appeals relating to rent officer determinations in non-LHA cases are dealt with differently (paras. 19.99-110)

The rights of a 'person affected'

19.6 Any 'person affected' by an appealable HB decision (para. 19.24) has all the rights identified in this chapter in relation to such decisions. Paragraph 16.8 identifies who counts as a 'person affected'. The term was considered by the Court of Appeal in *Wirral MBC v Salisbury Independent Living Ltd [2012] EWCA Civ 84.* It was held to include only those identified in the relevant regulations. This reversed an earlier decision (*[2011] UKUT 44 (AAC)*) that had extended the term to encompass others such as a landlord providing supported accommodation affected by a decision on the claimant's eligible rent. Note, however, that a person from whom an authority decides that an overpayment is recoverable (including the landlord) does have a right of appeal against the relevant decision (*[2012] EWCA Civ 84* at [13]). The right of appeal on an overpayment includes an appeal against the existence of the overpayment (i.e. the superseding decision or original decision as revised that causes the overpayment) *(R(H) 3/04* at [50]).

19.7   Whenever it makes an appealable HB decision the authority must notify each person affected of their:

- right to a written statement of the reasons for that decision;
- right to ask the authority to reconsider; and
- right to appeal to a tribunal (unless the decision is one which cannot be appealed: para. 19.25).

Written statement of reasons

19.8   A person affected (para. 19.6) may request a statement of reasons about anything that was not explained in the HB decision notice. Requests must be in writing and signed by the person affected or, if the person affected is a corporate body, by someone aged 18 or over on its behalf. They must be made within one month of the notification date of the decision. The authority should provide the statement within 14 days so far as this is practicable.

Reconsideration or appeal?

19.9   A person affected who disagrees with an appealable HB decision made by the authority has two options. They can:

- ask the authority to reconsider (i.e. revise) the decision; or
- appeal against the decision to an independent tribunal.

If they choose the first option, they can go on to the second option next. If they choose the second option, the authority can treat it as a request for a reconsideration (para. 19.21).

Asking the authority to reconsider

19.10   Any person affected (para. 19.6) can ask the authority to reconsider any HB decision it has made. In the case of an appealable decision they can do this either instead of or before making an appeal to an independent tribunal. Requests must be in writing and the normal time limit is one month (para. 19.11). The law calls this requesting a revision or supersession, but the person does not have to use these terms, and it is normally called requesting a reconsideration. If the authority needs information or evidence in connection with the person's request, see paragraph 19.16.

19.6   CPSA sch 7 paras. 3-4,6(3), 7-8, 23(2); NICPSA schedule 7 paras. 3-4, 6(3), 7-8, 23(2); DAR 3; NIDAR 3

19.7   DAR 10; NIDAR 10

19.8   HB 90(2),(4); HB60+ 71(2),(4); NIHB 86(2),(4); NIHB60 I 67(2),(4); DAR 10(2); NIDAR 10(2)

19.10   CPSA sch 7 para 3(1)(b),4(1); NICPSA sch 7 para 3(1)(b),4(1); DAR 4(1),(8),(9),7(2),(6),(7); NIDAR 4(1),(8),(9),7(2),(6),(7)

Time limit for requesting a reconsideration

19.11   A request is within the time limit if it is received by the authority within one calendar month of the date the decision was notified. In calculating this time limit:

- any time is ignored from the date the authority received a request for a statement of reasons (para. 19.8) to the date the authority provided the statement (both dates inclusive); and

- any time is ignored before the date on which the authority gave notice of the correction of an accidental error (para. 17.58); and

- the time limit may be extended by the authority as described below (para. 19.14).

19.12   If the request for a reconsideration is received:

- within the time limit, the authority must consider revising its decision (para. 19.13);

- outside the time limit, the authority must consider superseding its decision (para. 19.15) and may consider revising it under its own powers, for example where there has been an official error (para. 17.59).

19.13   If the request for reconsideration is received within the time limit, and the authority alters entitlement to HB, this takes effect from the date of the original decision. The one exception to this rule is where the authority determines that the original decision took effect from a wrong date, in which case it takes effect from the correct date. This is a revision. Whether or not the authority alters entitlement, the outcome must be notified (para. 19.17).

Extending the time limit for reconsideration requests

19.14   The one-month time limit is extended if:

- the person affected makes the request in writing and it is received by the authority within 13 months of the date on which the decision was notified; and

- the request says that the person is asking for it to be accepted late, and gives the reasons for the failure to request a reconsideration earlier; and

- the person gives sufficient details to identify the disputed decision; and

- the request for revision 'has merit'; and

- the authority is satisfied that there are or were 'special circumstances' as a result of which it was not practicable to request a reconsideration within the one month time limit. The longer the delay (beyond the normal one month), the more compelling those special circumstances need to be; and

- the authority is satisfied that it is reasonable to grant the claimant's request.

19.11   DAR 4(1),(4),10A(3); NIDAR 4(1),(4),10A(3)

19.13   CPSA sch 7 para 3(3); NICPSA sch 7 para 3(3); DAR 6; NIDAR 6

19.14   DAR 4(8),5(1)-(6); NIDAR 4(7),5(1)-(6)

In determining this, the authority may not take account of ignorance of the law (not even ignorance of the time limits) nor of the fact that the Upper Tribunal (in GB), the Commissioners (in NI) or a court has taken a different view of the law from that previously understood and applied.

Reconsideration requests received outside the time limit

19.15 If the request for reconsideration is received outside the one month time limit, and the authority refuses to extend this limit, the person affected has no right to ask it to accept a further late request to reconsider the same matter. However, the authority may nonetheless reconsider its decision and should consider making a superseding decision instead: (the details are in paras. 17.64-65).

Example: Late request for the authority to reconsider its decision

In May 2013 the authority notified a claimant of its decision on his claim. Among other things, the decision depended upon an assessment of the claimant's self-employed income.

In September 2013, the claimant asks the authority to reconsider its decision, as he forgot to tell them about part of his expenditure. He has no special circumstances for his delay. However, the authority accepts that (if it had known) it would have allowed that additional expenditure (and he would therefore have qualified for more HB).

The change is implemented from the Monday of the benefit week in which the claimant's request for a reconsideration is received by the authority. The claimant does not get his arrears. This is a supersession. (However, if the claimant has 'special circumstances' for the late reconsideration request, he may get his arrears: para. 19.14.)

Information and evidence

19.16 When reconsidering a decision, the authority may request the person to provide information and evidence it requires – and must take it into account if provided within one month, or longer if reasonable.

Notifying the outcome of the authority's reconsideration

19.17 In all the circumstances described in this section, the authority must notify the person(s) affected of the outcome of the request for reconsideration. The decision notice must include the following matters:

- whether the authority has changed its decision and, if it has, a statement of what it has altered;

19.15 DAR 5(7),7(2)(b); NIDAR 5(7),7(2)(b)

19.16 DAR 4(5), 7(5); NIDAR 4(4), 7(5)

19.17 DAR 10; NIDAR 10; HB sch 9; HB60+ sch 8; NIHB sch 10; NIHB60+ sch 10; CTB sch 8; CTB60+ sch 7; FTPR sch 1(c)

- the person affected's right to request a written statement of reasons, to request a reconsideration, and to appeal to a tribunal, and how and when to do these things.

Appeals to a tribunal

19.18   Any person affected (para. 19.6) can appeal an appealable HB decision to an independent tribunal. They can do this either instead of or after asking the authority to reconsider its decision. If there is more than one person affected by an appeal (for example both the landlord and the claimant in some overpayment cases) each is a party to the proceedings no matter which of them made the appeal.

The First-tier Tribunal (GB)

19.19   The First-tier Tribunal is an independent tribunal established under the Tribunals, Courts and Enforcement Act 2007. It is divided into a number of chambers. The Social Entitlement Chamber considers HB appeals as well as appeals on other social security benefits and certain other matters. The procedural rules of the Social Entitlement Chamber are set out in The Tribunal Procedure (First-tier Tribunal) (Social Entitlement Chamber) Rules SI 2008 No 2685.

The Appeal Tribunal (NI)

19.20   In Northern Ireland the composition of the tribunal to decide HB appeals is provided for in regulation 22 of the HB (Decisions and Appeals) Regulations (NI) S.R. 2001 No. 213. The procedural rules are set out in Chapters II to V of Part V of the Social Security and Child Support (Decisions and Appeals) Regulations (NI) 1999 S.R. 1999 No. 162 (subject to reg 23 of S.R. 2001 No. 213).

Revisions prompted by an appeal

19.21   When an appeal is received, the authority may consider whether the decision can be revised. If it can be revised to the advantage of the person affected, the authority should revise the decision and the appeal lapses (does not go ahead). This applies even though the person affected may not receive all that has been asked for in the appeal. Where a decision has been revised to the advantage of the person affected there is then a fresh decision with a fresh dispute period, and fresh rights to apply for a revision or appeal.

19.22   The appeal should automatically proceed to a tribunal if:

- the decision is not revised by the authority; or
- the decision is revised, but not in favour of the person affected; or
- the decision is superseded by the authority.

19.19   Part 1 of the Tribunals, Courts & Enforcement Act 2007, art 6(c) of SI 2010 No 2655, FTPR

19.21   CPSA sch 7 para 3(6); NICPSA sch 7 para 3(6); DAR 4(1),(6); NIDAR 4(1),(6)

19.23 If the authority revises the decision but not in favour of the person affected the appeal is deemed to be against the revised decision and the person affected is given an additional month in which to make further representations.

Which decisions can be appealed

19.24 A person affected has a right of appeal to a tribunal against an authority's decision on a claim for HB (including an original decision as revised) or a decision superseding a decision (or refusing to supersede *(R(DLA) 1/03* at [51])). Determinations relating to overpayments are also appealable. The legislation identifies certain decisions as non-appealable. These are mainly to do with claims, payments and certain overpayment matters (table 19.2).

Appeals against non-appealable decisions

19.25 If an appeal is made against a non-appealable decision (table 19.2), the authority should identify it as 'out of jurisdiction' when forwarding it to the tribunal. If the tribunal agrees, it should then be struck out by the tribunal so that the appeal does not go ahead. The appellant should have the opportunity to make representations on the matter. Note, though, that non-appealable matters can be the subject of a request for a reconsideration or judicial review (para. 19.10).

Making an appeal

How to appeal

19.26 To be properly made an appeal must:

- be in writing;
- be delivered, by whatever means (e.g. post, fax, e-mail, in person) to the authority;
- state the appellant's name and address;
- provide the name and address of any representative and an address where documents for the appellant may be sent;
- be signed by the person making the appeal;
- say what is being appealed;
- give their grounds of appeal; and
- be within one month or 13 months (paras. 19.30-35).

19.23   DAR 17(3),(4); NIDAR 17(3),(4)

19.24   CPSA sch 7 paras 1, 6(1), 6(6); NICPSA sch 7 para 1, 6(1), 6(6)

19.25   FTPR 8(2),(4); NIDAR99 46(1)(a),47

19.26   DAR 20(1); NIDAR 20(1); FTPR 23, sch 1

Table 19.2: Appealable and non-appealable HB decisions

Decisions about claims

Non-appealable

- Which partner in a couple is to be the claimant (para. 5.4)
- Who may claim when someone is unable to act (para. 5.5)

Appealable

- When and how a claim is made (paras. 5.8-12)
- Whether a claim is incomplete (para. 5.24)
- The date of claim and first day of entitlement (paras. 5.26-50)
- Backdating (paras. 5.51-61)

Decisions about payments

Non-appealable

- When and how benefit is paid (para. 16.19)
- Making a payment on account (para. 16.22)
- The frequency of payment of a rent allowance (paras. 16.27-30)
- Making payment to a person entitled (para. 16.15)
- Paying outstanding benefit after a death (para. 16.75)
- Suspending or restoring benefit (paras. 17.69-71)

Appealable

- Adjusting HB to correct a payment on account (para. 16.26)
- Who HB is to be paid to (e.g. claimant or landlord/agent) (paras. 16.31-56);
- Whether the landlord/agent is a 'fit and proper person' (paras. 16.57-61)
- Terminating benefit (para. 17.73)

T 19.2   CPSA sch 7 para 6; DAR 16(1) and sch; NICPSA sch 7 para 6 NIDAR 16(1) and sch

Decisions about overpayments

Non-appealable

+ What 'an overpayment' means (para. 18.4)
+ The exercise of discretion to recover or not (paras. 18.26-27)
+ The method of recovery (para. 18.38)

Appealable

+ Whether an overpayment is recoverable (paras. 18.11-14)
+ The amount of the overpayment (paras. 18.15-25)
+ Who an overpayment can be recovered from (paras. 18.28-37)

Other decisions

Non-appealable

+ The HB benefit cap (para. 6.31)
+ LHA figures and areas (paras. 8.36-44)
+ Rent officer figures in rent referral cases (but see para. 19.100)
+ The DWP's assessed income figure or 'AIF' (paras. 13.162-165) – though modifications to it are appealable (para. 13.166 and table 13.5)
+ Whether to run a local scheme for pensions for war disablement and war bereavement (para. 23.17)
+ A refusal to correct a mistake out-of-time *(Beltekian v Westminster CC reported as R(H) 8/05)*
+ Any figure laid down in the law (e.g. the capital limit)

Appealable

+ All other HB decisions

19.27 An appeal does not have to be on a form, though many authorities do have forms, sometimes based on the DWP's (form GL24). An appeal made in a letter should make it clear that it is an appeal to a tribunal (not a request for a reconsideration: para. 19.10).

Appeals that do not meet the conditions

19.28 If an appeal is incomplete, the authority can accept it if it contains enough information. If it does not, the authority must write requesting further details, or

19.28   DAR 20(2)-(8); NIDAR 20(2)-(8)

return it for completion, and allow the appellant 14 days to reply, or longer if the authority directs.

19.29   If the appellant does not reply within that time, the authority must send the documents to the tribunal (including any other documents it has by now received) for the tribunal to determine whether the appeal should go ahead.

The appeal time limit

19.30   An appeal should normally be received by the authority within one month of the date on which its decision notice was sent out. If a statement of reasons is requested within that time (para. 19.8) then the time limit is 14 days after the end of that month or the date on which the statement is provided, whichever is later. If an unsuccessful revision request has been made then the time limit is one month after notice of that decision is sent out. If the relevant time period runs out on a non-working day the appeal is still in time if it is received on the next working day. Appeals should normally be received by the authority at the latest by 5pm on the final day.

19.31   If the authority's decision notice is invalid because it fails to meet the relevant legal requirements (paras.16.11-12, 18.65-67 and table 18.6) the time for appealing does not start until the authority issues a valid notice: *CH/1129/2004*. The authority should refer disputes about this, or any other question about whether the appeal was within the time limit, to the tribunal.

Requesting acceptance of a late appeal

19.32   An appellant may, if they are outside the above time limit, write requesting acceptance of a late appeal, giving their grounds for lateness including details of any special circumstances. The request must be signed by the person who has the right of appeal and must be received within an absolute time limit of 12 months after the end of the last 'normal' day for appealing (19.30). An application for a late appeal can only be made once (for that appeal).

Accepting a late appeal

19.33   The authority may grant the request for a late appeal if it is in the interests of justice to do so. If it does not, it must forward the request to the tribunal. The First-tier Tribunal may grant the application for a late appeal under its case management powers in the context of the overriding objective to deal with cases fairly and justly, but must not extend the maximum time limit. In Northern Ireland a panel member must be satisfied that the appeal has reasonable prospects of success or that it is in the interests of justice for the late appeal application to be granted.

19.30   FTPR 12, 23, sch 1; NIDAR 18

19.32   DAR 20(1); NIDAR 20(1); FTPR 23(3)-(5)

19.33   DAR 19(5),(6),(8); FTPR 2(1),(3),5(3)(a),7(2),23(5),(8); NIDAR 19(3),(5),(6),(8),(10),(11)

'Interests of justice'

19.34   When the authority, or a tribunal in Northern Ireland, is determining whether to accept a request for a late appeal, only the following count as being in the interests of justice – and only if they meant that it was not practicable to make the appeal within the normal one month:

- the appellant or a partner or dependant of the appellant has died or suffered serious illness; or
- the appellant is not resident in the UK; or
- normal postal services were disrupted; or
- some other special circumstances exist which are wholly exceptional and relevant to the application.

19.35   Ignorance of the law (including the law about time limits) is ignored, as is any change in how the law is interpreted as a result of a decision of the Upper Tribunal, NI Commissioners or a court; and the longer the delay (beyond the one month time limit), the more compelling the special circumstances need to be.

Withdrawing an appeal

19.36   An appeal may be withdrawn by the appellant, or their representative, at any time before the appeal is decided, by giving notice in writing of withdrawal to the First-tier Tribunal (in Northern Ireland, the authority). In Great Britain withdrawal of an appeal at a hearing requires the tribunal's consent.

Death of a party to an appeal

19.37   If the appellant dies, the authority may appoint someone to act for them. Grant of probate, letters of administration, etc, have no effect on this appointment.

The authority's duties on receiving an appeal

19.38   When the authority receives an appeal, it should consider revising the decision appealed against (para.19.10). If it revises the decision in a way which is advantageous, the appeal lapses and no further action is taken on it.

19.39   In all other cases, the authority sends HMCTS/Appeals Service (NI):

- a notice of appeal completed by the authority (form AT37) along with the appellant's submissions; and
- the authority's response to the appeal (this is often referred to as its submission).

19.34   DAR 19(5A)-(9); NIDAR 19(6)-(9)

19.35   DAR 19(8)-(9); NIDAR 19(8)-(9)

19.36   FTPR 17(1)(a); NIDAR 20(9)

19.37   DAR 21; NIDR 21

19.39   FTPR 24(1)(b)

The authority also sends its response (with a covering letter) to the appellant and any third party. This should be done as soon as reasonably practicable.

19.40   The authority should tell HMCTS/Appeals Service (NI) (on form AT37) if eviction proceedings have begun so that the case can be heard urgently, and also if there are special reasons affecting the appellant which may delay their reply (para. 19.42).

The pre-hearing enquiry form

19.41   On receipt of the above, the HMCTS/Appeals Service (NI) sends a pre-hearing enquiry form to the appellant and a similar form to any third party. This asks the appellant whether they:

* want to withdraw their appeal;
* want a hearing (at which they and/or their representative can be present) or have no objection to the appeal being decided in their absence;
* have a representative and if so their name and contact details;
* agree to having less than 14 days notice if they have opted for a hearing;
* have dates they would be unable to attend a hearing; and/or
* need an interpreter or signer.

19.42   The appellant should return the completed form within 14 days – a period which may be extended for appropriate reasons.

The authority's response and the appellant's submission

19.43   In Great Britain the rules require the authority's response to include the following information and evidence:

* the name and address of the authority;
* the name and address of the authority's representative (if any);
* an address where documents for the authority may be sent or delivered;
* the names and addresses of any other respondents and their representatives (if any);
* whether the authority opposes the appellant's case and, if so, any grounds which are not set out in the documents before the tribunal; and
* any further information or documents required by a direction.

19.44   The authority must provide with its response:

* a copy of any written record of the disputed decision, and any statement of reasons for the decision, if not sent with the notice of appeal;
* copies of all documents relevant to the case in the authority's possession unless a direction says otherwise; and

19.41   (GB) Example enquiry form – www.justice.gov.uk/tribunals/sscs/appeals

19.42   FTPR 5(3)(a); NIDAR99 39(2),(3)

19.43   FTPR 24

◆ a copy of the notice of appeal and of any documents given by the appellant with the notice of appeal.

19.45 Additional DWP guidance on responses may be found in GM paras. C7.280-309. The appellant and any other respondent may make a written submission and supply further documents in reply to the authority's response. Unless directed otherwise, this should normally be done within a month of the authority sending out its response. Submissions, etc, on behalf of the appellant are often submitted later than this. If relevant they should be considered by the tribunal but if other parties have not been given adequate time to consider the material this may lead to the adjournment of a hearing.

How quickly should appeals be dealt with?

19.46 The authority should send its response to the tribunal as soon as reasonably practicable, but the law does not set a time limit. The DWP suggests a normal time scale of four weeks except for more complex cases (HB/CTB A20/2003, Appendix B, Annex C, para. A65). In cases of significant delay by the authority the appellant or their representative may make a written application to the First-tier Tribunal for a direction to be given requiring the authority to produce its response or listing the appeal for hearing (R(H)1/07 at [27]-[34]). The law also does not say how quickly an appeal is heard once HMCTS/Appeals Service (NI) receive the authority's response. The First-tier Tribunal has a responsibility to deal with cases 'fairly and justly'. This includes avoiding delay so far as compatible with proper consideration of the issues. In cases of urgency a written application may be made to the First-tier Tribunal for a direction to be given requiring an early hearing of the appeal.

The appeal tribunal

Membership of the tribunal

19.47 All tribunal members are independent of the authority. The tribunal normally consists of just one person, a judge or in Northern Ireland a panel member, who is legally qualified. In rare instances where difficult financial questions are raised (e.g. about company accounts) there may also be a member with relevant qualifications. An additional member may also be present to provide experience or to assist with the monitoring of standards. Tribunal Judges should be referred to as 'Sir' or 'Madam'.

Venues

19.48 The hearing normally takes place at a venue near to the appellant. HMCTS has around 140 venues across England, Wales and Scotland: information on venue locations and facilities can be found on its web site [www]. The Appeal Service

---

19.46   FTPR 2(2)(e),5,6,24(1)(h)

19.47   SI 2008/2835; SI 2008/2692; NIDAR 22(1),(2)

(NI) currently holds appeal hearings at 19 venues in towns and cities throughout the province [www].

Function

19.49 The tribunal's task is to reconsider the decision that has been appealed in a manner that is fair and just. It does not have to consider any issue that has not been raised but it does have the power to do so. The tribunal should not shut its eyes to things if to do so would cause an injustice. But it cannot take into account any circumstances that did not exist at the time the original decision was made. The tribunal may also give directions on its own initiative or on the application of one of the parties regarding a wide range of case management matters. The First-tier Tribunal also has the power to make a decision in the form of a consent order. This ends the proceedings and makes such other provisions as the parties have agreed. This is done at the request of the parties if the tribunal considers it appropriate. The First-tier Tribunal need not hold a hearing before making such an order or provide reasons.

The appeal hearing

Notice

19.50 Notice of the time and place of an (oral) hearing should be given to every party to the proceedings. This should be done at least 14 days before the hearing (beginning with the day on which the notice is given and ending on the day before it takes place). If notice has not been given to someone who should have been given it, the hearing may go ahead only with their consent or (in Great Britain) in urgent or exceptional circumstances. Appellants and representatives should note that where they have chosen not to have a hearing and the tribunal also considers that it is able to decide the matter without a hearing then the parties are not notified of the date on which the appeal is considered on the papers. They need to ensure that all relevant submissions and documents are sent to the tribunal without delay.

Postponement

19.51 The tribunal may postpone the hearing at any time before it starts. A request for a postponement must be made by a person affected in writing to the clerk stating the reasons for the request. If it is too late, an adjournment may be requested at the hearing, which the tribunal may grant or refuse as it thinks fit.

19.48   www.tribunals.gov.uk/qasvenuefinder.aspx
        www.dsdni.gov.uk/index/taser-appeals_service.htm

19.49   CPSA sch 7 para 6(9); NICPSA sch 7 para 6(9); FTPR 2,5,6,32

19.50   FTPR 27-29; NIDAR99 49(2)

19.51   FTPR 5; NIDAR99 51(1)

Public or private hearings

19.52   The presumption is that a hearing will be in public but in practice normally only the people involved are present. The tribunal may decide that the hearing (or part of it) should be in private. In Northern Ireland the rules set out that this may be done:

- in the interests of national security, morals, public order or children;
- for the protection of the private or family life of one of the parties; or
- in special circumstances, if publicity would prejudice the interests of justice.

19.53   Certain people such as trainee panel members or clerks may be present (whether or not it is in private), but they must not take part in the proceedings.

Deciding to proceed in the absence of a party

19.54   If one of the parties fails to appear, the tribunal may, having regard to all the circumstances including any explanation offered:

- proceed with the hearing if it is in the interest of justice to do so; or
- give directions to determine the appeal as it thinks proper.

19.55   If one of the parties has waived the right to be given 14 days notice of the hearing, the tribunal may proceed with the hearing despite their absence.

The parties' rights at the hearing

19.56   The procedure at the hearing is determined by the tribunal, but each party is entitled to be present and to be heard.

19.57   In law, parties entitled to be present at a hearing do not have to be physically present, but can attend by a live television link, e.g. a video conference facility, but only where the judge gives permission. The former Tribunals Service was working to extend the use of the video-link, mainly to enable appellants to attend their hearing from remote or rural areas.

19.58   A person who has the right to be heard at a hearing:

- may be accompanied; and
- may be represented by another person whether they have professional qualifications or not.

19.59   For the purposes of the proceedings at the hearing, any representative has all the rights and powers to which the person represented is entitled (except signing a witness statement). Once the tribunal and the other parties have been notified

---

19.52   FTPR 30; NIDAR99 49(6)
19.54   FTPR 31; NIDAR99 49(4)
19.55   NIDAR99 49(5)
19.56   FTPR 2,5,28; NIDAR99 49(1),(7)
19.57   FTPR 1(3) def 'hearing'; NIDAR99 49(8)
19.58   FTPR 11; NIDAR 49(8)

that a representative has been appointed they must provide the representative with any documents that should be provided to the person represented and need not provide them to that person. They may also assume that the representative remains authorised to act until they receive written notification that this is not the case from either the representative or the represented person.

19.60 Any person entitled to be heard at a hearing may:

+ address the tribunal;

+ give evidence;

+ call witnesses; and

+ put questions directly to any other person called as a witness.

Order of the hearing

19.61 The procedure for the hearing is determined by the tribunal within the framework set in the law, e.g. the need to ensure that the parties have the opportunity to put their case. Failure to observe proper procedures or the rights of the parties may leave the tribunal's decision open to appeal on grounds of natural justice (GM para C7.309) or the right to a fair hearing *(CJSA/5100/2001)*.

19.62 The way the tribunal hears the appeal varies according to the issue it has to decide. The appellant should expect to have those present introduced and their role explained at the start. The tribunal should also explain the procedure it wishes to follow and seek the agreement of the parties to going ahead in that way. The appellant may be asked to start by explaining why they think the decision is wrong. If the authority's presenting officer is present, they will be asked to explain the authority's decision. At some point the tribunal is likely to question both parties. Usually the appellant is offered the opportunity of having the final word before the tribunal goes on to consider its decision.

Directions

19.63 The tribunal may at any stage of the proceedings, of its own motion, or on a written application made to the clerk by any party to the proceedings, or by an oral request from any of the parties during a hearing:

+ give such directions as it considers necessary or desirable for the just, effective and efficient conduct of the proceedings; and

+ direct any party to the proceedings to provide such particulars or to produce such documents as may be reasonably required.

19.59   FTPR 11(5)-(6); NIDAR99 49(8)

19.60   NIDAR99 49(11)

19.61   FTPR 5,6; NIDAR99 49(1)

19.62   FTPR 2,5,6,8; NIDAR99 38(2)

19.63   FTPR 2, 5-6; NIDAR99 38(2)

Failure to comply with a direction from a First-tier Tribunal may result in an appeal being struck out. Where the authority fails to comply it may be barred from the proceedings or have all issues determined against it.

Adjournment

19.64 A hearing may be adjourned by the tribunal at any time on the application of any party to the proceedings or of their own motion. This might be, for example, to allow new evidence to be looked at.

Withdrawing an appeal

19.65 An appeal may be withdrawn by the appellant at the hearing (in GB if the tribunal consents). If this happens the clerk must send a notice in writing to any party to the proceedings who is not present when the appeal or referral is withdrawn, informing them that the appeal has been withdrawn.

The tribunal's decision

19.66 The tribunal reaches a decision once it has considered all the evidence. In reaching its decision the tribunal should:

* consider the relevant law applicable to the decision in question;
* identify the relevant facts – and where these are in doubt or dispute find them (if necessary on the balance of probability); and
* apply the law to the relevant facts to arrive at a reasoned decision.

Duty to follow decisions of the Commissioners, the Upper Tribunal and the courts

19.67 In its consideration of the legal issues the tribunal has a duty to follow past decisions of the Commissioners, the Upper Tribunal and the courts (para. 19.91) unless the case before the tribunal is distinguishable *(R(U)23/59)*. Northern Ireland decisions are of only persuasive authority in England, Wales and Scotland *(R(I)14/63)* and vice versa. Decisions of the First-tier Tribunal in Great Britain or Appeal Tribunals in Northern Ireland do not set any precedent.

19.68 There is an order of precedence to Upper Tribunal decisions (including the former Commissioners' decisions) *(R(I)12/75(T)* and *[2009] UKUT 4 (AAC)* at [37])*, as follows:

* decisions of the Upper Tribunal where a Three Judge Panel (formerly a Tribunal of Commissioners) heard the case are the most authoritative – whether reported or unreported;

19.64 FTPR 5,6; NIDAR99 51(4)

19.65 FTPR 17; NIDAR99 40(1)(a),(2)

- reported decisions come next. For many years these were given serial numbers by the year and identified by having the prefix 'R', e.g. *R(H)1/02.* However, since 1st January 2010 these are known as the Administrative Appeals Chamber Reports and are indicated (after a reference to the parties and a neutral citation number) by the year of reporting e.g. [2010]; the suffix (AACR) and the consecutive reporting number within that year's series, e.g. *[2010] AACR 40;*

- then come other decisions. These are identified by the file number, e.g. *CH/1502/2004* or a reference to the parties and a neutral citation number e.g. *JD v Leeds City Council [2009] UKUT 70 (AAC).*

19.69   If there appears to be conflict between two or more decisions the above hierarchy should be applied. If the conflicting decisions are of equal rank, the tribunal is free to choose between them. More recent decisions should be preferred to older decisions. If a more recent unreported decision has fully considered all the earlier authorities, and given reasons for disapproving one or more earlier reported decisions, the tribunal should generally follow the more recent unreported decision *(R(IS) 13/01).*

19.70   For details about on-line access to the decisions of the Upper Tribunal and NI Commissioners (and their predecessors) see para. 1.47 and appendix 2. Reported cases are kept at tribunal venues but unreported cases are not. If a party wishes to use an unreported decision in support of their case a copy should, where possible, be sent in advance, otherwise an adjournment may be necessary.

The written decision notice

19.71   If the appellant attends a hearing they may be given the decision on the day. It should be confirmed in writing as soon as practicable by the judge or (in NI) the legally qualified tribunal member or chair.

Communicating the decision

19.72   As soon as practicable after an appeal has been decided, a copy of the decision notice must be sent or given to every party to the proceedings. They must also be informed of:

- the right to apply for a statement of reasons; and
- the conditions governing appeals to the Upper Tribunal or (in NI) the Commissioners.

Implementing the decision

19.73   The decision notice is the legal document that enables the authority to correct and pay benefit in line with the tribunal's decision. The authority should action the tribunal's decision as soon as practicable and normally within four

---

19.71   FTPR 33(1); NIDAR99 53(1),(2),(5)

19.72   FTPR 33(2); NIDAR99 53(3)

19.73   CSPSA sch 7. para 13(3); DAR 11(2)(b); NICPSA sch 7 para 13(3); NIDAR 11(2)(b)

calendar weeks (HB/CTB A20/2003 Appendix B, Annex C, para. A70). An exception to this is where an appeal is pending against the tribunal's decision. In such cases the authority has the discretion to suspend payment in whole or in part (para. 17.70).

A 'statement of reasons'

19.74 A statement of reasons sets out the findings of fact and the reasons for the decision. If an appeal to the Upper Tribunal/NI Commissioners is being considered, a statement of reasons must be asked for.

Time limit for application for statement of reasons

19.75 A party to the proceedings may apply to the clerk for a statement of the reasons for the decision, at the hearing. Otherwise the application must normally be made within one month of the date the tribunal's decision notice was given or sent. If not made in time, the chance of appeal may be lost.

19.76 The First-tier Tribunal does have powers to extend the one month time limit for a statement of reasons if it would be fair and just to do so. In Northern Ireland late applications for the statement of reasons can only be accepted if the application is made in writing to the clerk within three months of the date the decision note was sent. Where a correction is made, or where set-aside is refused, the three month period is counted from the day notice of the correction or refusal is given.

19.77 The application should explain why the application is late, including details of any relevant special circumstances.

Requirement to supply written statement of reasons

19.78 Following receipt of an accepted application for a written statement of reasons the tribunal must:

- record a statement of the reasons; and
- send or give a copy of that statement to every party to the proceedings within one month of the date it received the application or as soon as practicable after that.

Record of tribunal proceedings

19.79 A record of the proceedings at an oral hearing, which is sufficient to indicate the evidence taken, must be made by the tribunal (Senior President's

---

19.75   FTPR 34; NIDAR99 53(4)

19.76   FTPR 2,5(3)(a); NIDAR99 54(1)

19.77   NIDAR99 54(3)

19.78   FTPR 34; NIDAR99 54(11)

19.79   NIDAR99 55(1),(2)
         www.judiciary.gov.uk/publications-and-reports/practice-directions/tribunals/tribunals-statements

Practice Statement (30th October 2008)) [www]. This record, together with the decision notice, and any statement of the reasons for the tribunal's decision, must be preserved for six months from the date it was created. Any party to the proceedings may apply in writing within that six month period for a copy, which should be supplied on request.

If a tribunal's decision is wrong

19.80   Once a tribunal has made and communicated its decision the decision may be:

*   altered if the authority supersedes the decision;
*   corrected, where there is an accidental error;
*   set aside on certain limited grounds;
*   appealed on a point of law to the Upper Tribunal or in Northern Ireland the NI Commissioners.

When may the authority supersede the tribunal's decision?

19.81   The decision of a tribunal may be superseded, either on application or on the authority's own initiative, where:

*   the decision was made in ignorance of a material fact; or
*   the decision was based on a mistake as to a material fact; or
*   there has been a relevant change of circumstances since it had effect.

When may a tribunal's decision be corrected?

19.82   The tribunal may at any time correct accidental errors such as a typing mistake or omission. A correction made to, or to the record of, a decision is deemed part of the decision or record of that decision. Any of the parties to the appeal can ask for a correction to be made. A written notice of the correction should be given as soon as practicable to every party to the proceedings. There is no right of appeal against a correction or a refusal to make a correction.

Setting aside decisions: Great Britain

19.83   If a tribunal decision is 'set aside' this means that the decision is cancelled and a new tribunal must be arranged. Any party to the proceedings may apply for a decision of a tribunal to be set aside. The tribunal may set aside a decision if it considers that it is in the interests of justice to do so; and

*   a document relating to the proceedings was not sent to, or was not received at an appropriate time by, a party or a party's representative;

19.81   DAR 7(2)(a),(d); NIDAR 7(2)(a),(c)

19.82   FTPR 36; NIDAR99 56(1),(2)

19.83   FTPR 37; 5(3)(a); NIDAR99 57(1)

- a document relating to the proceedings was not sent to the tribunal at an appropriate time;

- a party, or a party's representative, was not present at a hearing related to the proceedings; or

- there has been some other procedural irregularity in the proceedings.

19.84 A party applying for a decision to be set aside must make a written application to the tribunal so that it is received within one month of the date on which the tribunal sent notice of the decision to the party; though this time limit may be extended where it is fair and just to do so.

Setting aside decisions: Northern Ireland

19.85 In Northern Ireland a decision of a tribunal may be set aside where it appears just to do so in the first three circumstances set out above. In deciding to set aside a decision on the ground of a party's absence, the tribunal must consider whether the applicant gave notice that they wished to have an oral hearing. If not, the decision cannot be set aside unless the tribunal is satisfied that the interests of justice support the decision being set aside.

19.86 The application to set aside must:

- be made within one month of the date on which a copy of the decision notice is sent or given to the parties, or the statement of the reasons for the decision is given or sent in, whichever is the later;

- be in writing; and

- be signed by a party to the proceedings or, where the party has provided written authority to a representative to act on their behalf, that representative;

- contain particulars of the grounds on which it is made; and

- be sent to the clerk to the appeal tribunal.

19.87 A late application for set aside can be made up to one year after the end of the one month time limit (but only one such application can be made per decision). It must give the reasons for the lateness and is determined by a legally qualified panel member. Every party to the proceedings must be sent a copy and given a reasonable opportunity of making representations on it before it is determined. A late application for set aside is accepted if:

- it is in the interests of justice to do so (as described in paras 19.34-35); and

- there are reasonable prospects of success in the application to set aside.

19.88 Every party to the proceedings must receive a written notice of the

---

decision on an application to set aside as soon as practicable. The notice must contain a statement giving the reasons for the decision.

19.89   There is no right of appeal against the outcome of a set aside request. If the request is refused, however, the time limit for appealing to the NI Commissioners does not start until the notice of the set aside decision has been issued. The application to set aside may be treated as an application for a statement of the reasons, subject to the normal time limits (paras. 19.75-76).

Appeals to the Upper Tribunal/NI Commissioners

19.90   An appeal against a tribunal decision can be made to the Upper Tribunal or NI Commissioners, but only if:

- the person is entitled to appeal (para. 19.96); and
- their grounds of appeal are that the tribunal made an error of law (para. 19.95).

19.91   The Upper Tribunal/NI Commissioners give interpretations of the law which are binding on all decision makers and tribunals. Their judges/ commissioners are barristers, solicitors or advocates of not less than ten years' standing who are specialists in social security law, and have a legal status comparable to that of a High Court judge in their specialised area. The DWP gives good guidance on appeals to the Upper Tribunal (GM paras. C7.560 - 928). Detailed advice, along with copies of the forms, may be found online [www].

Permission to appeal and the appeal itself

19.92   If, having considered the statement of reasons, a party thinks that the tribunal's decision contains an error of law (para 19.95) they may apply to the tribunal for permission to appeal within one month from the date it was issued. This time limit may be extended by the tribunal. The tribunal may:

- decide to review the decision without the need to refer the case onwards. The case may be re-decided or heard again by a different tribunal;
- give permission for the appeal – in which case it can be sent on to the Upper Tribunal/NI Commissioners;
- refuse permission – in which case either party may then apply (normally within one month) directly to the Upper Tribunal/NI Commissioners for permission to appeal.

19.88   NIDAR99 57(5)

19.89   NIDAR99 57A(2)

19.90   CPSA sch 7 paras 8(1),(2),(7)(c),(8); NICPSA sch 7 paras 8(1),(2),(7)(c),(8); FTPR 38,39; UTPR 21; NIDAR99 58(1),(3); SSCPR 9,10,12,13; NISSCPR 9,10,12,13

19.91   www.justice.gov.uk/guidance/courts-and-tribunals/tribunals/aa/index.htm www.courtsni.gov.uk/en-GB/Tribunals/OSSC/Pages/OSSC.aspx

19.92   TCEA s9; FTPR 38-40; NIDAR 58

19.93   Direct applications for leave and appeals to the Upper Tribunal/NI Commissioners should be made on the appropriate forms (UT1, or UT2 for authorities, and the NI equivalent OSSC1) [www]. Direct applications for leave to appeal should normally be made within one month of refusal of leave by the tribunal but this may be extended. If leave is given then the appeal goes ahead.

19.94   Most appeals to the Upper Tribunal/NI Commissioners are determined on paper without a hearing. Parties make their submissions in writing. However, parties may ask for a hearing. These take place in London, Edinburgh and Belfast and can be arranged elsewhere.

What is an error of law?

19.95   An appeal to the Upper Tribunal/NI Commissioners can only be made on an error of law. An error of law is where the tribunal:

- failed to apply the correct law;
- wrongly interpreted the relevant Acts or Regulations;
- followed a procedure that breached the rules of natural justice;
- took irrelevant matters into account, or did not consider relevant matters, or did both of these things;
- did not give adequate reasons in the full statement of its decision (para. 19.74);
- gave a decision which was not supported by the evidence;
- decided the facts in such a way that no person properly instructed as to the relevant law, and acting judicially, could have come to the decision made by the tribunal.

These are examples, not an exhaustive list *(R(IS) 11/99)*.

Who can apply for leave to appeal?

19.96   The following can apply for permission to appeal:

- the claimant;
- any other 'person affected' by the decision against which the appeal to the appeal tribunal was brought or by the tribunal's decision on that appeal;
- the authority against whose decision the appeal to the tribunal was brought;
- the Secretary of State (the DSD in Northern Ireland).

19.93   UTPR 21; 5(3)(a); NISSCPR 9
http://hmctsformfinder.justice.gov.uk/HMCIS/FormFinder.do
www.courtsni.gov.uk/en-GB/Tribunals/OSSC/Pages/OSSC.aspx#Downloads

19.95   TCEA s11(2); NICPSA sch 7 para 8(1)

19.96   CPSA sch 7 para 8(2); NICPSA sch 7 para 8(2)

Appeals against the Upper Tribunal's/NI Commissioner's decision

19.97   There is a right to appeal against a decision of the Upper Tribunal/NI Commissioners to the Court of Appeal or the Court of Session in Scotland. An appeal can only be made on a point of law. Leave to appeal must be obtained from the Upper Tribunal/NI Commissioners or, if they refuse, from the relevant court. The time limit for applying for leave to appeal is three months, but it may be extended. If leave to appeal is refused the application may be renewed in the relevant court within six weeks.

19.98   Separately from the above, cases involving European Union law can be referred by the Upper Tribunal direct to the European Court of Justice.

Rent officer appeals

Appeals and errors in Great Britain

19.99   This section deals with appeals to the rent officer in non-LHA cases (chapter 10) in Great Britain. (For Northern Ireland see para. 19.110.) There is no right of appeal to a tribunal against the rent officer's figures. Instead, the following procedures apply. They have been considered by the courts to be sufficiently independent to comply with the Human Rights Act: *R (on the application of Cumpsty) v The Rent Service.*

Appeals by the claimant

19.100   If a claimant or other person affected makes signed representation about a determination by the rent officer (and does so within one month of being notified of any HB decision based on it), the authority must, within seven days, apply to the rent officer for a re-determination. This applies both to the claimant whose case was referred to the rent officer and to a later claimant at the same address to whom that determination applies. The authority must forward the claimant's representations at the same time. There are however limitations (in the next paragraph).

19.101   For any claimant and any dwelling, only one application to the rent officer may be made in respect of any determination (plus one in respect of any substitute determination: para. 19.107). This applies even if the authority itself has previously chosen to make an application for a re-determination.

19.102   However, a claimant who considers that a referral should or should not have been made in the first place, or that the wrong information has been provided by the authority to the rent officer, has the right to use the ordinary HB appeals procedure to challenge this. This is because the decision to refer a case

---

19.97   TCEA s.13(1); CPSA sch 7 para 9(3); NICPSA para 9(1)-(3)

19.100   HB 16; HB60+ 16

19.101   HB 16; HB60+ 16

to the rent officer and what information to provide is made by the authority
(*[2010] UKUT 79 (AAC), [2010] AACR 40*).

Appeals by the authority

19.103 The authority may itself choose to apply to the rent officer for a re-
determination. For any particular claimant and any particular dwelling, it may do
this only once in respect of any particular determination (plus once in respect of
any substitute determination: para. 19.107); unless a re-determination is
subsequently made as a result of an appeal by the claimant (para. 19.100), in
which case the authority may do this once more.

Rent officer re-determinations

19.104 In each of the cases described above (paras. 19.100-103), the rent
officer must make a complete re-determination. Even if the application for a
re-determination relates only to one figure, the rent officer has to reconsider all
matters pertaining to the case in question. All the assumptions, etc, applying to
determinations (para. 9.53 onwards) apply equally to re-determinations. Re-
determinations should be made within 20 working days or as soon as practicable
after that. The period begins on the day the rent officer receives the application
from the authority or (if he or she has requested this) on the day he or she
receives further information needed from the authority.

19.105 The rent officer making the re-determination (called a 're-determination
officer') must seek and have regard to the advice of one or two other rent
officers. In England, rent officers have set up independent re-determination
units. Reasons for their re-determinations should always be supplied to the
claimant and the authority [www]. Similar arrangements are in place in Wales
and Scotland. It would certainly be open to challenge if reasons were not given
(as happened fairly frequently in the past).

Rent officer errors

19.106 The rent officer has a duty to notify the authority, as soon as is practicable,
upon discovering that they made an error, other than one of professional judgment,
in a determination or re-determination (including a substitute determination or
substitute re-determination). The authority must then apply to the rent officer for a
substitute determination. The DWP advises (circular HB/CTB G5/2005) that only one
such application need be made covering all future cases (rather than the authority
applying on a case by case basis).

19.107 The authority must apply, on a case by case basis, to the rent officer for
a substitute determination (or substitute re-determination) if it discovers that it

---

19.104 HB 15; HB60+ 15; ROO 4, sch 3

19.105 www.voa.gov.uk/corporate/publications/Manuals/RentOfficerHandbook/HousingBenefitReferral/
Determination/r-roh-reasons-for-decision.html

19.106 ROO 7A; HB 17; HB60+ 17

made an error in its application as regards the size of the dwelling, the number of occupiers, the composition of the household or the terms of the tenancy. In all such cases, the authority must state the nature of the error and withdraw any outstanding applications for rent officer determinations in that case.

19.108   All the assumptions, etc, applying to determinations (paras. 9.71-73) also apply to substitute determinations/re-determinations.

The date the re-determination affects HB

19.109   Whenever the rent officer issues a re-determination, substitute determination, or substitute re-determination (for the reasons in paras. 19.109-111), the new rent officer figures apply as follows.

- If the new figures increase the eligible rent, the authority alters its original decision from the date it took effect (or should have). So the claimant gets his or her arrears. This is a revision.

- If the new figures reduce the eligible rent, the authority alters its original decision from the Monday following the date of the new determination. So the claimant (if the authority acts promptly) does not suffer from an overpayment. This is a supersession.

Appeals and errors in Northern Ireland

19.110   In Northern Ireland the NIHE sets the eligible rent. Such decisions cannot be appealed to a tribunal, but the claimant can ask the NIHE to reconsider in the normal way (para. 19.10). The new figures apply as follows:

- If the new figures increase the eligible rent, and the claimant made the request within one month of the original decision (or longer in special circumstances: paras. 19.11 and 19.14), the NIHE alters its original decision from the date it took effect (or should have). So the claimant gets his or her arrears. This is a revision.

- If the new figures increase the eligible rent, and the request was outside the time limit, the NIHE alters its original decision from the date of the claimant's request (paras. 17.64-65). This is a supersession.

- If the new figures reduce the eligible rent, the normal practice (except perhaps in the case of misrepresentation) is to treat the request as a change of circumstances (i.e. a change in the housing market) and alter its original decision from the date of the request (paras. 17.64-65). This is a supersession.

19.107 HB 17; HB60+ 17

19.108 ROO 4A(2)

19.109 DAR 4(3),7(2)(c),8(6),10

19.110 NIDAR 4(1) sch para 1

CTR appeals

19.111 The following paragraphs apply to England and Wales. In Scotland (as at the beginning of March 2013) CTR appeal procedures had yet to be confirmed. In particular, Scotland's independent valuation appeal committees had expressed a reluctance to play a role in CTR appeals.

19.112 In England CTR appeals are considered by the Valuation Tribunal for England [www]. Administrative arrangements are the responsibility of the Valuation Tribunal Service. In Wales appeals are considered by, and administered by, the Valuation Tribunal Service for Wales [www]. In Scotland CTR appeals were expected to be considered by independent valuation appeal committees – but as at March 2013 agreement had yet to be reached on this [www]. In England and Wales further appeals (on a point of law and if given permission) may be considered by the High Court.

Decision notices should include appeal rights

19.113 CTR decision notices sent to persons affected should explain how an appeal may be made and refer to the provisions in the authority's scheme about appeals. For CTR purposes a 'person affected' is defined in similar terms to the HB definition (para 16.10). CTR law then uses the term 'person aggrieved' in connection with appeals (paras. 19.115 onwards), presumably intending to have a similar meaning. This terminology reflects the fact that CTR appeals are dealt with in a similar way to appeals about council tax generally.

Written statement of reasons

19.114 A person affected may write to the authority to request a written statement that sets out the reasons for any decision in its notice. This request should be made within one month of the date of the decision notice. The authority should provide this written statement of reasons within 14 days – or as soon as reasonably practicable after that.

Appeals to the authority

19.115 Appealable CTR decisions are those which affect:

- the person's entitlement to a reduction under the scheme; or
- the amount of any reduction to which that person is entitled.

19.112 www.valuationtribunal.gov.uk/
www.valuation-tribunals-wales.org.uk/
www.scottish.parliament.uk/S4_Welfare_Reform_Committee/05032013_papers.pdf

19.113 CTP sch 8 para 12(4), (7)-(8), CTR 117(4), (7)-(8); CTPW sch 14, para 3; sch 13 para 9(7)-(8); CTRW sch 10, para 3, 115(7)-(8)

19.114 CTP sch 8 para 12(5)-(6); CTR 117(5)-(6); CTPW sch 13 para 9(5)-(6); CTRW 115(5) (6)

19.115 CTP sch 7 para 8(1); CTR sch 1 para 8; CTPW sch 12 para 8; CTRW sch 1 para 8; s16 of the Local Government Finance Act 1992

A person aggrieved by such a decision may write to the authority identifying the matter in dispute. They should also say why, e.g. the authority has established the wrong facts, considered the wrong law, has misapplied the law to the facts, etc. For the avoidance of doubt the appeal should identify itself as a 'notice of appeal under section 16 of the Local Government Finance Act 1992'. Neither the default scheme nor the prescribed requirements place time limits within which appeals should be made, but some local schemes do include such limits.

The authority's response to the appeal

19.116   The authority must consider the matters raised by the appeal. It should then write to the aggrieved person describing the steps it has taken to deal with the grievance. But if it thinks that the grounds for the grievance are not well founded, it should give its reasons for thinking this.

Further appeals to the valuation tribunal

19.117   Following receipt of the authority's written response, someone who is still aggrieved may appeal directly to the valuation tribunal. An appeal may also be made to the valuation tribunal if the authority fails to respond to the appeal within two months of receipt.

The Valuation Tribunal for England and the Valuation Tribunal for Wales

19.118   In England further appeals are considered by the Valuation Tribunal for England and administered by the Valuation Tribunal Service [www]. In Wales further appeals are considered and administered by the Valuation Tribunal for Wales [www]. The tribunal provides a free service and cannot award costs against the parties. Members of the valuation tribunal are volunteers. They are not required to have any relevant qualifications but should have received training. Normally three members sit on a hearing. A clerk who is a paid official advises on points of law and procedure. In England the power exists for members of the First-tier tribunal to act as members of the valuation tribunal in a CTR related appeal.

Procedural rules and practice statements/protocols

19.119   The tribunal's procedural rules are set out in regulations and supplemented by practice statements or protocols. In England the procedural rules are in the Valuation Tribunal for England (Council Tax and Rating Appeals) (Procedure) Regulations SI 2009 No 2269 as amended. SI 2013 No. 465 amends

---

19.116 CTP sch 7 para 8(2); CTR sch 1 para 9; CTPW sch 12 para 9; CTRW sch 1 para 9

19.117 CTP sch 7 para 8(3); CTR sch 1 para 10; CTPW sch 12 para 10 ; CTRW sch 1 para 10

19.118 www.valuationtribunal.gov.uk/
        www.valuation-tribunals-wales.org.uk
        s136, sch 11; para A18A of the Local Government Finance Act 1988

19.119 www.valuationtribunal.gov.uk/Attending_A_Hearing/PracticeStatements.aspx
        www.valuation-tribunals-wales.org.uk/en/best-practice-protocols/index.php

these rules to deal with CTR appeals. Relevant practice statements are on the web site [www]. In Wales the procedural rules are in the Valuation Tribunal for Wales Regulations SI 2010 No 713 as amended. SI 2013 No 547 amends these regulations to take account of CTR appeals. Relevant practice protocols are on the web site [www].

Time limits for further appeal to the tribunal

19.120 Appeals to the tribunal should normally be made within:

* two months of the date the authority responds to the initial appeal; or
* four months of the date the initial representation was made if the authority has not responded.

An out of time appeal may be allowed if the aggrieved person failed to initiate the appeal within the time limits due to circumstances beyond their control such as illness, absence from home or bereavement. A practice statement or protocol [www] sets out how such an application should be made and the relevant considerations.

Notice of appeal

19.121 An appeal to the tribunal is initiated by giving it direct written notice. Appeal forms are expected to be available from the relevant web site. The appeal notice should include the following information:

* the full name and address of the appellant;
* the address of the relevant chargeable dwelling – if different from the appellant's;
* the relevant authority's name – and the date on which the initial appeal was served on it;
* the date, (if any) that the appellant was notified of the authority's response;
* the grounds on which the appellant is aggrieved;
* brief reasons why the appellant considers that the decision or calculation made by the authority are incorrect.

If an equivalent HB appeal on the same matter has been made to the First-tier Tribunal, this should also be identified on the notice of appeal to the valuation tribunal. In Wales the HB appeal letter should also be included with the CTR notice of appeal. The clerk should acknowledge receipt of the appeal within two weeks and send a copy of it to the authority.

19.120 21(2)-(3), (6) of SI 2009/2269; 29(1)-(2),(5) of SI 2010/713
www.valuationtribunal.gov.uk/Libraries/Publications/
Practice_Statement_-_A1_Extension_of_times.sflb.ashx
www.valuation-tribunals-wales.org.uk/UserFiles/Documents/vtw-best-practice-protocol-1a-1.pdf

19.121 20A, 28(2) of SI 2009/2269; 30(1),(2), (5) of SI 2010/713

How appeals are dealt with

19.122 Appeals are normally heard but if all the parties agree and the tribunal considers it appropriate they can be dealt with on the written representations. In England, if a hearing is to be held each party is normally given at least 14 days notice of the time and place. In Wales, the equivalent time period is four weeks. In England shorter notice than the 14 days may be given in urgent or exceptional circumstances. Hearings are normally held in public so it is possible to attend a hearing as an observer to see a tribunal in action. A party may be accompanied to their own hearing by someone else. That other person may act as a representative or otherwise assist in presenting the case. The tribunal itself decides what form the hearing should take (subject to the rules of natural justice). It may give a decision orally at a hearing.

Decision notice and statement of reasons

19.123 The tribunal should provide a notice of its decision to the parties as soon as reasonably practicable. It should also explain the right to request a written statement of reasons (if not supplied with the decision) and any right of appeal. In Wales the decision notice should be accompanied by a statement of reasons.

19.124 In England, a request for a statement of reasons (if not supplied with the decision notice) should normally be received by the tribunal within two weeks of the date of the decision notice (though the tribunal does have the power to extend this period). The statement of reasons should be sent to the parties within two weeks of the request being made or as soon as reasonably practicable thereafter.

After the decision

19.125 The procedural rules enable the tribunal to correct clerical mistakes, accidental slips and omissions and also to review its decision in specific circumstances. A further appeal to the High Court may only be made on a point of law (para 19.95). It should normally be made within four weeks of the decision notice being issued or in England within two weeks of the statement of reasons being issued if later. Advice should be sought before embarking on this course of action.

19.122 2 29, 30, 31, 36(1) of SI 2009/2269; 33(1),(6); 34(1); 36, 37, 40(2) of SI 2010/713

19.123 36(2) of SI 2009/2269; 40(3) of SI 2010/713

19.124 37(3)-(7) of SI 2009/2269

19.125 39, 40, 43(1)-(2), of SI 2009/2269; 42, 44(1)-(2) of SI 2010/713

20 Migrants and recent arrivals

20.1 This chapter is about which persons from abroad are eligible for HB/CTR. It covers everyone, whether nationals of the British Isles, Europe or the rest of the world, and whether they are arriving in the UK for the first time or returning after a time abroad.

Which rules apply?

20.2 Three main rules affect which recent migrants are eligible for HB/CTR:

♦ the immigration control test;

♦ the right to reside test; and

♦ the habitual residence test.

Table 20.1 shows which of those rules apply to which claimants. There are also further rules for asylum seekers, refugees, evacuees and some others.

Table 20.1: Persons from abroad: eligibility for HB/CTR

Claims for HB

Nationals of	Test have to satisfy
The British Isles	Habitual residence
The EEA (table 20.2)	Right to reside (and in some cases also habitual residence)
Croatia, Macedonia and Turkey	Right to reside and habitual residence
The rest of the world	Immigration control and habitual residence

Claims for CTR

Nationals of	Test have to satisfy
The British Isles	Habitual residence
The EEA (table 20.2)	Right to reside (and in some cases also habitual residence)
The rest of the world	Immigration control and habitual residence

---

20.3 For clarity, this guide treats the above three tests as separate (though in the law they are intertwined: para. 20.17). The guide also avoids the term 'persons from abroad', because it is often used informally to describe anyone who has recently arrived in the UK (whereas in the law it has a narrower meaning).

Eligibility of nationals of different parts of the world

20.4 This section identifies which rules apply to nationals of which countries, followed by a straightforward example of each.

Nationals of the British Isles (the Common Travel Area)

20.5 The 'British Isles' (a geographical term, roughly meaning all the islands off the North-West of the continent) is also known in immigration law as the 'Common Travel Area'. They both mean:

- the United Kingdom (England, Wales, Scotland and Northern Ireland);
- the Republic of Ireland;
- the Isle of Man; and
- the Channel Islands (all of them).

To be eligible for HB/CTR a national of any part of the British Isles only has to satisfy the habitual residence test (paras. 20.38-52).

Table 20.2: The European Economic Area (EEA)

The EEA states (apart from Ireland and the United Kingdom) are:

Austria	Belgium	Cyprus
Czech Republic	Denmark	Estonia
Finland	France	Germany
Greece	Hungary	Iceland
Italy	Latvia	Liechtenstein
Lithuania	Luxembourg	Malta
Netherlands	Norway	Poland
Portugal	Slovakia	Slovenia
Spain	Sweden	Switzerland*
		(*treated as part of the EEA)

The A2 accession states (part of the EEA)

Bulgaria	Romania

T 20.2 and 20.6   EEA 2(1)

Nationals of the European Economic Area

20.6 Table 20.2 lists all the countries in the European Economic Area (EEA) plus Switzerland, which UK law treats as being part of the EEA. The EEA includes all of the European Union states and some others. Bulgaria and Romania, which joined the EEA on 1st January 2007, are known as the A2 accession states. The rules for eligibility for all EEA nationals are described in chapter 21.

Nationals of the rest of the world

20.7 In this guide this means any country not mentioned above (paras. 20.4-6). It also applies to any person who has applied for asylum or to enter the UK solely on humanitarian grounds whether or not their application has been determined.

20.8 To be eligible for HB/CTR, a national of the rest of the world has to satisfy the immigration control test (paras. 20.23-37) and also the habitual residence test (paras. 20.38-52).

Examples: Eligibility for HB/CTR

1. A British citizen

A British citizen has been living abroad for 12 years. During that time she gave up all her connections in the UK. She has now just come 'home' and has rented a flat here.

The only test that applies to a UK national is the habitual residence test. As described later, it is unlikely that the above claimant satisfies that test to begin with (unless she was living and working in an EEA state). She might well satisfy that test in (say) three months time. So for the time being she is not eligible for HB/CTR.

2. National of the EEA

An Italian national has been working in the UK for several years. He has recently taken a more poorly paid job.

He passes the right to reside test because he is working. So he is eligible for HB/CTR.

3. National of the rest of the world

An Indian national arrived in the UK six months ago to be with her family. She was given leave to enter and remain, and was granted leave by UKBA without any conditions, in other words her leave did not include a 'no recourse to public funds' condition, so she is able to claim benefits. She now claims HB/CTR.

The two tests that apply to a national of the rest of the world are the immigration control test and the habitual residence test. As described later, she passes both tests. So she is eligible for HB/CTR.

Decision-making

20.9   This section covers general matters relevant to this chapter and chapter 21, including decision-making and claims, and how the law and terminology work.

DWP and authority decisions

20.10   For HB only, a claimant in receipt of any of the following benefits is exempt from the habitual residence test (para. 20.38-52) and right to reside test (chapter 21):

* income-based jobseeker's allowance;
* income-related employment and support allowance;
* income support;
* any kind of state pension credit (guarantee credit or savings credit).

The above is true only if the DWP has decided (in full possession of the facts) that someone is eligible for one of the benefits mentioned (and not, say, in a case where a claimant wrongly continued to receive one of the benefits).

20.11   If the DWP has decided that someone is not eligible for one of the above benefits, this decision is not binding on the authority – but a considered decision by the DWP carries weight.

Claims and couples

20.12   Unfortunately, it can matter which partner in a couple is the HB/CTR claimant. The rules in this chapter apply to each partner individually. So if partner A is eligible under the rules, but partner B is not, it is necessary for partner A to be the claimant (for them to get HB/CTR at all). If the 'wrong' partner claims the authority must give a 'not entitled' decision; in such a case it would be good practice to explain this and invite a claim from their partner.

20.13   Once a claim is made by the 'correct' partner, the claim is assessed (e.g. income, applicable amount, etc) in the usual way.

Partners and national insurance numbers

20.14   For HB, an exception to the general rule (para. 5.16) that both members of a couple must have or have applied for a national insurance number, applies when one member of a couple requires 'leave' from UKBA (table 20.3 and paras. 20.24-26) but does not have it (for example if they have not applied for it or it has expired). In these cases, the general rule does not apply to that member. In such cases the DWP advises authorities that they should assign a dummy number (Circular A9/2009).

20.10   HB 10(3B)(k); HB60+ 10(4A)(k); NIHB 10(5)(l); NIHB60+ 10(5)(l); CTP 12(5); CTR 21(5)

20.12   HB 8(1)(b), 10(1); HB60+ 8(1)(b), 10(1); NIHB 8(1)(b), 10(1); NIHB60+ 8(1)(b), 10(1);
        CTP 12(1), sch 8 para 4(1); CTR 21(1), 109(1)

20.14   HB 4(c); HB60+ 4(c); NIHB 4(c); NIHB60+ 4(c)

20.15 The above is a rule only about eligibility for HB. This guide cannot guarantee that it is safe, in immigration terms, for that partner to be part of the claimant's HB claim.

HB/CTR claim forms

20.16 Most HB/CTR claim forms ask the claimant: (a) their nationality and (b) whether they have entered the UK within the past two years. These two questions are intended to act as a trigger for further investigation in appropriate cases. A person who is (a) a British citizen and (b) did not enter the UK within the past two years is unlikely to fall foul of these rules (since two years in the UK is almost always sufficient to pass the habitual residence test).

Law, terminology and how the tests overlap

20.17 The tests used in deciding eligibility for HB/CTR are contained in a mixture of immigration, European and HB/CTR law as follows.

20.18 The 'immigration control test' (para. 20.23) applies under the Immigration and Asylum Act 1999 (for the whole of the UK). It stops certain people from outside the EEA from getting HB/CTR (and many other benefits).

20.19 HB/CTR law (constrained by European law) then stops certain other people including EEA nationals from getting HB/CTR (and many other benefits):

a) The 'habitual residence test' (para. 20.38) is in HB/CTR law. For HB it treats them as not being liable for rent/rates and for CTR it treats them as not being in Great Britain – which means they do not qualify for HB/CTR.

b) The 'right to reside test' applies to EEA nationals (table 20.2). It is also in HB/CTR law, but what the right to reside means is in the Immigration (European Economic Area) Regulations 2006 (which apply to the whole of the UK). HB/CTR law says that if someone does not pass this test then they do not pass the habitual residence test (and so, as described in (a), they cannot get HB/CTR).

20.20 If someone passes the immigration control test then they also pass the right to reside test. There is one exception that applies to claims for HB only: nationals of Croatia, Macedonia and Turkey (para. 20.24) pass the immigration control test but do not pass the right to reside test unless they have 'leave' – 'temporary admission' (table 20.3) is not sufficient (*Yesiloz v LB Camden*). But without exception anyone who has a right of abode, right to reside or leave (table 20.3) passes both tests.

20.21 If someone passes the right to reside test then in most cases they also pass the habitual residence test – but there are a few exceptions: mainly those who are not in work or who have retired without having worked in the UK (see paragraphs 21.26-33).

Immigration law terms

20.22   A basic understanding of immigration law terminology is useful (particularly in relation to the immigration control test). Table 20.3 lists the key terms and defines them in a way that is useful for HB decision making.

Table 20.3: Simplified immigration law terminology

Immigration rules

The legal rules approved by parliament which UKBA officers use to decide whether a person should be given permission ('leave') to enter the UK.

UK Border Agency (UKBA)

The Home Office agency responsible for immigration control and determining asylum applications (including asylum support).

Leave and temporary admission

Leave is legal permission to be in the UK. Leave can be for a fixed period (limited leave) or open ended (indefinite leave). Both can be granted with or without a 'no recourse to public funds' condition, and this nearly always applies to limited leave. Leave can be varied if an application is made before it has expired (para. 20.26).

A person who has been granted open ended leave without any conditions is said to have 'indefinite leave to remain', also known as settled status.

Temporary admission is not in itself a form of leave, it is merely the discretion allowed by UKBA which allows time for that person to do something – such as apply for asylum or leave – without falling foul of the law. Since it is not a form of leave, it does not confer a right to reside.

Public funds

Nearly all tax credits and non-contributory benefits (including HB/CTR and passport benefits) count as public funds. So does a local authority homelessness duty or acceptance on their housing waiting list.

Sponsorship and maintenance undertaking

These terms go together. Someone (typically an elderly relative) may be granted leave to join a family member on the understanding that this 'sponsor' will provide for their support or accommodation.

Some (but not all) sponsors are required to sign a written agreement (a maintenance undertaking) as a condition of granting leave and if they do the person they sponsor is excluded from HB/CTR (but see para. 20.28 for exceptions).

> **Illegal entrant and overstayer**
>
> These both refer to someone who needs leave to be in the UK but does not have it and has not been granted temporary admission. An illegal entrant is someone who entered the UK without applying for leave and an overstayer is someone who was granted leave which has since expired.
>
> **Right of abode and right to reside**
>
> 'Right of abode' is a term that describes someone who is entirely free of any kind of immigration control. It applies to all British citizens and some citizens of Commonwealth countries, but not necessarily to other forms of British nationality. Non-British nationals can apply to have this status confirmed in their passport.
>
> 'Right to reside' is a wider term that describes anyone who has legal authority to be in the UK. It therefore includes everyone with the right of abode, plus anyone who has any form of leave (including those with 'no recourse to public funds') and any EEA nationals with a right of residence. 'Right to reside' is sometimes used informally to mean right of abode (because it sounds less archaic).

The immigration control test

20.23   Non-EEA nationals have to pass the immigration control test to get HB/CTR. (They also have to pass the habitual residence test: paras. 20.38-52.)

20.24   The purpose of the test is to stop someone getting benefit if:

- ♦ they require leave but do not have it – e.g. they are an illegal entrant or overstayer; or

- ♦ they have been granted leave but with a 'no recourse to public funds' condition (but in the case of HB see paras. 20.27-28 for exceptions); or

- ♦ they have been granted temporary admission while their application to UKBA is being decided – e.g. they are an asylum seeker.

People who pass the immigration control test

20.25   The following, regardless of nationality, pass the immigration control test:

- ♦ a holder of a passport containing a certificate of entitlement to the 'right of abode' (table 20.3) in the UK;

- ♦ a person who has 'indefinite leave to remain' (also called settled status);

- ♦ a person who has any form of leave whether limited or indefinite (table 20.3),

---

20.24 IAA99 115(9); CTP 13; CTR 22

but only if it is not subject to a public funds condition or a maintenance undertaking (table 20.3) – although certain exceptions apply (paras. 20.27-29);

- ◆ a person who has applied for asylum and has been granted refugee status, humanitarian protection or discretionary leave (paras. 20.33-34);
- ◆ a person (other than an asylum seeker) who has been granted exceptional leave by the Home Secretary.

The authority normally needs to see the claimant's passport or other Home Office documentation to confirm the above.

20.26   A person with limited leave can apply for it to be extended before it expires. Provided that the application is made in time and in the correct form, that person is still treated as having leave until 28 days after the decision is made on their application, and thus passes the immigration control test until then. Authorities often wrongly terminate benefit in these cases.

People with no recourse to public funds who are entitled to HB/CTR

20.27   The general rule is that a person who is the subject of a public funds condition or a maintenance undertaking fails the immigration control test (para. 20.24). The general rule applies to all claims for CTR or, in the case of HB only, with the exceptions in paragraph 20.28.

20.28   For claims for HB only, the following people also pass the immigration control test (and see also paras. 20.20 and 20.29):

- ◆ a national of Croatia, Macedonia or Turkey (but see paras. 20.20 and 20.24);
- ◆ a person admitted to the UK as a sponsored immigrant only as a result of a maintenance undertaking, who has been resident for five years or more;
- ◆ a person admitted to the UK as a sponsored immigrant only as a result of a maintenance undertaking, who has been resident for less than five years and whose sponsor (or all of their sponsors if there is more than one) has died;
- ◆ a person with limited leave whose funds have been temporarily disrupted: but only for up to 42 days in any one period of leave and only if there is a reasonable expectation that they will resume.

20.29   In the first three cases they are eligible for HB/CTR provided they are also habitually resident. In the fourth case they are eligible for HB/CTR without further conditions provided that the disruption to funds has not already exceeded 42 days when the claim is made *(CH/4248/2006)*.

Asylum seekers

20.30   An asylum seeker is someone who applies to be recognised as a refugee (para. 20.33) under the United Nations Convention because of fear of persecution in their country of origin (typically on political or ethnic grounds).

20.31 While their asylum application is processed they fail the immigration control test and are disqualified from HB/CTR: although there are some limited exceptions (para. 20.32). Those who are disqualified may be able to get help with their maintenance and accommodation from the UKBA asylum support scheme.

20.32 The following asylum seekers pass the immigration control test and so may be eligible for HB/CTR (although all of these cases are rare):

◆ a member of a couple where the other member is eligible (para. 20.12) – in this case any UKBA support counts as income (GM para C4.128);

◆ people who have been granted discretionary leave (para. 20.33) (e.g. an unaccompanied minor);

◆ people who are nationals of an EEA state (para. 20.6) in which case the rules in chapter 21 apply.

Refugees and others granted leave on humanitarian grounds

20.33 Following their application for asylum the Home Secretary may:

◆ recognise the person as a refugee (i.e. accept their claim for asylum) and grant leave; or

◆ refuse asylum but grant humanitarian protection (which is a form of leave) or discretionary leave (see circular HB/CTB A16/2006 for details of when these might apply); or

◆ refuse asylum and not grant leave.

20.34 If leave is granted in any of these cases it is normally for a period of five, six or ten years, after which they can normally apply for settled status. Any person who has been granted refugee status, humanitarian protection or discretionary leave passes the immigration control test. They also pass the habitual residence test. So they are eligible for HB/CTR from the date their status is confirmed. In the case of those granted refugee status (but not other cases), then their dependants are granted leave as well so they are also eligible for HB/CTR.

Evacuees

20.35 Evacuees are people who are allowed to enter the UK in response to a specific humanitarian crisis (e.g. war, famine, natural disaster) not covered by the asylum process (you cannot be persecuted by a volcano). In appropriate circumstances the government may decide to waive the normal immigration rules for those affected and grant leave (usually on a temporary basis).

20.36 These evacuees, because they have leave, pass the immigration control test but can only get HB/CTR if (or when they become) habitually resident. In the case of HB only, the following evacuees are exempt from the habitual residence test and so are eligible for HB/CTR:

20.34   HB 10(1),(3B)(g),(h); HB60+ 10(1),(4A)(g),(h); NIHB 10(1),(5)(g),(h); NIHB60+ 10(1),(5)(g),(h); CTP 12(1),(5)(d)-(f); CTR 21(1),(5)(d)-(f); CPR sch 4 paras 2 4; NICPR sch 4 paras 2-4

- evacuees from Montserrat. They must have left the island after 1st November 1995 but do not need to have travelled straight here;
- a person who entered the UK between 28th February 2009 and 17th March 2011 as part of the programme for vulnerable British citizens living in Zimbabwe.

Although there is no equivalent rule in CTR, such claimants are virtually certain to be habitually resident on the facts (paras. 20.45-52).

Others with exceptional leave

20.37   For claims for HB only, other people who apply for leave on humanitarian grounds outside the asylum process who are granted exceptional leave are exempt from the habitual residence test and are eligible for HB.

The habitual residence test

Who has to pass the habitual residence test?

20.38   The habitual residence test applies to nationals of:

- the British Isles; and
- the rest of the world (apart from the EEA).

It does not normally apply to nationals of the EEA except those not active in the labour market (e.g. not working or looking for work). All the rules concerning EEA nationals including these exceptions are dealt with in chapter 21.

20.39   The purpose of the test is to stop someone claiming benefit immediately they enter the UK (for example, if they have a right of abode in the UK but have never lived here or have not lived here for a long time).

CTR: Crown servants and members of armed forces

20.40   For CTR only, a person who is employed by the Crown or a member of HM armed forces who is performing their duties while overseas and who was habitually resident in Great Britain immediately before they were posted, continues to be treated as being resident in Great Britain and so remains entitled to CTR.

People deported to the UK from another country

20.41   A British citizen or a person with a right of abode or settled status (table 20.3) who is deported to the UK from another country is exempt from the habitual residence test and is eligible for HB/CTR.

20.36   HB 10(1),(3B)(h),(jj); HB60+ 10(1),(4A)(h),(jj); NIHB 10(1),(5)(h),(jj); NIHB60+ 10(1),(5)(h),(jj)

20.38   HB 10(2); HB60+ 10(2); NIHB 10(2); NIHB60+ 10(2); CTP 12(2); CTR 21(2)

20.40   CTP 12(6)-(8), CTR 2(1), 21(6),(7)

The meaning of habitual residence

20.42 To be eligible for HB/CTR a person must be 'habitually resident' in the British Isles (para. 20.5). Habitual residence is a 'question of fact' (a phrase used to mean that the term is not defined in the regulations). It is decided by looking at all the facts of a case; no list of considerations can be drawn up to govern all cases. The DWP gives general guidance on this (GM paras. C4.87-106).

20.43 There are two elements to the phrase 'habitual residence':

* 'Residence': The person must actually be resident, a mere intention to reside being insufficient; and mere physical presence is not residence.

* 'Habitual': There must also be a degree of permanence in the claimant's residence in the British Isles (GM C4.80), the word 'habitual' implying a more settled state in which the person is making their home here. There is no requirement that it must be their only home, nor that it is permanent, provided it is their genuine home for the time being.

Losing habitual residence

20.44 Habitual residence can be lost in a single day. This applies if someone leaves the UK intending not to return but to take up long-term residence in another country.

Gaining habitual residence

20.45 A person cannot gain habitual residence in a single day. A person who leaves another country with the intention to settle in the UK does not become habitually resident immediately on arrival. Instead there are two main requirements *(R(IS) 6/96)*:

* their residence must be for an 'appreciable period of time'; and
* they must have a 'settled intention' to live in the UK.

'Appreciable period of time' and 'intention to settle'

20.46 There is no fixed period that amounts to an appreciable period of time *(CIS 2326/1995)*. It varies according to the circumstances of the case and takes account of the 'length, continuity and nature' of the residence *(R(IS) 6/96)*.

20.47 Case law *(CIS 4474/2003)* suggests that, in general, the period lies between one and three months, and that a decision maker needs 'powerful reasons to justify a significantly longer period'. That time would have to be spent making a home here, rather than merely studying or on a temporary visit.

20.48 As suggested by the DWP (GM C4.85-86), factors likely to be relevant in deciding what is an appreciable period of time, though no one factor is the deciding factor in every case, include the person's:

* length and continuity of residence;
* reasons for coming to the UK;

- future intentions;
- employment prospects (para. 20.49); and
- centre of interest (para. 20.50).

20.49   In considering someone's employment prospects, their education and qualifications are likely to be significant *(CIS 5136/2007)*. An offer of work is also good evidence of an intention to settle. If a worker has stable employment here it is presumed that they reside here, even if their family resides in another state.

20.50   Someone's centre of interest is concerned with the strength of their ties to this country and their intention to settle. As suggested by the DWP (GM C4.105), this can be shown by:

- the presence of close relatives;
- decisions made about the location of their family's personal possessions (e.g. clothing, furniture, transport);
- substantial purchases, such as furnishings, which indicate a long term commitment; and
- the membership of any clubs or organisations in connection with their hobbies or recreations.

Temporary absence and returning residents

20.51   Once a person has attained habitual residence, the following general principles apply (in each case unless other circumstances over-ride them):

- for a UK or EEA national (only), it resumes immediately on return from a period of work in another EEA member state *(Swaddling v Chief Adjudication Officer)*;
- and, in all cases, it resumes immediately on return from a single short absence (such as a holiday or visiting relatives).

20.52   In considering whether someone regains their habitual residence following a longer absence, or repeated absences, the following points need to be considered:

- the circumstances in which habitual residence was lost;
- the person's intentions – someone whose absence was always intended to be temporary (even in the case of longer absences) is less likely to lose their habitual residence than someone who never originally had any intention of returning;
- the person's continuing links with the UK while abroad;
- the circumstances of their return. A person who slots straight back into a life they had before they left, is likely to resume habitual residence more quickly.

21 EEA nationals

21.1 This chapter is about which EEA nationals are eligible for HB/CTR. It also applies to the parents of a child who is an EEA national even if the parents are not EEA nationals themselves (para. 21.25). EEA member states are listed in table 20.2. To get HB/CTR, most EEA nationals only have to pass the right to reside test (paras.20.21 and 21.7-23). For all cases where further conditions may apply see paragraphs 21.24 onwards.

21.2 This chapter does not apply to nationals of the British Isles (para. 20.5) or European states which are not part of the EEA (para. 20.6).

Decision making and terminology

21.3 General matters applying to EEA nationals (as well as other cases) are in paragraphs 20.9-22, which cover decision-making and claims, and how the law and terminology work. In particular, an EEA national in receipt of a passport benefit is eligible for HB (paras. 20.10-11).

21.4 Case law on EEA nationals is developing rapidly (several new cases are covered in this chapter this year) and how the rules are interpreted is likely to continue changing.

21.5 EEA nationals have to pass the right to reside test to get HB/CTR. The purpose of the right to reside test is to stop someone with no intention of working from gaining the right to benefit simply by living in the UK. The details of the test are different for Bulgarians and Romanians (paras. 21.34-41) as opposed to other EEA nationals (paras. 21.7-33). Certain parents and self-sufficient people also have to pass the habitual residence test (paras. 21.24 and 21.26-32).

Differences for CTR claims

21.6 For claimants who are in work (except Bulgarians and Romanians) the rules are the same as for HB but there are some subtle differences for claimants who are out of work. In each of the cases described below, the claimant must pass both the right to reside and habitual residence tests (whereas for HB they are exempt from both). However, if they meet the conditions for HB (whether or not they claim it) then they have a right to reside and are entitled to CTR if they pass the habitual residence test (paras 20.45-52). A claimant has to pass the habitual residence test to qualify for CTR if they:

- are a EEA jobseeker in receipt of JSA(IB) (paras 21.26-27);

21.5   HB 10(3B)(a)-(f); HB60+ 10(4A)(a)-(f); NIHB 10(5)(a)-(f); NIHB60+ 10(5)(a)-(f); CTP 12(5)(a)-(c); CTR 21(5)(a)-(c)

- have a permanent right to reside only as a result of five years' residence (paras 21.19-20);
- are a Bulgarian or Romanian who is in authorised work (21.37-38) or exempt from worker authorisation (table 21.1).

Special rules apply to Crown employees and members of HM armed forces serving overseas (para. 20.40). In all other cases the rules are as described for HB (paras 21.7-41).

EEA nationals and the right to reside

21.7   This section (paras. 21.8-33) is about nationals of all EEA states apart from Bulgaria and Romania (but see paragraphs 21.35 and 21.39 for Bulgarians and Romanians who are self-employed or who have completed one year in authorised work).

The groups who pass the right to reside test

21.8   An EEA national (para. 21.7) passes the right to reside test (and so is eligible for HB/CTR) if they are:

- self-employed;
- a worker;
- a worker/self-employed person who has retained their worker status while temporarily out of work;
- a person who gained a permanent right of residence;
- in certain circumstances, a family member of the above; or
- in limited circumstances, a parent, a work seeker or a self-sufficient person.

Details of each are given in the following paragraphs, but in the case of the fourth item and claims for CTR, see also paragraph 21.6. In immigration law, the first three groups are sometimes called 'economically active'.

Self-employed people

21.9   An EEA national (para. 21.7) passes the right to reside test if they are self-employed (including Bulgarians and Romanians, see para. 21.36).

21.10   The self-employment must be 'real', and have actually begun, but unlike workers it seems that the ten-hour threshold (para. 21.15) does not apply and self-employed status can continue even where there is no current work, provided the person continues to look for it: *[2010] UKUT 451 AAC*. To be 'real' the activity must constitute self-employment. A recent case was about a Romanian national but seems likely to apply to all EEA nationals. The claimant was a seller of *The Big*

Issue, buying the magazine at half price and selling it on the street. The Upper Tribunal decided this constituted self-employment: *[2011] UKUT 494 (AAC).*

21.11 Anyone who is self-employed in the UK has a legal duty to register with HMRC within three months of starting the self-employment – even if they think they won't earn enough to pay tax/national insurance. However, registration does not mean that HMRC necessarily accepts that the person is self-employed (since their job is to collect money, without perhaps worrying unduly about the niceties of its origins). On the other hand, the fact that someone has not registered does not mean they are not self-employed: *CIS/3213/2007.*

Workers

21.12 An EEA national (para. 21.7) passes the right to reside test if they are a 'worker' (for Bulgarians and Romanians, see para. 21.34).

21.13 An EEA national qualifies as a worker if they are currently engaged in remunerative work in the UK, which is

- 'effective and genuine' and
- not 'on such a small scale as to be purely marginal and ancillary'.

'Remunerative' here has its ordinary English meaning (not that in para. 6.22).

21.14 The following are relevant to whether the work is effective and genuine:

- the period of employment;
- the number of hours worked;
- the level of earnings; and
- whether the work is regular or erratic.

21.15 The number of hours worked is not conclusive of worker status but is relevant: *CH/3733/2007.* Ten hours may not be enough when the other factors here are considered – and not doing ten hours does not automatically exclude a person. The factors always have to be considered together.

21.16 A low income from the job (or the fact of having to claim, say, tax credits) is not enough on its own to stop someone counting as a worker. A person can be a 'worker' even if they work 'cash in hand': *[2012] UKUT 112 (AAC).*

Examples: right to reside as worker

A Spanish national works in the UK as a cleaner in a garage for two hours a night on two nights a week. He is mainly in the country to study English. So he probably does not pass the right to reside test as a worker.

An Icelandic national works in the UK as a legal translator doing variable hours (depending on whether it is term time or holiday time) but averaging six hours a week over the year. She has been doing this for three years, and her hourly rate is substantial. It is therefore quite possible that she passes the right to reside test as a worker.

Retaining worker/self-employed status while out of work

21.17   An EEA national (para. 21.7) has the right to reside if they were previously in paid employment or self-employed in the UK, so long as they:

- are temporarily unable to work due to sickness or injury. 'Temporarily' is decided objectively (rather than solely by reference to the person's subjective intention): *De Brito v Home Secretary.* This excludes maternity, an exclusion which does not constitute unlawful discrimination: *JS v Secretary of State for Work and Pensions;*

- are on sick leave or maternity leave, with the right to return under their contract;

- have worked for more than a year (or have been unemployed no more than six months), and are currently registered with the DWP as a jobseeker;

- are involuntarily unemployed and have started vocational training; or

- are voluntarily unemployed in order to follow vocational training relating to their previous employment.

The first item relates to both former employees and self-employment and the remainder to former employees only. For Bulgarians and Romanians, see paras. 21.36-37.

21.18   'Unable to work due to sickness or injury' is not restricted to those who qualify for ESA *(CIS 4304/2007).* Likewise registering as a jobseeker is not restricted to those who are eligible for JSA or national insurance credits *(CIS 184/2008).* Small gaps between leaving employment and registering as a jobseeker can be ignored *(CIS 1934/2006).*

People with the permanent right of residence

21.19   An EEA national (para. 21.7) has the right to reside if they have a 'right of permanent residence' in the UK, as defined by the EEA regulations. They have this right if they:

- have lawfully resided in the UK for a continuous period of five years; or

- retired from working in the UK in a way which meets one of the conditions below.

But in the case of the first item and claims for CTR, see also paragraph 21.6

21.20   For the first rule above, 'residence' means residence under the right to reside: *McCarthy v Secretary of State for the Home Department.* And a period of residence counts as 'continuous' despite absences, so long as:

- in any one year, the total length of the absence(s) from the UK is no more than six months, and this can be longer if due to compulsory military service; or

21.17   EEA 6(2),(3); HB 10(3B)(c); HB60+ 10(4A)(c); NIHB 10(5)(c); NIHB60+ 10(5)(c); CTP 12(5)(a); CTR 21(5)(a)

21.19   EEA 5,15; HB 10(3B0(e); HB60+ 10(4A)(e); NIHB 10(5)(e); NIHB60+ 10(5)(e); CTP 12(5)(c); CTR 21(5)(c)

- the total absence is not more than 12 months – so long as the reason is pregnancy, childbirth, serious illness, study, vocational training, a posting in another country, or some other important reason.

Once acquired, the permanent right of residence can only be lost after an absence from the UK of more than two years.

21.21 For the second rule above (para. 21.19), the person must:

- have retired (at retirement age or at early retirement) after working in the UK for at least 12 months - and have been continuously resident in the UK for more than three years. In counting this 12 months, any period of involuntary unemployment registered with the Jobcentre, or period out of work due to illness, accident or some other reason 'not of [the person's] own making', is counted as a period of employment; or

- have retired (at retirement age or at early retirement) and their spouse or civil partner is a UK national; or

- have ceased working as a result of permanent incapacity; and either
  - the incapacity is the result of an accident at work or an occupational disease which entitles them to ESA, incapacity benefit, industrial injuries benefit or some other pension payable by a UK institution; or
  - they have continuously resided in the UK for more than two years; or
  - their spouse or civil partner is a UK national.

Family members of workers and the self-employed

21.22 Once someone has a right to reside (whether or not they claim HB/CTR) for any of the reasons given so far, then the right to reside is also acquired by:

- anyone who is their family member (as defined in para. 21.23)

- any family member of a worker or self-employed person who has died so long as:
  - at the time of death they had lived continuously in the UK for two years; or
  - the death resulted from an accident at work or an occupational disease;
  - or other special circumstances apply (e.g. their child is in education here).

In the first case, if the family member falls within (a) to (c) of paragraph 21.23 they are exempt from the habitual residence test and so entitled to HB/CTR. In the second case, or where that person qualifies as a family member under paragraph 21.23(d), then they must also be habitually resident to qualify for HB/CTR (which in most cases they will be).

21.20 EEA 3
21.21 EEA 5

21.23　For the above purposes, a family member means:

(a) a spouse or civil partner (until divorce/dissolution, not mere separation or estrangement);

(b) a child or grandchild (or further descendant) of the person or their spouse or civil partner, who is dependent on them or (regardless of dependency) under 21;

(c) a parent or grandparent of the person or their spouse or civil partner, who is dependent on them;

(d) anyone else who has been admitted to the UK on the basis that they are:

- the person's partner (in the benefit sense, not just a spouse or civil partner); or

- a dependant or household member (in terms of their country of origin), or so ill that they strictly require personal care from the person.

Parent of a child in education in the UK

21.24　An EEA migrant worker's child who is in normal education in the UK has the right to reside as does their parent. (This is sometimes referred to as an *'Ibrahim/Teixeira'* right after the cases that established it). To qualify, at least one parent must have been an EEA worker working in the UK when the child's education began. It does not matter that the EEA worker has since stopped working or left the UK, or if the parent claiming the right is not an EEA national. Anyone (including a Bulgarian or Romanian: *[2010] UKUT 347 AAC*) with this right to reside is entitled to HB/CTR provided that they are also habitually resident.

Non-EEA parents of a child who is a UK citizen

21.25　The non-EEA parents of a child who is a UK citizen have a right to reside under the EEA regulations. This right is sometimes referred to as a 'Zambrano' right after the case that established it. However, this right is excluded from conferring entitlement to HB/CTR by the HB/CTR regulations. The rules were changed to exclude entitlement to HB/CTB under this right from 8th November 2012.

EEA jobseekers

21.26　An EEA jobseeker is someone (as defined by the EEA regulations) who:

- enters the UK seeking work; and

- has a genuine chance of becoming employed.

21.22-23　EEA 7,8,14(2),15(1)(d),(c); HB 10(3B)(d); HB60+ 10(4A)(d); NIHB 10(5)(d); NIHB60+ 10(5)(d); CTP 12(5)(b); CTR 12(5)(b)

21.25　　EEA 15A(4A); HB 10(3A)(bb),(e); HB60+ 10(4)(bb),(e); NIHB 10(4)(bb),(e); NIHB60+ 10(4)(bb)(e); CTP 12(4)(b); CTR 21(4)(b)

21.26　　EEA 6(1),(4)

Note that in this context jobseeker applies to someone who enters the UK looking for work and not to someone who was previously employed in the UK and loses their job (para. 21.17).

21.27   EEA work-seekers are excluded from HB/CTR and all other passport benefits except JSA(IB). If they qualify for JSA(IB) they are entitled to HB (para. 20.10) but to qualify for CTR they must also be 'habitually resident' (paras. 20.45-52 and 21.6).

Students and other economically inactive but self-sufficient people

21.28   An EEA national passes the right to reside test if they were admitted to this country on the basis that they were self-sufficient. The rules for students and other economically inactive persons are similar but not identical. In both cases to qualify for HB/CTR that person must have a right to reside (paras. 21.29-32) and be habitually resident (paras. 20.38-52).

21.29   An EEA student has the right to reside if they:

* are currently studying on a course in the UK;

* have signed a declaration at the beginning of the course that they were able to support themselves without social assistance (which means HB/CTR and any passport benefit); and

* the declaration was true at the time it was signed and for the foreseeable future; and

* have comprehensive health insurance for the UK (although the right to access state healthcare may count: *[2010] UKUT 243 AAC*).

21.30   In practice, this means that the majority of EEA students are excluded from HB/CTR. However, it is possible for an EEA student to qualify if their circumstances have changed since they started their course (e.g. their source of funds has unexpectedly dried up) – but see also chapter 22.

21.31   Other economically inactive persons (i.e. non-students) have a right to reside if they:

* have sufficient resources not be an unreasonable burden on the social assistance system. Since 2nd June 2011, this does not automatically exclude someone whose income is so low that they would be eligible for social security benefits; and

* have comprehensive health insurance.

21.32   In practice, this means that the majority of such persons are excluded from HB/CTR. However, whether a person is an unreasonable burden is a matter of judgment and discretion (paras.1.48-49). DWP guidance acknowledges this

21.27   EEA 6(1),(4); HB 10(3A)(b); HB60+ 10(4)(b); NIHB 10(4)(b); NIHB60+ 10(4)(b); CTP 12(2)(3); CTR 12(2)(3)

21.29   EEA 4,6(1),14(1); HB 10(3); HB60+ 10(3); CTP 12(3); CTR 21(3)

21.31   EEA 6(1),(3),14(1); HB 10(3B)(a),(b); HB60+ 10(4A)(a),(b); NIHB 10(5)(a),(b); NIHB60+ 10(5)(a),(b); CTP 12(5)(b); CTR 21(5)(b); SI 2011/1247

and suggests that if a person has been resident in the UK for some time, the fact that they have been self-sufficient for some time will be a factor in the decision as will the length of time they are likely to be claiming (GM paras. C4.123). For example, a person whose funds were temporarily disrupted may qualify.

Transitional exceptions

21.33   In the case of claims for HB only, an EEA national (including a national of Bulgaria or Romania) is eligible for HB (without having to pass the right to reside test) if they were entitled to HB on 30th April 2004 (including a claim backdated to that date); and have remained continuously entitled since that date to one or more of: HB, CTB, IS or any kind of JSA or state pension credit. This is now rare.

Bulgarian and Romanian nationals

21.34   The remainder of this chapter is about nationals of Bulgaria and Romania, also known as the 'A2 accession states'. Like other EEA nationals they have to pass the right to reside test to get HB/CTR, but for them the test is stricter. These stricter rules expire on 31st December 2013. From 1st January 2014, the rules given earlier (paras. 21.7-33) will apply.

Right to reside

21.35   A Bulgarian or Romanian national has a right to reside (and so is eligible for HB) if he or she:

*   is self-employed (para. 21.36);
*   is working in authorised work (para. 21.37);
*   has completed their one year qualifying period in authorised work (para. 21.39) and would have a right to reside if they were not a Bulgarian or Romanian (paras. 21.7-33) (for example if they are working);
*   is working and exempt from worker authorisation in any of the ways listed in table 21.1; or
*   is, in limited circumstances, a parent (para. 21.24).

In the case of claims for CTR, a Bulgarian or Romanian national must also be habitually resident (paras. 20.45-52 and 21.6) to be entitled.

Self-employed people

21.36   The rules for self-employed Bulgarians and Romanians are the same as for other EEA nationals (paras. 21.9-11), since they do not require Home Office authorisation for this. The following additional points apply. A Bulgarian or Romanian must be currently self-employed; it is not enough that they were self-employed in the past: *R (Tilianu) v Secretary of State for Work and Pensions*. But

---

21.33   CPR sch 3 para 6(4); NICPR sch 3 para 6(3)

21.35   EEA 4(1)(a),(b), 6(1)(b),(c); SI 2006 No 3317 Reg 1(1)(t), 2(3),(4),(12), 6

they may remain self-employed despite the fact that their work has currently dried up: *[2010] UKUT 451 (AAC);* – even, in the short term, if they have claimed JSA: *[2011] UKUT 96 (AAC).* (Although the cases are about former 'A8 accession state' nationals, they appear to apply equally to Bulgarians and Romanians.)

Authorised work

21.37   Most Bulgarians and Romanians can only take up work which has been 'authorised' by the Home Office until they have completed 12 months in continuous employment in legal work. Authorised work is limited to certain specified occupations and in most cases the applicant must meet other further conditions. Except for applicants who are 'highly skilled', the numbers of applicants in each employment category are also subject to strict quotas.

21.38   It is not enough for a Bulgarian or Romanian to have been a worker in the past. To get HB/CTR, they must meet one of the conditions in paragraph 21.35.

Completing the 12 month qualifying period

21.39   After a Bulgarian or Romanian national has completed their 12 month qualifying period in legal work they are no longer required to be authorised and acquire the right to be treated as any other EEA national (paras. 21.8-33).

21.40   During this qualifying period work counts as 'legal' only if they hold the appropriate authorisation document and are complying with any conditions set out in it (*CIS/3232/2006* and *CJSA/700/2007*).

21.41   A person is treated as having completed their 12 month qualifying period if they are legally working at the beginning and end of that period and any intervening periods in which they were not legally working do not, in total, exceed 30 days.

21.37   SI 2006 No 3317 Reg 6

21.40   SI 2006 No 3317 Reg 2(3),(4),(12)

21.41   SI 2006 No 3317 Reg 2(12)

Table 21.1: Bulgarians and Romanians exempt from worker authorisation

A Bulgarian or Romanian national is exempt from worker authorisation if:

- they have leave to enter the UK (table 20.3) which is not subject to any condition restricting their employment;

- they have legally worked in the UK for an uninterrupted period (para. 21.39) of 12 months (whether that period started on, before or after 1st January 2007);

- they have dual nationality as a citizen of Britain or another EEA state, other than Bulgaria or Romania;

- their spouse or civil partner is either a UK national or a person with settled status (table 20.3);

- they have acquired a permanent right of residence (para. 21.19);

- they are a family member (para. 21.22) of an EEA national (other than a Bulgarian or Romanian who is subject to worker authorisation) who has a right to reside in the UK;

- they are the spouse, civil partner, or child aged under 18 of a person who has 'leave' to enter the UK (table 20.3) provided the terms of that leave allows them to work;

- they are the spouse, civil partner or direct descendant of a Bulgarian or Romanian who is subject to worker authorisation, provided that in the case of a direct descendant they are aged under 21 or dependent on that worker;

- they meet the Home Office criteria to enter the UK under the highly skilled migrant programme and hold a registration certificate that states that they have unrestricted access to the UK labour market;

- they are a student who works for no more than 20 hours per week and they hold a registration certificate which allows them to work for up to 20 hours per week; or

- they have been posted to work in the UK by an organisation that is based in another EEA member state.

T 21.1 SI 2006 No 3317 Reg 2(2)-(12); HB 10(3B)(f); HB60+ 10(4A)(f); NIHB 10(5)(f); NIHB60+ 10(5)(f); CTP 12(2),(3); CTR 21(2),(3); SI 2007 No. 3012; SI 2009 No. 2426

22 Students

22.1   This chapter describes the rules used in assessing HB and CTR as they relate to students.

It covers:

- who is a 'student';
- who counts as a 'full-time' student;
- which students can get HB and CTR; and
- how their income from loans, grants and other sources is assessed.

Dwellings wholly occupied by students are exempt from council tax (para. 10.12).

Working age claims

22.2   In the case of working age claims (table 1.4):

- students are eligible for HB and CTR throughout the UK if they are in the eligible groups (table 22.1),
- income from student loans and grants is assessed for HB and CTR as in this chapter (paras. 22.30-40);
- however the rules about both eligibility and assessment may vary for CTR in England (para. 10.25).

Pension age claims

22.3   In the case of pension age claims (table 1.4):

- students are eligible for HB throughout the UK;
- students are eligible for CTR in England and Scotland, but not Wales;
- income from student loans and grants is disregarded.

Figures

22.4   The figures given in this chapter (for loans, grants and disregards) are for the 2012-13 academic year. The HB disregards for books, equipment and travel have not been increased for this academic year. DWP circular A7/2012 paras 10-20 gives some background to the student support arrangements in 2012/2013. For more information on the available student financial support arrangements in this and subsequent years see the relevant student finance web site [www].

22.2-3 CTP 74, CTRW 72(1)(a), CTPW sch 11 para 3(1)(a)

22.4   www.direct.gov.uk/studentfinance NI: www.studentfinanceni.co.uk/
S: www.saas.gov.uk/ W: www.studentfinancewales.co.uk
NHS & Social Work: www.nhsbsa.nhs.uk/Students.aspx

Who is a student?

22.5   For the HB/CTR student rules to apply, the person in question must be a 'student'. The definition is given below. Other important terms are defined after that. Paragraph 20.20 compares these with the definitions used in council tax law, which are different.

Definition of 'student'

22.6   For HB and CTR purposes, a student is defined as any person 'who is attending or undertaking a course of study at an educational establishment'. It also includes someone on a prescribed employment-related qualifying course. It does not include someone in receipt of a prescribed training allowance, e.g. the allowances associated with certain government schemes such as Training for Work, Work-Based Learning or Employment Rehabilitation.

22.7   A 'course of study' includes courses for which no grant is awarded and sandwich courses. The term 'educational establishment' is not defined in the regulations. DWP guidance suggests that it should be taken to include not just schools, colleges and universities but also other education establishments 'used for the purposes of training, education or instruction' (DWP GM C2 Annex A para. C2.04).

Term-times, vacations and breaks in attendance

22.8   Once a course has started, a person carries on counting as a student until their course finishes, or they finally abandon it or are dismissed from it. So they do count as a student during all vacations occurring within the course. But they do not count as a student after the end of a course or between two different courses.

22.9   In sandwich courses (e.g. business studies where students spend time in industry) it includes the student's periods of work experience as well as their periods of study and holidays.

22.10   A student who takes time out (e.g. for illness or other personal reasons) continues to count as a student if they remain registered with their educational establishment: *O'Connor v Chief Adjudication Officer.*

Students in a couple

22.11   In the case of a couple, the HB and CTR rules vary depending on whether one or both are students and which partner makes the claim. Details are given as each rule is described (and see table 22.2).

22.6   HB 2(1),53,54,58; NIHB 2(1),50,51,55; CTR 2(1),73,74

22.7   HB 53(1); NIHB 50(1); CTR 73(1)

22.8   HB 53(2)(b) CTR 73(2)(b)

22.9   HB 53(1); NIHB 50(1); CTR 73(1)

22.11   HB 54,58; NIHB 51,55; CTR 74

'Full-time' versus 'part-time' students

22.12   Only full-time students are generally ineligible for HB/CTR. Some of the HB and CTR rules apply to both eligible full-time and part-time students; some apply only to eligible full-time students. Details are given as each rule is described.

General cases

22.13   There is no all-embracing definition of 'full-time' (or 'part-time'). Certain courses are defined as full-time (see the next few paragraphs). In all other cases the authority must decide whether a course is full-time by considering relevant factors such as: the nature of the course including the number of hours the student is required to attend, the view of the educational establishment and the amount and nature of any grant or loan received by the student (GM chapter C2, annex A, para. C2.08).

Courses funded by the Secretary of State for Education, the Chief Executive of Skills Funding or by Welsh Ministers

22.14   In England and Wales a course wholly or partly funded by the Secretary of State (Department for Education), the Chief Executive of Skills Funding or Welsh Ministers, that requires more than 16 guided learning hours per week is a full-time course. This requirement should be stated in the student's learning agreement signed on behalf of the educational establishment in England or in a document signed on behalf of the educational establishment in Wales.

Courses funded by Scottish Ministers at colleges of further education

22.15   In Scotland a course of study at a college of further education that is not higher education and that is wholly or partly funded by the Scottish Ministers counts as a full-time course if it involves more than 16 hours a week of classroom or workshop based programmed learning; or 21 hours a week in total of classroom or workshop based programmed learning plus hours using structured learning packages supported by teaching staff. In either case the requirements should be stated in a document signed on behalf of the college.

Sandwich courses

22.16   All students on sandwich courses count as full-time.

Modular courses

22.17   A modular course is one which contains two or more modules, a number of which have to be completed in order to complete the course. A student on a modular course counts as full-time only during the parts of the course for which he

22.13   HB 53(1); NIHB 50(1); CTR 73(1)
22.14   HB 53(1), CTR 73(1)
22.15   HB 53(1), CTR 73(1)
22.16   HB 53(1); NIHB 50(1); CTR 73(1)

or she is registered as full-time (so a student changing from full-time in her second year to part-time in her third would count as part-time in her third year).

22.18 The following applies only to the parts of modular courses that count as full-time. If someone fails a module or an exam in such a case, they continue to count as full-time for any period they continue to attend or undertake the course for the purposes of retaking the exam or module. (This includes any vacations within that period other than vacations after the end of the course.)

Other definitions

Further education and higher education

22.19 'Further education' means any education after the age of 16, up to and including GCE A Level or BTEC/SVEC National Diploma or National Certificate, whether or not leading to a qualification (i.e. up to level 3 [www]). 'Higher education' means any education beyond further education (i.e. levels 4-8), including all the following:

* first degree, postgraduate and higher degree courses;
* teacher training courses and courses for training youth and community workers;
* courses for the BTEC/SVEC Higher National Diploma (HND) or Higher National Certificate (HNC) or the Diploma in Management Studies.

Period of study and summer vacation

22.20 Some of the rules refer to a 'period of study' or 'summer vacation':

* the period of study for any course requiring more than 45 weeks study in a year (e.g. for many postgraduate courses) runs from the first day of the academic year to the day before the first day of the next academic year (the course is treated as not having a summer vacation);
* for courses of less than one year, the period of study is the whole of the course;
* in all other cases, the period of study runs from the first day of the academic year to the last day before the summer vacation (or in the final year of a course of more than one year, to the last day of the course). This usually means three terms plus the Christmas and Easter vacations;
* subject to the above points, for students on sandwich courses, periods of work experience are included in the period of study.

22.17 HB 53(2),(4); NIHB 50(2),(4); CTR 73(2),(4)

22.18 HB 53(3); NIHB 50(3); CTR 73(3)

22.19 HB 53,56; NIHB 50,53; CTR 73,75
https://www.gov.uk/what-different-qualification-levels-mean

22.20 HB 53(1); NIHB 50(1); CTR 73(1)

HB/CTR definitions and council tax definitions

22.21   The definition of a 'student' in council tax law is in category 6 in appendix 5. It can be different from the definitions in this chapter, though this is uncommon. Only the (benefit law) definitions in this chapter affect whether a student is eligible for HB or CTR. The council tax law definitions apply to council tax exemptions (para. 10.12) and discounts (para. 10.17). As appendix 5 illustrates (categories 5 and 6), a mixture of the two applies to non-dependant deductions (table 6.3) and second adult rebate (para. 6.35 onwards).

Which students can get HB and CTR?

22.22   To be eligible for HB or main CTR a student must satisfy the following rules. None of the rules prevents eligibility for second adult rebate in England or Scotland.

Which students are eligible?

22.23   Full-time students cannot get HB or main CTR unless they fall within certain groups:

- Students who are single claimants are eligible for HB and CTR only if they are in one (or more) of the groups in table 22.1.
- Students who are lone parents are in all cases eligible for HB and CTR.
- Couples are eligible for HB and CTR in all cases unless both are students and neither of them is in any of the groups in table 22.1. (See para. 22.24 for which partner should make the claim.)

Which partner in a couple should claim?

22.24   Table 22.2 explains which partner in a couple is eligible to claim HB and CTR on behalf of both. In all cases where a claim may be made, it takes into account the income, capital and applicable amount relating to them both.

Students who maintain two homes

22.25   Some students have to maintain two homes, one near their educational establishment and one elsewhere. There are special HB (and in Scotland CTR) rules for this:

- single claimants in the eligible groups (table 22.1) and lone parents get HB on only one home (para. 3.27);
- for couples, the rules are given in table 22.2 and paragraph 3.29.

The other rules about HB on two homes also apply (para. 3.7).

22.23 HB 8(1)(e),56(2); NIHB 8(1)(e),53(2); CTR 75(2)

22.24 HB 8(1)(e),56(2); NIHB 8(1)(e),53(2); CTR 75(2)

22.25 HB 7(3),(6)(b); NIHB 7(3),(6)(b); CTS 5(3), (6)(b); CTS60+5(3),(6)(b)

Table 22.1: Eligible student groups

1. Students on JSA(IB), ESA(IR) or income support.

2. Students who count as part-time rather than full-time (paras. 22.12-18).

3. Students under 21 where the course of study is not higher education (para. 22.19) and 21-year-olds continuing such a course.

4. Students under 20 on approved training which they began or were accepted on or enrolled on before the age of 19.

5. A student who has attained state pension credit age – or whose partner has (paras. 1.20-22) but note Welsh provision in relation to CTR (para. 22.3).

6. Student couples where both partners are full-time students, or lone parents, and in either case responsible for a child or young person.

7. Students who are single claimants responsible for a foster child placed with them by a local authority or a voluntary organisation.

8. Students who qualify for a disability premium or a severe disability premium in the assessment of their applicable amount (para. 12.20 and para. 12.35). This includes for example students who are registered blind, on disability living allowance or on incapacity benefit at the long term rate.

9. Students whose applicable amount would include the disability premium but for the fact that they are disqualified from incapacity benefit (i.e. treated as capable of work).

10. Students who are, or are treated as, incapable of work (as decided by the DWP) and have been so incapable, or have been treated as incapable, for a continuous period of not less than 196 days. Two or more separate periods separated by a break of not more than 56 days should be treated as one continuous period.

11. Students who have, or are treated as having, limited capability for work (as decided by the DWP) and have had, or have been treated as having, limited capability for work for a continuous period of not less than 196 days. Two or more separate periods separated by a break of not more than 84 days should be treated as one continuous period. The claimant should make a claim for ESA to trigger the limited capability for work test.

12. Students who have a UK grant which includes an allowance for deafness (from the date on which the request for the deafness related allowance is made).

13. Students unable to get a grant or student loan following an absence from their studies (with the consent of their educational establishment) due to illness or providing care. This applies only from the date the student ceases to be ill or stops providing care until the day before resuming the course (or, if earlier, the day their establishment agrees they can resume it) – and only up to a maximum of one year.

Table 22.2: Student rules for couples

An 'eligible group' means one in table 22.1.

Partner A	Partner B	Who can claim?	HB on two homes?
Student in an eligible group	Student in an eligible group	Either	Yes, if reasonable, and having two homes is unavoidable
Student in an eligible group	Student not in an eligible group	Partner A only	No, only on A's home
Student in an eligible group	Non-student	Either	Yes, if reasonable, and having two homes is unavoidable
Student not in an eligible group	Student not in an eligible group	Neither	No, not on either
Student not in an eligible group	Non-student	Partner B only	No, only on B's home

Halls of residence, student villages, etc

22.26 Most students who are eligible for HB can get it to meet the rent on halls of residence or other accommodation provided by the educational establishment they are attending. There are two groups of students that are excluded from getting HB on such accommodation during the period of study. These are:

- full-time students who would otherwise only be entitled to HB because they are waiting to return to the course after a period of illness or caring and are without a loan or grant; and

- part-time students – unless (if they were full-time students) they would be eligible to claim HB as one of the categories 3-12 identified in table 22.1.

Even these limited exclusions do not apply however if the educational establishment itself pays rent for the dwelling to someone else (except to another educational establishment, an education authority acting as such, or (in GB only) under a long tenancy, i.e. leased for more than 21 years). Finally, if it appears to the

T22.1 HB 56; NIHB 53; CTR 75
22.26 HB 57,58; NIHB 54,55

authority that the educational establishment has arranged for the accommodation to be provided by someone else to take advantage of the HB scheme there is no HB entitlement during the period of study. There are no similar rules for CTR (because such accommodation is usually exempt from council tax).

Absences during the summer vacation

22.27   Full-time students cannot get HB on term-time accommodation (if it is not their normal home) while they are absent from it during the summer vacation. This rule does not apply to part-time students; nor for absences in hospital for treatment.

Assessing student income

22.28   This section describes how student loans, grants and other income are assessed. Table 22.3 summarises the main rules. The main figures for maintenance loans in the 2012-13 academic year are in table 22.4.

For students depending upon the English support arrangements starting a course on or after 1st September 2012:

* universities, etc, can charge tuition fees of up to £9,000 (full-time);
* tuition fees loans are available to meet the higher fees;
* part-time students can apply for a tuition fee loan (replacing grants) for the first time up to £6,750.

22.29   In the case of eligible pension age claims (para. 22.3) all student grants and loans are disregarded. For working age claims, the rules in the following paragraphs apply.

Table 22.3: Assessment of student income

Type of student income	Treatment in assessing HB/CTR
• Maintenance loan ('student loan')	Assessed as income (table 22.4)
• Special support grant	Disregarded in full (table 22.5)
• Maintenance grant	Assessed as income (table 22.5)
• Fee loan	Disregarded in full (para. 22.31)
• Grants for extra expenses	Mostly disregarded (table 22.5)
• For CTR variations, see para. 22.2.	

22.27   HB 55; NIHB 52

22.29   HB60+29(1); NIHB60+27(1); CTR 39(1) – meaning of 'income': pensioners

Income from student loans

Who gets a student loan

22.30   UK students in higher education (para. 22.19) are generally eligible for a student loan. Exceptions include:

* part-time students who are excluded from maintenance loans for living costs;
* students on nursing and midwifery diploma courses;
* postgraduate students (unless they are studying for a Postgraduate Certificate of Education); and
* students aged 60+ at the start of the course or, in Scotland, 50+ at the start of the course unless under the age of 55 and intending to enter employment after completion of the course.

22.31   The student loan may include:

* an amount towards living expenses (called a 'maintenance loan'). This is treated as income (para. 22.32);
* an amount towards fees (called a 'fee loan'). This is disregarded.

Assessing the maintenance loan

22.32   In assessing HB and CTR, students who are eligible for a maintenance loan (including in Scotland any Young Students' bursary paid instead of part of the loan), independent student's bursary and any additional loan (up to £810 in 2012-13) are treated as receiving it at the maximum level applicable to them. This is done regardless of whether they apply for it, so long as they 'could acquire [a maintenance loan] in respect of that year by taking reasonable steps to do so'. The loan is then disregarded as capital but treated as income as shown in table 22.4, which also gives the main loan figures for 2012 13. If a condition of entitlement to a loan could not be met by the student taking reasonable steps then the authority should not treat the student as having a loan. In *CH/4422/2006* the fact that a Muslim student considered that they were prohibited from applying for a loan because of religious beliefs was not held to be an impediment to acquiring such a loan by taking reasonable steps.

22.33   If a maintenance loan is assessed on the assumption that the student or partner makes a contribution, the amount of that contribution is disregarded from the student's or partner's other income. Similarly, a parent who makes a contribution can have that amount disregarded in the assessment of their own HB or CTR (para. 13.135).

22.31   HB 64, 64A; NIHB 61, 62; CTR 81,81(6)

22.32   HB 53,59,64, sch 6 para 22; NIHB 50,56,61, sch 7 para. 23; CTR 73,76,81 sch 10 para. 27

22.33   HB 66(1),67; NIHB 64(1),65; CTR 83,84

22.34   If a student leaves part way through their course and was paid a student maintenance loan – or a grant for a dependant – during the year they leave in, the income continues to be assessed in the same way and for the same period as before for the period to which any instalments of loan received relate. The sole exception is that there is no £10 per week disregard from the loan (but otherwise all the other steps in table 22.4 for loans or table 22.5 for grants for dependants apply). See also DWP HB/CTB A14/2008 (revised) for the treatment of loan income paid other than quarterly when the course is not completed.

Repaying a student loan

22.35   If someone else repays a former student's student loan, that payment is disregarded as that former student's income. This includes government payments under the 'Teacher Repayment Loan Scheme' (DWP GM para. BW2.589) and any other such payments. However, when a student himself or herself repays a student loan this is not disregarded from their other income for HB/CTR purposes. There is no similar rule in Northern Ireland.

Income from student grants

22.36   The rules for assessing grant income apply to maintenance grants (table 22.3), and to any other kind of educational grant, award, scholarship, studentship, exhibition, allowance or bursary, whoever they are paid by.

Assessment

22.37   Grant income is assessed for HB and CTR purposes as shown in table 22.5. If a student leaves part way through their course, see also paragraph 22.34.

22.38   If a student's grant is assessed on the assumption that the student or their partner makes a contribution, the amount of that contribution is disregarded from the student's or partner's other income. Similarly, a parent who makes a contribution can have that amount disregarded in the assessment of their own HB and CTR (para. 13.135).

22.34   HB 40(7)-(9); NIHB 37(5)-(7); CTR 54(6)-(8)

22.35   HB sch 5 para 12; CTR sch 8 para 17

22.36   HB 59(1); NIHB 56(1); CTR 76(1)

22.37   HB 53,59,63,64; NIHB 50,56,60,61; CTR 73,76,80,81

22.38   HB 66,67; NIHB 64,65; CTR 83,84

Other income

Access funds and learner support funds

22.39   The following rules apply to payments from:

* 'access funds' (sometimes called 'hardship funds') made by educational establishments to students who fall within the student loan scheme (para. 22.30), postgraduates, and students aged 19 or more in further education;

* 'learner support funds' made by educational establishments from monies provided by the Secretary of State for Education or the Chief Executive of Skills Funding to students aged 16 or more in further education; and

* financial contingency funds made available by Welsh Ministers.

22.40   These payments are treated as follows:

* single lump sum payments are disregarded as capital for 52 weeks from the date of payment, unless they are for certain necessities (para. 22.41) in which case they are counted in full straight away;

* regular payments are disregarded as income, unless they are for certain necessities (para. 22.41) in which case £20 per week is disregarded (subject to the over-riding £20 limit on certain disregards: para. 13.160). However, even those payments are disregarded in full as income if they are made before the student's course begins or to tide them over until they receive their student loan.

22.41   The 'certain necessities' mentioned above (para. 22.40) are food, ordinary clothing and footwear, household fuel, eligible rent or in NI rates (apart from any amount attributable to non-dependant deductions), council tax or water charges – of the claimant or any member of the family.

Other earned and unearned income

22.42   If a full-time or part-time student receives earned or unearned income other than (or as well as) a student loan or grant, the ordinary earned and unearned income disregards apply to it (chapters 13-15).

The extra student income disregard

22.43   There is an extra disregard for student expenditure, which works as follows. If the student has loan or grant income, certain amounts are disregarded from it, as shown in tables 22.4 and 22.5. If the student necessarily spends more

---

22.39   HB 53(1); NIHB 50(1); CTR 73(1)

22.40   HB 65,68(2)-(4), sch 5 para 34; NIHB 63,66(2)-(4), sch 6 para 35; CTR 82, 85(2)-(3) sch 8 para 40

22.41   HB 65(3)-(4), NIHB 63(3)-(4) CTR 82(3)

22.43   HB 63; NIHB 60; CTR 80

on those items than the amounts indicated in the tables, the excess is disregarded from their other income – but it must be income which is 'intended' for this purpose: *CIS/3107/2003*.

Table 22.4: Student maximum maintenance loans: 2012-13 academic year

	Full year	Final year	Per extra week
English students who started course on or after 1st September 2009 and before 1st September 2012			
Courses in London	£6,928	£6,307	£106
Elsewhere	£4,950	£4,583	£83
English students who started on or after 1st September 2012			
Courses in London	£7,675	N/A	£106
Elsewhere	£5,500	N/A	£83
Welsh students			
Courses in London	£6,648	£6,053	£106
Elsewhere	£4,745	£4,396	£83
NI students			
Courses in London	£6,780	£6,170	£108
Elsewhere	£4,840	£4,480	£84
Scottish students			
Courses in London	£6,690	£5,905	£109
Elsewhere	£5,570	£4,945	£85

Reductions in main amounts

The maximum amount of maintenance loan is reduced if they also receive a maintenance grant. If the student started the course from 2009-10 onwards the reduction is £0.50 for every £1 of maintenance grant awarded. But claimants eligible for means-tested benefits should be claiming the special support grant instead.

Special cases

Lower figures apply to NHS-funded courses and some other courses (see table A1 in DWP HB/CTB A18/2009 (revised)).

Treatment for HB/CTR purposes

(a) Take the whole amount into account as income (even though it is in fact a loan). Include any amount for extra weeks. Treat any parental or partner's assumed contribution to it as being received (even if not actually paid).

(b) Disregard £693 in all cases. This is a standard amount including £303 towards travel and £390 towards books and equipment.

(c) Average the resulting amount over the period described below.

(d) Then disregard £10 from the weekly figure (in the case of a couple, disregard £10 from each one's weekly figure), subject to the over-riding £20 limit on certain disregards (para. 13.160).

Period over which the loan is averaged

General rule

Average over the period from the first Monday in September to the last Sunday in June. In 2012-13 this is 43 weeks: 3.9.12 to 30.6.13.

Exceptions

First years only: If the course begins after the first Monday in September, still average over the period described above, but then ignore it as income for the week(s) before the course begins *(CIS/3734/2004)*

Final years and one-year courses only: Average over the period from the first Monday in September to the last Sunday in the course.

Courses in Scotland: If any year starts before September, average over the period from the first Monday in the course to the last Sunday in June (or, in final year and one-year courses, the last Sunday in the course).

Courses starting other than in the autumn: From the whole academic year subtract the 'quarter' in which the longest vacation is taken, the 'quarters' (for these purposes) being January to March (three months), April to June (three months), July to August (two months), and September to December (four months). Average over the period from the first Monday to the last Sunday in the remaining three 'quarters'.

Example: Student income assessment: 2012-13 academic year

Information

A student who rents her home is in the second year of a three-year full-time university course in England (outside London). She is eligible for HB because she is disabled. No-one lives with her so her home is exempt from council tax.

Student loan and grant

She receives a maintenance loan at the maximum level available to her of £4,950, a special support grant, and a grant for her disability.

Assessment

The special support grant, and the grant for her disability, are wholly disregarded.

From her maintenance loan of £4,950 disregard the standard amount of £693 giving £4,257. Average this over the standard 43 weeks (3rd September 2012 to 30th June 2012) giving £99. Then disregard a further £10 giving £89.

So her total income during the 43 weeks from Monday 3rd September 2012 to Sunday 30th June 2013 inclusive is £98 per week (plus any other income she may have).

Note

Because she is a second year student, this income is counted even in weeks when she is not at university (such as the period from 3rd September 2012 to when the autumn term begins). If she was a first year student, the assessment would be exactly the same giving her a student income of £89 per week, but this income would be disregarded until her autumn term began *(CIS/3734/2004)*.

Table 22.5: Student grants: 2012-13 academic year

Treatment for HB/default CTR purposes

(a) Start with the whole amount of the grant (including the maintenance grant: table 22.3) and all allowances for the maintenance of a (child or adult) dependant. Treat any parental or partner's assumed contribution to it as being received (even if not actually paid).

(b) No standard disregard is made for travel or for books and equipment – unless the student neither receives nor is treated as receiving a student loan, in which case disregard £693.

(c) Disregard the following:

- all amounts because the student has a disability;
- all amounts for books and equipment and/or for travel (in addition to the standard £693 if appropriate);
- all amounts for child care (including a parent's learning allowance where paid under prescribed legislation, child care grant, etc);
- the special support grant (available to students eligible for means-tested benefits);
- education maintenance awards (EMA) and 16-19 Bursary Fund payments (which replaced EMA in England);
- the higher education grant;
- the higher education bursary for care leavers;
- £693 from the adult learning grant (DWP GM para C2.177);
- the National Assembly for Wales learning grant (but not for 'new style' full time undergraduates);
- tuition or examination fees;
- expenses for term-time residential study away from the student's educational establishment;
- two homes grant;
- additions for anyone outside the UK so long as the student's applicable amount does not include an amount for that person.

(d) Average the resulting amount over the period described below.

Period over which the grant is averaged

Students who receive or are treated as receiving a student loan

Average over the same period as the student loan (table 22.4: the general rule and exceptions all apply). This is how the maintenance grant (table 22.3) is treated.

Others

If the grant is attributable to the student's period of study (para. 22.20):
Average over the period from the first Monday to the last Sunday in that
period of study omitting, for sandwich students, any benefit weeks falling
wholly or partly within the period of work experience.

If it is attributable to any other period: Average over the period from the first
Monday to the last Sunday in that period.

Exceptions

Nursing and midwifery diploma students: They may get a bursary towards
their living expenses (and cannot get a student loan). Their bursary (after any
appropriate disregards, including the standard £693) is averaged over the full
calendar year (52/53 weeks).

NHS-funded students on degree courses: They may get a bursary towards
their living expenses (and can get a student loan at a lower rate than other
students). Their bursary (after any appropriate disregards, excluding the
standard £693) is averaged over the full calendar year (52/53 weeks) – and
their loan is dealt with as in table 22.4.

Care leaver's grant: Average this over the period from the first Monday to
the last Sunday in the summer vacation.

23 Local variations

23.1   This chapter sets out the local variations within, and from, the HB scheme in 2013-14. It describes:

* dIscretionary housing payments (DHPs);
* local HB schemes disregarding income from war pensions, etc;
* the HB payment demonstration projects;
* the benefit cap applied to certain HB awards; and
* the replacement of HB by universal credit – which in 2013 takes place in certain locations for a limited number of claimants.

Discretionary housing payments (DHPs)

Legislation

23.2   In Great Britain the government has the power to:

* make regulations providing for a scheme of discretionary housing payments (DHPs);
* pay grants to authorities for the cost of the scheme and impose a limit on the amount of each authority's total payments under the scheme.

23.3   In Northern Ireland the DSD has similar powers to run a DHP scheme

23.4   DHPs are an independent scheme administered by authorities that also administer HB but they are not a form of HB. The HB appeals procedures (chapter 19) do not apply. An authority on request may however review any decision it has made. Payment of DHPs is entirely discretionary. Authorities vary in their willingness to award them but central government funding for DHPs has been increased from an annual amount of £20m up to April 2011 to £155m in 2013-14 (DWP S1/2013 para. 2). While it is worth asking about and/or claiming DHPs, claimants should not rely on an authority making an award.

DWP guidance

23.5   Guidance for authorities is contained in the DWP's (draft) *Discretionary Housing Payments Guidance Manual* (April 2013) [www]. The guidance has been updated to reflect changes to the LHA rules from April 2011 onwards, the introduction of universal credit, the abolition of CTB, the introduction of the benefit cap and the social sector size criteria.

23.2   CPSA 69,70; SI 2001 No 1167; SI 2001 No 2340

23.3   NICPSA 60,61; NISR 2001 No 216

23.5   www.dwp.gov.uk/docs/discretionary-housing-payments-guide-draft.pdf

Circumstances in which DHPs may be made

23.6 DHPs are available to claimants who:

- in GB are entitled to HB or Universal Credit, have a rent liability, and 'appear to [the] authority to require some further financial assistance… in order to meet housing costs';

- in Northern Ireland are entitled to HB in respect of their rent which has been restricted as a rent referral case or under LHA rules and 'appear to [the] authority to require some further financial assistance… in order to meet housing costs'.

There is no requirement for the claimant's family circumstances to be 'exceptional', nor does there have to be 'hardship'.

Housing costs

23.7 The term 'housing costs' is not defined in the regulations. DWP draft Guidance (paras 1.11-13) says that the term may be interpreted to include not just rent (with certain exclusions) but also rent in advance, deposits and other lump sum costs associated with a housing need such as removal costs.

23.8 A DHP cannot be awarded to meet a council tax liability or make up any shortfall between an individual's council tax liability and their CTR. In England and Wales, however, an authority has a wide discretion to reduce any liability for council tax whether or not the person qualifies for HB or CTR (para 10.40).

Uses for DHPs

23.9 By way of example DWP draft Guidance (paras 2.2-2.17) says that DHPs may be used to cover such matters as:

- reductions in HB or UC where the benefit cap has been applied;
- reductions in HB or UC for under-occupation in the social rented sector;
- reductions in HB or UC because of local housing allowance restrictions;
- rent shortfall to prevent a household becoming homeless while the housing authority explores other options;
- rent officer restrictions such as local reference rent or shared room rate;
- non-dependant deductions;
- income tapers;
- a rent deposit or rent in advance for a property that the claimant has yet to move into if already entitled to HB for their present home.

23.10 DHPs cannot be awarded towards any of the following:

- service or support charges that are ineligible for HB (para. 8.17 onwards);

23.6 SI 2001 No. 1167 reg 2; NISR 2001 No. 216 rule 2

23.8 LGFA 13A(1)(c),(6),(7)

- any council tax liability;
- in Northern Ireland any liability to meet rates;
- increases to cover rent arrears which are not eligible for HB (para. 8.44);
- reductions in any benefit because of Jobseeker's sanctions, Child Support sanctions or sanctions following certain benefit related offences.

Maximum amount of DHP and period of award

23.11 The total weekly amount of a DHP, taken together with the claimant's award of HB, must not exceed the claimant's eligible rent calculated on a weekly basis (paras. 7.17-20 and 8.5-7).

23.12 The Court of Appeal has held that 'the limit placed on DHPs... does not prevent the Council from exercising its discretion to make DHPs for past housing costs (arrears of rent) on the ground that the applicant is currently receiving full housing benefit.' (*Gargett, R (on the application of) v LB Lambeth,* para. 32). The authority may award a DHP for any period (i.e. for a fixed period or indefinitely) that is appropriate for the circumstances of the case.

23.13 The maximum amount only applies where the DHP is calculated as a weekly sum – for example to meet a shortfall. Where the DHP is for a lump sum payment such as a deposit or rent in advance these limits do not apply (DWP draft Guidance para. 2.6) but the authority does have to take account of its overall DHP budget.

Claims, decisions, payments and overpayments

23.14 A DHP may be claimed by the person entitled or a person acting on their behalf if this appears reasonable. The authority may accept a claim in such form and manner as it approves. Some authorities have a separate DHP claim form. The authority should provide a written notice of its decision on a claim and the reasons for it as soon as is reasonably practicable. DHPs may be paid to the person entitled or to someone else the authority thinks appropriate. A person claiming or getting DHPs must provide the authority with details of the grounds of claim, information on any changes of circumstance that may be relevant and any other information required by the authority. The authority may stop making payments of DHP when it thinks fit.

23.15 The authority has the discretion to recover DHP payments when it decides that someone has misrepresented, or failed to disclose, a material fact and, as a consequence, a payment was made. DHPs may also be recovered where the authority decides that an error was made in deciding the application for payment which would not have been made but for that error.

23.10 SI 2001 No. 1167 reg 3; NISR 2001 No. 216 rule 3

23.11 SI 2001 No. 1167 reg 4; NISR 2001 No. 216 rule 4

23.14 SI 2001 No. 1167; NISR 2001 No. 216

DWP's limits and contribution to DHP expenditure

23.16 The DWP sets an annual limit on each authority's DHP expenditure and partly reimburses this expenditure through a system of grants (para. 24.48).

Local schemes to disregard war pensions, etc

23.17 The HB scheme described in this guide is one which authorities are required by law to run. However, authorities in Great Britain (not Northern Ireland) have the power to run an enhanced 'local scheme'. But the only enhancement authorities are now allowed to make is to disregard prescribed war disablement pensions and prescribed war pensions to surviving spouses or civil partners, in whole or in part, above the usual £10 disregard required by law (paras. 13.58-59). Many authorities also provide a total disregard for these benefits under their local CTR schemes.

23.18 The decision to run, end or vary a local HB scheme is made by a resolution of the authority. The question of whether an authority should run a local HB scheme is not open to the appeal procedure. All authorities provide some form of extra disregard (Commons Written Answers, 26th January 2010). Further information on subsidy payments for local HB schemes can be found in paragraphs 24.46-47 of this guide.

23.19 The war pensions that may be disregarded under a local HB scheme are set out in regulations. These payments are derived from numerous payments, pensions and allowances that make up the Armed Forces Pensions and Compensation Schemes. These include the scheme introduced in 2005 that replaced the War Pension Scheme for new beneficiaries. Included among the disregarded items are service attributable pensions (SAP), i.e. the element of occupational pensions under the Armed Forces Pensions Scheme 1975 which is paid due to injury or illness that is attributable to service on or before 5th April 2005 (HB/CTB A1/2010). The current rates of war pension etc are set out in DWP A2/2013 (Revised). More information may be found on the Service Personnel and Veterans Agency website [www].

HB payment demonstration projects

23.20 The universal credit arrangements include payment of benefit (including the housing element) to the claimant. There are six payment demonstration projects across the country testing different aspects of the direct payment of HB to council and housing association tenants (social sector tenants). Under these projects claimants, who would normally get HB by way of a rebate to a rent

---

23.17 AA s134(8)-(10), s139(6)-(8)

23.18 AA s134(8)-(10), s139(6)-(8)

23.19 SI 2007 No 1619, www.veterans-uk.info

23.20 www.dwp.gov.uk/newsroom/press-releases/2012/dec-2012/dwp135-12.shtml

account or by payment to the landlord, instead get monthly HB payments direct. The claimant is then expected to pay the money to the landlord.

23.21 The first projects started in June 2012 and are expected to run until June 2013 with the aim of clarifying what safeguards are necessary and to develop good practice. The projects involve the following partners: Dunedin Canmore Housing Association in Edinburgh, working in association with The City of Edinburgh Council (Scotland); Oxford City Council and Oxford Citizens, (part of the) Greensquare Group (Southern England); Shropshire Unitary County Council and Bromford Group, Sanctuary Housing and The Wrekin Housing Trust (West Midlands); Southwark Council and Family Mosaic (London); Torfaen County Borough Council and Bron Afon Community Housing and Charter Housing (Wales); Wakefield MDC and Wakefield and District Housing (Northern England). The findings from the projects are available on the DWP web site and more regular briefings on the CIH direct payments learning network [www].

The HB benefit cap

23.22 This section describes how the 'benefit cap' can reduce a claimant's HB so that the total of their HB and certain other 'welfare benefits' (para. 23.25 and table 23.1) does not exceed a fixed weekly figure (para. 23.24). The benefit cap only applies to working age claimants (paras. 1.20-22). Exceptions are given in table 23.1 and for exempt accommodation see paragraph 23.26. At the time of writing the benefit cap does not apply in Northern Ireland.

Phased roll out of the benefit cap

23.23 The benefit cap is being introduced on a phased basis (paras. 6.32-33) starting from 15th April 2013. The first authorities required to apply the cap are Croydon, Haringey, Bromley and Enfield (DWP G12/2012 paras 20-24). The cap is expected to be introduced in other authorities during the summer of 2013 and in place in all authorities by the end of September 2013.

The amount of the benefit cap

23.24 The benefit cap is:

♦ £350 per week for single claimants (para. 4.7);

♦ £500 per week for lone parents, couples and polygamous marriages.

23.21 www.dwp.gov.uk/docs/direct-payment-demo-figures.pdf
www.cih.org/directpaymentslearningnetwork

23.22 WRA ss96-97, SI 2012 No 2995, HB 75A-75G; www.nidirect.gov.uk/benefit-cap

23.24 HB 75G

The amount of the HB reduction

23.25   The reduction in the claimant's HB is calculated as shown in table 23.1.
(See example 1; and see paras. 6.30-33 for when a reduction takes effect. Table
23.1 lists all the welfare benefits included in the cap.

Where a 'welfare benefit' is received at a reduced rate because of sanctions,
recoveries of over-payments or third party deductions, the authority should base
its cap calculation on the gross amount payable before such deductions.

Table 23.1: Calculating HB benefit cap reductions:

For each benefit week (para. 5.29):

   (a) Start with the claimant's entitlement to HB in that week, using the
        amount of entitlement before any reductions for recoveries of
        overpayments or administrative penalties. But for exempt
        accommodation start with NIL (para. 23.26)

   (b) Add the claimant's and any partner's entitlement in that week to:

   - bereavement allowance
   - child benefit
   - guardian's allowance
   - income support
   - maternity allowance
   - widowed parent's allowance
   - employment and support allowance

   - carer's allowance
   - child tax credit
   - incapacity benefit
   - jobseeker's allowance
   - widowed mother's allowance
   - widow's pension
   - severe disablement allowance

   (c) If the total exceeds £350/£500 (para. 23.24) reduce the claimant's HB
        by the amount of the excess (subject to (d)).

   (d) This gives the claimant's entitlement to HB for that week except where
        the result is:

   - nil (or a negative figure); or
   - less than the minimum HB award (para. 6.13)

   in which case the minimum HB (para. 6.13) is paid so that claimant is
   entitled to claim DHP (para. 6.33 and 23.2).

23.25   HB 75A, 75C, 75D, 75G

T23.1   HB 75A, 75C, 75D, 75G

Exempt accommodation

23.26   The benefit cap applies to exempt accommodation (para. 9.2) but (as table 23.1 shows) the amount of the claimant's HB is excluded from the calculation. The DWP has advised that 'the vast majority' of exempt accommodation cases will therefore not be affected by the cap (Circular HB/CTB U5/2012). (See example 2.)

Exceptions

23.27   Table 23.2 lists the circumstances in which the benefit cap does not apply (and see also para. 6.32).

Table 23.2: When the HB benefit cap does not apply

The HB benefit cap reductions do not apply in any of the following cases:

- ◆ pension age claims (paras. 1.20-22);
- ◆ during an extended payment of HB (para. 17.42);
- ◆ When the claimant or any partner (including any partner in a polygamous marriage) is getting:
  - • universal credit (because a benefit cap will instead apply to UC itself),
  - • main phase ESA with a support component,
  - • disability living allowance,
  - • personal independence payments,
  - • industrial injuries benefit,
  - • a war pension,
  - • working tax credit (including people who are entitled to WTC but not receiving it);
- ◆ when a child or young person in the family is getting:
  - • disability living allowance, or
  - • personal independence payments.
- ◆ when any of the above would be getting disability living allowance, personal independence payments, attendance allowance or a war pension, but are not doing so because they are in hospital or a care home;
- ◆ During the 39 week 'grace period' after ending work: paras. 23.27-28.

23.26 HB 75C(2)(a)
T23.2 HB 72E, 73E, 75E

The 39 week grace period after ending work

23.28 The HB benefit cap does not apply during the 39 weeks beginning with the day after the claimant's or partner's last day of work if the following conditions are met (para. 23.28). Either the claimant or the partner must meet all the conditions; it is not enough for them to meet the conditions between them. The DWP calls this time limited exception a 'grace period'.

23.29 The conditions are that the claimant or a partner:

♦ has ceased work (including when this occurred before the benefit cap was introduced); and

♦ for at least 50 of the 52 weeks before their last day of work, that person was engaged in work for which payment was made or expected, and was not entitled to JSA, ESA or IS; and

♦ in their last full week of work they worked for 16 hours or more.

For these purposes, a person on maternity, paternity or adoption leave, or getting statutory sick pay, counts as being in work.

Applying and changing the benefit cap reductions

23.30 In any particular case, the authority need not apply the benefit cap or change the amount of any reduction until it receives notification from the DWP. The authority may however do either of these on its own initiative if it has the relevant information and evidence to do so (para. 6.33).

When benefit cap reductions take effect

23.31 A benefit cap reduction may be made as part of deciding an HB claim. Claims wrongly decided as to a reduction may be corrected at any time.

23.32 A benefit cap reduction may start, change or end during an award of HB. When it:

♦ starts or increases, HB changes from the date the authority makes the decision to do so (this prevents overpayments of HB occurring solely as a result of a reduction;

♦ reduces or ends, HB changes from the date entitlement to a relevant benefit (table 23.1) changed (so the claimant gets their resulting arrears of HB).

23.28 HB 72E, 73E, 75E
23.28-29   HB 75E(1)(b),(2), 75F
23.30 HB 75B
23.31 DAR 4(7H)
23.32 DAR 7(2)(r), 8(14F)

Examples: The HB benefit cap

1. The general rule

A single claimant aged 42 rents his home (but it is not exempt accommodation). Before the benefit cap is applied, he is entitled to:

HB	£210.00 per week
Other benefits listed in table 23.1	£170.00 per week

Because the total of £380 per week exceeds the benefit cap of £350.00 per week, his HB is reduced by the difference (£30.00 per week) to £180.00 per week.

2. Exempt accommodation

A single claimant aged 42 rents exempt accommodation. Before the benefit cap is applied she is entitled to:

HB	£290.00 per week
Other benefits listed in table 23.1	£130.00 per week

The amount of her HB is excluded from the calculation, and her other benefits do not exceed the benefit cap, so her HB is not reduced.

Introduction of universal credit

23.33   The government plans to introduce a new benefit, 'universal credit' (UC), between April 2013 and 2017. It is to be launched in stages for specific categories of claimants in particular geographical areas.

23.34   UC is for working age claimants. It replaces not only HB but also JSA(IB), ESA(IR) and IS and (slightly later) the tax credits (WTC and CTC). Pension credit (PC) continues for pension age claimants. Both UC and PC will include not only support for mortgage interest (chapter 25) but also support for rent. For social sector tenants this support is based on their actual rent and eligible service charges less any deduction due to under-occupancy. For private tenants it is the lower of actual costs or the LHA. HB therefore ceases as a separate benefit for claimants entitled to UC (except for those in exempt accommodation (para x.x)). In many respects, UC and PC resemble the former supplementary benefit scheme from which HB was extracted in 1982-83.

Legislative framework

23.35   The legal framework of the new benefit is set out in Part 1 of the Welfare Reform Act 2012 (and Part 1 of the Welfare Reform Bill NI – which at the time of writing has yet to receive royal assent). For GB the detailed rules are set out in statutory instruments. Those likely to be of particular interest to readers of this guide are identified in table 23.3.

UC – phased roll-out

23.36   The DWP is hoping to roll out awards of UC in three main phases [www]. Plans may change on the basis of experience. Latest updates are available on the DWP website [www].

23.37   Phase one (the pathfinder stage) is expected to start on 29th April 2013 with a restricted number of claimants resident in certain postcodes in Greater Manchester (Tameside, Warrington, Oldham and Wigan). The limiting criteria include not only that the claimant must be resident in the pathfinder locations but also single, available for work or in work with low earnings (but not have earnings from self-employment); not be getting existing benefits; not have capital above £6,000, not have children and not be homeless. Other limiting criteria also apply.

23.38   In phase two (between October 2013 and March 2014) UC awards are expected to be made available to a broader class of claimants in more places across GB. By April 2014 all new claims for HB (with the exception of supported accommodation) should have been phased out.

23.39   Phase three (between March 2014 and the end of 2017) is expected to see the migration of existing claimants to the new arrangements bringing an end (after 35 years) to the HB scheme.

23.36   www.dwp.gov.uk/docs/ucpbn-15-managing-claims.pdf
           www.dwp.gov.uk/local-authority-staff/universal-credit-information/universal-credit-updates
23.37   SI 2013 No 386

Table 23.3: UC – main statutory instruments

Title	Subject
UC (Transitional Provisions) Regulations SI 2013 No 386	Allows for introduction of UC in specific geographical areas (pathfinders) for a limited number of claimants.
UC Regulations SI 2013 No 376	Sets out the conditions of entitlement, the standard allowances and different elements a claimant may be entitled to including housing costs as well as the assessment of capital and income and the calculation of an award including a benefit cap.
UC, Personal Independence Payment, JSA & ESA (Decisions and Appeals) Regulations SI 2013 No 381	Ensures that the decision-making and appeals framework applicable to other benefits applies to UC. Includes new rules requiring claimants who wish to appeal to first apply for reconsideration by a DWP decision-maker.
UC, Personal Independence Payment and Working-age Benefits (Claims and Payments) Regulations SI 2012 No 380	Provides for claiming (mainly online) and paying UC – normally one month in arrears – direct to the claimant's bank or other account. Limited provision is also made for payment to someone else and for payment to third parties such as landlords in cases of rent arrears.
The Rent Officers (UC Functions) Order SI 2013 No 382	Sets out rent officers' functions in relation to UC including determination of broad rental market areas and LHA rates. Also requires rent officers to determine 'reasonable payments' in the social rented sector following a request from the DWP.
The Social Security (Overpayments and Recovery) Regulations SI 2013 No 384	Provides that all UC overpayments are recoverable, including those due to official error, how overpayments are calculated, who they can be recovered from and how, and the maximum rates of recovery direct from the claimant's benefit.

24 Subsidy

24.1   The DWP pays authorities most of their costs in administering and paying HB. This is called subsidy. This chapter explains how much subsidy the DWP pays. It applies to Great Britain only, and covers:

* who pays for HB;
* subsidy for benefit expenditure;
* the areas of expenditure which qualify for lower subsidy – especially overpayments and certain high eligible rents; and
* subsidy for benefit administration.

No subsidy is available for CTB expenditure or adjustments made on or after 1st April 2013 but the CTB element in an authority's subsidy claim for 2012-13 (due to be audited or certified by November 2013) should be met by the DWP (DWP S6/2012). At the end of this chapter is a note on the entirely separate method by which the cost of CTR is met.

Who pays for HB

24.2   An authority's expenditure on HB includes the following items, and the DWP pays subsidy towards part or all of these:

* benefit expenditure itself;
* ongoing administrative costs, e.g. staff salaries, accommodation costs, training, and computer running costs; and
* one-off costs e.g. to implement changes to the schemes.

24.3   Anything not met by the DWP is paid for by the authority itself, from its general fund, or in Wales from the council fund. For example, part or all of the cost of overpayments of HB is met by the authority itself (paras. 24.13-30), as can be part or all of the eligible rent of a claimant in 'exempt accommodation' (paras. 24.33-34).

Subsidy claims, payments and overpayments

24.4   Subsidy payments make up a large amount of authorities' total income, and also have a big effect on the way they run the HB scheme. Just as claimants need HB from the authority, authorities need subsidy from the DWP. Authorities may fail to get their full subsidy entitlement if they:

* fail to claim it, or claim it using the wrong procedures; or
* do not claim it on time (or do not ensure that their final subsidy claim is auditor certified by 30th November each year); or
* cannot provide the necessary information and evidence to support their claims.

24.5 If subsidy is overpaid to an authority, or there is some other breach of subsidy rules, the Secretary of State has the discretion to recover appropriate amounts (circular HB/CTB S1/2002) (see *R (Isle of Anglesey County Council) v Secretary of State for Work and Pensions* and *R (London Borough of Lambeth) v Secretary of State for Work and Pensions*).

Subsidy law and guidance

24.6 The Social Security Administration Act 1992 (sections 140A-140G) provides the legal framework for the payment of subsidies to authorities. The detailed legal rules are set out in the Income-related Benefits (Subsidy to Authorities) Order 1998 (SI 1998 No 562) as amended each year. The rules and rates for 2012-13 will be incorporated in an amendment to this Order, made towards the end of the year. However, most of these are known in advance as a result of DWP guidance.

24.7 The DWP gives guidance on subsidy arrangements in a Subsidy Guidance Manual which it reissues each year [www]. The DWP also issues the 'S' series of circulars to keep authorities up to date [www].

Benefit expenditure subsidy

24.8 The DWP pays authorities subsidy equal to their 'qualifying expenditure' on HB and in the case of CTB such expenditure incurred up to the end of March 2013. As described below, in practice this means the DWP pays back nearly all of the HB and CTB (up to the end of March 2013) authorities have paid out.

Qualifying expenditure

24.9 An authority's 'qualifying expenditure' is:

* the total of all HB and CTB lawfully paid (or treated as lawfully paid) by the authority during the relevant year;
* minus part or all of HB and CTB expenditure on certain items – as described in this chapter.

24.5   AA 140C(3)

24.7   www.dwp.gov.uk/local-authority-staff/housing-benefit/performance-and-good-practice/
       subsidy-guidance-manuals/
       www.dwp.gov.uk/local-authority-staff/housing-benefit/user-communications/hbctb-circulars/

24.8   SI 1998/562 art 11(2)

24.9   SI 1998/562 art 13

Correctly paid HB/CTB

24.10 Correctly paid HB and CTB (up to the end of March 2013) qualifies for 100% subsidy. In other words, the DWP meets the whole cost of all correct payments of HB (whether rent rebates or rent allowance) and CTB. Nowadays this includes backdated HB (para. 5.51) and extended payments (para. 17.42). That fact does not necessarily lead to authorities backdating HB with abandon, because subsidy claims for backdated HB are subject to the external auditor's certification that good cause has been established (DWP HB/CTB Subsidy GM, para. 307-308).

Penalised expenditure

24.11 To encourage authorities to monitor and control costs, certain areas of benefit expenditure are penalised which include certain overpayments and certain high eligible rents (in other words, the cost of these is not always met in full). But authorities must apply the benefit rules fairly, objectively and impartially. They must not allow the subsidy penalties to interfere with this duty; though where the authority has a discretion one factor it may take account of is its own financial position *(R v Brent LBC HBRB ex parte Connery)*.

Overpayments

24.12 Subsidy on overpayments of HB and CTB (up to the end of March 2013) varies depending on the reason for the overpayment. The DWP will not be seeking downward subsidy adjustments where CTB overpayments are identified after the end of March 2013 (DWP S6/2012 para 8). The main rules are given below.

Authority error/administrative delay overpayments

24.13 An 'authority error overpayment' means an overpayment caused by a mistake made, whether in the form of an act or omission, by an authority. It may be a mistake of fact or of law. It does not apply, however, if the claimant, a person acting on the claimant's behalf or any other person to whom the payment is made, caused or materially contributed to that mistake (see also paragraphs 18.11 and 18.13).

24.14 An 'administrative delay overpayment' means one which arises when:

- the authority is notified of a change of circumstances and has sufficient information and evidence to make a decision on it;
- the authority does not make the decision before the next day on which benefit is paid or allowed;
- the delay was not caused by a mistake of the authority; and

---

24.10 SI 1998/562 arts 13,14

24.13-18   SI 1998/562 art 18(1)(e),(6),(6A)

24.14   SI 1998/562 art 18(6ZA)

- the claimant, someone acting on their behalf, or the payee, did not materially contribute to the delay.

24.15　Authority error and administrative delay overpayments are combined for subsidy purposes. The amount of subsidy an authority receives in a year depends on its combined amount, as compared with its total correct payments of benefit (para. 24.10) in that year.

24.16　If in a year the percentage of authority error and administrative delay overpayments (as compared with correct payments) is:

- up to 0.48%, the authority gets 100% subsidy on all such overpayments;
- above 0.48% and up to 0.54%, the authority gets 40% subsidy on all such overpayments;
- above 0.54%, the authority gets 0% subsidy on all such overpayments.

24.17　The percentages (0.48% and 0.54%) are known as the 'lower threshold' and the 'higher threshold'. Reaching either threshold has a big impact on the authority's subsidy, as illustrated in the example. Reaching the lower threshold in a year is a horrible shock for an authority and it will often do all it can to avoid this, let alone getting anywhere near to the higher one – but see paragraph 24.30.

24.18　The DWP advises that an overpayment that arises as a result of administrative delay is always recoverable because it is not due to official error (A24/2008 para. 36). Authority error overpayments may also be recoverable if certain conditions are met (para. 18.14). In either case, the authority keeps any amount actually recovered (and keeps the subsidy too).

Example: Subsidy for authority error and administrative delay overpayments

An authority's annual expenditure on correctly paid HB and CTB in 2012-13 is £10,000,000.

So its 'lower threshold' is £48,000 for that year.
And its 'higher threshold' is £54,000 for that year.

If the total authority error and administrative delay overpayments in that year are £45,000, the authority gets subsidy of 100% of £45,000, which is £45,000.

If the total authority error and administrative delay overpayments in that year are £50,000, the authority gets subsidy of 40% of £50,000, which is £20,000.

If the total authority error and administrative delay overpayments in that year are £55,000, the authority gets subsidy of 0% of £55,000, which is NIL.

Departmental error overpayments

24.19   A 'departmental error overpayment' means an overpayment caused by a mistake made, whether in the form of an act or omission:

- by an officer of the DWP or of HM Revenue and Customs, acting as such, or a person providing services to that department or to HM Revenue and Customs; or
- in a decision of a First-tier Tribunal or an Upper Tribunal.

But an overpayment does not count as a 'departmental error overpayment' in either of the above cases if the claimant, a person acting on the claimant's behalf, or any other person to whom the payment is made, caused or materially contributed to that mistake.

24.20   Although there is no legal requirement to check with the DWP or HM Revenue and Customs that they consider the error is theirs, many authorities consider this is wise except in the most obvious of circumstances.

24.21   The authority receives subsidy equal to 100% of the amount of departmental error overpayments.

24.22   When a departmental error overpayment is recoverable (para. 18.14), the authority keeps any amount actually recovered – but (unlike all other cases) it has to return the subsidy. To put it another way, the authority receives subsidy equal to:

- 100% of the departmental error overpayments it identifies in a year;
- minus 100% of the departmental error overpayments it recovers in a year.

Some authorities might see this as incentive to never attempt to recover such overpayments – but see paragraph 24.30.

Claimant error/fraud overpayments

24.23   A 'claimant error overpayment' means an overpayment caused by the claimant, or someone acting on their behalf, failing to provide information they are required to provide. It also includes an overpayment caused by a third party such as a landlord or agent.

24.24   A 'fraud overpayment' means an overpayment where the claimant has:

- been found guilty of an offence, whether under a statute or otherwise; or
- made an admission under caution of deception or fraud for the purpose of obtaining benefit; or
- agreed to pay a penalty as an alternative to prosecution (para. 18.69), and that agreement has not been withdrawn.

24.25   Claimant error and fraud overpayments are combined for subsidy purposes. The authority gets 40% subsidy of the combined amount.

24.19-22   SI 1998/562 art 18(4)

24.23-26   SI 1998/562 art 18(4A)-(5A)

24.26　A claimant error/fraud overpayment is recoverable (para. 18.11). The authority keeps any amount actually recovered (and keeps the subsidy too).

Technical overpayments

24.27　Technical overpayments can only occur when:

- CTB was awarded up to the end of March 2013 for a future period to a claimant's council tax account; or

- HB is awarded (as a rent rebate) for a future period to a council tenant's rent account.

In those cases, a 'technical overpayment' means an overpayment which arises after that award, because of a change of circumstances or for some other reason. But it only includes the period from the Monday after the change was disclosed to the authority, or after the authority became aware of the overpayment. (General advice is in circular HB/CTB A24/2010.) The authority receives no subsidy for technical error overpayments. However, technical overpayments are recoverable (para. 18.12), and the authority keeps any amount it recovers.

Overpayments of payments on account

24.28　Overpayments of payments on account (para. 16.22) qualify for 100% subsidy, but only to the extent that they are not recovered (circular HB/CTB A14/2010).

Duplicate payments

24.29　Duplicate payments qualify for subsidy of 25%. A 'duplicate payment' occurs when a second instrument of payment is issued because the first was, or was alleged to have been, lost, stolen or not received.

Overpayments subsidy incentives and auditor certification

24.30　The overpayments subsidy arrangements described above can act, at least in part, as an incentive to authorities – sometimes to recover overpayments they have identified and sometimes not. Also, it has to be said, they could act as an incentive to authorities to close their eyes to having made an overpayment in the first place, or to categorise it in such a way that it receives a more favourable amount of subsidy. To counteract this, the authority's external auditors are instructed that 'testing of overpayments needs to provide assurance that overpayments are correctly classified and fairly stated, recognising that there is a subsidy incentive to misclassify overpayments, for example, to code a technical overpayment (nil subsidy) as an eligible overpayment (40% subsidy) or, at or near one of the LA error overpayment thresholds, not to code a local authority error at all' (Audit Commission, Certification Instruction BEN01 (06-07) para. 35).

24.27-28　SI 1998/562 art 18(7)

Limitations on eligible rent

LHA and local reference rent cases

24.31 The subsidy rules play no part in limiting eligible rent in these two types of case (described in chapters 9 and 10). Instead, limitations on eligible rent are imposed by a combination of:

* the local housing allowance (LHA) and local reference rent determinations themselves; and
* the over-riding power to restrict eligible rents (paras. 9.68 and 10.18).

24.32 However there is a subsidy limitation – for local reference rent cases only – which applies if:

* the authority is required to apply for a rent officer determination in a particular case during a year;
* but fails to do so before the date its final subsidy claim has to be submitted for that year.

In that situation, no subsidy is awarded for any of the HB awarded for that case. Several authorities have lost a significant amount of subsidy due to a failure to refer relevant cases to the Rent Service (see *R (Isle of Anglesey County Council) v Secretary of State for Work and Pensions* and *R (London Borough of Lambeth) v Secretary of State for Work and Pensions*).

Exempt accommodation cases

24.33 In 'exempt accommodation' cases (paras. 9.4-6), if the landlord is a registered housing association and the authority accepts the rent is reasonable (para. 7.13) there is no requirement to refer to the rent officer and so the authority receives full subsidy (and there is no restriction on the eligible rent). In any other exempt accommodation case (including if the authority considers the rent to be reasonable), the rent officer's figures are used in the calculation of subsidy (para. 24.34) even though they are not binding in the assessment of the eligible rent (para. 9.26).

24.34 If the authority has to set an eligible rent higher than the rent officer's significantly high rent or exceptionally high rent figure (paras. 9.59, 9.61):

* because of the protections for people who could formerly afford their accommodation and for bereavement (paras. 8.52-59 and 9.20), the authority gets 100% subsidy on the whole eligible rent;
* because the claimant falls into a vulnerable group (over state pension credit age, or with one or more children, or incapable of work: para. 9.21) and there is nowhere cheaper the claimant could reasonably be expected to

---

24.31 SI 1998/562 art 13

24.32 SI 1998/562 sch 4 para 6

24.33 HB 14(2)(b), sch 2 paras 3-12; HB60+ 14(2)(b), sch 2 paras 3-12

move to (paras. 9.22-23), the authority gets 100% subsidy up to the rent officer's figure, and 40% subsidy on the remainder;

- because there is no cheaper suitable alternative accommodation with which to make a comparison (para. 9.17-19), the authority gets 100% subsidy up to the rent officer's figure, and no subsidy on the remainder.

Housing association tenants

24.35   Except for exempt accommodation cases (para. 24.33) the subsidy rules do not limit eligible rent for tenants of registered providers of social housing (housing associations). But if the authority considers that the dwelling is unreasonably large or the rent is unreasonably high the case is referred to the rent officer and the local reference rent rules apply (para. 7.11).

Council tenants

24.36   The subsidy rules do not limit eligible rent for tenants of the authority itself (rent rebate cases), except that no subsidy is payable on any HB attributable to the following circumstances. For fuller details (and exceptions) see the Subsidy Guidance Manual (para. 24.7).

- The 'rent rebate subsidy limitation scheme' applies in England and Wales only. If an authority increases its tenants' rents by more than its central government guideline rent increase, no subsidy is payable on the HB attributable to the excess (DWP circulars S2/2012 and S3/2013).

- The 'disproportionate rent increase rule' applies in Wales and Scotland only. If an authority increases rents to its tenants on HB more than it increases its other rents, subsidy on the difference is restricted.

- Limitations on 'modular improvement schemes' apply throughout Great Britain. If an authority offers its tenants the right to select optional services, no subsidy is payable on the amount of HB attributable to these.

- Limitations on 'rent payment incentive schemes' apply throughout Great Britain. If an authority makes payments (in cash or kind) to reward tenants for paying their rent on time, the total value of such payments is deducted from the amount of subsidy paid to the authority.

Temporary accommodation for homeless people

24.37   The DWP intends to 'reform' arrangements to support people living in temporary accommodation but as at April 2013 HB subsidy for all temporary accommodation cases continues to be paid on the basis of the arrangements introduced in April 2011 (circular G10/2012 para. 14-18 – see also Annex A). These rules apply to the calculation of subsidy on HB for claimants living in certain types of temporary or short-term accommodation (table 24.1) provided

---

24.34   SI 1998/562 sch 4 paras 7, 10

24.36   SI 1998/562 art 15, 15A, 19, 20A, sch 4A

by an authority, or by a registered housing association following an arrangement with an authority, to meet a duty to the homeless under specific legislation. The relevant legislation is:

+ Part 7 of the Housing Act 1996; or

+ Part 2 of the Housing (Scotland) Act 1987; or

+ Part 3 of the Housing Act 1985 (which is now repealed but still applicable for applications made before 20th January 1997!).

24.38 The rules are described in detail in DWP Circulars S1/2011 and S5/2011. They do not apply to supported housing that is 'exempt accommodation'. Subsidy in such cases is calculated as set out in paras. 24.33-34.

24.39 The subsidy payable in the cases identified in this section is an amount equivalent to the lowest of:

+ the claimant's weekly HB entitlement;

+ the maximum weekly subsidy amount (table 24.1) ; or

+ the upper cap limit of £500 (where the accommodation is in one of seven London Broad Rental Market Areas i.e. Central, Inner East, Inner North, Inner South East, Inner South West, Inner West, and Outer South West) or £375 elsewhere

24.40 Licensed accommodation is accommodation which the authority has a right to use under an agreement, other than a lease, with a third party. For the purposes of this subsidy arrangement accommodation is not self-contained if the claimant has to share a kitchen, bathroom or toilet with another household.

24.41 Board and lodging accommodation is accommodation:

+ where the charge is inclusive of the provision of at least some cooked or prepared meals which are both cooked or prepared and consumed in that accommodation or associated premises; or

+ accommodation provided in a hotel, guest house, lodging house or similar establishment.

It excludes accommodation in a residential care home, nursing home or a hostel (paras. 2.23 and 9.45).

24.42 The DWP has told authorities that the use of the January 2011 LHA rates continues in 2013-14 (G10/2012 para 18 and S1/2011 para 3). The LHA used is the one applicable to the broad rental market area in which the accommodation is situated. In deciding the appropriate January 2011 LHA rate the maximum rate is the five bedroom rate. And in deciding the number of bedrooms where the total number of rooms suitable for living in and bedrooms in the property is

---

24.37-39   SI 1998/562 art 17,17A,17B,17C

24.40   SI 1998/562 art 17,17A,17B,17C

24.41   SI 1998/562 art 11(1)

24.42   SI 1998/562 art 17,17A,17B,17C

between two and five at least one of those rooms is treated as a room suitable for living in. For example, in accommodation with five rooms the maximum appropriate LHA rate for subsidy purposes is the four bedroom LHA because one of the rooms in the accommodation must be treated as a room suitable for living in. Where the total number of rooms suitable for living in and bedrooms is six or more then at least two of those rooms must be treated as rooms suitable for living in. So in the case of accommodation with seven rooms, the maximum appropriate LHA rate for subsidy purposes is the five bedroom LHA because two of the rooms must be treated as rooms suitable for living in.

Table 24.1: The maximum weekly subsidy for different types of temporary or short-term accommodation

Type of accommodation	Maximum weekly subsidy
LA or HA licensed accommodation (non-self-contained); and LA or HA board and lodging accommodation	• The January 2011 LHA for one-bedroom (self-contained) accommodation.
LA leased accommodation (non-self-contained) • in England held outside the LA's housing revenue account on a lease not exceeding 10 years; or • in Scotland or Wales all non-self-contained LA leased accommodation. HA (non-self-contained) leased or owned accommodation	• 90% of the January 2011 one-bedroom LHA rate for self-contained accommodation; plus • £40 if the placing LA is in London, or £60 elsewhere (as a contribution towards management costs).
LA or HA licensed accommodation (self-contained) LA leased accommodation (self-contained) • in England held outside the LA's housing revenue account on a lease not exceeding 10 years or • in Scotland and Wales all such LA leased accommodation). HA (self-contained) leased or owned accommodation	• 90% of the appropriate January 2011 LHA figure (based on the number of bedrooms and the location of the property); plus • £40 if the placing LA is in London or £60 elsewhere (as a contribution towards management costs).

Note: The January 2011 figures continue to be used: para. 24.42.

Example of reduced subsidy available on rent rebates awarded on short-term leased accommodation

An authority outside London houses a family in a short-term leased three-bedroomed house in London. The authority accounts for the property outside its housing revenue account.

The January 2011 LHA for the property (not the number of occupiers in the claimant's household) is £180 a week.

The extra management cost element for an authority outside London is £60 a week. Note the £60 a week management costs element applies although the property is in London (it is the location of the placing authority that determines the amount).

The claimant's HB entitlement is £260 a week.

Subsidy is calculated as follows:

90% of the LHA (£180)	=	£162
The management element	=	£60
£162 + £60	=	£222

Subsidy of £222 a week is claimed (90% LHA + £60 is less than the claimant's HB entitlement of £260 a week). The HB paid that is above the £222 figure (£38) attracts nil subsidy.

Benefit administration subsidy

Subsidy to help with on-going administrative costs

24.43 The DWP pays subsidy to authorities towards their administration costs via a 'cash-limited specific grant'. For 2010-11 the total amount of administration subsidy allocated for all authorities was £515.4 million (HB/CTB S6/2009); for 2011-12 it was £488.4 million (HB/CTB S5/2010), a reduction; and for 2012-13 it is £464.7 million (HB/CTB S9/2011) – a further reduction. While CTR support from April 2013 is the responsibility of the Department for Communities and Local Government (DCLG) and the Scottish and Welsh Governments, the DWP has agreed to maintain administrative subsidy at comparative levels to 2012-13 to limit disruption to local authority finances (S5/2012 para 2). For 2013-14 the total distributed amount of administration subsidy is £444m (S5/2012 para 4).

Subsidy to help with 'one-off' costs

24.44 The DWP also pays subsidy to authorities to help with the introduction of various new schemes and unforeseen events. Recent examples (with totals for all authorities) are: £22 million in 2013-14 to assist authorities with the additional

T 24.1 SI 1998/562 art 17,17A,17B,17C

administrative costs associated with the economic downturn (HB/CTB S5/2012 – see S9/2011, S5/2010, S6/2009 and S2/2009 for the additional subsidy awarded for this reason in previous years).

Other grants towards expenditure

24.45   The following items of local authority expenditure (paras. 24.46-49) are not part of the subsidy scheme but are partly reimbursed through a separate system of grants.

Local schemes for war pensioners

24.46   Local schemes for war disablement and bereavement pensions allow authorities to disregard all of these, or at least more than £10 per week (paras. 13.59 and 23.17).

24.47   Benefit expenditure attributable to a local scheme does not qualify for subsidy (and does not count as part of the benefit correctly paid: para. 24.10). Instead, the authority receives an addition of 0.2% to its annual subsidy up to the value of 75% of the cost of the scheme to the authority.

Discretionary housing payments (DHPs)

24.48   No HB subsidy is paid towards DHPs because they are not a form of HB (paras. 23.2-16). The DWP sets an annual limit on each authority's DHP expenditure and partly reimburses this expenditure through a system of grants. The financial arrangements are set out in the Discretionary Housing Payments (Grants) Order SI 2001/2340. Each authority's grant entitlement and annual DHP expenditure limit for 2013-14 is set out in Appendix A of DWP Circular S1/2013 (Revised).

24.49   The authority's annual DHP limit is set at 2.5 times its grant entitlement. Prior to 2011-12 the national annual financial limit on DHP expenditure had been set at £50m towards which the DWP contributed £20m. This was distributed among authorities on the basis of their past DHP expenditure. In 2011-12 the figures were increased to £75 million and £30 million (S2/2011 para. 4) and in 2012-13 to £150m and £60m. For 2013-14 the figures are £387.5m and £155m. The purpose of the additional money is to provide authorities with more flexibility to help claimants who face a shortfall in rent and may need to move because of the reductions in HB entitlement arising from the LHA reforms, the social sector size criteria and the benefit cap. The increases have been allocated between authorities as described in S1/2013, paras 3-9. There is no requirement that authorities spend up to their limit. Indeed, in the past a number of authorities have spent less on DHPs than even the amount they would be directly paid back by the DWP. Authorities must make their grant claim by 31st May each year. Claims for grants do not need to be audited.

24.46   AA s.140B(4A)(a), SI 1998/562 sch 1

24.48-49   s.70 CPSA, SI 2001/2340

Money for CTR expenditure

24.50   Responsibility for supporting CTR expenditure lies with the CLG and the Scottish and Welsh Governments. The introduction of CTR is accompanied by:

◆   a 10% reduction in central funding against forecast subsidised CTB expenditure for 2013-14; and

◆   a change from demand led to fixed budget controlled funding.

This is expected to result in savings for the UK Government of £470 million [www]. On 16th October 2012 the Government announced transitional funding for English local authorities of £100m to 'support them in developing well-designed council tax support schemes and maintaining positive incentives to work' [www]. For the central support available to help with administrative costs, see para. 24.43.

Wales

24.51   In January 2013, the Welsh Government announced that it would provide an extra £22 million to cover the shortfall in funding in 2013-14. This additional funding allowed it to increase the initially proposed maximum level of support from 90% to 100% [www].

Scotland

24.52   So that those previously getting CTB were protected from the 10% cut in funding the Scottish Government and COSLA agreed to cover this £40 million in 2013-14, the Scottish Government providing £23 million and COSLA £17 million.

24.50   www.gov.uk/government/uploads/system/uploads/attachment_data/file/8358/2146648.pdf
www.gov.uk/government/news/government-gives-out-transition-funding-for-council-tax-support

24.51   wales.gov.uk/about/cabinet/cabinetstatements/2013/counciltaxsupport/

24.52   www.scotland.gov.uk/News/Releases/2012/04/counciltax19042012

25 Support for mortgage interest

25.1 This chapter sets out the rules for help with mortgage interest or similar costs that are excluded from the HB scheme (paras 2.14-26). Help with these costs is available through JSA(IB)/ESA(IR)/IS/guarantee credit which are paid by the DWP.

25.2 This chapter covers:

* common rules and differences from the HB scheme and terminology used in this chapter;
* the basic eligibility rules for JSA(IB)/ESA(IR)/IS/guarantee credit and how housing costs are included as part of these benefits;
* waiting periods and time limiting rules;
* which kinds of housing costs are eligible for help;
* how help with housing costs is calculated;
* other matters, such as making claims, administration, payment and appeals.

25.3 There are many complicated transitional rules for help with mortgage interest for certain older claims. This chapter describes the rules only for new claims made on or after 1st October 2010. Certain other housing costs apart from mortgage interest are also payable through JSA(IB)/ESA(IR)/IS/guarantee credit (such as rent for Crown tenants) but are not fully described in this chapter.

25.4 The rules described in this chapter stand alone and are not part of the HB scheme. In some cases the rules are identical to HB and reference is made to these as and when they arise.

Terminology and common rules with HB

25.5 Help with housing costs such as mortgage interest are paid as part of JSA(IB)/ESA(IR)/IS/guarantee credit – in this chapter we also refer to these as qualifying benefits. Although help with housing costs is an integral part of each of these benefits, the rules for each type of claim are similar enough to be referred to generically (in much the same way that there are many rules common to HB and CTR). Any differences in each of the passport benefits are identified as they arise.

What is this type of support called?

25.6 Although a number of different types of housing costs are eligible for help, in the vast majority of cases the claimant receives help with mortgage interest on their home loan. Because there are many common rules (para. 25.5) and most claimants receive help with mortgage interest, this type of housing cost support is generally referred to as Support for Mortgage Interest (SMI) regardless of the type of housing cost covered – and this is the term we use in this chapter.

Differences from and similarities to the HB scheme

25.7   There are many features of the SMI scheme that are similar – or even identical to – the HB scheme, such as the method of assessment of most sources of income. But there are many differences too. It is beyond the scope of this guide to describe them all in detail but the main differences are set out in the next paragraph and described further in this chapter.

25.8   The main differences from the HB scheme are:

♦ administration and assessment is by the DWP rather by the local authority/ NIHE;

♦ eligible housing costs (together with any personal allowances and additional amounts) form part of the overall applicable amount;

♦ no support is payable if the claimant's assessed income and capital exceeds their applicable amount;

♦ there is no upper capital limit for pension credit claims;

♦ there are other numerous small differences in the assessment of income and capital and the applicable amount;

♦ for working age claims, support is only available if the claimant is out of work;

♦ for most working age claimants there is a waiting period at the start of the claim during which benefit is not payable;

♦ for JSA claimants, SMI is time limited (i.e. all support ends after a set time period).

25.9   In addition, unlike HB cases for tenants in low cost housing (chapter 7), but more like LHA tenants (chapter 8), eligible housing costs in mortgage interest cases are based on a standard rate, rather than what the home owner actually pays and are also subject to an overall limit. As in the HB scheme, not all housing costs are eligible so the amount of SMI payable may not reflect what the occupier pays.

Eligibility for SMI qualifying benefits

25.10   To be entitled to SMI the claimant must be in receipt of a qualifying benefit – or would be once their housing costs have been included. The qualifying benefits are JSA(IB), ESA(IR), IS and guarantee credit. Therefore, to be entitled to SMI the claimant must meet the qualifying rules for the particular benefit they are claiming.

Basic qualifying rules for JSA/ESA/IS/guarantee credit

25.11 It is beyond the scope of this guide to describe in full the qualifying rules for each of these passport benefits. The basic rule is that the claimant's income and capital must be low enough (paras. 25.17-21) and either:

- the claimant (or their partner if they have one) must have attained state pension credit age (para. 1.20); or
- in the case of a claimant (and their partner if they have one) who is/are under state pension credit age:
  - the claimant (or their partner) must not be in remunerative work (para. 25.13); and
  - they must be in one of the qualifying groups entitled to claim JSA, ESA or IS.

Note that certain claimants who meet these basic conditions are nevertheless excluded from entitlement (para. 25.12).

25.12 The two main groups of claimants excluded from IS/JSA/ESA are working age students and certain migrants and recent arrivals in the UK: the rules are similar to those that apply to HB but there are some differences (chapters 20-22)

25.13 In the case of the claimant, remunerative work has the same meaning as it does for HB (para. 6.22), or in the case of the claimant's partner the same meaning except that the minimum number of hours worked is 24 instead of 16.

Who is entitled to JSA and ESA?

25.14 To qualify for JSA the claimant (and in some cases both the claimant and their partner) must meet the labour market conditions. Broadly these are that they must be 'available for work' and 'actively seeking work' and not be disqualified (for example if they gave up a job without good reason). To qualify for ESA the claimant must be accepted by the DWP as being incapable of work (para. 12.24).

Who is entitled to Income Support?

25.15 Income Support is a residual benefit for those people who, in most cases, are capable of work (with some exceptions) but who are not expected to meet the labour market conditions for JSA. A claimant is entitled to income support if he or she is:

- entitled to statutory sick pay;
- a lone parent with a youngest child aged under 5;
- not a member of a couple and fostering a child aged under 16;
- pregnant and either incapable of work due to the pregnancy or there are 11 weeks or less before the baby is due;
- a woman who has given birth to a baby not more than 15 weeks ago;
- a person aged under 19 (in some cases aged under 21) in non-advanced

full-time education who has no-one acting as parent for them or who, in certain circumstances, is unable to live with their parents;

◆ a carer entitled to carer's allowance, or caring for a person who has claimed attendance allowance or disability living allowance in the last 26 weeks;

◆ a refugee learning English (in certain circumstances);

◆ a person subject to immigration control but whose funds have been temporarily disrupted (para. 20.28);

◆ a prisoner on remand or awaiting sentence (only eligible for the housing costs element of IS);

◆ a juror or witness required to attend court or a tribunal.

This is not an exhaustive list: there are other less common categories, including certain other sick or disabled people who would have met the qualifying conditions prior to April 2011 (i.e. transitional cases).

How to start a claim for JSA/ESA/IS/guarantee credit

25.16   Most claims for qualifying benefits are started by a telephone call to the national number: 0800 055 6688 for JSA/ESA/IS; 0800 99 1234 for pension credit. Claims for JSA/ESA/IS can also be started online [www]. In Northern Ireland, claims for these benefits must be made in writing at the local Social Security Agency office.

Assessing income and applicable amounts

What are the capital limits and how is capital assessed?

25.17   To be entitled to JSA/ESA/IS the claimant's capital must not exceed the upper capital limit. If the claimant's capital exceeds the lower capital limit but not the upper limit a tariff income applies. The upper and lower limits and tariff income are the same as for working age HB claims (paras. 13.13-14).

25.18   There is no upper capital limit for pension credit claims but if the claimant's capital exceeds the lower capital limit a tariff income applies. The lower limit and tariff income are the same as for pension age HB claims (paras. 13.13-14). Capital is assessed in a similar way to HB (chapter 13) although there are some differences.

How is income assessed?

25.19   Income is assessed in a similar way to HB (chapters 13-15) – although there are some differences. The main ones are identified in table 25.1.

26.16   www.dwp.gov.uk/eservice

Table 25.1: Assessment of income – main variations from HB

This table sets out the main variations in the assessment of income and capital from the rules as set out in the rest of this guide. Except where otherwise stated, rules that apply to working age claims apply to IS/JSA/ESA and pension age claims to pension credit.

Earned income

* Self-employed earnings are averaged over one year or a more appropriate period. Reasonable expenses include debts.

Earnings disregards

* There is no child care disregard or additional disregard (paras. 14.17 and 14.30). The lone parent disregard is £20 (IS/JSA/PC). For ESA, the main disregard is £20 (work as a councillor, partner works part-time or in one of the special occupations (para. 14.38), and some other rare cases) but the higher £99.50 disregard may apply if the claimant is in permitted work. For pension age claims there is no access to the £20 disregard through either long-term incapacity or limited capability for work (i.e. national insurance credit cases).

Income from social security benefits and tax credits

* For working age claims only, statutory sick pay, statutory maternity pay, etc (para. 14.50 and table 14.2) count as unearned income and therefore do not attract an earnings disregard. Arrears of any benefits only count from the moment they are paid for the same length of time as the period they cover. For pension age claims (including pension age claims for JSA/IS) the rules are the same as for HB.

* Child tax credit is disregarded in full. There is no carry over of any unused earnings disregard to working tax credit (para. 13.47).

* Only £10 is disregarded from widowed parent's allowance (para. 13.56).

Other income

* Maintenance for an adult counts in full.

* Payments made by a mortgage protection policy to cover costs not covered by SMI are ignored completely.

What is a low income and how much is the award?

25.20   The claimant's assessed income is compared with their applicable amount to determine whether or not they are entitled to benefit. The applicable amount is calculated in a similar way to HB (chapter 12) – but with the following important differences:

- there are no personal allowances or additional amounts payable in respect of any child, and there is no family premium (this is because children are covered by child tax credits which are not counted as income);
- the only premiums payable are the carer and severe disability premiums together with any additional amounts identified in table 25.2 for JSA/ESA/IS claims;
- in cases where the claimant (or their partner if they have one) has attained state pension credit age (para. 1.20), the personal allowance is always the same rate, £145.40 for a single person, £225.05 for a couple for 2013-14 (strictly speaking for JSA/ESA/IS claims the applicable amount comprises the appropriate working age personal allowance rate plus a pensioner premium but the result is the same);
- the claimant's eligible housing costs form part of the overall applicable amount for the appropriate benefit (in other words, the amount is added to any personal allowance and additional amounts);
- deductions are made from the eligible housing costs in respect of any non-dependant; the same rules apply as for HB including cases where no deduction is made (para. 6.18). The rates of deduction are the same as for HB in table 6.4 except where the non-dependant is on ESA in which case:
  - for IS, JSA and pension credit: if the non-dependant is under 25 and on any kind of ESA no deduction is made except where it is ESA(IR) paid with a work related activity or support component;
  - for ESA: if the non-dependant is on ESA(IR) no deduction is made except where it is paid with a work-related activity or support component.

25.21 The rules about converting an amount of income for a particular period into a weekly amount are the same as for HB (para. 6.49) except that payments received on a yearly basis are always divided by 52 (i.e. including working age claims).

Table 25.2: Additional amounts in JSA/ESA/IS

This table sets out the additional premiums and components payable in the calculation of the applicable amount for JSA/ESA/IS (in addition to those set out in paragraph 25.20). The weekly rates (table 12.1) and qualification rules are the same as in chapter 12.

Income support and income-based JSA

- Disability premium
- Enhanced disability premium (adults only)

> **Income-related ESA**
>
> + Work related activity component*
> + Support component*
> + Enhanced disability premium (adults only)
>
> *Except for pension age ESA claims

Deciding which period a payment belongs to

25.22 The rules about deciding which weeks a particular source of income belongs to are broadly the same as for HB (para. 13.24) but there are some differences. Payments are generally treated as paid on the first day in the benefit week in which it is due, or the date it was due if this was before the date of the claim.

25.23 The benefit week is the seven days ending on the pay day for JSA, or the day before pay day for IS and ESA(IR). For pension credit the benefit week is the seven days ending on the day on which pension credit is paid if it is paid in arrears, or starting on that day if it is paid in advance. The pay day for DWP benefits is determined by the last two digits of the claimant's national insurance number as follows (although there are some exceptions for older claims):

+ 00 to 19 – Monday
+ 20 to 39 – Tuesday
+ 40 to 59 – Wednesday
+ 60 to 79 – Thursday
+ 80 to 99 – Friday

The amount of JSA/ESA/IS/guarantee credit payable

25.24 The amount of the JSA/ESA/IS/guarantee credit award is simply the claimant's applicable amount less their assessed income. If the assessed income is equal to or exceeds the applicable amount there is no entitlement. Note that in some cases the claimant only qualifies for an award which is less than their eligible housing costs (i.e. if their income exceeds their basic personal allowance and premiums).

Differences in overall support levels between HB/CTR and SMI

25.25 In some cases even a small award can make a significant difference: the payment acts as a passport benefit for CTR and the amount of CTR could be significantly more as a result because:

+ eligible housing costs are not taken into account in CTR and so they do not reduce the claimant's excess income (see example);
+ in pension credit cases where the claimant has more than £16,000 capital,

entitlement to CTR would otherwise be zero.

However, because of major differences between the HB/CTR and SMI calculations, the total amount of support from all benefits varies according to the household type. Broadly, households with children (especially larger families) can often still qualify for maximum CTR even when their SMI has expired, because the child personal allowance and family premium more than offset the increased income from child tax credits (child benefit being disregarded): see example.

Minimum benefit

25.26 The minimum payment for JSA/IS/PC is 10p per week – although in the case of pension credit if the amount is less than 10p the claimant will have underlying entitlement and so will be entitled to maximum CTR.

Examples: Calculation of SMI and effect on CTR

Maximum housing costs covered: ESA(IR)

A claimant and his wife are homeowners. They are buying their home with a mortgage of £71,625; the current interest rate on their home loan is 4%. The SMI standard interest rate is 3.63%. Nine months ago the claimant gave up work due to very severe health problems. He has claimed ESA and is entitled to contribution-based ESA of £106.50 per week which includes the support component. His wife has no income. Their council tax is £1405.25 per year (payable over 365 days in 2013-14) = £26.95 per week.

Their income for ESA(IR) is £105.05.

Their applicable amount for ESA(IR) is calculated as follows:

Personal allowance:	£112.55
Enhanced disability premium	£21.75
Support component	£34.80
Eligible housing costs	£50.00
Total:	£219.10

The housing costs element is calculated as follows:
£71,625 x 3.63% = £2599.99 a year. Divide by 52 = £50.00 (rounded).

They are entitled to £219.10 minus £106.50, which is £112.60 ESA(IR) which includes £50.00 per week housing costs element which is paid direct to their lender. Because they get ESA(IR) they are entitled to maximum CTR = £26.95 per week

Partial housing costs covered: ESA(IR)

The claimant's wife starts part-time work for 12 hours per week at £10.35 per hour (too low for tax and national insurance).

Their assessed income is now £106.50 + £124.20 − £20.00 disregard = £210.70.

They are now entitled to £8.40 ESA(IR) and even though it is solely on account of their housing costs they are still entitled to maximum CTR of £26.95 per week.

Ineligible for SMI

The claimant's wife increases her hours from 12 to 13 per week. Their assessed income is now £106.50 + £114.55 = £221.05. Their income exceeds their ESA(IR) applicable amount by £1.95 so they do not qualify for any ESA(IR) including help with their housing costs.

Their applicable amount for CTR is the same as for ESA(IR) except that it would not include a housing costs element so would be £169.10.

For CTR the excess income is not £1.95 but £51.95 so their CTR will be £26.95 − £51.95 x 0.2 = £16.56.

Note, however, that if they had one child they would still be entitled to maximum CTR because their CTR applicable amount would include a child personal allowance and family premium (£65.62 + £17.40) which would more than offset the £1.95 plus the maximum possible income from child tax credit of £62.62 which counts as income for CTR (para. 13.46).

Eligible housing costs

25.27   There are three main types of eligible housing costs. These are:

*   interest on a loan taken out to purchase a home (e.g. a mortgage or other loan);
*   interest on a loan taken out to pay for certain repairs and improvements on a home;
*   other miscellaneous housing costs not eligible for HB (ground rent, rent for Crown tenants, certain service charges payable by leaseholders etc).

The following paragraphs (paras. 25.28-37) set out these rules in more detail.

Eligible mortgages and home loans

25.28   A loan is eligible if:

*   it is taken out to buy the home the claimant and their family normally occupy (para. 3.3) or to increase their share of the equity (such as buying out the share of a former partner or a sitting tenant or purchasing the freehold of a leasehold property);
*   it is taken out to repay a loan that would have qualified as above.

However, even if the loan meets these requirements, all or part of it may be disqualified (para. 25.29).

Disqualified home loans

25.29   Even for a qualifying loan, the following are not eligible:

* any part of the loan above and beyond what was taken out with the immediate intention to buy the home (e.g. any part of the loan that was used to purchase other goods, or to repay accrued interest); or

* any loan that was taken out or increased while on benefit (para. 25.30) though in this case there are some exceptions (paras. 25.32-34).

Taking out or increasing a loan while on benefit

25.30   Loans taken out or increased during a period on benefit are disqualified if they were taken out during a 'relevant period'. A relevant period is a period:

* when the claimant was entitled to JSA(IB)/ESA(IR)/IS/pension credit;

* when the claimant was living as a member of a family of someone who was entitled to JSA(IB)/ESA(IR)/IS/pension credit; or

* up to 26 weeks between two of either of the above periods.

The above rules are modified according to the type of qualifying benefit claimed, as described in the next paragraph.

25.31   The rules about a relevant period are modified as follows:

* for IS claims it does not include periods on pension credit;

* for JSA(IB) claims it does not include periods on pension credit, but it does additionally include periods on JSA(C) (although DWP guidance suggests it should not when the claimant or the family member they were living with was entitled to JSA(C));

* for ESA and PC, 'member of family' means partner only.

However, some new or increased loans are eligible even if they are taken out during a relevant period.

Eligible new or increased loans

25.32   Certain new or increased loans are eligible for assistance even if they were taken out during a relevant period (para. 25.30). A new or increased loan is eligible if:

* it was used to buy a home that is better suited than the former home to the special needs of a disabled person. The disabled person need not be a member of the family but they must qualify as disabled at the time the loan was taken out;

* it was used to buy a new home because it was needed to provide separate sleeping accommodation for two children of the opposite sex aged 10 or over but under 20 who are members of the family;

* it was used to pay off the original loan (e.g. a remortgage);

◆ the original home was sold to pay off an eligible loan and the loan was taken out to buy a new home even if this was some time later; or

◆ it was used to buy a home and in the week before, that person was in receipt of HB or 'other' housing costs on their JSA/ESA/IS/pension credit that were not for a home loan (e.g. ground rent, etc);

In the case of the last three items, although the loan will be eligible, the amount of SMI payable will be subject to a maximum limit (paras. 25.33-34).

25.33 If a loan was taken out to repay the original loan or after the original home was sold then any increase in housing costs is not eligible. For example, if the original loan was for £50,000 and the new loan is for £60,000 then only £50,000 of housing costs are eligible.

25.34 If the loan was taken out immediately after being on HB or help with other housing costs, then to begin with the amount of help is limited to the amount of support the claimant was previously receiving (e.g. if they were getting £50.00 HB per week this would be the maximum help they could receive). However, if the standard rate of interest increases they become entitled to a proportional increase.

Loans for repairs and improvements

25.35 Help with housing costs is not available to cover the cost of repairs or improvements (i.e. any bills for those repairs), nor for variable service charges in leasehold accommodation.

25.36 However, a loan taken out to cover the cost of certain qualifying repairs and improvements (including a loan to cover a leasehold variable service charge) is eligible. Any type of borrowing is eligible but it must be used to pay for the repairs or improvements within six months of being taken out.

Qualifying repairs and improvements

25.37 A loan for repairs and improvements only qualifies if the works undertaken are to maintain the fitness of the home for human habitation and it is for one or more of the qualifying repairs or improvements in table 25.3. If a loan is also for other repairs and improvements not listed in table 25.3, only the proportion that is in respect of qualifying items will be covered.

Table 25.3: Qualifying repairs and improvements

The following items are qualifying repairs and improvements for the purpose of paragraph 25.37.

Measures to provide

◆ a bath, shower, wash basin, sink or lavatory, and necessary associated plumbing, including the provision of hot water not connected to a central heating system;

- ventilation and natural lighting;
- drainage facilities;
- facilities for preparing and cooking food;
- insulation;
- electrical lighting and sockets;
- storage facilities for fuel or refuse.

Repairs

- to an existing heating system;
- of unsafe structural defects.

Other measures

- damp proofing measures;
- the first two bullet points in paragraph 25.32.

The amount of eligible housing costs

25.38   Once any eligible housing costs have been identified the amount of weekly eligible housing cost is calculated and is included as part of the claimant's applicable amount. The calculation is as follows:

- Any eligible loans are added together (e.g. separate loans for home purchase and eligible repair).
- A restriction is made if the total exceeds the upper limit (para. 25.39) or if the costs are otherwise considered excessive. If there is more than one eligible loan and together they exceed the upper limit the restriction is applied proportionately to each.
- Each loan (or each restricted loan) is multiplied by the standard rate of interest and then divided by 52 to give a weekly amount and, if there is more than one, they are added together.
- From this total the appropriate deductions are made for any non-dependants (para. 25.20).
- The resulting figure is included in the calculation of the applicable amount (i.e. added to any personal allowance and additional amounts) (para. 25.20).

The upper limit on eligible loans

25.39   The upper limit on eligible loans is:

- £200,000 in the case of claims for JSA, ESA or IS.
- £100,000 in the case of claims for pension credit.

Prior to 4th January 2009, the upper limit was also £100,000 for JSA/ESA/IS and the rules are expected to revert to this position from April 2015 (as announced in the 2012 Autumn Statement).

Restrictions on excessive costs

25.40   Whether or not the upper limit applies, housing costs can be restricted if:

+ the dwelling occupied is larger than is reasonably required by the claimant and their family (including any foster children) and any non-dependants, having regard to any suitable alternative accommodation;

+ the area in which the home is located is more expensive than other areas in which suitable alternative accommodation exists; or

+ the amount that is eligible is higher than the cost of suitable alternative accommodation in the area.

In reaching a decision about any of the above, the area over which a comparison is made should not be too wide and the capital value of the property must be ignored. In certain circumstances a restriction cannot be applied or must be delayed (paras 25.41-43).

25.41   A restriction must not be made even if suitable accommodation is available, if it is not reasonable to expect the household to look for other accommodation. In deciding this, similar considerations apply as in HB exempt accommodation cases (paras. 9.22-23).

25.42   If it is reasonable to expect the household to move, housing costs cannot be restricted for the first 26 weeks if the claimant was able to meet the repayments when they were entered into. This can be extended for a further 26 weeks if the claimant is using their 'best endeavours' to find somewhere cheaper. In calculating the 26 week period, the 12 week linking rule applies (para. 25.53).

25.43   If a restriction applies, any excess over the amount of loan the claimant would need to obtain suitable alternative accommodation is disallowed. So if the equity in the home is sufficient to buy a new home outright, there may be no entitlement.

The standard rate of interest

25.44   As at 1st April 2011 the standard rate of interest is 3.63% (and has been since 1st October 2010). The standard rate of interest is set in line with the Bank of England average mortgage rate. Future changes will only be triggered when the standard rate and the Bank of England published average mortgage rate differ by at least 0.5%.

25.45   The standard rate applies to all claims covered in this chapter, regardless of whether the actual interest rate paid by the claimant is more or less. If the standard rate is more than the actual interest rate, any excess payments are nonetheless credited to their mortgage account.

Waiting periods and time limit of awards

What is the waiting period and when does it apply?

25.46   For JSA/ESA/IS claimants only, even if there is entitlement to help with housing costs then these costs will not normally be met during the first 13 weeks of the claim (known as the 'waiting period').

25.47   Prior to 4th January 2009, the waiting period was 39 weeks (in certain rarer cases 26 weeks). It is expected that the waiting period will revert to the pre-January 2009 position from April 2015 (as announced in the 2012 Autumn Statement).

25.48   The waiting period does not apply if:

* the claimant's partner has attained the qualifying age for state pension credit or, for JSA only, the claimant has;
* the claim is for payments as a Crown tenant, under a co-ownership scheme or for a tent.

25.49   If the claimant is entitled to JSA/ESA/IS during their waiting period without their housing costs included (i.e. because their income is less than their personal allowance plus any premiums and components) then the award is superseded when the waiting period ends.

25.50   If the claimant is only entitled to JSA/ESA/IS once their housing costs are included then the 'nil award' can be superseded at the end of the waiting period and housing costs included provided they are treated as entitled, otherwise a fresh claim will be required. The claimant will be treated as entitled if throughout that period they were entitled to contribution-based JSA/ESA, incapacity benefit or statutory sick pay or awarded national insurance credits for sickness or unemployment – but there are other exceptions also.

What is time limiting and when does it apply?

25.51   For JSA claimants only there is a maximum limit on the length of an award of housing costs. This limit does not apply to claims for JSA which began before 4th January 2009 including any linked claim (para. 25.53) where different rules apply.

25.52   The maximum length of a housing costs award for a claim that began on or after 4th January 2009 is 104 weeks. In calculating the 104 week limit the 13 week waiting period is ignored. This means that the earliest date a housing costs award could be terminated by time limiting was 3rd April 2011. Any two or more periods that are linked to an award that first began on or after 4th January 2009 will count as a continuous award (see example).

> **Example: Time limiting and linking rules**
>
> Joese Baker claims JSA on 8th April 2013. She is awarded JSA(IB) initially without any housing costs element during her waiting period. After 13 weeks her award is superseded and maximum housing costs are included. After a further 39 weeks her JSA ends when she takes a full time temporary job for eight weeks. When the job ends she reclaims JSA and is awarded a housing costs element immediately because the claims are linked. However, for the same reason she is only entitled to a housing costs element for a further 65 weeks (104 – 39 = 65).

Linking rules

25.53 Except in the case of state pension credit, breaks in entitlement to a qualifying benefit can affect entitlement to SMI (para. 25.46 and 25.51). However, there are special rules (known as the 'linking rules') by which the claimant can be treated as being continuously entitled to benefit. There are two main linking rules (and a number of less common linking rules) that affect the payment of SMI. These are:

- where a repeat claim for a qualifying benefit is made within 12 weeks (104 weeks in the case of a 'welfare to work beneficiary': table 12.2), the claims are linked and treated as being continuous (whether or not the waiting period had been served when the earlier claim ended);

- where SMI was previously in payment and the claimant or their partner moves into work (or certain kinds of training such as New Deal) a 52 week linking period applies, and they are treated as having been continuously in receipt of SMI from day one of any repeat claim.

25.54 In addition to the main rules above, periods on JSA(IB), ESA(IR) and IS are treated as entitlement to each other and so, for example, if the claimant moved off ESA(IR) and onto JSA(IB), any time spent on ESA(IR) would be treated as time on JSA(IB). Likewise, any periods spent on these benefits by the claimant's partner or former partner will also count. There are a number of other more obscure linking rules which are beyond the scope of this guide.

25.55 These linking rules have two main effects on the payment and qualification for SMI:

- any linked claims count as time served towards the waiting period and if SMI was already in payment at the end of the previous claim SMI can be paid immediately; and

- they prevent jobseekers who have exhausted their 104 weeks' entitlement from re-qualifying for a further 104 weeks' entitlement by simply breaking their claim and reclaiming.

25.56 The only way that a JSA claimant can re-qualify for SMI once their 104 week entitlement has been exhausted is to:

- leave JSA for over 12 weeks if they are not working, or over 52 weeks if they move off benefit and into work; and

- make a new claim for JSA and serve a new 13 week waiting period for SMI.

If both of these conditions are met a new 104 week period of entitlement can begin.

Other matters

Moving home, two homes and temporary absence

25.57   As with HB, there are rules about when the claimant can claim for two homes, during a temporary absence and during a move into a new home:

- SMI is payable for certain people during a move into a new home. The rules are the same as in paragraphs 3.18-23 (waiting for disability adaptation or social fund payment, and leaving care);

- SMI is payable for up to 13 or in some cases 52 weeks during a temporary absence. The rules are the same as in paragraphs 3.32-35 and table 3.1;

- SMI is payable in some cases on two homes. The rules are same as in paragraphs 3.8-17 and 3.27-29 (unavoidable liability, fear of violence, students and trainees).

Mortgage interest run-on

25.58   The mortgage interest run-on scheme mirrors extended payments for HB/CTB for JSA/ESA/IS claimants (paras. 17.42-49). The qualifying conditions are the same as for 'qualifying income related benefits' in table 17.7 except that, instead of the fourth bullet, any qualifying benefit received must have included an amount for housing costs within the applicable amount. Payment is automatic provided the claimant notifies the DWP/Jobcentre Plus office that they have started full-time work.

25.59   If the claimant is entitled, payment is for four weeks. The amount payable is the same as any housing costs previously paid with the claim, or the amount of JSA/ESA/IS payable if lower (i.e. if the claimant's income exceeded their basic personal allowance plus premiums and components). Payment is an award of the relevant benefit, so maximum CTR is payable.

Payment

25.60   Payment of SMI is normally direct to the lender – except in the case of an SMI run-on which is made to the claimant. Lenders can opt out of the direct payment scheme but this is virtually unheard of.

Appeals

25.61   Most decisions about SMI can be revised or appealed to a tribunal. The rules about appeals – including the basic one month time limit – are similar to those described in chapter 19, although there are many minor differences that are beyond the scope of this guide.

Appendix 1: HB/CTR legislation

HB: England, Wales and Scotland

Main primary legislation (Acts)

The Social Security Contributions and Benefits Act 1992

The Social Security Administration Act 1992

The Child Support, Pensions and Social Security Act 2000

The Welfare Reform Act 2007

The Welfare Reform Act 2012

Main secondary legislation (Regulations and Orders)

SI 2006/213	The Housing Benefit Regulations 2006
SI 2006/214	The Housing Benefit (Persons who have attained the qualifying age for state pension credit) Regulations 2006
SI 2006/217	The Housing Benefit and Council Tax Benefit (Consequential Provisions) Regulations 2006
SI 1997/1984	The Rent Officers (Housing Benefit Functions) Order
SI 1997/1995	The Rent Officers (Housing Benefit Functions) (Scotland) Order
SI 2001/1002	The Housing Benefit and Council Tax Benefit (Decisions and Appeals) Regulations
SI 2001/1167	The Discretionary Financial Assistance Regulations

Recent secondary legislation (Regulations and Orders)

The following is a list of amendments made (or otherwise relevant) to the main regulations made since 1st April 2012. This list is up to date as at 1st April 2013.

SI 2012/646	The Rent Officers (Housing Benefit Functions) Amendment Order 2012
SI 2012/646	The Rent Officers (Housing Benefit Functions) (Amendment) Order 2012
SI 2012/1267	The Social Security and Child Support (Supersession of Appeal Decisions) Regulations 2012
SI 2012/1483	The Social Security (Information-sharing in relation to Welfare Services etc) Regulations 2012

SI 2012/1651	The Welfare Reform Act 2012 (Commencement No. 3, Savings Provision) Order 2012
SI 2012/2994	The Benefit Cap (Housing Benefit) Regulations 2012
SI 2012/2587	The Social Security (Habitual Residence) (Amendment) Regulations 2012
2012/2946	The Welfare Reform Act 2012 (Commencement No. 5) Order 2012
SI 2012/3040	The Housing Benefit (Amendment) Regulations 2012
SI 2012/3090	The Welfare Reform Act 2012 (Commencement No.6 and Savings Provisions) Order 2012
SI 2013/41	The Social Security (Information-sharing in relation to Welfare Services etc) (Amendment) Regulations 2013
SI 2013/178	The Welfare Reform Act 2012 (Commencement No.7) Order 2013
SI 2013/384	The Social Security (Overpayments and Recovery) Regulations 2013
SI 2013/443	The Social Security (Miscellaneous Amendments) Regulations 2013
SI 2013/454	The Social Security (Information-sharing in relation to Welfare Services etc) Amendment and Prescribed Bodies Regulations 2013
SI 2013/477	The Tribunal Procedure (Amendment) Rules 2013
SI 2013/546	The Benefit Cap (Housing Benefit) (Amendment) Regulations 2013
SI 2013/574	The Social Security Benefits Up-rating Order 2013
SI 2013/665	The Housing Benefit (Amendment) Regulations 2013
SI 2013/666	The Rent Officers (Housing Benefit Functions) Amendment Order 2013
SI 2013/1036	The Transfer of Tribunal Functions Order 2013

HB: Northern Ireland

Main primary legislation (Acts and Acts of Northern Ireland Assembly)

The Social Security Contributions and Benefits (Northern Ireland) Act 1992

The Social Security Administration (Northern Ireland) Act 1992

The Child Support, Pensions and Social Security Act (Northern Ireland) 2000

The Welfare Reform Act (Northern Ireland) 2007

Main secondary legislation (Statutory Rules and Orders)

NISR 2006/405 The Housing Benefit Regulations (Northern Ireland) 2006

NISR 2006/406 The Housing Benefit (Persons who have attained the qualifying age for state pension credit) Regulations (Northern Ireland) 2006

NISR 2006/407 The Housing Benefit (Consequential Provisions) Regulations (Northern Ireland) 2006

NISR 2008/100 The Housing Benefit (Executive Determinations) Regulations (Northern Ireland) 2008

NISR 2001/213 The Housing Benefit (Decisions and Appeals) Regulations (Northern Ireland) 2001

NISR 2001/216 The Discretionary Financial Assistance Regulations (Northern Ireland) 2001

Recent secondary legislation (Statutory Rules and Orders)

The following is a list of amendments made (or otherwise relevant) to the main regulations made since 1st April 2012. This list is up to date as at 1st April 2013.

NISR 2012/157 The Housing Benefit (Executive Determinations) (Amendment) Regulations (Northern Ireland) 2012

HB Northern Ireland

NISR 2012/380 The Social Security (Habitual Residence) (Amendment) Regulations (Northern Ireland) 2012

NISR 2013/67 The Social Security (Miscellaneous Amendments) Regulations (Northern Ireland) 2013

NISR 2013/69 The Social Security Benefits Up-rating Order (Northern Ireland) 2013

CTR: England, Wales and Scotland

Main primary legislation (Acts)

The Local Government Finance Act 1992

The Local Government Finance Act 2012

Main secondary legislation (Regulations)

SI 2012/2885 The Council Tax Reduction Schemes (Prescribed Requirements) (England) Regulations 2012

SI 2012/2886 The Council Tax Reduction Schemes (Default Scheme) (England) Regulations 2012

SSI 2012/303 The Council Tax Reduction (Scotland) Regulations 2012

SSI 2012/319 The Council Tax Reduction (State Pension Credit) (Scotland) Regulations 2012

SI 2012/3144 The Council Tax Reduction Schemes and Prescribed Requirements (Wales) Regulations 2012

SI 2012/3145 The Council Tax Reduction Schemes (Default Scheme) (Wales) Regulations 2012

Amending secondary legislation (Regulations)

The following is a list of amendments made (or otherwise relevant to) the main regulations. The list is up to date at 1st April 2013.

SI 2013/215   The Council Tax Reduction Schemes (Transitional Provision) (England) Regulations 2013

SI 2013/358   The Welfare Reform Act 2012 (Commencement No.8 and Savings and Transitional Provisions) Order 2013

SI 2013/458   The Council Tax Benefit Abolition (Consequential Provision) Regulations 2013

SI 2013/465   The Valuation Tribunal for England (Council Tax and Rating Appeals) (Procedure) (Amendment) Regulations 2013

SI 2013/501   The Council Tax Reduction Schemes (Detection of Fraud and Enforcement) (England) Regulations 2013

SI 2013/502   The Local Authorities (Contracting Out of Tax Billing, Collection and Enforcement Functions) (Amendment) (England) Order 2013

SSI 2013/48   The Council Tax Reduction (Scotland) Amendment Regulations 2013

SSI 2013/49   The Council Tax Reduction (State Pension Credit) (Scotland) Amendment Regulations 2013

SSI 2013/87   The Council Tax (Information-sharing in relation to Council Tax Reduction) (Scotland) Regulations 2013

2013/63   The Council Tax (Demand Notices) (Wales) (Amendment) Regulations 2013

2013/111   The Council Tax Reduction Schemes (Transitional Provisions) (Wales) Regulations 2013

2013/112   The Council Tax Reduction Schemes (Prescribed Requirements and Default Scheme) (Wales) (Amendment) Regulations 2013

2013/588   The Council Tax Reduction Schemes (Detection of Fraud and Enforcement) (Wales) Regulations 2013

2013/695   The Local Authorities (Contracting Out of Tax Billing, Collection and Enforcement Functions) (Amendment) (Wales) Order 2013

2013/ 547   The Valuation Tribunal for Wales (Wales) (Amendment) Regulations 2013

Appendix 2: Table of cases cited in guide

The following table lists all cases cited in the guide in the order they appear. It does not include cases which are subsequently reported by the social security commissioners. Where possible the table indicates where a free on-line case transcript can be accessed. Where none is available both free and on-line the table provides a reference for a recognised published law report.

Upper Tribunal decisions cited in this guide are not included in this table. For further details on the status of Upper Tribunal decisions and how to access them, see paras. 1.46-47 and 19.67-68.

Para	Case
2.29	*R v Poole BC HBRB ex p Ross* 05/05/95 QBD 28 HLR 351
T 2.3	*R v Sutton BC HBRB ex p Partridge* 04/11/94 QBD 28 HLR 315
T 2.3	*R v Sheffield CC HBRB ex p Smith* 08/12/94 QBD 28 HLR 36
T 2.4	*R v Sutton LBC ex p Keegan* 15/05/92 QBD 27 HLR 92
T 2.4	*R v Solihull MBC HBRB ex p Simpson* 03/12/93 QBD 26 HLR 370
T 2.4	*R v Manchester CC ex p Baragrove Properties* 15/03/91 QBD 23 HLR 337
2.43	*R (Painter) v Carmarthenshire CC HBRB* 04/05/01 HC [2001] EWHC (Admin) 308 Admin *www.bailii.org/ew/cases/EWHC/Admin/2001/ 308.html 308*
2.45	*Secretary of State for Social Security v Tucker* 08/11/01 CA [2001] EWCA Civ 1646 *www.bailii.org/ew/cases/EWCA/Civ/2001/1646.html*
2.55	*The Governors of Peabody Donation Fund v Higgins* 20/06/83 CA [1983] 1 WLR 1091
3.36	*R v Penwith DC HBRB ex p Burt* 26/02/90 QBD 22 HLR 292
4.14	*Crake and Butterworth v Supplementary Benefit Commission* 21/07/80 QBD [1982] 1 All ER 498
4.32	*R v Swale BC HBRB ex p Marchant* 9/11/99 CA 32 HLR 856 *www.casetrack.com* Subscriber site case reference: QBCOF 1999/0071/C
4.45	*Kadhim v Brent LBC HBRB* 20/12/00 CA [2000] EWCA Civ 344 *www.bailii.org/ew/cases/EWCA/Civ/2000/344.html*
5.13	*R v Liverpool CC ex p Johnson (No 2)* 31/10/94 QBD [1995] COD 200

Para	Case
5.17	*R v Penwith DC ex p Menear* 11/10/91 QBD 24 HLR 115
5.17	*R v South Ribble HBRB ex p Hamilton* 24/01/00 CA [2000] EWCA Civ 518 *www.bailii.org/ew/cases/EWCA/Civ/2000/518.html*
7.19	*Burton v Camden LBC* 17/12/97 CA 30 HLR 991
7.20	*R (Laali) v Westminster CC HBRB* 08/12/00 QBD *www.casetrack.com* Subscriber site case reference: CO/1845/2000
7.21	*R (Naghshbandi) v Camden LBC HBRB* 19/07/02 CA [2002] EWCA Civ 1038 *www.bailii.org/ew/cases/EWCA/Civ/2002/1038.html*
8.7	*R (Laali) v Westminster CC* See 7.20 above
8.21	*R v Swale BC HBRB ex p Marchant* See 4.32 above
8.46	*R (Heffernan) v the Rent Service* 30/07/08 HL [2008] UKHL 58 *www.publications.parliament.uk/pa/ld200708/ldjudgmt/jd080730/ heffer-1.htm*
T 9.1	*R(S) v Walsall MBC* 19/12/08 HC (Admin) [2008] EWHC (Admin) 3097 and 03/09/09 HC (Admin) [2009] EWHC (Admin) 2221 *www.bailii.org/ew/cases/RWHC/Admin/2008/3097.html www.bailii.org/ew/cases/RWHC/Admin/2009/2221.html*
9.16	*R v Swale BC HBRB ex p Marchant* See 4.32 above
9.18	*R v Beverley DC HBRB ex p Hare* 21/02/95 QBD 27 HLR 637
9.18	*Malcolm v Tweedale HBRB* 06/08/91 CS 1994 SLT 1212
9.19	*Malcolm v Tweedale HBRB* See 9.18 above
9.22	*R v East Devon DC HBRB ex p Gibson* 10/03/93 CA 25 HLR 487
9.23	*R v Sefton MBC ex p Cunningham* 22/05/91 QBD 23 HLR 534
9.24	*R v Westminster CC HBRB ex p Mehanne* 08/03/01 HL [2001] UKHL 11 33 HLR 46 *www.publications.parliament.uk/pa/ld200001/ldjudgmt/ jd010308/mehann-1.htm*
9.24	*R v Beverley DC HBRB ex p Hare* See 9.18 above
9.24	*R v Brent LBC ex p Connery* 20/10/89 QBD 22 HLR 40
9.27	*R v Brent LBC ex p Connery* See 9.24 above
9.64	*Heffernan (No.2) v The Rent Service* 01/12/09 HC (Admin) [2009] EWHC (Admin) 3539 *www.bailii.org/ew/cases/EWHC/Admin/2009/3539.html*

Para	Case
T 13.2	*Minter v Hull City Council* 13/10/2011 CA [2011] EWCA Civ 1155 *www.bailii.org/ew/cases/EWCA/Civ/2011/1155.html*
13.131	*R v Doncaster MBC & Another ex p Boulton* 11/12/92 QBD 25 HLR 195
16.6	*R v Liverpool CC ex p Johnson (No 1)* 23/06/94 QBD unreported
16.7	*Waveney DC v Jones* 01/12/99 CA 33 HLR 3 *www.casetrack.com* Subscriber site case reference CCRTF 1998/1488/B2
16.20	*R (Spiropoulos) v Brighton and Hove CC* 06/02/07 QBD [2007] EWHC 342 (Admin) *www.bailii.org/ew/cases/EWHC/Admin/2007/342.html*
16.24	*R v Haringey LBC ex p Ayub* 13/04/92 QBD 25 HLR 566
16.38	*R v Haringey LBC ex p Ayub* See 16.24 above
16.71	*Bessa Plus PLC v Lancaster* 17/03/97 CA *www.bailii.org/ew/cases/EWCA/Civ/1997/1260.html*
18.8	*R v Cambridge CC HBRB ex p Sier* 08/10/01 CA [2001] EWCA Civ 1523 *www.bailii.org/ew/cases/EWCA/Civ/2001/1523.html*
T 18.1	*R v Cambridge CC HBRB ex p Sier* See 18.8 above
T 18.2	*R v Liverpool CC ex p Griffiths* 14/03/90 QBD 22 HLR 312
18.27	*R v South Hams DC ex p Ash* 10/05/99 QBD [1999] EWHC Admin 418 *www.bailii.org/ew/cases/EWHC/Admin/1999/418.html*
18.33	*Warwick DC v Freeman* 31/10/94 CA 27 HLR 616
T 18.5	*R v Haringey LBC ex p Ayub* See 16.24 above
18.51	*Secretary of State for Work and Pensions v Payne* 14/12/11 [2011] UKSC 60 *www.supremecourt.gov.uk/decided-cases/docs/UKSC_2011_0007_Judgment.pdf*
18.61	*Ghassemain v Kensington and Chelsea LBC* 09/06/09 CA [2009] EWCA Civ 743 *www.bailii.org/ew/cases/EWCA/Civ/2009/743.html*
T 18.6	*R v Thanet DC ex p Warren Court Hotels Ltd* 06/04/00 QBD 33 HLR 32 *www.casetrack.com* Subscriber site case reference CO/523/1999
T 18.6	*Warwick DC v Freeman* See 18.33 above
T 18.6	*Godwin v Rossendale BC* 03/05/02 CA [2002] EWCA Civ 726 *www.bailii.org/ew/cases/EWCA/Civ/2002/726.html*
T 18.6	*Haringey LBC v Awaritefe* 26/05/99 CA [1999] EWCA Civ 1491 *www.bailii.org/ew/cases/EWCA/Civ/1999/1491.html*
T 18.6	*Waveney DC v Jones* See 16.7 above

Para	Case

T 18.6 *Norwich CC v Stringer* 03/05/00 CA 33 HLR 15 *www.casetrack.com*
Subscriber site case reference FC2 99/7400/B2

19.99 *R (Cumpsty) v The Rent Service* 08/11/02 HC [2002] EWHC 2526 Admin
Admin *www.bailii.org/ew/cases/EWHC/Admin/2002/2526.html*

20.51 *Swaddling v Chief Adjudication Officer* 25/02/99 ECJ C-90/97
*http://europa.eu.int/smartapi/cgi/sga_doc?smartapi!celexapi!prod!
CELEXnumdoc&lg=EN&numdoc=61997J0090&model=guichett*

21.17 *De Brito v Home Secretary* 30/05/12 CA [2012] EWCA Civ 709
www.bailii.org/ew/cases/EWCA/Civ/2012/709.htm

21.17 *JS v Secretary of State for Work and Pensions*
13/07/11 CA [2011] EWCA Civ 806
www.bailii.org/ew/cases/EWCA/Civ/2011/806.html

21.20 *McCarthy v Secretary of State for the Home Department*
25/11/10 ECJ C-434/09
*http://eur-lex.europa.eu/LexUriServ/LexUriServ.do?uri=
CELEX:62009CC0434:EN:HTML*

21.25 *Harrow LBC v Ibrahim and Secretary of State for the Home Department*
23/02/10 ECJ C-310/08) *http://eur-lex.europa.eu/LexUriServ/
LexUriServ.do?uri=CELEX:62008J0310:EN:HTML*

21.25 *Teixeira v Lambeth LBC and Secretary of State for the Home Department*
23/02/10 ECJ C-480/08 *http://eur-lex.europa.eu/LexUriServ/
LexUriServ.do?uri=CELEX:62008J0480:EN:HTML*

22.10 *O'Connor v Chief Adjudication Officer* 03/03/99 CA [1999] EWCA
Civ 884 *www.bailii.org/ew/cases/EWCA/Civ/1999/884.html*

23.12 *R (Gargett) v Lambeth LBC* 18/12/08 CA [2008] EWCA Civ 1450
www.bailii.org/ew/cases/EWCA/Civ/2008/1450.htm

24.11 *R v Brent LBC ex p Connery* See 9.42 above

24.32 *R (Isle of Angelsey County Council) v Secretary of State for Work and
Pensions* 30/10/03 QBD [2003] EWHC 2518 Admin
www.bailii.org/ew/cases/EWHC/Admin/2003/2518.html

24.32 *R (Lambeth LBC) v Secretary of State for Work and Pensions* 20/04/05
QBD [2005] EWHC 637 Admin
www.bailii.org/ew/cases/EWHC/Admin/2005/637.html

Abbreviations used in this appendix

AC	Appeal Cases, published by The Incorporated Council of Law Reporting for England and Wales, London
All ER	All England Law Reports, published by Butterworths
BC	Borough Council
CA	Court of Appeal for England and Wales
CC	City Council
ChD	High Court (England and Wales) Chancery Division
COD	Crown Office Digest, published by Sweet & Maxwell
CS	Court of Session, Scotland
DC	District Council
ECJ	European Court of Justice
EWCA Civ	Court of Appeal Civil Division for England & Wales (neutral citation)
EWCA Crim	Court of Appeal Criminal Division for England & Wales (neutral citation)
EWHC Admin	High Court for England & Wales, Administrative Court (neutral citation)
HBRB	Housing Benefit Review Board
HC (Admin)	High Court for England and Wales, Administrative Court
HL	House of Lords
HLR	Housing Law Reports, published by Sweet & Maxwell
LBC	London Borough Council
MBC	Metropolitan Borough Council
QBD	High Court (England and Wales) Queens Bench Division
SLT	Scots Law Times, published by W. Green, Edinburgh
UKHL	House of Lords, UK case (neutral citation)
UKSC	Supreme Court (neutral citation)
WLR	Weekly Law Reports, published by The Incorporated Council of Law Reporting for England and Wales, London

Appendix 3: Overview of welfare benefits

This appendix lists the welfare benefits which have particular relevance in the assessment of HB and CTR. It is for ready reference, uses simplified descriptions, and does not attempt to give all the rules. In this table:

✔ **'Passport benefits'** are the ones which mean the claimant gets maximum ('full') HB/CTR.
'Income-related' means entitlement to the benefit depends on income (as well as other things).
'Contributory' means the person must have paid enough national insurance contributions at some point.

Housing benefit and **Council tax rebate**
These help lower income people with rent, rates and council tax.
Income-related; non-contributory.

Universal credit
The benefit for working age claimants (paras. 1.21-22) being introduced from this year onwards (para. 23.33).
Income-related; non-contributory.

✔ **Pension credit guarantee credit** (or just Guarantee credit)
The last resort benefit for pension age claimants (paras. 1.21-22).
Income-related; non-contributory.

Pension credit savings credit (or just Savings credit)
The benefit that says 'thank you' to 65+s who made some provision (not too much) for retirement.
Income-related; non-contributory.

✔ **Income-based jobseeker's allowance**
The last resort benefit for working age claimants (paras. 1.21-22).
who are expected to work so have to sign on.
Income-related; non-contributory.

Contribution-based jobseeker's allowance
The benefit (which lasts for up to 26 weeks) for people who are expected to work so have to sign on.
Not income-related; contributory.

✔ **Income-related employment and support allowance**
The last resort benefit for working age claimants (paras. 1.21-22)
who cannot work because they have a limited capability to do so. Starts
with **assessment phase** for 13 weeks, followed by **main phase.**
Income-related; non-contributory.

Contributory employment and support allowance
The benefit for people who cannot work because they have a limited
capability to do so. Starts with **assessment phase** for 13 weeks, followed
by **main phase.**
Not income-related; contributory.

✔ **Income support**
The last resort benefit for working age claimants (paras. 1.21-22) who do
not qualify for JSA or ESA – for example, lone parents with at least one
child under 5.
Income-related; non-contributory.

Incapacity benefit
This was replaced by ESA for new claimants from 27th October 2008 (and
from October 2010 existing IB recipients are gradually being transferred
onto ESA). It is for people who cannot work because of incapacity.
Not income-related; contributory.

Disability living allowance – has two elements:
• **Care component** is for people needing personal care; awarded at the
  lowest, middle or highest rate.
• **Mobility component** is for people with difficulty walking or who can
  walk but who need supervision to ensure they are safe; awarded at the
  lower or higher rate.
Not income-related; non-contributory.

Attendance allowance
The equivalent of DLA middle or higher rate care component for 65+s.
Not income-related; non-contributory.

Working tax credit and **Child tax credit**
The benefits for lower to middle income people who have at least one child
(CTC) and/or who are in paid work of 16/30 hours per week (WTC).
Income-related; non-contributory.

Carer's allowance
The benefit for people who are prevented from working by caring
responsibilities.
Not income-related – non-contributory (but with maximum earnings limit).

Appendix 4: Selected benefit rates from April 2013

Attendance allowance	£
Higher rate	79.15
Lower rate	53.00

Bereavement benefits	
Widowed parents allowance (standard rate)	108.30
Bereavement allowance (standard rate)	108.30
Reduction in standard rate for each year aged under 55 (approx)	7.58

Child benefit	
Only or older/oldest child	20.30
Each other child	13.40

Carer's allowance	
Claimant	59.75

Disability living allowance	
Care component	
Highest rate	79.15
Middle rate	53.00
Lowest rate	21.00
Mobility component	
Higher rate	55.25
Lower rate	21.00

Employment and support allowance	
Personal allowances	
Under 25/lone parent under 18	56.80
18 or over/under 25 (main phase)	71.70
Couple both under 18 with child	85.80
Couple both over 18	112.55
Components	
Work-related activity	28.45
Support	34.80

£

Guardian's allowance   15.90

Incapacity benefit

Short-term lower rate (under pension age)	76.45
Short-term higher rate (under pension age)	90.50
Long-term rate	101.35
Spouse or adult dependant (where appropriate)	58.85
Increase for age higher rate (under 35)	10.70
Increase for age lower rate (35-44)	6.00

Industrial disablement pension

20% disabled	32.32
For each further 10% disability up to 100%	16.16
100% disabled	161.60

Jobseekers allowance (contribution-based)

Aged under 18 to 24	56.80
Aged 25 or more	71.70

Maternity and paternity pay and allowance

Statutory maternity, paternity and adoption pay	136.78
Maternity allowance	136.78

Retirement pension

Single person (basic rate)	110.15
Couple (basic rate)	176.15

Severe disablement allowance

Basic rate	71.80
Age-related addition	
Higher rate	10.70
Middle rate	6.00
Lower rate	6.00

Statutory sick pay

Standard rate	86.70

For details of other benefit rates from April 2013 (including means-tested benefits, tax credits and war pensions) see Circular A2/2013 (Revised).

Appendix 5: Non-dependant categories

For the following categories of non-dependant, this appendix describes:

* whether there is a non-dependant deduction for them in HB and CTR (paras. 6.18-20, and see para. 6 17 for CTR variations);
* whether they are a 'disregarded person' for second adult rebate purposes – because a disregarded person cannot be a second adult (paras. 6.37-38).

1. People on JSA(IB), ESA(IR) or income support

HB	No non-dependant deduction if aged under 25 – but for ESA(IR) this is true only in their ESA 'assessment phase' (first 13 weeks)
CTR	No non-dependant deduction.
Second adult rebate	Not 'disregarded persons'.

This means anyone receiving JSA(IB), ESA(IR) or income support, including people who would get JSA(IB) or ESA(IR) except that they are currently subject to a sanction or in their 'waiting days' (first three days).

2. People on pension credit

HB and CTR	No non-dependant deduction.
Second adult rebate	Not 'disregarded persons'

This means anyone receiving guarantee credit or savings credit (or both).

3. People under 18

HB and CTR	No non-dependant deduction.
Second adult rebate	'Disregarded persons'.

This means anyone under 18 whether a member of the claimant's family or not.

4. People under 20 for whom child benefit is payable

HB and CTR	No non-dependant deduction.
Second adult rebate	'Disregarded persons'.

This means anyone under 20 for whom someone receives or could receive child benefit – e.g. at school and shortly after leaving school. See also category 7.

5. Full-time students (benefit law definition)

HB	No non-dependant deduction (with exceptions during the summer holidays: table 6.3)
CTR	No non-dependant deduction
Second adult rebate	'Disregarded persons'.

This means:

+ a student in further education (para. 22.19) who is normally expected to undertake more than 16 guided learning hours per week; or
+ a student in higher education (para. 22.19) on a course which is regarded as full-time by the academic establishment and/or the local education authority; or
+ a student on a sandwich course.

6. Students (council tax law definition)

HB	Whether there is a non-dependant deduction depends on whether they fall within category 5.
CTR	No non-dependant deduction
Second adult rebate	'Disregarded persons'.

This means:

+ a student in further or higher education in the UK or EU (para. 22.19) – who is on a course of at least one academic or calendar year's duration, and is normally required to study at least 21 hours per week for at least 24 weeks per year; or
+ a student under 20 in further education in the UK or EU (para. 22.19) – who is on a course of at least three months' duration, and is normally required to study at least 12 hours per week in term times; or
+ a student nurse studying for a first inclusion in parts 1 to 6 or 8 of the nursing register; or
+ a foreign language assistant who is registered with the British Council.

7. Education leavers under 20

HB	A non-dependant deduction applies.
CTR	No non-dependant deduction.
Second adult rebate	'Disregarded persons'.

This only applies from 1st May to 31st October inclusive each year. It means anyone who leaves any of the types of education described in category 6 within that period. It lasts until that person reaches 20 or until 31st October, whichever comes first. See also categories 3 and 4.

8. Youth trainees

HB and CTR   No non-dependant deduction.

Second adult rebate   'Disregarded persons' if aged under 25.

This means people doing youth training funded by the Learning and Skills Council for England or equivalent bodies in Wales and Scotland.

9. Apprentices

HB   A non-dependant deduction applies.

CTR   No non-dependant deduction.

Second adult rebate   'Disregarded persons'.

This means someone who:

- is in employment for the purpose of learning a trade, profession, vocation or similar; and
- is studying for an accredited qualification; and
- is paid no more than £195 per week.

10. Carers for whom the claimant or partner is charged

HB and CTR   No non-dependant deduction.

Second adult rebate   'Disregarded persons' only if they fall within categories 11 or 12.

This means carers caring for the claimant or partner, who are provided by a charitable or voluntary body which charges the claimant or partner for this.

11. Carers of people receiving certain benefits

HB   A non-dependant deduction applies unless they fall within category 10.

CTR   No non-dependant deduction.

Second adult rebate   'Disregarded persons'.

This applies to someone if:

- they are providing care or support for at least 35 hours a week; and
- they reside with the person receiving the care or support; and
- that person is not a child of theirs under 18, nor their partner; and
- that person is entitled to the highest or middle rate of the care component of disability living allowance, or attendance allowance, or equivalent additions to industrial injuries and war pensions.

12. Carers introduced by an official or charitable body

HB   A non-dependant deduction applies unless they fall within category 10.

CTB   No non-dependant deduction.

Second adult rebate   'Disregarded persons'.

This means someone who:

+ is employed by someone to provide them with care or support for at least 24 hours a week; and

+ is paid no more than £44 per week; and

+ resides (for the better performance of the work) in premises provided by or on behalf of that person; and

+ was introduced to them by a local authority, government department or charitable body.

13. People who are 'severely mentally impaired'

HB   A non-dependant deduction applies.

CTB   No non-dependant deduction.

Second adult rebate   'Disregarded persons'.

This means someone who has 'a severe impairment of intelligence and social functioning (however caused) which appears to be permanent'; and has a medical certificate confirming this; and is receiving one or more of the following (or would do so apart from the fact that he or she has reached pension age):

+ the highest or middle rate of the care component of disability living allowance, or attendance allowance or equivalent additions to industrial injuries and war pensions; or

+ incapacity benefit, or severe disablement allowance; or

+ income support or JSA(IB) (or his or her partner is) – but only if it includes a disability premium awarded because of the person's incapacity for work.

14. Members of religious communities

HB   A non-dependant deduction applies.

CTR   No non-dependant deduction.

Second adult rebate   'Disregarded persons'.

This means someone who:

+ is a member of a religious community whose principal occupation is prayer, contemplation, education, the relief of suffering, or any combination of those; and

+ has no income (other than an occupational pension) or capital; and

+ is dependent on the community for his or her material needs.

15. International bodies and visiting forces

HB   A non-dependant deduction applies.

CTR   No non-dependant deduction.

Second adult rebate   'Disregarded persons'.

This means someone who is a member of certain international headquarters and defence organisations and certain visiting forces (plus in some cases their dependants).

16. Non-British spouses and civil partners

HB   A non-dependant deduction applies.

CTR   No non-dependant deduction.

Second adult rebate   'Disregarded persons'.

This means someone who is not permitted to work or claim and is the husband, wife or civil partner of:

+ a student in category 6; or

+ an education leaver in category 7; or

+ a person in category 15.

17. Long-term hospital patients

HB and CTR	No non-dependant deduction.
Second adult rebate	'Disregarded persons'.

This means someone who has been in an NHS hospital for more than 52 weeks (adding together stays in hospital if the break between them is four weeks or less).

18. People in prison or other forms of detention

HB	No non-dependant deduction.
CTR	No non-dependant deduction unless detained only for non-payment of a fine or (in England and Wales) council tax.
Second adult rebate	'Disregarded persons' unless detained only for non-payment of a fine or (in England and Wales) council tax.

This means someone in any kind of detention (whether on bail, on remand or serving a sentence).

19. Absent members of the armed forces

HB	No non-dependant deduction.
CTR	A non-dependant deduction applies (unless they fall within another relevant category).
Second adult rebate	Not 'disregarded persons'.

This means anyone in the armed forces (regular or reserve) who is away on operations.

20. Other people not resident in the dwelling

HB and CTR	No non-dependant deduction.
Second adult rebate	'Disregarded persons'.

This means anyone who is not normally resident in the dwelling including, for example, a visitor or a student returning just for the holidays.

21. Any other non-dependant

HB and CTR	A non-dependant deduction applies.
Second adult rebate	Not 'disregarded persons'.

This means anyone who does not fall into any of the previous categories.

Appendix 6: Rent arrears direct scheme

This appendix describes how the DWP/DSD can pay part of a claimant's JSA, ESA, IS or pension credit to their landlord towards their rent arrears. These are called 'direct payments' or officially 'third party payments'. They are additional to the rules about paying HB to a landlord (paras. 16.31-56). Indeed, they are not HB rules at all, but they so often arise in HB cases that they are included here for reference.

The law is in schedule 9 to the Social Security (Claims and Payments) Regulations SI 1987/1968 (as amended) or in Northern Ireland NISR 1987/465 (as amended). For DWP guidance see GM paras. D1.570-689.

Qualifying conditions for direct payments

The power to make direct payments is discretionary even if all the qualifying conditions are met. The qualifying conditions are that the claimant or their partner must be:

- in receipt of a 'qualifying benefit' (see overleaf); and
- in receipt of HB (or claimed HB in the case of a hostel resident); and
- resident in the property for which the direct payments are to be made; and
- either:
  - they have rent arrears and meet one of the rent arrears conditions (overleaf); or
  - (regardless of whether they have rent arrears or not) they live in a hostel (para. 9.45) for which the overall charge includes payment for one or more of the following services: water; a service charge for fuel; meals; laundry or cleaning (other than communal areas); and the DWP/DSD determines that direct payments should be made.

Qualifying benefits for direct payments

The qualifying benefits from which deductions can be made are:

* income support;
* state pension credit (savings credit or guarantee credit or both);
* income-based jobseeker's allowance;
* income-related employment and support allowance;
* contribution-based jobseekers' allowance if there would be entitlement to income-based jobseekers' allowance but for the fact that contribution-based jobseeker's allowance is being paid at the same rate;
* contribution-based employment and support allowance if there would be entitlement to income-related employment and support allowance but for the fact that contribution-based employment and support allowance is being paid at the same rate.

In addition, in the case where any of the first three qualifying benefits are in payment and the amount is insufficient for deductions to be made, deductions can also be made from any contribution-based jobseekers' allowance, incapacity benefit, retirement pension or severe disablement allowance that they also receive (whether or not it is paid in a combined payment with the qualifying benefit).

What are the rent arrears conditions?

There must be 'rent arrears' of at least four times the gross weekly rent and either:

* the rent arrears have accrued or persisted over a period of at least eight weeks and the landlord requests that deductions are made; or
* the rent arrears have accrued or persisted over a period of less than eight weeks but in the opinion of the DWP/DSD it is in the overriding interests of the family that payments should be made.

In calculating the four weeks' arrears and any period over which those arrears have accrued, any arrears which have arisen due to the tenant's failure to pay a non-dependant charge must be ignored.

What counts as rent and rent arrears?

For these rules 'rent' and 'rent arrears' includes:

* any charge which is covered by HB;

* any water charges or service charges payable with the rent which are ineligible for HB;

* fuel charges included in the rent provided the charge does not vary more than twice a year;

* any other inclusive charge paid with the rent, whether or not it is eligible for HB, except any unpaid non-dependant charge.

Note that because of the requirement for residence (see qualifying conditions) direct payments cannot be made towards former tenant arrears.

Rate of payment

In the case of direct payments for a hostel, the amount of the payment equals whatever amount of the charge is ineligible for HB for water, fuel, etc.

In the case of direct payments for rent arrears the rate of payment is, subject to any maximum amount:

* £3.60 per week (the standard amount), plus, if it applies,

* the weekly charge for any fuel or water charged as part of the rent, provided that the qualifying benefit is at least equal to that charge.

When all of the rent arrears have been cleared, weekly payment of the amount for fuel or water can continue if it is in the 'interests of the family'.

Maximum deductions for rent arrears cases

In the case of direct payments for rent arrears, the rate of deduction from any qualifying benefit is subject to the following rules:

◆ There must be at least 10 pence of any qualifying benefit(s) remaining after any deduction.

◆ If the standard amount together with any ongoing fuel/water exceeds 25% of their qualifying benefit applicable amount (or where child tax credit is payable, 25% of their applicable amount plus child tax credit and child benefit) then the deduction cannot be made without the claimant's consent.

◆ If there are standard deductions for several items such as rent, fuel, water, council tax, child maintenance and fines, the total cannot exceed £10.80.

◆ If there are deductions for various other debts such that the total would reduce the qualifying benefit to less than 10p, then they are paid in the following order of priority:

- 1st   rent arrears;
- 2nd   fuel;
- 3rd   water;
- 4th   council tax;
- 5th   unpaid fines;
- 6th   child support;
- 7th   repayments of a refugee integration loan;
- 8th   loan repayments to certain qualifying affordable credit lenders (e.g. credit unions);
- 9th   tax credit overpayment debts and tax self-assessment debts.

Appendix 7: Qualifying age for state pension credit

Date of birth	Date qualifying age for state pension credit is reached
Before 6th April 1950	On reaching age 60
6th April 1950 to 5th May 1950	6th May 2010
6th May 1950 to 5th June 1950	6th July 2010
6th June 1950 to 5th July 1950	6th September 2010
6th July 1950 to 5th August 1950	6th November 2010
6th August 1950 to 5th September 1950	6th January 2011
6th September 1950 to 5th October 1950	6th March 2011
6th October 1950 to 5th November 1950	6th May 2011
6th November 1950 to 5th December 1950	6th July 2011
6th December 1950 to 5th January 1951	6th September 2011
6th January 1951 to 5th February 1951	6th November 2011
6th February 1951 to 5th March 1951	6th January 2012
6th March 1951 to 5th April 1951	6th March 2012
6th April 1951 to 5th May 1951	6th May 2012
6th May 1951 to 5th June 1951	6th July 2012
6th June 1951 to 5th July 1951	6th September 2012
6th July 1951 to 5th August 1951	6th November 2012
6th August 1951 to 5th September 1951	6th January 2013
6th September 1951 to 5th October 1951	6th March 2013
6th October 1951 to 5th November 1951	6th May 2013
6th November 1951 to 5th December 1951	6th July 2013
6th December 1951 to 5th January 1952	6th September 2013
6th January 1952 to 5th February 1952	6th November 2013
6th February 1952 to 5th March 1952	6th January 2014
6th March 1952 to 5th April 1952	6th March 2014
6th April 1952 to 5th May 1952	6th May 2014
6th May 1952 to 5th June 1952	6th July 2014

App 7   Pensions Act 1995 schedule 4; Pensions Act 2011 s1; SI 1995 No. 3213 (NI 22) schedule 2; Pensions Act (Northern Ireland) 2012 s1

6th June 1952 to 5th July 1952 . . . . .6th September 2014

6th July 1952 to 5th August 1952 . . . . .6th November 2014

6th August 1952 to 5th September 1952 . . . . .6th January 2015

6th September 1952 to 5th October 1952 . . . . .6th March 2015

6th October 1952 to 5th November 1952 . . . . .6th May 2015

6th November 1952 to 5th December 1952 . . . . .6th July 2015

6th December 1952 to 5th January 1953 . . . . .6th September 2015

6th January 1953 to 5th February 1953 . . . . .6th November 2015

6th February 1953 to 5th March 1953 . . . . .6th January 2016

6th March 1953 to 5th April 1953 . . . . .6th March 2016

6th April 1953 to 5th May 1953 . . . . .6th July 2016

6th May 1953 to 5th June 1953 . . . . .6th November 2016

6th June 1953 to 5th July 1953 .6th March 2017

6th July 1953 to 5th August 1953 . . . . .6th July 2017

6th August 1953 to 5th September 1953 . . . . .6th November 2017

6th September 1953 to 5th October 1953 . . . . .6th March 2018

6th October 1953 to 5th November 1953 . . . . .6th July 2018

6th November 1953 to 5th December 1953 . . . . .6th November 2018

6th December 1953 to 5th January 1954 . . . . .6th March 2019

6th January 1954 to 5th February 1954 . . . . .6th May 2019

6th February 1954 to 5th March 1954 . . . . .6th July 2019

6th March 1954 to 5th April 1954 . . . . .6th September 2019

6th April 1954 to 5th May 1954 . . . . .6th November 2019

6th May 1954 to 5th June 1954 . . . . .6th January 2020

6th June 1954 to 5th July 1954 .6th March 2020

6th July 1954 to 5th August 1954 . . . . .6th May 2020

6th August 1954 to 5th September 1954 . . . . .6th July 2020

6th September 1954 to 5th October 1954 . . . . .6th September 2020

6th October 1954 or after . . . . .On reaching age 66

Appendix 8: Equivalent Scottish and Welsh references

This table shows the equivalent references in the footnotes for CTR law in Scotland and Wales. See also key to footnotes at the front of this guide.

'See text' means the equivalent reference is in the footnote for that paragraph (usually because the law is unique to that country). **'Not CTR'** means there is no CTR reference (usually because the law applies to HB only). **'No equiv'** means there is no equivalent law in that country.

Para	Scotland		Wales	
	CTS	**CTS60+**	**CTPW**	**CTRW**
Chapter 1	See text	See text	See text	See text
Chapter 2	See text	See text	See text	See text
3.3-3.30	Not CTR	Not CTR	Not CTR	Not CTR
3.32	5(11)-(17) 14(3)(b),(15)	5(11)-(17),14(3)(b),(15)	24	17
3.34	5(11),(13),(16), 15(3)	5(11),(13),(16), 15(3)	24(2)	17(2)
T3.1	2(1), 5(16), 15(4)	2(1), 5(16), 15(4)	24(3),(6)	17(3),(6)
3.40	5(14),(15), 15(5),(6)	5(14),(15), 15(5),(6)	24(4),(5)	17(4),(5)
3.41	15(4)(a)	15(4)(a)	24(3)(a)	17(3)(a)
3.43		69(6)	sch 13 para 7(6)	113(6)
3.45-50	Not CTR	Not CTR	Not CTR	Not CTR
4.7	2(1)	2(1)	2(1),(4)	2(1),(4)
4.8	2(1)	2(1)	6	6
4.9	2(1)	2(1)	2(1)	2(1)
4.11	2(1)	2(1)	2(1),(4)	2(1),(4)
4.12	2(1)	2(1)	2(1)	2(1)
4.20	2(1),8	2(1),8	5	5
4.21	11(1)	11(1)	8(1)	8(1)
4.24	2(1)	2(1)	2(1)	2(1)
4.25	4	4	2(1),6	2(1),6
4.26	4	4	2(1),6	2(1),6
4.31	10	10	7	7
4.34	11(1)	11(1)	8(1)	8(1)
4.35	11(2),(3)	11(2),(3)	8(2),(3)	8(2),(3)
4.36	11(4)	11(4)	8(4)	8(4)
4.37	11(1)	11(1)	8(1)	8(1)
4.41	3(1),(2)	3(1),(2)	9(1),(2)	9(1),(2)

Para	Scotland CTS	CTS60+	Wales CTPW	CTRW
4.42	3(3)	3(3)	9(3)	9(3)
4.48	3(2)(e)	3(2)(e)	9(2)(e)	9(2)(e)
4.49	sch 4 para 26(2)	2(1)	2(1)	2(1)
4.52	3(2)(e),(3)	3(2)(e),(3)	9(2)(e),(3)	9(2)(e),(3)
4.58	3(2)(f)	3(2)(f)	9(2)(f)	9(2)(f)
5.2	2(1)	2(1)		
5.3	SI 2013/48	72	SI 2013/111	
5.4	82	61	sch 13 para 1(1)	107(1)
5.5		sch 13 para 1(2)-(7)	107(2)-(7)	
5.8	2(1), 83, 84, 91	2(1), 63, 64, 71	sch 12 paras 2,3,12-14	sch 1 paras 2,3,13-14
5.12	87, 88	67, 68	sch 13 para 6	112
5.13	86(1),(4)	66(1),(4)	sch 13 para 5(1),(4),(6)	111(1),(4),(6)
5.15	86(2),(3)	66(2),(3)	sch 13 para 5(5),(7)	111(5),(7)
5.16	No equiv	No equiv	sch 13 para 5(2),(3)	111(2),(3)
5.20	83(1),(6), 84, 91	63(1),(6), 64, 71	sch 12 paras 2,3,13	sch 1 paras 2,3,13
5.22	83(2)-(5), 84(4)-(6)	63(2)-(5), 64(4)-(6)	sch 12 paras 4-7, sch 13 paras 2(3)-(5), 5(4),(6)	108(3)-(5), 111(4)-(6), sch 1paras 4-7
5.24	83, 84	63, 64	sch 13 para 2(3)-(5)	108(3)-(5)
5.25	83(1), 91(4)	63(1), 71(4)	sch 12 paras 3, 13(7)	sch 1 paras 3, 13(7)
5.26	80(1),(2)	58(1),(2)	sch 1 para 39	104
5.28	91(5)	71(5)	sch 12 para 15	sch 1 para 15
5.29	2(1)	2(1)	2(1)	2(1)
5.30	85	65	sch 13 para 2	108
5.31	85(1)(d)	65(1)(d)	sch 13 para 2(f)	108(1)(f)
5.33	85(1)(c)	65(1)(c)	sch 13 para 2(e)	108(1)(e)
5.35	85(1)(a),(2),(9)	65(1)(a),(5)	2(1), sch 13 para 2(a),(c),(2)	108(a),(c), (2),(8)
5.37	85(1)(b)	65(1)(b)	sch 13 para 2(b),(d)	108(1)(b),(d)
5.39	85(1)(e)	65(1)(e)	sch 13 para 2(g)	110(1)(g)
5.41	85(3),(5),(6)	65(2),(3)	sch 13 para 2(6),(7)	108(6),(7)
5.43	See text	See text	See text	See text
5.45	80(1)	58(1)	No equiv	No equiv
5.46	Not CTR	Not CTR	Not CTR	Not CTR
5.47	80(2)	58(2)	No equiv	No equiv
5.54		62	sch 13 para 3	109
5.56	85(7),(8)		sch 13 para 4	110
6.4	66(1)	47(1)	sch 1 para 2(1), sch 6 para 4(1)	27(1)

6.6	14(5)(a),(8)	14(5)(a),(8)	20, 22, sch 1 para 4(2), sch 6 para 6(2)	13, 15, 29(2)
6.7	42	40	28	21
6.9	14(5)(b)	14(5)(b)	21(f), 23(f)	14(f), 16(f)
6.11	14(5)(b),(8)	14(5)(b),(8)	21,23, sch 1 para 4(3), sch 6 para 6(3)	14, 16, 29(3)
6.16	3	3	9	9
6.18	3(2), 67(7),(8)	3(2), 48(6),(8)	9(2), sch 1 para 3(7),(8), sch 6 para 5(7),(8)	9(2), 28(7),(8)
6.19	2(1), 67(6)	2(1), 48(7)	2(1), sch 1 para 3(6), sch 6 para 5(6)	2(1), 28(6)
6.20	67(1),(2)	48(1),(2)	sch 1 para 3(1),(2), sch 6 para 5(1),(2)	28(1),(2)
6.21	67(1)(a)	48(1)(a)	sch 1 para 3(1)(a), sch 6 para 5(1)(a)	28(1)(a)
6.22	6(1),(5)	6(1),(5)	10(1),(5)	10(1),(5)
6.23	6(6)-(8)	6(6)-(8)	10(6)-(8)	10(6)-(8)
6.24	67(1),(2)	48(1),(2)	sch 1 para 3(1),(2), sch 6 para 5(1),(2)	28(1),(2)
6.25	6(4),(5)	6(4),(5)	10(4),(5)	10(4),(5)
6.26	6(3)	6(3)	10(3)	10(3)
6.27	2(1), 67(9)	2(1), 48(9)	2(1), sch 1 para 3(9), sch 6 para 5(9)	2(1), 28(9)
6.28	67(3),(4)	48(3),(4)	sch 1 para 3(3),(4), sch 6 para 5(3),(4)	28(3),(4)
6.29	67(5)	48(5)	sch 1 para 3(5), sch 6 para 3(5)	28(5)
6.30		59(10)-(13)	sch 1 para 40(10)-(12)	105(10)-(12)
6.33	14(6),(7), 79, sch 2 para 4	14(6),(7), 57, sch 5 para 4	No equiv	No equiv
6.34	14(7)(a)	14(7)(a)	No equiv	No equiv
6.35-37	14(3),(6),(7), (8)(c),78(1), sch 2 paras 1,4	14(3),(6),(7), (8)(c),56(1), sch 5 paras 1,4	No equiv	No equiv
6.38	sch 2 paras 2,3	sch 5 paras 2,3	No equiv	No equiv
6.39	78(2),(3)	56(2),(3)	No equiv	No equiv
T 6.5	sch 2 para 1	sch 5 para 1	No equiv	No equiv
6.40	14(9)	14(9)	No equiv	No equiv
6.44	66(1)(b)	47(1)(b)	sch 1 para 2(1)(b), sch 6 para 4(1)(b)	27(1)(b)
6.45	33(1)	31(1)	sch 1 para 11(1), sch 6 para 13(1)	37(1), 47(1)
Chapter 7	Not CTR	Not CTR	Not CTR	Not CTR
Chapter 8	Not CTR	Not CTR	Not CTR	Not CTR
Chapter 9	Not CTR	Not CTR	Not CTR	Not CTR
Chapter 10	See text	See text	See text	See text
Chapter 11	Not CTR	Not CTR	Not CTR	Not CTR

Para	Scotland CTS	CTS60+	Wales CTPW	CTRW
12.4	21, 22	20	sch 1 para 1, sch 6 paras 1,2	23, 24, 25
12.6	23	No equiv	sch 6 para 3	26
12.11	21, sch 1 para 1	20, sch 1 para 2	sch 1 para 1, sch 2 para 1, sch 6 para 1, sch 7 para 1	23, 24, sch 2 para 1, sch 3 para 1
12.13	sch 1 para 3	sch 1 para 3	sch 2 para 2, sch 7 para 3	sch 2 para 2, sch 3 para 3
12.14	sch 1 paras 5-7	sch 1 para 5	sch 2 para 4, sch 7 paras 5-7	sch 2 para 4, sch 3 paras 5-7
12.15	sch 1 para 4	sch 1 para 4	sch 2 para 3, sch 7 para 4	sch 2 para 3, sch 3 para 4
12.17-19	sch 1 paras 18-22	No equiv	sch 3 paras 18-22	sch 1 paras 18-22
12.20	sch 1 para 9	No equiv	sch 7 para 9	sch 3 para 9
12.21-26	sch 1 para 10	No equiv	sch 7 para 10	sch 3 para 10
12.28-30	sch 1 paras 25-29	No equiv	sch 7 paras 25-29	sch 3 paras 25-29
12.31	sch 1 para 13	sch 1 para 9	sch 2 para 8, sch 7 para 13	sch 2 para 8, sch 3 para 13
12.32-34	sch 1 para 12	sch 1 para 8	sch 2 para 7, sch 7 para 12	sch 2 para 7, sch 3 para 12
12.35-38	sch 1 para 11	sch 1 para 7	sch 2 para 6, sch 7 para 11	sch 2 para 6, sch 3 para 11
12.39-40	sch 1 paras 8(2), 14	sch 1 paras 6(2), 10	sch 2 paras 5(2),9, sch 7 paras 8(2), 14	sch 2 paras 5(2),9, sch 3 paras 8(2), 14
12.41				
12.43	sch 1 para 16	sch 1 para 12	sch 2 para 11, sch 7 para 16	sch 2 para 11, sch 3 para 16
12.44	sch 1 para 16	sch 1 para 12	sch 2 para 11, sch 7 para 16	sch 2 para 11, sch 3 para 16
12.46	sch 1 para 15	sch 1 para 11	sch 2 para 10, sch 7 para 15	sch 2 para 10, sch 3 para 15
12.47	sch 1 paras 8,16	sch 1 paras 6,12	sch 2 paras 5,11, sch 7 paras 8,16	sch 2 paras 5,11, sch 3 paras 8,16
12.48	2(1)	2(1)	2(1)	2(1)
12.49-51	sch 1 para 10		sch 7 para 10	sch 3 para 10
12.52	2(1), sch 1 para 8(1)	2(1), sch 1 para 6(1)	2(1), sch 2 para 5(1), sch 7 para 8(1)	2(1), sch 2 para 5(1) sch 3 para 8(1)
12.53	22	sch 1 para 2	sch 2 para 1, sch 6 para 2	25, sch 2 para 1
12.54	2(1), sch 1 paras 10-14	2(1), sch 1 paras 1,7-10	sch 1 para 1(2), sch 2 paras 6-9, sch 6 para 1(2), sch 7 paras 10-14	23(2), 24(2), sch 2 paras 6-9, sch 3 paras 10-14
13.3	sch 3 para 14, sch 4 paras 8,9, sch 5 paras 7,8	24	sch 1 para 6, sch 8 para 14, sch 9 paras 9,10, sch 10 paras 8,9	32, sch 7 paras 8,9, sch 9 paras 8,9
13.5	24, 44	23	sch 1 para 5, sch 6 paras 7,26	30, 60(4)

13.7	25	22	sch 1 para 6, sch 6 para 8	31
13.8	27, 31(1), 35, 37, 39	27, 31	sch 1 paras 10,11, sch 6 paras 12(1), 15,17,20,24	36,37,46,49, 51,54,58
13.13	42, 51	27(2), 40	sch 1 para 31, sch 6 paras 25,28,33	37, 68, 69
13.15	43	41	sch 1 para 25, sch 6 para 26	60
13.16	46	42	sch 1 para 26, sch 6 para 28	62
13.19	50	46	sch 1 para 30, sch 6 para 32	67
13.22	27, 31, 39	28	sch 1 para 18, sch 6 paras 12,17,20	46, 51, 54
13.24	27(1)	28(1)	sch 1 para 18(1), sch 6 para 20(1)	54(1)
13.25	31(2), 81(8),(9)		sch 6 paras 12(2), 46(8),(9)	46(2), 105(8),(9)
13.26	sch 4 para 3	31(12)	sch 1 para 11(13), sch 9 para 4	37(13), sch 7 para 4
13.29	31(1)	27(1)	sch 1 para 10(1), sch 6 para 12(1)	36(1) 46(1)
13.30	31(2)	31(6)	sch 1 para 11(7), sch 6 para 12(2)	37(7), 46(2)
13.31	81(9)	31(6)	sch 1 para 11(7), sch 6 para 46(9)	37(7), 105(9)
13.32	sch 5 para 11	sch 4 paras 18,21,22	sch 5 paras 18,21,22 sch 10 para 12	37(7), sch 8 paras18, 21,22, sch 9 para 12
13.33	39(3)	27(3),(4)	sch 1 para 10(2),(3), sch 6 para 17(3)	36(2),(3), 51(3)
13.34	39(3)	27(3),(4)	sch 1 para 10(2),(3), sch 6 para 17(3)	36(2),(3), 51(3)
13.35	2(1), 39(5)		2(1), sch 6 para 17(5)	2(1), 51(5)
13.36	sch 4 para 52	27(1)(j)	sch 1 para 10(1)(j), sch 9 para 53	36(1)(j), sch 7 para 53
13.37	sch 4 paras 7,8,11, sch 5 para 11	24, 25, 41(3), sch 4 paras 21,22	sch 1 paras 7,8,25(3), sch 5 paras 21,22, sch 9 paras 8,9,12, sch 10 para 13	32, 33, 60(3), sch 7 paras 8,9,12, sch 8 paras 21,22, sch 9 para 12
13.40				
13.41	sch 4 para 42	27(1)(j)	sch 1 para 10(1)(j), sch 9 paras 42,57	36(1)(j), sch 7 paras 52, 57
13.42	sch 5 para 11	sch 4 paras 21,22	sch 5 paras 21,22, sch 10 para 13	sch 8 paras 21,22, sch 9 para 12
13.43	sch 4 para 62		sch 9 para 64	sch 7 para 64
13.45	sch 4 para 38, sch 5 paras 24,25	27(1)	sch 1 para 10(1), sch 9 para 38, sch 10 para 25	36(1), sch para 38, sch 9 para 25
13.46	32	27(1)(b), 30	sch 1 para 10(1)(b),21, sch 6 para 22	36(1)(b), 56

Para	Scotland		Wales	
	CTS	**CTS60+**	**CTPW**	**CTRW**
13.47	27(1),(2), sch 4 para 56, sch 5 para 11		sch 1 paras 8(1),(2), 22(e), sch 9 para 58, sch 10 para 13	54(1),(2), 57(e), sch 7 para 58
13.48	45(9), sch 5 para 11	41(3), sch 4 paras 18,21	sch 1 para 25(3), sch 5 paras 18,21, sch 6 para 27(10), sch 10 para 13	60(3), 61(10), sch 8 paras 18,21, sch 9 para 12
13.49	sch 4 paras 51,64	27(1)(j)	sch 1 para 10(1)(j), sch 9 paras 52,66	36(1)(j), sch 7 paras 52, 66
13.50	34(1)(j)	27(1)(j)	sch 1 para 10(1)(j), sch 6 para 14(1)(j)	36(1)(j), 48(1)(j)
13.52	sch 4 paras 10-13	27(1)(j), sch 4 para 21	sch 1 para 10(1)(j), sch 5 para 21, sch 9 paras 11-14	36(1)(j), sch 7 paras 11-14, sch 8 para 21
13.53	sch 5 para 11		sch 10 para 13	sch 9 para 12
13.54			sch 5 para 27	sch 8 para 27
13.55	sch 4 para 38	27(1)(j)	sch 1 para 10(1)(j), sch 9 para 38	36(1)(j), sch 7 para 38
13.56	sch 4 para 20		sch 4 paras 7,8, sch 9 para 21	sch 5 paras 7,8, sch 7 para 21
13.57		27(1)(j)	sch 1 para 10(1)(j)	36(1)(j)
13.58	sch 4 paras 11-13,19,52-54	27(1), sch 3 paras 1-5, sch 4 paras 21,22	sch 1 para 10(1), sch 4 para 1-6, sch 5 paras 21,22, sch 9 paras 14,20,53-55	36(1)(j), sch 5 paras 1-6, sch 7 paras 12-14, 20,53-55, sch 8 paras 21-22
13.63	sch 4 paras 53-55, sch 5 para 42		sch 9 paras 54-56, sch 10 para 42	sch 7 paras 54-56, sch 9 para 42
13.65	sch 4 paras 30,31	27(1)	sch 1 para 10(1), sch 9 paras 31,32	36(1), sch 7 paras 31-32
13.66	sch 4 para 29	27(1)	sch 1 para 10(1), sch 9 para 30	36(1), sch 7 para 30
13.67	sch 4 paras 30,32,33,57, sch 5 paras 22,62-64	27(1), sch 4 para 29	sch 1 para 10(1), sch 5 para 28, sch 9 paras 31, 33,34,59,sch 10 paras 23,60-62	36(1), sch 7 paras 31,33,34,59, sch 8 para 28, sch 9 paras 23,60-62
13.68	sch 4 para 63, sch 5 para 61	27(1)	sch 1 para 10(1), sch 9 para 65, sch 10 para 59	36(1), sch 7 para 65, sch 9 para 59
13.71	sch 5 para 3	sch 4 para 26	sch 5 para 26, sch 10 para 4	sch 8 para 26, sch 9 para 4
13.72	sch 5 para 6(a)	sch 4 para 4(a)	sch 5 para 4(a), sch 10 para 7(a)	sch 8 para 4(a), sch 9 para 7(a)
13.73	sch 5 paras 4,32,33		sch 10 paras 5,32,33	sch 9 paras 5,32,33
13.75	sch 5 para 31	sch 4 para 7	sch 5 para 7, sch 10 para 31	sch 8 para 7, sch 9 para 31
13.76	sch 5 para 30	sch 4 para 6	sch 5 para 6, sch 10 para 30	sch 8 para 6, sch 9 para 30

13.77	sch 5 para 6(b)	sch 4 para 4(b)	sch 5 para 4(b), sch 10 para 7(b)	sch 8 para 4(b), sch 9 para 7(b)
13.79	sch 5 para 13(a)		sch 10 para 14(a)	sch 9 para 14(a)
13.80	sch 5 paras 5,13(a)		sch 10 paras 6,14(a)	sch 9 paras 5, 14(a)
13.81		sch 4 paras 18,20(a)	sch 5 paras 18,20(a)	sch 8 paras 18, 20(a)
13.83	sch 5 para 9	sch 4 para 5	sch 5 para 5, sch 10 para 10	sch 8 para 5, sch 9 para 10
13.84	sch 5 para 37	sch 4 para 32	sch 5 para 30, sch 10 para 37	sch 8 para 30, sch 9 para 37
13.86	sch 5 paras 13,41	sch 4 paras 18,20(b)	sch 5 paras 18,20(b), sch 10 paras 14,41	sch 8 paras 18,20(b), sch 9 paras 14,41
T 13.3	sch 4 paras 24,26	27(1), sch 3 paras 8,9	sch 1 para 10(1), sch 4 paras 10,11, sch 9 paras 25,27	36(1), sch 5 paras 9,10, sch 7 paras 26,27
T 13.4	45(4), sch 4 para 21(1),(2)	27(1), sch 3 para 22	sch 1 para 10(1), sch 4 para 24, sch 6 para 27(5), sch 9 paras 21(1),(2)	36(1), 61(5), sch 5 para 23, sch 7 para 22(1),(2)
13.87	sch 5 para 26	27(1)	sch 1 para 10(1), sch 10 para 26	36(1), sch 9 para 26
13.88	sch 4 para 34	27(1)	sch 1 para 10(1), sch 9 para 35	36(1), sch 7 para 35
13.89	sch 5 para 12	sch 4 paras 18,19	sch 5 paras 18,19, sch 10 para 13	sch 8 paras 18-19, sch 9 para 13
13.91	sch 5 para 14	sch 4 para 8	sch 5 para 8, sch 10 para 15	sch 8 para 8, sch 9 para 15
13.94	34(2), 39(11), sch 4 para 3, sch 5 para 35	27(1)(x), 31(12), sch 4 para 24	sch 1 para 10(1)(x),11(13), sch 5 para 24, sch 6 para 14(2),17(10), sch 9 para 4, sch 10 para 35	36(10(x), 37(13), 48(2), 51(10), sch 7 para 4, sch 8 para 24, sch 9 para 35
13.95	43(1)	41(1)	sch 1 para 25(1), sch 6 para 26(1)	60(1)
13.97	45(4)	sch 3 paras 21,22	sch 4 paras 23,24, sch 6 para 27(5)	61(5), sch 5 paras 22-23
13.98				
13.100	sch 5 para 20	sch 4 para 11	sch 5 para 11, sch 10 para 21	sch 8 para 11, sch 9 para 21
13.101	No equiv	Not CTR	No equiv	Not CTR
13.102	sch 5 para 15	27(1)	sch 1 para 10(1), sch 5 para 31, sch 10 para 16	36(1), sch 8 para 31, sch 9 para 16
13.103	40(2), sch 5 para 15	27(1), sch 3 para 10, sch 4 para 33	sch 1 para 10(1), sch 4 para 11, sch 5 para 31, sch 6 para 18(2), sch 10 para 16	36(1), 52(2), sch 5 para 11, sch 8 para 31, sch 9 para 16
13.104		27(1)(w),(6)	sch 1 para 10(1)(w),(5)	36(1)(w),(5)
13.105	sch 5 para 18	sch 4 para 31	sch 5 para 29, sch 10 para 19	sch 8 para 29, sch 9 para 19

Para	Scotland CTS	CTS60+	Wales CTPW	CTRW
13.106	sch 5 para 9	sch 4 para 5	sch 5 para 5, sch 10 para 10	sch 8 para 5, sch 9 para 10
13.111		sch 4 para 34	sch 5 para 32	sch 8 para 32
13.112		sch 3 para 11	sch 4 para 12	sch 5 para 12
13.113	sch 4 para 18	sch 3 para 11	sch 4 para 12, sch 9 para 19	sch 5 para 12, sch 7 para 19
13.114	sch 5 para 17	sch 4 para 17	sch 5 para 17, sch 10 para 18	sch 8 para 17, sch 9 para 18
13.115	sch 5 para 16	sch 4 para 17	sch 5 para 17, sch 10 para 17	sch 8 para 17, sch 9 para 17
13.116	sch 5 paras 50,51	sch 4 para 17	sch 5 para 17, sch 10 paras 48,49	sch 8 para 17, sch 9 paras 48,49
13.117	40(5)	sch 3 paras 13,14	sch 4 paras 14,15, sch 6 para 18(5)	52(5), sch 5 paras 14,15
13.118	sch 4 para 41, sch 5 paras 29,38,59	27(1), sch 4 para 14	sch 1 para 10, sch 5 para 14, sch 9 para 41, sch 10 paras 29,38,57	36(1), sch 7 para 41, sch 8 para 14, sch 9 paras 29,38,57
13.120	2(1), sch 4 para 41, sch 5 para 29	sch 4 para 16	2(1), sch 1 para 10(1), sch 5 para 16, sch 9 para 41, sch 10 para 29	2(1), 36(1), sch 7 para 41, sch 8 para 16, sch 9 para 29
13.121				
13.122	sch 4 para 19(g), sch 5 paras 58,60	27(1)(m), sch 3 para 1(g), sch 4 paras 13,15	sch 1 para 10(1)(m), sch 4 para 1(g), sch 5 paras 13,15, sch 9 para 20(g), sch 10 paras 56,58	36(1)(m), sch 5 para 1(g),sch 7 para 20(g), sch 8 paras 13,15, sch 9 paras 56,58
13.124				
13.125	sch 4 para 49	27(1)(o)	sch 1 para 10(1)(o), sch 9 para 50	36(1)(o), sch 7 para 50
13.126	sch 4 para 48	sch 3 para 19	sch 4 para 20, sch 9 para 49	sch 5 para 20, sch 7 para 49
13.127	2(1), 45(7), sch 4 paras 1,2,17,50, 58,60, 61, sch 5 paras 1,2 10,39,		2(1), sch 6 para 27(8), sch 9 paras 2,3,18,51,60, 62,63 sch 10 paras 11,39,46,47,51	2(1), 61(8), sch 7 paras 2,3,18,51,60, 62, 63, sch 9 paras 2,3,11,39,46,47,51
13.128	2(1), sch 4 para 59, sch 5 para 54	27(1)	2(1), sch 1 para 10(1), sch 9 para 61, sch 10 para 52	2(1), 36(1), sch 7 para 60, sch 9 para 52
13.129	45(6), sch 4 para 18, sch 5 para 38	27(1)	sch 1 para 10(1), sch 6 para 27(7), sch 9 para 19, sch 10 para 38	36(1), 61(7), sch 7 para 19, sch 9 para 38
13.130	39(1), sch 4 para 27	27(1)	sch 1 para 10(1), sch 6 para 17(1), sch 9 para 28	36(1), 51(1), sch 7 para 28
13.131	39(1), sch 4 para 27	27(1)	sch 1 para 10(1), sch 6 para 17(1), sch 9 para 28	36(1), 51(1), sch 7 para 28

13.132	sch 4 paras 45-47, sch 5 paras 43-46	27(1)	sch 1 para 10(1), sch 9 paras 46-48, sch 10 paras 43-45	36(1), sch 7 paras 46-48, sch 9 paras 43-45
13.133		27(1)	sch 1 paras 10(1), sch 9 para 44	36(1), sch 7 para 44
13.134	sch 5 para 52	27(1)	sch 1 para 10(1), sch 9 para 15, sch 10 para 50	36(1), sch 7 para 15, sch 9 para 50
13.135	sch 3 para 13, sch 4 paras 22,23	sch 2 para 7, sch 3 paras 17,18	sch 3 para 7, sch 4 paras 18,19, sch 8 para 13, sch 9 paras 23,24	sch 4 para 7, sch 5 paras 18,19, sch 6 para 13, sch 7 paras 23,24
13.136	sch 4 para 15, sch 5 para 55	27(1)	sch 1 para 10(1), sch 9 para 16, sch 10 para 53	36(1), sch 7 para 16, sch 9 para 53
13.137	34(2)(c), sch 4 para 5	32(2)(f)	sch 1 para 12(2)(f), sch 6 para 14(2)(d), sch 9 para 6	38(2)(f), 48(2)(c), sch 7 para 6
13.138	40(4), sch 4 para 17	27(1)	sch 1 para 10(1), sch 6 para 18(4), sch 9 para 18	36(1), 52(4), sch 7 para 18
13.139	sch 4 para 16	27(1)	sch 1 para 10(1), sch 9 para 17	36(1), sch 7 para 17
13.142	40(1), sch 5 para 21		sch 6 para 18(1), sch 10 para 22	52(1), sch 9 para 22
13.143	47, sch 5 para 28	43, sch 4 para 23	sch 1 para 27, sch 5 para 23, sch 6 para 29, sch 10 para 28	63, sch 8 para 23, sch 9 para 28
13.144	sch 4 paras 28,39, sch 5 para 19	sch 3 paras 15,16	sch 4 paras 16,17, sch 9 paras 29,39, sch 10 para 20	sch 5 paras 16,17, sch 7 paras 29,39, sch 9 para 20
13.145	sch 4 para 4	27(1)	sch 1 para 10(1), sch 9 para 5	36(1), sch 7 para 5
13.146	41(9),(10)	44(5)	sch 1 para 28(5), sch 6 paras 19(9),(10),30(7)	53(9),(10), 64(9)
13.147	41(1), 48(1)	31(8), 44(1)	sch 1 paras 16(9),28(1), sch 6 paras 19(1),30(1)	42(9), 53(1), 64(1)
13.149				
13.150	49	45	sch 1 para 29, sch 6 para 31	65, 66
13.152		2(1), 38	2(1) sch 1 para 16	2(1), 42
13.153	41		sch 6 para 19	53
13.155	41(3)(a),(11), 48(4)	39	sch 1 para 17, sch 6 paras 19(3)(a),(11), 30(4)	43, 53(3)(a),(11), 64(6),(7)
13.157	41(5)	38(11),(12)	sch 1 para 16(13),(14), sch 6 para 19(5)	42(13),(14), 53(5)
13.158	41(6),(7)		sch 6 para 19(6),(7)	53(6),(7)
13.159	48(5),(6)		sch 6 para 30(5),(6)	64(7),(8)
13.160	sch 4 para 40	sch 3 para 11(3)	sch 4 para 12(3), sch 9 para 40	sch 5 para 12(3), sch 7 para 40

Para	Scotland CTS	CTS60+	Wales CTPW	CTRW
13.162		25(1)	sch 1 para 8(1)	33(1)
13.163				
13.166		25(2),(3)	sch 1 para 8(2),(3)	33(2),(3)
13.167		25(4),(5)	sch 1 para 8(4)	33(4)
13.168		25(6)	sch 1 para 8(5)	33(5)
13.169	26	No equiv	sch 6 para 9	34
14.3			30, 31, 32	
14.4	2(1)	2(1)	2(1)	2(1)
14.7	2(1), 29	2(1), 31	2(1), sch 1 para 11, sch 6 para 10	2(1), 37, 44
14.8	29	31	sch 1 para 11, sch 6 para 10	37, 44
14.9	35	33	sch 1 para 13, sch 6 para 15	39, 49
14.10	35	33	sch 1 para 13, sch 6 para 15	39, 49
14.11				
14.12	35	33	sch 1 para 13, sch 6 para 15	39, 49
14.14	35(2), sch 3	33(1), sch 2	sch 1 para 13(1), sch 3, sch 6 para 15(2), sch 8	39(1), 49(2), sch 4, sch 6
14.15	sch 3 para 16	sch 2 para 11	sch 3 para 11, sch 8 para 16	sch 4 para 11, sch 6 para 16
14.17	28	29	sch 1 para 19, sch 6 para 21	55
T14.1	sch 3 paras 1-12	sch 2 paras 1-8	sch 3 paras 1-8, sch 8 paras 4-12	sch 4 paras 1-8, sch 6 paras 4-12
14.18	27(3)	28(3)	sch 1 para 18(3), sch 6 para 20(3)	54(3)
14.19	27(1)(c)	28(1)(c)	sch 1 para 18(1)(c), sch 6 para 20(1)(c)	54(1)(c)
14.20	28(10)	29(10)	sch 1 para 19(10), sch 6 para 21(10)	55(10)
14.21	28(2)-(4), (15)-(17)	29(2)-(4), (15),(17)	sch 1 para 19(2)-(4), (15)-(17), sch 6 para 21(2)-(4),(15)-(17)	55(2)-(4),(15),(17)
14.26	28(11)	29(11)	sch 1 para 19(11), sch 6 para 21(11)	55(11)
14.27	28(7),(8)	29(7),(8)	sch 1 para 19(7),(8), sch 6 para 21(7),(8)	55(7),(8)
14.29	28(6),(14)	29(6),(14)	sch 1 para 19(6),(14), sch 6 para 21(6),(14)	55(6),(14)
14.30	sch 3 para 18	sch 2 para 10	sch 3 para 10, sch 8 para 18	sch 4 para 10, sch 6 para 18

14.31	sch 4 para 56	sch 3 para 20	sch 4 para 21, sch 9 para 58	sch 5 para 21, sch 7 para 58
14.34	34(1)	32(1)	sch 1 para 12(1), sch 6 para 14(1)	38(1), 48(1)
14.35	81(9)	59(9)	sch 1 para 40(9), sch 6 para 46(9)	105(9)
14.36	45(2)		sch 6 para 27(2)	61(2)
14.37	40(3)		sch 6 para 31(3)	66(3)
14.38	45(1)		sch 6 para 27(1)	61(1)
14.39	34(1)(l)	32(1)(g)	sch 1 para 12(1)(g), sch 6 para 14(1)(l)	38(1)(g), 48(1)(l)
14.43	34(1)(f),(2)(b), sch 4 para 6	32(1)(f),(2)(b)	sch 1 para 12(1)(f),(2)(b), sch 6 para 14(1)(f),(2)(b), sch 9 para 7	38(1)(f),(2)(b), 48(1)(f),(2)(b), sch 7 para 7
14.45	sch 4 para 6	27(1)	sch 1 para 10(1), sch 9 para 5	36(1), sch 7 para 5
14.47	45(5)		sch 6 para 27(5)	61(5)
14.48	34	32	sch 1 para 12, sch 6 para 14	38, 48
14.49	34(1)(d), 45(3)	32(1)(d), sch 2 para 9	sch 1 para 12(1)(d), sch 3 para 9, sch 6 paras 14(1)(d),27(3)	38(1)(d), 48(1)(d), 61(3), sch 4 para 9
14.50	2(1), 34(1)(j),(k)	32(1)(h)-(k)	2(1), sch 1 para 12(1)(h)-(k), sch 6 paras 14(1)(j),(k),15(3)	38(1)(h)-(k), 48(1)(j),(k), 49(3)
14.51	34(1)(e)	27(1), 32(1)(e)	sch 1 paras 10(1),12(1)(e), sch 6 para 14(1)(e)	36(1), 38(1)(e), 48(1)(e)
14.52		27(1)	sch 1 para 10(1)	36(1)
T14.2	sch 3 para 1(c),2		sch 8 para 1(c),2	sch 6 para 1(c),2
14.53	34(1)(b)	32(1)(b)	sch 1 para 12(1)(b), sch 6 para 14(1)(b)	38(1)(b), 48(1)(b)
T14.3	34(1)(e),(g),(h), sch 3 para 1(b),2	32(1)(e),(g),(h), sch 2 para 9	sch 1 para 12(1)(e), sch 3 para 9, sch 6 para 14(1)(e), (g),(h), sch 8 para 1(b),2	38(1)(e), 48(1)(e),(g),(h), sch 4 para 9, sch 6 para 1(b),2
15.4	2(1)	2(1)	2(1)	2(1)
15.6	36(1)-(2)	35(1)-(2)	15(1)-(2), 16(1)-(2)	41(1)-(2), 50(1)-(2)
15.7	sch 3 para 3, sch 5 para 10	sch 4 para 9,10	sch 5 paras 9,10, sch 8 para 3, sch 10 para 11	sch 6 para 3, sch 8 paras 9,10, sch 9, para 11
15.9	2(1); 30;	2(1); 34	2(1), sch 1 para 14, sch 6 para 11	2(1), 40, 45
15.18	36(1), 37(1)	35(1), 36(1)	15(1), 16(1), 23(1), 24(1)	41(1), 50(1), 58(1)
15.2	36(1)	35(1)	15(1), 16(1)	41(1), 50(1)
15.21	37(3)(a), (4), (7)	36(2)(a), (3), (6)	23(2)(a),(3), (6), 24(3)(a), (4), (7)	58(3)(a), (4), (7)
T 15.1	37(3)(a), (4), (7)	36(2)(a), (3), (6)	23(2)(a),(3), (6), 24(3)(a), (4), (7)	58(3)(a), (4), (7)

Para	Scotland CTS	CTS60+	Wales CTPW	CTRW
15.27	37(9),	36(8)	23(8), 24(9)	58(9),
15.28	37(1),(3)-(4)	36(1)-(3)	23(1)-(3), 24(1),(3)-(4)	58(1)-(4)
15.29	37(1)(b),(4)	36(1)(b), (3)	23(1)(b),(3); 24(1)(b)(c),(4)	58(1)(b),(c), (4)
15.32	37(10)	36(9)	23(9), 24(10	58(10)
15.34	38	37	24	59
15.35	38	37	24	59
15.36	38	37	24	59
15.37	37(11)-(12)	36(10)-(11)	23(10)-(11); 24(11)-(12)	58(11),(12)
15.4	37(1),(3);	36(1)-(2)	23(1)-(2), 24(1),(3)	58(1),(3)
15.41	36(3)-(4)	27(1)(q)(r), 31(4)-(5)	10(1)(q)(r); 11(5)-(6); 16(3)-(4)	36(1)(q)-(r), 37(5)-(6); 50(3)-(4)
15.42	N/A	31(4)	11(5)	37(5)
15.43	36(4)	N/A	16(4)	50(4)
16.2	No equiv	No equiv	sch 13 paras 8,9(1)(a)	114, 115(1)(a)
16.3	No equiv	No equiv	sch 13 para 8	114
16.4	No equiv	No equiv	sch 13 para 9(1)(b)	115(1)(b)
16.9	No equiv	No equiv	sch 13 para 9(1)	115(1)
16.10	No equiv	No equiv	sch 13 para 13(7),(8)	115(7),(8)
16.11	No equiv	No equiv	sch 13 para 9(2),(3), sch 14 paras 2,3	115(2),(3), sch 10 paras 2,3
16.12	No equiv	No equiv	sch 13 para 9, sch 14	115, sch 10
T16.1	No equiv	No equiv	sch 13 para 9(2),(3), sch 14	115(2),(3), sch 10
16.13	No equiv	No equiv	sch 13 para 10(1)	116(1)
16.14	No equiv	No equiv	sch 13 para 10(2),(3)	116(2)-(4)
16.15-75	Not CTR	Not CTR	Not CTR	Not CTR
17.3	89(1),(4)	69(1),(4)	sch 13 para 17(1)	113(1)
T17.1	89	69	sch 13 para 7	113
T17.2	89(2),(3)	69(2),(3)	sch 13 para 7(3),(4)	113(3),(4)
17.5	89, 90, 91	69, 70, 71	sch 12 para 13, sch 13 para 7(2)	113(2), sch 1 para 13
17.7			sch 13 para 7(2)	113(2)
17.10-14				
17.16	86(1)	66(1)	sch 13 para 5(1)	111(1)
17.17			sch 13 para 1(b),(2)-(4), sch 14	115(1)(b),(2)-(4), sch 10
17.24	81(2),(3)	59(2),(3)	sch 1 para 40(3),(4), sch 6 para 46(3),(4)	105(3),(4)
17.25	81(2),(3)	59(2),(3)	No equiv	No equiv
T17.3	81(2),(3)	59(2),(3)	sch 1 para 40(3),(4), sch 6 para 46(3),(4)	105(3),(4)
17.21	81(1),(5),(6)	59(1),(5),(6)	sch 1 para 40(1),(5),(6), sch 6 para 46(1),(5),(6)	105(1),(5),(6)

17.27		60	sch 1 para 41	106
T17.4		60	sch 1 para 41	106
17.30	81(1)	59(1)	sch 1 para 40(1),(2), sch 6 para 46(1),(2)	105(1),(2)
T17.6	81(1)	59(1)	sch 1 para 40(1),(2), sch 6 para 46(1),(2)	105(1),(2)
17.35			sch 1 para 22, sch 6 para 23	57
17.38				
17.39	81(4)	59(4)		
17.40	81(7)	59(7)	sch 1 para 40(7), sch para 46(7)	105(7)
17.42	68, 73	49	2(1), sch 1 para 32, sch 6 paras 34,39	85, 86, 92, 93
17.43	See text	See text	See text	See text
17.45	69,70, 74, 75	50, 51	sch 1 paras 33,34, sch 6 paras 35,36,40,41	87, 88, 94, 95, 99, 100
17.47		54		
17.48	72, 77	53	sch 1 para 36, sch 6 paras 38,43	90, 97, 102
17.49	71, 76	52	sch 1 paras 35,38, sch 6 paras 37,42,44	89, 96, 101, 103
17.50		55	sch 1 para 37	91
17.50-56				
Chapter 18	Not CTR	Not CTR	Not CTR	Not CTR
19.1-110	Not CTR	Not CTR	Not CTR	Not CTR
19.111-125	See text	See text	See text	See text
20.14	83(1), 84(2), 86(1)	63(1), 64(2), 66(1)	sch 13 para 5(2),(3)	111(2),(3)
20.24-28	See text	See text	See text	See text
20.34	16(1),(5)(d),(e)	16(1),(5)(d),(e)	26(1),(5)(d),(e)	19(1),(5)(d),(e)
20.36	No equiv	No equiv	No equiv	No equiv
20.38	16(2)	16(2)	26(2)	19(2)
20.40	16(5)(g)	16(5)(g)	26(5)(g)	19(5))(g)
21.5	16(5)(a)-(c)	16(5)(a)-(e)	26(5)(a)-(c)	19(5)(a)-(c)
21.8	16(3),(5)	16(3),(5)	26(3),(5)	19(3),(5)
21.17	16(5)(b)	16(5)(b)	26(5)(b)	19(5)(b)
21.19-26	See text	See text	See text	See text
21.27				
21.29-41, T21.1	See text	See text	See text	See text
22.4	2(1), 53	2(1);	29(2), sch 11 para 1(1), para 2	2(1), 70(1), 71
22.5	2(1)	2(1)	sch 11, para 1(1)	70(1)
22.6	2(2)(b)	2(2)(b)	sch 11, para 2(b)	70(2)(b)
22.7	2(1)	2(1)	sch 11, para 1(1)	70(1)

Para	Scotland CTS	CTS60+	Wales CTPW	CTRW
22.9	53		sch 11, para 2	71
22.11	2(1)		sch 11, para 1(1)	70(1)
22.12	2(1)		sch 11, para 1(1)	70(1)
22.13	2(1)		sch 11, para 1(1)	70(1)
22.14	2(1)		sch 11, para 1(1)	70(1)
22.15	2(2), 2(4)	2(2), 2(4)	sch 11, para 1(2), para 1(4)	70(2),(4)
22.16	2(3)	2(3)	sch 11, para 1(3)	70(3)
22.17	2(1), 20	2(1)	sch 11 para 1(1), sch 11 para 3	70(1), 72
22.19	52		sch 11 para 1(1)	70(1)
22.23	20(2)-(3)		sch 11, para 3(2)	72(2)
22.24	20(2)-(3)		sch 11, para 3(2)	72(2)
T22.1	20		sch 11, para 3	72
22.29	N/A	27(1)	sch 1, para 10(1)	36(1)
22.31	59, 60	N/A	sch 11, paras 9-10	78, 79
22.32	52, 54, 59, sch 5 para 27		sch 11 para 1(1), para 4, para 9 sch 10 para 27	70, 73, 78 sch 9 para 27
22.33	62, 63	N/A	sch 11 para 12, para 13	81,82
22.34	39(7)-(9)	N/A	sch 6 17(6)-(8)	51(6)-(9)
22.35	sch 4 para 16	N/A	sch 9 para 17	sch 7 para 17
22.36	54(1)	N/A	sch 11 para 4(1)	73(1)
22.37	52, 54, 58, 59	N/A	sch 11 para 1(1) sch 11 para 4, para 8, para 9	70, 73, 77, 78
22.38	62, 63	N/A	sch 11 para 12, para 13	81, 82
22.39	52	N/A	sch 11 para 1(1)	70(1)
22.40	52, 64(2)-(3), sch 4, para 40	N/A	sch 11 para 11 para 14(2)-(3); sch 11, para 11(3)	80, 83(2)-(3) sch 7 para 40
22.41	61(3)	N/A	sch 11 para 11(3)	80(3)
22.43	58	N/A	sch 11, para 8	77
Chapter 23	Not CTR	Not CTR	Not CTR	Not CTR
Chapter 24	Not CTR	Not CTR	Not CTR	Not CTR
Chapter 25	Not CTR	Not CTR	Not CTR	Not CTR

Index

References in the index are to paragraph numbers (not page numbers), except that 'A' refers to appendices, 'T' refers to tables in the text and 'Ch' refers to a chapter.